PRAISE FOR *COMPASS OF THE SOUL*

"The presentation [is a] rich, lucid, illuminating, and ultimately convincing and heartening demonstration, reminding us of the significance of the functional couplings and reinforcing their place in the landscape of both Jungian psychology and *MBTI*®-style typology."

JULIE BENESH

"This is an important book for two communities: the Jungian community that values Jung's work on typology, and the world of typology as represented by the *MBTI*® [theory of type.] . . . Giannini is willing to take on the difficult questions and to challenge other theoreticians in both the Jungian and *MBTI* camps."

HARVEY HONIG, PhD

"For students of the human psyche, organizations, and social systems, *Compass of the Soul* provides a wealth of insight which to my knowledge is provided in no other publications."

LAURENCE J. QUICK, PhD
W. Edwards Deming Center for Ethical Leadership

"In *Compass of the Soul* John Giannini provides readers with a concentration of wisdom that carries a reader into surprising depths of intelligence and meaning—and that awakens a creative energy of immediate relevance for one's work in the world. As one reads this book, hope for the entire human enterprise blooms in one's soul."

BRIAN SWIMME
California Institute of Integral Studies

COMPASS OF THE SOUL

COMPASS OF THE SOUL

Archetypal Guides
to a Fuller Life

JOHN L. GIANNINI

Center for Applications of Psychological Type, Inc.

Gainesville, Florida

Published by
Center for Applications of Psychological Type, Inc.
2815 NW 13th Street, Suite 401
Gainesville, FL 32609
352.375.0160

CAPT, the CAPT logo, and Center for Applications of Psychological Type are trademarks of the Center for Applications of Psychological Type, Inc., Gainesville, FL.

Myers-Briggs Type Indicator, Myers-Briggs, and MBTI are trademarks and registered trademarks of the Myers-Briggs Type Indicator Trust in the United States and other countries.

Introduction to Type is a trademark and registered trademark of the Myers-Briggs Type Indicator Trust in the United States and other countries.

Printed in the United States of America.

Cover design concept by Scott Lewis, Chicago, IL.

Library of Congress Cataloging-in-Publications Data

Giannini, John L., 1921–
Compass of the soul : archetypal guides to a fuller life /
John L. Giannini.
p. cm.
Includes bibliographical references.
ISBN 0-935652-70-1
1. Typology (Psychology) 2. Temperament. 3. Myers-Briggs Type Indicator. I. Title.

BF698.3.G53 2003
155.2'64--dc21

2003046190

This book is dedicated to all those who have sought and who seek a wisdom whose two central truths were reportedly carved on the wall of Apollo's temple at sacred Delphi in Greece, and are certainly inscribed by God in the heart and soul of every human being, namely: "Know thyself" and "All in moderation." These two truths are at the center of Carl Jung's psychology and its extension in the Myers-Briggs Type Indicator® instrument.

TABLE OF CONTENTS

FIGURES

Chapter 7

Chapter 8

Chapter 9

Chapter 10

SECTION 3: The Function Couplings in Society

Chapter 12

FOREWORD

IN THE EIGHTY YEARS since *Psychologische Typen* was published in 1921, many people have accepted Jung's intuitive vision that four "functions" of differentiated psychic activity—sensation, thinking, feeling, and intuition—offer the most practical way to describe and orient to the unfolding miracle that analytical psychology calls "consciousness." By 1931, Jung himself had realized that the "four functions are somewhat like the four points of a compass; they are just as arbitrary and just as indispensable"—indispensable, that is, if one wants to make headway in "psychological voyages of discovery" of the kind he pioneered. These are voyages of human individuation, journeys in which consciousness evolves in individually characteristic ways. For the voyagers—individuating people—the function types have proved reliable as a way to identify their emerging capacities to make sense of inner and outer realities. Psychologists trying to keep up with the consciousness explosion produced by all these individual discoveries have also found Jung's types helpful, as a way of understanding how it happens that people are able to develop "psychologies" at all, that is, their individual abilities to discriminate for themselves what psyche can mean in their lives. Evidently, Jung's has been a fertile as well as seminal model.

In the United States, after 1956, the theory of psychological types received an unexpected boost from the reach and popularity of one assessment tool, the *Myers-Briggs Type Indicator® (MBTI®)* instrument. This extraordinary tool, available to professionals since 1975, has created a new, enthusiastic cadre of career counselors, teachers, personnel recruiters, and management consultants who have recognized that type theory is the key to different styles of effectiveness in work and study situations. There is now an Association for

Psychological Type made up of people who are qualified to administer this instrument, and its members now outnumber the Jungian analysts in the world.

John Giannini, the author of this volume, is highly qualified to bridge these two worlds of type, that of the Jungian analyst and that of the *MBTI* practitioner, because he has exposed himself to every continent within them and knows where the places of intersection lie. What he has provided in this volume, however, goes well beyond this marriage of the perspectives of the analyst and the type counselor. He has achieved nothing less than a full survey of the meaning of the type problem for our time, and in this way updates Jung's project for a contemporary audience.

There have been many good books on type since 1921—van der Hoop's *Conscious Orientation* in 1939, von Franz and Hillman's *Lectures on Jung's Typology* in 1971, Isabel Briggs Myers' *Gifts Differing* in 1980, and Angelo Spoto's *Jung's Typology in Perspective* in 1989 come immediately to mind—but no book previous to Giannini's has succeeded in keeping Jung's original vision of the four-function compass so front and center in the course of exploring the contemporary implications of Jungian and post-Jungian type theory. He accomplishes this by circulating the light of Jung's typological mandala along the ever-curving line of its own contour. One gets in this volume a holistic sense of how type theory is used in the United States today and how useful it can be in fostering the development both of individuals and of cultures. With consummate relatedness and considerable skill, Giannini circumambulates the character of type theory itself without ever losing sight of Jungian typology's central concern, the integrity of human consciousness.

John Beebe
President
The C. G. Jung Institute of San Francisco

PREFACE

JOHN GIANNINI AND I MET IN JULY 1995 at the International conference of the Association for Psychological Type in Kansas City where we began to talk about a book he was writing based on the work of C. G. Jung. We shared an interest in Jung as I had for some time used a Jungian instrument called the *Myers-Briggs Type Indicator*® (MBTI®). I met the author, Isabel Briggs Myers, in 1969 and under her tutelage had learned the theoretical and psychometric complexities of her instrument. Although my graduate degree in clinical psychology had focused on Freud and ignored Jung, my work with Isabel Myers, taught me much about Jung's typology, and I eventually read his *Psychological Types* but ignored the rest of his complete works.

In 1975 Isabel Myers and I had created a non-profit organization in Gainesville, Florida. She named it Center for Applications of Psychological Type and gave it the mission to promote "the constructive use of differences." In the twenty years before I met John Giannini, I had been consumed with *MBTI* research and training.

As John Giannini progressed with writing *Compass of the Soul*, we talked often and corresponded. The letters described below show how he opened up aspects of Jung's work to which I had never paid attention. Through our communication my understanding and appreciation of the full body of Jung's work has deepened. I was so impressed with the book that I told Mr. Giannini CAPT would be pleased to publish it.

From the beginning of my review of John Giannini's manuscript, *Compass of the Soul*, I struggled with two issues in his writings: (1) that types, particularly the couplings, are archetypes; and (2) that Giannini seemingly was demonizing ESTJ-type persons.

Regarding my first concern—the types as archetypes—I found it difficult to assimilate an idea that puts the types into the very center of Jung's system and brings analysts and typologists closer together. Much earlier in my study of Jung, I was told that many analysts ignored his typology because they understood he had disowned it. I have since found that this belief is not universal. In particular, C. S. Meier, an early associate of Jung, who has written a book entitled *Personality: The Individuation Process in the Light of C. G. Jung's Typology,* wrote me that this was not true and that Jung saw typology as essential to individuation. John Giannini agreed. Individuation, he reminded me, is itself an archetypal process; that is, its patterns are inborn and universal even as its particulars are unique to each person. This same archetypal identity is true of each type; each is inborn and exists as a common structure in every society and in every age. I had not realized that understanding the nature of the archetypes, as large universal givens, was a stage in Jung's development of his theory. Giannini adds the idea that Jung and analysts have focused on the archetypes' primordial imagery. Because of this form as great images, I felt the pragmatic structures of the couplings somehow diminished the archetypes. However, the images need to be described as having specific qualities, which the couplings provide. So I have finally understood why the couplings as archetypes have been central for Giannini, and why he sees—as did Myers—the "combinations of perception and judgment" as the most important type groupings. The couplings as archetypes are universal givens made up of images and traits.

In a 1992 article in the *Bulletin of Psychological Type,*[1] I explained that an enormous variety of persons in many diverse roles and professions were interested in the types because Jung's theory was based on perception and judgment, "two words that should be printed with flashing lights around them to remind us how basic they are." Jung classified us, I wrote, not in terms of the traditional variables of sociology; but instead sorted people by the four tools of our minds— that is, the two perceiving functions and the two judging functions, which also constitute the four function pairs. The reason there are so many applications of psychological type is that every waking hour we are either perceiving or judging—taking in information or making decisions. I realize now that this was my way of describing the archetypal work of the function couplings.

As to my second concern, the possible demonizing of ESTJ persons, we typologists have learned from Isabel Briggs Myers the importance of a normal psychology, in contrast to the usual patholo- gized ways of understanding persons. I have learned that Jung also sought to stress the normal rather than the abnormal problems of the human experience. However, even Myers describes possible type dis- functions in her *Introduction to Type,* particularly when one has not developed the secondary or auxiliary function in any coupling. For example, ENFP types, whose dominant function is intuition, will ignore the feeling function to their peril. Myers writes: "*If* their [feeling] judgment is undeveloped, they may commit themselves to ill-chosen projects, fail to finish anything, and squander their inspirations by not completing their tasks." Myers zeroes in on a more ominous possibil- ity in typology, the ignorance of and misuse of any inferior function. She writes the following about the ESTJ type: "ESTJ people use their thinking to run as much of the world as may be theirs to run." Such persons are challenged to explore their inferior function, which is feel- ing. She continues: "If feeling values are ignored too much, they may build up pressure and find expression in inappropriate ways."

However, it was only when Giannini helped me realize that an *entire cultural atmosphere* can be characterized in a typological way that I began to understand what he calls in chapter 12 our "ESTJ cultural pathology." Giannini's letter to me in 1998 helped me realize the extent of this collective type's destructive atmosphere. It can be described as a one-sided warriorlike patriarchy. Jung held that any type, whether realized individually or collectively, could become barbaric when it is too one-sided. In chapter 3, Giannini discusses Jung's observation in the first pages of his *Psychological Types* that our Western culture had developed an EST bias by the Second Century, A.D. Young monks were to ignore as satanic the intuitive chaos of dreams; a collective sensate spirituality was preferred. Theology became thinking dominant in its logical theorizing, and spiritual practices became more extroverted. Such decisions and practices, Jung concluded, "exemplified how far our Western religious culture had lost the idea of psychic reality and the sacredness of Soul as an introverted intuitive feeling experience." I gradually learned from Giannini to distinguish between an ESTJ person with this type's normal and healthy traits and an ESTJ public environment, which he holds has become, too often, demonic. Watch for this distinction as you read the book.

In this context, I have come to appreciate Giannini's antidote to this cultural woundedness that he finds in the organizational philosophy of William Edwards Deming. Giannini reports, with support from Deming, that because too many individuals and corporate leaders have a materialistic bias, capitalism is not an unadulterated benefit—it can be cruel. As I write, the collapse of our national economy, fueled by fraudulent financial reporting by many companies, supports this tragic observation and its distorted ESTJ assumptions. Giannini's plea is for a world where all the functions and attitudes are valued and used. I agree with his warning of the dangers we have faced and still face from our one-sided viewpoint in the present day world. More of us need to read and assimilate Deming in his books and in the last chapter of this book. A concluding summary at the end of that chapter brought tears to my eyes.

Finally, Giannini has raised a concern in this book which I have puzzled over for a long time and which might need a Deming-like wisdom to resolve. For decades, Myers and I pursued our work on the types with practically no input from analysts. Sometimes we even experienced antagonism. At one point in our communication, Giannini sent to me what he called a "Summary Interlude," which is now included in his chapter 11. In that chapter, entitled "Jung's Divided Family: Analysts and Typologists," he lays out many historical and attitudinal factors which have contributed to this impasse in both professions. What a wonderful gift! I do not know the analyst's side well enough to evaluate it, but it brings together so many strands I did not before understand even though I have certainly lived through many of them.

I had first seen Giannini's vision at an intellectual level, but it finally came alive to me. This book will be a rich resource, bringing together the threads of many aspects of Jung's theory and weaving a powerful understanding of types more complete than before available. To me a major practical issue for the book is its usefulness for the two different audiences it addresses. It gives a rich review of theory and integrates the approaches of both analysts and type practitioners who interpret and implement Jung's theory in different ways. No one else has done such a valuable work. Giannini also makes the book come alive by using the rich experience from his work as an analyst over the years. How well will he have succeeded in the difficult task of reaching the scholarly and popular audiences at the same time? Time will tell.

Early in our correspondence he wrote that he had three main agenda in mind in writing this book: (a) developing the archetypal nature of the types, especially the couplings; (b) bringing the analyst and *MBTI* communities to a better understanding of each other; and (c) adding to type theory more of the richness of Jungian thought that is often overlooked in *MBTI* writings, e.g., dreams, imagination, literature. I believe the book is on target with all three. In reference to the second agenda, I once wrote the following that, I believe, succinctly describes my hope for this book, that, as one family originating from the psychology of Carl Jung, we may more fully activate our unrealized potential:

> In psychology we talk about the clinician-research model.
> As clinicians, we see patterns and come up with hunches.

As researchers, we turn our hunches into hypotheses and test them. Jung was a good example of this model: he began by observing patterns and validating them in his clinical work. Isabel Myers studied Jung's work and tested his observations for twenty years by studying her family and friends. Then she became a researcher. Starting from Jung's work, she set herself the task of creating a tool to validate his work and apply it. Together, they became one of the most creative clinician-researcher teams in the history of psychology.[2]

Notes

1. McCaulley, Mary. "Applications of Type: Filling in the Jig-Saw," in the *Bulletin of Psychological Type,* 15:3, Summer, 1992, p. 20. I give here a homey example of the archetypal richness of each type, when I describe four ESTJs: "one may enjoy looking at the foundations of a bridge, another at the balance sheet of a business, the third at the carburetor of a car, and the fourth at the broken bone of an athlete. They seem to have chosen widely different careers, but they have a bond: all enjoy the evidence of their senses."

2. McCaulley, Mary. "Applications of Type: Filling in the Jig-Saw," in the *Bulletin of Psychological Type,* p. 20. I quote Jung here from the Preface of the 7th edition of *Psychological Types*, in which he addresses the book's critics who "commonly fall into the error of assuming that the types were, so to speak, fancy free and were forcibly imposed on the empirical material." Instead he says: "All my formulations are based on the experience in the hard course of my daily professional work. What I have to say in this book, therefore, has been tested a hundredfold."

ACKNOWLEDGMENTS

I WANT FIRST TO THANK FATHER VICTOR WHITE, a Dominican monk and my first Jungian analyst, who told me in 1956 that I had been living the wrong type for thirty-five years. I asked, "What is a type?" He answered, "Carl Jung's system of understanding human differences." That was the beginning of my psychology education, the seeds of which have grown into this book and my realization that typology is not peripheral to but intimately woven into Jung's entire system. I thank Jane and Joseph Wheelwright, whose Gray-Wheelwright Type Survey fueled my interest in typology as a training analyst. This interest received further impetus when I was certified in the *Myers Briggs Type Indicator*® (*MBTI*®) instrument in the early 1980s. The rest of this evolving consciousness is in this book.

I thank most of all the hundreds of clients, family members and friends for whom I have scored the *MBTI* over the last twenty years. Their scores, in the context of their life stories, work interests, and social struggles, have strengthened my conviction that typology is not just a set of traits but the archetypal ground of their personalities and their unique journeys of individuation. Just the insights typology has given me into the individual qualities of members of my immediate family would have been sufficient reasons for writing this book. Amy (INFP) delights in meaningful children and adult stories as mother and teacher; Julie (ISFJ) treasures existential order and facts in life and literature; Marty's big-picture view (ENTP) informs his ideas, music and organizational philosophy; Ricky (ISTJ) easily learns systems such as anatomy and computers; Scott (ENFP) engages many facets of life from marketing music to research in childhood pathologies; and Rita (INTJ) sees the subtle clues in mystery movies I invariably miss and with deft and often painful strokes, cuts out the fat and builds missing bridges in sentences and paragraphs I write.

I thank the following persons from many disciplines who have read and commented on my initial manuscript and its many variations: Harvey Honig, Ph.D.; David Dalrymple, D.Min; Garey A. Malek, M.D.; Gail Roen, Ph.D.; Angelo Spoto, M.A.; Katherine Benziger, Ph.D.; Ned Herrmann; Walter Lowen, Ph.D.; David Rosen, M.D.; Dick Simpson, Ph.D.; Lawrence Quick, Ph.D.; Bryan Swimme, Ph.D.; Father Matthew Fox; Joan McKiel, M.A.; Boris Matthews, Ph.D.; Robert Moore, Ph.D.; Pierre and Binnie Ferrand; John Beebe, M.D.; Mary McCaulley, Ph.D.; Charles Fleetham; and Eleanor K. Sommer. I also need to recognize the many groups both among analysts and typologists with whom I have shared the substance of this book in courses and workshops throughout this country. Their living accounts of both their life stories and worldviews have strengthened my understanding of the breadth and depth of the types as archetypes.

Among the above persons, several demand special acknowledgments. Joan McKiel is responsible for the artistic construction of the book's many diagrams after patiently reviewing my clumsy drawings. In the process she helped me better articulate texts which explained the diagrams. Lawrence Quick introduced me to William Edwards Deming's organizational philosophy of profound knowledge, which enabled me to connect typology to organizational systems. Among analysts, John Beebe is one of the few who has creatively worked with typology in both the analysts' and the MBTI worlds; so his encouragement of my initial writing significantly strengthened my resolve to continue. Mary McCaulley, a legendary, renowned authority in type circles, scrutinized carefully and critically every aspect of the book that dealt with typology. She was an intimate friend and collaborator with Isabel Briggs Myers, with whom she founded the Center for Applications of Psychological Type (CAPT). When Dr. McCaulley suggested that CAPT would publish this book, I knew immediately that a dream I'd had about the book had been synchronistically answered. Boris Matthews, commissioned to review this book's overall

Jungian methodology, gently and persistently prodded me into doing some serious rethinking of the type system, especially relative to the feeling and intuitive functions. Eleanor Sommer, my editor at CAPT, patiently coordinated many unfinished aspects of the book. Elayna Rexrode and Christy Freeman coordinated the art work, reproduction of the diagrams and the final production of the book.

Finally, I want to acknowledge the hidden work of the Self in the unconscious, the invisible spiritual atmosphere in which we all live. Out of this psychic realm, many synchronistic events have emerged in the writing of this book the many aspects of which I could never have anticipated.

Typology and the Hunger for Identity

The four functions are somewhat like the four points of the compass; they are just as arbitrary and just as indispensable. Nothing prevents our shifting the cardinal points as many degrees as we like in one direction or the other. . . .

But one thing I must confess. I would not for anything dispense with this compass on my psychological voyages of discovery. This is not merely for the obvious, all-too-human reason that everyone is in love with his own ideas. I value the type theory for the objective reason that it provides a system of comparison and orientation which makes possible something that has long been lacking, a critical psychology.[1]

C. G. Jung

 THERE IS A HUNGER FOR DIRECTION and meaning in all of us, particularly since we all live, in various degrees, in chaotic, passionate times. We have a longing, first, to understand and esteem ourselves as unique persons, and, second, to understand others in our complex and fast-changing human society. Without personally nurturing self-understanding and self-esteem, we live secretly desperate lives devoid of security. If we fail to understand others who are different both in personal agendas and larger viewpoints, we suffer the pains of isolation, perplexity, and anguish when they do not appreciate us and

challenge our perceptions and judgments. Nothing hurts us more than the lack of a caring connection with our spouses, our children, our friends, our bosses, and our fellow workers, among others. We feel joy, gratitude, and relief when we connect with our sense of Self and when we are sufficiently understood and valued by others. But complex personal and societal forces make a reasonable satisfaction of this hunger very difficult.

One avenue to the understanding and acceptance we desperately need is through typology. Typology is a systematic method of assessing and describing our innate personality, which, as Jung suggests in the above quotation, can include both ordinary conscious as well as wide-ranging theoretical viewpoints. This system is based on the psychology of Carl Jung and the follow-up work of Katharine Briggs and Isabel Briggs Myers in their development of the *Myers-Briggs Type Indicator®* (*MBTI®*) instrument. The popularity of the *MBTI* has led to a massive data bank of research. The research, extensive literature, professional associations, and many regional and international conferences have validated the survey's accuracy and widespread usefulness. Occasionally it is criticized for its perceived "one size fits all" use.

What does account for its popularity? Angelo Spoto, for example, explains its extensive use and widespread following as partially attributable to a "typological frenzy" stemming from an all too human need for too rigid "an archetype of order," from some practitioners using a cookbook approach to type assessment, and from excessive marketing strategies.[2]

Valid as this criticism is, Spoto also recognizes a hidden meaning behind this frenzy: a hunger for a wise and comprehensive understanding of human differences and their larger sociocultural dimensions. For typology is not a mere measuring instrument useful for naming of personality traits, but rather a practical, dynamic system of vital interactive structures that constitute the complex pattern of outer human relationships and internal depth factors that Jung called the Compass of the Soul. Typology honors both a rich order and a creative disorder that emerges from the Soul's mysterious depths. True, typology does name our differences, not in order to nullify the complexity of personality but as a way of encouraging individuation and relationships.

John O'Donohue, a Celtic artist and philosopher, in telling about the nature of creativity and language, captures the inadequate but essential way in which we struggle to attain maturity through the medium of language and the behavior it suggests. His words may better explain typology's attraction. He writes:

> Everyone is an artist. Each person brings sound out of silence and coaxes the invisible to become visible. . . . An unknown world aspires toward reflection. Words are the oblique mirrors that hold your thoughts. You gaze into these word-mirrors and catch glimpses of meaning, belonging and shelter. Behind their bright surfaces is the dark and the silence. . . . If we become addicted to the external, our interiority will haunt us. We will become hungry with a hunger no image, person or deed can still. To be wholesome, we must remain truthful to our vulnerable complexity.[3]

It is this depth of spirit and understanding that knowingly or unknowingly attracts many to typology and that moves me to write this book. Since typology is so easily useful as a practical system, we can "become addicted to the external," to a stereotypical language of traits. So most typologists treat the types as purely outer behaviors and cognitive traits. However, typology is also a sacred language that describes "our vulnerable complexity," and encompasses a far-reaching theory with its multiplicities of human understanding and complex behaviors. Most of all, it represents in qualities and images the mystery and darkness of the Compass of the Soul's depth, which haunts us and from which we each hunger to authentically actualize all of the types. All these dimensions, in my view, account for the immense, passionate interest and wide-ranging popular and professional literature that the Jung/MBTI instrument generates, which is unique among all personality surveys. Yet this depth is rarely acknowledged both in typological and in larger psychological circles.

HISTORICAL AND PERSONAL INFLUENCES
THAT SPAWNED TYPOLOGY

Typology itself developed its living flesh and bones out of the intense life experiences of its originators. Jung, Briggs, and Myers suffered the angst of misunderstanding and saw other people experiencing the same suffering. Jung recognized that psychological type affects us internally by determining our worldview, and hence our theory about relationships with everyone and everything that surrounds us externally.

Jung had seen Sigmund Freud and Alfred Adler articulating different psychological theories because of their type differences. He had also recognized that any pure type, when isolated from others due to a lack of what he called "the principle of imagination," led to "a wholly one-sided development."[4] For example, how many readers remember as little children sitting quietly and even fearfully in the back of the room while other more aggressive children sat in the front and sought the attention of the teacher? The introverted children in the back need to develop some of the assertiveness of the front-desk children, but in turn the more extraverted or outgoing children need to discover their quieter side. Otherwise, the former may never have an impact on society and the latter may quickly burn out in life.

Jung's own typology—especially his introversion—contributed to a difficult split from Freud, his psychological mentor. That split profoundly changed his life and shaped his subsequent work. One of Jung's responses was to go into a deeply isolated review and emotionally turbulent transformation of his life in and through the "principle of imagination," a transformation that gave him the raw material for his psychology. In his deep introversion he discovered the Self, the fundamental pattern of identity and the primal source of our energy, creativity, and all of the dimensions of psychological types. It was the Self, he later realized, that had guided him in his intense plumbing of the psyche's depth.

The Self (or Soul) is so powerful, so determined to become wholly conscious, that it continually haunts and prods us. We crave its depth and breadth. But the Self is not only personal, not only bounded by our skin, but transpersonal, a veritable matrix that contains us and all other people and even the whole creation as well, and tries to actualize various aspects of itself through us and other people according to our innate talents. We cannot fully realize the fullness of our personal types without plumbing this Self or Soul consciousness. Realizing this depth consciousness is a central concern of this book. Consistent with this centrality of the Self as the archetype of wholeness and health, if we live out wrong types, which Jung calls "a falsification of type," we betray the Self's health-giving potential, we betray our authentic energy and identity. As a result, we usually suffer, according to Jung, neuroses and often an "acute exhaustion."[5] Others, particularly Katherine Benziger, point to the possibility of even serious physical illnesses.[6]

Jung's other response in seeking to understand his split with Freud was to publish in 1921 a comprehensive book on human differences, which he called *Psychological Types*. These types are a way of understanding and categorizing common human differences. Jung first explored large attitudinal differences between private, inward people he called introverts (I) and outer public-minded people he called extraverts (E). Then he began to recognize more specific behavioral differences within each attitude, which he called the four functions. sensation (S) and intuition (N) are the perceiving functions; thinking (T) and feeling (F) the judging functions. Some people (sensing types) value knowledge as practical and others (intuitive types) value knowledge as original insights and possibilities emerging from the unconscious. Secondly, given this knowing or perceptive spectrum, some (thinking types) use knowledge in a logical, objective way and others (feeling types) in a subjective, relational way. Jung said of these four functions:

> These four together produce a kind of totality. Sensation establishes what is actually present, thinking enables us to recognize its meaning, feeling tells us its value, and intuition points to possibilities as to whence it came and whither it is going in a given situation. . . . the four functions are somewhat like the four points of the compass.[7]

For Jung, recognizing the four functions and two attitudes served a dual purpose. As a way of categorizing common observable differences, typology serves the practical purpose of orienting and understanding ourselves in relationship to other individuals, or as Jung puts it, "with respect to the immediate world."[8] Typology serves another larger purpose. Jung writes in the opening quotation that he values "the type theory for the objective reason that it provides a system of comparison and orientation which makes possible something that has long been lacking, a critical psychology."[9] A critical psychology is a comprehensive system of thought that establishes an objective basis for understanding other systems of thought. Jung, for example, holds "that every philosophy that is not just a history of philosophy depends on a personal psychological premise,"[10] based on type characteristics. This premise applies to all theoretical and practical systems. Closer to home, Jung developed his typology in order to reconcile the differences in other psychologies with his own, beginning with Sigmund Freud's and Alfred Adler's.[11]

Jung's work inspired Katharine Briggs to pursue the subject of typology and motivated her daughter, Isabel Briggs Myers, beginning in the forties, to develop the *MBTI* as a personality instrument and research tool. In subsequent decades, this instrument, used by millions and researched by many, spread Jung's theory of typology around the globe. In a 1950 letter, Jung assessed Myers' work on the survey and encouraged her, against considerable professional opposition she was experiencing, to continue her research, improve the Indicator, and to rethink his type theory.[12]

In 1962, Myers began to describe an additional aspect of Jung's typology: the complementary interplay between the four perceptive/judging function combinations. These couplings became the bases of Myers' sixteen types and her extensive research. Developing the larger implications of these couplings is one of my main objectives in writing this book. It is my hope that elaborating the theory of the function couplings, identifying their place in the body of Jung's theory and practice, and recording the many ways these combinations manifest in our lives will further the pioneering work of Jung, Briggs, and Myers, as well as satisfying each reader's hunger for self-awareness.

THE FUNCTION PAIRS AND THEIR PLACE
IN JUNG'S PSYCHOLOGY

The unifying theme of this book and its many variations is that the function couplings are the four archetypal modalities through which the Soul perceives and judges the "outer" and "inner" worlds. The couplings together constitute the four directions of the type mandala, or, borrowing Jung's language, the Compass of the Soul. As major interactive patterns or archetypes, they direct our daily lives both in our minds and hearts and in our social relationships. Understanding how our combinations of attitudes and functions contribute to our sense of meaning and purpose in life shapes our experience of society and feeds our Soul in all endeavors as we work, love, play, and pray by ourselves and with others.

Jung first discussed the couplings—sensation-thinking (ST), sensing-feeling (SF), intuiting-feeling (NF), and intuiting-thinking (NT)—in the last chapter of his *Psychological Types,* when he considered the relationship between the dominant and auxiliary function.[13] The dominant function is that cognitive preference by which we basically guide our individual lives, and the auxiliary is its helper and assistant. Jung gave birth to the function couplings and held that they were at the core of his entire type system, but then treated them like orphans. After discussing these coupled combinations in a provisional way, he never expanded on their significance, turning instead to other areas of his general psychology in which the concept of the archetype dominated. His entire type theory languished until the advent of the *MBTI,* as most Jungian analysts ignored typology and concentrated on archetypes.

The coupled relationship, realized in four perceptive/judging combinations, became the cornerstone both theoretically and practically in the creative work of Isabel Briggs Myers and Mary McCaulley, the founders of the Center for Applications of Psychological Type, who developed, researched, and lived the *MBTI.* Their work with Jung's types serves as the cornerstone of this book. This is apparent as we consider the many variations on our theme and the many ways these couplings emerge as a foursome in theoretical and practical systems, in many instances in our life journey, in waking moments or in dreams, and in the great human dramas that so enrich, deepen, and clarify our personal lives.

In order to bring the couplings back into the Jungian fold and thereby integrate typology as a whole within Jung's entire theory and practice, we need to consider the meaning of archetypes and then establish the archetypal nature of all the types, but particularly of the couplings. While Jung only peripherally discussed types as archetypes and never did so systemically, the archetypal nature of the individual functions and attitudes, the coupled functions, the type table, and the type compass is, upon examination, quite clear. This clarity is particularly evident as we see the function combinations emerge in so many variable yet consistently similar ways, so typical of archetypes.

Thus, to fully understand types we must understand archetypes. This is not easy for those who are skilled in typology but unacquainted with Jung's psychology. Types—that is, the four functions, two attitudes, the couplings, and sixteen *MBTI* formulations—understood as archetypes will also bother many Jungian analysts who have customarily kept these concepts separate. But to fully understand typology we must understand archetypes, although in most of his writings Jung kept the two ideas—type and archetype—distinct.

In layman's terms, an archetype is first of all an inherited, potential pattern in the unconscious, somewhat like a hidden organ in our body, such as the lungs. Jung calls this potential pattern the *archetype as such*, meaning that the very essence and ground of this psychic and spiritual organ is unknowable and unrepresentable as it subsists in the depth of the Self or Soul. We know it only by the effects that it produces, just as we know a crystal by its six-sided, axial appearance, or a snowflake by its six-pointed structure. We do not know the pattern of the archetype until it manifests in two particular ways: first, as archetypal or universally shared images and qualities, and, second, as personally and uniquely experienced memories of events, images, and emotions that we call complexes. The first, universal images, are found to be similar among all peoples and are unlearned experiences received directly from the unconscious; the second, complexes, are expressions of the archetype that are learned historical experiences unique to each individual. An example of the first would be the mother as a goddess image or as mother nature. The journey of life is another, for example as envisioned by Jung as a two-stage process in which typical events and felt experiences occur to all of us, such as birth, growth to adulthood, illness, success, failure, and death. Other common archetypal images, received from nature but experienced as metaphorical images in dreams and stories, are earth, mountain, valley, lake, ocean, tree, forest, wind, air, fire, and animals and plants, from the primordial ones to the tamed and cultivated. When we encounter these images, they are understood to be internalized experiences and not merely observed things in nature. Other archetypal images are such human behaviors and ideas as work, love, play, pray, communion, competition, warrior, lover, magician, and king/queen.

Second, the archetype as such also organizes our experiences over time into "units." Such units of experience, made up of remembered or forgotten configurations of images, events, and words centered in a specific emotion, are called complexes. An example of a complex is the many memories of events and emotions associated with our own mother. Another is the idiosyncratic experience of the life journey by each individual. As either an archetypal image or quality or as a complex, we usually experience the effects of the archetype as a mix of negative and positive qualities, depending on how we have been treated from inception. Our lifelong challenge, aided always by the Self as our God-image and creative companion, is to overcome the negatives and fully actualize the positives.

The Self, or Soul, as our common principle of identity as human beings and yet as unique in each of us, is an archetype as such. This hard-wired pattern in the unconscious is the principle of life that pervades every aspect of our person, the master playwright that organizes and directs our body, emotions, mind, societal relationships, and spirituality. Out of this universal, but also personal archetype (the Self), emerges countless other archetypes, beginning with the patterns of mother and father, and extending even to that of the entire human race. It can manifest archetypally as a Godlike figure or as a pattern of wholeness called a mandala, such as the compass of the Soul. It manifests in each of us as the individuality of consciousness, the ego, or, as Jung called it, the "ego complex."

In the first nine chapters of Jung's *Psychological Types,* he describes types primarily as symbolic, archetypal concepts that are revealed in many cultural stories, systems, and examples given by great scholars of life, and reserves classification of the types for his chapter 10. Jung often complained that his classification of types, rather than their larger symbolic archetypal concepts, seemed to attract most readers of his book. But is this the fault of only the reader? Or did Jung himself not make sufficiently clear the relationship between the archetypal nature of the functions and attitudes and their expression in persons with certain type preferences? Jung himself used the word "type" in two senses: sometimes he referred to people as certain "types," and at other times he writes about functions and attitudes. Mary McCaulley reports that as late as April 8, 1960, a year and a few months before he died, Jung wrote in this regard to a young man who was involved in an *MBTI* type research. After asserting that the classification of normal or pathological individuals "was not my original tendency," but rather "the discovery of conceptual means deriving from experience . . . by which I could express . . . the peculiarities of an individual psyche and the functional interplay of its elements," he then wrote, "Classification did not interest me very much . . . the classifying application," though legitimate as such, had become "the first and almost exclusive way, in which my book was understood." Jung continued:

> My book, as a matter of fact, was written to demonstrate the structural and functional aspects of certain typical elements of the psyche. That such a means of communication and explanation could be used also as a means of classification was an aspect which I was rather afraid of.

Later in the letter Jung admitted:

> your statistical line of research is perfectly legitimate, but it certainly does not coincide with the purpose of my book, which in my humble opinion aims at something more vital than classification. . . . I hold the conviction

that for the purpose of any classification one should start with fundamental and indubitable principles and not with empirical notions, i.e., with almost colloquial terms based on mere rules of thumb. My concepts [the types] are merely meant to serve as means of communication through colloquial language. As *principles* [my italics], however, I should say that they are in themselves immensely complicated structures which hardly can fulfill the rule of scientific principles. Much more important are the *contents* [my italics] conveyed by language than their terms.[14]

This "something more vital than classification," these "*principles* . . . that are in themselves immensely complicated structures," and "the *contents*" are expressions of the archetypal nature of the types embedded in the Soul. However, Jung contributed to the focus on "classifications" since he never adequately and systematically clarified their archetypal nature and, as already noted, tended in his writings to keep types and archetypes apart.

Yet, types, whether individual, couplings, or *MBTI* configurations, are both traits and images. The extraverted children in the classroom can be consistently described in trait terms, as socially comfortable, confident in speaking, and assertive in relationships. Extraversion also enters our consciousness as we describe such outward oriented children as archetypal images in imagination, behavior, and story. Both traits and images are embraced by the same invisible principle that Jung called the *archetype as such,* such that as "principle" it is a primal hidden energy in the unconscious and as "content" it is a potential source of wisdom.[15] The latent archetype is like an invisible but palpably present mother, holding both trait and image. The traits describe prosaic aspects of the archetypes that can be classified in measurable ways. The images are the larger immeasurably varied containers of the traits, which are experienced in dreams and visions, in myth and fairy tale, in great novels and sacred liturgies. The types as traits ground the archetypal images. The types as archetypal images enable the type traits to expand and grow in depth and breadth. Both traits and images—for example, the extraverted childrens' assertiveness and their actions—are distinct *inborn* aspects of the same hidden psychic entity, the archetype of extraversion.

The function pairs—couplings—as archetypal manifestations constitute one of the most immediately practical and universal aspects of Jung's psychology, in contrast to the individual functions, which, according to Jung, hardly ever occur "in such pure form in actual life."[16] People all over the world distinctively live both practically and theoretically in one or more of the perceptive/judging combinations: ST, SF, NF, and NT. Let us assume that the extraverted children in our previous example in the classroom also prefer sensing and thinking (ST). These children, consciously as well as unconsciously, embrace facts as sensing types and systematize those facts as thinking types. Moreover, as thinking types, they also filter out those facts that fit a thinking function's logical and name-giving qualities.

Like these children, we constantly use our own functions as perceptive/judging combinations. For, whether we realize it or not, all of us continually accumulate knowledge either through the outer senses (sensing) or inner imaginings (intuition), and decide what to do about that information either through logical processes (thinking) or relational evaluations (feeling). This innate and patterned functioning locates the functions as archetypes squarely in the prosaic consciousness of everyday life, as we have noted in the possibilities of our classroom children. The types as archetypal patterns are also portrayed in fairy tales, myths, drama, art, ritual, and literature.

Forty-one years after the publication of Jung's *Psychological Types* book, Isabel Briggs Myers first brought the four couplings to a public consciousness when she described them, in a deceptively simple way, as four "Effects of Combinations of Perception and Judgment."[17] In basic verbal and imaginative strokes, like those of a Matisse or a

Picasso, she painted primal designs of four universal archetypal structures, though she did not use the term archetype for them. In her 1980 book, *Gifts Differing,* she wrote that "Each of these combinations produces a different kind of personality, characterized by the *interests, values, needs, habits of mind and surface traits that naturally result* [italics, Myers] from the combination."[18] Note the term, "a different kind of personality." This is the language of archetypes, as innate predispositions to certain attitude and function preferences. In this same place, Myers discusses the difficulty people with different couplings have with one another in all the facets of life and thought.

Since archetypal themes predictably reappear in many variations, it is not surprising that these type couplings manifest in other people's writings. Staying with the sensation-thinking (ST) theme, Jung describes this personality as the practical thinker (see chapter 3). Myers conceives of it as the practical/analytical team (see chapter 5). An ensemble of typologists I call the Osmond group names this archetype the "structural" and the "map maker," and Robert Moore and Douglas Gillette describe its cultural manifestation as the warrior, as the disciplined doer (see chapter 5). In Ned Herrmann's Whole Brain Theory, ST characteristics are associated metaphorically with the left cortex of the brain; Herrmann calls this ensemble the logical organizer (see chapter 8). In human development, Walter Lowen relates the ST to the child's fine motor phase. In Erik Erikson's model of the eight ages of life, the virtues of the third age, initiative versus guilt, and the fourth age, industry versus inferiority, are typical ST features (see chapter 9). On the largest stage of all, our earlier and contemporary Western cultural history, Jung initially sees the societal consequences of the pathological side of the ST coupling when the ST characteristics emerged as a one-sided and rigidly organized societal tradition that feared and stifled imagination, dreaming, and any innovative insight (see chapter 3).

I recognize much of that same shadow warrior pervading many

facets of our American life today, in psychology itself, in religion, in politics, and in organizations of every kind. The overwhelming prominence of the ST qualities in society and the need to rebalance our societal typology can be viewed from the perspective of William Edwards Deming's popular quality control management, particularly with the "Understanding of Systems," one of the four disciplines of Deming's organizational philosophy. His overall system provides both a philosophy and practice that can help restore the balance of our ST culture (see chapter 12). But lest it sound as though there is nothing good in the sensing-thinking coupling, I will later show the important place of this ST coupling in both the creative process and in the stages of life.

I develop each of the other three couplings in the various sources and places mentioned above. All of the couplings have their special value both as strengths and weaknesses. Each coupling moves us from a natural inborn ground in a direction that first fulfills its own type potentialities, after which we need to explore the other archetypal couplings to achieve a fuller life. This is the rich typological feast that leads to individuation. Throughout this book we will consider the contributions of Jungian analysts as well as leading typologists, who have contributed to this communion that explicitly existed in Jung's mind when he wrote the *Psychological Types* book.

OTHER SUBSIDIARY INTENTIONS OF THIS BOOK
Besides pursuing the theme of the couplings and their variations, I address several additional themes in this book. Throughout I will reflect on the reasons for the separate development of the two world-wide Jungian communities, the analysts and the type practitioners. Such a fracture diminishes the effectiveness of Jung's psychology among the participants in both communities. Why in effect do we have such a divided Jungian family? These two communities' use and description of contrasting symbols clearly illustrate their differences.

Jung pictured the types as a circular or compasslike symbol, in harmony with his intuitive function's holistic perception (see figure 1.3, page 34). Although an intuitive like Jung, Myers took a more pragmatic sensing approach by presenting her extensive research in her famous Type Table and in statistics (chapters 1 and 7). Also by virtue of her lucidly simple prose, she brought Jung's original complex insights down to earth for the ordinary person. Bringing typology back into the whole of Jung's psychology could contribute to a renewed dialogue between the two communities.

Following Jung's depth psychological approach, we must, along with considering the everyday differences among people with the various functions and attitudes, also plumb these types as polarities that can only be deeply reconciled in the Self. Individual differences are played out in society in ordinary ways when persons recognize and honor types other than their own, even though they may consciously resist or struggle with differences. However, when we hit an impasse in societal situations, when differences among peoples seem to be irreconcilable, we must turn to our own comparable but nondominant attitudes and functions in the depth of the unconscious, still hidden and seeking verbal and experiential articulation. Recognizing our opposites can never occur by intellectual insight and willpower alone. We must seek, watch for, and feel bodily and emotionally those illusive opposites from the Self or Soul, as revealed in dreams, intelligible insights, deep meditations, and serendipitous events, that will make possible reconciliation and significant growth. This task, as most of us are learning or will learn, is most difficult and painful.

As to other kinds of dynamics, the type couplings also describe four moments in the life cycle (see chapters 6, 9, 10, and 12). The couplings can also picture phases in the creative process (see chapters 4, 6, and 8). Finally, typology also describes specific human cultures. In this regard, we will especially plumb the ESTJ makeup of our Western culture (see chapters 3 and 12).

I will also respectfully argue with differing reflections on the *MBTI* by analyst James Hillman (in chapters 3 and 6); analysts June Singer and Mary Loomis, who created the Singer-Loomis Indicator of Personality (SLIP), another type instrument (in chapter 10); David Keirsey and Marilyn Bates, typologists who developed four archetypes based on the ancient temperaments and the *MBTI* types (in chapter 10); and with the belief among some type practitioners, led by Ted and Noreen Guzie, that types and archetypes are totally distinct (in chapter 5). Finally, I will disagree with Jung about certain limits he places on the intuitive and feeling functions (chapter 4).

A BRIEF DESCRIPTION OF THE BOOK'S STRUCTURE AND CHAPTERS

The book is divided into three sections. Section 1, "Prelude to the Function Couplings," contains the first four chapters; section 2, "The Function Coupling Theme and Variations," contains chapter 5 through chapter 10; and section 3, "The Function Couplings in Society," concludes with chapter 11 and chapter 12.

In section 1, chapter 1, "The Birth of Typology in a Chaotic, Passionate Time," we begin to understand the difficult circumstances, contexts, hurdles, and personal struggles that attended the birth of typology itself in the mind of Jung, and the professional resistance that Briggs, Myers, and McCaulley encountered in developing and marketing the *MBTI*.

In chapter 2, "Jung, Typology, and Taoism," we consider Jung's passion for and understanding of Chinese Taoism, where he found many structures and dynamics that parallel his discoveries in typology, as well as the archetypal polar characteristics of the types as they emerge from the Self. Given this large perspective, we realize that Jung's entire typological psychology is just as archetypal as the ancient Taoist spiritual philosophy and psychology.

Chapter 3, "Jung's Historical Research and Intimations of the Types as Archetypes," outlines from Jung's 1921 book, *Psychological Types,* some of his prolific historical researches into cultural systems and earlier theories, such as in theology, poetry, education, and psychopathology, which provided Jung seminal intimations of the archetypal nature of human differences. Jung describes, for example, the polar larger-than-life qualities of two brothers in literature— Prometheus, the "forethinker," and Epimetheus, the "afterthinker"— as introverted and extraverted, respectively. Finally, we begin to see how Jung began to identify our Western culture as mainly extraverted, sensing, and thinking.

Chapter 4, "The Nuts and Bolts, the Fuel and Mobility of Typology," seeks to outline imaginatively the six elements of Jung's original type theory: introversion and extraversion, sensation and intuition, and thinking and feeling. This view of the two attitudes and the four functions strengthens for the reader the breadth and depth of the sixteen *MBTI* types and their grounding in the four archetypal couplings, to be developed in the next section.

In section 2, I consider the main theme of the book: the type couplings, their variations in different thinkers and systems, and their natural fit in Jung's entire psychology. Chapter 5, "The Type Compass' Four Archetypal Directions: The Osmond Group; Isabel Briggs Myers; Robert Moore and Douglas Gillette's Adult Archetypes," teaches the reader that when we identify and develop the application of an archetypal system, such as the function pairs and the type circle, we deepen our understanding of ourselves and others. We also experience a significant increase in intelligence, order, energy, creativity, and meaning that the Soul provides through the coupled functions for the enhancement of our personal lives in work and love and in the sciences and the arts.

Chapter 6, "Playing with the Function Couplings," gives many examples of dreams that reveal constructive and destructive mini-dramas of couplings that correspond to outer relational conflicts and inner unrealized potentials in waking life. Recognizing these mini-dramas helps readers discover the playful contributions of the couplings to understanding their dreams, their intimate relationships, the dimensions of their work, their creative processes, and their stages of life, and aids therapists in recognizing the typological biases and characteristics of many other therapeutic systems, all within the quadrants of the type compass. Above all, we will better understand the hidden influence of the Self or Soul as source and organizer of all the functions, attitudes, and couplings.

Chapter 7, "Strengthening Jung's Typology: The *Myers-Briggs Type Indicator*," outlines the important contributions in theory and research that Myers, Briggs, and McCaulley have made to Jung's type theory and specifically to our consciousness of the couplings. The reader will understand the basis for recognizing and describing the perceiving (P) and judging (J) spectrums, and the work of P and J in identifying the dominant function and producing the sixteen types. Most of all, the *MBTI* creators pursued an application of the couplings that was totally ignored by analysts: the congruence of the couplings to different areas of work.

Chapter 8, "Creative Breakthrough: Herrmann's Metaphorical Whole Brain Model," reviews Herrmann's theory, formulated independently of typology, of the metaphorical quadrants of the brain, which, in fact, coordinate with the four individual functions and the four couplings. Readers will discover in Herrmann's work (and in a subsequent related work by Katherine Benziger) that most people actualize any two adjacent quadrants (and therefore couplings) in the Compass. Finally, by recognizing the counterclockwise movement of the compass, readers can better appreciate why persons in the coupled quadrants differ in their awareness of creativity itself, time, decision-making processes, and even clothing styles. Benziger contributes a crucial added awareness of the many pathologies that arise from adapting a type in opposition to our innate preference.

Chapter 9, "Enlarging the Archetypes: Walter Lowen's Child Development and Erik Erikson's Ages of Life," reviews Lowen's *Dichotomies of the Mind,* a difficult yet rewarding attempt to show the developmental phases of the child, based on the four couplings and extended to all sixteen *MBTI* types. Lowen's model makes possible a productive connection between the four couplings and Erik Erikson's eight ages of life. In this chapter we see how the most critical moments in one's life cycle, including the midlife crisis, are usually experienced as a plunge into the NF's frightening, dark, yet fruitful waters. This dynamic, supported by Erikson's adolescent fifth age and intimacy's sixth age of life (which are actually archetypal stages of development), helps readers understand the surprising challenges, sudden changes, and hopeful outcomes experienced in such a fall.

Chapter 10, "Freezing and Unfreezing the Compass' Dynamics: The Five Factor Model, the Keirsey Bates Model, and the Singer-Loomis Model," reviews three interesting challenges to the Jung/*MBTI* theory and practice. First, I consider the response of type researchers to the Five Factor Model in academia; then I show how the Keirsey Bates model violates the type Compass and the couplings' integrity and dynamics, and how, by rejecting the Compass, the Singer-Loomis Inventory of Personality (SLIP) also obliterates the couplings.

The third part of the book, "The Function Couplings in Society," addresses in typological terms some important issues in societal life. Chapter 11, "Jung's Divided Family: Analysts and Typologists," considers many historical and personal factors that slowly separated analysts and typologists. Readers can better understand how such historical factors and attitudes, acting cumulatively over time in these two communities, also can effect comparable collective, intimate, and personal splits in their own lives.

Chapter 12, "Our ESTJ Pathology and the Healing Possibilities of William Edwards Deming's System of Management," initially considers the mean-spirited attitude that any one-sided use of any type preference, in this case, the ESTJ viewpoint, can bring to our national life. I review how American society's bias toward the ESTJ negatively affects five populations: ordinary American families in general; the poor and immigrants on welfare; criminals and the justice system; doctors and patients in health care; and employers and workers in downsizing industries. In this context we review the fertile work of William Edwards Deming, who was instrumental in re-creating Japan's postwar industrial economy as well as invigorating some American companies when they adopted the four disciplines of Deming's organizational system. Readers will also see how Deming's personal typological makeup contributes to the development and understanding of his four disciplines and how these disciplines are organizational extensions of the four couplings.

Overall, this book is an attempt to give a larger frame to typology within our personal lives and within the psychology of both Jung and the *MBTI* around the theme of the function couplings. I have incorporated the *MBTI*, the varied and in-depth dimensions of Jung's psychology, competing theories within typology, and many corresponding systems that deepen and widen the meaning of typology. For readers just beginning in the field of typology, I recommend you first read chapters 1, 2, 4, 5, 6, 7, 8, 11, and 12. In my view, chapters 3, 9, and 10 and chapter 4's discussion of intuition and feeling are the most theoretical, and so can be more readily understood if read last. A general index of attitudes, functions, couplings, the sixteen *MBTI* preferences, and other key Jungian terms is provided to assist the reader.

The Jung/*MBTI* type theory turns out to be more complex than meets the eye, but understanding the many uses of the types, their archetypal nature, their coupling structures, and the integration of typology into Jung's overall psychology has rich rewards for both individuals and society. I hope the readers will find that their personal difficulties in understanding and living their typology resonate with the struggles and fruitful outcomes that the creators experienced in birthing this remarkable psychology.

Notes

1. Carl G. Jung, *The Collected Works of C. G. Jung* (hereafter cited as CW), vol. 6, *Psychological Types,* English edition, translated by H. G. Baynes (1923; rpt., Princeton NJ: Princeton University Press, 1971), paras. 958–59.

2. Angelo Spoto, *Jung's Typology in Perspective,* revised edition (Wilmette IL: Chiron Publications, 1995), pp. 17–20.

3. John O'Donohue, *Anam Cara: A Book of Celtic Wisdom* (New York: Cliff Street Books, 1997), pp. xv–xvi.

4. Jung, *CW,* vol. 6, *Psychological Types,* para. 91.

5. Ibid., paras. 560–61.

6. Katherine Benziger, *Falsification of Type: Its Jungian and Physiological Foundations and Mental, Emotional, and Physiological Costs* (Rockwall TX: KBA Publishing, 1995). Her new version of her 1989 book, *The Art of Using Your Whole Brain,* will contain further discussions of this subject: *Thriving in Mind: The Art and Science of Using Your Whole Brain* (Rockwall TX: KBA Publishing, chapter 8. Benziger will be discussed further in chapter 8.

7. Jung, *CW,* vol. 6, *Psychological Types,* para. 958.

8. Ibid.

9. Ibid., para. 959.

10. Ibid., para. 846.

11. Ibid. Jung spoke in September 1913 at the Psychoanalytical Congress in Munich on "A Contribution to the Study of Psychological Types." There he discussed many differences between Sigmund Freud's and Alfred Adler's psychological theories, and ended with these words: "The difficult task of creating a psychology which will be equally fair to both types must be reserved for the future" (para. 882).

12. Frances W. Saunders, *Katharine and Isabel: Mother's Light, Daughter's Journey* (Palo Alto CA: Consulting Psychologists Press, 1991), p. 121.

13. Jung, *CW*, vol. 6, *Psychological Types,* paras. 666–67. I will develop the characteristics and archetypal qualities of the couplings in the part of chapter 3 entitled "Intimations of the Types as Archetypes," and I will expand on the archetypal nature of the couplings in the entire second section of this book. I designate chapter 10 as the last chapter of Jung's book because chapter 11, "Definitions," while including some types, marked the beginning of his entire subsequent psychology. It was followed only by a short epilogue.

14. Mary H. McCaulley, "Why Did C. G. Jung Create his Typology?" *Bulletin of Psychological Type* 21, no. 5 (Late Summer 1998): p. 20. The letter also appears in the *C. G. Jung Letters,* vol. 2, 1951–61 (Princeton NJ: Princeton University Press, 1975), pp. 550–52. The letter was in response to a man named Erich A. von Fange, the dean of students at Concordia College, Edmonton, Alberta, Canada, who, according to the editors, "was writing a thesis on the statistical evaluation of types and asked for Jung's comments."

15. Jung, "On the Nature of the Psyche," *CW*, vol. 8, *The Structure and Dynamics of the Psyche* (Princeton NJ: Princeton University Press, 1960), para. 417. Jung writes: "The archetypal representations (images and ideas [read also traits] mediated to us by the unconscious should not be confused with the archetype as such. They are varied structures which all point back to one essentially 'irrepresentable basic form. . . . The archetype as such is a psychoid factor [a transcendent but real dimension of psyche that is also bodily and instinctual] that belongs, as it were, to the invisible, ultra-violet end of the psychic spectrum. It does not appear, in itself, to be capable of reaching consciousness."

16. Jung, *CW*, vol. 6, *Psychological Types,* para. 666.

17. Isabel Briggs Myers, *Introduction to Type: A Description of the Theory and Applications of the Myers-Briggs Type Indicator* (Palo Alto CA: Consulting Psychologists Press, 1962), p. 28.

18. Myers, Isabel Briggs, with Peter B. Myers, *Gifts Differing: Understanding Personality Type* (Palo Alto: Consulting Psychologists Press, 1980), p. 4.

SECTION 1

PRELUDE

TO THE FUNCTION COUPLINGS

CHAPTER 1

The Birth of Typology in a Chaotic, Passionate Time

Freud's view is essentially extraverted, Adler's introverted. The extraverted theory holds good for the extraverted type, the introverted theory for the introverted type. Since a pure type is a product of a wholly one-sided development, it is also necessarily unbalanced. . . . Both theories reject the principle of imagination.[1]

Carl Jung

I dream that long after I am gone, my work will go on helping people.[2]

Isabel Briggs Myers

HE INTENSE STRUGGLES and sufferings that accompanied the developers of typology, Jung, Briggs, and Myers, in their creative efforts is the subject of this chapter. Their success in living their own personality type while working to create the Jung and *Myers-Briggs Type Indicator®* (*MBTI®*) type theories and practices can be an inspiration for each of us. I will also look at my own introduction to typology in a time of crisis, the knowledge of which changed my life and eventually led to the writing of this book.

JUNG'S STRUGGLE WITH FREUD AS CONTEXT FOR HIS DISCOVERY OF TYPES

In the first decade of this century, Carl Jung and Sigmund Freud cooperated in developing the revolutionary psychology called "psychoanalysis."

They also cooperated in founding the International Psychoanalytic Association, where they shared their new exciting theories about the nature and mystery of the human Soul. Jung's quiet words, quoted above, point to the crucial idea we have been exploring: namely, that a vibrant archetype of order, the type Compass as the Soul's fourfold archetypal way, is revealed daily in all of us in our dialogues and conflicts.

Jung's theory of typology was the final blow that permanently severed relationships between himself and Freud. Though Jung for a time had been Freud's designated heir, he was quite different from Freud. In heritage, Freud was born into a Jewish family whose ancestors had suffered ethnic persecution in Christian Austria. Jung was the son of a Swiss Protestant minister, who himself stood in a lineage of ministers. Freud saw religion as a vestige from the past, whereas Jung valued religion as an essential function of the Soul. Freud's understanding and use of mythology was limited to the Oedipus and Narcissus stories from Greece; Jung sought out and understood tales from many lands. Freud demanded a rigid obedience to his theories, while Jung passionately followed his own vision of a transpersonal inner authority. However, the most important difference between them may have been in their psychological types, which, as Jung points out in the above quote, account for entire theoretical systems and world-views. Of the two, Jung's mental orientation was inward (in type terms, introverted) and fiercely individualistic, qualities valued in his Swiss heritage. His psychological theory and practices are oriented to inner or psychic reality. Freud's attitude, valued by the outgoing Viennese as well as his fraternal associates, was more socially oriented (extraverted), and so is his theory of sexuality.

The differences between them finally resulted in a split, possibly brought to a head because of Jung's theory about human differences. In the Fourth International Association Congress, held in Munich in September 1913, where these two pioneers met for the last time but never spoke, Jung, the president of the association, lectured on "A Contribution to the Study of Psychological Types." In his talk, he focused on the difference between extraversion and introversion. He first compared hysteria and schizophrenia, holding that the former is "centrifugal," or extraverted, and the latter, "centripetal," or introverted. He ended the talk by comparing the psychological theories of Freud and Alfred Adler, ascribing their differences to personality type, Freud being extraverted and Adler introverted. He writes:

> While the dominant note in Freudian psychology is a centrifugal tendency, a striving for pleasure in the object, in Adler's it is a centripetal striving for the supremacy of the subject, who wants to be "on top," to safeguard his power, to defend himself against the over-whelming forces of existence."[3]

He concludes with a terse but prophetic sentence: "The difficult task of creating a psychology which will be equally fair to both types must be reserved for the future."[4]

Later, Jung acknowledged in his autobiography that the book "sprang originally from my need to define the ways in which my outlook differed from Freud's and Adler's."[5] This sentence absurdly understates the fire and ice, the warmth and cold, the enlightened sharing and the spiteful accusations that characterized the relationship between Freud and Jung.

The split pushed Freud and his group to consolidate their position in the association and eventually control it under Freud's watchful eye. As reported by John Kerr in A Most Dangerous Method, Freud even set up a "secret committee" that scrutinized any of its members' deviant behavior.[6] Meanwhile, Jung plunged into a depressed, anxious, yet formative period that lasted from 1912 to 1916, which has been aptly called a "creative illness," but can also rightfully be viewed as a midlife crisis. During this time, Jung discovered his native typology as an introverted intuitive; in the past he had considered himself an introverted thinking type, evidence that he himself had been caught in a typological complex.

In terms of an archetypal/complex theory of the psyche, Jung had been born innately intuitive. However, for whatever reason, probably because our Western culture is so thinking oriented and the Swiss so dominated by sensation and thinking, Jung had erroneously adopted thinking as his dominant type. This meant that his ego complex was caught in a type complex not native to him, while his true intuitive type sat in a secondary and despised place in his intuitive thinking (NT) coupling and haunted him as a semi-unconscious complex, representing not his inferior orientation, but his natural possibilities. During this time, he finally followed his intuitive capacities and let himself fall into the frightening imagery and emotions of his psychic depth.[7] When he began to emerge from this inner, isolated journey, he wrote in 1916 "The Ego and the Unconscious," the first thoroughly innovative theoretical essay that began to describe his own theory.[8]

Later in the same decade, he began studying alchemy and Taoism, both of which he intuitively understood as philosophical and spiritual explorations. Breaking the code of alchemy helped him conclude, "the unconscious is a process, and the psyche is transformed or developed by the relationship of the ego to the contents of the unconscious." He notes that this idea was reflected also in "various religious systems and their changing symbols." Thereby, he concludes, "I arrived at the central concept of my psychology: *the process of individuation*," his name for life as the dynamic journey of self-fulfillment in which typology plays a significant role.[9] Typology must be understood as part of this dynamic process of the Soul in the context of Jung's theory of psychic energy. Jung wrote his types at a time when he was becoming aware of all kinds of psychic opposites within the flow of energy. He considered this awareness the culmination of his book *The Psychology of the Unconscious*. He wrote in this regard: "With this duality in the cosmic principle, the book ends. It leads up to the pair of opposites, that is, to the beginning of the *Types*."[10] He further strengthened this understanding of typology when he wrote "We are part of the general energic process, and it is psychology looked at with this fact in mind that I have tried to present in the *Types*."[11]

Throughout the inner journey in his own psychic depths, freighted with frightening experiences and complex emotions, Jung worked on his psychological theory. Some eight years after his break with Freud, Jung published *Psychologische Typen*, a major contribution to the "difficult task" he had identified in his 1913 address to the Fourth International Association Congress. One of Jung's assistants, H. G. Baynes, translated *Psychologische Typen* into English, publishing it in 1923, with the subtitle "The Psychology of Individuation," which was removed in later editions. Decoupling typology from individuation—one of Jung's most important concepts—attests to the diminished energy that Jung and most of his followers have given to typology since the 1920s. Given the creation of typology in the context of Jung's most formative year in which he formulated the essentials of his psychology, I am puzzled as to why subsequently he and analysts generally placed typology at the periphery of his overall system.

In the midst of this turbulent and creative period, a young woman, Sabina Spielrein, appeared, first as a client and medical student and later as a psychoanalytic associate of both Freud and Jung, and, finally (according to some sources) as Jung's lover. Sabina's presence in this drama gives even more emphasis to the many currents of emotion and thought in which Jung birthed typology. Although her fascinating story as told in John Kerr's exciting book, *A Most Dangerous Method*, is beyond the purvey of this book,[12] we can note from the perspective of today that her feminine presence in the midst of the struggle between Freud and Jung in the first decade of the twentieth century might be an important clue for understanding the importance of typology for our time. It is the feminine in us that is capable of discerning subtle differences in persons so as to maximize cooperation, a necessary requisite for our social survival as we live in this twenty-first century. Hence it is fitting that three women, Briggs and Myers and later Mary McCaulley, took up and further developed Jung's original work on types.

In the very last extant letter sent by Jung to Spielrein on October 7, 1919, Jung refers to and even draws several diagrams representing type differences in persons. One compares himself, Freud, and Bleuler, Jung's Swiss mentor, and another compares Goethe, Kant, Schopenhauer, and Schiller. Kerr continues:

> Then there follows without explanation a mysterious third diagram composed of an outer circle labeled with the symbol of masculinity and an inner circle labeled with the feminine symbol. Two x's mark the top and bottom of the inner circle: the top x is labeled "Spielrein consc." while the bottom half of the diagram as a whole is labeled "uncs." The diagram has a vertical and horizontal line which cross at the middle, seemingly to indicate that Jung's theory of types is implicated here too. Jung's only comment is that perhaps Spielrein was once more extraverted than she is now.[13]

We do not understand the content of Sabina's "consc.," a common shorthand for consciousness, except to note that Jung is implying she was becoming more introverted than extraverted at this point in her life. However, beyond their issues, this diagram, with its circle and its horizontal and vertical lines, lays out the essentials of typology's quadrated mandala or psychological Compass, a primal circle of energies and structures. Jung's enigmatic commentary highlights the overall tenor of this book: namely, that typology is not just a simple language describing different human traits. Rather, its deep structures and dynamics are an ongoing, subtly changing force in every person's life. Typology affects the dark as well as the light, the spiritual and the prosaic, the inner and the outer, the chaotic and the ordered, the feminine and the masculine aspects of the Soul. Knowing typology helps us meet our pragmatic needs as well as enhancing our Soulfulness.

Though Jung never continued his research in this typology, he occasionally mentioned it and how practitioners and the public understood it. He never failed to point out that his intention was never to "classify human beings into categories" but to shed light on interpersonal differences as well as differences in psychological theories based on the theorists' types. From the beginning, both in experience and theory, Jung never intended that typology be considered purely a conscious psychology, as he sometimes described it, but one that is present in every dimension of Soul.

Jung gives further context to typology in his 1925 seminar, the first he gave to a fast developing group of followers after his long years of inner search. In that seminar, he sketched diagrams of the basic type mandala and of the type mandala at the center of two cones, one representing the past, the other, the future.[14] He suggests that the past attracts one type and the future another type. Obviously he was concerned that his typology not be seen just as a conscious psychology, for then he writes, "So far, these pictures have disregarded the unconscious." To correct this, he pictured a dominant thinking type, with the two auxiliaries as "half conscious and half unconscious, and in whom feeling is in the unconscious."[15] Here we begin to see to what extent Jung viewed the types as dynamic interrelated vectors in the psyche's Compass. (See figure 1.1, p. 34.)

Jung added that feeling, as the inferior function in a person such as the diagram describes, is available to consciousness in a minimal way, but that usually such a person's "feeling is not under his control, but eruptive in character, so that normally it is not in the picture at all, and then all of a sudden it quite possesses him."[16] This autonomy of the inferior function clearly shows that its emergence has all the

The Conscious and Unconscious Aspects of the Type Mandala
in a Dominant Thinking Type According to Jung

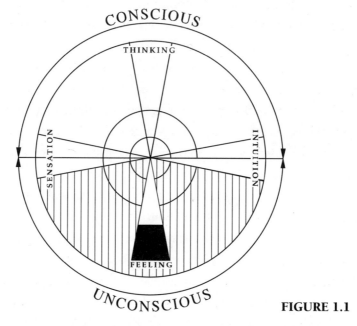

FIGURE 1.1

From: C. G. Jung's Analytical Psychology: Seminar Notes 1925, *p. 128*

characteristics of a complex, which Jung called an "autonomous complex," with all of its fearful, potentially destructive—as well as creative—possibilities.

Jung assumes that our psychological type is both inherited and innately rooted in archetypes; hence we must pay attention to an inner knowing and wisdom from the unconscious if we are to individuate, that is, actualize our inborn potential. If we ignore the Soul's purposeful dynamism and function by embracing another type and not our native one, we inwardly constellate a negative complex that can be destructive to both mind and body, to inner relations as well as outer social relationships, as Jung himself learned. He called this development, as noted in the introduction, a "falsification of type." Because of early wounds, many of us spend too much time copying someone else's lifestyle or personality. Instead, we are called to live our own unique identity, and we can do that only by living our native type. The instruments that have been created to better understand our types have significantly advanced the possibility of our living authentically.

Since the publication of the English translation of *Psychological Types* in 1923, several people have developed survey methods to determine an individual's typology based on Jung's work: the Grey Wheelwright or Jungian Typology Survey (JTS), the Singer Loomis Inventory of Personality (SLIP), and the more widely used *Myers-Briggs Type Indicator* instrument.[17] Although each deserves special attention, I will consider primarily the *MBTI*, because millions of people have taken it; because it has proven to be a consistent and reliable indicator; because it extends Jung's theory of types; and because its construction assumes the bipolar and complementary relationship between types. In addition, the *MBTI*'s extensive research program, now including over one million scored type surveys, is based on the four coupled functions, in contrast to the JTS and SLIP, which, respectively, ignore and eliminate the four couplings. Also, its extensive data on the consistent relationship of the couplings to certain vocational areas strongly support the archetypal nature of typology. Moreover, the *MBTI* research informs and supports a sound theory for understanding our dominant culture and its typological counterculture. Finally, those who take the *MBTI* need to understand its connections with Jung's psychology, which teaches that a typological dynamic enters into the deepest threads of the Soul's intricate and mysterious weavings.

The *MBTI* is the fruit of a mother-daughter collaboration. Katharine Cook Briggs and Isabel Briggs Myers took Jung's basic ideas and developed an instrument used around the world. Without them, Jung's typology might well have remained a brilliant but obscure and neglected appendage to Jung's psychology. In their story, we can follow the evolution of typology beyond Jung's pioneering work.

THE TRIALS AND SUCCESSES OF BRIGGS AND MYERS

Katharine Cook Briggs, the original inspirer of the *MBTI* and a student of Jung's psychology even before he wrote *Psychological Types,* was passionately interested in human differences. By persistently discussing this subject of types, Briggs eventually awakened the same intense passion in her brilliant daughter, Isabel Briggs Myers.[18] Myers was strongly shaped and influenced not only by her very intelligent mother, but also by her equally brilliant and successful father, who eventually became the head of the National Bureau of Standards in Washington, D.C. Her relationship with her husband, Clarence Myers, provided the solid ground for the many challenges she had to face and master in the pursuit of her life mission, the Indicator.

Briggs was a prolific writer. Although a tough disciplinarian and a strongly opinionated person, she was also far ahead of her time in seeking the highest possible education for herself, her daughter, and all other women in her extended family. Briggs, an introverted, intuitive, feeling, and judging (INFJ) type, was first of all attracted to human differences, because she was interested in understanding the personalities of famous people in biographies and utilizing different characters in her fiction.[19]

When Briggs read the English translation of *Psychological Types* in 1923, she "allegedly responded, 'This is IT.'" She wrote Jung, telling him that his chapter, "The Type Problem in Biography," was her favorite. She subsequently wrote him five more times, reportedly about a medical case history of a person Katharine knew and presumably counseled.[20] Jung replied twice. In 1937, when Jung was in the United States to give the Terry Lectures at Yale, Katharine visited Jung, bringing her daughter, Isabel, as a reluctant companion.

Isabel Briggs Myers had become a phenomenal success as a teenage and young adult author of articles and poems, easily overshadowing her mother. She attended Swarthmore College, earned top honors, and was elected to Phi Beta Kappa. At age thirty-one, she combined caring for her two babies with writing a mystery novel, *Murder Yet to Come*, which became a best-seller in 1930 and brought her considerable fame.[21] However, Isabel experienced a lot of grief in the course of both her marital and professional lives. Early in her marriage, she lost two children: a stillborn son and a premature girl who died in her arms. Two healthy children were finally born to her and Clarence, Peter and Ann, both of whom as adults married and then divorced. Four years after Katharine died in 1968, Ann, newly in love, died suddenly.

However, in the years of their collaboration, these two remarkable women, Briggs and Myers, expanded Jung's type theory and developed their now famous instrument, the *MBTI*. In 1942, Isabel began to construct the first survey and completed it in the next year; other surveys followed over the years. Biographer Frances Saunders succinctly summarizes the key developments in their collaboration after 1943:

> Over a period of three decades, the project would progress from Isabel's dining room table, to a cottage industry, to the auspices of Educational Testing Service, to Consulting Psychologists Press, its current publisher. In due course, the Indicator would become internationally known and would be translated into sixteen different languages.[22]

As mother and daughter worked over those years, they never forgot from whom they received their inspiration for, as well as the substance of, typology. Before traveling to Europe in 1950, Myers wrote Jung asking to see him, and also sent him a three-page description of the "'Briggs-Myers Type Indicator,' for which the 'psychological insight has been my mother's, the labor and validation of proof has been mine.'"[23] Jung responded on July 1, indicating that he had been ill and could not see her. However, he graciously commented on the

MBTI, stating in conclusion "that for any future development of the Type-Theory your Type Indicator will prove to be of great help."[24]

Jung's reply inspired and supported Myers in the many trials she would later endure. In academic and professional circles she faced resistance to Jung's ideas, to her lack of credentials, and to her supposed lack of competence. However, because of her stubborn persistence and even evangelical spirit, as well as the help of her father as the director of the National Bureau of Standards, Myers successfully undertook substantial research in medical schools and high schools. In 1957 her work finally attracted the Indicator's first publisher, Educational Testing Services, which opened more avenues for research and feedback. However, professionals at ETS constantly sparred with Myers over procedures and suppositions. Probably the best example of the professional criticism was voiced by John Ross, an Australian Psychometric Fellow, who appraised the Indicator, suggested more research and the writing of a manual, then added:

> A veil of suspicion hangs about it. It had an unorthodox origin, it is wedded to a somewhat unfashionable theory [Jung's], and the enthusiasm it has aroused in some people has provoked sterner opposition in others.

Isabel, angered by another ETS critic, accused him of cutting "off the dog's tail behind the ears." She then added, "The dog might just turn out to be a champion."[25] She continued, however, to write and rewrite the text of the manual. Junuis A. Davis, her supervising clinical psychologist at ETS, wrote of her:

> Mrs. Myers has dedicated her life and that of her family to the concept of type; she believes it to be a profound and extremely important social discovery. . . . The woman has worked day and night for . . . [many] years with this goal overriding all other personal goals; she is a kind of modern Joan of Arc, and her cause is as sacred; she simply doesn't anticipate being trapped and bound at the stake.[26]

When interviewed in 1987, Davis said that "she had such utter faith in [the Indicator] and was so profoundly convinced of its integrity that to her it was 'almost god-like in its power.'" In more secular terms, Davis acknowledged that "her work has been timely, appropriate, sound and responsible."[27] David Saunders of ETS and husband of the author of *Katharine and Isabel* held that Isabel "had an intuitive grasp of statistics that psychology hasn't caught up with yet."[28]

While Isabel acknowledged that ETS had allowed her to add to her research, use more sophisticated procedures, receive valuable feedback and write a manual, she complained of its poor management and its failure to push the instrument. Her missionary zeal was such that some of the men on staff, tainted with antifeminism according to Frances Saunders, called her "that horrible woman" and "the little old lady in tennis shoes."[29] When one considers the ESTJ (extraverted, sensing, thinking, and judging) mental environment at ETS, and Myers' INFP (introverted, intuitive, feeling, and perceiving) type, we can better understand that these typological opposites had to conflict. Meanwhile, before ending her contract with ETS in 1975, "the little old lady" had suffered the death of her father, her mother, and her daughter, and had experienced recurring cancer.

A final crucial organizational development was Myers' professional association, beginning in 1969, with Mary McCaulley, a clinical psychologist who set the *MBTI* on a more solid course. McCaulley aided Myers in systematizing her research, computerizing her data, applying for grants, involving faculty and graduate students at the University of Florida (an affiliation that spawned many theses and dissertations), setting up a nonprofit corporation in Gainesville, Florida, the Typology Laboratory (which eventually became the Center for Applications of Psychological Type), and, finally, organizing the first national *MBTI* conference in Gainesville in 1975.

In the 1970s, Myers, now in a firm new alliance with McCaulley, heard that a new ETS vice president saw her Indicator as "a very small fly on the wall."[30] When McCaulley heard "quite by accident" that ETS intended to discontinue the *MBTI*, Isabel agreed that Mary should find another publisher. In 1975, Mary contacted Consulting Psychologists Press (CPP), a promising new publishing company in Palo Alto, California. With McCaulley and Myers doing research in Florida and New England respectively and CPP publishing and promoting the *MBTI* from California, the instrument quickly flourished.

In 1977, Isabel was again found to have cancer, this time of the liver. With her son, Peter, she urgently began to rework a neglected manuscript that described in a nontechnical way the Jung/Myers theory of types. They completed the book, *Gifts Differing*, a short time before Isabel died in 1980—fifty-nine years after *Psychological Types*. Jung would have recognized the book as a gentle and wise interpretation of his ideas as well as the only overall creative addition to his type theory up to that time. Isabel wrote a friend that *Gifts Differing*, only half the size of her two mystery novels, was her "pride and joy" and her "contribution to the future."[31] The *MBTI* Conference III, held in October 1979 in Philadelphia, honored Isabel for her monumental work. When asked about her dream for the future, she said, "I dream that long after I am gone, my work will go on helping people."[32]

INTEGRATING TYPE THEORY

The history of the development of typology among *MBTI* practitioners would not be complete without at least briefly recognizing three additional persons whose work has contributed to reintegrating typology into Jung's typology in substantive ways: Henry Thompson, Naomi Quenk, and Angelo Spoto.

Henry Thompson's small book, *Jung's Function-Attitudes Explained*,[33] contains a rich assortment of quotes from Jung on all of the eight individual types. Thompson's fertile mind views the eight attitude-function combinations in innovative language, such as the "sensuosity" of the extraverted sensing type and the "surreal" landscape of introverted sensing.

In her crucial book, *Besides Ourselves,* Naomi Quenk[34] provides a well-rounded picture of the many facets of Jung's dynamic psychology, but focuses on the inferior function, the most undeveloped part of our personal Compass. Noting the relatively scattered approach which Jung took to the inferior function's nature, she considers the conditions that lead to its eruption in each of the eight types, its role in self-regulation, and its importance in the midlife crisis.

Angelo Spoto's *Jung's Typology in Perspective*[35] conceptualizes the types as archetypes and presents a wealth of theoretical and practical support for locating typology in the body of Jung's theory and practice. His book, above all others, most immediately complements what I am doing here. Robert Johnson's foreword to the book notes that in this work "we have an excellent perspective on the place of typology within Jung's broader analytical work, clearly written for those interested in deepening their use of typology."[36]

None of these writers, however, develop the couplings as archetypes, describe their recurring appearances in many facets of human life, integrate them into Jung's system, analyze ideas in typology competing with them, or discuss their contributions to our personal lives. I hope this book's discussion of the four couplings will do so.

In concluding this historical chapter, it is only fair to share with the reader how I became fascinated with Jung's and others' ideas on psychological types, which have been of such great importance in the course of my life.

MY ROMANCE WITH TYPOLOGY

While the originators of typology created a theory in the context of the emotional ups and downs of their lives, and somewhat in response to what they experienced, countless beneficiaries of their work have also discovered and studied typology in similar stormy circumstances. I cut my Jungian baby teeth on typology at a time of great personal pain and confusion that launched me on my individuation process, my journey with the Soul.

I began Jungian analysis in the 1950s because of depression and anxiety. At the time I was studying to be a priest in the Dominican Order at St. Albert's College in Oakland, California. I left the monastery for two weeks' rest with medication. That did nothing to alleviate my spiritual anguish. When I returned, I began working with Father Victor White, an analyst from England and the first significant theologian who saw in Jung's psychology the possibility of a radical transformation of Christianity. White never spoke of his friendship and differences with Jung. It was only when I read the *C. G. Jung Letters*,[37] published in the 1970s, and later Ann Lammer's *In God's Shadow: The Collaboration of Victor White and C. G. Jung*[38] that I was able to understand what had happened between them. I have since speculated that part of their problem might have been that they were too similar, sharing the same difficulties with fathers, similar introverted, intuitive, thinking, and judging preferences, and, therefore, common shadow problems.

The first dream a client tells an analyst is called a presenting dream. It is usually of great importance in describing one's suffering and indicating a course of recovery and growth. In my presenting dream:

> I enter the office of the House of Studies and open a file drawer. I am supposedly beginning to do some work for a particular brother seminarian. Suddenly a series of valentines pop up, one of which especially fascinates me. It is a large red heart, with many shades and hues in it. As I am looking, this seminarian comes in with some papers under his arms. He's angry because I am not filing away his papers.

White asked me to tell him about this student brother. This particular student was a scholar who appeared extraverted, confident, cocky, highly intelligent, devoid of feeling, and seemingly so out of touch with his body that we jokingly wondered whether he ever went to the bathroom. White immediately began to speak of Jung's "typology," a word that I had never heard of before. He said that my emotional difficulties resulted from trying to be an extraverted, sensate, thinking man, represented by this student. Instead, he continued, the heart image in the dream (and some knowledge of my early life) told him that I was the opposite to this person, that my nature was much more introverted, intuitive, and feeling. Hence, as indicated by the type persona of this student as symbolically depicted in the dream, I was trying to be what I was not. I, like Jung, had been caught in powerful complexes. Thus, from the beginning of my Jungian work, I learned of the centrality and demanding dynamics of types and their imaginal representations in dreams.

Further, the dream held cultural implications, since my initial childhood difficulties were not so much with my parents as with being an Italian child in an Anglo environment. I could not speak English when I began my first year of grammar school. That experience was so traumatic that I had several childhood illnesses and became a first-year dropout. When I returned for my next year of school, I became a determined young scholar, and, eventually, a driven student and athlete.

After my presenting dream, I began to face my childhood cultural problem through other dreams and memories. The heart's message expanded to symbolize the warmer, softer Mediterranean culture in which I had been raised in our Italian neighborhood, as opposed to the more heady and intellectual cultures typical of the United States. Thus, from the beginning of my analysis, my understanding of Jung's typology was linked to both personal and larger cultural issues of national orientation: the Italian culture tends to be extraverted feeling in contrast to, let us say, the English tendency toward introverted thinking or the American to extraverted thinking. I began to experience Jung's typology not just as an isolated aspect of individual psychology but as a participant in every pattern and movement of psyche in both personal development and cultural contexts. The creative travail that led Jung, Briggs, and Myers to develop the psychology of types in the larger transforming containers of psyche and societal life had helped release me from my own painful entrapments.

The drama that gave shape, substance, and vitality to the original theory and practice of typology and the consciousness-raising impact it made on my life has recurred in practically every client with whom I have worked, as well as in the members of typology classes I have taught. In various degrees, it has touched the lives of literally millions who have taken any of the type surveys. It is this personal impact which makes typology so important.

Jung tells us repeatedly, both implicitly and explicitly, that by virtue of type differences, any personal or theoretical stance is necessarily relative. This does not mean that our views and commitments are unsubstantial. Rather, our personal typological ground makes them relative, never absolute. Jung's anger at Freud's authoritarian attitude and his fear of a collective mentality lingers at the edges of Jung's relativistic view, but this view also affirms his belief in the value of type differences. He holds that, by virtue of knowing and living our personal type—our typological identity—rather than another's type, we are to be a light that shines with, not against, others in a family or an organization. This is a light that is also with the ultimate Other in us, that is, the Self, the Soul, which Jung describes as "God within Us."[39]

As I have said several times, it is important to see typology as a central component in the body of Jung's psychological theory and practice. To further this integration, which in turn enhances our understanding of the significance of typology for individuation—that is, for actualizing our innate potential and living fully and authentically—we must explore the relationship between Jung, typology, and Taoism, the subject of the next chapter.

Notes

1. C. G. Jung, *CW*, vol. 6, *Psychological Types,* English edition, translated by H. G. Baynes (1923; rpt., Princeton NJ: Princeton University Press, 1971), paras 91, 93.

2. Frances Wright Saunders, *Katharine and Isabel: Mother's Light, Daughter's Journey* (Palo Alto CA: Consulting Psychologists Press, 1991), p. 179.

3. Jung, *CW*, vol. 6, *Psychological Types,* para. 881.

4. Ibid., para. 882.

5. Jung, *Memories, Dreams, Reflections* (Princeton NJ: Princeton University Press, 1961), p. 208.

6. John Kerr, *A Most Dangerous Method, The Story of Jung, Freud and Sabina Spielrein,* New York: Vintage Books, 1993). "The sole purpose of this group [the secret committee] was to guard against future deviations from Freud's view within the psychoanalytic movement. Explicitly, Freud was to tell them where to stand and they would stand there" (p. 452). The committee was initially made up of Jones, Ferenczi, Abraham, Sachs, and Rank, and its existence has been known, according to the author, since 1944. This book is both brilliant in its insights and deeply moving in its drama.

7. Jung, *Memories, Dreams, Reflections,* pp. 170–99.

8. Ibid., p. 207.

9. Ibid., p. 209.

10. Jung, *Analytical Psychology: Notes of the Seminar Given in 1925* (Princeton: Princeton University Press, 1989), p. 28.

11. Ibid., p. 78. Gary V. Hartmann's article, "Typology's Distractions and Opposites' Attractions," *Spring*, pp. 42–55, is devoted to this subject, that typology can only be understood as an energic system and therefore, by implication, is an integral part of Jung's psychology.

12. Kerr, *A Most Dangerous Method.* Kerr includes the last of a series of letters written by Spielrein and Jung, so that the Spielrein relationship with and influence on Jung is found in many pages of his book.

13. Ibid., p. 492.

14. Jung, *Analytical Psychology,* pp. 123, 127.

15. Ibid., p. 128.

16. Ibid., p. 128.

17. I have had the privilege of knowing and valuing the founders of two of the three of the Grey-Wheelwright's creators, Jane Wheelwright, and her late husband, Joseph Wheelwright. They gave enormous personal encouragement to those of us who trained in the Inter-Regional Society of Jungian analysts during the 1970s and the 1980s. June Singer and Mary Loomis, the creators of the Singer Loomis Inventory of Personality (SLIP), have even been more closely connected to my life. June was one of my personal analysts, one of the co-founders of the Inter-Regional, a writer of note, beginning with a perennial favorite in the articulation of an American and personal approach to Jung's psychology and practice, *Boundaries of the Soul*. I was one of several trainees to whom June explained and on whom she tested the SLIP. Mary Loomis did her Ph.D. on the problems of type testing creative people, which led to the SLIP. Mary has also written a book on types, as related to the Cherokee Native American Medicine Sundance Teachings, of which she has been a long-time student, entitled *Dancing the Wheel of Psychological Types,* which I will discuss in chapter 10.

18. Saunders, *Katharine and Isabel.* All my knowledge about these two women comes from this book, except for personal conversations with Mary McCaulley.

19. Ibid. Katharine read biographies endlessly in order to understand human differences, and wrote an unpublished manuscript entitled "Notes on the Art of Creating Character" (p. 58). Her major attempt at fiction was entitled "The Guesser," in which "she had tried to interweave a love story with Carl Jung's theories of personality, and the emphasis had turned out to be more on Jung than on love." The book "survives, unpublished, in the family archives as a monument to Katharine's unfailing belief in Jung's theory of personality types" (pp. 80–81). However, she managed to get many short pieces on child raising and education published (p. 21) in the second decade of the twentieth century and other later pieces, one of which was serialized and considered for use in films (p. 72).

20. Saunders, *Katharine and Isabel*, p. 59.

21. Ibid., chapter 12, "Acclaimed Writer."

22. Ibid., p. 3.

23. Ibid., p. 120.

24. Ibid., p. 121.

25. Ibid., p. 134–135.

26. Ibid., p. 137.

27. Ibid., p. 138.

28. Ibid., p. 154.

29. Ibid., p. 155. Myers was typologically different from the ETS's corporate ESTJ typology. As an intuitive, she "did some things that would shock a conventional statistician," but she "had good reason for what she did." However, among typical ESTJs, she simply "broke the rules," which their mental outlook simply would not abide (p. 154).

30. Ibid., p. 153.

31. Ibid., p. 173.

32. Ibid., p. 179.

33. Henry Thompson, *Jung's Function-Attitudes Explained* (Watkinsville GA: Wormhole Publishing, 1996).

34. Naomi L. Quenk, *Besides Ourselves: Our Hidden Personality in Everyday Life* (Palo Alto CA: Consulting Psychologists Press, 1995).

35. Angelo Spoto, *Jung's Typology in Perspective* (Wilmette IL: Chiron Publications, 1995).

36. Ibid., p. x.

37. Jung, C. G. *Jung Letters,* 2 vols., edited by Gerhard Adler (Princeton NJ: Princeton University Press, 1973). Jung's letters begin to reveal their theoretical and practical differences, but we get only a glimpse of White's letters and responses.

38. Ann Lammer, *In God's Shadow: The Collaboration of Victor White and C. G. Jung* (New York: Paulist Press, 1994). For the first time the full personal story as well as the many facets of the theological/psychological struggle between Victor White and Carl Jung has been revealed. Lammer was allowed by the Jung family and the Dominican Order in England to review all the letters written by White and Jung to each other. White met Jung in the first half of the 1940s. In 1947, White was asked to be a member of the originating analysts of the Jung Institute in Zurich. In 1951, after Jung published his *Answer to Job,* his most controversial book, White's and Jung's differences began to heat up on two important issues: the nature of evil and the shadow or evil in God. Thus the title of Lammer's book. They reconciled before White died in 1960.

39. Jung, *CW,* vol. 7, *Two Essays on Analytical Psychology* (Princeton NJ: Princeton University Press, 1953–56). Jung continues: "The beginnings of our

whole psychic life seem to be inextricably rooted in this point [the Self], and all our highest and ultimate purposes seem to be striving towards it" (para. 399). Later he adds: "So too the self is our life's goal, for it is the completest expression of that fateful combination we call individuality, the full flowering not only of the individual, but of the group, in which each adds his portion to the whole [i.e., the Compass of the Soul]" (para. 404). See the similarity here to Paul in the New Testament, as in 1 Cor. 12.

CHAPTER 2

Jung, Typology, and Taoism

The book on types yielded the insight that every judgment made by an individual is conditioned by his personality type and that every point of view is necessarily relative. This raised the question of the unity which must compensate this diversity and it led me directly to the Chinese concept of the Tao.[1]

C. G. Jung

The Tao of Jung *regards spirituality as the primary ordering principle in psychology. The essential task in analytical psychology is individuation, a process toward wholeness, which like Taoism is characterized by accepting and transcending opposites. The basic tenets of Jung's psychology are also central to Taoism: the downfall of the prime ego position and a rekindling of humility in the face of the Self occur as one proceeds along the Eternal Way of the Tao.*[2]

David Rosen

N HIS AUTOBIOGRAPHY, Jung acknowledges a general affinity between typology and the Chinese philosophy of Taoism that gets to the core of his psychology. Both promote health. Both find the source of health in the unconscious and its hidden order of personal identity and cosmic unity, called respectively the Self and the Tao. In Taoism, the symbol of Yin and Yang imaginatively captures the polarities that can be harmonized and even transcended through the Tao,

just as in Jung's psychology, the reconciliation of type opposites can lead to individuation. In a letter, Jung expands on the relationship between his typology and Taoist ideas because he wants the West to better understand the psychological reality and "the underlying truth" that grounds Taoism:

> Taoism formulates psychological principles which are of a very universal nature. . . . The truth is one and the same everywhere and I must say that Taoism is one of the most perfect formulations of it I ever became acquainted with.[3]

In his psychology, Jung expresses the truthfulness of the Tao in terms of the Self, the reconciler of all opposites.

Given these connections, two major goals inform this chapter: to show how Jung's total view of his own life, as mirrored in the body of his psychology and as specified in his typology, was significantly influenced by Chinese Taoism, and to demonstrate how Taoism and typology are archetypal systems in both their wholeness and in their parts.

TAOISM'S INFLUENCE ON JUNG

Jung's 1921 *Psychological Types* not only helped him heal his split with Freud but also aided him in formulating a solid understanding of the Self, the archetype of identity and wholeness and the ultimate reconciler of the type opposites, as inspired by his growing consciousness of the Tao. During the preceding years, as a result of his split from Freud and associates who allied themselves with Freud, Jung felt alienated from society, as he reported in his autobiography, *Memories, Dreams, Reflections*. In his solitude and inward search, he drew daily mandalas, which he saw as pictures of his Soul. In 1928, he drew one with a building that for him felt Chinese. A short time later, he received *The Secret of the Golden Flower* from Richard Wilhelm. This book on a Taoist alchemical meditation text included an image of a temple as symbolizing the immortal body. This was another instance in which Jung was discovering that others had trodden a similar spiritual path. For the radically introverted Jung, this synchronistic event helped him reconnect not only with his Soul but also with the extraverted world.[4]

Taoism is dedicated to health and healing. Taoist doctors were paid to keep people from illnesses, rather than just treat them when they were ill. Jung learned that the Taoist practitioners maintained a client's health by teaching alchemical disciplines, in which, through the imagination, bodily energy functions were changed into spiritual ones, such as breath into spiritual energy, the *Chi*.[5] Taoist students, for example, who imagine breathing down the spine as they physically breathe, experience sensations of a spinal energy flow. Jung perceived his psychology as promoting health through an analogous transformational process. He taught an alchemical-like healing process called active imagination, which works with emotionally laden dreams or consciously evoked symbols. Similar transformations can occur when feelings are honestly expressed within interpersonal interactions.

Typology is another avenue of this transformative process of health and healing when it reveals, in dreams and conscious experiences, the type direction in which a person should move through careful inner work. In typology, an individual often understands the psyche's need to embrace or avoid certain type behaviors. In turn, when typology is understood not in terms of any individual's traits but as a way of describing the universal lifelong steps toward individuation, it explains some of the healing practices in Jungian dream work and Taoist exercises, as we shall see later in this book.

Jung was profoundly introverted, which helps explain the subjective intrapsychic ways in which he explained many dream experiences following his break with Freud. His critics, including Jungian analysts, rightfully point out that many of his dreams from that time contained clear references to more personal relational material, especially referring to his painful break with Freud. However, that was an extraverted event and in itself carried little weight for the ultimately private Jung. Reading the Taoist *The Secret of the Golden Flower* in the late 1920s, as noted above, helped Jung heal the breach that he felt with society as a whole, but this healing emerged from a deeply private place in his soul. Jung also saw both typology and Taoism as heralding a more friendly and healing society and cosmos.

In analytical (Jungian) psychology, the essential task is individuation, which David Rosen describes as "a process toward wholeness, which like Taoism, is characterized by accepting and transcending opposites."[6] Analytical psychology and Taoism share the same basic tenets: "The downfall of the prime ego position and a rekindling of humility in the face of the Self occur as one proceeds along the Eternal Way of the Tao."[7] In typological terms, this means surrendering some aspects of a dominant function or coupling, and learning to value the other types in your personal compass of the Soul. Like Taoism, typology's "psychological principles"—functioning as type opposites and complementarities—are of a "universal nature," and can lead each of us toward individuation. Like Taoism, typology challenges us to live a full life in which conscious successes must be balanced by a "rekindling of humility in the face of the Self."

The traditional symbol of Taoism, as in figure 2.1, must have had a significant impact on Jung's vision of his type psychology. This figure's circumference with its inclusive area symbolizes the Tao. The Tao's central polarities are pictured as the dark, feminine Yin and the light, masculine Yang. The Tao and its Yin and Yang constituents are archetypes or universal patterns in the truest sense of the word. Taoism's greatest cultural and spiritual achievement, the ancient *I Ching* oracle, is made up of sixty-four archetypal situations, each of which is made up of Yin and Yang elements. We will discuss its makeup and its use as we proceed. Jung writes of this oracle's numerical method for depicting the Yin and Yang patterns:

These, as representatives of Yin and Yang, are found both

in the unconscious and in nature in the characteristic form of opposites, as the "mother" and "father" of everything that happens, and they therefore form the *tertium comparationis* between the psychic inner world and the physical outer world.[8]

Jung called this meaningful connection the principle of correspondence or synchronicity. In the religious tradition, synchronicity is called providence, which is understood as the hand of God working in human life. It can also be understood in Jungian terms as a hidden intuitive order of archetypal patterns and energies in the unconscious that guides us inwardly and societally, as we will discuss further in chapter 4. Jung recognized this same order in Taoism, which confirmed his embryonic ideas on and encouraged his development of typology as a whole as well as the individual and coupled types, as discussed in the introduction. We shall see that the types, while usually evident as ordinary behaviors and attitudes to type practitioners in the "physical outer world," also show up as dream symbols in dreams and as actors in great stories in "the psychic inner world."

Jung and Taoism share a circular and polar view of the Soul as

The Taoist Symbol

FIGURE 2.1

symbolized in figures 2.1 and 2.2. Figure 2.2 (created by Jung, to which the author has added the couplings) pictures the Soul as a maternal circular mandala that embraces all of the type polarities, individual as well as coupled, within its circumference. The four quadrants, also characteristic of so many mandalas, are symbolic spatial depictions of the four type couplings.

This ancient Taoist system spiritually influenced Jung's personal

Jung's Diagram with Couplings Added

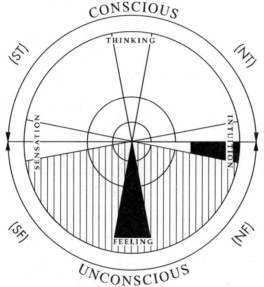

FIGURE 2.2

life even before it became the inspiration for his typological theory. In *The Tao of Jung,* Rosen interviewed some of Jung's closest followers, who held firmly that Jung was a natural Taoist even before Jung knew of the existence of this ancient system. He shared the Taoist's acute observations and exquisitely felt affinities with nature. For example, Jung, as a child, felt so at one with nature that he recalled wondering, while sitting on a rock, whether he was the rock or the person sitting on the rock. As an adult, he built his tower at Bolingen because he needed to concretize in stone what he experienced in his own Soul and because he needed to experience the surrounding trees, earth, and water in silence.

Jung's natural attraction to Taoism, however, did not supplant Jung's Christian heritage. *Psychological Types* begins with an exploration of human differences within a Christian classical and medieval theology. Jung was both Judaic-Christian and Taoist, a spiritual pragmatist and a secular mystic. There was no conflict between his Western spirituality and a Taoist spirituality. As a scientist he wished to explore every means of healing his patients, as he asserted in a September 1944 letter. In that same letter, he wrote the following about his Christian background and his scientific profession:

> As a scientist, I have to guard against believing that I am in possession of the final truth. . . . As a Christian, of course, I take my stand on the Christian truth. . . . Though I know little of Catholic doctrine, that little is enough to make it an inalienable possession for me. And I know so much about Protestantism that I could never give it up.[9]

Jung's interest in Catholicism centered on the rich symbolic nature of its sacraments and its tradition of mysticism. His commitment to Protestantism was fed by his Swiss-German heritage that valued the private consent of faith that Jung called "The Protestant Principle." More evidence of Jung's cultivated religious heritage is revealed in his fascination with the Old Testament and with his many commentaries on some of its major figures, especially in his *Answer to Job*.[10] His Judaic-Christian commitment, however, did not prevent him as an eclectic thinker and intellectual explorer from a certain spiritual pragmatism as he sought out the fundamental truths in all religions and philosophies to deepen his understanding of the human soul. In this context, he was able to declare, as in the above quotation, that

"Taoism is one of the most perfect formulations" of the truth.

The truth for Jung could not be contained only in theoretical systems. He was first of all a person who needed to know through experience, who even as a child could not understand his minister father's religious commitment in which the personal experience of God was ignored. Jung's psychology was totally based on life events, beginning with his own. (We shall see in chapter 5 that a Princeton-based group called his type theory "Experiential Typology.") So when he writes, "I'm chiefly concerned with the ways and means by which one can make the Western mind aware of the psychological facts underlying the concept of the Tao," he may well have been thinking of his typological system and its down-to-earth characteristics as practical equivalents to Taoism.

The Tao for Jung is, like the nature of the Self/Soul, a mysterious source with many characteristics, such as power, flow, and hidden structure. Jung writes that it is, like the Western view of God, "the prime cause of all phenomena, the right, the good, the moral order," but also has a changing, unpredictable, and dynamic quality.[11] It cannot be pinned down: "The Tao that is told is not the eternal Tao," writes Lao Tzu.[12] Jung says substantially the same about the Self, the archetype of identity, and the source of all of the archetypes. We can say of the Tao and the Self what is said in scripture: "The Spirit bloweth as it will," and still it is ordered. The Tao is the source of freedom. Yet, as the Taoist symbol metaphorically suggests, it is also the disciplining container of all of life and its dynamic life-affirming polarities.[13] The Tao is the begetter of all paradoxes. So Lao Tzu writes:

> The Tao is like a well: / used but never used up. / It is like the eternal void: / filled with infinite possibilities. / It is hidden but always present. / I don't know who gave birth to it. / It is older than God.[14]

PRACTICAL SIMILARITIES BETWEEN
TAOISM AND TYPOLOGY

As I mentioned above, Taoism is based on a principle that Jung calls synchronicity; that is, that all things are connected in the hidden, holistic dimensions of our personal lives and the natural world. By virtue of this abiding principle, meaningful coincidences often occur. Even more important, a constant depth consciousness develops in us if we live by this "thinking in terms of the whole," as Jung characterized Taoism. By virtue of this consciousness (which clearly originates in the intuitive function), the Taoist master, Chuang Tzu says that "you use your inner eye, your inner ear, to pierce to the heart of things, and have no need of intellectual knowledge."[15] Thus Taoists see the affinities between outer events and inner attitudes in the sixty-four hexagrams that make up the I Ching as manifestations of synchronicity, which act as the principle of correspondence.

Students of Jung see similar meaningful correspondences occurring between outer events, persons and types and their corresponding symbols in dreams. Types as traits and emotional energies in individuals correspond with their related images and emotional energies in dreams and great stories. Examples of this often occur in analytical work. For example, one of my clients, a woman, was afflicted with serious allergic responses to wheat, milk products, and green beans. She dreamt that as she was being ejected from the house by her parents, her drunken mother was carrying a pot of buttered green beans. Then outside the house, the dreamer was attacked by a wild woman. She realized that the wild woman represented the assertive sensate, thinking (ST) behaviors of the mother, which were very different from her intuitive, feeling (NF) sensitivities. She further realized that her allergens, in this case butter and green beans, represented the body's symptomatic correlatives to the symbol of the attacking and controlling mother. She knew that to heal and to grow into some needed ST traits, she needed to face bodily felt emotions and images of the wild woman many times in her imagination.

Taoism's structures and forms are subservient to the dynamic flow of the Tao's hidden energy, the Chi. Likewise, the type structures are innate channels or pathways for the flow of psychic energy which manifests itself as preferences and interests as well as related emotions. We need to experience this natural overall flow more than the specifics of behaviors. The flow of psychic energy (which is what Jung meant by libido) is relatively effortless when it acts according to a person's natural type preferences. This means, for example, that a thinking type is interested in and energized by an objective view of a situation, and a feeling type by a personal, subjective view.

Taoism is based on polar opposites—the forces and structures of Yin and Yang. Similarly, Jung's typology is based on the play between opposites. Without these polarities, Jung holds, there is no flow of life, just as electricity does not move through a battery unless both the negative and positive poles are connected. When we are psychologically healthy, the opposites do what is natural: flow in harmony with one another. However, if we are overly developed in any psychic structures, life will often providentially challenge us to develop an ignored function or coupling. For example, an intuitive type with less consciously developed sensing may often have a strongly felt aversion to detail (the sensing function mediates this aversion). However, the sensing function will force its way into the intuitive's life, perhaps as the dominant function in a significant other, especially a spouse. We are egged on by fate and its emotionally loaded images to assimilate our undeveloped potentials. (In chapter 6 we will see more complicated examples of intrapsychic and interpersonal resistance that blocks our individuation and challenges us to develop the complementary type through further type development.)

The Tao is the middle way and the synthesizing depth in this flow of opposites,[16] just as in Jungian psychology the Self is the reconciling ground of all opposites. Taoism insists in its book of oracles, the I Ching, also called The Book of Changes, that individuals, within themselves and as representatives of social institutions, "must go down to the very foundations of life," so as to move beyond conventions and superficialities.[17] So the task faced by every person, whether extraverted or introverted, is not just to consciously understand one's type differences and fight the resistance to moving toward opposite types, but to seek help from the Self's depth through prayer, dream work, or spontaneous insights in order to realize a more inclusive type consciousness. The allergic NF woman knew that besides overcoming her mother's angry, violent ways, she also had to assimilate aspects of her mother's sensate, thinking makeup.

Jung found other venerable traditions, such as Hinduism, that also value this middle and deepest place of Soul. He writes in *Psychological Types*:

> The natural flow of libido, this same middle path, means complete obedience to the fundamental laws of nature, and there can be no positively higher moral principle than harmony with natural laws that guide the libido in the direction of life's optimum. The vital optimum is not to be found in crude egoism. . . . [A]s we study the philosophy of the Upanishads, the impression grows on us that the attainment of this path is not exactly the simplest of tasks. Our Western superciliousness in the face of these Indian insights is a mark of our barbarian nature, which has not the remotest inkling of their extraordinary depth and astonishing psychological accuracy. . . . And because we are still such barbarians, any trust in the laws of human nature seems to us a dangerous and unethical naturalism.[18]

Jung's contention reveals something of his introverted frustration with and his sensitive historical understanding of our outer-oriented culture. His calling our culture "barbaric" meant for him its one-sided extraverted sensing thinking that feared and even abhorred an inward intuitive feeling approach. Jung also knew that the Eastern cultures had their limitations, especially in social justice for the poor and weak. Nevertheless, these weaknesses did not diminish his view of the essential worth of the Hindu tradition that recognizes that the laws of nature are written in our bodies, hearts, and minds in the Soul's original script from the moment we are conceived.

The *I Ching* itself provides various metaphorical comparisons with the types' polar dynamics. Each hexagram in the *I Ching* is constructed from any two of eight basic trigrams, which represent the book's main metaphors consisting of analogous relationships between nature and an inner attitude. The trigrams are made up of three parallel lines: all Yang, all Yin or a mixture of Yang and Yin. Each hexagram, constituted of six parallel lines, in turn, is made up of an upper and lower trigram acting like type polarities.

Taoists and others come to the *I Ching* for meaning. Casting lots to determine the proper hexagram, they expect that the results will synchronically shed light on the nature of their problem or question. They learn that the meaning of each hexagram is based on the interaction of the upper and lower trigrams. Many hexagrams, for example, are composed of trigrams that are opposed or attracted to the other. At times, reconciling the opposites is represented as easy, as beautifully illustrated in the *I Ching's* Hexagram 11 named Peace, in which the trigrams, Heaven (all Yang lines) and Earth (all Yin lines), are turned toward one another, as if they were embracing. Couples with significantly different type makeups can experience a similar peace, if they are securely grounded in their own type and each can, therefore, hold and internalize the partner's differences. On the other hand, in Hexagram 12 called Standstill, Heaven and Earth are turned away from one another; so that they are antagonists. In a comparable situation with a married couple or friends, it is as though they have turned their backs on one another. Harmony in this case becomes practically impossible until each person does much inner or outer work toward reconciliation. A couple in this painful condition might expect to receive Hexagram 12 when they inquire about the cause of their afflictions. One couple I was counseling turned to the I Ching. He was an NT husband who had difficulty demonstrating affection and sharing concerns with his NF spouse. In turn, his spouse had difficulty understanding his intense commitment to a creative scientific pursuit, which is so attractive to his wide-ranging NT personality. Hexagram 12 aptly summarized the work they needed to do.

In our own personal or intrapsychic life, we flow effortlessly in the direction of our dominant inherited type or coupling and somewhat easily toward our secondary type or coupling. However, when we seek to consciously develop our opposite inferior function or coupling, we struggle against a natural psychic gravity. We are in the condition comparable to Hexagram 12. For many whose early childhood experiences were painful and conflicting, the undeveloped pole acts as a warlike opposition. While some persons born in the middle of a particular type polarity easily flow both ways, most must work consciously, even heroically, on their inferior function before beginning to move comfortably between the dominant/inferior opposites. If, for example, I am a dominant thinking type, I need to experience the fearful chaos and creative paradox of my inferior feeling function, as I seek that function at the edge of my consciousness. This can be done by going, in the imagination, to the brink of one's imagined inner earth and saying to the unconscious abyss (or to God, depending on one's theology), "Let the inferior function appear in my presence." At first, some frightening and confusing images will usually appear. The inferior feeling function may also appear in a dream, for example, as an attractive siren or a ghastly monster.

In Taoism and in intrapsychic terms, the Yang archetype is masculine and the Yin is feminine. The epitome of these opposites in the I Ching is found in Hexagrams 1 and 2. The first hexagram, entitled "Heaven" and "The Creative," is made up of all six Yang, or masculine, lines. The second, entitled, "Earth" and "The Receptive," is made up of all six Yin, or feminine, lines. These archetypally masculine and feminine qualities are shared in many variations by both men and women. All the other hexagrams are various combinations of Yang and Yin.

Similarly, among the sixteen type families of the *MBTI*, the ESTJ type, with its ST coupling, is made up of conventionally assumed "masculine" qualities: tough, differentiating, and highly defined. The INFP, with its NF coupling, is made up of so-called feminine aspects: soft, embracing, and relating. All the other *MBTI* types are mixtures of these characteristics.

Moreover, understanding that both sexes share ST and NF features can help us avoid stereotyping men and women as to social roles and personal characteristics. For example, I counseled a husband, who is an INFP literature and writing professor, and his wife is an ESTJ top-level business executive. I had both of them take the *MBTI*. Knowing their different typologies has made them more comfortable with their vocational choices and family roles. He enjoys being a house husband during the day and a professor in the evening, and she pursues her business career without experiencing a socially imposed maternal guilt. As he internalized some undeveloped sensate, thinking behaviors of his own through dream work, he has also learned to handle her assertive power when they differ on personal issues.

In summary, Jung's study of Taoist wisdom in the first decades of the twentieth century helped him heal the breach that he felt within himself and with society as a whole. Taoism, as an archetypal system, influenced his development of typology's archetypal structures and dynamics as a series of different attitudes and functions that are also flexible polar attractions. In turn, Jung saw that his type theory and practice translates and grounds this Eastern worldview, whether his types are used by Orientals or Occidentals. Jung then asked, what allows for both type diversity and unity within polar preferences, such as thinking and feeling? Synchronically, he became aware of the

Chinese concept of the Tao. This "reconciler of all opposites," figuratively expressed in Taoism as a containing circular mandala, became an analogy for the archetype of the Self, which is also symbolized as a circle and, specifically in typology, as the type compass. In this large context, each of us can heal any breach within ourselves and with society as we work toward our own individuation.

It is for this reason that I have felt compelled, following Jung's lead, to construct or borrow many circular type diagrams that Mary McCaulley called "circumplexes." Hopefully they will help elucidate the interactive dynamics of the types in the compass of the Soul (which can be obscured or ignored in type tables), especially as expanded into the four central archetypal couplings.

Before we pursue this book's main theme, we will consider Jung's account of his discovery of the types in chapter 3 and some imaginative reflections on each individual type in chapter 4, always looking for intimations of the type couplings.

Notes

1. C. G. Jung, *Memories, Dreams, Reflections* (New York: Pantheon Books, 1961), pp. 207–8.

2. David Rosen, *The Tao of Jung: The Way of Integrity* (New York: Viking Arcana, 1996), p. 10.

3. Jung, *Jung Letters,* vol. 1 (Princeton: Princeton University Press, 1973), p. 560.

4. Jung, *Memories, Dreams, Reflections,* p. 197.

5. Jung, "Commentary on the Secret of the Golden Flower," *CW,* vol. 13, *Alchemical Studies* (Princeton NJ: Princeton University Press, 1967). This writing came to Jung from Richard Willhelm, who also compiled the *I Ching.* The healing exercises are only generally developed in the "Secret" as also in Hexagram 52 in the *I Ching.* The reader should seek out Mantak Chia's series of books that describe the Taoist exercises in detail.

6. Rosen, *The Tao of Jung,* p.10.

7. Ibid., p. 10.

8. Jung, "Synchronicity: An Acausal Connecting Principle," *CW,* vol. 8, *The Structure and Dynamics of the Psyche* (Princeton NJ: Princeton University Press, 1960), para. 865. By *tertium comparationis,* Jung means that the unconscious' Self, as structure and as energizing dynamic, acts as the "reconciler of all opposites." See additionally Jung, *CW,* vol. 5, *Symbols of Transformation* (Princeton: Princeton University Press, 1956), paras. 329, 422.

9. Jung, *Letters,* p. 346.

10. Jung, *CW,* vol. 11, *Psychology and Religion: West and East* (Princeton NJ: Princeton University Press, 1958/1969), paras. 355–470.

11. Jung, *Psychological Types,* English edition, translated by H. G. Baynes (1923; rpt., Princeton NJ: Princeton University Press, 1971), para.. 358: "The meanings of *tao* are as follows: way, method, principle, natural force or life force, the regulated processes of nature, the idea of the world, the prime cause of all phenomena, the right, the good, the moral order. Some translators even translate it as God, not without some justification, since *tao,* like *rta,* has a tinge of substantiality."

12. Lao Tzu, with Stephen Mitchell's new English version, *Tao Te Ching,* New York: Harper Perennial, 1988), no. 1.

13. Chaos scientists are reporting similar phenomena of apparent chaos and hidden patterns. For example: (1) James Gleick, *Chaos: Making a New Science* (New York: Viking Penguin, 1987); (2) Jim Briggs and F. David Peat, *Turbulent Mirror* (New York: Harper and Row, 1989).

14. *Tao Te Ching,* no. 4. The Tao therefore is like Godhead in the theology of Meister Eckhart. Jung knew of this similar distinction in Eckhart, that God is not Godhead. He quotes Eckhart: "God is begotten of the Soul, and his Godhead he has of himself. God comes into being and passes away." Jung notes "that Eckhart distinguishes between God and Godhead. Godhead is All, neither knowing or possessing itself, whereas God is a function of the Soul." *Psychological Types,* paras. 428–29. God is a human way of understanding the Divinity, that is, Godhead, which is total mystery, total incomprehension.

15. Jung, *CW,* vol. 8, *The Structure and Dynamics of the Psyche,* paras. 924–25.

16. *I Ching,* p. 50: "Not neglecting what is distant/not regarding one's companion:/Thus one may manage to walk in the middle." Richard Wilhelm, translated into English by C. F. Baynes with a foreword by Jung, *I Ching* (London: Routledge and Kegan Paul, 1968).

17. Ibid., p. 186. See also Hexagram 22, in regard to the aversion that Taoists had toward superficial living.

18. Jung, *Psychological Types,* paras. 356–57.

CHAPTER 3

Jung's Historical Research and Intimations of the Types as Archetypes

Unlike Freud, who after a proper psychological start reverted to the ancient assumption of the sovereignty of the physical constitution, trying to turn everything back in theory into instinctual processes conditioned by the body, I start with the assumption of the sovereignty of the psyche.[1]

C. G. Jung

In the foregoing description I have no desire to give my readers the impression that these types [the eight attitude/function combinations] occur at all frequently in such form in actual life. . . . Closer investigation shows with great regularity that, besides the most differentiated [i.e., principal] function, another, less differentiated function of secondary importance is invariably present in conscious-ness and exerts a co-determining influence.[2]

C. G. Jung

N THIS CHAPTER WE WILL LOOK at Jung's 1921 book, with four interwoven ideas in mind: we will attempt to understand the historical influences that led to Jung's formulation of his type theory; we will gain an appreciation of the importance he attached to the creative functions of symbols as they emerge from the "sovereignty of the psyche" in shaping the types; we will discuss Jung's initial perceptions

of the typological Compass and the individual types as archetypes; and we will note his first tentative constructions of the type couplings as combinations of perceiving and judging functions in which each type has a co-determining influence.

To illustrate the pervasive reach of typology, figure 3.1 shows Jung's four levels of psyche: the ego/persona level, the shadow level, the anima/animus level, and the self-image level, all rooted in the sovereign Self or Soul. Jung considered the Self the abiding principle or source of life and identity, as well as the goal of wholeness and comprehensive consciousness. Individuation consists in as full a realization and actualization of the Self as humanly possible.

Some Correlations with Psyche's Four Levels

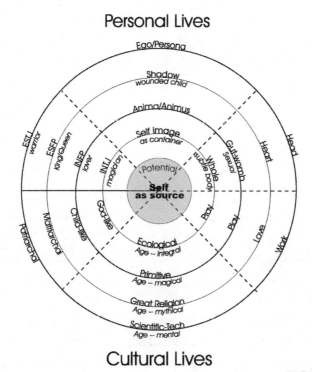

FIGURE 3.1

It is difficult to visualize the complex interactions suggested by Jung's type theory, not to mention some of the corresponding personal and cultural effects of each type on the four levels of the psyche depicted in figure 3.1. This figure also shows these correspondences functioning in the most basic polarity in each of us: the relationship between consciousness and the unconscious, or between the ego and the Self. Notice that all of the levels and relationships are ultimately contained in and moved by the Self, which is both the center and circumference of the circle. Typology, seen in this context, is capable of comprehending the breadth, depth, and heights of our individual and cultural makeup. Typology helps us understand the normal, healthy aspects of these human structures and their interactions, as well as the individual aberrations or pathologies I will discuss throughout the book.

Typology first of all provides a language for discussing the healthy and pathological features of our culture in both its conscious and unconscious aspects as we consider Jung's view of our Western history. The historical eras have proceeded, in the scheme of human evolution, from the shamanic/primitive, to the great religions and to our present scientific age. In figure 3.1, I have suggested a typological perspective for the four cultural periods with their corresponding human behaviors. For example, we see that our present "Scientific-Technological Era" is associated with the ST coupling, where "work" and the "head" provide the body metaphors, and the "Warrior" and the concomitant familial connection as "Patriarch" are the major cultural archetypal figures. As the deepest (fourth) level, I suggest the Ecological and its relationship to the Self image as, hopefully, our future age that transcends yet comprehends the other three historical eras.

MY PERSONAL EXPERIENCE
OF THE PSYCHE'S FOUR LEVELS

An understanding of typology can be the basis for significant personal insights. I have already explained how I, like most of us, developed many aspects of an ego-consciousness and persona (first level) that were contrary to my innate endowment. I developed an ego "complex" informed more by the dominant society than by the Self. I was caught in a wrong consciousness or a negative ego complex which eventually I had to face.[3] Persona is the archetypally based complex structure by which we play out various social roles, for example, as student, parent, or teacher. A persona can be positive if one's role is congruent with one's innate typological preference and relevant to the authentic needs of society, but a persona can have negative or damaging effects when because of familial or societal pressures one assumes a life role that violates one's typology. The persona is an important part of and is adjunct to the ego, the locus of consciousness and the agency through which the Self incarnates in the world.

I developed an extraverted persona informed by sensation, thinking, and judging (ESTJ), at odds with my own typology and the typology of my native Italian culture. In the heart dream which led to my understanding of my typology, the Dominican brother represented an assertive, confident ESTJ behavior (that I will relate to the warrior archetype in chapter 5). In turn, my ESTJ persona covered over an implicit cultural message I had internalized—being an Italian feeling type was bad, and I needed to repress my true self (fourth level). My cultural inferiority complex (second level) functioned as a destructive shadow that has often appeared in my memory and dreams in the form of big, blond men who scoff and laugh, or as a frightened Italian kid in his first classroom. These figures have acted as repressed sub-personalities that block the persistent urgings of my innate nature and heritage. For me, blond men represented our culture's dominant ESTJ preference that has, in fact, become one-sided and therefore destructive.

If I appear in this book to demonize the ESTJ cultural dominance, I would suggest that one-sidedness of any kind is destructive. Jung, as we will see below, described the early emergence of such a societal distortion in our history. I also ask readers, whether familiar or not with typology, to distinguish between individuals with their typological preferences and this generalized societal type. When a person identifies with the typological one-sidedness that dominates his or her society, the identification will usually create a complex that opposes, inhibits, and damages the individual's innate, normal type preferences. However, the same complex can also provide a person with a significant challenge and opportunity to grow in consciousness. As we learn in depth psychology, the negative power of the ESTJ shadow, represented, for example, in my dreams by a large, angry blond man, can change significantly. If the dreamer, when awake or in the dream state, confronts the negative shadow complex and consistently works with it in active imagination, it will eventually transform into an inner mentor, friend or even lover. A person may experience this transformation as a capacity to confidently utilize the evolving ESTJ abilities. In dreams, an inner transformation of this sort will often appear as the birth of a child from the union of a male and female figure.

Confronting such a powerful inner antagonist assumes that one has first begun to claim one's innate type preferences (one's original birthright) and has developed an authentic ego complex. In my case, by reexperiencing my heart dream in my body, emotions, and mind, I could begin to claim the heart as the core of my innate makeup. In typological terms, the heart represented my innate, potential identity as having a balance between extraversion and introversion as well as preferring intuition, feeling, and perceiving (E/INFP), a potential that I was finally able to realize. But only after grounding myself in this typology was I able to seek a more healthy integration of my opposite type, ESTJ, as represented in the heart dream by the brother, and in many other dreams by male antagonists. My dreams and their waking implications, representing the fated imperatives of my life, prodded me to actualize these new potentials.

Victor White, my analyst, once said to me, "John, you will never make a systematic theologian or systematic anything. Yes, work on developing it. But acknowledge that your heart hungers first for pastoral or people-oriented spiritual concerns that are the stuff of feeling types. You need to write and live more out of your experience, out of your intuitive feeling core than out of a thinking, abstract basis." Victor's words gave me great comfort and relief. Later I learned that, because of my clear innate intuitive preference, my inferior sensation function was weak, and when overtaxed could quickly lead to frustration and anger. It was no accident that I had developed a reputation as the absentminded professor. My inferior sensation often was the basis of losing things and resisting any work that involved many details.

In analysis I also began to discover my sexuality, which I had repressed in childhood and had suppressed by my choice of a vocation as a celibate priest. In dreams I became aware of the inner lover archetype, what Jung calls the anima in the male and the animus in the female (third level in figure 3.1, page 68). As I reflected on my life and my dreams, I found that typology had a lot to do with the women I had previously chosen to love. In some significant respects they were always typologically different from me. This contrasexual part of us, whose typology may be similar or opposite to our conscious type preference, has crucial significance in our development, not only interpersonally and socially in relation to the opposite sex, but also in the world of our imagination and fantasy. All of this led to my eventual marriage.

I learned early on that typology was linked to all of the levels and structures of psyche that we have been discussing here. In recent years, as I have begun to recognize the archetypal structures of the functions, I have concluded that typology has or should have a central place in Jung's psychology, and that it permeates every aspect of personal and social life.

As great numbers of people have learned about their typology through the *Myers-Briggs Type Indicator*® (*MBTI*)®, they have also become, in varying degrees, aware of Jung's psychology. Now, these people need to see the various functions and the attitudes as substantive elements in Jung's understanding of the psyche and in our everyday behaviors, as well as in the larger arena of cultural issues and theories. Both personal and cultural dynamics involve the interactions among persona, ego, and shadow, between complex and archetype, consciousness and the unconscious, and outer and inner forces. Typology contributes significantly to our deeper understanding of all these interactions.

ESTJ: THE DOMINANT TYPOLOGY
OF OUR WESTERN CULTURE

In *Psychological Types,* Jung examined the typical attitude and functions of our Western culture in depth by tracing the development of society into a tough, extraverted ST warriorlike cultural preference so familiar to us today. Few, even among professional psychologists, have appreciated that this book is one of Jung's most penetrating critiques of our culture.

Jung showed how very quickly the Christian society, following the regressive Greek and Roman influences that dominated European thought in the first centuries, began to separate body and psyche by emphasizing abstract spirituality and intellectualism. Jung examined Tertullian and Origen as examples of early Christians who struggled with the splitting of spirit and body, and feeling and thinking. Tertullian, an introvert, sacrificed the prowess of his thinking function in society to nurture the inwardness of Soul with his feeling function. In contrast, Origen, truly extraverted and a natural feeling-sensation type, sacrificed the feeling function in favor of a disembodied intellect by actually castrating himself. Tertullian, on the other hand, proclaimed, "the soul is naturally Christian,"[4] which, for Jung, meant "innately religious" and, I hold, spontaneously relational. Jung wrote that Tertullian "reached a depth of religious feeling that we miss in Origen."[5] Typologically this means that the "emotional value" we experience (Jung's description of the feeling function) must above all serve our sacred task of consciously connecting with the Soul and with one another. The feeling function binds together the quaternity of functions in the Soul's configurations of archetypal images and traits both within and without.

Jung saw that the patriarchal dominance of our Western Christian culture was oriented toward the objectivity of extraversion and abstract thinking. Further, the Christian view chose to look at the human condition as essentially wicked from birth due to the concept of original sin. Augustine, the greatest Christian intellectual of the first centuries, popularized this position. In following an extraverted view that places so much emphasis on objects and the other (rather than on oneself), Augustine insisted that we Christians could only be saved or redeemed by the other-worldly intervention of God in the person of Jesus and by the institutional Church with its sacraments. In other words, we are saved by the extraverted "outside" or "other," an other that is both Deity and Church. Jung had bitter words for this viewpoint, which he saw as a negative cultural complex:

> In this scheme of things, the value of man stands very low.
> He is really nothing but a miserable rejected creature, who
> is delivered over to the devil under all circumstances,
> unless through the medium of the Church, the sole means
> of salvation, he is made a participator in divine grace.[6]

Augustine's opponent Pelagius represented an Irish Celtic Christian view that looked inward and saw all of nature, including our own, as good. In effect, he defended the rightness of the feeling function in its preference for a personal and universal harmony with one another and with nature. Pelagius concluded that Jesus was a reminder of the God-given health that is in all of nature from the beginning of time, including ours. Jung commented that with Pelagius' view, "there arises ever anew the feeling of man's freedom and moral value—a feeling that will not long endure suppression whether by insight, however searching, or by logic however keen."[7] This Celtic view, typical of other societies living close to the earth, reveals a mix of the sensation feeling and intuition feeling couplings.

Jung gives another interesting example of our culture's preference for sensate thinking: the communion debate of the ninth century shows how a symbolic, intuitive view of communion yielded to the sensation-oriented doctrine that the wine and host are transformed into the actual blood and body of Christ. Jung called this "an extreme concretization of a symbol" and "the concretization of religious experiences." Scotus Erigena, who, as Jung wrote, was a solid thinker (and I would add, an intuitive type), saw this doctrine as unreasonable. His own monks killed him for opposing the sensation thinking tendencies of his age.[8] Tragically, a theology oriented by sensation and thinking won out in Christianity as a whole because psychic reality, with its inner, intuitive, symbolic and sacred way of knowing had effectively been lost except in the private experiences of the rare and unacknowledged mystic.

We begin to see an interesting implicit picture: Jung was constantly connecting extraversion (E) with sensation and abstract thinking (the ST coupling), and introversion (I) with intuition and feeling (the NF coupling). In his 1936 article entitled "Psychological Typology," found in the appendix of *Psychological Types,* Jung sketches a broader picture of the development of culture that goes beyond the Christian influence. The materialism of his time, he thought, was made possible by mankind's evolving from the spiritual mind/body unity of primal peoples (in a cultural first stage of life) to abstract thinking and the present-day extraverted, surface-of-life outlook. However, this materialistic view "gave the body first place and relegated the psyche to the rank of something secondary and derivative."[9]

The modern development differed from the attitude of primal peoples who live mainly by emotion, and who understood mind as "phren," or breath, that is located in the "diaphragm" as well as in the heart.[10] Jung adds that it was the early Greek philosophers who first assigned the seat of reason to the head (developmental fourth level in figure 3.1, page 68). Jung quotes a Pueblo Indian Chief who told him that "only madmen think with their heads."[11] The positive aspect of our heady, thinking orientation is that it awakens "humanity out of the irresponsible and innocent half-sleep of the primitive mentality."[12] Later we will see that this differentiating ST process in which feeling yields to logical behavior describes the indispensable first-stage life task for individuals as well as societies. Note that I am speaking here of a (personal and cultural) developmental process involving sensation and thinking as part of a life cycle that must not be confused with our individual type preferences. However, in the second stage of life we must consciously realize a primal as well as culturally sophisticated human ground, an NF mentality, without losing our pragmatic consciousness and our scientific/technological mental skills.

This first stage in cultural development evolved, according to Jung, into modern science, which has led us to our understanding of the material world. While conceding the value of this process, Jung disagreed with its assumption, as well as with Freud's—that psyche arises from matter. Instead, he wrote that he started "with the assumption of the sovereignty of the psyche,"[13] with all the dynamics of self-generation, healing, personal-cultural identity, and typological inheritance that sovereignty implies. The Soul's endless invention of new symbols in dreams and great cultural stories are the language of this psychic sovereignty and its individuating fruits that include a comprehensive type consciousness.

SYMBOLISM IN PSYCHE AND TYPE

Symbols come to us from the archetypal potentials of the Self (or Soul), which always seeks to resolve the tension created by opposites and thereby encourage growth. Opposites are energies and structures that arise as the individual and the collective cultural consciousness develops. When personal or societal resistances cause us to become stuck in one-half of a pair of opposites, our ego complex becomes, according to Jung, "barbaric."[14] This one-sidedness leads to intrapsychic and interpersonal violence. To be stuck in either of the poles is a kind of death wish and a quick way to grow old. However, between opposites there can be a vitalizing dynamic tension. Attraction is inherent in opposites, including opposite types. I have observed, for example, that the dreams of my clients constantly present archetypal symbols as well as the client's actualized complexes of INFP qualities that seek to compensate for our ESTJ cultural dominance. Symbols, Jung teaches, reveal the damaging effects of a rigid one-sidedness, the natural inborn attractions of the type opposites that lead to healing and growth, as well as the element that reconciles conflicting opposites.

Jung argues that there is an autonomous, creative faculty in the psyche, independent of our conscious will, that continually unites opposites. This faculty—fantasy, or imagination—is "a vital process, a continually creative act."[15] Fantasy, Jung continues, operates through all the four functions. Fantasy is "the clearest expression of the specific activity of the psyche," the preeminent creative activity that "fashions the bridge between the irreconcilable claims of subject and object, introversion and extraversion."[16] Jung examines the power of autonomous fantasy (or imagination) in the context of discussing the medieval philosophical conflict between nominalism (the primacy of the idea that Jung equates with introversion) and realism (the primacy of things that Jung equates with extraversion). Abelard attempted to reconcile these two positions with his argument for "conceptualism." Jung, however, suggests that a better term than "conceptualism" could be found, since idea and thing come together in the human psyche through the autonomous activity of fantasy. Rather than calling this resolution "conceptualism," Jung suggests the term *"esse in anima"* ("existence in the soul"). It is the autonomous fantasy—or imaginative—activity of the psyche that unites the sensory impressions of things with the abstractness of the idea.[17] In other words, autonomous fantasy or imagination unites extraversion (things) and introversion (ideas).

Fostering the personal and collective sensitivity to and consciousness of symbols as the Soul's language, however, depends on the culture. The relation of the individual to his or her symbolic life "is very largely conditioned by his relation to the unconscious in general, and this in turn is conditioned by the spirit of the age." Unfortunately, Jung continues, "Christianity, like every closed system of religion, has an undoubted tendency to suppress the unconscious in the individual, as much as possible, thus paralyzing his fantasy activities."[18] Religion tends to stereotype symbols because this leads to easier collective conformity among church members. But by demanding a literal acceptance of established symbols, the Church ignores our creative depths and our individual potential for wisdom and truth. We have also experienced in Jung's depth psychology, as well as in any lived spirituality, that the literalizing and stereotyping of a symbol destroys the very vitals of psychology and spirituality. We forget, for example, that all scriptures are first and foremost symbolic records of humankind's encounters with God and with one another, and only secondarily recorded history and established dogmas.

Jung surmises that, tragically, the voice of the unconscious as intuitive and feeling fantasy became, for the early Christians, the voice of the devil. The devil as the so-called "father of lies," Jung muses, may often represent the frightening and strange images of the unconscious, and so may be speaking the truth. Jung then gives an amusing account of a monk's active imagination dialogue with the devil. At first addressing the monk, Satan speaks the truth about his downfall due to the power of God and his Son. Then he wonders why Christians heap such abuse on him, for, he says, "It is not I who trouble them but it is they who trouble themselves." The monk responds: "How does it happen that whilst thou hast been a liar on every other occasion, at this present the truth is spoken by thee?" Satan leaves only when the word "Christ" is spoken.[19] Christians had not learned or had forgotten the subtle message in the Old Testament's book of Job that Satan can, paradoxically, in his "evil" be the guide to a greater good under God's wise dominance.

What is the meaning of this story? The devil puts the responsibility for our fate, our destructive views and our damaging choices where it most often lies: in our own devilish aspects. Each of us is like Pogo, who said, "I met the enemy, and the enemy is us." We are challenged to realize that the devil is, first of all, our own sinful tendencies, in which we ignore our unfinished or distorted aspects. Following Jung's view of this story, Satan represents "the voice of the anchorite's own unconsciousness, in revolt against the forcible suppression of his nature."[20] Confronting and dialoguing with this inner darkness would have benefited the monk enormously. The scriptural Job challenges God in His guise as Satan, providing our model for depth psychological and depth theological work. However, in the monk's active imagination dialogue, naming the literalized historical Christ destroys the symbolic experience of the monk's dark side and obscures the truth of psychic reality, namely, that salvation must first come from within, and secondarily from traditions, dogmas, religious practices, and spiritual mentors and friends. Typologically, the outer-oriented, concrete, and logical ESTJ mentality supplanted the inner-oriented, symbolic INFP attitude in many early Christians and in much of early Christian society. The later development of the sciences also "excluded the standpoint of feeling and fantasy [intuition] and indeed it was absolutely necessary for them to do so," since "the intellect [thinking] is the sovereign of the scientific realm."[21] Again we see our cultural development dominated by science and technology's extraverted sensation thinking approach and tending to exclude the more introverted intuitive feeling poles of the Soul's compass.

Psychologies, continues Jung, try to be hard sciences. They cannot be, though, for in psychology, science has entered the sphere of "practical application" within the mystery of each person. Here, "intellect" must be at the "service of creative power and purpose" (read the dynamics of the unconscious). In psychology, "creative fantasy is given prior place."[22] Psychological science must then include both intellect and feeling. It is wrong to be one-sided and to say, like Faust, that "feeling is all," even as our society tends to say "thinking is all." For Jung, the bridge between feeling and thinking is "creative fantasy"[23] that must be used "within just bounds," or it "can degenerate into the rankest growth." Jung means that the creative contents of the unconscious demand conscious reflection and containment. We recall in this regard what Jung says about the inferior function: its images are inevitably wild, frightening, and yet potentially creative. Jung also notes that we cannot integrate the inferior function unless we surrender some of the energy of the dominant function and relinquish some of its hegemony over consciousness. In other words, we cannot transform an inferior function directly into a superior one. We have to help the inferior function become conscious.[24]

Jung found the approaches of both Freud and Adler to be one-sided. Freud, as we know, focused on sexuality, and Adler on power. Freud's extraverted interest was in "establishing the strongest relation between subject and object;" Adler's introverted preference needed to break the spell created by that same energy flow "in order to save the ego from suffocating in its own defensive armor."[25] Freud focused his psychology on the problem of instincts, and Adler dealt with the problem of power in "ego-superiority."[26] Jung recognized that for Freud, sexuality was the basic formula; sexuality expressed the most powerful bond between two people. For Adler, the subject's power made him effective against the object.

In Jung's view, each in his one-sidedness repressed the other's point of view. However, even though Freud reduced fantasy to infantile instinct and Adler reduced it to the power drive, the two psychologies could have been reconciled via the motive force of unconscious symbolism. Now Jung gives us one of his greatest insights—one that addresses the depth to which typology takes us—namely, the third level, the Soul's play behavior as creative spontaneity.

Jung argues that both Freud and Adler rejected the principle of imagination by seeing it as a disguised replay of once-known material. Hence in their view, imaginative activity could not bring forth anything new. Jung, however, recognizes that fantasy—the manifestation of the psyche's imaginative capacity—expresses what lies outside the purview of consciousness, that is, an extraverted consciousness that represses introversion experiences and introverted fantasies, and an introverted consciousness that represses outer experiences and extraverted fantasies. The undeveloped, and hence archaic, embryonic function, whether feeling, sensation, intuition, or thinking, gets repressed (because it is a minimal embarrassment to the conscious personality), but expresses itself in involuntary fantasies. This inferiority vis-à-vis the developed function(s) is what makes these sorts of spontaneous fantasies unacceptable or frightening. *"And yet we know,"* Jung reminds us, *"that every good idea and every creative work are the off- spring of the imagination,* and have their source in what one is pleased to call infantile fantasy," and "The dynamic principle of fantasy is *play*[27] (emphasis added). All creativity, not just that seen in the works of artists, is born of the imagination, of fantasies we catch and develop. But fantasies in their raw form are only a potential. We must develop them further to realize their worth, and that development comes not through taking them apart to expose their "infantile" roots, but in synthesizing them "by means of a constructive method"[28] such as active imagination, a process in which we consciously strive to dialogue with images that emerge spontaneously from the unconscious.

In the psyche, extraversion and introversion are inseparable from one of the functions, whether that be sensation, intuition, thinking, or feeling. For example, if extraversion is repressed, it represses the function that is naturally extraverted. Jung calls this the "repressed function," the "unrecognized unconscious function," or the "inferior function." This repressed function, while often frightening to the most developed (and hence conscious) function, is also the pregnant opening to the creative, chaotic depths, to the inventive play of fantasy, without which "no creative work has ever yet come to birth."[29] We are reminded here that such creative fantasy is available to all in the form of dreams—the evidence of the playful, childlike nature of the unconscious (figure 3.1, page 68, third level), and of the wholesome awe and wonder about this creativity, which is the essence of prayer (fourth level).

By means of what he calls the "constructive method," Jung describes the dialogue between our reflective consciousness and what emerges into consciousness from the unconscious (e.g., a dialogue between our dominant and inferior functions). For example, conscious work with the emotionally charged images of dreams and spontaneous insights carries the dream forward and transforms dream images into effective psychic organs that serve life in the world. There is no creative work without a disciplined and differentiated consciousness that does not drown in dream images, but can dialogue spontaneously in serious play with the felt symbols from the unconscious. In typological terms, we can say that without a pragmatic consciousness doing ST and SF work, we will not realize the potential NT and NF creativity of play.

Jung found that many scholars, philosophers, and artists had discussed human differences, which he saw as evidence of typology. For example, Friedrich von Schiller's ideas helped Jung formulate his concept of dominant and inferior functions. Schiller had identified a kind of feeling/sensation function (which Jung later identified as feeling on one hand, and thinking on the other) which he thought demanded reconciliation via "the play instinct." He also identified two kinds of poets, the "naive," who are extraverted and sensate oriented, and the "sentimental," who are introverted and intuitively disposed.[30]

In Nietzsche's two dimensions of Greek life, the Apollonian and the Dionysian, Jung found additional support for the distinction between introversion and extraversion. The Apollonian is an introverted mixture of the intuitive and feeling functions based on an inner perception of beauty that produces a psychological state, which Nietzsche called "dreaming." The Dionysian is characterized by a streaming outward akin to Goethe's distole and Schiller's world-embracing extraversion, producing a psychological state that Nietzsche called "intoxication," thus evoking the idea of the sensation function.[31]

In his drama, "Prometheus and Epimetheus," Carl Spitteler described twin brothers. Jung recognized the introverted attitude in Prometheus, the "forethinker," and the extraverted attitude in his twin, Epimetheus, the "afterthinker."[32] Prometheus, the introvert, reflects before acting; Epimetheus, the extravert, acts first and only later reflects. Spitteler imagined a uniting symbol, an image that would join the two brothers and the two attitudes of introversion and extraversion, as a middle or unifying way in the form of a savior or a Messiah.[33] Jung notes that such uniting symbols are found in many cultures—for example, the pair of opposite faces in Brahmanism, and the Chi energy that unites the extraverted yang and the introverted yin in Taoism. The function of analytical psychology, Jung writes, is to balance psychic opposites, such as the outward thrust of sexuality in Freud and the inner thrust of power in Adler, through what Jung calls "the domestication of the libido."[34]

Jung teaches that symbols are always relative to something else and thus are never isolated. This means that the Soul assimilates both inside and outside objects and transforms them into meaning through the process of symbolization. Jung points to the work that Dante did in the *Divine Comedy,* in which he eventually transformed Beatrice, the young woman who was his inspiring muse, into the Mother of God.[35] A similar symbolic transformation occurs in "Shepherd of Hermas," a story from the early centuries of the Church, in which Hermas, sensually attracted to a woman, changed her through fantasy into a guiding inner feminine figure and finally into Mother Church in the form of a tower he helped construct as a devoted lifelong servant.[36] Sensuality, at one end of the body-spirit opposites, is transformed into and enhanced by spiritual symbols.[37] This sort of reconciliation of opposites and the assimilation and transformation of objects, events, and persons through symbols strengthens the soul with meaning, purpose, creativity, and spirituality.

The symbol can transform the power we invest in persons in the world as well as the power that inner images exert over us. The effect of the mediating symbol is to free us from the spell of the inner or outer other, and raise our consciousness to a new level where we experience our deeper sense of identity and self-esteem. By doing this we free the Self, too often inaccessible because of the control of the outer object, and are then better able to make authentic choices (i.e., choices in accord with our innate potentials). We will learn throughout this book that such changes never occur unless we work with the emotions that symbols and images present to us in dreams.

To see more clearly how this process can work, let us consider the common experience of one who fears the extraverted mother or father, experienced and internalized in childhood, who appears in memories and dreams as an overpowering parental figure. A person with overpowering parents would project these internalized parents on outside authority figures. Through the determined, conscious inner work of facing, dialoguing, or wrestling with the imaged powerful figures, this person can slowly transform the childhood giants into a sense of personal power, and from this introverted ground function more confidently in society.

For example, a young man with introverted, intuitive, feeling, and perceiving preferences came to me depressed because he knew he was in the wrong field of work and felt powerless to leave it because his well-known stepfather favored this occupation. He began to seek help from the unconscious to free himself. He dreamt:

> I see the Empire State Building in all its glory, reminding me of my stepdad. Suddenly, a great cascade of water descends down on the building, melting it down until it disappears below the surface of a lake that had formed. At this moment I decide to buy the land and the lake and am beginning to plan the construction of my own building.

Human artifacts in dreams are invariably symbols of our conscious work. The fact that the symbol of power, the Empire State Building, is a human construction tells us that the dreamer, in striving to imitate his ESTJ (extraverted, sensate, thinking, and judging) stepfather, had contributed consciously to the development of his entrapped condition. His unconscious responds with a natural symbolic antagonist to the building: the great flood of water that dissolves his unwanted structure, symbolizing his unhappy life in an inappropriate occupation. In the dream, he intends to erect his own building, telling us that our young man is beginning to consciously build his own destiny based on his innate typology and overall character.

Symbols in dreams reconcile and integrate typological as well as other opposites. The most powerful symbolic figure in a dream is a God figure. Jung understood such a figure as an inner experience—that is, as a symbol—rather than as the God of metaphysics or faith. We do not know the Godhead directly, Jung argued, but we do experience this ultimate mystery in human ways that we call God. Jung drew his inspiration for this viewpoint from the spiritual theology of Meister Eckhart, the thirteenth-century German mystic.[38] Both Meister Eckhart and Jung experienced God as an inner force. God and humankind were not wholly cut off from each other; on the contrary, each was dependent on the other. From the viewpoint of psychology, Jung saw the God-image as a symbolic expression of a particular function of the psyche that has absolute ascendency over the will of the individual. What the God-image dictated, the ego was constrained to do.[39]

According to Jung and Eckhart, God is a negative factor in our life when His power is experienced mainly in an outer sacred figure, religious practice, or church dogma that we internalize as a constricting and punishing psychic authority. We also experience God as negative when historical figures, such as a Hitler, assume the prerogatives of God by massacring millions of people. Conversely, God is a positive factor when we recognize Soul or Self as the true locus of the God experience in ourselves. We can then begin an inner dialogue with God as our mysterious depth to realize our fullest possibilities as individuals in the process of what Jung calls individuation.

The dialogue with God (i.e., with our inner experience and image of God) has typological overtones. For example, an introverted thinking type may unhappily give too much power or undue respect to an extraverted feeling person, treating that person as if he were possessed of a superhuman strength or insight. After all, extraverted feeling is the introverted thinker's inferior function and it assumes an inner power that evokes awe and terror, as does a naive experience of an externally perceived God. Eckhart held that he was not happy when he was taught that he existed only *in* God. He was not happy when he perceived God as an object external to him. "I am happy only when God is *in me*," he exclaimed, meaning that God is *in* him when he is not cowering before divinity, but humbly and courageously experiencing God's inner friendship.[40] In typological terms, our introverted thinking type must, with the help of the Godlike support of the Soul, move toward individuation first by integrating his innate introverted thinking, and, second, by effectively confronting and making some use of his inferior extraverted feeling. This corresponds to Eckhart's felt happiness when God is in him.

JUNG'S PSYCHOLOGY OF THE INDIVIDUAL

We can now better understand how it is that Jung's psychology is considered the preeminent psychology of the individual: all fundamental change in society, Jung taught, occurs in the individual. Jung's view of history is similar to that of Carlyle, who held that history is essentially biography. Arnold Toynbee, reading of the preeminent importance of the individual in *Psychological Types,* added this vital principle to his historical method and research. He acknowledged his gratitude to that which opened up for him, in his words, "a new dimension in the realm of Life."[41] Of course, social and cultural and even geographical forces do impinge on the individual. But in the final analysis, it is the individual who assimilates the strengths and overcomes the limitations of society and then contributes to the further development of that society. For example, the face of America changed when two individuals voiced their rage at years of suffering and oppression. First, Rosa Parks challenged segregation by refusing to move to the back of the bus in Birmingham, Alabama. In that same city, a young preacher and legendary orator, Martin Luther King, Jr., began leading freedom marches.

In this context, we will consider Jung's often nebulous thoughts in *Psychological Types* on the types as archetypes. We have touched on this subject in the introduction, and have noted that Jung never *consistently or systemically* made up his mind in this regard. As discussed in his last writing, *Man and His Symbols,* Jung kept discussions of the types and the archetypes explicitly separate in considering their impact on and appearance in dreams. Yet in the same book he implicitly described types as archetypes. In the following section we shall see that, in *Psychological Types* and in other writings, Jung gave more direct indications of the archetypal nature of types and the type couplings than he did in his last article and most of his writings.

INTIMATION OF TYPES AS ARCHETYPES

Jung did not give a definition or even a description of archetypes in chapter 11, "Definitions," of *Psychological Types*. His editors note that the notion of the archetype was always implicit in Jung's thought, but that he formulated the concept only in the course of time.[42] However, intimations of the types—the four functions and the two attitudes—as archetypes abound in all of Jung's writings, particularly as he describes all the familiar major elements we use in describing the functions and attitudes. For example, he includes the term "Self" in his "Definitions" chapter.[43] Besides being symbolized in literature by great figures such as a king or a hero, the Self appears in the form of *totality symbols, such as the circle, square, squared circle, cross,* etc. The Self can appear as a duality or a union of opposites, such as the interplay of yang and yin in Taoism. The square and circle are all examples of the mandala, a major archetype in the Jungian corpus and "the totality symbol" by which Jung has represented his typological system. We have also seen in chapter 2 that Taoism is an archetypal system that inspired Jung's development of typology. The squared circle connotes a figure of four equal sides within a circle. Jung referred often to the archetypal nature of circular quaternities as symbols of spiritual completeness. We can deduce, therefore, that the type Compass as a total system is an archetype.

Jung strongly suggests that the four functions constitute such an archetypal foursome. By means of consciousness we adapt and orient ourselves to the inner and the outer worlds. Jung found empirically that there were four basic functions that sufficed to account for the ability of our consciousness to adapt and orient us to the inner and the outer worlds.[44] A complete orientation would need to employ all four functions, further strengthened by the attitudes. Thinking facilitates cognition and judgment; feeling tells us the value of something; sensation informs us of concrete reality through our tactile, visual, auditory, gustatory, and kinesthetic senses; and intuition reveals the inherent possibilities that may be hidden in the background.[45] For Jung this quaternity makes up "a complete picture of a given situation," another way of describing a substantial pattern that we call an archetype.[46] Jung writes of the cross as another mandala-like way of picturing the functions: one axis of the cross is "rational" (feeling and thinking), the other is "irrational" (intuition and sensation). The combination of cross and circle produces the type mandala with its four quadrants. Then Jung characterizes the type circle and its quadrants as a compass by means of which we orient ourselves, a compass for our psychological voyage of discovery "that provides a system of comparison and orientation which makes possible something that has long been lacking, a critical psychology."[47]

The magnetized needle of the compass always points to the magnetic north pole. This makes possible the establishment of the three other directions: south as directly opposite the needle, west to the left of north and east to the right of north. The type compass functions in a comparable way in that the dominant function (and, as I will later argue, the dominant coupling) points one's Soul on both conscious and unconscious levels toward its strongest energies, its most constant preferences, and its most consistent interests. If that dominant function is, say, thinking, and is represented on the top of a vertical axis, then its opposite psychic direction is the inferior function, feeling. The two other functions, sensation and intuition, are depicted on the horizontal axis, one of which will be the first auxiliary and the other, the second auxiliary.

Jung uses another term to refer to and yet not name the archetypal quality of the four functions: he speaks of their "numinal accent."[48] This "accent" refers to the sudden sense of awe and excitement emanating from the unconscious that often accompanies the discovery of our own type and which is typical of an archetypal experience. Numinal comes from "numen," which, according to *Webster's,* in Roman mythology refers to the "presiding spirit" and "divine will" that suggests a sacred imperative. In the context of psychological types, this means living according to our innate typological constitution that emerges from that mysterious depth that is the Self—what Jung characterized as "God within us." As archetypes, the types "have a numinous character which can only be described as spiritual.[49] James Hillman comments on this quality, particularly in the four functions: "We begin to see that the four types are more than mere manners of functioning. There is something more at work in them, something numinal. . . . And surely when in the grips of our typical set, as we cannot help but be when we imagine ourselves typologically, the structuring power of the type is like that of an archetype or mythologem."[50] We can deduce that Jung perceived the archetypal nature of the types, though he never explicitly said so in any organized way.

As a matter of fact, Jung's *very first* definition of archetypes (in 1919) evoked the types. He called the archetypes "the *a priori,* inborn forms of 'intuition'" and "necessary *a priori* determinants of all psychic processes."[51] Simply put, since Jung describes intuition as a perception of future possibilities by way of the unconscious, it follows that the archetypes as innate potentials are a kind of inexhaustible intuitive well of possibilities that make up our original human endowment. Jung adds that the instincts and the archetypes together constitute the "collective unconscious" (that he later also called the "objective psyche").[52] For Jung, "collective" meant not the contents of the personal unconscious which are personal and idiosyncratic, but those patterns which are universal and appear everywhere in human cultures. So the archetypes are inborn and "necessary *a priori* determinants" of our human nature that exist universally in all human beings. On the other hand, they are not inborn specific ideas but only potential sources of such ideas. Jung also uses the term "primordial images" to describe archetypes. This refers to consistent kinds of images and behaviors that a given archetype may produce. These are specific expressions of the archetypes that we hear and see; the "archetypes as such" are silent and invisible intuitive potentials.

If the archetypes are also described as "*a priori* determinants" in the unconscious, the types fit this description. They are "inborn forms" of the consistent traits, images, and behaviors found in persons throughout the world. The archetypal nature of typology is further shown by the way that types describe and articulate the figures in fairy tales and myths, which are archetypal stories found in every culture.

Jung's unfinished yet implicit consciousness of types as archetypes is evident in another passage in *Psychological Types,* although he does not include the term "archetype" in chapter 11, "Definitions." However, by using the index of the book, I learned that Jung had written directly of the archetypal nature of introversion. He first states that this type is "normally oriented by the psychic structure." Psychic structure, which is hereditary, is not the same as ego structure, which is formed in the course of early development.[53] Here Jung attributes to introversion the characteristic of all archetypes: they are inborn in the Soul, and they originate in the Soul's "psychic structure," which Jung called the Self. Jung then relates the archetypes to the instincts in the collective unconscious and the Self:

> The psychic structure is . . . what I call the "collective unconscious." The individual self is a portion or segment or representative of something present in all living creatures, an exponent of the specific mode of psychological behavior, which varies from species to species and is inborn in each of its members. The inborn mode of *acting* has long been known as *instinct,* and for the inborn mode of psychic apprehension I have proposed the term *archetype.* I may assume that what is understood by instinct is familiar to everyone. It is another matter with the archetype. What I understand by it is identical with the "primordial image."[54]

For Jung, introversion is both instinct and archetype, a bodily as well as a psychic reality. The archetype is the intelligent describer of the instinct of introversion that is rooted in the body as a speechless, spontaneous activity. According to Jung, this intelligence appears in consciousness as a "primordial image" that originates from its "inborn mode of psychic apprehension" in the unconscious and corresponds with its bodily instincts. In a later essay, Jung uses the analogy of the color spectrum, infrared to ultraviolet, to describe the relationship, respectively, of instinct with archetype, so that the two seem to be distinct yet united in one psychosomatic reality. By virtue of this innate, unconscious intelligence, we consciously recognize in ourselves and others consistent patterns of action, bodily responses, story, image, and emotion, which make up our introverted awareness in this case.[55]

Although he does not use the term archetype, Jung confirms the archetypal nature of the functions and attitudes in a backhanded way when he discusses archetypes in preferential, that is, typological terms. After stating that the archetype is a "symbolic formula," he continues: "The contents of the collective unconscious are represented in consciousness in the *form of pronounced preferences and definite ways of looking at things*" [emphasis added].[56]

In his 1925 seminar Jung characterizes the thinking function as archetypal when he says that thinking is based only indirectly on the empirical world. The stronger influence in the mind of the person who prefers thinking is "certain general or collective ideas" that "go back to archetypal origins."[57] Thus substantial evidence exists, however scattered and indirect, for the conclusion that Jung understood the types as archetypes.

Another indirect evidence of the archetypal nature of the types is found in Jung's discussion of complexes in *Psychological Types* and elsewhere. We have already noted that a complex is a concrete internalization or incarnation of the archetype; for example, the mother archetype and its universal images and traits are collective roots of the mother-complex's internalized, specific configurations of one's experience of the mother. This complex could not exist if it were not rooted in the mother archetype, just as the assimilation of food could not occur without the existence of the intestinal organs. Jung writes elsewhere that "The mother archetype forms the foundation of the so-called mother-complex." On the other hand, we would never know the existence of the mother archetype without the experienced evidence of both archetypal images and traits and the images and characteristics of the mother-complex.[58]

In appendix 3 of *Psychological Types*, entitled "A Psychological Theory of Types," Jung discusses his "theory of complexes" as "emotionally-toned contents, having a certain amount of autonomy," which are therefore "psychic entities which are outside of the control of the conscious mind."[59] Usually, they appear as negative in the sense of their being "sore spots" or "skeletons in the cupboard" in sudden fantasies, memories and dreams.[60] These sorts of complexes are considered inferior, Jung continues, but only in the sense "that something discordant, unassimilated, and antagonistic exists, perhaps as an obstacle, but also as an incentive to greater effort, and so, perhaps, to new possibilities of achievement."[61] The root of the word complex is the Latin *complexus* (*com* = with, and *plectare* = to weave). The adjectival form, complicated, means "to encircle, embrace." The center of this circle is a specific emotion that functions like a magnet, attracting memories, images, events, ideas, and type characteristics. A complex is somewhat unconscious but also haunts the fringes of our consciousness. Given Jung's penchant for circles, we can represent the complex as circular, like the mandala and the type compass.

Each type, as inherited and universal, is archetypal. However, as an individual experience of personality, each type or configuration of types is a complex, having both negative and positive dimensions, usually depending on the differences or congruences the child experiences between its inherent typological endowment and the parent's typology, or between one's typology and our dominant ESTJ culture. Further, within each assemblage of types, either as an attitude/function duo, a perceiving/judging coupling, or any of the sixteen *MBTI* types, the individual types are operative in an interactive circle, and, as Henry Thompson has written, are nonlinearly transformative and not the sum of linear parts.[62]

Jung points out that "complexes are infinitely varied," yet are constituted from a "small number of primary forms," based on one's "innate . . . individual disposition," meaning the archetype.[63] Hence every type discussed in this book, whether individual or coupled, dominant, auxiliary, or inferior, or one of the *MBTI* sixteen, or a type functioning as a cultural phase of life, a creative moment, and so forth, is both an inherited archetype and a learned complex. Therefore, persons with the same typological preferences are both similar, and yet uniquely varied.

In a 1934 lecture, "A Review of the Complex Theory," Jung sees an even larger meaning for the complexes, beyond revealing and concretizing the archetypes.[64] He points out first that Freud must be given credit for discovering the unconscious and pointing to dreams as the *via regia,* or "royal road," to "those dark places." But, he continues, the royal road is not the dream as Freud thought, but the complex "which is the architect of dreams and symptoms," and therefore the way to health and creativity—signposts on the road to individuation.[65] When we pursue the complex, Jung warns, we enter into dark places in the Soul as well as in society, like "the storm of indignation" that arose among many when Freud's discoveries became known. We encounter the sacrosanct, the *numinosum,*[66] the frightening sacredness of the unconscious archetypes. The complex was so important to Jung that he even called his system and psychoanalysis in general "complex psychology."[67]

All that I am saying here about the painful but rewarding aspects of the complexes has already been said and will be said about the types that are unfamiliar to our consciousness, including their "numinal accent," which we can experience either as our response to an opposite attitude or a tertiary or inferior function, or as the disturbing influence of people whose types are different from ours.

This frustrating pursuit of the archetypal and complexlike character of types would not have been necessary if Jung had clearly and systemically addressed this important subject. Jung kept types and archetypes distinct even in what I call his "Last Will and Testament," a 94-page lead article in the book *Man and His Symbols,* which he completed only a short time before he died. Yet he discussed types there as if they were archetypes: they are inherited potencies emerging from the unconscious, they appear in consciousness as patterns, and, as we have already discussed above about archetypes, they are cognizant of instinctual forces. As in all archetypes, if they are not honored and dialogued with, we will become ill in mind and body.[68]

However, no person, even one as abundantly creative as Jung, can complete everything in a lifetime. Many of us are now attempting to fill this gap in his type theory.

JUNG'S DESCRIPTION OF THE COUPLINGS

This archetypal base is true of all type combinations, such as those combining attitudes and functions with those making up the judging and perceiving couplings, which form the four directional patterns of the type compass. This is important not only because of the intrinsic importance of the couplings, but for another reason. In chapter 10 of this book, when we begin to see differences between the Jung and the *MBTI* systems and three oppositional systems of typology, we will understand what it means to lose a coupling consciousness in understanding human differences.

Jung touches on the couplings whenever he discusses the one-sidedness of any type, whether as attitude or function. He has held that any one-sidedness is barbaric from the beginning chapter of *Psychological Types.* By implication, the coupling of the dominant function and attitude and its auxiliary and attitude is constantly called for, to avoid such one-sidedness. He acknowledges in many places that the opposites in any spectrum, the E–I, the S–N, and the T–F, are constantly battling. But he also holds that this same polarity of opposites is the basis of life; paradoxically, opposites attract, mate, and propagate new life both biologically and psychically. It is in this context that we can look at the very last three pages of his chapter 10, "General Description of the Type," where he talks about the "Principal and Auxiliary Functions."[69]

Here Jung writes more directly, even if only embryonically, about couplings when he shows that one function is "principal" and another function is its "auxiliary," thus sowing the seeds of a larger psychology based on these combinations. Subsequently, he never watered those seeds. I know of no analysts, including myself, who have watered them since. The editors of *Psychological Types* do not even show the terms "principal" and "auxiliary" in the index.

The seminal idea about the couplings remained dormant for forty-one years until Myers nurtured it in 1962, and a typological team I call the Osmond Group gave it further sustenance in 1977. As I will illustrate and develop in chapter 5, these two writings fired my interest in the late eighties. When I went again to Jung's three pages on the principal/auxiliary combinations, I read the sentences in a new light. It was as if I was reading them for the first time, especially the first paragraph. There, I read Jung's disclaimer of the individual types, which he had just finished describing: "In the foregoing descriptions I have no desire to give my readers the impression that these types occur at all frequently in such pure form in actual life." Then he wrote a sentence which is the primary seed for all subsequent developments of the couplings:

> Closer investigation shows with great regularity that, besides the most differentiated [principal] function, another, less differentiated [auxiliary] function of

secondary importance is invariably present in consciousness and exerts a co-determining influence.[70]

Later, in a private conversation with Mary McCaulley, I learned that Myers considered this sentence, especially with its idea of "a co-determining influence," to be an important quote and inspiration for her creative advance of a coupling consciousness. Here, too, is the basis for my thoughts that the two members of each coupling are like themes in a piece of music. There is, in their "co-determining" relationship, the intimation of what we all regularly experience, that we are always perceiving and then deciding in every moment of life.

Jung insists, however, in stressing the dominance of one of the functions, and so he rules out "the presence of a second function of equal power." That second function must instead have a "secondary importance" and it "comes into play more as an auxiliary or complementary function."[71] The term "complementary" resonates more than "secondary" with the reality of the couplings, in which one is indeed dominant and the other is auxiliary and yet both must learn to live with one another in a close partnership. Jung presents this idea of partnership in a backhanded way when he explains that though their natures and tasks are different, they are not thereby "antagonistic."[72] Thus the perceiving functions give "welcome assistance" to thinking as a judging function, for example. However, the auxiliary *"serves,"* without any claim to autonomy separate from the dominant function. It is also always linked to the opposite attitude, so that a person with an introverted principal needs an extraverted auxiliary function and vice versa. Moreover, according to Jung, the auxiliary function serves two other needs: it links one's consciousness to the inferior function and the unconscious, and it protects one's consciousness from the potential chaos, and even madness, of the unconscious inferior type.[73]

In the midst of all of this, Jung plays with the couplings in a more integral and complementary way, though retaining the dominant-auxiliary focus. He writes:

The resulting combinations present the familiar picture of, for instance, practical thinking, allied with sensation, speculative thinking forging ahead with intuition, artistic intuition selecting and presenting its images with the help of feeling-values, and philosophical intuition systematizing its vision into comprehensible thought by means of a powerful intellect, and so on.[74]

It is interesting that Jung sees in each of these an affinity between the adjective ascribed to each dominant function and its auxiliary function. Thus the "practical" thinking is allied with "sensation," which of its very nature is earthy, detailed, and practical. This is further evidence of communality and cooperation between the two functions, according to Jung. Further, he sees the possibility of the opposite couplings in the type circle. He writes:

The unconscious functions likewise group themselves in patterns correlated with the conscious ones. Thus, the correlative of conscious practical thinking may be an unconscious, intuitive-feeling attitude, with feeling under a stronger inhibition than intuition.[75]

Feeling is under a "stronger inhibition" in relationship to thinking than intuition is with its opposite, sensation, because thinking as the dominant function has such an immediate superiority in influence and energy in the judging spectrum. On the other hand, in focusing on the couplings, Jung indicates that practical thinking [ST] is opposite the intuitive feeling [NF]. We can, therefore, imagine Jung's provisional type mandala as looking like figure 3.2. The reason why eight couplings are shown is that Jung, unlike Myers, had not learned to depict the couplings as they actually appear in our everyday experience: first, in the process of perceiving, then in a decisive action, irrespective of which function is dominant.

A Provisional Mandala of the Type Couplings

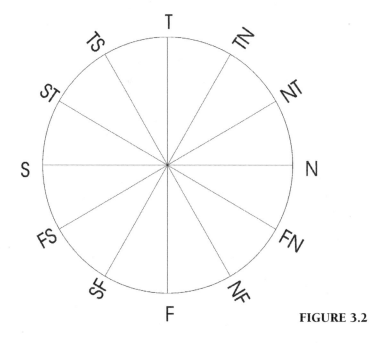

FIGURE 3.2

We are reminded that this diagram represents the final formal work that Jung did with the *Types* book. In his 1925 lectures, he does place typology into the broader context of all his current theories, focusing particularly on his theory of opposites. He made one diagram which shows the four couplings but only as links to the individual types on the type circle.[76] It is my view that if he had written a second book on types, he would have developed the psychology of the couplings. Instead, it was left to the genius of Isabel Briggs Myers to significantly further this development forty-one years later.

No analysts have written about the couplings, though some have written extensively about certain aspects of typology. Maria-Louise von Franz and James Hillman have done outstanding work in writing, respectively, of the inferior function and the feeling function in their important book, *Jung's Typology*.[77] We have already noted Hillman's understanding of the types as archetypes in his 1980 lecture when he pointed to Jung's recognition of the "numinal accent" of each type. However, he discussed the individual types and their polarities only as images. He wrote "that typological polarities are themselves an image: an image of a sliding scale along a straight line." By virtue of seeing types exclusively as images, Hillman continues, we don't have "to multiply instances to prove the type"; rather, "the type multiplies images out of itself." For example, "a typical introvert is not conceptually defined or described as a cluster of traits. It is my younger brother sunk in thought on the beach under the sea gulls."[78]

I value Hillman's wanting to focus on the imaginal descriptions of each type, since very little thought has been given to this. However, I also value the fact that they are "a cluster of traits." All archetypes can be described as images and complex patterns in great stories, as well as a complex of specific characteristics, seen in such books on archetypes as Jean Shinoda Bolin's *Goddesses in Every Woman* and Moore and Gillette's *King, Warrior, Magician, Lover.* Traits and images do not exclude one another, any more than sensation's prosaic details and intuition's inventive pictures do. Hillman, as a strong intuitive, is naturally attracted to the types as images, and presents a good example of how we experience the "numinal accent" of our own type. He gets too caught up in the power of his intuition's energies and images— overall, its archetypal pull—and so can get myopically one-sided about any sensing aspect of the types.

Another valuable aspect of Hillman's work is his discussion of the feeling function and its deeper archetypal meaning. Jung has written that the feeling function exhibits "redemptive features" in our healing and growth.[79] Each of the functions has its own unique archetypal function and awakens the unconscious when acting as the inferior one in the psyche. However, according to Jung and Hillman, only the feeling function as the numinous emotional value in any relationship provides the indispensable healing and the maturing linchpin between the consciousness and the unconscious. Grounded in it, we are in an authentic self love, and then capable of loving others. I will show in this book that this also applies to the intuitive/feeling (NF) combination.

Now we are ready to consider the individual types imaginally and their implications for couplings before proceeding to the characteristics of the couplings themselves.

Notes

1. C. G. Jung, *The Collected Works of C. G. Jung* (hereafter cited as *CW*), vol. 6, *Psychological Types,* English edition, translated by H. G. Baynes (1923; rpt., Princeton NJ: Princeton University Press, 1971), para. 968.

2. Ibid., para. 666.

3. Jung, "A Review of the Complex Theory," in *CW*, vol. 8, *The Structure and Dynamics of the Psyche* (Princeton NJ: Princeton University Press, 1960). Dealing with complexes became so important for Jung that, after noting the importance of Freud's discovery of them, he wrote: "The *via regia* to the unconscious is not the dream, as he thought, but the complex, which is the architect of dreams and of symptoms" (para. 211). Given Jung's overall theory, he means here that the complex is the architect only because it functions as agent for the Self, as chief architect of all complexes and archetypes.

4. Jung, *CW*, Vol. 6 *Psychological Types,* para. 28.

5. Ibid., para. 26.

6. Ibid., para. 33.

7. Ibid., para. 34.

8. Ibid., para. 36.

9. Ibid., paras. 961–62.

10. Ibid., para. 963.

11. Ibid., para. 963.

12. Ibid., para. 964.

13. Ibid., para. 968.

14. Ibid., paras. 346 and 357.

15. Ibid., para. 78.

16. Ibid., para. 78.

17. Ibid., paras. 77–78.

18. Ibid., para. 80.

19. Ibid., para. 82.

20. Ibid., para. 82.

21. Ibid., para. 84.

22. Ibid., para. 84.

23. Ibid., paras. 85–86.

24. Ibid., para. 131.

25. Ibid., para. 91.

26. Ibid., para. 90.

27. Ibid., para. 93.

28. Ibid., para. 93.

29. Ibid., para. 93.

30. Ibid., paras. 215–19.

31. Ibid., paras. 234–39.

32. Ibid., para. 276. Jung is at first somewhat tentative in ascribing these meanings to the names. Webster's dictionary is quite forthright in doing so.

33. Ibid., para. 326.

34. Ibid., para. 372.

35. Ibid., paras. 376–77.

36. Ibid., paras. 381–91.

37. Ibid., para. 391.

38. Ibid., paras. 407–33.

39. Ibid., para. 412.

40. Jung's translation is as follows: "For so long as God, the highest value, is not in the soul, it is somewhere outside. God must be withdrawn from objects and brought into the soul, and this is a 'Higher state' in which God himself is blissful." Ibid., para. 421.

41. Barry Ulanov, *Jung and The Outside World* (Wilmette IL: Chiron Publications, 1992), p. 221. Ulanov traces on pp. 220–28 the important impact that all of Jung's psychology had on this important historian in the writing of his *A Study of History*. On pp. 226–27, Ulanov notes how Toynbee even classified various religions according to the two attitudes and the four functions. For example, he considers Hinduism and Buddhism introverted and the two religions that have emerged from Judaism, Christianity and Islam, as extraverted.

42. Jung, *CW*, vol. 6, *Psychological Types*, para. 684.

43. Ibid., paras. 789–91.

44. Ibid., para. 958.

45. Ibid., para. 899.

46. Ibid., para. 900.

47. Ibid., para. 959.

48. Ibid., paras. 982–84.

49. Jung, "On the Nature of the Psyche," *CW*, vol. 8, *The Structure and Dynamics of the Psyche,* para. 405. Jung continues: "Consequently, this phenomenon is of the utmost significance for the psychology of religion. . . . It can be healing or destructive, but never indifferent."

50. James Hillman, "Egalitarian Typologies versus the Perception of the Unique," *Eranos Lectures,* no. 4 (Dallas TX: Spring Publications), p. 21. Hillman already has acknowledged here the genius of Jung in creating this "fourfold system" as a mandala. He writes: "That is, it belongs to the rhetoric of the archetypal perspective of fourness to present itself as a systematic whole, a mandala with an internal logic by means of which the system defends itself as all-encompassing. . . . Typology and mandala both serve the same purpose of ordering irreconcilable conflicts" Yet, Hillman adds, "Despite their mandala structure, Jung does not give his types archetypal significance as such. A closer look at the way Jung speaks of the types, however, suggests that they too are archetypal" (pp. 18–21).

51. Jung, "Instinct and the Unconscious," *CW,* vol. 8, *The Structure and Dynamics of the Psyche,* para. 270 (emphasis added).

52. Jung, "On the Nature of the Psyche," *CW,* vol. 8, *The Structure and Dynamics of the Psyche,* para. 414.

53. Jung, *CW,* vol. 6, *Psychological Types,* para. 623.

54. Ibid., para. 624.

55. Jung, "On the Nature of the Psyche," *CW,* vol. 8, *The Structure and Dynamics of the Psyche,* for example in para. 414. Jung progressively moved toward an understanding of the archetype as being a bodily and mental spectrum. Using the color spectrum, he relates the bodily instincts to infrared and the corresponding mental archetypal images to ultraviolet. He then addresses the inner dynamism of the archetype: "The dynamism of the instinct is lodged as it were in the infra-red of the spectrum, whereas the instinctual *image* lies in the ultra-red part" (emphasis added).

56. Jung, *CW,* vol. 6, *Psychological Types,* para. 625.

57. Jung, *Analytical Psychology: Notes of the Seminar Given in 1925* (Princeton NJ: Princeton University Press, 1989), p. 123.

58. Jung, (1959) "Psychological Aspects of the Mother Archetype,"in *CW,* vol. 9:1, *The Archetypes and the Collective Unconscious* (Princeton NJ: Princeton University Press, 1959), para. 161. He continues: "My own experience leads me to believe that the mother always plays an active part in the origin of the disturbance [read, complex], especially in infantile neuroses. . . . In any event, the child's instincts are disturbed, and this constellates archetypes which, in their turn, produce fantasies [archetypal as generalized images of the mother archetype, such as an "animal or witch,"or actual mother-like images based on the experience of the mother, thus the complex] . . . that come between the child and the mother as an alien and often frightening element." Such a disturbance of the instinct, and therefore of the archetype, is often expressed in the lived experience as typological differences between the child and the parent.

59. Jung, *CW,* vol. 6, *Psychological Types,* para. 923.

60. Ibid., para. 924.

61. Ibid., para. 925.

62. Henry L. Thompson, *Jung's Function-Attitudes Explained* (Watkinsville GA: Wormhole Publishing, 1996). Noting the dominance of our culture's "linear version," Thompson writes: "A common application of the linear

approach to Type is to imply that ENFJ=E+N+F+J. Implicit in this linear, additive model is that one will understand an ENFJ if one understands the individual components. . . . As we enter the 21st century, . . . the study of nonlinear systems has become one of the hot topics of the 80's and 90's. A hot topic not only from a mathematical perspective, but from a human and organizational understanding" (pp. 113–14).

63. Jung, *CW*, vol. 6, *Psychological Types,* para. 927.

64. Jung, "A Review of the Complex Theory," *CW,* vol. 8, *The Structure and Dynamics of the Psyche,* p. 210.

65. Ibid.

66. Ibid., p. 216.

67. Ibid., para. 215.

68. Jung et al., eds., *Man and His Symbols* (Garden City NY: Doubleday, 1964), p. 53.

69. Jung, *CW,* vol 6, *Psychological Types,* paras. 666–71.

70. Ibid., para. 666.

71. Ibid., para. 667.

72. Ibid., para. 668.

73. Ibid., para. 670.

74. Ibid., para. 669.

75. Ibid., para. 670.

76. Jung, *Analytical Psychology,* p. 119.

77. Marie Louise von Franz and James Hillman, *Jung's Typology* (Irving TX: Spring Publications, 1979). Von Franz wrote on the "The Inferior Function," in which we are reminded that this function is the fourth function, so that its qualities, as located in the chaos and creative possibilities of the unconscious, is like the fourth dimension. We are reminded that the four functions together constitute an archetypal system, that is, one that exists in every human being. Moreover, we learn that it is by virtue of the fourth function that "In dreams, the inferior function relates to the shadow, the animus or anima and the self," in other words, to all the levels of the psyche (p. 111). On the other hand, when it remains unconscious, we project its primitivity in negative ways on others and entire peoples. Hillman, in his article, "The Feeling Function," notes also the fourfold archetypal nature of the functions, but shows, in beautiful writing,

the varied nature of their expressions in human culture, with a focus on the feeling function. He reminds us of one of the most important tasks of this function, to relate consciousness to the unconscious. He writes: "the cooperative relationship between ego-consciousness and the unconscious dominants—is, as a relationship, largely a function of feeling" (p. 83).

78. Hillman, "Egalitarian Typologies versus the Perception of the Unique," pp. 16–17.

79. Ibid., p. 22. He refers the reader to various sources of this viewpoint in Jung, such as CW, vol 14, paras. 328–34, CW, vol. 16, paras. 488–91, CW, vol. 13, para. 222, and CW, vol. 8, para. 668. He also refers the reader to William Willeford's article, "The Primacy of Feeling," *Journal of Analytical Psychology* 31 (1976): pp. 115–33, where Willeford "argues for a special place for the feeling function beyond Jung's polar equalities." Further because Hillman sees feeling as "the function of the 'subjective sphere' [an idea which brings us again to Jung's early identification of feeling with introversion] he is suggesting that its relation to soul is different and more important than that of the other functions." John Beebe refers to Willeford's book, in which he has further expanded his ideas about the feeling function. The book, published in 1987, is called *Feeling, Imagination, and the Self: Transformation of the Mother-Infant Relationship* (Evanston IL: Northwestern University Press). I refer the reader to the specific discussion of the feeling function in section 2.5.

CHAPTER 4

The Nuts and Bolts, the Fuel and Mobility of Typology

The typological system I have proposed is an attempt, grounded on practical experience, to provide an explanatory basis and theoretical framework for the boundless diversity that has hitherto prevailed in the formulation of psychological concepts.[1]

C. G. Jung

N ORDER TO MAKE SOME SENSE of the "boundless diversity" that Jung perceives in the field of psychology, we need to first understand each of the six building blocks of typology—the two attitudes and the four functions. We need to recognize them as ordinary, everyday, conscious experiences. We also need to understand them as archetypes and know that they exist in us before we experience them in consciousness, know that they are inborn potentials and universal patterns hidden, seedlike, in the human soul. As archetypes, we may feel their effects in sacred and strangely felt events, an effect that Jung calls "numinous." Jung writes that all archetypes—including the six building blocks of typology—have, as discussed in chapter 3, a "numinal accent," his term for the archetypal "energy charge." This charge powers an individual's preferred attitude and function as well as his or her despised or feared inferior attitudes and functions, which attract us or challenge us from the Soul's depth.[2]

However, our American culture so deeply values the force of the sensation and thinking functions that such a cultural preference seems to have led typology practitioners, as Jung pointed out in his *Psychological Types,* to value primarily the use of his typology as a system for classifying people.[3] Moreover, the extraverted bias in our culture beguiles even introverted researchers and practitioners, who may then ignore the deeper dimensions of the Soul's four functions and two attitudes. Our use of typology can be of limited value or may even be destructive unless we balance it with an introverted, intuitive, and feeling approach to personality. Further, the failure among the now large numbers of users and professional practitioners to recognize the functions and attitudes as archetypes greatly reduces their impact. Jung tells readers in later reflections on his *Types* book (as we noted in the previous chapter) that they should not turn immediately to his chapter 10, in which he describes each type as a conscious specific complex of characteristics. Rather, he says that readers should first study the earlier chapters, in which he discusses the larger cultural and historical contexts and dynamics out of which his type theory emerged. In these chapters Jung is implying the archetypal character of the functions and attitudes.

The functions and attitudes as archetypes govern the dynamics of relationships: with one's Soul, other people, and nature. They focus our attention, and in their flowing, fluid manner that defies simple categorization, they are the energies that determine the ways we know and decide. The attitudes and functions are not just the nuts and bolts but the fuel that energizes us and enables us to be cognitively and decisively mobile. We must look imaginatively at these six building blocks as vigorous energies and preferences, as shaping consistent yet personally unique patterns and richly varied stories of relationships, and as offering the occasions for numinous experiences. We must remember that these six building blocks are primarily rooted in the Soul's mystery, which tirelessly and wisely seeks to help us individuate, to realize our personal inborn potential. We must look at them as the expansive, deep, and yet practically useful archetypes that they are.

By giving archetypal names to the four functions and the two attitudes, Jung and Jungian analysts have, at least implicitly, acknowledged the archetypal nature of the building blocks of typology. For example, Jung found two figures in literature, Prometheus ("Forethought") and Epimetheus ("Afterthought"), who correspond exactly to introversion and extraversion. In other words, extraverts act first and later reflect whereas introverts act only after much reflection. Many analysts have popularly attached the collective names to the four functions: thinking as Logos, feeling as Soul, intuition as Spirit, and sensation as Matter.[4] Finally, as we shall see in chapter 10, analysts have traditionally connected the four cosmic elements to functions: Air with thinking, Earth with sensation, Water with feeling, and Fire with intuition. In this chapter and throughout the book, I argue that each building block is an inherited, archetypal capacity of the Soul that we can develop as a conscious function to be used as needed, *not just a consciously acquired set of traits*. We will raise the archetypal issue only when it is necessary to clear up misunderstandings or correct limited perceptions of the four functions and two attitudes.

Two sets of factors condition and distinguish us: the societal/environmental and the typological. The first set is made up of our societal histories beginning with our parents and continuing with siblings, friends, and work associates, as well as all our environmental influences from culture to nature, from the smallest atom to the farthest stars. Because of these societal and historical determinants, we are each as different as our fingerprints. The other set, our typological dispositions, also differentiates us: we are born with individual preferences for certain ways of knowing and acting that are as distinguishable as our history. These differences emerge from the unconscious where the Self/Soul is the master archetypal playwright, who gives us our unique, inborn introverted and extraverted preferences for perceiving and judging. We are wise, therefore, to live in accordance with the numinal accent of the function type and attitude that naturally and innately move us. Then we're in the Tao, in the flow of life.

Jung's goal in setting forth his theory of typology was to establish for each of us the basis for claiming our own authority, an inner power and an identity of which he became aware early in childhood. Even as a young boy, he felt that while he lived out the role his society prescribed for children in his "Personality No. 1," in his introverted "Personality No. 2" he was an old man of the 18th century who "wore buckled shoes."[5] Typologically, Jung was forced by the demands of school, his later medical studies, and our Western culture in general to take on an extraverted, sensate, thinking style in his Personality No. 1, and only occasionally to realize the introverted, intuitive dominance of his Personality No. 2, which he finally began to claim after his break with Freud.

Meanwhile, Jung, like all of us, had to first awaken to an initial mature self-awareness, which usually occurs around puberty and which transcends type preferences. The moment Jung first recognized the autonomous nature of his individuality occurred one day as he was walking to school; he suddenly came out of what he called a "dense cloud," after which he writes:

> I knew all at once: now I am *myself*. . . . Previously I had existed, too, but everything had merely happened to me. Now I happened to myself . . . now I willed. This experi-ence seemed to me tremendously important and new; there was "authority" in me.[6]

Just listen to that: "there was authority in me." Whether I prefer introversion or extraversion, I have authority when I first know that I know, and when I act decisively in accordance with that knowledge. Knowing my typology helps me be reflectively conscious and effective in living my authentic, innate preferences. Usually it takes a lifetime of persistent effort to finally free ourselves completely from living a typology that is wrong for us and to begin to realize both the full implication of our inborn preferences and to cultivate the other functions and attitude we need to develop fully.

Thus far we have looked briefly at the couplings as structures, and we have discussed the archetypal roots of all the types as revealed in Chinese Taoism. In this section of the book, "Prelude to the Function Couplings," we have considered some initial ideas about the building blocks: that each function and attitude is an archetype, and, as Jung perceived, each function and attitude evokes a numinal accent that is characteristic of archetypes. In the previous chapter on Jung's *Types* book, we considered other vast cultural resources from which Jung gleaned his typological psychology.

Now we need to describe the two attitudes and four functions—introversion, extraversion, thinking, feeling, sensation, and intuition—that constitute the main building blocks of typology. However, no one attitude or function ever acts separately from the other attitude or the other functions. We are reflecting on the parts of a whole only in order to better understand the whole.

CULTURE, THE STAGES OF LIFE AND TYPOLOGY: PROBLEMS OF TYPE FALSIFICATION

Many of us are interested in how our typological makeup fits into the overall patterns of differences within our own country, particularly since such patterns can easily cause one to live the wrong types. It is instructive in this context to get a quick picture of the most recent authoritative research on the individual type distributions in the United States based on the 1990 census. In a lead article in the *Journal of Psychological Type*, the authors give us this summary:

> Introverts slightly outnumber extraverts, about two thirds
> of people prefer sensing, about two thirds of men prefer

thinking, while more than six in ten women prefer feeling, and up to six in ten people prefer judging. . . . While not perfect, these norms are now the best estimate of the type distribution in the general adult population of the US.[7]

The approximately equal number of introverts and extraverts is surprising, considering the general American cultural typology—that is, the ESTJ type that dominates the media and most facets of our American life. I doubt that any American would question the observation that our mass cultural expressions—especially in television, movies, corporate atmospheres, and lifestyles—primarily demonstrate an extraverted, sensing, thinking, and judging behavior. Except for the surprising number of introverts, the research results just cited support this view. Sensing and judging dominate, as does thinking, since most leaders of our cultural organizations are men. Also, there are strong extraverted aspects in our society's use of sensing and thinking (as Jung already implied about the older Christian culture in *Psychological Types*). Moreover, following the findings of Briggs and Myers, a collective judging dominance indicates that thinking will be extraverted in our culture; the reason for this deduction will be examined and discussed in chapter 7. So the extraverted bias of our American culture could be expected even if the numbers of extraverts and introverts in the country are approximately equal. Societal traditions and cultural leaders can establish a typological emphasis that differs from and can override individual type preferences.

The type characteristics are often set up in our typological literature with ESTJ types in the left column and INFP types in the right column, as follows:

extraverts (E)	introverts (I)
sensing types (S)	intuitive types (N)
thinking types (T)	feeling types (F)
judging types (J)	perceiving types (P)

We see this arrangement, for example, in Myers' *Introduction to Type,* from which I selected the above lineup, and Keirsey and Bates' *Please Understand Me.* This alignment represents a wise unconscious choice. The ESTJ type, the contemporary culture's ST "head consciousness," suggests the left brain; and the INFP, the counter-culture's NF "heart and gut consciousness," suggests the right brain. The heart and gut are associated, in Jungian terms, with the feminine and the childlike, or in William James' terms, "the tender-minded," while the head is associated with the masculine or "tough-minded."[8] ESTJ toughness is based on the assertiveness of the E, the pragmatic facticity of the S, the objectivity of the T, and the finality of the J. INFP tender-mindedness is based on the inwardness and privacy of the I, the hunger for wholeness in the N, the need for harmony in the F, and the open-mindedness of the P.

The left column also suggests the societal masculine characteristics of our Western culture, and to some extent, most major world cultures for the last five thousand years; this is a cultural one-sided overlay in which males control public life, and masculine consciousness dominates our emotional, mental, and spiritual lives. This one-sided ESTJ typology has had a profound influence on our collective and individual lives. Jung saw this societal typology developing early in the Christian era, and by implication the earlier Greek and Roman eras. In my view we are now in a cultural midlife crisis in which a balance is required that will emerge from realizing a more feminine, childlike, and right brained INFP makeup.

The above ESTJ and INFP lineup also suggests another typological overlay: Jung's two-stages-of-life view of individual development in which each of us must realize an ESTJ first stage of life consciousness, followed by the challenging but seldom realized INFP second stage awareness, no matter what our individual typology may be. While Jung did not discuss the stages in typological terms, we can clearly see them as such. He discusses in *Psychological Types* "the general attitude of consciousness," in which we move from an introverted unconscious life as children to an extraverted adult consciousness.[9] This process requires an outer adaptation to societal demands in school and work that makes up the first half of life. In his later article, "The Stages of Life," Jung saw this first stage as also needing sensing thinking (ST) strengths and the second stage as needing introverted intuitive and feeling (INF) capabilities.[10] He uses the metaphor of the sun to illustrate the first-stage movement from an inner darkness to a noonday outer awareness.[11] The tasks, clearly illustrating ESTJ traits, include "Money-making, social achievements, family and posterity,"[12] along with "efficiency" and "the shrewd steering of offspring into suitable marriages and good positions."[13] These considerable successes occur both "within oneself as well as outside" as a transcending of "stubbornly childish illusions and assumptions."[14] However, Jung reminds us, "the social goal is attained only at the cost of a diminution of personality."[15] Jung assumes that a second stage of life is necessary in order to realize "personality," a term clearly synonymous with individuation.

Jung theorizes that a midlife crisis inevitably marks the end of the first stage, which often produces "mental depression in men about forty" and morally rigid attitudes in anyone in their middle years.[16] Such a crisis leads to a necessary second stage, "Attitude of the Unconscious," which has an "introverting character." Here our energies turn toward "subjective factors" which we have ignored in life's first stage.[17] This exploratory inwardness of mind and emotion can be characterized as INFP in its makeup. Jung returns to the metaphor of the sun in his "Stages" article: "The sun falls into contradiction with itself. It is as though it should *draw in* its rays instead of emitting them."[18] The second half of the life-task is fearsome in its inner images and emotions, involving "unknown and dangerous tasks," and possibly "the fear of death."[19] This stage challenges each of us to develop "the art of life," an older age "wisdom" and a spiritual "supermundane goal."[20]

I submit that these are all inward-oriented INFP challenges.[21]

Overall, "the afternoon of human life must also have a significance of its own and cannot be merely a pitiful appendage to life's morning."[22] Notice that Jung is suggesting that these stages have a significance of their own, which transcends the specific type and related personal tasks of the individual. For example, an introverted individual is obviously not comfortable with the first stage of life's extraverted demands. However, while nurturing and valuing his own introversion, he also must in his own quieter way meet those first-stage extraverted requirements, such as giving verbal reports in class.

I am stressing these collective cultural and individual stages of life-influences because they have a powerful impact on our own type consciousness, as we have seen in the case of Jung and as I have reported of my own life. *These influences can most often be significant factors in causing us to develop a "falsification of types."* When this takes place, Jung writes, "the individual becomes neurotic later, and can be cured only by developing the attitude consonant with his nature."[23] Reversal, or falsification of type, "often proves exceedingly harmful to the physiological well-being of the organism, usually causing acute exhaustion."[24]

THE TYPES IN GENERAL

Beyond statistics and cultural tendencies, we must also discuss the qualities and stories associated with each typological preference. We begin with the observation that each can initially be described in one or two terms. I suggest the following:

- inwardness and ego consciousness for introversion;
- outwardness and assertiveness toward objective others (people or events) for extraversion;

- imagination and possibility for intuition;
- detail and concreteness for sensation;
- objectivity and systemizing for thinking;
- subjectivity and relationship for feeling;
- openness and looseness for perceiving;
- completion and order for judging.

We begin here where Jung began, with the orientations or attitudes, and then we will discuss the four functions. We will end this chapter with an initial discussion of the function couplings.

EXTRAVERSION AND INTROVERSION

Although it is true that everybody has to deal with the outside world as well as with his or her inner reaction to it, one person will tend to embrace what the world offers while relegating the inner reaction to secondary status, and another person will deal first with the inner reaction and only secondarily with the outer reality. These differences arise from two opposed attitudes: extraversion and introversion.

Jung defines "attitude" as "a readiness of the psyche to act or react in a certain way." A psychological attitude is an "*a priori* orientation to a definite thing, no matter whether this be represented in consciousness or not."[25] Our *native* or *natural attitude* is fundamentally not under the conscious control. Hence our whole view of ourselves, our outlook on life and the actions we take or do not take are oriented in accordance with our native attitude.

Introversion and extraversion, Jung points out, are not "mere idiosyncrasies of character peculiar to individuals." Rather, we find introverted and extraverted attitudes in types among both sexes and in all strata of society. "Such a widespread distribution could hardly have come about if it were merely a question of a conscious deliberate choice of attitude . . . but must be due to some unconscious, instinctive cause." Jung suggests that the polar contrasting character of these two attitudes, as a general psychological phenomenon, "must have some kind of biological foundation."[26] (We saw in chapter 3 the instinctual nature of introversion.) Since our natural attitude is innate and not of our conscious choosing *and* typically either extraverted or introverted, we are justified in regarding these two attitudes as archetypal.

The attitudes of extraversion and introversion are overall ways of orienting ourselves to "outer" and "inner" worlds. We need both attitudes as we evolve in life and as specific life challenges present themselves. Metaphors from a larger context help us here. Mother Nature herself metaphorically goes through cycles of introversion and extraversion: the inwardness of autumn and winter, followed by the bursting forth of spring and summer. On a more personal level, each night begins with the introversion of sleep, proceeds in the morning awakening to the external demands of daily life, and in turn is followed by a slowing and quieting introverted orientation at dusk and evening, which progresses once more into sleep. The extravert is more likely to neglect times of reflection while the more introverted person is apt to neglect extraverted relationships with others. Nature and human life demand both introversion and extraversion.

Jung saw in nature a direct analogy to extraverted and introverted persons in their adaptation to the world. He writes that extraverts are like one form of nature that "consists in a high rate of fertility with low powers of defense and short duration of life for the single individual." Introverts are like another form of nature that "consists in equipping the individual with numerous means of self-preservation plus a low fertility rate. *This biological difference, it seems to me, is not merely analogous to, but the actual foundation of, our two psychological modes of adaptation.*" He concludes: "The one [the extravert] achieves its end by a multiplicity of relationships, the other [the introvert] by monopoly."[27]

It is important to remember that besides the native, typically extraverted or introverted general attitude of consciousness, there is also an attitude of the unconscious, that part of the psyche that is beyond conscious control. In Jung's view of the psyche, the attitude of the unconscious is compensatory to consciousness. Accordingly, as the conscious attitude becomes more extreme and one-sided, the unconscious becomes more extreme in an opposed direction in its attempt to maintain balance and equilibrium. (I will have more to say about this in the following discussions of the two attitudes.)

Extraversion

When the attitude of the psyche is extraverted, attention naturally flows outward into the world toward persons, things, events, and so forth. Jung writes:

> Now when orientation by the object predominates in such a way that decisions and actions are determined not by subjective views [an introverted orientation] but by objective conditions, we speak of an extraverted attitude. When this is habitual, we speak of an extraverted type. . . . Naturally, he has subjective views too, but their determining value is less than that of the objective conditions. Like Epimetheus, his inner life is subordinated to external realities.[28]

Jung and Myers list some of the preferences of the extravert as outwardly oriented, strongly assertive, sociable, and flexible. This type of person is also described as liking variety and action, deciding before reflecting, using teamwork, communicating in conversations, and liking (or at least, not minding) being in crowds. But we need to be aware of some negative traits when this type becomes one-sided, such as being excessively loud, aggressively invasive, impulsive, driven by time and speed, and having an intense need for diversity and high living.

Extraversion is the norm in our very outer-oriented Western society. It has been arguably the emerging norm since patriarchy began dominating the West five thousand years ago, according to Riane Eisler's *The Chalice and the Blade*.[29] She describes several patriarchal cultures from different parts of the world and from different eras, such as the Aztecs of Meso-America, the Japan of the Samurai, Hitler's Germany, and Khomeini's Iran. She writes:

> All these otherwise widely different societies are not only rigidly male dominant but also have a generally hierarchic and authoritarian social structure and a high degree of social violence, particularly warfare.[30]

Jung also realized that Christian Europe, as part of this larger history, developed along extraverted and related sensate and thinking (ST) lines.

I am suggesting that the features Eisler attributes to such societies are typical of the exaggerations of extraversion, when societies are thus too one-sided. There have been cases in introversion where some very reserved individuals have suddenly become violent toward others, as is also the case of the introverted earth cultures. However, the assertiveness of most introverts occurs primarily when they are defending their private turf. They are usually not interested in aggressively conquering the territory or the psyche of another. When the introvert becomes too inner oriented, he typically, according to Jung, becomes even more wary of the outer world: "His fear of objects develops into a peculiar kind of cowardliness; he shrinks from making himself or his opinions felt, fearing that this will only increase the object's power. He is terrified of strong affects in others, and is hardly ever free from the dread of falling under hostile influences."[31] However, a one-sided extraversion is equally or even more destructive. "The more complete the conscious attitude of extraversion is," Jung writes, "the more infantile and archaic the unconscious attitude will be. The egoism which characterizes the extravert's unconscious attitude goes far beyond mere childish selfishness; it verges on the ruthless and the brutal."[32]

Americans, among all of the Western nations, seem to be most oriented toward this particular typology. We have noted this popular assumption before, and yet we have learned that the 1990 census indicates extraverts and introverts are about equal in numbers in the general population. Yet in our popular cultural forms, there is an extreme extraverted dominance. We are constantly assailed on television and in movies by a noisy emotional outer environment. In addition, our leadership in every area, from religion and education to commerce and politics, is dominated by this mentality. Positively, this characteristic accounts for the development in Europe and the United States of the scientific method and worldwide explorations that sought a conquest of nature for the first time. This is also the energetic quality of the frontier and the main impetus for the European development of this continent in the seventeenth century, the quick development of an enterprising, assertive group of states, and this country's fast westward expansion. Probably by virtue of this type, we, like many other European countries, also developed an inventive, curious eye, which eventually led to the development of the scientific/technological age. A generally extraverted Western society spawned, appropriately, an outer technology, in contrast to the more internal sciences of the East. Negatively, it is the basis for our reputation as the Ugly American tourists and hard-driving conquerors in international industry.

The preoccupation of the extravert with the objective world lends itself to aggression and dominance when it becomes exaggerated. Eisler and many other women scholars such as Carolyn Merchant, Ruth El Saffar and Gerda Lerner,[33] have made a strong case for a far-reaching cultural extension of this extraverted pathology.

Sprawling modern cities with their boisterous, exciting energies are good symbols of extraversion. Skyscrapers, the scattered melodies of fast-paced jazz songs, the bawdy, sensual, driving rhythms of rock and perhaps the fast-changing images of multimedia also symbolize extraversion. Extraverts often feast on variety and excitement—the big play in sports and fast-moving action movies. Aggressive figures from politics, dynamic personalities from the arts, fast-talking stand-up comedians, flamboyant salesmen, and gutsy women such as Mae West of the twenties and Rosanne Barr of recent TV fame are all extraverted cultural icons.

Locations symbolizing extraversion and introversion often show up in dreams as metaphors of our interpersonal challenges. One client dreamt constantly of a safe, private, maternal summer place in which he had grown up in Italy. When he dreamt and thought of Rome, he felt isolated and traumatized, and yet knew that in Rome he had to deal with the competitive demands of school, love, and work.

In our often-pathologized extraversion, we become manic and hysterical. We are a nation of fast-moving people, driven by time. David Elkind's *The Hurried Child* shows how our demanding and aggressive society savagely affects children in their sports, academics, and dating.[34] Another result is our society's *Addiction to Perfection,* the title of Marion Woodman's book.[35] Perfection does not mean excellence or wholeness, which develops in peaceful, reflective, and organic ways, but instant success and the quick fix from medicine to scholastics, from pleasure to religion.

Medically, this extraverted pathology leads to heart attacks in so-called Type A people, particularly when expressed through their angry work- and time-driven behavior. Friedman and others who have written about Type A behavior have found few introverts in this group.[36] Healing occurs when Type A persons learn to integrate their work with the values of love, play, and prayer that together result in Type B behavior, which leads to healthy, spiritual living (see the four levels of figure 3.1, page 68).

Driven extraverted types usually resist a dream wisdom that

invariably advises them to take it easy. One such person, living out a learned extraversion, did respond. She dreamt that Nazis, symbolizing her working pathology, surrounded her house every time that she sought to escape. I challenged her to invite them into her room in active imagination. She did, and they turned into human-sized grasshoppers who surrounded her bed while pointing flashlights at her. She was frightened, but asked, "Who are you?" They responded in unison, "WE ARE YOUR.BIG EXPECTATIONS." We realized that in the famous Aesop's fable of the "The Ants and the Grasshopper," the latter symbolized the easygoing life and the ants were the relentless, primordial workaholics. So even her grasshoppers, inflated to human size, had been invaded by her compulsive overworking. The dreamer's compulsiveness had significantly limited her capacity to play (Level 3). The dreamer stayed with her awesome images in active imagination. Eventually, they became normal-sized grasshoppers in her fantasy, but she was still afraid to have them around because of their helter-skelter, playful jumping. Finally, one day a very small, feminine grasshopper, a dancer, landed on her hand, smiled at her, and proceeded to teach her to dance. Jung has reminded us that the extravert's resistance to introversion is so strong because an inferior attitude and its related function can be frighteningly archaic. When these undeveloped and unused capacities initially erupt in unsophisticated or even primitive ways they are frightening indeed.

The Soul, which is so sensitive to the universal web of life, knows that growth within also needs to be realized without. In terms of individual development, there can be no wholeness unless we can call on both introversion and extraversion, unless we can live both private and public lives. We are each unique, yet we are also part of the greater Tao, the universe story. Our very inwardness (the introverted attitude) leads us to the collective unconscious with its implications for our connectedness to our society (the extraverted attitude), demanding that we be part of the societal process, the human community.

Introversion

When introversion is our natural attitude of consciousness, the structure of the psyche "prior to any ego-development," rather than the ego or the conditioned personality, orients us inwardly rather than outwardly. Just as the extravert asks, "How do I fit in the outer world of objects, the introvert asks, "How does the outer world of objects fit into my inner world, which has its own psychic structure." Jung writes: "The introverted attitude is normally oriented by the psychic structure, which is in principle hereditary and is inborn in the subject. . . . The psychic structure is . . . what I call the 'collective unconscious,'"[37] the "objective psyche" where all the possible archetypes reside. Introverts live comfortably and intimately with this inner world of conscious objects and unconscious potentialities.

The contents of the collective unconscious, the objective psyche, appear in consciousness as pronounced preferences and definite ways of looking at things. The introverted individual may be tempted to believe that the object occupying conscious attention determines the attitude, but this is not the case. Rather, conscious impressions are determined by the structure of the psyche as expressed through the various archetypes. Jung writes, "They are stronger than the object's influence . . . their psychic value is higher, so that they superimpose themselves on all impressions."[38] The introvert is ruled by inner values, not outer ones.

In his foreword to O.A.H. Schmitz's *Märchen vom Fischotter,* Jung writes that discovering the psyche as something that really exists inside of us changes a person's life and work:

> For those who are vouchsafed such a discovery, the psyche appears as something objective, a psychic non-ego. This experience is very like the discovery of a new world. The supposed vacuum of a merely subjective psychic space becomes filled with objective figures,

having wills of their own, and is seen to be a cosmos that conforms to law, and among these figures the ego takes its place in transfigured form. This tremendous experience means a shattering of foundations, an overturning of our arrogant world of consciousness, a cosmic shift of perspective, the true nature of which can never be grasped rationally or understood in its full implications."[39]

Hence the "subjectivity" of introversion is not eccentricity but rather the expression of structures in the psyche (i.e., archetypes) over which the individual has no conscious control. Because introverts are considered "oddballs" in our outward society, an introverted person must strive heroically to value his inwardness.

Jung and Myers, in turn, list some of the conscious preferences of the introvert as inward, subjectively oriented, private, intense, concentrated. The introverted person reflects before deciding, communicates better in writing, works alone, and is quiet and threatened by extraverted aggressiveness. We can add reserved, private, slow-paced, and quiet in voice. Extreme introversion can also lead to isolation and painful depression.

Introverts mull things over and generally prefer solitude. They need psychic space, sometimes even resenting telephone calls, seeing them as an intrusion. Keirsey calls this "territoriality."[40] Introverts also often have a quiet demeanor, unless pushed by life to develop a more vociferous persona. They have difficulty claiming authority among extraverts. These types enjoy small groups. They are not usually on center stage at a party, unless their extraversion should emerge, usually with the aid of alcohol. But they will fight like a mother tiger if their private integrity is threatened. Jung once wrote humorously about a clearly introverted professor, "He . . . must be approached with the politeness due to animals in the bush."[41] Introverts like to read quietly, need long vacations or many short ones, and generally have to have private time and quiet or they become irritated and angry—an extraverted partner is likely to unknowingly violate those needs. Introverts also fear psychic invasions. Dreams of being raped or burglarized are common dream motifs for introverts.

Introverts face a serious dilemma in our culture. Their privacy is not valued, yet when they make clumsy attempts to reach outward they are often derided. One male INTJ's story is painfully typical of a childhood in which a parent thwarted his tenuous but resolute attempt to develop some extraversion. His mother was a controlling extravert who would slap him across the face if he argued with her. He had this dream in therapy:

> I enter a private room of a train. There I see a pre-adolescent boy sleeping. The child has no mouth, nose, ears or eyes. He lives entirely within himself. The mother, in a pleading way, shows me some photographs of when he was a little boy, in which he had all of his facial features.

The dream reveals how difficult it is for an introvert to develop an outer or extraverted face, a persona, a role that affects others, especially when one is treated so as a child.

Although this man is creative (NT) in his profession, he has difficulty selling himself professionally. He recounted a childhood in which his parents neither saw nor heard him. One example involved his attempting to show them some chemistry experiments, but they did not respond. He finally gave his chemistry set away. He is typical of quiet NT types who have difficulty working out relationships with people, particularly with women. Predictably, he married a domineering, probably ESFP woman, whom he finally divorced.

Another introverted client, an INFP type, felt that she was never understood by her domineering mother, who always worried about what the neighbors would think. Her powerless, introverted father would often explode in rage. The mother's influence over the quiet husband and daughter appeared in one of her dreams, in which her parents were getting a divorce; the dreamer rejoiced because then both she and her father would be free. She was beginning to experience some psychic separation from her mother. She had been so fused to her mother that at age twelve, she had made up her mind that because she considered herself evil, she would always be the servant of her mother, her father, and her siblings, of whom she was the oldest.

A male INTP client reported that when he was a pre-adolescent and wanted to be alone in his room, his father, a driven extravert, would sometimes throw open his door and shout, "This is no god-damed hotel!" His father couldn't stand his sensitive son's quiet demeanor; consequently, he was much closer to his mother. He dreamt the following:

> I am with my mother on the lower levels of a building. I know that my mentor (an academic father figure) is teaching in a room up above. I go up the stairs and find outside the room sport coats that one must wear in order to enter. None of them fit. I return to mother.

This introvert's difficulty in developing an extraverted persona is represented by not finding a sports coat that fits. The dream also implies his mildly depressive state: he feels like the low person on the social totem pole, undeserving of any power in society. However, in waking life this man is professionally successful, writes poetry in private, and calls his mild depression, so typical of introverts, "the place of my sad poet." He shows here what all introverts must first do: value their privacy and quiet demeanor that an extraverted society rarely understands.

Angel at My Table, based on the autobiography of the New Zealand novelist and poet Janet Frame, is an outstanding movie for introverts.[42] Painfully shy from birth, this woman would probably be an INFP. She was practicing teaching when a supervisor came unannounced to her classroom. Janet froze, could not even speak, and walked out of the room in total confusion. Her favorite professor, whom she trusted, suggested that she spend some time in the local mental hospital because she had developed some anxiety. As a result, she was in and out of hospitals for many years and was treated as a clinical depressive. Her medical certificate stated that she was schizophrenic.[43] Here is her brave response to that diagnosis:

> I knew that I was shy, inclined to be fearful, and even more so after my six weeks of being in the hospital and seeing what I had seen around me, that I was absorbed in the world of imagination, but I also knew that I was totally present in the "real" world and whatever shadow lay over me, lay only in the writing on the medical certificate.[44]

Meanwhile, she wrote poems and stories, which she sent to her mentor. He said of her: "You are suffering from the loneliness of an inner soul," and he compared her work to Van Gogh and Hugo Wolf. Both, she discovered, had probably suffered schizophrenic breaks. To keep her mentor's interest, she kept him believing that her imaginative explorations were diseased. She developed this "formidable schizophrenic repertoire" because he was newly interested in Freud, and, in her words, because he was the "link with the world [she] had known and because [she] wanted these 'talks' to continue."[45] In a final hospitalization she was almost subjected to a lobotomy. She was saved because the superintendent of the hospital read that her first book, *The Lagoon,* had won the "Hubert Church Award for the best prose!"[46] I know of no other story that better illustrates our tragic misunderstanding and mistreatment of introverts.

Emily Dickinson, very likely an INFP personality as well, is another of our gifted modern introverts. She lived her entire life in Amherst, Massachusetts, a quiet New England village, from her birth in 1830 until her death in 1886. One collator of her poems, Robert Linscott, wrote of her in his introduction:

Here she lived a life, outwardly uneventful, inwardly dedicated to a secret and self-imposed assignment—the mission of writing "a letter to the world" that would express, in poems of absolute truth and of the utmost economy, her concept of life and death, of love and nature, and of what Henry James called "the landscape of the soul."

Unpublished in her lifetime, unknown at her death in 1886, her poems, by chance and good fortune, reached, at last, the world to which they had been addressed. . . . She had a demure manner which brightened easily into fun where she felt at home, but among strangers, she was rather shy, silent, and even deprecating.[47]

Here are two of her poems which point to her introverted makeup.

I'm nobody! Who are you?
Are you nobody too?
Then there's a pair of us—don't tell!
How dreary to be somebody!
How public like a frog
To tell your name the livelong day
To an admiring bog.[48]

And another:

To fight aloud is very brave,
But gallanter I know,
Who charge within the bosom,
The calvary of woe.
Who win, and nations do not see,
Who fall and none observe,
Whose dying eyes no country
Regards with patriot love . . .[49]

Both Frame and Dickinson illustrate in their lives and writing how our society's immense ignorance about the inward life inflicts pain and injury on introverts. In all of my years of counseling, two major problems have stood out in the lives of my analysands: patriarchy first, and, related to this first, introversion. Introverts are placed in a particularly uncomfortable position because society both fears them and yet is also secretly attracted to them. Dickinson describes their poignant plea for recognition and worth in a poem Linscott alludes to:

> This is my letter to the world,
> That never wrote to me,—
> The simple news that nature told,
> With tender majesty.
>
> Her message is committed
> To hands I cannot see;
> For love of her, sweet countrymen,
> Judge tenderly of me![50]

Dickinson pleads for all of nature's interiority, which includes my Soul and yours, as well as all the suffering entailed in our unique journey of identity. We are particularly challenged, in the words of Janet Frame's mentor and the Taoists of old, to suffer through "a loneliness of the inner soul."

However, we must not forget the potential for pathology in introversion. One obvious possibility is the combination of isolation and depression. In some respects both can be healthy components of this type, giving rise to poetry such as that of Emily Dickinson and Janet Frame. On the other hand, this depression and isolation can be so debilitating as to reduce one to a pathological state, or, according to Dr. Lawrence LeShan, a psychologist and internationally known cancer expert, can contribute to a serious condition such as cancer.[51]

Serious paranoia, fear of open spaces, and a paralyzing isolation also fit this kind of inward person. Such pathologies, in league with cruel parenting and chronic low esteem, could be the basis of extreme antisocial or sociopathic behavior, even serial killing. Neighbors will often reminisce how quietly and peacefully such killers lived while deceptively carrying a virtual arsenal of explosive fears and hatreds within. An inferior extraversion, repressed in a tragically wounded life, can burst forth in all its pent-up fury in such killers.

THE PERCEIVING FUNCTIONS:
SENSATION AND INTUITION

The attitudes, introversion and extraversion—the directions of our natural energy flow within or without—are just one element of typology. We also have the four functions, the more specific cognitive aspects of typology that have their own kind of innate flow. Jung noticed that, although there was a big division between introverts and extraverts, there also were significant differences between the functions. First, he reasoned, we have different ways of accumulating knowledge that was generally called perception. He noted that some people depended on the outer senses for their knowledge of anything from atoms to people, whereas others depended on their inner senses, particularly their imagination. He called the former sensates and the latter intuitives. As in introversion and extraversion, he realized that we are always a combination of both, with one dominating.

Jung calls the perceiving spectrum "irrational." By this he means that all of us are constantly bombarded by overwhelming and unsought information. Jung wrote that both sensation and intuition by themselves "lack all rational direction." Students of the *Myers-Briggs Type Indicator*® (*MBTI*)® recognize here the intimations of the perceiving orientation (P) that Briggs and Myers added to the type categories. Jung continues: "For this reason I call them irrational functions, as opposed to thinking and feeling (J), which find fulfillment only when they are in complete harmony with the laws of reason."[52]

Sensation

According to Jung and Myers, a number of characteristics typify an individual's preference for sensing: consciousness of detail; the need to be concrete in expression; the preference for experiencing rather than reflection; finding comfort in routines; orientation to the present; realistic, methodical, and steady work habits; stability; awareness of the body and sensuality; and an attachment to possessions. When sensing is exaggerated, it will express itself in a mistrust of the imagination and change, and a rigidity, even compulsion, in its handling of everyday activities and tasks.

We'll let these qualities work on us like structural sketches as we seek to describe the sensate more dynamically and imaginatively in three large aspects. First, sensation serves a pragmatic and even prosaic function. Second, it contributes crucially to human etiquette and style. Finally, it operates in conjunction with artistic creativity and the drama of human history. As to its earthy pragmatism, sensation seems to be the first function that is operative on an instinctual level in the fetal child and infant, especially via the sense of smell. Grounding us in and around our mother's body, sensations remain in memory and dream as the homing function, reminding us of joyful or sorrowful events in childhood. These early concrete impressions reconnect us subtly with the atmospheres experienced in the body as emotion and the physical sensations of touch, smell, sound, and taste, which may haunt us our entire lives, sometimes experienced as nostalgic and other times as hauntingly frightening. Our conscious work with these experiences can prove to be most fruitful in both healing and maintaining our spiritual health.

In considering the sensing type or the sensing part of ourselves, intuitive types may exclaim, "Dullsville." Intuitive types are easily bored with detail, with the hard-nosed demands of life that keep us from turning to exciting new things. For the intuitive type, the sensing function immediately means the old and everyday, the tried and true of the past. Yet we are often brought down to earth and into this present moment by the fundamental sensing question, "What are the facts?" It is the sensing function in us that says, "Don't jump to conclusions. Let's first get grounded in the details."

Sensing types are often very practical people, devoted to their crafts and hands-on arts, such as pottery or knitting. They usually enjoy work in hands-on occupations such as massage, interior decoration, nursing, and other practical helping and art professions. They often do the hard-nosed, detailed, and necessary work of accountants, secretaries, mechanics, farmers, plant workers, and managers.

In the realm of etiquette and style, the sensation function observes, and by observing, enables us to compare present choices (e.g., in etiquette and style) with the cultural canon, thereby serving to maintain the matrices of social conformity. Certainly most of us are aware of many books written on etiquette in everyday life, such as in table manners and the myriad other conventional demands. John T. Molloy's work on clothing, found in *New Dress for Success,* shows dramatically the shorthand sensate code which operates in a culture.[53] Of his findings Molloy writes:

> This research is based on the very reasonable premise that the two great behaviorists Pavlov and Skinner are right. We are preconditioned by our environment—and the clothing we wear is an integral part of the environment. The way we dress has a remarkable impact on the people we meet professionally or socially, and greatly (sometimes crucially) affects how they treat us.[54]

The introverted intuitive feeling part of us might cringe at this assessment of the social implications of proper dress, yet such imperatives must be taken seriously. For example, it is widely accepted that a dark grey, black, or blue-striped suit gives the coded message that one is powerful. Sensory impressions create a powerful impact, and intuitive types must keep this in mind as they deal with everyday life.

People who prefer intuition often do not conform to the conventional structures of their culture, a fact which sensation-oriented corporate leaders need to keep in mind if they value the particular creative flair of this type. At one point, one major Fortune 500 company made room for mavericks they called "Wild Ducks," creative individuals who were unorthodox in their dress. When the Wild Ducks were replaced with power-suit counterparts, the company made some very conservative mistakes that left them lagging in their fast-developing market. As result, corporate management went through a considerable reappraisal and overhaul of their attitudes and requirements.

The movie, *The Age of Innocence,* set in nineteenth-century New York, shows both the beautiful detail and the tragic pathologies of the rigid stylistic demands of a conventional society. Movie director Martin Scorsese captures the typological atmosphere described in Edith Wharton's book on which the movie is based: exquisite details of furniture and paintings and, especially, formal table settings with flowers and candelabra framing each person at the table. The story also records the sad consequences of a rigid societal style that prevents two passionately involved people from realizing their rightful union.

What possible value could dull detail have for the creativity of the Soul and its flowing, amorphous, and sublime Tao? Jung answers this snobbish question in his foreword to Wilhelm's translation of *The I Ching.*[55] There he discusses the nature of the Chinese Taoist mind, how its psychophilosophical view paints magnificent pictures of the subtle correspondences of inner and outer events, of large spiritual meanings, of time as quality and of chance's hidden patterns. But Taoism's great teachers have also been practical observers of the workings of both inner and outer nature, providing humankind with a wise system of body-mind care and spirituality through Taoism's disciplines, all of which take sensate details very seriously. In Bill Moyers' TV study of alternative medicines, we see individual dishes being prepared in a hospital kitchen for each patient, based on precise physical yang-yin needs, an approach not found in the West. There, sensation is utilized at its creative and healing best. Taoism's description of energy flow, the Chi, is based on thousands of years of precise attention paid to bodily sensations.

Jung writes that Taoism, as presented in *The I Ching*, integrates a highly intuitive spiritual approach with an equally exquisite sensate awareness. He writes:

> While the Western mind carefully sifts, weighs, selects, classifies, isolates, the Chinese picture of the moment encompasses everything down to the minutest nonsensical detail, because all the ingredients make up the observed moment.[56]

In other words, whereas the West uses the sensing function to examine individual details and the thinking function to name and explain, the Chinese approach embraces each detail within the large, intuitive, holistic view of the cosmos and the microcosm that is every one of us. Somehow each detail, each sensate aspect, fits into the large picture. I find this to be true also in doing dream work. A detail in a dream can be the key to its deepest meaning. In other dreams, repeated images of sensual impressions can depict crucial aspects of an entire life story that demand contemporary resolution.

For example, I mentioned one of my clients' repetitive dreams of the Italian countryside. That dream motif represented this person's powerful memory of a beloved land, a maternal ground, and his emotionally fused state with several women from his youth. The women are imaginally captured in the dreams in their evocative glances, haunting smells, and innocent sensual explorations. He is challenged both to love those women and to free himself from this inner feminine aspect and take on the practical challenge of the other Italy symbolized by Rome.

The great artist sees the unfolding of the fullness of the human drama in things and in existential, earthy moments, like Blake's seeing the universe in a grain of sand. In *Writing Down the Bones,* Natalie Goldberg notes, "Life is so rich, if you can write down the real details of the way things were and are, you hardly need anything else."[57] She points to the importance of the individual in death as in life. The Jerusalem memorial to the Holocaust, *Yad Vashem,* catalogues the names of each of the six million martyrs, with as many particulars about each person as organizers could assemble. She continues, "These people existed and they mattered. *Yad Vashem,* as a matter of fact, actually means 'memorial to the name.' It was not nameless masses that were slaughtered; they were human beings."[58]

In line with this kind of vision, the promoters of the Vietnam Memorial in Washington accepted, in a stroke of genius, a design that recorded the name of each of the American war dead instead of erecting the usual heroic statues. The existential grounding of the memorial in the names of the dead has given the American people the first true wailing wall in our history. This felt, caring attitude is a combination of sensing and feeling (SF).

A master teacher of meditation and healing, Dr. Lawrence LeShan leads students to meditate on such mundane things as a matchbox. Eventually the matchbox begins to shine, to exude, as it were, its energy from its matter. Related to this, Einstein's imaginative exercises led him in his intuitive genius to discover the relationship between matter and energy and thus to the mightiest of sensing realities: the power in one tiny atom. In every sensate detail we can find its opposite, the fire of intuition. This agrees with the classical Taoist diagram pictured in figure 2.1, page 53, showing that each opposite has the seed of its polar partner within it.

The creative power of the sensing function is vividly depicted in two other great contemporary films: *Like Water for Chocolate* and *Babette's Feast*. In both, food touches people's lives for good and ill, humorously and tragically. In the first, the sensual details of cooking and eating act out a sensuality that is otherwise stifled by culture and tradition. The second movie tells of a quiet, SF type servant woman, formerly a famous chef, who wins a lottery and spends her money on a sumptuous meal for her benefactors and their Christian community. An Army general, visiting his mother in this parish, presides over the meal. His sensitive tastes and appreciative remarks about the exquisite cooking and wines turn the sour and sullen Christians into a loving, gentle, and happy community.

The sensing function does, however, pose some dangers. When the "pursuit of sensation becomes all-consuming," Daryl Sharp quotes Jung's remark that sensing types can become "crude pleasure-seekers, unscrupulous aesthetes, and gross hedonists."[59] Of course, the same fate can befall us if the sensing function overpowers the other three functions. In this context Jung could also have mentioned the compulsive person haunted and obsessed by detail. When the inferior intuition comes sneaking out, sensates can be caught up, according to Jung, in a phobia, in grotesque morality, in magical superstition, in blatant stinginess and meddlesome officiousness. People who prefer sensation can become misers, penny-pinchers, money-mongers, but their inferior intuition can make them susceptible to religious cults and other forms of fanaticism, the implications of which they do not foresee.

Intuition

Jung and Myers identify several characteristics of intuition. Persons who use intuition extensively are imaginative, inventive, and ingenious. They fantasize, see possibilities, enjoy new challenges and skills. They may be research oriented and may promote improvements, get bored by repetition and precision, and work in enthusiastic bursts. They respond to inspirations, hunches, and special freedoms; they see opportunities and leap to conclusions. When intuition is exaggerated, a person can become too theoretical, too caught up in fantasy, or, as popular culture puts it, function like a space cadet or an airhead. Intuition gone amuck can also account for some of the loose thinking and fantasizing of psychotics.

Most persons interested in Jung's psychology in general and his typology in particular are intuitive types either in their primary or secondary functions. I have noted this fact from many years of teaching, from research showing that 80 percent of Jungian analysts have reported this preference, and from reading that the Association for Psychological Type reports a similar percentage of intuitive types combined with feeling or thinking in its membership records. However, intuitive types may often take their preferred function for granted, probably more than other types, because of their dominance in analytical and type circles, or may not give much thought to intuition's breadth and depth. For that reason, I will explore this function in a way that distances intuitives from themselves and at the same time expands the work of intuition through a system that is usually strange to the Western mind. That system is Chinese Taoism, which, as discussed in chapter 1, deeply influenced Jung's life and his type theory.

Taoism is a philosophical and spiritual tradition based on intuitions about the ties between objective reality and subjective consciousness. Jung called this connection *synchronicity*. Intuition is more easily, as well as comprehensively, seen through the concept and experience of synchronicity. I can state the connection between intuition and synchronicity in the following general way: intuition, according to Jung, is a perception by way of the unconscious.[60] However, Jung writes in a letter that the unconscious

. . . is more like an atmosphere in which we live than

something that is found *in* us. . . . it does not by any means behave merely psychologically; in the cases of so-called synchronicity, it proves to be a universal substrate present in the environment rather than a psychological premise.[61]

Therefore, intuition as a perceptive function is coextensive with the unconscious as the "universal substrate" that embraces both our inner and outer relationships. Intuition is the function that is at work when we experience a synchronistic event, such as when an eager and concerned student is looking in library stacks for a book on a specific subject and, while returning one book to a shelf, causes another one to fall out. When the student picks it up, he sees that it deals exactly with his pursued subject. It seems that intuition, therefore, includes not only consciousness as the searching and perceiving subject, but also the potential content of the book, the object that is received.

Such specific synchronistic events, having their origin in this connecting substrate between subject and object, occur in highly charged emotional moments of our lives that are, according to Jung, mediated by archetypes.[62] In the case of the student, his felt need for the book and his anxious state are the emotional stimuli. Archetypes, as Jung points out, appear in such "practical experiences" as "both images and emotions."[63] Archetypes are both perceived events and unconscious content, whether they appear in synchronistic events or not. Archetypes, as Jung has so often written, are both invented and discovered. As discovered, they exist as *a priori* or potential entities in the unconscious, like gold in the earth. As invented, they are consciously developed aspects of consciousness, like the miner who is an expert at looking for signs of gold and fully expects to find it. Intuition, therefore, is both an intentional and expected aspect of consciousness and an autonomous set of capabilities in the unconscious.

Further, intuition participates in the emergence of every archetype. We are justified in making this latter assertion because, as we saw in chapter 3, archetypes were first described by Jung as "*a priori* forms of 'intuition,' namely the *archetypes* of perception and apprehension." Intuition, therefore, participates in all archetypal activities that the Self spawns. But intuition is also a specific archetype, described variously as "Spirit" and as "Fire." Jung is more specific when he characterizes intuition as birdlike "thoughts and the flight of thought." He continues, "Generally it is fantasies and intuitive ideas that are represented thus (the winged Mercurius, Morpheus, genii, angels)."[64]

Another example will help us concretize such abstract yet also practical considerations. As I wrote in the introduction, I suffered childhood dual culture traumas. My father, a respected man in the Italian community, was not at all comfortable in the larger American society. I lacked a mediator and guide to lead me into this prevalent society. A dream figure filled that gap many years later at a time when I was experiencing a painful crisis. The figure was a godfather who acted in the dream as both an Italian spiritual leader and a successful American businessman. He gave me many gifts, all of which signified a healing of my dual culture problem. Seeing the Self through intuition provided the healing synchronistic link between my father's social inadequacy, my related childhood fears, my emotional, needy state when the dream occurred, and the dream godfather's psychic success in both cultures.

We need to delve more deeply into the heart of synchronicity and its connection with intuition. In his foreword to *The I Ching,* Jung juxtaposes synchronicity with causality. By causality, he means the immediate, measurable, or observable relationship between cause and effect. This is mechanical causality, which, because of its pragmatic parts and rational approach, is the realm of sensation and thinking (ST). It structures the patriarchal and Newtonian worldview prevalent today. Furthermore, Jung also notes in his foreword to *The I Ching* that causality deals with "statistical truth . . . a working hypothesis of how events evolve one out of the other"[65]—that is, facts linked to facts, logically and linearly.

In contrast, synchronicity is "acausal," as Jung says, and he names his article on this subject in *Collected Works,* volume 8, "Synchronicity: An Acausal Connecting Principle."[66] When this principle appears in consciousness, it is expressed as a "coincidence of events" that meaningfully links a psychic awareness and an outer event in a manner that transcends space, time, and causality. How does intuition participate in all three aspects of Jung's definition of synchronicity?

Consider the first term, "acausal." This word carries a negative meaning. As noted above, acausal means for Jung "non-mechanical" causality. That is, there can be no physical connections between the elements of synchronistic events, such as a person's dream of a cousin's illness and the actual reported ill cousin the next morning. Jung says a "formal" causality connects such an inner event with the historical event. According to *Webster's,* "form" as an object means "shape, figure, image," and as a verb it means, "to think of." This implies a knowing or an intelligence. Synchronicity, therefore, is an *intelligent* connecting principle according to Jung, for he says that in any meaningful coincidence, such as the dream of the sick cousin, there is a shared knowledge in the dreamer and in the sick relative that the dreamer intuitively realizes. This kind of knowledge, as Jung explains in one of his letters and as already noted, comes from the depth of the unconscious, which is not just under our skin but is an "atmosphere in which we live."[67]

In his article on synchronicity, Jung writes that synchronicity, besides being necessarily a formal cause, is also a final causality, since such a cause "postulates a *foreknowledge of some kind.*"[68] According to Henricus Cornelius Agrippa, it is "an inborn 'knowledge' or 'perception' in living organisms." It is not a conscious knowledge, writes Jung, "but rather a self-subsistent 'unconscious' knowledge which I would prefer to call 'absolute knowledge,'"[69] so that the dreamer's knowledge, evoked by emotion-laden archetypal images and traits of intuition, includes the cousin's condition.

In *Psychological Types* Jung describes intuition in a similar way, as already noted above, as a knowledge that comes to us not from outer senses, as in the case of sensation, but "a perception by way of the unconscious, or perception of unconscious contents."[70] Intuition is a synchronistic knowing, a knowing that defies mechanistic causality as well as space and time, because its vehicle is imagination—that spontaneous imaging in insights, visions, dreams, inventions, poetry, and prose that knows no bounds, and yet, like the synchronicity principle, discerns meaning and knows connections. However, in the experienced event, the intuitive meaning is subjective or personally perceived, and yet is rooted in the synchronistic atmosphere's objective meaning, that is, an atmosphere that is simply "out there," over which the subject has no control but in which the subject nevertheless participates.

Synchronistic events often occur in moments of creative insights. For example, in describing how she wrote her novel, *The Color Purple,* Alice Walker said in a radio conversation that she heard inner voices when she was living in New York, saying "What is this high rise shit?" She moved to San Francisco. The voices said the same thing. She finally moved into the country far north of San Francisco, where her inner country folk began to tell their stories. She knew intuitively that she had come to the right place as her imaginatively experienced stories tumbled out. In Walker's inner knowledge, there was a meaningful correspondence or connection between these inner folk and the country environment to which she had come. She was now able to hear them and work with them, as they emerged out of her artistic unconscious. The entire experience was a synchronistic event, mediated through and understood in the intuitive function.

This idea of "correspondence" brings us to another meaning of intuition as related to the principle of synchronicity. Synchronicity is the intelligent *connecting* principle. This connecting occurs by way of "correspondences." This is why Jung also calls synchronicity the "principle of correspondence." Correspondence, like the term analogy, means that two events, things, or ideas are linked together as both similar and different. For example, one might dream of a friend as an inner helper. The inner image contains particular traits of the outer person, but obviously the flesh-and-blood friend and dream image are different: the dream friend as intrapsychic reality is an aspect of the dreamer's inner life, and the friend in waking life is a separate and sovereign human being.

However, correspondence is not limited to similarity of structures. It has even more to do with the dynamic of relationships. This is illustrated by the Taoist's ancient spiritual tradition: "When the student is ready the master will come." Or, as a contemporary Jungian analyst might say in relating inner and outer possibilities, "When the inner lover is ready, the outer beloved will follow." Practically speaking, if I constantly think and feel negatively, negative events will follow. On the other hand, the unconscious' healing dynamic, in spite of our negative attitude, tirelessly tries to correct and heal this negativity by sending us compensatory dreams and outer synchronistic opportunities.

Intuition constantly relates inner and corresponding outer events. For example, a veteran actress of several decades, an INFP, who was loath to make legitimate demands for herself, dreamt that a union leader (probably an ESTJ), whom she had not thought of for years, was joining the cast. In waking reality, this woman had been an assertive union stewardess when she worked in New York chorus lines. The dream image implied that an ESTJ power, corresponding to the union leader's actual power, was what the INFP dreamer needed. This strongly introverted, feeling type woman needed the extraverted thinking strength of her former union stewardess. Dreams and meaningful insights that link inner and outer events are synchronistic or intuitive events. The dream is the realization of the intuitive function in every one of us, no matter what our dominant function may be.

Intuition makes connections in the realm of perception, just as feeling does so in the domain of judging. Intuition is the *holistic* knowing function of the entire psyche. Jung writes, "In intuition a content presents itself as whole and complete, without our being able to explain or discover how this content came into being."[71] While we can picture sensing as a *dot,* as something very specific such as a fact or an extended sensory experience, we can imagine intuition as a *circle,* embracing and containing many sensate details in an intelligible whole. In fact, this function is a container that can imaginatively unite all the other functions and attitudes. Jung writes in this regard: "The peculiarity of intuition is that it is neither sense perception [S], nor feeling [F], nor intellectual [T] inference, although it may also appear in these forms."[72] Jung could have included introversion and extraversion. None of the other type functions or attitudes have intuition's organizing capacity that can embrace all the types.

It is for these reasons that we say that intuition is the basis of the organizing dynamic of complexes. Jung discovered the complex during his early association experiences, in which subjects hesitated too long in responding to certain words.[73] He began to see that these words pointed to some common emotional factor that bound them all together in an "unconscious conflict or 'complex.'"[74] Conflict implies a negative complex, such as one based on fear. However, the term is applied also to positive aspects of psychic configurations. Even the ego is called a complex by Jung and other analysts.[75] As we saw in the introduction, the complex is a historical experience and a particularized manifestation of an archetype. A complex is a concrete incarnation of each archetype. For example, the mother complex, as a personal realization of the mother archetype, pulls together and stores in our memory many psychic factors that are both positive and negative about our experience of the mother, such as type differences between mother and child, memories, images, ideas, and even synchronistic events, all centered around a strong emotion, around that powerful dynamic reality that we experience both in the body and in the mind.

This consideration leads to a final understanding of intuition, based on the definition of synchronicity as the intelligent, connecting *principle*. *Webster's* describes "principle" as "the ultimate source, origin, or cause of something." The matrix out of which synchronicity arises is the Self or Soul, the source of our individual identity, our relationships with all persons and things, the alpha and omega of our individuation, and the creative principle of life. We must, Jung writes, consider synchronicity's "causeless events" as "*creative acts,* as the continuous creation of a pattern that exists from all eternity, repeats itself sporadically, and is not derivable from any known antecedents."[76] Intuition is the compass of the Soul's unique perception of the Self's "continuous creation."

Is a dream a product of intuition? Given the above, I hold that a dream is a product of intuition. Intuition helps us perceive the Soul's meaning delivered to us in the seeming chaos of a dream. Every dream is a spontaneous, playful outburst from the depth of the Soul, synchronistically occurring in this moment of time, yet often encompassing past connections and future possibilities. It would seem, therefore, that the content of a dream is also the product of intuition.

Jung did not agree with this conclusion in his early writings and some analysts who I have consulted concur—others do not. In *Psychological Types* Jung held that only "*Active* fantasies are the product of intuition" because "they are evoked by an attitude" in consciousness "directed to the perception of an unconscious contents." In intuition, consciousness is *actively* expecting a message from the unconscious; Jung called this "intuitive expectation." On the other hand, Jung argued, a dream's content is "*passive* fantasy," during which the conscious subject is "wholly passive" and, therefore, is not expecting the dream. Unlike active fantasies, the dream does not involve the entire personality, but represents, "mainly the standpoint of the unconscious personality." So he does not attribute its unconscious content to intuition.[77] According to Jung, intuition comes into play, therefore, whenever we seek to dialogue with an inner imagined or dreamt figure that we treat as autonomous, as if this figure were a sovereign person in waking life. Jung calls this "active imagination," which the editors of the *Types* book equate with "*active* fantasy."[78]

Robert Johnson gives us an example of an active imagination. In one of his taped lectures, Johnson reported an active fantasy at a time in his life when he felt very stuck and trapped in workaholism and in too much thinking behavior. In his imagination, he went to the edge of his inner earth and asked the unconscious to send him a healing figure. The figure who emerged was an easygoing, sensing, and feeling beachcomber who taught him to enjoy and play more in life. It is clear that in such active imaginings, intuition embraces this content originating from the unconscious.

I disagree with Jung's conclusion that dreams are not a product of intuition for several reasons. (1) He came to this conclusion very early in the development of his psychology as a whole and his typology theory, at a time when he acknowledged the tentativeness of some of his views. At that time he was thinking of all of the four functions as only conscious perceptions, and was not thinking of them systematically, but only sporadically, as archetypes, as innate and universal patterned contents in and emerging from the unconscious, as we saw in chapter 3. (2) Intuition as the function of creativity must include the creative potentials of dreams. How is it possible that intuition, as the creative function *par excellence* and as that perception that knows from the unconscious, according to Jung, analysts, and typologists, is divorced from dreaming, whose contents are all expressions of the unconscious and are the primitive creative processes which every human being experiences? (3) The process of active imagination and its "active fantasy" demonstratively includes, along with spontaneous dialogue, drawings, and dance, what is called dream induction.

(4) Given this context, isn't it possible that a consciousness that is centered in the ego complex, which in turn is rooted in the archetype of the Self, is at least implicitly and existentially intending help and wisdom from the unconscious in what we might call an implicit active fantasy? Accordingly, I want to expand on these four points.

(1) Jung's contention that a dream content is not included in intuition appeared in *Psychological Types,* published in German in 1921. This was an early time in his theorizing, a time in which he did not even give a definition of an archetype in his "Definitions" chapter. He was viewing the types as mainly cognitive patterns in consciousness, though he also acknowledged that they existed first in the unconscious as innate *a priori* patterns. However, because he left this part of his work unfinished, he never systematically developed the types as archetypes, which by definition are innate *a priori* patterns and contents in the unconscious. Remarkably, when he did define archetypes for the first time, he characterized all of them in intuitive terms, as already noted in chapter 3. Because of the importance of this issue on dreaming, I want to give his complete quotation here. (Preceding the quotation, Jung first described the personal unconscious as including "all more or less intentional repressions of painful thoughts and feelings.") He continued:

> But, over and above that, we also find in the unconscious qualities that are not individually acquired but are inherited, e.g., instincts as impulses to carry out actions from necessity without conscious motivation. In this "deeper" stratum we also find the *a priori* inborn forms of "intuition," namely the archetypes of perception and apprehension, which are the necessary *a priori* determinants all psychic processes.[79]

So Jung in his discussion of intuition and dreaming had not yet considered the fact that all archetypes including the Self are "*a priori* inborn forms of 'intuition,'" namely the archetypes of perception and apprehension. He also did not consider there the archetypal nature of intuition itself, which includes both conscious intentions and unconscious universal imaginal contents that emerge into consciousness. Yet elsewhere in the Jungian literature all the types have been described as archetypal. Hillman did so, calling intuition "Spirit," and Jung, as noted above, called this function the "Winged Mercurius, Morpheus, genii, angel." So it seems that, from an archetypal standpoint, the dream, originating as it does from the Self and its archetypes, participates in both the "conscious and the unconscious personality of the subject," which Jung attributes to "active fantasy."[80]

(2) How does one account for the creative nature of the dream, if Jung does not allow the dream in intuition? Must we assume that the dream's inventive content comes directly from the Self, since such imaginative outpourings do not come from the other function? This assumption begs the question: what content, what structure, and what dynamic of psyche in the entire conscious-unconscious spectrum and in the compass of the Soul does *not* come from the Self? We have learned that the Self as playwright calls upon every archetype to play out its specific role on the immense human stage. Which function, if not intuition, provides the creative matter, the felt insights and dramatic lines in the creative episodes of our life journey and story? We attribute the following characteristics, among many others, to intuition: a recognition of possibilities in any life situation, a preference for the new, a reaching into the future, a comfort with chaos, and a playful behavior. These are all attributes of creativity. As Jung has noted, no other function can include the other functions in its boundaries, so that it selects from sensation the needed detail, from thinking the necessary logical clarity, and from feeling the passionately moving dialogue? It is for this reason that intuition's symbol is the circle, which as a mandala is also symbolic of the Self. Yet intuition and Self are, of course, distinct.

My contention here also anticipates the place of intuition in the type compass' four major coupling archetypes, the subject of section 2 of this book. Beginning with chapter 5, we learn that the intuitive feeling (NF) coupling is the Creative Artist and Lover and the intuitive thinking (NT) pairing is the Creative Scientist and Magician. Further, we see in chapter 6 (as well as in chapter 9) to what extent in the second half of life a creative healing and transformation occurs in the oft-bewildering chaos, the frightening darkness, and saving hidden order of the intuitive feeling's Oceanic place. We also learned in chapter 3 that psychology as an experiential science is ruled by "fantasy and emotion," which are, respectively, intuitive and feeling qualities. This NF combination is the formative structure of dreams, although the contents of those dreams can include any of the attitudes and functions, which, as we have seen, is also true of intuition. So that both in the second half of life as well as in the very core of psychology as Jungians understand it, consciousness explicitly and implicitly expects the creative contribution from dreams. Is there, thereby, any limit to the active fantasy that is associated with intuition?

(3) The editors of the *Collected Works* equate active fantasy to what Jung came to call "active imagination." After Jung discussed a term he called "imaginative activity," which he identified with simply a neutral "flow of psychic energy" in nature in which all four functions participate, the editors write: "Imaginative activity is therefore not to be confused with active imagination, a psychotherapeutic method developed by Jung himself. Active imagination corresponds to the definition of *active fantasy* in paras. 712–714."[81] Jung perceived the artist as also doing active imagination when he wrote: "Because active fantasy is the chief mark of the artistic mentality, the artist is not just a *reproducer* of appearances but a creator and educator."[82]

Given the above, what if, instead of engaging in a conscious dialogue with an image from the unconscious as Robert Johnson did when he received his beachcomber, or the artist actively engaged in his artistic process, I ask the unconscious before sleep for a dream that will answer a need and actually receive an answer in what is called an induced dream? In my personal experience and in the experience of many of my clients, we can induce dreams. We can call for a dream that responds to a particular issue and often—not automatically—such a dream will occur. This process is another form of active imagination, just as is spontaneous painting, doodling, and dancing.

Here are two examples, one from a client and one of my own, of the process for making dreams one of the ways of active imagination. I have learned in decades of dreamwork that the latent compensatory intention of a dream of an inner attacking antagonist is that the dreamer is challenged to consciously claim the undeveloped areas of one's personality that the enemy represents. One male client finally faced before sleep a frightening male pursuer he had experienced in many dreams. I had challenged him to do so either consciously or in a dream. In his dream that followed, the dreamer stopped and faced the pursuer who also stopped, fell backward, and turned into a pregnant woman. My client at this time was beginning to consciously lose his lifelong and one-sided masculine self-image and persona. He, a celibate priest, was falling in love. The dream's symbol of transformation with its feminine and pregnant possibilities aided this realization, and he eventually did marry. In the case of my dream, in which I was attacked by a powerful male figure, I intuited that, given the particular stormy and critical events of my waking life in which the dream appeared, I needed more strength, more assertive power. The dream was responding to an explicit need and from an implicit expectation that emerged from that period's critical circumstances. I first wrestled with the antagonist in a conscious active imaging. Then that night I asked for a dream response in which I would claim the dream enemy's power. The dream that came depicted me as the owner and president of a new merchandising company. Flanked by assistant managers, I was exhorting and teaching hundreds of my employees as they sat in a grandstand in front of the building. I had received warrior and leadership power. These dream responses are as valid as examples of active imagination as Robert Johnson's beachcomber that came to him spontaneously outside of dreaming.

(4) I hold, considering the above, that the dream must be considered an implicit as well as explicit active fantasy rather than a passive fantasy. Active fantasy, Jung argued, requires an expectant awareness directed to the "perception of unconscious contents." How focused must consciousness be in relationship to any content from the unconscious, given the difficulty in understanding the nature of conscious processes and also given the explicit as well as implicit need for healing when one is in a deeply felt existential pain? Is a sudden insight that occurs in such needy times also outside the purview of intuition, if one is not actively seeking it? If the ego complex is rooted directly in the Self and the Self and all of its archetypes are "*a priori* inborn forms of intuition" and "are the necessary *a priori* determinants of *all* psychic processes," it would seem that our consciousness, with its many levels of explicit and implicit expectations from life, is always in some manner in a synchronistic dialogue with the unconscious through insights, visions, and dreams. In an intentional as well as in a subliminal way, our consciousness continually needs the unconscious as its wise, spiritual companion on the journey of individuation. In turn, the unconscious responds with what has become the most fundamental function of dreams for Jung: compensation. The idea of compensation, as a corrective to a one-sided conscious attitude, as well as a deep support for an authentic conscious position, is always in an implicit dialogue with consciousness.[83] This compensatory function tells us that the unconscious is always paying attention to and is in dialogue with the needs of the consciousness, and often satisfies those needs through visions and dreams. Nearly four decades after writing *Psychological Types,* Jung wrote the following about active imagination in relation to compensation.

> This [active imagination] is a method which is used spon-

taneously by *nature herself* or can be taught to the patient by the analyst. . . . Such a situation is bound to arise when the analysis of the psychic contents of the patient's attitude and particularly of his dreams has brought the compensatory or complementary images from the unconscious so insistently before his mind that the conflict between the conscious and the unconscious personality becomes open and critical.[84]

Jung did not hold here that such a process occurs only in critical moments in analysis and in learned active imagination. That is why he also wrote that such a method is "used spontaneously by nature herself," namely, our own unconscious as it responds to all of life's critical moments, not just those arising in analysis or explicitly expected in an active dialogue. Jung called such messages from the unconscious *vox Dei* or "the voice of God.[85] Such a voice also points to the idea of "vocation," that we each have a destiny that is known by the Self and mediated through the creative work of intuition in insights, dreams, and visions. In summary, for all the above reasons, our consciousness is haunted by the wise and ethical demands of the unconscious, so that one can argue that our awareness is always in an implicit active fantasy that expects dreams.

An example from a male client might be of help for those who are unfamiliar with a Jungian analytic intervention. He was in a deep angst, a profound grieving process, because his lover had moved out. He loved her for her own uniqueness, but he also knew that he was reliving his ancient disjointed relationship with a very demanding mother. He didn't ask for this particular dream, but he desperately needed some relief from his anguish and desolation. He dreamt that he and two companions stole a car from one of his professional mentors, an arrogant man in waking life. In his house of origin where he was hiding, he was suddenly attacked by several members of a mafia gang, all of whom he repelled. Then a powerful godfather showed up, who, instead of attacking him, pointed toward the painting of a famous artist who had painted many scenes from Rome, a city that is beloved to the dreamer. Suddenly, he saw a great arch. He knew that he was in Rome. Next, he realized that near the arch, a lovely young woman awaited him.

I hold that this dream is an active imagination spontaneously induced by nature and given to him to help him in his time of anguish. The dream is a product of the archetype of intuition responding to his conscious pain and his implicit hope and expectation that his unconscious would help him.

Other writers besides me view intuition as a reality that is already potentially present in one's depth, beyond being only a perceiving function. The analyst Daryl Sharp writes that extraverted intuitives see "under the surface." In contrast to a more pragmatic sensing type's view of "'a thing' or 'a person,' the intuitive sees its soul."[86] Soul has arche-typal content. Sonia Chaquette writes in her book, *The Wise Child: A Spiritual Guide to Nurturing Your Child's Intuition,* that we need to awaken "our children's intuitive hearts."[87] "Hearts" refers to a given content of the Soul. In the new and also very old profession of healing body as well as mind through psychological and spiritual alternatives, Maurie Pressman, M.D., writes about the need for humility and wisdom in the "true teacher." We protect ourselves from a false teacher by giving "obedience to our intuition, *the inner guide*."[88] The idea of an inner guide implies that intuition, like all archetypes, has an *a priori* knowledge and therefore a potential content. In these various ways, we experience the Soul expressing itself synchronistically as the intelligent connecting *principle,* as realized in these cases through intuition as one of the Self's archetypes.

The pathologies of intuition, when combined with introversion, revolve around its tendency to lose contact with everyday life. As Jung notes, such a person even "has little consciousness of his own bodily existence or of its effect on others."[89] For example, in a highly intuitive normal person, this tendency may appear as daydreaming and unrealistic imaginings. When faced with too much daily routine and detail, the intuitive easily gets bored and can suddenly ignore or walk away from his fellow workers. As Jung points out, the intuitive who is also extraverted can "abandon them cold-bloodedly, without any compunction."[90] He continues: "Consideration for the welfare of others is weak. Their psychic well-being counts as little with him as does his own . . . and on this account he is often put down as an immoral and unscrupulous adventurer."[91] On the other hand, in this one-sided intuition, he "may fritter away his life on things and people" too readily, and then others will profit from his labors. Jung concludes: "In the end he goes away empty."[92] In severely ill mental patients as described in the *Diagnostic and Statistical Manual of Mental Disorders IV*, intuition's pathology emerges as delusions and hallucinations.

THE JUDGING FUNCTIONS: THINKING AND FEELING

We have considered the two attitudes, introvert and extravert, which establish our inward and outward orientations respectively, and the two perceptive functions, sensation and intuition, whereby we gather knowledge. We decide and act on this information through thinking and feeling, which Jung called rational functions. Jung called sensation and intuition irrational functions, meaning that the mind is constantly bombarded with information-carrying impressions from "the general flux of events."[93] Thinking and feeling, however, as the decision-making functions, help us by way of "reflection," to, as it were, stop the "flux of events," so that we can consciously focus on specific information and make decisions. The rational functions, in turn, filter the information, so that thinking tends to organize the data logically and feeling selects the relational aspects of the information. Jung continues: "They function most perfectly when they are in the fullest possible accord with the law of reason."[94] In ordinary talk, this means that we have a certain degree of willpower that enables us to consciously organize specific data and act on it, while letting go of or bracketing out other more extraneous information. We'll first consider feeling.

Feeling

Jung and Myers list these feeling preferences: responding subjectively and empathetically to others; having strong likes and dislikes and personal and social values; valuing and working for harmony and sensitivity in relationships; enjoying some praise; avoiding unpleasantries; seeking stories to explain life; and translating raw emotion into useful values. Some characteristics of a one-sided feeling function are being overly generous, exhibiting an inability to say no, and, conversely, becoming rabidly judgmental.

I previously suggested certain symbols as representing the following qualities for the perceiving functions: the dot for the sensate's penchant for facts and the circle for the intuitive's need to be holistic. Notice the congruity of the dot and circle on this perceptive spectrum. When we come to the thinking function, I will suggest that its symbol is the straight line, implying that this function is a straight shooter in its logic. I suggest the curved line for feeling, because feeling, despite its name, is also rational and also discriminating. Notice also in this judging spectrum the similarity of the straight line and curved line. The curve can be uneven in feeling's undulations, suggesting the more dramatic qualities of this kind of rationality and its decision-making capacities.

The curve suggests a story, or a process, in which we experience the ups and downs and the emotional flux in human relationships. Feeling types, or the feeling aspect in us, loves the narrative as a basis for action, rather than the logic which thinking prefers. Feeling involves more than relatedness with other people. In the intrapsychic realm, its playful, vibrating lines connect consciousness with the symbols of the unconscious and the collective stories of humankind—

its myths, fairy tales, and biblical narratives. Jung says very strongly that the maturing, storylike process he calls individuation is not possible without this work of the feeling function as "affective value" in relating us to both society and the depth of Soul.[95] Feeling, as a matter of fact, is the relational function *par excellence.* The analyst William Willeford writes of feeling, "It evaluates in the forming, maintaining, and breaking of relationships on behalf of the ego."[96] Willeford also agrees with both Jung and James Hillman that the fullest realization of feeling is love in its highest and most creative forms.[97]

Jung had difficulty defining feeling's uniqueness, knowing that in our common speech, we can loosely confuse it with both sensation and intuition.[98] We can say, "I feel pain," and "I have a feeling that it will rain tomorrow." The former is a particular sense perception; therefore, it is sensate awareness. The latter posits a future possibility; this is intuition. Our feeling function is neither of these. Feeling, Jung wrote, is not a perception, as are sensing and intuiting; it is a judging and decision-making process based not on logic but on equally precise good or bad evaluations.

Principally because of the above confusions, Jung also found it difficult to show that feeling is, along with thinking, a rational function. Yet feeling is as pointed, direct and consistent in its own way as thinking. However, in its mode of operating, it is not logical but evaluative. Whereas, according to Jung, thinking's aim is "to establish conceptual relations" having an objective quality,[99] and while thinking judges contents or relationships dispassionately, feeling "is primarily a process that takes place between the ego and a given content, moreover, that imparts to the content a definite value in the sense of acceptance or rejection ('like' or 'dislike')." Such a value may be in the form of a mood that captures the emotional climate of an entire situation, writes Jung. Even "indifference" is a form of evaluation, says Jung.[100] The crucial difference between thinking and feeling is that one is objective and logical and the other subjective and evaluative.[101]

Thus, the former does not enter into intimacy as such, whereas the latter revels in it.

Seeking a resolution to the relationship between emotion and feeling. It is also difficult to think of feeling as rational because emotions are involved in its every expression. Jung described feeling as articulating "likes and dislikes." Yet, Jung argued, feeling and emotion are not the same. Still, in the language of experienced typologists, there is often a haunting presence of emotions in their description of feeling. Myers wrote in *Gifts Differing* of such "feeling traits" (in contrast to thinking characteristics) as "tender-hearted, more tactful, more social . . . more inclined to take things personally," and states that feeling types "value sentiment above logic."[102] Such subtle intimations of emotion do not appear in the other three functions, because emotionality simply does not belong in any intrinsic way in their structures and dynamics. However, emotions, of course, can *accompany* any function, just as they can accompany any human behavior. The question here has to do with the *substantive* presence of emotion in the feeling function, such that this function would not be complete without emotion.

Jung seemed to be quite ambivalent about the presence of emotions, or affects, within feeling in *Psychological Types*. He wrote, "When the intensity of feeling increases it turns into an affect." On the other hand, he continued, "feeling is distinguished from affect, by the fact that it produces no perceptible physical innervations, i.e., neither more nor less than in ordinary thinking process."[103] Elsewhere Jung clearly established a connection between emotions and feeling when he wrote that some people "conspicuously neglect thinking in favor of *emotional factors,* that is, of feeling."[104]

Jung acknowledged that such uncertainties at that time in the first quarter of this century were indicative of the youthful nature of psychology, noting that the field "is virgin territory, and its terminology has still to be fixed."[105] Jung never resolved this issue nor did psychologists in general, as he indicated in his last writing before his death.[106] The relationship between emotion and feeling continues to be very difficult to discern. William Willeford, certainly one of the most astute and penetrating explorers of this topic, holds that "theories of 'feeling and emotion' make up the most confused subfield within psychology." So Willeford does not "try to employ a single, rigorously self consistent vocabulary in discussing both feeling and emotion."[107]

Willeford helps us resolve this issue by concluding that "feeling is emotional but not synonymous with emotion. . . . There is, I assume, a distance, often slight between feeling and emotion."[108] Obviously the feeling function is not to be identified with the raw spontaneity and irrationality of any of the emotions. Emotions as such are involuntary, uncontained energies, acting as wildly on the body and mind as water plunging down great falls. Yet, as *Webster's* indicates, "emotion" comes from the Latin, "emovere," meaning "to move out, stir up, agitate." Emotions move us, either destructively in their primitive spontaneity or in a higher form that can give impetus and meaning to any human behavior. Somehow, they must be transformed, in order to participate in the decision-making and initiating capacities of the feeling function, if Jung's description of the feeling function as "emotional value" has any validity.[109] Jung writes elsewhere of the feeling function as "affective value, as already noted," and also as "a certain intelligence of the heart."[110]

How is crass emotionality transformed into "emotional value" or into "the intelligence of the heart?" Neither Jung nor Willeford directly solves this problem. I want to suggest the following solution, based on Jung's description of the way in which the energies of the natural instincts—and, therefore, I add, the emotions associated with the instincts—are transformed into useful energies via symbols. In his article "On Psychic Energy," he speaks of the "canalization of libido" as "the process of energic transformation or conversion" and as "a transfer of psychic intensities or values from one content to another, a process corresponding to the physical transformation of energy." Such physical transformations occur in a steam engine's process of changing heat into steam and then "into the energy of motion."[111] He rather favors—and so do I—a better basis for understanding the transformation of crass emotions into value, the human inventiveness by which a power plant's pipes and turbines transform a waterfall's turbulent waters into useful electrical energy "capable of manifest applications." The psychic equivalent of such a transformation changes "natural instincts, which would otherwise follow their gradient without performing work, into other dynamic forms that are productive of work."[112]

Jung identifies the psychic equivalent of the power plant as the symbol, with its many corresponding levels and nuances, that, acting as a "psychological mechanism," "transforms energies" from potentially destructive ones into useful ones."[113] For example, appropriate symbolic actions and images transform the natural instinct of survival with its potentially damaging emotions of fear and anger, into energies of practical or creative achievements. A dimension of survival certainly participated in my above-discussed nightmare of the attacking man. My holding and confronting this fearful and angry figure led to its transformation into useful assertive ideas and actions in waking life, comparable to my imagined strong leadership in the responding dream.

A comparable transformation of any involuntary emotionality occurs through feeling's archetypal symbolic representations and evaluative nature. The archetypal essence of feeling is its evaluative powers, which exist in a potential form in the Self. Willeford writes in this regard: "Feeling relates the ego to the pathic ground and so to the self, its evaluative aspect."[114] The feeling function, in its primary archetypal aspect and symbols, transforms as *value* the crudeness of any emotion into its likes and dislikes, into symbols and experiences of the precious and sacred quality of loving relationships, as well as the despised and prosaic aspects of existence. Feeling contains and transforms the chaotic emotions the way a power plant's dam and generators transform the fall's waters into useful electricity.

Here is an example from the life experience of a client, a woman of great stature and intelligence with whom I have worked for many years. Usually self-composed, she became enraged and deeply saddened for weeks because a friend had betrayed her. As a result she decided to break off the friendship, following her feeling function bent. We were aware that such feelings of betrayal were deeply rooted in her childhood experiences. She could not overcome these emotions with willpower or prayers. She finally sat in her anger and her sorrow as I suggested, imagining the emotions as a dirty pool of water. Suddenly she was enveloped by a fearful metallic blackness so thick that no existing element could account for it. She sat there, sad and rageful, seeing and hearing nothing. Finally, she heard cracking sounds and the blackness changed to a sadly felt grey, a grey as impenetrable as the black. She sat in this depression until she heard a cracking again, after which the greyness changed to natural light and she opened her eyes. She was unable to reevoke the anger and depression that had so haunted her, she personally felt stronger, and she finally reestablished a relationship with her old friend. Thus the feeling function can lead us to tough confrontations and transformations, which reward us with substantial change.

We need to reflect on the extent to which our lives are filled with emotional components that influence, for good or ill, our evaluation of life and our human relationships. A recent First Advent liturgy illustrated this for me. I experienced singing in a congregation led by a large choir and a brass ensemble and watching a liturgical dance. The congregation experienced the collective moral, aesthetic, and religious values of the music, dance, sermon, and prayers for the parish's dead and ill, and the call for justice and compassion for the world's hungry and displaced persons. The elements and events in our lives often move us to value ourselves, others, and life in general through the more civilized emotions contained in the feeling function.

Feeling at the subjective level has to do with personal experiences of relationships, and is therefore inseparable from both love and hate. Love and hate are the ultimate dynamic stuff of our drama of individuation. Within these affective polarities we play out a myriad of emotions, all having to do with relationships and therefore with the feeling function. That all these humanly contained emotions might be outside the feeling function's guidance is inconceivable. For example, Erik Erikson's daughter, Sue Erikson Bloland, has written a powerful description of her famous father's impact on her life. The article is loaded with a rich tapestry of emotions, all of which have touched both her self-esteem and self-loathing. For example, she writes, "It has sometimes been a source of great pride to be Erik Erikson's daughter, but more often it has overwhelmed my sense of myself—been demoralizing, diminishing, even paralyzing."[115]

The goal of this complex and anguished process of maturation is always the Self. Jung speaks of the Self in a way that resonates with our understanding of feeling as the function that relates us even to a cosmic value and meaning. He writes of the Self:

> This "something" is strange to us and yet so near, wholly ourselves and yet unknowable, a virtual center of so mysterious a constitution that it can claim anything— kinship with beasts and gods, with crystals and with stars. . . . This "something" claims all that and more, and having nothing in our hands that could fairly be opposed to these claims, it is surely wiser to listen to this voice.
>
> I have called this center the Self. . . . It might equally well be called "God within us." The beginning of our whole psychic life seems to be inextricably rooted in this point, and all our highest and ultimate purposes seem to be striving toward it.[116]

This immeasurable "kinship," a familial relating to all the universe as a dynamic aspect of the Self, is one of the prime characteristics of feeling. Put in another way, the Self constitutes our highest value; and since feeling is the function of value, then the Self is feeling's "highest and ultimate" purpose. In terms of an authentic self-love, the ego's conscious feeling as seeker is romancing the Self's unconscious feeling as beloved attractor, and that attractor is found in everyone and everything. From a Taoist's view, the dramatic play of Self and the ego in seeking a mutual harmony is the Tao.

William Willeford puts this ultimate work of feeling in this way:

> Feeling relates the ego to the pathic ground and so to the self, its evaluative aspect. By "pathic ground" I mean the indissoluble rootedness of our experience in emotionality that is ultimately unconscious and always at least semi-autonomous with respect to conscious volition . . . it is itself a ground because it is the basis of the unconscious empathy found among humans as well as in infrahuman species as when a school of fish suddenly rush in the same direction. . . . The pathic ground is the basis of emotional life. It is also a fundamental aspect of the self, since all knowledge of the self is emotional.[117]

Given the assumption that emotion has been incorporated into the evaluative work of feeling, we can then appreciate the fact that there can be no growth in consciousness without emotions, as Jung argues. In his article on "The Psychology of the Mother Archetype," Jung speaks of "the stirring up of conflict," and links it to fire. He says,

> the fire of affects and emotions, and like every other fire it has two aspects, that of combustion and that of creating light. On the one hand, emotion is the alchemical fire whose warmth brings everything into existence and whose heat burns all superfluities to ashes. . . . But on the other hand, emotion is the moment when steel meets flint

and a spark is struck forth, *for emotion is the chief source of consciousness.* There is no change from darkness to light or from inertia to movement without emotion.[118]

"Movement" implies the feeling function's judging task as the emotionally contained mover and shaker.

The pathologies of the feeling function are many. Keeping in mind that one of this function's main traits is one's behavior in relationships, an outstanding one is codependency, acted out through either a submissive servant role or a rejecting rebel role that we decide, consciously or unconsciously, to play out. I have worked in analysis with a woman, an introverted, intuitive, feeling type, who decided at a young age that she was going to be a servant to her mother for life, and another client, another similar type, who decided at age fourteen that he would never let another person get close to him. Both have overcome being fused codependents, one from a subservient servant role and the other, from an alienated rebel role. Both have been in "stuck" relationships, one out of fear and the other out of anger.

While these clients demonstrate personal pathologies, general societal pathologies of the feeling function are common. Paranoia, while a pathology of introversion, is also a pathology of the feeling function on a larger scale when society scapegoats a particular or a general segment of society. Distorted feeling becomes judgmental and prejudicial. We have all experienced this in Americans' treatment of the blacks. The Jews were so treated under the Nazis and generally in distressed periods in the last 2000 years of our European history. People with liberal leanings suffered the effects of this type of paranoia in the McCarthy era and still fall victim to it today. On the other hand, political conservatives are subjected to emotional stereotyping by liberals. The distrust by any significant segment of a population, such as classical anarchists, toward any kind of government control is another form of paranoia.

Another pathology of the feeling function is sentimentality often invested in the past. How many get carried away, for example, by a nostalgia for the past's seemingly golden years? Such nostalgia can be fun and even satisfying, if one does not get stuck in it and does not ignore the living challenges of the present moment. Two forms of this pathology are a spirituality, in which one focuses only on the sweetness of God and religion in general, and its opposite, a dreary, masochistic subservience to a punishing religion and a severe God. This happened in the Catholic church when a harsh patriarchal hierarchy was offset by a maudlin devotion to the Virgin Mary and the saints, and by masochistically harsh disciplines in the supposed service of the suffering Christ. Such excesses often can be overcome by the unique, more objective qualities of the thinking function and by refining and educating the feeling function. The Second Vatican Council's recovery of the ancient ideas of the Church as the People of God and as the spiritual Body of Christ, as collective expressions of the feeling function, has significantly changed Catholicism on a parochial level.

Thinking

Jung and Myers note that the thinking function lends itself to objectifying, systematizing, categorizing, naming, being logical, responding to ideas, seeking just treatment, observing hierarchies, being firm and tough-minded, being easily able to dismiss subordinates, enjoying policy-making and strategizing, seeking dignity and authority, and generally preferring to lead than follow. Some of its negative traits are crude name-calling, cold-blooded decision-making, and an inability to empathize. As previously mentioned, if the dot and the circle could respectively symbolize sensation and intuition, then the curved line and the straight line could respectively symbolize feeling and thinking. Only a thinking type could come up with this definition: "A straight line is the shortest distance between two points." The thinking aspect in us not only knows how to define and construct linear thought, but knows also how to structure information in a way that helps to quicken decision-making. Thinking types readily construct outlines and construct diagrams built of clear concepts and their well-defined interconnections. Those who are intuitive, feeling writers or artists need first to work from intuition's felt visions, which act as provisional maps or general configurations about a given subject. Then in revision, we need Thinking's ladder, the outline, in order to give structural bones to the writing's living flesh.

Jung holds in *Psychological Types* that "our age and its most eminent representatives know and acknowledge only the extraverted type of thinking." However, there is another kind of thinking type, an introverted type, who is oriented, contrary to the extraverted thinking type, neither "by immediate experience of objects nor by traditional ideas."[119] When we reflect on our dreams or our spontaneous insights, obsessions, and worries that have minimal connections with the outer world, we are operating with introverted thinking. "This thinking is neither determined by objective data nor directed to them; it is a thinking that starts from the subject and is directed to subjective ideas or subjective facts."[120]

Metaphorically, thinking types are straight shooters and knife-wielders. They know how to get to the point and also how to quickly slice a jungle of ideas into clear concepts. They give clarity to the otherwise jumbled perceptions as well as nebulously articulated decisions of the feeling function. Thinking types do for the world of concept and decision-making what the sensate person does for detail. The sensate, thinking types are very practical and logical.

There is an objective toughness to this approach, so much so that feeling types will often characterize thinkers as "cold-blooded people." Thinking types spend their mental time on high, distant promontories of the Soul that enable them to see and map the larger scenario, both without and within, more clearly. In order to effectively live our first stage of life, we must develop some of the thinking qualities. We recall that when Jung entered college and, especially, proceeded into medicine, he put aside his mythic inner introverted personality No. 2 in favor of the more practical, thinking stance of our outer contemporary society that he called his personality No. 1. After he broke with Freud, he had to abandon this identification with the rational collective expectations and collapsed into and worked with the unconscious' fearful images and emotions. Jung reports that he was also able to return to the high place of the thinking function, so as to reflect on these experiences with the unconscious. He writes in his autobiography that he "was able to take an *objective view* of that whole experience" (emphasis added). In this thinking state of mind, he wrote his first significant article after his break with Freud, "The Relationship between the Ego and the Unconscious." Then he added, "Simultaneously, I was busy with preparatory work for *Psychological Types*."[121] Jung's article eventually became one of the two that make up his *Two Essays on Analytical Psychology, CW,* volume 7, which together with *Types,* represent his professional and intellectual break with Freud.

Thinking types are the strategists of both war and peace, of industry and art. They see clearly what policies should guide a course of action, what standards need to be established for performances, and what criteria are needed for different areas of thought. Thinking types see principles clearly, so that those principles become primary rungs on the ladder of thought and action. Thinking types are our law-givers. The law makes possible the rational and ordered functioning of society, just as bones and sinews hold together the flesh. Feelings are not allowed in the courtroom, since the focus is on facts and abstraction. Ben Sells, a psychotherapist and lawyer, and the author of *The Soul of the Law,* makes clear that the law is, most of all, the province of thinking when he describes the law itself, legal training, and the typical characteristics demanded by lawyers in the schools and in the courts.[122] The author, in exploring the imaginative, archetypal basis of the law, establishes without question that in the legal profession, thinking is king. In articulating this function, he lays out its many facets as "the hallmarks of the analytical mind," basically contained under the rubric of "objective rationality."

This outlook informs not only the law, but also "mathematics, philosophy, or science," as we already have seen in Jung's appraisal of these areas of thought in the previous chapter.[123] Such a cool mental judgment does not allow the presence of feeling in both assessing a client's case and in the courtroom's procedures. Judging objectively implies not only a knowledge and action from a distance, but also a consideration of only the facts as "objects of study." The facts in turn are gathered into a "case" within abstract and rational parameters.[124] The case must epitomize a "bedrock belief in reason and logic," and its presentation in the courtroom reveals "the craving for process, rules, and regulations."[125] This rational and factual mentality also increasingly leads legislators to overload laws with minute rules and procedures,[126] a subject we will take up in chapter 12. The line as the symbol of the thinking function becomes, in the realm of the law, the sword as well as the scale.[127] The sword means that the thinking type individual must always sharply and clearly conceptualize reality. As to the symbol of the scale, Sells seems to look at it from only a negative side, that is, that it represents the lawyers' fear of being upset, of fearing the turbulent realms of emotions and the humane demands of equity. However, we know from extensive typological literature that one of the strong attributes of the thinking function is the sense of justice, demanding that there must be a balancing of personal and collective forces and energies in life and in governance. It is no accident that a democratic society seeks a balance between the three branches of government—the executive, the legislative, and the judicial. In conclusion, there is no doubt that the thinking function, as it reaches its zenith in the law, focuses on, and is even obsessed about, "order and obedience." As Sells writes, "'Law' and 'Order' are so linked in our common imagination that they seem to follow as one breath follows another."[128]

Because thinking's distancing and detachment imply, metaphorically, being in a high place, this function is correlated with an attachment to a hierarchical viewpoint. So the court system has higher and lower courts, legal offices have various strata of partners, and corporation lawyers are comfortable with the idea that the more one is vested with authority "the higher one goes."[129] Sells associates this thinking trait with "a religious tenet of wide belief . . . that Power Rests On High."[130] One thinking type dreamt that he came down from a high place in a building to attend a musical event. He knew the dream was inviting him to awaken and utilize his inferior feeling function. He was a politician, who sometimes became rather inflated in his views. His wife would challenge him by remarking: "Get off of your high horse, Dude." However, she also valued the clarity and sense of justice of her husband's thinking dominance.

Given this picture of the law and its thinking strength, we can see some of the thinking function's pathologies. Lawyers and other professionals oriented especially toward sensation and thinking dominance, can be lonely people, cut off from the generality of society, and inclined toward depression and even suicide.[131] This practical thinking diet feeds the head, as it were, and not the heart and guts, so that intimacy, or a soulful relationship with another person, can be very difficult to realize. The tough-minded and objective approach in the law does not easily adjust to an empathic and tender-minded attitude in family life and in friendships. The lawyer, as well as other professionals such as doctors, soldiers, policemen, and accountants, who must naturally or adaptively abide by the thinking function's demands, finds it difficult to enter into the community's chaotic and oceanic demands.[132]

The thinking function is dedicated to bringing order to the chaos of our personal and social life. On the other hand, if this function becomes rigidly one-sided, one is forced to deal with the more messy images of intuition and feeling, of life and death concerns, and of raw fear, frustration, and rage. These represent healing possibilities that, if not attended to, will invite a more fearful chaos. One thinking type, trying hard to maintain order and to control every social relationship, suddenly collapsed psychologically. He trashed his office and his apartment and was eventually hospitalized. With the help of medication, he returned to himself and resumed his controlling behavior. But he had many dreams of garbage dumps, of swimming in filthy waters, of being force-fed rotting food. Another thinking type, a male, had to face in a dream a group of dogs that tore like Tasmanian devils at a man's body lying in a churning, muddy pool. In type terms, both clients needed to be open to the messiness of both their intuitive and feeling functions. Chaotic images symbolize the intuitive function and dogs, as "man's best friend," are often images of the feeling function in dreams and myths.

The unconscious is relentless in its attempt to help the thinking type find intimate and loving relationships. If its efforts are not honored, then the Soul of the thinker may be captivated and consumed, as was the professor in the movie, *The Blue Angel*. Professor Unrath, played by Frederic March, meets a vampish, exciting woman, played by Marlene Dietrich, in a nightclub. The professor's feeling side, long stifled by his thinking function, bursts forth in an obsessive, inappropriate hunger for a meaningful relationship. He is repeatedly and abjectly humiliated by the woman. If the thinking type, whether male or female, does not heed the necessity of developing the feeling function, such a person will be constantly beset by dream images that force the issue. One thinker, a hard-driving business professional, overwhelmed by the rational and time-driven demands of his job and struggling to understand his relations with women, dreamt that he was home alone in his parents' house, locking every door and window for fear of some outside frightening presence. In the dream he heard a knock at the back door, and from a window he saw an old bag lady. He awakened in a panic, moaning and gasping for air. He returned to the door in active imagination and let her in. Without words, she beckoned him to follow as she opened all doors and windows, letting in, thereby, the feeling function's openness to life that he so badly needed. He was ethically challenged by this dream to realize feeling's capacity for surrender—to his spouse and to his developing role in the human community.

We have concluded our view of each of the types as the nuts and bolts, the fuel and mobility, of the psyche. Generally we have bracketed out their relationship to other types, except when we could briefly suggest their coupling connections.

THE FUNCTIONS IN THE COUPLINGS

The four functions we have been discussing are the constituent types that make up each coupling. We will see in section 2 that the coupling's two functions are always distinct from one another in their structural traits and their dynamic functions, and we need to be conscious of their specificity. The distinctive traits of each individual type will persist in the couplings, even though the couplings play out archetypal wholes. Also, one of the functions in each coupling, as dominant, is in charge and the other, the auxiliary, acts as an assistant. Finally, in this minidrama, one function will have an extraverted role and the other an introverted role.

It is interesting to note that of the four attitudes and the four functions discussed in this chapter, the two that have been the most difficult to describe and the most controversial in psychology in terms of meanings and boundaries have been intuition and feeling. Late in his life, Jung wrote that the "scientific mind" has difficulty with both. This mind-set cannot square "symbolic ideas" or intuitions with "intellect and logic," and cannot pin down "the phenomenon of 'affect' or 'emotion' . . . with a final definition. The cause of the difficulty is the same in both cases—the intervention of the unconscious."[133] One can, thereby, conclude that they are the most undifferentiated of the types and most closely associated with the creativity of the unconscious. Appropriately, therefore, their union in the intuitive feeling coupling has been named "Oceanic," "Creative Artist," and "Lover," and this archetype is associated with times of crisis and chaos as well as opportunity and inventiveness. Also, Jung held, as we saw in chapter 3, that in psychology, thinking is no longer king and must yield to "fantasy and emotion," that is, to intuition and feeling. This combination thrives more in the ambiguous and uncertain realms of the Soul and is associated with that edge of the Psyche in which the known and the unknown connect. So the dream, in its emotion-laden imagery, is an NF structure, though its content can include any of the type compass' four quadrants, as we have noted above.

Given their parts, each coupling has its own unique characteristics, energies, preferences, and roles within and without each of us. Consider one coupling, the sensing thinking combination, bracketing out for now whether one function is extraverted or introverted or one is dominant or auxiliary, as Myers did when she described the couplings in her *Introduction to Type*.[134] Sensing collates information through the outer senses, and thinking logically and systematically appropriately selects as well as uses these sensing perceptions. The two functions are distinct, but only in the sense that individual musical notes are distinct from the overall structure of a musical piece, which is experienced as a harmonious totality. The thinking's naming of ideas flows into the sensing's assembling of facts, very much like watercolors' different colors flow into one another to create a total picture. As we noted above, one of these functions will in fact dominate and the other will be an aid. The two functions act like the left and right hands and arms of the body, one of which will dominate yet they work together in the one body. So the two functions form one entity, the ST archetype.

Some critics of the functions correctly note that the perceiving and judging functions are not as distinct as the literature claims. One can argue that there are judging aspects in sensation and in intuition, since sensation decides to collect things in boxes, metaphorically speaking, and intuition decides to see reality in interactive configurations. Both "boxes" and "configurations" establish limits, which is a judging function. In turn, it is clear that the two judging functions, thinking and feeling, embrace cognitive fields; they know as well as judge. Yet it is clear from experience and the extensive *MBTI* research that the perceiving functions can remain limitless *within* their established parameters, and so need the judging functions to move from an endless knowing to an actual doing, which stops the flow of perceptions and completes the task. Furthermore, the fact that the couplings, as combinations of perceiving and judging functions, are always present in all of life puts this issue to rest. What works are the interplay of the functions in the combinations, not their isolated traits and images.

Finally, we need to remind ourselves that the unity of the two functions is based on the underlying principle of the psyche, the Self or Soul, as the overall archetype of wholeness. Henry L. Thompson, a leading typological thinker and organizational development person, writes in this regard:

> When the psyche comes into existence, it is as if a bubble forms (a "sphere," wrote Jung) in the collective unconscious with the self as both the boundary and the center. . . . The overall psyche system is under the influence of a strange attractor [the Self] that pulls the system into a dynamical type pattern of observable behavior and actions that we call "psychological types."[135]

It is by virtue of the Self that each individual type unites to form any of the couplings, and in turn the four couplings, under the aegis of the Self, point us in the direction of undeveloped traits that form the typological circle, the compass of the Soul, and, together, help us constantly strive for wholeness and a fuller life.

Now we are ready to consider the full and complex actualization of the types as couplings on the typological compass, which is the subject of section 2 and the centerpiece of this book.

Notes

1. C. G. Jung, *The Collected Works of C. G. Jung* (hereafter cited as CW), vol. 6, Psychological Types, English edition, translated by H. G. Baynes (1923; rpt., Princeton NJ: Princeton University Press, 1971), para. 987.

2. Ibid., paras. 982–84.

3. Jung, foreword to the Argentine edition, *CW*, vol. 6, *Psychological Types,* p. xiv.

4. James Hillman, "Egalitarian Typologies versus the Perception of the Unique," *Eranos Lectures,* no. 4 (Dallas TX: Spring Publications 1980, p. 21.)

5. Jung, *Memories, Dreams, Reflections* (Princeton NJ: Princeton University Press, 1961), p. 33f.

6. Ibid., p. 32f.

7. Allen L. Hammer and Wayne D. Mitchell, "The Distribution of *MBTI* Types in the U.S. by Gender and Ethnic Group," *Journal of Psychological Type* 37 (1996): p. 2.

8. Jung, *CW*, vol. 6, *Psychological Types,* para. 507.

9. Ibid., paras. 563–67.

10. Jung, "The Stages of Life," *CW*, vol. 8, *The Structure and Dynamics of the Psyche* (Princeton NJ: Princeton University Press, 1960), pp. 387–403.

11. Ibid., p. 778.

12. Ibid., paras. 771 and 787.

13. Ibid., para. 789.

14. Ibid., para. 771.

15. Ibid., para. 772.

16. Ibid., para. 773.

17. Jung, *CW,* vol. 6, *Psychological Types,* paras. 568–70.

18. Jung, "The Stages of Life," *CW,* vol. 8, *The Structure and Dynamics of the Psyche,* para. 778 (emphasis added).

19. Ibid., paras. 777-78.

20. Ibid., paras. 788-90.

21. Jung clearly sees even the P as more operative in this more introverted second stage. He writes: "Generally speaking, a judging [J] observer will tend to seize on the conscious character [obviously more outer oriented], while a perceptive [P] observer be more influenced by the unconscious character, since judgment is chiefly concerned with the conscious motivation of the psychic process, while perception registers the process itself" (Jung, *CW,* vol. 6, *Psychological Types,* para. 576).

22. Jung, "The Stages of Life," *CW,* vol. 8, *The Structure and Dynamics of the Psyche,* para. 787.

23. Jung, *CW,* vol. 6, *Psychological Types,* para. 560.

24. Ibid., para. 561.

25. Ibid., para. 687.

26. Ibid., para. 558. Jung adds: "But that is not all; on the contrary, the types seem to be distributed quite at random. In the same family, one child is introverted, the other extraverted."

27. Ibid. para. 559 (emphasis added).

28. Ibid., para. 563. Epimetheus, as we recall in chapter 3, means "after-thinker," a typical characteristic of the extravert, that is, to act and then reflect.

29. Riane Eisler, *The Chalice and the Blade* (San Francisco: Harper and Row, 1987).

30. Ibid., p. xix.

31. Jung, *CW,* vol. 6, *Psychological Types,* para. 627.

32. Ibid., para. 572.

33. Carolyn Merchant, *The Death of Nature: Women, Ecology, and the Scientific Revolution* (San Francisco CA: Harper and Row, 1980); Ruth Anthony El Saffar, *Rapture Encaged: The Suppression of the Feminine in Western Culture* (New York and London: Rutledge, 1994); Gerda Lerner, *The Creation of Patriarchy* (New York

and Oxford: Oxford University Press, 1986).

34. David Elkind, *The Hurried Child: Growing Up Too Fast, Too Soon* (Reading MA: Addison Wesley, 1981, 1989).

35. Marion Woodman, *Addiction to Perfection: The Still Unravished Bride* (Toronto: Inner City Books, 1982), p. 51.

36. Meyer Friedman and Ray H. Rosenman, *Type A Behavior and Your Heart* (Greenwich CT: A Fawcett Crest Book, 1974), p. 270.

37. Jung, *CW,* vol. 6, *Psychological Types,* paras. 623–24.

38. Ibid., para. 625.

39. Jung, "On the Tale of the Otto," *CW,* vol. 18, *The Symbolic Life* (Princeton NJ: Princeton University Press, 1954), p. 1720.

40. David Keirsey and Marilyn Bates, *Please Understand Me: An Essay on Temperament Styles* (Del Mar CA: Prometheus Nemesis Books, 1978), p. 25.

41. Jung, *C. G. Jung Letters,* Vol 1: 1906–1950 (Princeton NJ: Princeton University Press, 1973). Jung writes here to Heinrich Zimmer about Walter Eugene Clark, a professor of Sanskrit at Harvard University. Jung continues: "that is to say, one must act as if one had not seen him and must talk softly and slowly, so as not to scare him off. He has a very nice wife who is the exact opposite" (p. 222).

42. Janet Frame, *Janet Frame: An Autobiography* (New York: George Braziller, 1989). The movie, based on Frame's life, made in 1990 in New Zealand and directed by J. Campion, was rated by the *Chicago Tribune* movie critic, Michael Wilmington, one of the best movies of the century (Section 13, "The Arts," March 19, 1995).

43. Frame, *Janet Frame: An Autobiography,* p. 196.

44. Ibid.

45. Ibid., p. 201.

46. Ibid., pp. 222–23.

47. Emily Dickinson, *Selected Poems and Letters of Emily Dickinson,* edited by Robert N. Linscott (New York: Doubleday Anchor Books, 1959), from the introduction.

48. Ibid., p. 75.

49. Ibid., pp. 41–42.

50. Ibid., p. 102.

51. Lawrence LeShan, *You Can Fight For Your Life, Emotional Factors in the Causation of Cancer* (New York: A Jove/HBJ Book, 1977).

52. Jung, *CW*, vol. 6, *Psychological Types,* para. 776.

53. John T. Molloy, *New Dress for Success* (New York: Warner Books, 1988).

54. Ibid., p. 2.

55. Richard Wilhelm, *The I Ching or, The Book of Changes,* translated into English by Carl F. Baynes, with a foreword by C. G. Jung (London: Routledge and Kegan Paul, 1968).

56. Jung, foreword to *The I Ching,* p. xxii.

57. Natalie Goldberg, *Writing Down the Bones* (Boston: Shambhala, 1968).

58. Ibid., p. 43.

59. Daryl Sharp, *Personality Types: Jung's Model of Typology* (Toronto: Inner City Books, 1987). Sharp quotes Jung, p. 57.

60. Jung, *CW*, vol. 6, *Psychological Types.* Jung writes: "It is the function that mediates perceptions in an *unconscious way* (emphasis, Jung's). . . . In intuition, a content presents itself whole and complete without our being able to explain or discover how this content came into existence"(para. 770).

61. Jung, Letter to Fritz Kunkel in *C. G. Jung Letters,* vol. 1, p. 433.

62. Jung, "Synchronicity: An Acausal Connecting Principle," *CW,* vol 8, *The Structure and Dynamics of the Psyche* (Princeton: Princeton University Press, 1960). The archetypes, as "formal factors," writes Jung, "express themselves as [numinous] affects, which lower our consciousness." This lowering has contents, which are "often of an inferior or primitive nature and thus betray their archetypal origins." Thus, "certain phenomena of simultaneity or synchronicity seem to be bound up with the archetypes" (para. 841).

63. Jung et al., eds., *Man and His Symbols* (Garden City NY: Doubleday, 1964), p. 87. Jung continues: "One can speak of an archetype only when these two aspects are simultaneous."

64. Jung, "Individual Dream Symbolism in Relation to Alchemy," *CW,* vol. 12, *Psychology and Alchemy* (Princeton: Princeton University Press, 1968). Jung adds that these quoted symbols of intuition and others he discusses in the text, "depict the conscious-transcending fact we call the self" (para. 305). Intuition, as both a conscious perception and as a potential content in the unconscious, is in the service of the Self.

65. Wilhelm, *The I Ching*, p. xxiv.

66. Jung, "Synchronicity: An Acausal Connecting Principle," *CW,* vol. 8, *The Structure and Dynamics of the Psyche,* pp. 417–519.

67. Jung, letter to Fritz Kunkel, *C. G. Jung Letters,* vol. 1, "the collective unconscious . . . is more like an atmosphere in which we live than something that is found *in* us. Also, it does not by any means behave merely psychologically; in the case of so-called synchronicity, it proves to be a universal substrate present in the environment rather than a psychological premise" (p. 433).

68. Jung, "Synchronicity: An Acausal Connecting Principle," *CW,* vol. 8, *The Structure and Dynamics of the Psyche,* para. 931 (emphasis, Jung's).

69. Ibid.

70. Jung, *CW,* vol. 6, *Psychological Types,* para. 899.

71. Ibid., para. 770.

72. Ibid., para. 770.

73. Jung, "A Review of the Complex Theory," *CW,* vol. 8, *The Structure and Dynamics of the Psyche,* para 196.

74. Jung, *Two Essays on Analytical Psychology, CW*, vol. 7 (Princeton: Princeton University Press, 1966), para. 432.

75. Jung, "The Stages of Life," *CW,* vol. 8, *The Structure and Dynamics of the Psyche,* para. 208.

76. Jung, "Synchronicity: An Acausal Connecting Principle," *CW,* vol. 8, *The Structure and Dynamics of the Psyche,* para. 967.

77. Jung, *CW,* vol. 6, *Psychological Types,* paras. 712–15; Jung, "Instinct and the Unconscious," *CW,* vol. 8, *The Structure and Dynamics of the Psyche,* para. 270.

78. Jung, *CW,* vol. 6, *Psychological Types,* para. 722, note 45.

79. Jung, "Instinct and the Unconscious," *CW,* vol. 8, *The Structure and Dynamics of the Psyche,* para. 670. The editors of this book state in a note: "This is the first occasion on which Jung uses the term "archetype" (emphasis, Jung's).

80. Jung, *CW,* vol. 6, *Psychological Types,* para. 714.

81. Ibid., para. 722 and note no. 45 (emphasis, editors').

82. Ibid., para. 720 (emphasis, Jung's).

83. Jung, "On the Nature of Dreams," *CW*, vol. 8, *The Structure and Dynamics of the Psyche,* para. 546.

84. Jung, *CW,* vol. 14, *Mysterium coniunctionis* (Princeton NJ: Princeton University Press, 1963–70), para. 705 (emphasis added).

85. Jung, *Man and His Symbols,* p. 93. Jung notes here that, whereas our Christian heritage teaches us that there are *somnia a Deo missa* (dreams sent by God) and that *vox dei* (the voice of God) might be perceived in a dream, most Christian preachers and theologians ignore our world of dreams.

86. Sharp, *Personality Types,* p. 59.

87. Sonia Choquette, *The Wise Child: A Spiritual Guide to Nurturing Your Child's Intuition* (New York: Three Rivers Press, 1999), p. 233. The awakened intuitive "heart," as she writes, includes dreams.

88. Maurie Pressman, "Discernment, Discrimination, and Judgment in Energy Medicine," in *Bridges,* the quarterly magazine of the International Society for the Study of Subtle Energies and Energy Medicine 10, no. 2 (1999): pp. 1, 4 (emphasis added).

89. Jung, *CW,* vol. 6, *Psychological Types,* para. 658. Jung added: "The extravert would say: 'Reality does not exist for him, he gives himself up to fruitless fantasies.'"

90. Ibid., para. 613.

91. Ibid., para. 613.

92. Ibid., para. 615.

93. Ibid., para. 787.

94. Ibid., para. 787.

95. Jung, *Aion, CW,* vol. 9:2 (Princeton NJ: Princeton University Press, 1959). "What lay further away from waking consciousness and seemed unconscious assumes, as it were, a threatening shape, and the affective value {feeling} increases the higher up the scale you go: ego-consciousness, shadow, anima, self" (para. 53). The term "higher up" is misleading since Jung then notes that this emergence of feeling is especially evoked in "transition from waking to sleeping," and in the emergence of primitive energies in one's plunge into the more instinctual *"abaissement du niveau mental* levels of the unconscious. Further, it is impossible to individuate without the feeling function, which makes possible a marriage of the feminine and masculine opposites within ourselves in "a *conjunctio oppositorum.* This is an indispensable prerequisite for wholeness" (para. 58).

96. William Willeford, *Feeling, Imagination, and the Self* (Evanston, IL: Northwestern University Press, 1987). The author continues: "I am here using relationship to mean eros-connectedness, and I am assuming that the ego can be related in this sense to intrapsychic contents and processes—including ideas—as well as to persons and objects in the outer world. . . . the term *eros* makes love cognitive." So Plato and Aristotle, as well as Thomas Aquinas, see eros as love as the highest realization of truth. Dante regarded love "as the ultimate motive of poetic creation" (p. 41).

97. Hillman, "The Feeling Function," in *Jung's Typology* (1958), p. 88. Hillman summarizes Jung's ideas from, at that time, unauthorized seminar notes in *Dream Analysis,* vol. 2, 3rd ed. (Zurich: Psychological Club), pp. 292–93, to the effect that "Jung makes some distinctions between the feeling function, love, and eros. He points out that any of the functions can be under the influence of eros. . . . Yet he does tend to consider the highest development of the feeling function to be manifested by the quality of love." Willeford agrees:"Rather, feeling can be thought to aspire, from the outset, to universal values known personally, through love" (p. 41).

98. Jung, *CW,* vol. 6, *Psychological Types,* para. 951.

99. Ibid., para. 725.

100. Ibid.

101. Ibid. "Feeling, therefore, is an entirely *subjective* experience. . . . feeling is a kind of *judgment* differing from intellectual [thinking] judgment in that its aim is not to establish conceptional relations but to set up a subjective criterion of acceptance or rejection" (para. 725).

102. Isabel Briggs Myers with Peter B. Myers, *Gifts Differing: Understanding Personality Type* (Palo Alto CA: Consulting Psychologists Press, 1980), pp. 66, 68.

103. Jung, *CW,* vol. 6, *Psychological Types,* para. 725.

104. Ibid., para. 950.

105. Ibid., para. 952.

106. Jung, *Man and His Symbols.* He writes that just as "symbolic ideas" trouble "the scientific mind," so do the "phenomena of 'affect' or emotion, which evades all of the attempts of psychologists to pin it down with a final definition" (p. 80). He remains mixed, as he writes in one place that "feeling according to this definition [as a judgment of value] is not an emotion (which, as the word conveys, is involuntary)" (p. 49). Then, as already noted, he writes elsewhere that feeling can be described as "emotional value" (p. 90). In my

view, emotion is no longer involuntary when it is assimilated into value.

107. Willeford, *Feeling, Imagination, and the Self*, p. 39.

108. Ibid., p. 44.

109. Jung, *Man and His Symbols*, pp. 89–90. Here Jung writes of the "main task of dreams" as getting to one's "most primitive instincts," which can happen only through symbols. Symbols in turn must not be merely understood intellectually but in their "numinosity," which for Jung represents "the value of an archetypal event." He continues: "This emotional value [which he identifies with the feeling function] must be kept in mind and allowed for throughout the whole intellectual process of dream interpretation."

110. Jung, "On the Nature of Dreams," *CW*, vol. 8, *The Structure and Dynamics of the Psyche*, para. 543. Mary Ann Mattoon discusses the importance of interpreting dreams using all of the types including the feeling function as, per Jung, "the intelligence of the heart," in her book, *Understanding Dreams* (Dallas TX: Spring Publications, 1984), p. 109.

111. Jung, "On Psychic Energy," *CW*, vol. 8, *The Structure and Dynamics of the Psyche*, para. 79.

112. Ibid., para. 82.

113. Ibid., para. 88. Jung adds: "I mean by this a real symbol, not a sign." A symbol is a form of communication that points to an unknown dimension in the Soul. A sign is a form of communication that points to something known, such as a barber shop sign.

114. Willeford, *Feeling, Imagination, and the Self*, p. 41.

115. Sue Erikson Bloland, "Fame: The Power and Cost of Fantasy," *Atlantic Monthly* (November 1999): p. 51. She records the impact that her father's developing fame had on him and the family. On the one hand, the world admired and fawned on him. On the other hand, few understood how poorly he esteemed himself. He obviously had great love and compassion for both his family and people generally. However, he suffered great anguish in family life because he was unable—to the point of feeling a terrible grief—to personally comfort even his children when they were in mental pain. He called on his wife to take over. It seems clear to me that he was an NT type who had difficulty getting to his feeling function when he was faced with intimate family challenges.

116. Jung, *Two Essays on Analytical Psychology*, paras. 398–99.

117. Willeford, *Feeling, Imagination, and the Self*, pp. 41–42. He also writes

on page 40: "It makes sense that affectivity—with its implications for liking and disliking—and emotionality or emotion should at least overlap, since emotion plays such an important part in the evaluative system of the organism."

118. Jung, "Psychological Aspects of the Mother Archetype," *CW*, vol. 9:1, *The Archetypes and the Collective Unconscious*, para. 179 (emphasis added).

119. Jung, *CW*, vol. 6, *Psychological Types*, para. 578.

120. Ibid., para. 579.

121. Jung, *Memories, Dreams, Reflections*, pp. 206–7.

122. Benjamin Sells, *The Soul of the Law: Understanding Lawyers and the Law*, with a foreword by Thomas Moore (Boston MA: Element Books, 1994).

123. Ibid., p. 103.

124. Ibid. Sells gives the example of a rape case in which he suddenly realized that "something was being left out. The horror was missing. The violence and brutality of this particular human tragedy had been replaced by an intellectual exercise" (p. 41).

125. Ibid., p. 103.

126. Ibid., p. 29.

127. Ibid., p. 178.

128. Ibid., pp. 29-30.

129. Ibid., p. 57.

130. Ibid., p. 58.

131. Sells, "Reports from the field: Lawyers are almost four times more likely to be depressed than the population at large. Researchers in Washington and Arizona found one-third of all lawyers suffering from either clinical depression or substance abuse, both at twice the general prevalence rates for these disorders. In a survey of 105 occupations, lawyers ranked first in experiencing depression" (p. 99).

132. Sells, *The Soul of the Law*, p. 95.

133. Jung, *Man and His Symbols*, p. 80.

134. Isabel Briggs Myers, *Introduction to Type: A Description of the Theory and Applications of the Myers-Briggs Type Indicator* (Palo Alto CA: Consulting Psychologists Press, 1987), pp. 27–28. We will expand on this work by Myers in both chapters 5 and 7.

135. Henry L. Thompson, "The Personality Landscape," *Bulletin of Psychological Type* 21, no. 2 (Early Spring): pp. 1, 4.

SECTION 2

THE FUNCTION COUPLING

THEME AND VARIATIONS

CHAPTER 5

The Type Compass' Four Archetypal Directions

The Osmond Group; Isabel Briggs Myers; Robert Moore and Douglas Gillette's Adult Archetypes

---

Whatever a person's particular combination of preferences [the couplings] may be, others with the same combination are apt to be the easiest to understand and like. They will tend to have similar interests, since they share the same kind of perception, and to consider the same things important, since they share the same kind of judgment. On the other hand, people who differ on both preferences will be hard to understand and hard to predict.[1]

Isabel Briggs Myers

E HAVE CONSIDERED Jung's historical explorations that led to his discovery and formulation of his type theory; we have discussed the basic individual elements of typology with a focus on their dynamic and imaginal representations in our minds, in creative writers and poets, in dreams and movies. These individual elements are the building blocks of Jung's entire system and the basis for the *Myers-Briggs Type Indicator®* (*MBTI®*) as well as for related research. In *Psychological Types,* Jung focused primarily on individual functions.

However, in the last three pages of that book he briefly discussed the importance of the couplings under the heading "The Principal and Auxiliary Functions." There he wrote again, echoing what we have already recorded in chapter 3, that typology usually functions in pairs:

> For all the types met within in practice, the rule holds good that besides the conscious primary function there is a relatively unconscious, auxiliary function, which is in every respect different from the nature of the primary function.[2]

He then proceeded to give the couplings names, thus beginning to recognize their unique nature. For example, he called the ST pair "practical thinking allied with sensation."

Jung then unfortunately dismissed the theoretical, and most of all, the practical importance of his observation of the function couplings: "These peculiarities are of interest only for one who is concerned with the practical treatment of such cases."[3] However, the specific combination of functions, implied by his system but barely explored, holds the most important characteristic constellations of personality.

In this chapter, we get to the core of this book: we consider the type couplings not only as a major contributor to personal understanding, but also as making it possible to reconcile the dynamic social tensions between individuals and nations. This has enormous implications for typology as a larger conscious and unconscious framework for living a fuller life on both an individual and a societal level. Typology offers a framework with the potential for allowing new ways to accommodate differences among individuals as well as groups and societies. It helps ameliorate misunderstandings and combat indifferences that otherwise lead to violence in every stratum of human life.

Disregarding for the moment whether they are introverted or extraverted, we first need to see more clearly the intrapsychic and

The Functions' Intrapsychic Dynamics

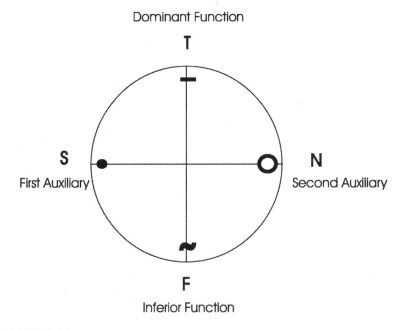

FIGURE 5.1

inner relationships, as well as oppositions, among the functions that produce an elemental type cross, as we saw earlier in Jung's diagram (figure 1.1 page 34).

Whenever I teach typology and make reference to the elemental type mandala, I have habitually constructed (figure 5.1), with the thinking function at the top, the sensation function at the left, and intuition at the right on the crossbar. The feeling function occupies the bottom. This is exactly how Jung diagrammed his type compass (figure 1.1), so that in such a setup thinking is dominant, sensation and intuition are the auxiliary functions, and feeling the inferior function. We will see when we work with the whole brain theory, child development, the Native American's Wheel of Healing, and William Edwards Deming's philosophy of management how perfectly Jung's intuitive arrangement fits the various theoretical constructions in these disciplines.

As discussed in chapter 3, there are four and only four functions that Jung represented as an archetypal structure called a mandala or compass. The mandala is a figure made up of four interrelated aspects, as is common to many human symbolic constructs; for example, the four seasons, the four directions, the four gospels, the four horsemen of the Apocalypse, and the four figures in Ezekiel's wheel. As Jung's research proceeded, he began to discover the symbolic quaternities in all the great cultures.[4] In this archetypal context, he found that the quaternity of functions encompassed the basic modes for both perceiving and judging.

The dynamic interplay of the four functions seems so simple that many therapists and other professional practitioners often overlook or superficially explore typology.[5] However, Jung often said that the most simple thing, the *res simplex,* was also the most difficult to deeply discern and realize.[6] Those who research and use typology consistently discover in the two attitudes and four functions complex and profound dimensions of personal and interpersonal behaviors that we will explore in the rest of this book. The individual functions and their interplay explain so much of human behavior that therapists and analysts who ignore typology seriously limit their understanding of themselves as well as their interventions with clients. An understanding of typology can help everyone, not simply those in the psychological professions, and to discount such insight can limit growth in love and life relationships. This holds true to an even greater degree for understanding the function couplings because of their crucial importance as central structures of personality.

THE TYPE COUPLINGS AS THE SOUL'S FOUR ARCHETYPES
The work of several people has significantly contributed to my understanding of the type couplings and the soul's four archetypes and the

genesis of this book. Since their work is so important, not only to me but to our fuller view of the couplings and the four archetypes, I devote the remainder of this chapter primarily to the contributions of the Osmond group, Isabel Myers, and Robert Moore and Douglas Gillette.

THE OSMOND GROUP

A 1977 article by a group of type practitioners led by Humphrey Osmond enormously enlarged my consciousness of the field of typology and led to the writing of this book.[7] Their research emerged, as they put it, not because Jung's description of the individual functions makes it easy to distinguish one function type from another, but rather because his characterizations *do not* adequately do so. We have seen that Jung never intended his type theory as a facile categorization of people.[8] Jung's position was that "a typology is a great help in understanding the wide variations that occur among individuals."[9] Jung wanted us to understand our human differences because they lead to differing assumptions, life styles, intrapsychic and interpersonal strategies, vocational interests, philosophies, and psychological methodologies—all of which demand a "critical psychology," that is, his typology.[10]

Jung documented examples of individual type preferences in historical figures and characters in literature in the first nine chapters of *Psychological Types,* and then in chapter 10 developed a phenomenology of each function type. However, Osmond and his group saw that in describing the function types in that chapter, Jung had "shifted his emphasis from the polarity between individuals [in the interpersonal realm] to the polarity within each person," so that his type system became a "tool for the development of the individuating person."[11] Hence "typing" people "reliably" meant little compared to "the relationship of forces or 'functions' within [the individual's] . . . psyche."[12] Although Jung's typology describes personality structures that affect others, Jung charts a relatively private path for individuation in chapter 10 of *Psychological Types.*

However, individuation assumes a deep, committed connection with all society. Therefore, Osmond continued, we are still left with the problem of conflict between individuals that, as Jung showed, is solved only by a view or an understanding of human differences that overcomes private, egocentric imprisonment. Individuation is not just personal—it is social. Osmond and his colleagues suggested expanding one's understanding of typology from focusing, for example, on the interplay of dominant and auxiliary functions within an individual to looking at, say, either the NT or the TN simply as pairs or couples, ignoring which one is dominant. Further, they argued:

> Suppose . . . that instead of asking what a thinking-sensation and a thinking-intuitive have in common, we ask what a thinking-sensation and a sensation-thinking have in common. The schema then looks like this:

thinking-sensation	feeling-intuitive	intuitive-thinking	feeling-sensation
sensation-thinking	intuitive-feeling	thinking-intuitive	sensation-feeling

> The categories are the same, but the focus is now different: it is on pairs of functions rather than on a first and second or auxiliary function. The four groupings in the new schema can be taken to be as representing four new entities, which we shall call "umwelts" or self-worlds, after the manner of the ethnologist, Jakob von Uexkull. These entities turn out to have a nature and attributes importantly different from those of the functions. Unlike the functions which tell one what a person is experiencing— thoughts, feelings, sensations, intuitions—the umwelts tell one how the person experiences the world. The functions give one the contents of consciousness, the umwelts the form of consciousness.[13]

When I read this article in the late 1970s, I began to realize for the first time that these authors were talking about the functions as archetypes. I realized that the pairings were more comprehensive and viable avenues for Soul-making than the individual function types, both in inner work and in interpersonal relations. Archetypes, as Jung pointed out, are forms or formal potential structures existing in all persons that are revealed through their manifest images and traits. These four couplings began to emerge in my mind as the essential archetypes of human conduct.

Figure 5.2 depicts how the couplings look within the structure of the typological compass, with the symbolic depiction of each type combined in each of the four couplings. The Osmond group named the couplings "Ethereals" for the NTs, "Oceanics" for the NFs,

The Osmond Group's Couplings as Archetypes

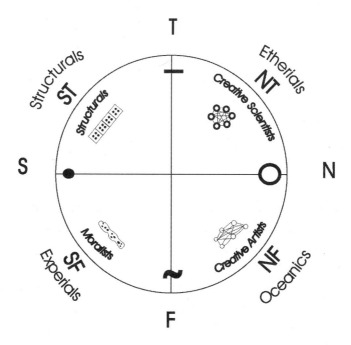

FIGURE 5.2

"Experials" for the SFs and "Structurals" for the STs. (Note that they show each coupling with the perceiving function first followed by the judging function. Figure 5.2 also shows some alternate names of my choice within the circle.

DISCOVERING THE OSMOND GROUP'S SOURCE: ISABEL BRIGGS MYERS

This shift in my conception of typology led me further when I read "Effects of Combinations of Perception and Judgment" in Myers' booklet, *Introduction to Type*.[14] I realized that the Osmond group had undoubtedly picked up their idea of the couplings from this source, first published by Myers in the 1962 *MBTI Manual,* although she did not receive credit in their original article.

I learned from Mary McCaulley that Humphrey Osmond had lectured at the 1983 International Conference on Typology. Osmond and others were the first typologists to recognize and advance the significance of Myers' creative contribution to the type theory, and I was curious about the origin of this group. I found the answer in Michael Malone's book, *Psychetypes*.[15] Malone writes that he learned a system called *experiential typology* from a Dr. Harriet Mann, whom he met in 1970 in Cambridge: "As I understand its origins, experiential typology was first developed at Princeton by Dr. Mann, Dr. Humphrey Osmond, and Mrs. Miriam Siegler."[16]

The Osmond group saw the table (figure 5.3) in both the *Manual* and in *Introduction to Type*. The first line shows both ST and SF types as "People who focus their attention on . . . realities," and the NF and NT types as people who focus their attention on "possibilities." Clearly, the perceiving functions—sensation and intuition respectively—are the basis of these differences: sensation looks at facts and intuition looks at possibilities. As in Jung, we look at the perceiving functions first: we acquire knowledge before we use it. Examining the type circle in figure 5.2, page 191, we see that the left side deals with realities and the right side, with possibilities.

The *MBTI* Couplings:
"Effects of Combinations of Perception and Judgment"

Effects of Combinations of Perception and Judgment

	ST	SF	NF	NT
People who prefer:	Sensing & Thinking	Sensing & Feeling	Intuition & Feeling	Intuition & Thinking
focus their attention on:	Realities	Realities	Possibilities	Possibilities
and handle these with:	Objective analysis	Personal warmth	Personal warmth	Objective analysis
Thus they tend to become:	Practical & analytical	Sympathetic & friendly	Enthusiastic & insightful	Logical & analytical
and find scope for their abilities in:	Technical skills with objects & facts	Practical help & services for people	Understanding & communicating with people	Theoretical & technical developments
for example:	Applied science Business Administration Banking Law enforcement Production Construction	Health care Community service Teaching Supervision Religious service Office work Sales	Behavioral science Research Literature Art & music Religious service Health care Teaching	Physical science Research Management Computers Law Engineering Technical work

FIGURE 5.3

Myers pointed out another kind of differentiation in the couplings based on the judging functions (see figure 5.3). The ST types handle *realities* with "objective analysis" and the NT types handle *possibilities* with "objective analysis." Clearly, "objective analysis" is found to be characteristic of the thinking function, a preference common to each of these couplings. On the other hand, the SF and the NF types respond with "personal warmth," thereby emphasizing the feeling function's influence in these couplings on the bottom half. Based entirely on the perceiving and judging functions, an archetypal phenomenology of the four couplings is taking shape here that is considerably more complex than the individual functions.

Myers then pointed to a specific effect that each of these couplings exerts on individuals: the ST type person tends to become "practical and analytical"; the SF type, "sympathetic and friendly"; the NF type, "enthusiastic and insightful"; and the NT type, "logical and analytical." The practicality and the analytical capacities of the ST coupling, based on the earthy sensation and the heady thinking make up a "tough-minded" archetype. The "sympathetic and friendly" aspects of the SF coupling are an amalgam of the specific hands-on, concrete qualities of the sensation function and the feeling function's capacity for empathy. The "enthusiastic and insightful" facets of the NF, due to intuition and feeling, produce the most "tender-minded" as well as the most spontaneously creative configuration of the four couplings. However, Myers' description of the NT as "logical and analytical" is the least satisfactory of the four descriptions. She ignored the inventive capacities of intuition and overemphasized the logical and analytical qualities of thinking (I would call this combination "imaginative and analytical"). In the 1962 version of the couplings, according to a personal correspondence with Mary McCaulley, Myers had called the NT "logical and ingenious," a description which is still retained by the *MBTI Manual*.[17]

In *Introduction to Type* (figure 5.3, page 193), we see that Myers connected each function with its own particular vocational preferences: the STs find "scope for their abilities in . . . technical skills with objects and facts"; SFs provide "practical help and services for people"; NFs are good at "understanding and communicating with people"; and NTs excel in "theoretical and technical developments." She concluded by listing specific types of work that each prefers. Myers helps us see the outlines of archetypal structures and dynamics that underlie the behavioral traits that the Osmond group describes so well in their four "umwelts" and which analysts have barely considered.

I began to see a dynamic occurring in this structure when I looked at figure 5.2, page 191, and considered the left and right sides as in brain hemispheres. The realities of the left side focus on the techniques of a creative process and the possibilities of the right side focus on the art of a creative process. I also began to wonder about the first stage of life as being more practical and the second stage as more exploratory and philosophical, so that one could envision a clockwise development of a circle of life based on the four couplings of the type mandala, beginning with the feeling function. Finally, as we will consider in the next chapter, I discerned in Myers' lineup of the four couplings the emergence of a counterclockwise process (see again figure 5.2, page 191) beginning with ST and ending with NT, which I began to characterize as the creative process.

THE OSMOND GROUP'S FOUR ARCHETYPES

The ST Structural. Building on these insights by Briggs and the larger *MBTI* research, the Osmond group describes each of its couplings. The ST Structurals are pragmatic and objective: "The Structural cannot directly experience his subjective self; it is like a spot on the back of his head that he knows is there but cannot 'see.'"[18] As their name implies, they like blueprints and clear pictures of life. The clarity that this archetype imparts follows from the sharp particularity of the sensation function's attention to detail and the incisive reasoning of the thinking function. The Osmond group cited Freud as an example of this type, so that when his seduction theory collapsed, he "wrote Fliess that he did not know how he was going to treat patients any more."[19] He had to create a new and clear theory before he could go on. Freud's temperamental shortcomings in interpersonal relationships and the brilliant lucidity of his writing also point to the ST type.

Supporting this view of Freud, Daniel Yankelovich and William Barrett in their landmark book, *Ego and Instinct,* discussd the dual nature of Freud as both a scientist and as a humanist.[20] As a scientist, he felt that he had to meet the concretist and abstract criteria of Scientific Materialism. This helps to explain Jung's later view of Freud's typology. In a letter dated February 18, 1957, Jung wrote to his colleague, Ernest Hanhart, that when he first met Freud he perceived him as being "originally an introverted feeling type with inferior thinking. When I got to know him in 1907 this original type was already neurotically blurred. . . . Freud, then as later, presented the picture of an extraverted thinker and empiricist." In effect, Freud had adopted the persona of an extraverted sensation thinking type, whereas, according to Jung, he was probably more authentically an introverted intuitive feeling type.[21]

Jung's view is possible, but questionable. Yankelovich and Barrett showed that the sensation thinking pattern of nineteenth-century scientific materialism and Freud's theory fit together perfectly, point for point: Freud's basic psychosomatic building blocks correspond to the ultimate particles of existence; his rational reality principle and the object-oriented, extraverted nature of his sexual theory are attempts at rational systemization as well as objective measurement.[22] Freud's clear and precise prose confirms the characteristics of a person who prefers sensation and thinking. Also, John Kerr depicted Freud as a consistently aggressive, tough-minded EST in articulating his theory, in demanding strict loyalty to himself and his precise views, and in wresting political dominance of the psychoanalytic movement from Jung and the Zürich school. Beyond authority issues, Freud saw his theory as allowing the individual in a rational society to build a balancing structure for the "chaos" of the Id, a quality that easily can be applied to the ST's opposite on the typological cross; the NF Oceanic. Florence Nightingale, like Freud, is another person who was probably a Structural and who stubbornly built the nursing profession as a well-defined system.[23]

The Structurals shine wherever systematic fact-gathering is needed, such as in accounting and computer data processing. They also make tough, disciplined workers such as mechanics, shop foremen, and marine sergeants. Structurals are seen positively by other types as "orderly, reasonable, capable . . . dependable, protective" and, negatively, as "dry," "rigid," domineering" . . . not "sensitive to others' feelings" or not "overly imaginative."[24] These are the negative aspects of both the sensation and thinking functions: sheer facts and pure logic do not prevail with either the context that intuition can supply or the sense of human values that the feeling function provides. In the realm of pathology, the DSM-4's description of the Obsessive Compulsive Personality Disorder reveals psychic distortions in both the sensation and thinking functions.

Malone called the ST combination "Territorial," but adds that the term "Structural" best describes this archetype. The Territorial ST focuses more on the structure of reality rather than its substance.[25] Such people hate being "fenced in." Malone mentions Humphrey Bogart as an example of such a Structural. Although Structurals take hierarchies seriously, they simply want to be independent and private within such structures.

The NF Oceanic. NF Oceanic types, as their name implies, are opposite the ST Structurals in the type compass because of their fluid, unstructured ways. Oceanics experience life as "a seamless whole" since the feeling function seeks harmony among all and intuition embraces wholeness. "Oceanics learn to handle impersonal problems by subjectifying them, just as Structurals learn to handle personal problems by objectifying them."[26] This characterization reveals the inward, personalizing tendency of both the N and F in the Oceanic, and the outward, distancing orientation of the S and T in the Structural. People of other types may perceive the Oceanic's capacity to embrace others as "receptive," "flexible," "romantic," and "mystical," or they may interpret them as "helpless," "moody," and "cruel." Holden Caulfield in Salinger's *The Catcher in the Rye* is an Oceanic who is "moody, dreamy, constantly caught up in his own imaginings," both the gift and curse of the intuitive function.[27] No wonder this book has been condemned in our American society—a society that prides itself on its ST cultural pragmatism! Further, "Oceanics have the capacity to bend where others break," and often "win over other types by 'creating confusion' as in Lord Nelson's battle tactics." Gandhi, Churchill, D. H. Lawrence, and Hamlet, among others, exemplify this type.[28] Chairman Mao would likely have been an NF, because he found chaos "positively exhilarating."[29]

The Oceanic is found in most fields where creative thinking and personal relating combine, such as in spiritual and psychological teaching and counseling, in writing novels and biographies, and in the fine arts. Another name for this archetype might be "Creative Artist." Generally, Oceanics also want to make a total commitment to work that advances human understanding. Myers and Briggs were both Oceanics, as was McCaulley.

Malone also called this coupling of intuition and feeling "Oceanic." Whereas the territoriality of the Structural implies "boundaries, limits, organized, and defined space," the "ocean is one of undifferentiated, uncontained, undefined, boundless expanses."[30] The philosophy of Zen Buddhism, of Chinese Taoism, and the messages of Eastern mystics exemplify Oceanic values. Our civilization only minimally holds such values because "they are not the attitudes that make for conquest, industrialization and upper mobility, for imperialism. . . . As a consequence, there are fewer Oceanics in our history books than individuals with other primary areas, Winston Churchill and Robert E. Lee being two of the preeminent exceptions."[31] The hippie movement was led by Oceanics, asserting ideas of freedom and passivity with phrases such as, "Do your own thing," "Go with the flow," and "Let it be." They are less apt to blame other people than are persons of a different type. However, the distortions of the intuitive and feeling functions in the Oceanic are associated with emotional upheavals, anxiety, and dark, rageful sadness or depression.

The NT Ethereal. A cosmic inner and outer reality informs the umwelt or archetype of the NT Ethereal. Through intuition, an NT Ethereal experiences the inner universe as being as real as the outer universe of social and material realities. The term "Ethereal" aptly applies to this personality. *Webster's* defines the "ethereal" as "relating to the regions beyond the earth . . . celestial, heavenly, unworldly, Spiritual." William Blake's statement, "Everything possible to be believed is an image of truth," is an apt description of the NT world.

Einstein, an Ethereal, used his intuitive imagination to embrace both "the universe and the observer,"[32] just as Jung, another Ethereal, began to develop the synchronicity principle that encompasses the subject and the object, the inner and the outer, the person and the universe, the present, past, and future. Jung's description of Taoism in his foreword to Wilhelm's *I Ching* makes clear that the Taoist philosophical system is preeminently an Ethereal worldview.

However, the Ethereal's umwelt is not wholly mystical. The Ethereal's intuitive function is always constrained by the sharp distinctions and organizing powers of the thinking function. Paradoxically, the Ethereal type is also very deeply interested in "facts because of the possibility that they may sustain a theory."[33] For these reasons another name for this type, in more pragmatic terms, would be the "Creative Scientist." The NT Ethereal is found wherever creative systematizing is needed, such as in architecture, innovative research and high-tech creativity, and management.

People of other types may experience the Ethereal type's intuitive organizing and incisive talk and writing as "brilliant, witty, imaginative," or the Ethereal's flights of fantasy, as "impractical, visionary . . . unfeeling."[34] The Osmond group saw Franklin D. Roosevelt, John F. Kennedy, Napoleon Bonaparte, Benjamin Franklin, and Arthur Conan Doyle's Sherlock Holmes as Ethereal types. Malone wrote that when the word "Ethereal" comes to mind we usually think of the "absent-minded professor," his head in the clouds, musing over philosophical conundrums, as he walks past his wife without recognizing her. However, some Ethereals have been politicians; for example, John F. Kennedy and Franklin D. Roosevelt. They cared less for the way things were than the way things *could* be or *ought* to be. Ralph Waldo Emerson's Transcendentalism is another example. "For all ethereals want to *transcend*, transcend the body for the mind, the real for the ideal, the present for the future."[35]

C. G. Jung, "an Ethereal par excellence, made explicit the view that

the psyche was a source of infinite riches, a treasure-house of imagery"
from which the Ethereal enriches us. The Osmond group bemoaned
the fact that Jung didn't turn types from the "rich hoard of unstrung
pearls" found in *Psychological Types* "into a coherent theory" that would
have enhanced even more the understanding of human differences.[36]
This lament echoes my conviction that Jung never treated his typology
systematically as an archetypal pattern. In truth, as is typical of most
NT Ethereals, Jung gave only an inkling of how to resolve differences
with other types, such as his differences with Adler and Freud. The
Osmond group gave more substantial hints, since they described more
fully these basic type patterns; the *MBTI*, because so much of its
research is based on the four couplings, provides the basis for further
work along this line.

The consistency of the NT's ethereal archetypal patterns are found
even in psychopathology's grandiose delusional and hallucinatory
systems such as schizophrenia and in post traumatic stress disorders.

The SF Experial. This SF Experial archetype is opposite to the
Ethereal. This strange new word—"Experial"—was coined by the
Osmond group, and comes from "experience" that *Webster* associates
with "experiment" and the Latin word, experiri, "to try, to put to test."
These connections fit, since the person informed by this archetype is
described as seeing reality as the "concrete, direct, personal experience
of things as they happen minute by minute and day by day."[37] SFs live
each moment with their sensation function engaging the moment's
particulars and their feeling function enclosing those particulars in
warm, caring responses to others. A drawback for SFs is that they find
it difficult to disentangle themselves "from the environment in which
they are involved,"[38] because the S in this configuration hates changes
in nesting environments and the F simply finds separations difficult.

"To put to test" also has moral connotations, hence the Osmond
group also calls Experials "moralists." Experials are our practical
moralists, such as Sam Ervin in the Watergate hearings. They tie their

ideas and moral principles directly to experience, as they combine the feeling function's compassion with the sensation function's pragmatics. George Washington could have been an Experial. He was described by Jefferson as a man whose "integrity was most pure, his justice the most inflexible I have ever known."[39] As scientists (Konrad Lorenz, for example), they derive principles of behavior from large, detailed observations. In everyday life they are most effective in concerns that include personal services, such as those provided by nurses, teachers, salespeople of pragmatic wares, and craftsmen.[40]

Malone called the SF the Volcanic, meaning not the "explosive, eruptive aspects of this personality" but its "in-rootedness."[41] They love their connection with the earth and its fruits; illustrating this bond, Walt Whitman wrote, "I will make my poems of materials for I think they are to be the most spiritual poems."[42] SF Experials do not like theory. This is most fitting, since in the type compass the theoretical NT is their exact opposite. The Experial/Volcanic says, "I felt it. I saw it. That's how I know it's true." They live in this moment and value action, not contemplation. Since they are great lovers of order, the pathologies to which this archetype might predispose an individual would be adjustment disorders or any other disorder that surfaces in reaction to the demands of significant change or new adaptations.

A REFLECTIVE INTERLUDE

Both the Osmond group as experiential typologists and the researches of the *MBTI* describe four basic archetypal structures. What is the value of this finding? First, this awareness of the archetypal nature of the four couplings places typology much more into the center of the entire Jungian enterprise, from which it has been effectively excluded by most Jungian analysts.[43] In fact, since the typological compass is the only holistic depiction of Jung's psychology, its four archetypal couplings seem to embrace every aspect of Jung's system, especially culminating in a lifetime individuation process. Second, it provides a bridge to Jung for people trained in the *MBTI*. Third, the four archetypal function couplings, the many applications of which will be discussed in the rest of this book, provide more comprehensive behavioral templates than the individual functions for organizing, understanding, and categorizing individuals, societies, and intellectual systems in our often chaotic personal and social worlds. Fourth, as we shall see throughout this book, the function couplings help ground the archetypal images in everyday life, even as the images enlarge and expand the gestalt of the couplings' characteristics and fields of aware-ness. Finally, they help us understand more accurately our own psychic anatomy, our relationships, and our work preferences.

The Osmond group's descriptions and the *MBTI* couplings are archetypal patterns traceable throughout cultural history. When one looks at the description of the Greek gods and goddesses, or at any other of the many pantheons, we can see connections with the type couplings. Both Apollo and Athena, as cultural inspirers of intellectual and artistic pursuits, fit into the NT Ethereal group. In their emotional but creative excesses, Dionysius and Aphrodite are both NF Oceanics. While Hestia is more introverted and Hera more extraverted, both are certainly related to the SF Experial in their heroic commitments. Aries, the god of war, and Artemis, the goddess of the moon, wild animals, and hunting, meet the rugged criteria of the ST Structural.[44]

This theory of the four function coupling archetypes stands in contrast to Hillman's view that by virtue of the imagination an indefi-nite number of archetypes is always available to us. Quantity is never a substitute for quality and depth. In the function coupling theory, imag-ination works within the four archetypes to enlarge and deepen our understanding of the Soul's Compass and provides some, albeit expan-sive, order in the bewildering vagaries of nature and the complexities of human life. Like chaos science, the seemingly formless unconscious reveals configurations. Most people cannot traverse the forests of the mind without a map and a direction finder.[45] Some intuitive types, like Hillman, appear to explore without a compass, but reject conventional markers only to replace them with idiosyncratic ones.[46]

One friendly critic of this book's thesis who is a follower of Hillman charges that the type quaternity, with its circle and cross, is a "Christian fantasy." However, countless traditions have developed mandalas that are often quadrated circles, which we find, for example, in Hinduism, Buddhism, Taoism, Judaism, and Native American traditions. Neolithic cities were usually constructed in the form of a quadrant with the temple in the middle. This quaternary "fantasy" is a common one with deep roots in the soil of the human psyche.

In the depth psychological tradition, dreams commonly make use of quaternity. A young analysand of mine, who was seeking to develop a more specific path for himself in both love and work, had a quaternity dream:

> An angel guided him into a valley. There she pointed to four hills, on the top of which he saw four figures. When through her magic he brought them to four positions around him, there was a king in front of him, a child to his left representing a lover, a warrior behind, and a magician to his right. When he struggled to face the warrior, the warrior complained about the weak leadership of the king [signifying the lack of direction and decision-making the dreamer was feeling about himself]. The child and magician said nothing. Meanwhile, the angel [symbolizing the integrating Self] hovered above.

The positioning of the warrior had to do with the psyche's need to comment on the lack of focused direction in this man's life: that his kingly moral values needed strengthening with the help of the warrior's sharply defining sword. Subsequently, the dreamer has been developing his king potential. This dream with its four archetypes provides the bridge between the Osmond group's and Myers' work on the couplings, and the social archetypes as rediscovered and reconstituted by Moore and Gillette, which I will discuss next.

The Four Traditional Adult Archetypes

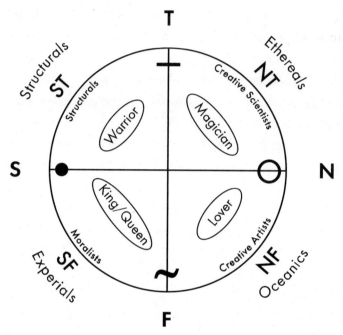

FIGURE 5.4

MOORE AND GILLETTE'S FOUR SOCIAL ARCHETYPES

Robert Moore and Douglas Gillette have popularized the ancient pattern of four archetypes in their book, *King, Warrior, Magician, Lover.*[47] They focused on this subject in a number of other books as well, not simply because they want to delineate human differences, but because they are also interested in reawakening initiatory processes in adults comparable to those practiced by primal peoples, which helped boys and girls become adults. Although their emphasis is on male initiations, modern women as well as men must discover these same patterns and these rituals of growth within themselves as well as in familial, church, neighborhood, and professional societies. Figure 5.4

pictures these four archetypes in conjunction with those of the Osmond group.

The SF King/Queen Archetype. The first archetype is the King and the Queen. The King and Queen are moralists. As such, they are exemplars of the SF Type or the Experial in the larger cultural realm and in the types' differences and dynamics in any group of persons.

The King/Queen archetype fits perfectly the SF Experial archetype in the Osmond description: "Experials provide the social glue which holds societies together."[48] In the *MBTI* view, persons informed by this coupling find "scope for their abilities in . . . practical help and services for people."[49] Here, the qualities of the SF help fill out this archetype that Moore and Gillette have identified from cultural sources. SFs as extraverts proclaim aloud their parental values, and as introverts quietly communicate these values to others. They are open-minded and sensitive to others but stick staunchly to their own loyalties. They are suited to parental-type work that requires "both devotion and a large measure of adaptability."[50]

The King's energy is father energy, just as the Queen's is mother energy. The King and the Queen are the lawmakers as well as the ones who fertilize the entire society (and the human psyche) and bless sons and daughters. In ancient Egypt the great gods or goddesses were named the "Right Order," similar to the Chinese meaning of the Tao. Hence the Chinese emperor had to live by the "Mandate of Heaven," again, the "Right Order."[51] The parental energies and structures here are working on a large stage.

Ideally, the sense of order embodied in this archetype flows into the imperatives of morality that these royal persons transmit to their subjects, children, or fellow workers. They are charged with the vital task of blessing those under them who live out those laws of humanity and the universe, especially in their "fertility and blessing" of offspring, be they actual children in a family or persons whom they are charged to ethically inspire. Moore and Gillette give many cultural examples of this kind of nurturing leadership. The King and the Queen, as father and mother, as leaders in any organization, are the ethical leaders whose moral atmosphere permeates the entire organization. If they are morally sound, the family, the nation, and the organization will be morally sound.

The Shadow King and Queen, on the other hand, are destructive, vindictive tyrants, such as a King Herod who seeks to kill the new king, the new creative life and principle of order emerging in society that threatens his fragile sovereignty.[52] In family life, they are the parental tyrants who demand absolute obedience, who rule the family with iron fists. Such parents find it impossible to bless their children, to praise them for their own thoughts and achievements. The father of one of my clients would hold court each night over drinks. Whenever some-one, his wife or his children, would report a mild success, he would incessantly question them until he found something to criticize. He acted incessantly as a judge, not as a caring parent. Such parents never admit they are wrong, never apologize for mistakes they have made, and to their dying day are unable to say to their children, "You are okay. You have done well." Such parenting damages not only the immediate family but also the larger human family. These attitudes reemerge in business and government leaders who tyrannize entire organizations and nations.

In dreams, the King may appear as a figure in charge of a large company with offices in skyscrapers, and the Queen may appear as the wise leader of a clan. Images such as a river valley with its quadripartite town like those in the Neolithic agricultural period have appeared in dreams, recapturing a historical era when the goddess and her queen ruled. In a woman's dream, a ruler appeared as a despot sitting on a hilltop, taunting the mother and her children crawling toward him. Sometimes, the shadow parent in dreams may be experienced as an invisible, ghostlike presence or as a lethal atmosphere, representing the poisonous climate of a sad and fearful childhood.

The NT Magician Archetype. The Magician archetype stands opposite the King, not as a moralist, but as the one who knows. As Moore and Gillette show, this kind of person or aspect within us has a "secret knowledge," like an Obi-Wan Kenobi, mentor of young hero Luke Skywalker in the *Star Wars* adventure, or like Merlin, King Arthur's strategist in both war and peace.[53] In the Old Testament story, King David, who covets Bathsheba, has her husband killed in battle; David is confronted by the prophet Nathan, who knows in his inward wisdom that David has committed this crime. Because of inner knowledge, the Magician is often the critic of the King, the only one who can scold the King, sometimes as a teasing trickster. The fool in the medieval courts also played this role.[54] Whatever the role, the Magician is most of all the link between the spirit world and the human world.[55]

Along with inner knowledge, the Magician is also a kind of magical technician who knows the incantations and other practices that lead to the inner world. Moore and Gillette feel that this high-tech age of subatomic physics and depth psychology (as well as computers and their subsequent language, I would add) is "the age of the Magician."[56] Both see below the surface of life. The authors note, however, the lack of ritual elders who are capable of guiding young people into mature depth living, into dangerous yet blessedly rewarding inner spaces. I would add that the ritual elder is not necessarily an external person. It can also be the function of the Magician within, that is, the Self, the inner, all-wise Soul with its dream language.

Moore and Gillette imply that the NT Magician in each of us awakens a unique spirituality that is especially contemplative and systemic. The authors speak of the "observing ego" as that aspect of our consciousness that, in concert with this archetype in the unconscious, "doesn't live life" but "watches life," stimulates the emergence of necessary life energies, and keeps in balance "the overwhelming power of the other archetypes."[57] Through the observing ego that is informed by the Magician, the Self as Magician now realizes itself consciously.

On this level, the ego, as the incarnation of the Self, knows the depths, even as it is known by the Self, the God within. This level of consciousness has many names: absolute subjectivity, pure awareness, unconditional love. It embraces all polarities. In classical philosophy, it is the consciousness of Being, which is not a concept, rather, it is an experience of existence that embraces the mystery that is God and the mystery of everything that is. In spiritual terms, reflecting both the Old and New Testaments, the spirit of God in consciousness seeks out the spirit of God in the depths, often depicted as in the great waters or soft wind.

In our typological approach to archetypes, the Magician is clearly the NT Ethereal, according to the Osmond article. Jung as Magician, in effect, described the psyche as "a treasure-house of imagery into which one only had to dive to pull up pearl after pearl."[58] That part of the psyche that we call the unconscious—as symbolized, for example, by Avalon in the Arthurian tales, with its lakes, misty valleys and deep forests, and the home of Merlin and the goddesses—is the source of the Magician's inner knowledge. In Taoist terms, the unconscious is the Tao, which in itself is indescribable, and the Chinese sage is its Magician.

All dreams reveal this magicianlike wisdom of the unconscious in their precise, creative, and transforming images and affects. Dreams often specifically provide inner mentors that complement, consolidate, or supplant the teachings of outer magicians. One young man's father could not teach him to consolidate, or supplant, the teachings of outer magicians. His father could not teach him the creative function of anger that empowers one to take initiative because the father displayed his anger in drunken rages. In earlier analytical work, the client could neither express his anger nor acknowledge it when it appeared in life or in dreams. The following dream provided the necessary mentoring:

> I am standing in waist-deep ocean water alongside a very
> powerful woman. She hands me a knife, points to a near-
> by fish and says quietly: "kill it." I look at the soulful eyes
> of the fish and return to her saying, "I can't." She looks at
> me with great power and shouts, "KILL IT." I realize that
> this is an important initiation. I not only kill the fish but
> cut it into pieces for cooking and hand them to her on a
> platter.

Just as the Magician stands opposite to the King as critic and mentor in the history of cultures, so in the typological cross and circle the NT Ethereal or Creative Scientist stands opposite to the SF Experial or Moralist. When one moves back into the Jungian and *MBTI* type dimension of this archetype, NTs, according to Myers, "find scope for their abilities in . . . theoretical and technical developments." Further, "People with INTJ preferences [such as Jung] are relentless innovators in thought as well as action. . . . Their faith in their inner vision can move mountains."[59]

If we look at the play of the two functions in this archetype—that is, the N (intuition) and the T (thinking)—we immediately see the typological ground for the Ethereal or Magician: intuition delves into the depth, as its etymology indicates, as inner prober and guardian. It knows instantaneously through the imagination. It is the creative and innovative function, the curious inner child in the adult. Then, drawing on thinking, the NT integrates inventiveness with technology or large intellectual systems. Merlin in the Arthurian legends not only had a deep, inventive wisdom but also had the wizard's techniques for accessing that knowledge. We now begin to get a sense of how the imaginative aspects of the archetype enlarge consciousness, as well as the ways conscious exercise of the function or coupling grounds the archetypal images in everyday life. Isabel Myers, herself an NF, wrote:

> People with ENTP preferences are ingenious innovators,
> who always see new possibilities and new ways of doing

things. They have a lot of imagination and initiative for starting projects and a lot of impulsive energy for carrying them out. They are sure of the worth of their inspirations and are tireless with the problems involved. They are stimulated by difficulties and most ingenious in solving them. They enjoy feeling competent in a variety of areas and value this in others as well.[60]

All of this is in tune with one of Moore and Gillette's culminating statements: "The Magician, then, is the archetype of thoughtfulness and reflection."[61] This inward-turning energy is not necessarily introversion as such (which is not a function, but an attitude); rather, it is the introverted tendency of intuition itself that depends on the inner senses for its knowledge, which, as Jung reminds us, is perception via the unconscious. When this knowing is combined with introversion, as in Jung's type, INTJ, an inward knowing is enhanced.

The ST Warrior Archetype. The Warrior is the primordial doer and fighter. He is the disciplined arm of the King or Queen. When this archetype is activated in culture and in us, we are able to carry out the policies shaped by the leaders' values and mores for the family, the organization, and the realm. The (mature) Warrior is too easily and superficially identified in our culture with the Shadow Warrior, the rage-filled killer that has produced such violence in our cities and that has been dramatized in our popular arts. This sort of Warrior emerges out of an infantile rage, so typical of a pathologized patriarchy, which is discussed further in chapter 12.

The mature Warrior can direct his or her aggression to constructive ends, striving mightily to plan, organize, and complete a task. The Warrior archetype is the innate pattern in us that, when activated and informing consciousness, gets things done. Societally, the Warrior is the defender of people. Intrapsychically, the Warrior marshals the psychic power to stand up for oneself, and psychosomatically, the immunizing power to protect against invading bacteria, viruses, and allergens. The Warrior is the doer and fighter, but also a respecter of the limits of Self and other. The Warrior energy is concerned with skill, power, and accuracy, and with control, both inner and outer, psychological and physical.[62] Moore and Gillette give a colorful twist to this propensity: "Often, in life, we need to 'step back,' we say, from a situation in order to gain perspective, so that we can act. The Warrior needs room to swing his sword."[63] But like all the archetypes, the Warrior should not be separated from the other three archetypes lest it become a Shadow Warrior, a barbarian or mercenary. The Warrior must serve the ideals of the King or Queen, know the inner wisdom of the Magician, and be connected with the compassion of the Lover.[64] (We will pursue these connections further when we consider the dynamics of the typological cross and circle in the next chapter.)

In the Osmond research, the Warrior is the Structuralist. The Structuralist turns all consciousness into "objective reality." There is a difference, however, in the emphasis of these two groups. Moore and Gillette stresses objective action;[65] the Osmond group stresses the interest that the Warrior has in structure, in making "maps, blueprints, tool and die casts."[66] However, by virtue of the blueprinting and mapping, the Structuralist becomes the activist and builder. When the first wartime nurse, Florence Nightingale, saw doctors in the Crimea ignore her and her nurses, she ordered her nurses to do no medical work. She knew that the doctors sorely needed the systemic functions her nurses performed. The doctors relented, "and a new profession was born."[67]

In the language of Myers and Jung, the ST Warriors "find scope for their abilities in . . . technical skills with objects and fact."[68] The typical ST, whether introverted or extraverted, is "logical, analytical, and objectively critical" and is "not likely to be convinced by anything but reasoning based on facts." These are the thinking characteristics in the Warrior that produce both plans and results. Warriors are good with their hands, like sports and the outdoors, and "have a firm grasp on the realities of any situation," based on the fact-getting of sensation and the systematizing of thinking. They are interested in how and why things work "and are likely to be good at applied science, mechanics, or engineering."[69] ST Structurals can be tough, but they can be weak in their feeling function, which may express itself in inappropriately destructive rages.

In his tapes on the cultural archetypes, Moore points to one of the great arenas of Warrior activity in our times: driving. In the car, truck, SUV, or plane, the driver feels the motive power of the Warrior. He experiences in this competence the power of effective and disciplined functioning which can be available to him in any area of life. In dreams, the Warrior may show up as an airplane pilot or driver of another vehicle. How a person handles a vehicle in a dream and how well the vehicle is constructed are both symbols of the strength or weakness of the Structural aspects of the Soul, the strength or lack of one's determination and character in finishing a task or pursuing a worthwhile goal. Also, someone else in a dream is very often handling a car in a dangerous way, and when the dreamer takes control, it signals that he is developing this particular archetype and thereby taking charge of life both within and in society. Negative Warrior energy will often manifest itself as threatening characters in cars who are trying to run the dreamer over, or are wielding knives or guns with the intent to steal, rape, or kill. Such inner characters, representing societal threats, if confronted, will lead to greater Warrior powers for the dreamer.

The NF Lover Archetype. The Lover archetype, according to Moore and Gillette, embraces the full range of loves: *agape* or "brotherly love"; *eros* as "phallus or sexual love"; *amor* as "the complete union of one body and soul with another body and soul"; and the psychological term, *libido*, which Jungians identify as a "general appetite for life."[70] They associate this archetype with the collective unconscious and with a connection to all living things. We realize this connectedness not through intellect but rather "through feeling."[71]

Using different terminology, the Osmond group writes of this archetype in a similar vein: "What Oceanics have in common is that they experience life as a seamless whole; all events which are subjectively important to them come effortlessly together."[72]

The Lover is often an artist, and thereby experiences all of life as art. This archetype includes the mystic, who feels not only the exquisite joys of life, but the awful pains of humankind. "Here, we have the image of Jesus weeping—for his city, Jerusalem, for his disciples, for all of humanity."[73] Under the influence of the Lover archetype, a person "does not want to stop at socially created boundaries. . . . His life is often unconventional and 'messy'—the artist's studio, the creative scholar's study."[74] The Lover's compassion and messiness are evidences of the feeling and intuitive type makeup of this creative artist archetype.

In spite of the great value of the Lover, there has been a tension between the Lover and the other archetypes that often oppose the artist, innovator, creator, psychic, and mystic.[75] As a result, our society has been afflicted by the "Shadow Lover," the addicted and impotent seeker of drugs, work, alcohol, food, and any other addiction that replaces true love of Self, God, and others. This addictive aspect of the hurt Lover is one of Moore and Gillette's finest insights.[76]

Blame for our sad cultural state today must fall on the Shadow Warriors and Shadow Kings who have dominated our patriarchal culture for five thousand years. Anthropologist Riane Eisler makes clear in her book *The Chalice and the Blade* that these archetypes have created our male-controlled culture, which is based on the Warrior's sword of logic, duty, and work, and the King's aggression and victory-at-any-cost.[77] In a lecture on June 26, 1995, at the C. G. Jung Institute of Chicago, Ms. Eisler pointed out that a society dominated by archetypally masculine values seeks to control what one can do with one's body in two areas: a woman in relationship to her pregnancy, and young men (and now, young women) in regard to warfare. Eisler has extended her critique to include the effects of centuries of a dominant type culture on the area of sex and spirituality.[78]

Our cultural history arises directly from our dominant typological makeup. Accordingly, it is no accident that in the typological cross and circle, the Structuralist or Warrior is opposite and farthest from the Oceanic or Lover. Yet in the sacred economy of the Soul, these opposites of Lover and Warrior are deeply attracted to one another, as we see, for example, in the Greek myth of Aphrodite (Venus) and Aries (Mars).

When Moore and Gillette write that the Lover is in touch with an "underlying 'oceanic' connectedness,"[79] they unknowingly resonate with the Osmond group's description of the Oceanic or Lover. NFs swim in chaos, revel in the soup of life, and find there hidden patterns. This umwelt sensitively envisions a new enterprise and easily captures large pictures and the main outlines of a story or of a poem. In any creative work, vision is the first order of business, and the NF Lover most clearly perceives its manifold aspects. Then comes the revision, the linear and clear stuff of the thinking function belonging to the NT Creative Scientist or the ST Warrior. The Lover's undifferentiated tendencies (hence one of its names, the Oceanic) often need the balance of the ST Warrior's structures.

Although it is implied in the idea of the Oceanic, neither the Osmond group nor the *MBTI* directly considers the sensual and passionate aspect of the Lover, a characteristic that Moore and Gillette point out. This dimension of passion is experienced through "feeling" realized in a "primal hunger" and a "deep knowing." They continue: "Being close to the unconscious means being close to the 'fire'—to the fires of life and, on the biological level, to the fires of the life-engendering metabolic processes. Love, as we know it, is 'hot,' often 'too hot to handle.'"[80]

Besides feeling, the authors are also implicitly defining its companion, intuition, in the NF Lover when they speak of this archetype's perceptive knowing as "being close to the unconscious." They also allude to the sensation function when they state that the Lover "notices colors and forms, sounds, tactile sensations and smells."[81] However, sensation is only experienced here as a secondary, if necessary, aspect of the larger configuration of the Oceanic's feeling and intuitive functions.

In life and in dreams, the NF Lover often feels battered like a tender plant in a violent storm, or feels reduced again to childlike help-lessness. In one dream an NF client was confronted by his shadow mother suddenly standing as tall as a doorway in the midst of an enjoy-able walk with his beloved. Mother functioned in life as an ST Warrior. In the dream, Mother shamed him by reminding him that he should have been caring for his drunken father. Standing before her towering body and pierced by her accusations, he felt as small and helpless as when in childhood he attempted to hold together his emotionally fragmented parents.

Another NF client dreamt of a uniquely constructive way of expressing her innate passionate feeling. She was lying fully dressed on a hospital cot. A so-called sex technician, clearly an ST Warrior, came to her saying he had to check her out. He proceeded to roughly push at her body with his fingers in a supposedly systemic and dispassion-ate way. Finally she said, "Why don't you undress me and we'll make love." The dream, while revealing a passionate nature, also reflected the dreamer's personal feelings about the usual coldness of the medical profession and the compassion and creativity it needs in its care of patients. Here, too, we see the polarity of the Lover's eros and the Warrior's aggressiveness that is consistently experienced in life and psyche, as well as so clearly depicted in the typological mandala. In the dream, the Lover seeks reconciliation with and a healing of the Warrior.

In turn, the Lover's highly flexible combination of intuition and feeling can cause such a person to get lost in a quest for meaning in an other-worldly outlook without the solid earthly and tough grounding of its archetypal opposite, the ST Warrior.

Isabel Myers describes NFs as deeply interested in people, passionately committed to their ideas, seeking the new and innovative and gifted in "being able to see value in other people's opinions."[82] They are committed to harmony among family members and between friends, and can become neurotic in overly serving others. They see possibilities beyond the present. "They are twice as good when working at a job they believe in, since their feeling puts added energy behind their effort." On the other hand, Myers writes, NF's often feel inadequate in our culture because "they may feel such a contrast between their ideals and their actual accomplishments."[83]

I believe their discomfort is more than intrapsychic. It emerges, first of all, from a mismatch between their NF makeup and the ST characteristics of the dominant culture. We are reminded of what Moore and Gillette have said of the Lover: "Christianity, Judaism and Islam—what are called ethical or moral religions—have all persecuted the Lover," namely, the "artists, innovators and creators" and "psychics and mediums, people who along with artists and others live very close to the image-making unconscious, and hence to the Lover."[84]

In Taoism, the NF Lover's compassion and imagination are beautifully exemplified in the Taoist Chi Kung exercise, the Inner Smile.[85] As in all Taoist exercises, the imagination, or intuition, is called forth. The meditator evokes the loving energy of the heart (the feeling function) by visualizing that energy moving from the heart through slightly smiling lips, and from the lips to the interior sight. In this interior seeing, which is intuition, the imagination sends loving energy to every system of the body as a compassionate, imaged flow, a healing balm for every organ, gland, and structure of the body and mind. This exercise has an ancient tradition, as Chia notes:

> In ancient China, the Taoist masters recognized the power
> of smiling energy. They practiced an Inner Smile to

themselves, which moved Chi energy and produced a high grade of Chi [spiritual or subtle energy], and achieved health, happiness and longevity. Smiling to oneself is like basking in love, and love can repair and rejuvenate.[86]

We must not, however, forget the shadow side of the Lover. We have already seen that this NF combination is especially sensitive to emotional mistreatment in childhood. If the lack of loving attention in childhood is not redressed, then the Lover in us can too readily fill this spiritual gap by turning to addictions, becoming attached to impossible ideals and causes, or taking on codependent relationships.

A CONTRAST BETWEEN MOORE AND GILLETTE'S QUATERNITY AND TONI WOLFF'S FOUR FEMININE ARCHETYPES

We have seen in our work with both the Osmond group and Isabel Briggs Myers' formulations that the four pairs of coupled functions are archetypal and flow naturally out of the inner structure and dynamic of the four functions. (We will explore further implications of this inner dynamic when we consider all sixteen types of the *MBTI*.) However, Moore and Gillette did not arrive at their quaternity through typology, but through their study of cultures. These four cultural archetypes have been in the air in Jungian circles for a long time, especially since 1934 when Toni Wolff published her essay, "Structural Forms of the Feminine Psyche."[87]

Wolff names these feminine archetypes the Mother, the Hetaira (as companion and friend), the Amazon, and the Medium. She locates the first two on the vertical, "personally connected" line and the last two on the horizontal, "impersonally connected" line (figure 5.5, page 218). She writes:

> *In common with the psychological functional types,* their axes are directly opposed (i.e., personally or impersonally

Toni Wolff's Structural Forms of the Feminine Psyche

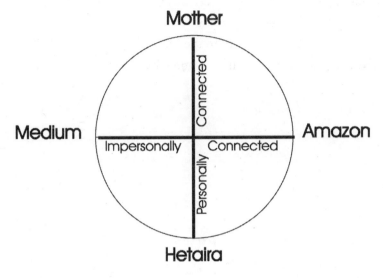

Mother

Medium

Amazon

Connected

Impersonally   Connected

Personally

Hetaira

FIGURE 5.5

connected), with the result that generally one form dominates, a second may become attached to it, and the third
and fourth are at first unconscious and only become
conscious and integrated with great difficulty in later life.
As all four forms are found throughout cultural history,
they are probably archetypal in nature. They also
correspond to aspects of a man's anima.[88]

In his 1925 *Seminar,* Jung alludes to two of Toni Wolff's four
feminine archetypes when he writes: "As you know, I think of women
as belonging in general to two types, the mother and the hetaira. The
hetaira acts as a mother for the other side of men's thinking."[89] In
Wolff's writing and as supported here by Jung, we have the first
indication in our Jungian history, as far as I know, of a quaternary
archetypal system related to and including the four functions. Jung
diagrams the four type couplings in this same seminar, and even names

them: speculative thinking (NT); the intuitive feeling (NF); empirical thinking (ST); and emotional feeling (SF).[90] However, since he does this only to show them as bridges to the individual functions, his couplings remain subservient to the individual types and also remain in the intrapsychic realm. In his commentary on this text, he does not discuss the couplings at all but speculates on the possibility of "a complete consciousness of all the functions," which is never realized "in reality."[91] Incidentally, I would not call SF "emotional feeling" since, as we have already seen, Jung has called feeling "emotional value." Rather, I would call this coupling "practical feeling."

In her essay, Wolff does not show the connection between the four archetypes of the feminine and specific functions, except to note that these four archetypes have the same internal, dynamic relationship to one another as do the four functions. It has been suggested in Jungian circles that these archetypes represented Wolff's initial attempt to restate the function types in more feminine terms. One axis is impersonal, like the rational judging axis, and one is personal, like the irrational perception axis. One archetype will overshadow the others, like the dominant function, and one will act as the auxiliary, or secondary, archetype. However, we can strongly argue that Wolff implies the four couplings since the four archetypes of the feminine resemble the type mandala in their circular affinity to one another, and their added complexity as perceptive–judging combinations suggests that they are substantial archetypal patterns. She does not explore this connection with Jung's couplings, though.

Notice, however, the different juxtapositioning of the archetypes in the psychic compass if we assume, as do Moore and Gillette, that the Mother refers to the Queen, the Hetaira to the Lover, the Amazon to the Warrior, and the Medium to the Magician. In Wolff's configuration, the Mother-Queen and Lover are opposed, as are the Magician and Warrior. There is nothing intrinsically wrong with Wolff's positioning, but it conflicts with corresponding positions in the type mandala when we begin working with the couplings. Others would argue that Wolff's structure is more feminine, in contrast to the oppositional masculine lineup. We'll pursue this issue further as we go along.

Edward Whitmont takes up these four archetypes in his well-known book, *The Symbolic Quest*,[92] in which he accepts Wolff's positioning in the mandala. However, when he describes each archetype, he gets closer to Moore and Gillette's descriptions, especially when he describes the Mother as having an impersonal aspect like the Queen, and the Hetaira as carrying the lover qualities of an Aphrodite. Then he assumes rightly that these four feminine patterns have their counterpart in the male psyche as Father, Son, Hero, and Wise Man, which can be translated into King, Lover, Warrior, and Magician.

Whitmont identifies some of the same key concepts that Moore and Gillette describe. For example, the Father is the archetypal leader, the voice of collective authority, the figure concerned with hierarchical order, whose word is law, hence the Lord, King, and Protector, but also potentially the Tyrant. The Son as Lover is "Adonis, Attis or Peter Pan . . . the eternal Friend but also the challenging Enemy," and as "the Knight Errant [he is] the eternal seeker." The Hero is the "soldier or go-getter type," and the Wise Man, "the scholar, teacher, sage, seer and philosopher."[93] We have here, respectively, the SF, the NF, the ST, and the NT.

Tad Guzie and Noreen Monroe Guzie draw on and amplify the work of both Wolff and Whitmont by developing a straightforward and rich description of what they call eight "Great Stories" about the four female archetypes and the four male archetypes.[94] They also follow Wolff's diagram with its impersonal and personal axes and its juxtaposition of Mother (Queen) and Companion (Lover), and of Warrior and Sage (Magician). The Guzies specifically ask in their appendix if there is any correlation between the four individual functions and the four archetypes. They find none, appropriately so, since they do not consider Jung's typological cross with its four couplings. They do not notice the significance of Myers' description of the four couplings in the *Manual, Introduction to Types,* and *Gifts Differing* as virtual archetypes, and they were probably unaware of the Osmond group's naming the couplings "umwelts," or archetypes.

As a result, their theorizing about types and archetypes is incorrect, yet because they are influential in *MBTI* circles, their argument must be seriously considered here. They believe that the function types arise from the personal unconscious, but that archetypal stories or myths and all the other archetypes come from the collective unconscious.[95] On the other hand, Jung and Jungian scholars and analysts generally believe that the personal unconscious is made up of contents that we acquire throughout life in contrast to inherited contents, such as the functions, that are found only in the collective unconscious' deep strata. This theoretical assumption is at the core of my thesis: namely that the four functional couplings constitute four archetypes that manifest in personal, interpersonal, and collective ways. I have also discussed the archetypal nature of all four functions. In the introduction and in chapter 2, I discussed Jung's conception of the functions in two archetypal worldviews: alchemy's energic vitality and Taoism's primordial polarities and spiritual energies. In chapter 3, I developed Jung's observation that each function evoked in consciousness a "numinal accent," a sacred felt-sense that comes only from the archetypes of the collective unconscious. (As a result, Hillman acknowledges the archetypal nature of each individual function.) We saw in that same chapter that Jung connected introversion, intuition, and thinking with archetypal roots.

The Guzies make a further distinction: "Psychological types and the *MBTI* help to explain *how* we communicate. Archetypes, the Great Stories, help to explain *what* we communicate."[96] This contradicts the position of the Osmond group, who said of the individual functions that they tell us *what* is communicated, and the archetypal couplings, *how* we communicate. "Hows" and "whats" are a confusing basis for determining what is or is not archetypal. The Osmond group comes up with a better basis for identifying archetypes: the individual functions reveal the "content" of human differences whereas the couplings lay out the "form," or the fundamental intelligence, of human differences.

Form is a synonym for archetype and is also associated with the *numen,* the "fiery sparks of the soul," according to Jung.[97] As we have noted before, Jung complained that people, while ignoring the large cultural and archetypal perspectives and the Western historical picture associated with the types as he developed them in the first nine chapters, could never really understand his typology if they stuck only with chapter 10 of *Psychological Types,* where he describes types as specific traits. The Guzies persist in doing this when, in contrast to viewing the types as archetypes, they write:

> The types have to do with inborn traits which are respon-
> sible for the way our energy flows, outward or inward (E
> and I), and the way we gather (P) and organize (J) every-
> day information in a variety of perceiving and judging
> ways (S or N, T or F).[98]

This sort of description, valid in itself, is like analyzing a poem simply by its subject, verb, and object or a Mozart piece by its mathematical precision. The Guzies are reflecting the obvious fact that so much of the *MBTI* literature has dealt with types in this way. This view supports the necessity of a new alliance between the professional analysts and *MBTI* practitioners. However, aside from their denial of the functions as archetypes, the Guzies' book contains solid down-to-earth descriptions of the four basic archetypes, showing many subtle and even significant differences between men and women in each.

Moore and Gillette did not base their work on that of Wolff and her followers, or even explicitly on Jung's function couplings. Rather they looked directly at archetypal qualities and their four-fold relationships in a mandala that kept reappearing within human consciousness, surfacing in a number of ways in different cultures and psyche, beyond the explicit Jungian tradition. They write in *The Magician Within* that they arrived at their quaternity of archetypes both in males and females not through an *a priori* assumption about the psyche, but through inductively discovering them in human cultures and experientially finding their counterparts in the psyche. They added: "Later we were astounded and gratified to find that others had struggled to decode the same diamond body"—that is, their metaphorical diagram of four male archetypes and four female archetypes, pictured in a diamond-shape.[99] Their support of their finding of a "dialectical opposition" between "eros and aggression" [read the NF Lover versus the ST Warrior] and ruler and sage [read SF King/Queen versus the NT Magician] came from psychology. They continue: "Freud focused of course on the eros/aggression dialectic and Adler on the ruler/sage. . ."[100]

Contrary to the positioning of the four archetypes in Wolff's circle, Moore and Gillette argue that in cultural stories, the Warrior and Lover and the King/Queen and Magician are naturally opposed. They seek the support of two of the founders of modern psychology to support their view. They show that Freud's two opposing energies, eros and aggression, agree respectively with the opposition of the NF Oceanic/Lover and the ST Structural/Warrior; in Adler's psychology, the superiority of the ruler versus the social interest of the Sage agrees with the opposition between the SF Experial/King/Queen and the NT Ethereal/Magician. In establishing these oppositional dynamics in their archetypes, Moore and Gillette are also supporting the type mandala, and in turn, the type mandala, with its four coupling archetypes, supports their cultural research.

In contrast to their actual manifestations in life's stories and in dreams as specific images (such as those of Warrior or Lover), archetypes as such are implicit or potential structures in the psyche. We infer their existence from universally observed behaviors. As we have already noted, Jung held that the type compass, as well as individual functions, were archetypal in nature. Until Myers and Osmond, no one had linked those behaviors to type couplings and their dynamics. Given the fact that millions of people have experienced the Jungian function types as reasonable descriptions of their life preferences and interests, that knowledge of one's typology significantly adds to one's sense of identity, and given the fact that the *MBTI* is considered in psychological research circles to be one of the most reliable testing instruments, we can say Moore and Gillette's picture of the "diamond body" from the standpoint of type images and traits is well supported. The diamond body is another term for the Self, which can be depicted by the side-by-side presence of four permanent psychic forms or archetypes for both male and female, thus making up an "octahedral self."[101]

In further reflections in *The Magician Within,* Moore and Gillette express a viewpoint about the relationship between the archetypes and the types that demands our attention here. They write: "While the relation of the four foundational archetypes to Jung's theory of typology has yet to be researched, there does not seem to be any one-to-one correspondence." This was written before Robert Moore began to review *Compass of the Soul.* Now he agrees that, given the four couplings within the *Compass of the Soul,* the correspondences do exist. They write further on Freud and Adler's contributions to the foundational archetypes: "Jung was not entirely correct to ascribe Freud and Adler's conflict purely to psychological differences. The two were focusing on different structural dynamics inherent in the deep structures of the Self."[102] For one thing, as we have seen in chapter 3, Jung saw the type difference between these two men as purely between Freud's extraversion and Adler's introversion. Here the authors are simply not perceiving introversion and extraversion as archetypes, which we now know they are, but only as surface-of-consciousness traits. Further, we perceive the congruency of the King, Warrior, Magician and Lover with the SF, the ST, the NT, and the NF respectively, so that we can say of Freud and Adler, ascribing type language to them, that Freud was focusing on the inner differences between the NF Lover and the ST Warrior, and Adler was stressing the SF Ruler and NT Sage aspect of the Soul's type compass. As to the typology of Freud and Adler, I believe that Freud functioned with a false persona as an extraverted sensate thinking type as he sought to control his followers and to create a scientific theory that satisfied an ESTJ scientific world. He may have covertly and authentically been an INFJ, whereas Adler was probably an introverted sensate feeling type.

The authors' revision of the names of Wolff's four archetypes helps clarify and deepen their implication for the foundational type couplings. Wolff's Mother archetype and its equivalent Father form in the male are not as inclusive as the Queen and King. Moore and Gillette hold, for example, that "The Mother's focus is on a single family" and the care of children, in contrast to the "Queen, from whom the earth itself derives its fecundity."[103]

They also point out that the Greek name, Amazon, negatively limits the personality of the Warrior, particularly since these female fighters often turned against "the services of the royal couple," whose ideals the integral Warrior fiercely implements. Wolff's language, they contend, too readily brings to mind these female fighters' anti-male attitude and their often sadistic treatment of men.[104] The Osmond research shows the equivalent archetype, the ST Structural, as positively and stubbornly serving, if not royalty, some high ideals, such as Freud did with his sex theory and Florence Nightingale did with the medical vocation of nurses.[105]

In contrast to the creative and expansive Lover, Moore and Gillette see Wolff's Hetaira, like the Amazon, as culturally bound. In their view, the Hetaira functioned in Greece like a Japanese geisha. Further, "In Wolff's system, the Hetaira displays both aspects of the Lover's bipolar Shadow, the Addict and the Impotent Lover."[106] This is unnecessary criticism, because each archetype has its own shadow aspects. Besides, Wolff also describes the healthy Lover in many positive ways, such as giving the man she loves "personal value quite apart from collective values" and moving him "beyond his male responsibilities into his total personality." Further, "her instinctive interest is directed towards the individual elements of a relationship in herself as well as in her man," for the "relationship is decisive . . . beyond everything else" for the Hetaira Lover.[107] However, the NF Lover, as the Oceanic or Creative Artist, is restricted less by culture. The Osmond group portrays Oceanics as moody, dreamy persons, or as rugged lovers who stand tall and unbowed before the storm. Lord Nelson described himself as "a reed among oaks, who bows while the oak is laid low." He is an example of a Creative Artist in the art of war. Another example of the Lover and Oceanic is the Dutch woman Betsie ten Boom who despite imprisonment by the Nazis, "gave thanks for all the circumstances in the barracks" and rose "to great spiritual heights even while her body wasted away."[108]

Finally, Moore and Gillette acknowledge, "To the extent Wolff's final type, the Medial, approaches the concept of the shaman, it is an appropriate and full expression of the Magician." That aspect of each of us "may serve as a spiritual guide to others" as we enter "into the mysteries of adult responsibilities and joys."[109] The Medial has an affinity with the NT Ethereal and Creative Scientist, who, as the Osmond group points out, experiences "the limitless possibilities of the mind."[110]

In summation, my work, following Moore and Gillette and the Osmond group, acknowledges Toni Wolff's recognition of the four fundamental archetypes. Moore and Gillette modify the dynamic relationships of Wolff's archetypes by placing Mother (Queen) ·

opposite the Medial (Magician) and by situating the Hetaira (Lover) opposite the Amazon (Warrior), based on consistent cultural traditions and because of Freud and Adler's psychological polarities. I modify Wolff's quaternity in order to attune them to the inner dynamic relationship of the four functions which Jung so creatively envisioned in the type compass.

These reflections on the four archetypes by Moore and Gillette and Toni Wolff are based mainly on a mainline Jungian cultural tradition that has envisioned practically no connections with the type couplings. On the other hand, we have already seen in the typology work of Isabel Myers and the Osmond group that the archetypes emerge directly from a consideration of the function couplings.

Finally, we can look at spirituality from the viewpoint of the four function couplings. Peter Tufts Richardson focuses in his book, *Four Spiritualities,* on the couplings as four worldwide spiritual styles that, in effect, recognize the couplings' universal patterns as archetypes, although he does not use the term archetype.[111] The ST spirituality manifests as a journey of works and responsibility; the SF as a journey of devotion and service; the NF as a journey of harmony and experiment; and the NT as a journey of unity and clarity.[112] Richardson's main chapters explore each of these varieties of spirituality; and then he devotes his chapter 8 to the subject, "Deepenings," where he begins to show a connection among them. He gives the example of the creation of a temple which the NF inspires, the NT designs, the ST runs (and I would add, builds), and the SF celebrates.[113] Here we find an intimation of a counterclockwise, playfully creative process in the relationship between the types that I will be exploring in the next and subsequent chapters.

Notes

1. Isabel Briggs Myers with Peter B. Myers, *Gifts Differing: Understanding Personality Type* (Palo Alto CA: Consulting Psychologists Press, 1980), p. 4.

2. C. G. Jung, *CW*, vol. 6, *Psychological Types,* English edition, translated by H. G. Baynes (1923; rpt., Princeton NJ: Princeton University Press, 1971), para. 669.

3. Ibid., para. 670.

4. Jung, "The Phenomenology of the Spirit in Fairytales," *CW,* vol. 9:1, *The Archetypes and the Collective Unconscious* (Princeton: Princeton University Press, 1959), paras. 422–26.

5. Naomi L. Quenk's book, *Beside Ourselves,* is a solid exception, along with some sections of Angelo Spoto's *Jung's Typology in Perspective,* and the article by Marie-Louise von Franz in *Jung's Typology.* Ms. Quenk's work is unique because she is the first, as far as I know, to extensively develop the inferior function for all the sixteen types, which she characterizes as "our hidden personality." She brings to this book over thirty years of wise and intense work with typology as a psychological practitioner and as an *MBTI* trainer.

6. Jung, *CW,* vol. 14, *Mysterium coniunctionis* (Princeton NJ: Princeton University Press, 1963–70). "From ancient times the adept knew that he was concerned with the *'res simplex,'* and the modern man too will find by experience that the work does not prosper without the greatest simplicity. But simple things are always the most difficult," para. 750.

7. Humphrey Osmond et al., "Typology Revisited: A New Perspective," *Psychological Perspectives* (Fall 1977): pp. 206–19.

8. Jung, *CW,* vol. 6, *Psychological Types,* pp. xiv–xv.

9. Ibid., para. 986.

10. Ibid., paras 959, 986.

11. Osmond et al., "Typology Revisited: A New Perspective," p. 206.

12. Ibid.

13. Ibid., pp. 207–8.

14. Myers, *Introduction to Type: A Description of the Theory and Applications of the Myers-Briggs Type Indicator* (Palo Alto CA: Consulting Psychologists Press, 1962), p. 28.

15. Michael Malone, *Psychetypes: A New Way of Exploring Personality* (New York: Dutton, 1977). Malone dedicates the book to "Dr. Harriet Mann, whose book this is." Apparently she was his significant teacher and mentor at Cambridge University.

16. Ibid., p. xi.

17. Myers and Mary McCaulley, *Manual: A Guide to the Development and Use of the Myers-Briggs Type Indicator* (Palo Alto CA: Consulting Psychologists Press, 1985), pp. 33–35.

18. Osmond et al., "Typology Revisited: A New Perspective," p. 209.

19. Ibid.

20. Daniel Yankelovich and William Barrett, *Ego and Instinct: The Psychoanalytic View of Human Nature* (New York: Random House, 1970). They opt for Erik Erikson, as influenced initially by Heinz Hartmann, as the new architect of the psychoanalyst edifice of the late twentieth century, even though they concede that Jung, like Erikson, had developed a whole-life view of psychological development.

21. Jung, *C. G. Jung Letters,* vol. 2 (Princeton NJ: Princeton University Press, 1975), pp. 346–48. It is only fair to note here that the younger Jung had succumbed to the thinking function, just as had the older Freud, as we have already seen in Jung's 1925 Seminar notes.

22. Yankelovich and Barrett, *Ego and Instinct,* pp. 195–97.

23. Osmond et al., "Typology Revisited: A New Perspective," p. 210.

24. Ibid., p. 209.

25. Malone, *Psychetypes,* p. 75.

26. Osmond et al., "Typology Revisited: A New Perspective," p. 211.

27. Ibid.

28. Ibid., p. 212.

29. Ibid., p. 210.

30. Malone, *Psychetypes,* p. 89.

31. Ibid., p. 90.

32. Osmond et al., "Typology Revisited: A New Perspective," p. 213.

33. Ibid.

34. Ibid., p. 214.

35. Malone, *Psychetypes,* p. 52.

36. Osmond et al., "Typology Revisited: A New Perspective," p. 213.

37. Ibid., p. 214.

38. Ibid.

39. Ibid., p. 215.

40. Ibid.

41. Malone, *Psychetypes,* p. 65.

42. Ibid., p. 64.

43. According to Plaut's research, "only half the number of analysts reply-ing found the typology helpful in analytical practice" (p. 143). In my discus-sions with fellow analysts, and especially among trainees, there is a general suspicion and even careful avoidance of typology. Why? One clinical psychol-ogist and Jungian analyst believes that we tend to avoid any kind of clinical classification as a group of people. Also, the *MBTI* as an instrument is the most-used test in clinical psychological practices. It sells by the millions each year. Moreover, the Jung/*MBTI* theory has become a very popular psychological guide. Maybe Jungians are simply not popularists!

44. Jean Bolen, *Goddesses in Every Woman* (New York: Harper and Row, 1984).

45. My figure 4, chapter 2, "Some Correlations with Psyche's Four Levels," also shows a quaternity of levels, coordinated with four somatic metaphors and with four human behaviors: work, love, play, and prayer. (Freud well under-stood the first two, but not the last two.) Matthew Fox has identified four spiritualities in Meister Eckhart's sermons and other writings, and I have identified four periods of humankind, with the last, the ecological or earth age, being one in which we must now enter or perish. I have also realized that there are four brain rhythms and levels: Beta for ordinary consciousness; Alpha for a relaxed consciousness; Theta for a relaxed, fluctuating, and creative consciousness (that is consistent with the level of the new or creative child and the behavior of play); and finally, Delta, the condition of sleep that for many adepts is also another state of consciousness and the condition for creative dreaming.

46. For decades, Hillman has been rejecting Jung's concept of the Self as a central archetype and matrix of the other archetypes. He finds the idea of the Self equivalent to and as repugnant as the concept of the one God in theology, in contrast to the many gods. In his 1996 book, *The Soul's Code: In Search of Character and Calling* (New York: Random House), he introduces as a central concept the idea that the Soul is like an acorn, as metaphor for the unique and precise potentials in each of us. The acorn has been around for a long time in Jungian circles as a metaphor for the Self.

47. Robert Moore and Douglas Gillette, *King, Warrior, Magician, Lover: Rediscovering the Archetypes of the Mature Masculine* (San Francisco: HarperSanFrancisco, 1990). Another analyst has written a book that refers to the qualities of the couplings in the type circle's four quadrants without naming them. See Gareth Hill, *Masculine and Feminine: The Natural Flow of Opposites in the Psyche* (Boston: Shambhala, 1992).

48. Osmond et al., "Typology Revisited: A New Perspective," p. 215.

49. Myers, *Introduction to Type,* p. 28.

50. Ibid., p. 16.

51. Moore and Gillette. *King, Warrior, Magician, Lover,* pp. 56–57.

52. Ibid., pp. 63, 67.

53. Ibid., p. 98.

54. Ibid., p. 100.

55. Ibid., p. 99.

56. Ibid., p. 102.

57. Ibid., p. 107.

58. Osmond et al., "Typology Revisted: A New Perspective," p. 213.

59. Myers, *Introduction to Type,* pp. 28, 24.

60. Ibid., p. 22.

61. Moore and Gillette. *King, Warrior, Magician, Lover,* p. 108.

62. Ibid., p. 83.

63. Ibid., p. 86.

64. Ibid., pp. 86–87.

65. Osmond et al., "Typology Revisited: A New Perspective," p. 209.

66. Ibid., p. 209

67. Ibid., p. 210.

68. Myers, *Introduction to Type,* p. 28.

69. Ibid., p. 12.

70. Moore and Gillette, *King, Warrior, Magician, Lover,* p. 120.

71. Ibid., pp. 121–22.

72. Osmond et al., "Typology Revisited: A New Perspective," p. 211.

73. Moore and Gillette. *King, Warrior, Magician, Lover,* p. 125.

74. Ibid.

75. Ibid., p. 126.

76. Ibid., pp. 131–40.

77. Riane Eisler, *The Chalice and the Blade: Our History, Our Future* (Cambridge MA: Harper and Row, 1987).

78. Riane Eisler, *Sacred Pleasure: Sex, Myth, and the Politics of the Body* (San Francisco: HarperSanFrancisco, 1995).

79. Moore and Gillette. *King, Warrior, Magician, Lover,* p. 122.

80. Ibid.

81. Ibid., p. 120.

82. Myers, *Introduction to Type,* p. 15.

83. Ibid., p. 17.

84. Moore and Gillette. *King, Warrior, Magician, Lover,* p. 126.

85. Mantak Chia teaches such exercises in *Taoist Ways to Transform Stress into Vitality: The Inner Smile, Six Healing Sounds* (Huntington NY: Healing Tao Press, 1985).

86. Ibid., p. 29.

87. Toni Wolff, "Structural Forms of the Feminine Psyche," *Psychological Perspectives,* issue 31 (Spring-Summer 1995): pp. 77–90.

88. Ibid., p. 80 (emphasis added).

89. Jung, *Analytical Psychology: Notes of the Seminar Given in 1925* (Princeton

NJ: Princeton University Press, 1989), p. 33. The editors note that Wolff had added two other archetypes, "the Amazon and the medial woman," to thus create a quaternity.

90. Ibid., p. 119.

91. Ibid., p. 120.

92. Edward Whitmont, *The Symbolic Quest: Basic Concepts of Analytical Psychology* (New York: Harper and Row, 1969), chapter 2 generally, entitled "Male and Female," but specifically on the archetypes, pp. 178–83.

93. Ibid., pp. 181–82.

94. Tad Guzie and Noreen Monroe Guzie, *About Men and Women: How Your "Great Story" Shapes Your Destiny* (New York: Paulist Press, 1986). Tad Guzie has functioned as president of the Association for Psychological Type.

95. Ibid., p. 153.

96. Ibid., p. 155.

97. Jung, "On the Nature of the Psyche," *CW*, vol. 8, *The Structure and Dynamics of the Psyche* (Princeton NJ: Princeton University Press, 1960), para. 388. Jung continues: "These formae correspond to the Platonic ideas, from which one could equate the *scintillae* [divine sparks] with the archetypes on the assumption that the Forms 'stored up in a supra celestial place' are a philosophical [read intellectual] version of the latter.

98. Guzie and Guzie, *About Men and Women*, p. 153.

99. Moore and Gillette, *The Magician Within: Accessing The Shaman in the Male Psyche* (New York: William Morrow and Company, 1993), p. 238.

100. Ibid.

101. Ibid., p. 255.

102. Ibid., p. 238.

103. Ibid., p. 249.

104. Ibid., p. 251.

105. Osmond et al., "Typology Revisited: A New Perspective," p. 210.

106. Moore and Gillette, *The Magician Within*, p. 252.

107. Wolff, "Structural Forms of the Feminine Psyche," pp. 82–83.

108. Osmond et al., "Typology Revisited: A New Perspective," pp. 211–12.

109. Moore and Gillette, *The Magician Within,* pp. 252–53.

110. Osmond et al., "Typology Revisited: A New Perspective," pp. 213.

111. Peter Tufts Richardson, *Four Spiritualities: Expressions of Self, Expressions of Spirit* (Palo Alto CA: Davies-Black Publishing, 1996).

112. Ibid., p. 188.

113. Ibid., p. 190.

CHAPTER 6

Playing with the Function Couplings

Not the artist alone, but every creative individual whatsoever owes all that is greatest in his life to fantasy. The dynamic principle of fantasy is play, a characteristic also of the child, and as such it appears inconsistent with the principle of serious work. But without this playing with fantasy no creative work has ever yet come to birth.[1]

C. G. Jung

No longer am I the image I embody. I have become identified with what is not unique, my resemblance with others. My image has been fed to the type. My sense of image lost, my identity seeps out; and so I seem to have no specific shape that can be grasped individually. . . . Persons in bins can only resemble one another in their communality. So we would climb out into individualism by heroic acts of rugged will. Ego is the phantom risen, the idol erected, when the image cannot be seen.[2]

James Hillman

LL THE TYPE COUPLINGS as archetypal expressions belong to each of us, though we are naturally oriented toward one or two. The one that is most natural to us is the dominant coupling. The second coupling, almost as natural, is the first auxiliary. The third is the second auxiliary and the fourth is our inferior coupling. The couplings operate very much like the individual functions. However, no matter what

seems natural to us, all couplings are part of our potential and all are important for our lives. Learning to play with all of them enhances our lives, particularly in the two vocational areas of work and love.

Freud understood the structures of work and love, but ignored the need to play and pray, thus seriously diminishing his view of humanity. Play is spontaneous behavior and the basis of creativity. Prayer is an expression of spirituality, the essence of which is valuing the mystery and wonder of life. Without play and prayer, work and love lose both their depth and breadth of meaning. For a full life we need to work, love, play, and pray. Although play is the focus of this chapter, it is never separable from prayer, since play's creative character and mysterious ground evoke a reverence for the fertility of nature and the fruitful mystery of existence itself. The metaphorical geography of psyche, as illustrated in figure 3.1 (page 68), shows that the human behavior of play is located below work and love, and is associated with the new or creative child, the metaphorical bodily area of gut/womb, and the primitive, magical era of human history. Play calls forth spontaneities of the Soul in image and vitality often tragically ignored in our time-driven, compulsively active society. Without play and prayer, the sacred callings of work and love become arid and deathlike, with work degenerating into workaholism and love into servitude. The addition of play and prayer to our understanding of types should satisfy criticisms, such as that of James Hillman (page 235), that this typological field is too rigidly structured.

PLAYING WITH WORK

Imagine an artist looking at our quadrants. Where would the artist locate artistic technique such as the pragmatic understanding and use of the artist's medium? Clearly in the left quadrants, in the left brain, where sensation's pragmatic particularity is the central function at the horizontal axis, flanked by both feeling and thinking. Without technique, the art will not have a suitable medium for creatively coming into being. Artistic creativity, on the other hand, is located in the right brain quadrants with intuition as the central function of innovation, and with the intuitive, feeling (NF) ensemble as the artistic font and the NT combination as the creative systematizer.

Eventually, both hemispheres must work together. For example, one client has been a student of the master piano teacher, Abby Whiteside. He reported that she stresses the enormous importance of the upper arms, which, in line with the body as a whole, effortlessly direct the hands and fingers. Whiteside calls this bodily awareness and practice "a basic rhythm" which is "the most important factor in the creation of a beautiful performance."[3] This student, an NF Lover and Creative Artist, described this "basic rhythm" as a felt sense in the body as a whole and in unison with the piano, as a movement from the center of the body to the peripheries of the hands and the fingers on the keys. If the process is right, he commented, the "fingers will do the walking" in a magnificent unfolding of the art. In this description, technique is constituted through combining sensation with both thinking and feeling (ST and SF). The musical artistry is attained through combining intuition with both feeling and thinking (NF and NT), as the artist attunes his basic bodily rhythm to the artistic and spiritual rhythm and breadth and depth of the music. The artist's learned technique must be wed with a mysteriously felt, intuitive grasp of the medium—then powers of the unconscious are tapped first through the indispensable combination of feeling and intuition. Technique and art have flowed into one.

Another NF Creative Artist was worrying about an upcoming concert, her most important since college graduate recitals. She asked the I Ching for help in handling her anxiety. The answer she received, Hexagram 48, was startlingly relevant. Hexagram 48, the Well, is one of only two of the sixty-four hexagrams that are human constructs. The well in China is made of wood siding that closely hugs the earthen hole. The pole for pulling up the water in the clay bucket is also made of wood. Human ingenuity and nature's rich largesse of cool water hidden in the earth's deep recesses combine to assuage people's thirst. Political parties may change, says the hexagram, "but the life of man with its needs remain eternally the same." For any political institution and any individual human life to be worthwhile, "We must go down to the very foundations of life." We must draw from "the inexhaustible wellspring of the divine in man's nature."[4]

Translated into the pianist's personal concern, the hexagram suggests that she is already capable of effectively performing, since its text shows such a dramatic affinity between the conscious effort of technique on one hand, symbolized by the wood structures (ST and SF) and, on the other hand, the inexhaustible life-giving art, depicted by the earth's water supply. As previously mentioned, the pianist is an NF Creative Artist who doubted her other capacities: a secondary NT strength as her vision of the composer's music and her ST strength as her disciplined practice. Trusting in the ultimate factor that unites and transforms all the types, the creative Soul, she did well and her performance was masterful.

I have worked with another NF musician, an organist, who dreamt of a coordination between her art and technique. In the dream she saw two women (herself) playing on both levels of a two-level stage. On the top, she was practicing her technique. On the bottom, she was playing passionately, vibrating with the felt bodily sense of her art and its subtle but solid partnership with the learned rhythms of her hands, feet, and the rest of her body. She also felt that this consolidation of all of her typological strength was resonating in her art of living. Her former husband, an ST, had scoffed at her artistry as well as her need to know herself. Now she was also reclaiming her capacities as a Lover, first, through dreams of inner lovers that affirmed her femininity and then with a new man in her life, who loves both her artistry and her person.

The Whiteside student, an INFP, had developed a futile survival technique designed to keep any person from entering his inner "eminent domain" during a period of truly ineffective living. "I succeeded very well in maintaining this 'noble' alienated goal with the use of alcohol, drugs, and stoically supporting my often crumbling wall of fear, particularly my fear of surrender." In recent years, through analysis and Alcoholics Anonymous, he has been learning to surrender, learning to respond to both the needs and gifts of his ex-wife and children, as well as his new companion, a successful woman in her own right. He is also experiencing "a renaissance" of his art. He had a dream that spoke directly to him about his capacity to live life well. In the dream he let himself fall into a soft containing mother earth place. Then, lying in a coffin, he was able to look through a slit at a woman's sensual leg. He was told by a dream voice to listen to this woman, in whom he experienced, for the first time in his life, an integration of sensuality and spirituality, of vulnerability and strength. He realizes that in waking life he can, in active imagination, listen to his inner woman, while connecting harmoniously to an art of living and, artistically, to his musical muse. His dream "tomb" has become a womb, a place of continuing rebirth, as he has allowed himself to surrender and trust in his archetypal mother and lover. Against mighty resistance, he has occasionally, in an active imagination exercise, let her hold him, and has experienced tears of mixed joy and pain and feelings of ravenous satisfaction and unrequited sadness. He is learning to trust the fullness of what he is: an NF Artist and Lover.

THE COUPLINGS IN THE CIRCLE OF LIFE AND WORK

In terms of our compass with its four typological archetypes and as a circle of life's two stages (figure 5.5, page 218), this client, from the age of fourteen on, had become a drug-and-alcohol-using Shadow Warrior, an angry rebel in both love and war. In the first quadrant of the SF Moralist, he struggled with minimal love from his parents. The mother was a powerful narcissist who never praised him for school or musical successes, and the father was weak and alcoholic. With a family life that was more a prison of despair and rage than a royal palace of love and guidance, he passed through his first stage of life, haunted by his parents while he struggled to attain some ST Warrior qualities in order to differentiate from family, peers, and fellow workers and compete in the world. He joined the Army in order to realize some ST discipline, and subsequently struggled vocationally both as a musician and as a high school teacher. At sixty in the depth of a depression, he sank into the muddy, frightening emotions and fearsome images of the NF place and mentally and physically hit bottom. His rigid ego structures collapsed and he almost died. He received deep insights from the NT quadrant in both an inner Magician's warnings and an AA sponsor's guidance, which led him to the beginning of an authentic self-love and a successful return to his beloved piano.

However, AA support and a new Warrior determination were not enough. He needed to enter more fully into an intuitively felt depth beyond his music. This happened in analysis when, in many conscious inner encounters with the archetypal woman of his dream, she became a wise old woman, a Magician (NT), and a motherly Queen figure who consistently blessed and supported him (SF). In the NF quadrant he began to learn to surrender and to be childlike, as the dream image also became more of a Lover. In experiencing each of the four typological quadrants, he was realizing his individuation. He was realizing that individuation is a lifelong, repetitive, and circular process that each of us idiosyncratically must pass through no matter what our inborn types may be. For example, a dominant ST male with whom I worked was challenged to experience and realize his NF inferiority in the chaotic NF quadrant. His key dream involved his coming down from a high place in a building to a musical setting in which he began to dance with abandon. On the other hand, a dominant NF woman had to face her ST inferiority in that same NF place. In many dreams she had to confront dangerous men who sought either to rob or kill her.

Typology gives distinct yet related meaning to our life's journey and our individual uniqueness. In the two stages of life's creative process and circle, each of us must grapple with our typological weaknesses to fully live. Jung touched on a similar four-quartered life process, but only in relationship to the 180 degree arc of the sun.[5]

A young man in his twenties had a dream which represented his struggle with type potentials not yet developed. In the dream, he was on a sailboat controlled by his father, while he sat in the bow, experiencing the motion of the swelling, dangerous sea with fear and excitement. His father was handling the vessel skillfully. Then the dreamer attempted in a quieter and shallower sea to catch some fish as well as pull out a woman who had fallen in the water.

In his historical life, his parents had divorced years before and he felt afraid of and estranged from his father. This estrangement was symbolized in the dream by the father in the stern and he in the bow. So because his childhood—his SF Parental phase—had been difficult, he was now facing dangerous waters in adjusting to the pragmatic ST challenges of life, particularly in seeking a profession. In spite of his emotional difficulties with his father, however, he had still received a strong practical ST boost from this parent, who, though a failure in love, was successful in work. These successes, symbolized by the father's skillful maneuvering of the boat and internalized in the young man's Soul as indicated in the dream, helped him look confidently in the midst of fearful waters to a successful professional future. Further, he needed a Magician's NT knowledge, imaged as probing the inner depth of the unconscious (the water) for elemental strength (the fish). Finally, in terms of the NF Lover quadrant, he needed a connection with his inner feminine (the woman in the water), in order to complete his circle of life.

Another example is a young woman client who is an NF. The four quadrants are helping her develop a typological understanding of the various elements of her work as a real estate agent. She feels that her

NF strength allows her to be sensitive to the many aesthetic and comforting amenities of houses, and be responsive to the match between the buyer and these qualities of a house. She feels that in her SF quadrant, she is capable of building a trustful, parental relationship with clients. She knows also that she can develop, as the NT realm assumes, an appraiser's intuition as well as a systemic view of a neighborhood. Her greatest challenge is in the ST quadrant: her need to memorize a lot of the details about each house and the multitude of facts and strategies involved generally in real estate work.

The four type quadrants have also enlightened a young psychiatrist who has been working with a difficult patient. The patient, formerly a successful contractor, has become psychotically obsessed with a grandiose scheme of becoming a world-renowned movie producer and director. Along with this preoccupation, he has become obsessive-compulsive about minute thoughts and details of his life. These heavy preoccupations eventually exhaust his consciousness, and he falls into major depressions. Such pathologies have so affected his personal and family life that he has been forced into a retirement in which, fortunately, he is economically comfortable. Our psychiatrist has located his obsessive-compulsive behavior in the ST quadrant with its otherwise normal attention to facts and cognitive particulars, his grandiose scheme in the NT with its large visionary outlook, and his amorphous depressive state in the appropriately Oceanic NF place. The doctor is realizing that the patient is beginning to recover by becoming attached to both gardening and pottery. These crafts are located in the grounded and well-ordered SF quadrant.

The couplings have been of great assistance to another young client, who has been hired to be an assistant producer on a television advertising team, the members of which are highly creative people from photography and other visual art areas. She is an NT, but immediately began to realize that much of her work on this team would be in handling detail in the ST area of the work, in conjunction with her immediate boss, the coordinator, an ST Structural. She also began working closely with the producer, whom she observed to be a "Magician" in both his large perception of the task, and his capacity to grasp its many details. The producer functions in the NT area as the coordinating person between, on one hand, the advertising agency and the client and, on the other hand, the director. The initial inspiration for the advertisement comes from artistically minded people in the ad agency, in the NF quadrant's inventive font. When the producer finalizes a contract between his team and the agency representing the client, the coordinator goes to work amassing all the necessary materials, from cameras, trucks, and walkie talkies to hotels, food, keys, and notebooks—the ST quadrant. Finally, all the persons and all the psychic quadrants come together in the director, who functions as the top manager of the production itself. He is the SF King as well as the NF Creative Artist, the one who must create the final product on film, that which all the others could only imagine. To realize this goal, he is responsible for hiring the creative staff, such as the stylist, the cameramen, the electrical technicians, and the coordinators. Seeing these aspects of her job from the perspective of the type compass is useful for her, especially in functioning more effectively on the team.

TYPES IN THE CREATIVE PROCESS
IN BOTH WORK AND LOVE

This archetypal circle (figure 6.1, page 244), if we imagine ourselves as moving along it in a counterclockwise direction, is a metaphor for the elemental creative process which includes every aspect of typology. Counterclockwise is always associated in the mythic world with the "sinistra," etymologically with the "left," with the "sinister" chaotic dark side, which is the condition of creativity.

The creative process begins with an ST question that the person or life itself asks, which phalluslike, penetrates the Soul's feminine depth. This question incubates in the caring arms of the SF Parent,

The Creative Process in Our Inner Work

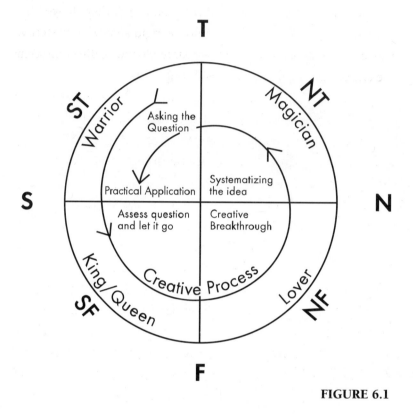

FIGURE 6.1

followed by the inspired fertilizing breakthrough and answer in the NF Creative Artist. This creative but rudimentary response is developed and systematized by the NT Creative Scientist, and then put into practice or production by the ST Warrior/Structural. Eventually, another question will follow from the more tough-minded ST, and if one trusts in the unconscious, another creative answer will emerge. Mary McCaulley, in a letter examining this process, suggests that each quadrant typically asks specific questions: the ST—what is it?; the SF—what matters?; the NF—what might be?; and the NT—how might it all fit? All these questions can be held in the SF incubator followed by the breakthrough in the deep NF dimension of the Soul. We also saw in chapter 4 that Peter Richardson's description of the creation of a temple began for him in the NF place and from there flowed in a counterclockwise direction. We cannot be rigid about the mysterious creative potentials of the Soul, yet its counterclockwise direction seems to be a necessary containing requisite.

All dream work seems to proceed in this circular direction, in which life poses a question, we sleep on it, then the answer emerges as a spontaneous and emotionally filled dream image in the NF quadrant. In waking life, we are then challenged to integrate the dream into a large NT vision. Dreams are the elemental creativity of the Psyche. Every dream is a creative attempt on the part of the Soul to help us realize our potential and to help us love ourselves, the bases of both our natural psychological health and the Golden Rule of our spiritual ethic. Then, we are challenged to do a critical reflective work on the dream's moral imperatives, and apply its just demands to everyday life.

The creative circle can also help us harmonize the realms of work and love that make up a family life. Sometimes we can hear all the voices in our typological mandala that make this harmony possible, but we often need a soul mate who hears differently than we do. Such a situation can work well but also needs to be carefully worked through. An example of one couple who were joined both in work and love illustrates the difficulties of different but complementary strengths and weaknesses. The woman is an extraverted ST, and he is an introverted NT. In the circular mandala, they sit side-by-side, she in the Warrior quadrant and he in the Magician quarter. Because he is oriented to inner knowledge, he seeks Jungian analysis, a Magician's enterprise. She seeks couple work, in which she takes the aggressive lead in pushing the interpersonal relationship. At work, she does all the tough organizational and data work, and he uses his creative organizing to explore new professional possibilities. He also has technical proficiency. Their partnership works well, yet he is discovering that he must muster, from his quiet introverted depth, a capacity to aggressively dialogue with his partner, whom he calls a "pit bull" when she brings her extraverted ST teeth to bear on an issue.

In this respect she evokes memories of his mother, who literally would slap his mouth as a child when he spoke out of turn. He was the client discussed before who dreamt of a faceless nine-year-old boy sleeping in a railroad car, with the mother plaintively showing photos of her child of earlier years with a face. Though his partner and he are located side-by-side on the mandala, her aggressive ESTJ type and his quieter, introspective INTJ makeup are miles apart in the realm of love. Can perspectives gained from this picturing of the type/archetype mandala help these two awaken a more loving commitment? She has, along with her ST Warrior, the beginnings of an SF parenting sense and he, along with his NT creative scientist's capacities, is beginning to experience in dreams the passionate feelings of the Lover, which he has stifled most of his life. She is challenged to be more responsive to his quiet, private needs and to seek help from her own unconscious in relating to his introverted, artistic sensitivities. He is challenged, in dream and imaging work, to evoke his awakening Lover, even while he is learning to claim his rights in the SF King and ST Warrior quadrants where she is so strong.

MINING THE DEPTH

To show this need to work deeply in claiming unrecognized potentials, it is helpful to reconfigure our diagram to include the element of depth by showing the circle as the surface of the cone, at the base of which is the Self. Figure 6.2 illustrates the fact that typological archetypal work must be understood integrally from the standpoint of the Self, which is both the hidden source of all archetypes, the embracing arms of both consciousness and the unconscious, and the basis of any fundamental transformation of one's sufferings and limitations. Most typology books, in showing individual differences and methods of integrating differences with others, merely describe a cognitive learning process

The Self as Source and Container of the Archetypes and the Total Life Process

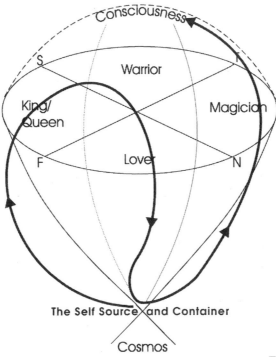

FIGURE 6.2

with little acknowledgment of the difficulties that one encounters when one goes against one's natural propensities. Both Naomi Quenk's *Besides Ourselves* and Angelo Spoto's *Jung's Typology in Perspective* attempt to correct this tendency by showing the emotional resistances encountered in integrating, for example, the inferior function, which is closely allied with the Self's potentials.

Figure 6.2 pictures the Self as the creative, integrating, and healing source of the entire typological and archetypal compass. In this three-dimensional view, the term "hitting rock bottom" is metaphorically very apt. Such a crisis describes one way in which a person is forced to enter into psychic depths and confront the Self. We begin to see that our pianist was pulled down to the bottom of his Soul, not just because he was an alcoholic but because, as in all of us, the deepest intention of the Soul is to open us to its limitless creative and healing resources and remind us that individuation is an endless journey. This client was stuck in his ST Shadow Warrior, desperately defending himself against any Lover intrusion. He could not leave this prison simply through willpower or intellectual understanding.

We also recall, in line with this subject, that Jung was referring in chapter 3 of this book to the Soul's depth and healing potential when he talked about the tragic consequence of the conflict between Freud's extraversion and Adler's introversion. They could not understand that their attitudinal opposite, represented by the other, resided also in their hidden Self, so they were unable to bear one another's opposite attitude and accompanying functions. Adler was probably an introverted SF and Freud, as we have discussed, an extraverted ST.

In most societies, people are often encouraged to read about an inspirational example as a way to the Self, based on the implicit theory that if one sufficiently lives the story of a famous artist or a great warrior, one will become like that person. While such stories do make an impact and can stimulate the process of individuation, we do not take on admirable characteristics just by reading biographies. Instead, we must find our own inner archetypal ideal as King or Queen, our own inner Magician as mentor, our own inner Warrior as a stimulus to achievement, and our own inner Lover as a teacher of intimacy. Inside mentors from dreams and inspirations are necessarily primary; outside mentors must always be subordinate to these inner guides. Besides, if one is too caught up in any one archetype, the Soul often presents an emotional and cognitive initiation into one of the other archetypal realms. So our pianist needed the dream that the Soul, in its Magician's wisdom, sent him, in which he was learning to surrender to the inner Lover and Parent, in the figure of the woman who sat beside him as he lay in his tomb. He also needed to do much inner imaginative work in order to feel grounded in the inner feminine and comfortable with outer females.

PLAYING WITH TYPE CONFLICTS IN THE REALM OF LOVE

Typological interactions can also be useful in understanding conflicts in the realm of love. For example, I have seen in analysis a married couple, in which John is the tough ESTJ Warrior and Jane the equally strong INFJ Lover. John had a difficult time surrendering to his feelings, to falling into his more feminine NF Lover anima capacity, which Jungian-oriented typologists also call his inferior archetype. Surrender for him, as for many men in our culture, meant only defeat. However, his Soul was constantly sending him dreams, in which he was challenged to relate empathically to women. In one, he was on a commercial airplane which a female pilot landed on a vast, high ridge. From there, he not only saw a modern city, but also his beloved summer place with its leisurely atmosphere, its great river, and his boat. In this dream, he felt he was touching his opposite, the NF Lover. In a later dream, he and this woman were copilots in a plane stripped of all luxuries and heading toward a common goal.

In another dream, a woman came to John's door and demanded immediate entrance. He argued logically with her while at the same time feeling the absurdity of his argument. He knew intuitively she had a right to come in, to be recognized as representing his feeling function. Meanwhile, her two little girls were playing behind her. Suddenly, they swished through his legs like tiny balls of energy, and he saw them in the room behind him. The young, playful feminine, the young Lovers, had come into his consciousness, even though his fearful Shadow Warrior resisted mightily. I wondered if his powerful masculine ST consciousness, which heretofore had dominated his private and professional life, could sufficiently surrender inwardly in order to be flexible and understanding in his relationship with his wife.

Meanwhile, John's NF wife, Jane, faced often by his anger and fear of intimacy, dreamt of dangerous males and angry masculine environ-ments. They also represented her angry, alcoholic father, as well as the dominant patriarchal culture that she saw destroying the natural world she loved. In one dream, she swam into the future:

> It is as if I am suddenly swimming into a time two thousand years hence. The water is very clear and I begin to see on the bottom countless numbers of what appear to be female mannequins all with their eyes wide open and staring up at me. I know that they were all once alive, all sensually alive women. But the culture has drowned them in these waters. I also begin to see that all the land around me is barren. It is a waste land. I see a few people on a pier, and I shout to them, warning them to change before it is too late.

While Jane's sensitive Soul was picking up the enormous societal issue of a patriarchy wasting Mother Earth as well as reducing women to mannequinlike creatures, she was also challenged personally in this dream, as an NF Lover, to confront in verbal or nonverbal dialogues and transform the opposing ST Warrior animus energies into her own inner powers and awaken her lifeless mannequins. This couple even-tually separated, then filed for divorce. They were unable to work out their typological differences and overcome their typological weak-nesses within this relationship.

THE SELF AND SYMBOLS OF TRANSFORMATION

Our diagram, which added the depth of the cone to the circle of types and archetypes, provides a plan for another category of psychic processes. These are symbols of transformation, in which negative, destructively uncontained or useless energies and images are changed into positive, containeds and useful energies and images. These symbols will often occur in dreams and in active imaginations. Sometimes the changes occur despite the dream ego's resistance or a waking state's inattentiveness, whereas in other instances, the changes occur in conjunction with significant dialogical work by the dream ego or the waking consciousness with the unconscious. The transformation itself, however, always occurs spontaneously in the unconscious, and enters consciousness with often abrupt and frightening strangeness. Consciousness, therefore, must be strong enough to contain this often fearful process of change. Typologically, this demands enough extraverted, sensate thinking differentiation and objectivity to toughen, so to speak, the ego's skin, so as to contain the change without being sucked into its powerful unconscious dynamics. One important assumption is central to this dynamic, an assumption based not just on Jungian psychology, but on the ancient wisdom found in the sacred stories in scripture, myths, and fairy tales: that when one faces one's inner enemy, the all embracing Self/Soul is ready to transform so-called negative experiences with the enemy into positive ones. The "enemy" that appears in these stories and in our dreams as representing addictions, compulsions, repetitive fears, and failures is striving to be our teacher, mentor, and source of additional inner authority and self-esteem.

The story of Jacob in the Old Testament (Genesis 32) is an example of this process. After years of exile Jacob decides to return home and face his brother, Esau, from whom he has stolen his birthright. The night before he meets his irate brother, he dreams that he is wrestling with an angel, symbolically representing God and his angry brother, as well as the related guilt he felt. In Jungian terms, the Godlike angel is a visitation from the unconscious and its divine source, demanding that Jacob face his sin and seek healing. In the language of typology, the sensitive Jacob, as an NF Lover, is also seeking to realize something of his tough-minded potential, found in his ST Warrior brother. Jacob will not let his adversary go until he receives a new name from him, Israel, reminding him that his life's calling has a larger cultural and spiritual significance. The angel also wounds him in the hip as a reminder of his human vulnerability. Most of all, Jacob is so changed internally that when Esau sees him he experiences his strength and holy presence and they embrace.

Let's play with some contemporary examples. One woman we'll call Betsy recalled that at age seven, her father walked into the house with another woman and coldly announced that he was leaving her and her mother. Her mother had a nervous breakdown, and Betsy had to live with her grandparents until her mother recovered. Later in life, Betsy entered analysis complaining of enormous rages that she called explosions. She exploded at everyone—bosses, lovers, her mother and father, her friends, and me, her analyst. She also had many dreams in which she endured seemingly life-threatening explosions. We talked about a needed conscious effort on her part to hold and contain her anger so that this raw emotion might change into its true essence— initiative. Anger is the emotion of initiative, of the thrusting, differen- tiating power of extraversion and assertion. In her outer life, she needed to accept her father and overcome her ancient rage. In her symbolic internalization of him, she needed to claim and transform what he internally represented, an extraverted, sensate, and thinking inner Warrior, who constantly exploded in anger in her waking and dream encounters.

Finally, after many months of work in analysis, Betsy dreamt that someone put a live bomb in her cupped hands. She held it, instead of dropping it and running. Suddenly it changed in the dream into a piggy bank with money in it. We spent weeks discussing this symbolic process of transformation. She painted the piggy bank several times with water colors. She was encouraged over and over again to get in touch with her initial fright in the dream and yet stay with the bomb and feel its change, from an instrument of destructive communication to the aesthetic NF creation of the piggy bank and the pragmatic ST earning of money—two creative ways to seize initiative. Both art and money talk. She had translated the ST Warrior antagonists, symbolically representing her father and others, into a more contained femininity of the piggy bank, which united the positive Warrior and the Artist/Lover who also knew how to make money. Through the process she was learning to integrate her ST and NF opposites in a symbolic experience of transformation. She was experiencing the meaning and healing value of what Jung described as symbols of transformation, these imaginal figures that change damaging emotions into constructive psychic factors. She was learning that developing typological potentials can occur somewhat in a conscious effort and reflection, but also more radically demands the creative transforming ground of our mysterious inner companion, the Soul, and its universal symbolic language.

Another client, a young man we'll call Tony, an INFP and a quiet, gentle person, was entering the Jesuit order, a vocational call that would demand much more ST Warrior energy than he felt he possessed. He asked the unconscious and prayed to God for this new capacity. He finally had this seminal dream:

> I am with a woman companion and many others. The two of us decide we want to be alone in a forest. We're enjoying our companionship when suddenly a tree grabs her in its branches, as if it were going to swallow her. I frantically try to pull her away. The branches become quiet and I look in to see against the trunk a large cocoon. I know she is in it. I pull it out, rip it apart and a young man my age emerges. In the next instant, we're standing side by side looking into a mirror and an older man, a mentor, is standing behind us and placing his hands on our two adjacent shoulders.

We will not fully understand this dream unless we first understand that, as an INFP Lover, Tony was most comfortable, though a male, with a sensitive consciousness that William James has characterized as tender-minded. The woman in the dream, therefore, was not to be understood as simply his inner bisexual opposite, called by Jung the Anima, but as his feminine alter ego. The symbolic transformation from feminine to masculine companion, supported further by the male mentor who touched their adjoining shoulders, helped Tony feel that he was ready for his new venture into the strongly masculine world of the Jesuit order, often called the marines of the Catholic Church. In typological terms, his natural INFP was now incorporating an added consciousness, an ESTJ confidence that he could meet the more tough-minded demands of the Jesuit order. He realized that such a dream represented a substantial seed for this needed development. This seed needed to be constantly nurtured with awareness and appropriate decisions in order for its type fruits to emerge fully in a mature INFP and ESTJ combined consciousness.

We examine yet another client, Helen, whose life and one transforming dream succinctly exemplify both life's new possibilities and past-based resistance. At a young age, she was tormented by destructive male relationships, beginning with her father and then emerging later with lovers. She was a successful student in engineering, and so was at home in her dominant sensate thinking strength. She clearly needed to acquire a capacity to love herself more deeply. Her sister had introduced her to Jung's thought, and she came to me for analysis when she was twenty-one. One of the turning points in her analysis came when she had the following dream:

> I am standing in a kitchen talking to my sister. There are other women there cooking food. Suddenly in the adjacent hallway, a young girl, probably about fourteen years old and wielding a knife in her right hand, announces she is there to kill my sister. I awaken frightened.

I asked if she had tried to confront and/or dialogue with this inner girl. She said she had not. I suggested that she try in the session. She closed her eyes and remained quiet for a few minutes. Then she reported what had happened in active imagination:

> I decided immediately to charge her, faking toward her head, then dropping low. As I did, I grabbed her knife arm and fell on top of her, hugging her tightly with my right arm. As I held her, she began to get smaller and smaller until she was a weeping five-year-old. I brought her to the ladies in the kitchen to feed her. Another surprising change had occurred: her knife had changed into a large key.

The girl with the knife and angry threat revealed the dreamer's aggressive state of mind that she had developed around ages twelve to fourteen, a time in which we come to realize an adult conceptual consciousness. When the dreamer, however, confronted and contained this inner adolescent figure, she became a whimpering, needy child, the typical remnant of a dysfunctional family life. This child needed the food of love, which the Soul, symbolized by the wise older women, provided in the dream.

However, a question remained: why had she had this dream at all? At this point, I asked Helen to tell me what was going on in her life. She told me that she had been thinking of quitting analysis. This admission began to shed further light on the dream, specifically, the knife that had changed into a key. Her sister had introduced her to this inner work. Her decision to quit was then metaphorically depicted in the dream as an attempt to kill the sister's inner counterpart. The knife, as her symbol of self-destructive anger, had changed into a key, a symbol of constructive initiative. The sister had been the "door" that had led the dreamer into this inner work. The transformation of the knife into the key indicated that she needed to continue therapy. Typologically, she was moving from her strongest ST Warrior quadrant to the NF Lover through the NT Magician's work in therapy.

TYPES AS PROBLEM AREAS IN THERAPY

All the examples given above have involved struggles that clients them-selves have experienced in working toward individuation through the development of both their preferred and less preferred types. I learned as a therapist that understanding and interpreting their struggles within the framework of typology gave us a safe, coherent, interactive space in which to seek necessary change. Most of my clients have been NFs and NTs, some SFs and, rarely, STs. This mix is similar to the type distribution found in our classes at the Jung Institute as well as in the membership of the Association for Psychological Type. Very often, ST clients come into therapy only reluctantly, because of the insistence of their lover or spouse. I am very conscious that I must stay in a practi-cal dialogue with STs, though very often their dreams pull them into SF Parental and NF Lover realms, as in the aforementioned case of the husband with his dreams of a female pilot. In such cases, STs begin to learn the language of the dream, even though, unlike clients from the three other couplings, these Warriors prefer ordinary language that is specific, logical, and to the point. They are resistant and uncomfort-able with the more turgid imagery of symbols. This means that ST clients present problems for therapists who seek to work in depth.

My personal typological consciousness, including my own E/INFP makeup, has evolved slowly over a long period of time, and I am aware that some former clients would have profited more from our work if I had had, at the time, a better understanding of types. Yet with only a limited knowledge of types, I began to realize that my NF preference made it easier to work with clients who preferred intuition or feeling in the SF, NF, and NT couplings. However, even given some typologi-cal harmony, I had difficulties with some clients in which type under-standing was crucial. I want now to present two examples of such difficulties. In the first case with Carol, an NF, I did not sufficiently understand the complexities and depth of her personal struggle and its typological factors. In the second case of Jason, an NT, I learned only slowly and painfully why, given his conscious type makeup, he so resisted understanding both the chemical cause of his pathology and the pharmacological basis of his healing.

In Carol's case, I worked with this client roughly between 1977 and 1979, before I was using the *Myers-Briggs Type Indicator®* (*MBTI®*). At this time I was beginning to understand individual type characteristics as factors in therapy, but was totally unaware of the value of the couplings. Carol was one of those clients whose sensitive nature both perplexed and intrigued me. After some time in analysis, I concluded she was an introverted intuitive and feeling type, following my usual analytical training. She was a third-year student in medicine, facing her impending work on a hospital floor with considerable panic. As a student, she would be required to diagnose patients and recommend treatment under the watchful eyes of the supervising physician and fellow students. This shook her intensely introverted nature, both in her fear of outward functioning before critical professionals and in inward devalued aspects of her intuitive and feeling functions.

She came into therapy because of her high anxiety about this extraverted challenge. Adding to her anxiety, she was in her late twenties, at a time of life in which her father had mentally collapsed. Carol was afraid that her life would parallel her father's. Before she came to me, she had been in a short Freudian analysis that she had found unsatisfactory because the analyst had refused to deal with her spiritual concerns or her fantasies.

Her fantasies were surprisingly intense, and our mutual decision to consider them seriously provided one of the major themes of our analytic work. She reported an ongoing daydream, in which on weekends she would lie for hours watching, as she put it, "my inside soap opera." In her teen years, this inner drama was centered on four fictional characters: a mother, father, brother, and sister. In college and medical school, the quaternity had changed to the brother, sister, and their two spouses.

We realized that this inner imaginal work would bear fruit for her only if she could begin an active conscious contact with the four characters and their other companions. This represents a therapeutic procedure that is called active imagination in Jungian psychology. As her work with active imagination and our therapeutic alliance progressed, I began to realize that the four characters in her "soap opera" each symbolically represented one of the four functions. (At this point in my consciousness I was not working with the couplings.) Her four functions were aligned as shown in figure 6.3: her dominant function as IF; her first auxiliary as EN; her second auxiliary as IS; and her inferior function as ET. I realized much later this figure pictured her INFP makeup exactly. Her subsequent work with each of the characters helped her deal with the strengths and weaknesses of her type makeup.

Carol's Individual Type Mandala and Her Inner Figures

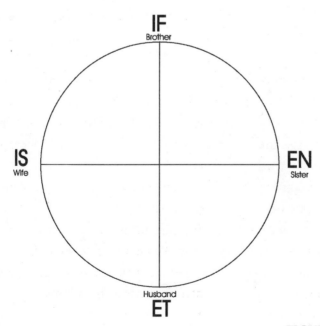

FIGURE 6.3

She began her work with the inner brother, who I thought was an extraverted feeling type, representing the kind of boldness she needed in her work. I was recently in contact with Carol, now almost twenty years after our work together. Today, she believes that the brother was an introverted feeling type like her, but more confident in relating to society. In her active imagination work with her inner story, she would walk down stone steps and meet the imaginary brother in an underground place. There he took on an increasingly shamanic or Magician's NT role. He constructed a shield for her, on which a powerful hawk was painted, sitting sideways and looking with piercing eyes straight at the observer. We considered this shield a symbol of a tough-skinned warrior persona, which she needed in order to handle societal and other extraverted challenges. After developing an inner relationship with the brother, she dealt with the fantasy character, the sister, who I believed was the first auxiliary, her extraverted intuitive function, even though this character lacked some of the imaginative vitality so typical of such a type. Following the sister, Carol met with the wife of the brother in this drama, who, in her ethereal ways, was Carol's introverted sensate function and the second auxiliary or tertiary function.

Finally, the story moved to the husband of the inner sister, who was a doctor and, as an extraverted thinking type, represented Carol's inferior or least developed function. We saw already in the introduction, in conjunction with figure 1.1 (page 34), that the inferior function plays itself out as a very archaic, clumsy, tenuous subpersonality that can often appear in dreams and fantasies as dangerous, invasive, or challenging figures. However, like all negative psychic factors, it is also at the cutting edge of an emergent creative life, like the dramatic floral outbursts in the aftermath of a forest fire. At this point in her imagined story, disaster struck both in Carol's inner drama and in her outer life. In the interior scenario, the doctor became ill, and as a result, the entire inner community became sick. Carol, in her frightened reaction, discontinued attending to her daydream and our therapeutic relationship reached a critical stage. Carol was threatening to quit medical school as well as therapy. At this point, common sense, compassion, and my own values dictated that I encourage her to complete the last few months of school.

Accordingly, I counseled Carol to continue her inner work so as to strengthen her capacity to finish school. Also, a resolution had begun to occur in her fantasy world in which members of the community began to minister to the doctor. Carol's soul seemed to be at peace, and she completed her medical studies.

Carol's present memories include her recollection of a significant dream at this critical stage of her story. She dreamt that, while in a boat in the company of an old man who had rescued a woman from the water, the boat sank and Carol, as dreamer, was swept into a dangerous section of the water. It was a "very scary, ugly swamplike area under another large dock." No one, including the old man, was available to help her. I did not remember the dream this way. Instead, I recalled a dream, maybe in my own fantasy, in which Carol pushed an old man off the dock, representing her rage against medicine but also claiming her own powers. I also felt that the old man in both cases might have represented something of my own inadequacies and her anger toward me during this very stressful time in her life and in our work.

However, Carol now feels that I was mistaken in urging her to complete her last few months in medical school. In any event, her subsequent residency in California quickly turned into a disaster. During this residency, a young man, who had been in therapy with her for four months and with whom she felt a strong empathic connection, committed suicide. Carol says that "his suicide was such that it has affected the whole rest of my life," which led not only to her leaving the medical profession, but also to letting go of friends, ignoring dream work, and cutting "my soul off from everything except my children for the next ten years."

Carol now feels that the swamp dream was in effect commenting on her complete incompatibility with medicine. She wrote in her recent letter that it also "was an image of what was happening in therapy to me at that time. My real inner nature was not being supported and I was, in effect, being swept away by unconscious forces which I couldn't control." I, as the therapist, might have been represented by the old man who had coaxed her into the boat and then could not save her.

As she now looks back at our work, she feels that while she learned very much about the value of her imaginative powers, I had encouraged her too strongly to complete her studies and graduate. The sickness of the doctor in her fantasy, then, had not only to do with what we had perceived to be her inferior extraverted thinking function but also represented her rage toward the medical profession that had seriously devastated her father and which demanded, in her words, an "extraverted, thinking, sensation type of work," that was totally alien to her INFP nature. I, as her "doctor," was also implicated in this generalized anger.

The suicide of her patient, which affected Carol so deeply, should not in any way be connected to Carol's painful process of medical training. This self-induced death was a tragic behavior on the part of the young man, which can haunt all those in the helping professions, even though we do all that we can to counter such outcomes. When such tragedies occur, and many therapists including myself have experienced them, one can only be with and grieve with the family, and grieve also at the recognition of our own limitations.

Also, I feel that Carol, looking back, read too much negativity into the swamp dream. Given the events that occurred during her last months in medical school, the dream represented the inner and outer chaos that accompanied her encounter with her inferior thinking function and her ST coupling, an encounter that included her resistance to and dissatisfaction with her medical studies and her fearful experiences with the doctor in the inner soap opera. Further, the Soul's dynamism never ends with images of death, illness, or drowning. Life, health, and buoyancy follow in other dreams and in life if one persists in the darkness, in what we traditionally call the *dark night of the Soul*. Carol did persist, the inner doctor was healed, and she graduated, confirming her own healing potentials.

Today, Carol feels that, within her NF central personality, she has always been a dominant intuitive, rather than the dominant feeling type which we had both believed. Following the inner dynamic of the *MBTI*, this would make her an INFJ. She felt that she had covered up her intuitive strength in favor of her feeling function because she feared that the loose, fluid perceptions of intuition "would lead into madness, as [they] did for my father." When I asked her whether her intuitive strength favored the feeling or thinking function as its coupling partner, she opted emphatically for feeling. Again, she confirmed her basic NF strength.

Two significant observations arise from this discussion. First, the dominance of N or F is not as important as the expanded archetypal meaning of the NF coupling, in which her imaginative perceptions richly combine with her strong feelings in realizing meaningful human relationships and, above all, creative work. Carol now realizes that she has always been called to be an artist rather than a psychiatrist. She is beginning to write. Secondly, the introverted intuitive and feeling combination is in itself a typological synonym for a highly sensitive person, one who can get too readily swamped by the experiences of others. It is no wonder this coupling was named the Oceanic by the Osmond group. As therapists, therefore, we must be exceedingly conscious of the help that an INFP or an INFJ needs to build a stronger defense against fusion with others, as Carol's inner brother was trying to do in providing her a shield. Today, knowing what I now do about typology, I would have encouraged Carol more in this regard.

Let us now briefly consider Carol's social stresses and inner family dynamics from the standpoint of the couplings. Had I been more conscious of the couplings as significant archetypal structures, I would have come up with the configuration in figure 6.4.

Carol's NF combination, as her dominant archetype, brought her into a painful, conflicting struggle with the medical profession's rigid ST Structural approach. The inner doctor as an ST was and is representative of her inferior coupling, so understandably she dealt with this inner fantasy figure last. Carol began her imaginative work with her soap opera brother who demonstrated NF and NT features in his artistic and shamanic roles. In his NF capacities, the brother created for her a protective shield against a feared ST society. He also articulated for her an NT's supportive theoretical bridge to her ST potentials, so she could complete her studies and deal more effectively with the

Carol's Inner Figures as Coupling Archetypes

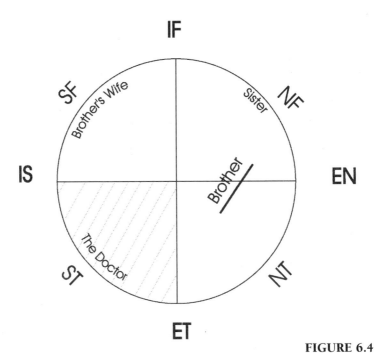

FIGURE 6.4

ongoing pragmatics of life. I see the sister now as representing Carol's NF strength, which she has steadily learned to claim, and the brother's wife as an SF, thus completing the quaternity and the inner play of the couplings in her personal compass.

Looking back over twenty years at my interaction with this early client, I wish I had had more of the insights available through typology and Jungian psychology's overall wisdom to have helped her understand what was necessary to have withstood the vicissitudes of her life and her own typological limitations. Now I am more sensitive to the implications of typology for my clients, even when specific psychosomatic factors, such as substance abuse, might deflect my attention from typological issues. Jason, a recent client, is such a case.

Jason is an extraverted intuitive thinking perceptive (ENTP) type, whom I saw two years ago. All studies of these ENTP types show them to be confident leaders in any area that they pursue, as long as they can be in charge and as long as they can find continual variety and new challenges. In childhood, they are strong-willed individuals, and as typical NTs they very quickly challenge authority. They easily negotiate school tasks with practically no help from parents.

Jason was a leader from the beginning. Sometimes, however, given his strong assertive propensities, he alienated friends by reacting arrogantly or impatiently to their limitations in grasping his big picture of life. Then Jason explored LSD for the first time and had a "bad trip." He was somewhat innocent, since what was supposed to have been a minimal amount turned out to be of unusual strength. Its potency broke open his usual barriers and filters between consciousness and the unconscious, and he experienced many effects: fear of dying, the felt presence of a powerful Godlike figure who both frightened him and fascinated him, hallucinations, paranoiac/psychotic feelings and images, pain, extreme fatigue, and insomnia. He finally entered a hospital where he received an antipsychotic drug and then was quickly released. He stayed on the drug until he took a trip to South America.

When he returned home, he remained in a kind of twilight zone. A Freudian-oriented analyst dismissed his drug-related experiences of God as an "infantile hallucination." The psychiatrist did, however, help him get in touch with his feelings and his SF parental, empathic concerns, which his NT consciousness, as opposite to the SF in the Soul's circle, usually had a difficult time touching. However, he suddenly quit therapy, again abandoned his antipsychotic drug and, after another hospitalization, came to see me.

I could not get him to discuss his feelings. He only minimally acknowledged that the LSD had influenced his behavior, and would not agree that the antipsychotic drug had been the main factor in clearing his mind in two hospitalizations. We painstakingly reviewed his behavior after each hospital stay. He was confronted with the fact that, without the medication, he consistently lost conscious control and could not make decisions or hold a job. He finally talked about his hallucinations, in which he felt his mind had been synchronistically in touch with and controlling many other persons. I helped him see that the objective content of the unconscious is holistic and synchronistic, as all of the great religions teach, but that his ego could not be the originator of this awareness. In typological terms, it was difficult getting him to climb down from his strong ENTP place and acknowledge that the LSD's subtle sensing effects had brought him to his knees.

I realized that one's dominant type gives a therapist a specific picture of such a client's normal state of mind and behavior, and helps the therapist look beyond a client's normal conscious borders to the unconscious and see its resistances and psychic blinders, noting the inferior function and the inferior archetypal coupling.

In Jason's case, given his ENTP traits, he could not concede that a small amount of mineral, LSD, had brought him low, and that a small amount of the antipsychotic drug had helped him regain his sanity. The LSD was not responsible for the content of his unconscious, but only for opening a psychic dam which allowed powerful images to flood his ego. Along with humbly taking the corrective medicine he also faced a spiritual challenge: to find, in a deep and dark ground, some other aspects of himself.

Jason's deep, dark ground is typologically both his inferior function, introverted sensing, and his inferior coupling, the SF King/Moralist. The particulars of his IS inferiority clearly demonstrate why he was unable to concede the power of both the LSD and the corrective drug. In this case, IS is actually a psychic "place" that is hidden within the body, in the sensations of Jason's nerves and muscles, sensations which work quietly and almost invisibly, like germs. But given a powerful hallucinogen like LSD, these primitive sensations and their corresponding emotions, usually well contained within bodily and mental complexes, emerge as monsters and specters to the unsuspecting and frightened ego. Jason's extraverted intuitive and thinking coupling, with its large perspectives, could usually successfully battle weaker or equal adversaries in the visible outer society or in obvious inner mental counterparts. However, his Magician's mind, which can easily conceive of large internal truths, could not or would not recognize the power of the minute material ingredients which make up both the LSD and the antipsychotic drugs.

Also Jason was spiritually challenged to discover the deeper meaning of his inferior sensing feeling coupling—its moral imperatives. He would use it in a cocky, clumsy, moralistic way to put down friends and family. Now, he was challenged to embrace an authentic humility as expressed in a series of dreams. In one, he was told to lie in the mud like a pig, and enjoy the feeling of the mud, the humus, from which, as we learn from *Webster's,* the word "humble" is derived. In another dream, he tried to climb to a high place on a cliff to be with both his well-established father and a beloved mentor, people who were secure in love and work. Jason, for the first time in his life feeling wretched and insecure, could not negotiate the last vertical wall. He was implicitly being told to go down and get grounded in the nearby sand and the ocean, from which the cliff arose. Finally, the dream message from the unconscious, which Jung has called the vox Dei, "the voice of God," was even more explicit. He realized that at the end of a vague series of events he was standing on the ground and at the bottom rung of a ladder. He could only go up, but he had to start, humbly, at the bottom of his Soul. As among AA followers, he was challenged to surrender his NT consciousness and trust God in the low-down places of his Soul. There, his authentic holistic identity with all the types as well as his preestablished relationships with all beings and with the Divine were to be found.

In the above two cases of Carol and Jason, I shared with both a common dominant intuition, although Carol's was combined with a strong introversion and mine with a mild extraversion. All three of us shared a common sensate inferiority. I, like Carol, am an NF, so we needed to avoid fusion and not turn the therapeutic relationship into a mutual admiration society. The same difficulty was more remote with Jason, though we still shared a common intuition as we sat side-by-side, NT and NF, on the circle. More serious difficulties arose when I, as an NF, worked with an ST such as John in the case of him and his wife. For one thing, we sat opposite to one another on the Compass. Moreover, John had suffered serious abandonment from his very cold mother, and I had experienced warmth and containment from mine. In the circle of life, beyond our individual types, I was grounded in a strong SF quarter of life, but suffered a more fearful confrontation with the ST world when I tried to mimic it. John was a successful engineer and I had been a failed one in our ST society. On the other hand, I learned, after many fearful and confusing meanderings, to welcome my breakdown and plunge into the NF chaos. John resisted with all his might this fearful feminine and childlike place. He would rage at me when he felt I was not containing him with sensing warmth as a mother would. I would get impatient with his reluctance to spend therapeutic time in the Oceanic NF place to which all of his dreams' feminine and childlike figures were calling him. Also, because he knew I was an NF, he felt he was surrendering his powerfully defended ST ego to me. Our therapeutic alliance ended in an uncomfortable truce and inconclusiveness when he had to move.

A SHORT THEORETICAL INTERLUDE

With Carol, we see a person who has great NF sensitivities and capacities, has beautifully developed her SF parenting, has NT glimmerings, but is considerably hostile to an ST worldview. With Jason, we see a young man who is only beginning to assimilate his SF function, with its mentoring and parenting possibilities. He has had particular difficulty with his introverted corporeally grounded sensing function, particularly when he experienced this function as both damaged and healed by small amounts of chemicals. John, on the other hand, was bitter in both his inferior feeling and his inferior SF coupling because he felt that his mother, Jane, and I had abandoned him in the final analysis. His Soul, however, was striving for healing to the last.

However, all these typological and archetypal perspectives should not obscure the fact that the Soul, also called the Self, as the fundamental principle of life, is the center, source, and container of the entire Compass, and is, above all, the dramatic playwright of all of its personalities. Jung says the Self is the "complex of all opposites," the reconciler of all the typical and archetypal resistances and polar tensions that the above persons have experienced. These reconciliations do not necessarily follow the usual dominant, auxiliary, and inferior function linear dynamic. As we will see in chapter 9, the Self in adulthood does not push us linearly, but invites us in its circle of life to use the types we need in a given moment of time. The psyche, with its creative dreaming, is not just a balancer of opposites but also a promoter of growth. If a particular type or archetype is not sufficiently developed, the Soul seeks its growth and awakening. Overall, Jung's total psychology and his typology demonstrate that the Self is consistently striving to work dynamically toward individuation, which demands a balance between all aspects of the personality. So Carol has discovered herself as an NF artist, Jason needs to be sensitive to his SF order and temptation to be moralistic, and John needs to find an inner self-love.

In struggling to express this central core belief, Jung found similarities between the metaphors of alchemy and Taoism. As mankind's first attempt at the science of chemistry, alchemy both explored processes for physically transforming base substances into precious metals, and saw this chemistry as an allegory of spiritual transformation occurring in the interplay of opposites. Taoism, as we have seen in chapter 2, shares this allegorical imaging within ever-present Yang/Yin archetypal poles. Taoism works directly in focused meditations with the physical energies of the body, so as to transform them into the revitalizing spiritual energies called the Chi.

In 1928, as recorded in his autobiography, *Memories, Dreams, Reflections,* Jung was beginning to realize the similarity in alchemy, Taoist meditations, and his psychological processes of transformation. He received from his friend Richard Wilhelm a Chinese Taoist alchemical meditation treatise called *The Secret of the Golden Flower.* Jung wrote that this "was the first event which broke through my isolation. I became aware of an affinity. I could establish ties with something and someone."[6]

After his break with Freud, Jung had begun a slow recovery from his self-imposed isolation by publishing his *Psychological Types* book in 1921. He says in his 1925 Seminar that his book attempted to show the slowly evolving and even confusing consciousness of the human psyche. He was groping for an understanding that went beyond the manifest reasons he gave for writing *Psychological Types*. These reasons included his split with Freud and the type differences he observed between Freud and Adler in both their personalities and their theories. He continues:

I could perfectly well say this was the way the book came about and make an end of it there. But there is another side, a weaving about among mistakes . . . which is always difficult for a man to make public.[7]

He records further that in the book that led to his 1913 split from Freud, *The Psychology of the Unconscious,* he had studied and interpreted quite consciously a young woman's mythlike fantasy, which had emerged from her unconscious. Then, after his break with Freud, he had begun to be "interested in the material of the unconscious," which led him to realize that "this is the only way to get at myth-formation"[8] and to understand humanity's Great Stories. This conviction had evolved particularly since in his "creative illness" he had experienced the unconscious' dark, oceanic depths within himself. In his painful explorations, he experienced a "weaving about among mistakes" that led eventually to his grand schema of the holistic psyche. His schema evolved out of

empirical material from my patients, but the solution of the problem I drew from the inside, from my observations of the unconscious process. I have tried to fuse these two currents of outer and inner experience in the book of the *Types.*[9]

However, Jung needed a more objective affirmation that he was on the right track, and Taoism provided an ancient social support. As we saw in chapter 2, typology and Taoism became closely linked in Jung's life. When in 1929, he wrote a "Commentary on The Secret of the Golden Flower," he noted the general alchemical transformations that are reported in that Chinese text, such as dark into light and heavy physical energies into lighter, spiritual energies.[10]

Those who practice Taoist Chi Kung exercises know from experience these transformations.[11] For example, the Inner Smile meditation directs one to change the physical (sensing) energy of the heart, through visualizing a golden stream (intuition) into a spiritual loving (feeling) energy. Through such imaginings and an accompanying belief in this theory and practice, real physical changes occur. In these exercises, when one is imaginatively breathing healing energy from the universe into a specific organ, the crass action of breathing in oxygen and breathing out carbon dioxide is changed into Chi, into a spiritual energy that is often intensely felt. When one imagines breathing the Chi down the spine, for example, or into one's eyes, one can feel the flow of energy. The Chi is unseen but very real. The transformation via the imagination from physical breath to Spirit (meaning breath, from the Latin, spiritus) is physically felt. The sensing function's experience of physical breathing is changed in and through the imaginative powers of intuition and the loving capacities of feeling into subtle energy. These exercises, invented within an NT/Taoist philosophy, are practiced in the NF Lover realm of the Soul's compass. In exercises for enhancing sexual powers, the process of imaginatively controlled breathing changes the energy in the sexual organs into a sensual Chi that is consciously fed, again by the imagination, to all systems of the body. The various organs are, in effect, told by the meditating person: "I am sexually alive. Awaken and participate in this healthful, spiritual, and sensual living."

Typology shows how our human energies, as captured in the individual and coupled types, are dynamic factors and aspects of personality similar to the structures and energies of alchemical Taoism. When the energy of a misused dominant coupling leads to an unbalanced and destructive life, the psyche seeks to rebalance us and further growth through dreams, through the appropriate loving interventions or observed examples of friends and family who are often of different types, and through the experiences and interpretations of even synchronistic or providential events. These interventions often lead to the transformation of energies, which make possible wholeness and balance between the various parts of the personal compass.

Jung's entire system finds echoes in the principles and metaphors of alchemy and Taoism, while firmly rooting itself in the Judaic-Christian spiritual tradition. Typology is an entering point in understanding all of these archetypal and playful processes of transformation, as we have sought to show in this chapter.

A COMPARATIVE LOOK AT PSYCHOLOGICAL THEORIES WITHIN THE TYPE COMPASS

The second quotation at the head of this chapter by James Hillman leads us to consider his thought-provoking ideas about typology. He rightfully rejects any rigid type categorizing as blocking the flux, incongruities, and images of a uniquely personal individuation. Hillman criticizes the specificity of scoring traits, of naming and measuring of traits in opposition to imaging and experiencing the archetypal mystery of each type. So he is opposed to any instrument that measures human traits. His criticism of typology in this regard, as already noted elsewhere, given as part of the distinguished Eranos lectures at Ascona, Switzerland in 1980, deserves further thought as we now imagine playing with the different psychological theories within the compass' couplings.[12]

Jung would certainly have agreed with Hillman when Jung told readers to spend time with chapters 2 and 5 of *Psychological Types* to truly understand the dynamics of types. However, the structures and testing of types are like paint to the artist, a rather crass medium that can have ordinary or sublime results. Jung understood the potential for the misuse of typology, but when he had the opportunity he did not remove chapter 10, which describes the types as traits, from later publications of his book. He said, in effect, that categories are all right as long as they are, like bones to flesh, that which gives specific order to the uniqueness of each person and the dynamics of relationships. Besides, the type circle would be bereft of its wholeness and of its integrity without the traits, tests, research, and pragmatic systematizing which are characteristics of the ST mentality. This is why Jung spoke so favorably of Myers' work in his 1950 letter, which effectively anticipates and corrects Hillman's idiosyncratic dismissal of a types technology.

I suggest here that Hillman's view of the *MBTI's* work suffers the same difficulty that two other Jungians, June Singer and Mary Loomis, display when they reject the typological cross and circle, with its four types, as too restrictive in understanding human potential (see chapter 10). All these criticisms of the *MBTI* have to do with a broader issue of the general estrangement between Jungian analysts and *MBTI* researchers and practitioners. Only a few Jungians have ever read Myers' *Gifts Differing* or have known of her and her mother's communications with Jung, and the depth of their dedication to and passion for Jung's theory and their instrument. Further, few Jungians know that Briggs and Myers, as well as Mary McCaulley, in spite of their introverted intuitive feeling preferences, acquired a mountain of research over five decades that substantiates the Jung/*MBTI* theory. Even though their makeup is hardly a typological fit for such an enterprise, they have heroically pursued this work because of their concern for a human society in which too much needless, tragic suffering occurs due to a lack of understanding of human differences.

This long-term, damaging split between Jungian analysts and typologists gives further perspective to the following discussion, raised by Hillman, of the place of types in understanding different theories.

As a broad prelude to this discussion, we need to consider what Jung wrote in the epilogue to *Psychological Types* about both the uniformity and the uniqueness of the human makeup in general:

> I myself am so profoundly convinced of the uniformity of
> the psyche that I have even summed it up in the concept
> of the collective unconscious, as a universal and homoge-
> neous substratum whose uniformity is such that one finds
> the same myth and fairy tale motifs in all corners of the

earth. . . . But this fundamental homogeneity is offset by an equally great heterogeneity of the conscious psyche. What immeasurable distances lie between the consciousness of a primitive, a Periclean Athenean and a modern European! . . . Quite apart from the differences among individuals whose innermost natures are separated by stellar differences, the types, as classes of individuals, are themselves to a very large extent different from one another, and it is to the existence of these types that we must ascribe the differences of views in general.[13]

Jung makes a distinction between, on one hand, the homogeneity of the collective unconscious, the consequential similarity of human stories throughout the world and the "classes of individuals" or types, and the different theories that issue from such "classes," and, on the other hand, the heterogeneity, the endlessly idiosyncratic ways in which each individual consciously lives out his common nature. Heterogeneity balances homogeneity. So, by extension, we could say that Jung would value both the *MBTI*'s shared traits and Hillman's imaginal variations. Jung could have added that, even though the collective unconscious has a certain uniformity, it gives birth to endlessly creative ways of imaging and experiencing that uniformity.

Hillman marshals another argument against typing individuals, besides his abhorrence of categorizing human uniqueness. He holds that typology does not necessarily apply to individuals at all, but only to the differences in human theories in psychology and in any field of human thought. Hillman writes:

Jung did not intend his typology to be used for typing persons. Precisely the way in which his types are used and experimented with in the Grey-Wheelwright and Briggs-Myers tests—the clinical scientism—is what Jung expressly did not intend.[14]

Hillman holds, therefore, that the only intention of Jung's *Psychological Types* book is to "provide a critical psychology . . . first and foremost . . . for the research worker" as a means of understanding different psychological systems. But Hillman leaves out Jung's other reasons, recorded in the same paragraph, for writing his *Psychological Types* book. Jung says it is "a great help in understanding the wide variations that occur among individuals," as well as "an essential means for determining the 'personal equation' of the practicing psychologist, who, armed with an exact knowledge of his differentiated and inferior functions, can avoid many serious blunders in dealing with his patients."[15] Jung was emphasizing here that typology was not intended as an excuse to "classify human beings into categories" or "to stick labels on people at first sight." Instead, Jung stresses the importance of the intrapsychic and relational dynamics that occur within and between individuals who are different from one another. Jung then says of therapists that they are to be armed with "an exact knowledge of . . . differentiated and inferior functions," that is, their traits. While the traits and categories are subservient to the dynamics of the relationships, they are there, as alive and as present as type images. Further, Jung writes in *Psychological Types* that the very genesis of the book came from his work with individuals, not with theories:

> This book is the fruit of nearly twenty years' work in the domain of practical psychology. It grew gradually in my thoughts, taking shape from the countless impressions and experiences as a psychiatrist in the treatment of nervous diseases, from intercourse with men and women of all social levels, from my personal dealings with friend and foe alike, and, finally, from a critique of my own psychological peculiarities.[16]

Hillman also neglects Jung's discussion in the *Psychological Types* epilogue of how individual typologies are the source of every system of human thought. Jung says there quite clearly that every human theory—he specifies philosophies at that point—is dependent on the typology of its creator and that the theory's followers must to some extent be the same type so as to harmonize with the creator of the theory: "every philosophy that is not just a history of philosophy depends on a personal psychological premise." Then Jung adds:

> the standpoint of a particular philosopher often has a considerable following. It is acceptable to his followers not because they echo him without thinking, but because it is something they can fully understand and appreciate. . . . The peculiarity of the standpoint which is understood and acknowledged by his followers must therefore correspond to a *typical* [italics, Jung's] personal attitude, which in the same or a similar form has many representatives in a society.[17]

Therefore, Jung insists that viewing both the individual and human theory through the perspective of typology is useful. Further, following the major theme of this book, rather than focusing on the individual functions and their vectorlike relations, the couplings unfold a kind of field theory which makes typology even more valuable as a tool for understanding differences. The couplings clarify how typology both forms the basis of "a critical psychology"[18] and "furnishes a clue to the fundamental differences in the psychological theories."[19] When Jung was writing, those psychological theories in his mind were mainly Freudian, Adlerian, and his own. Today, because psychologies have proliferated over the many intervening decades, it is even more valuable to recognize how various theories fall into different typological quadrants.

Moving around the type circle (figure 6.5), we can locate each theory in one dominant and in several subordinate quadrants. Jung's psychology fits primarily into the NT quadrant, because of its holistic worldview, based on the microcosmic Self as a spiritual, creative, and autonomous source and inner connector with the Cosmos. It also fits

Psychological Theories in the Quadrants

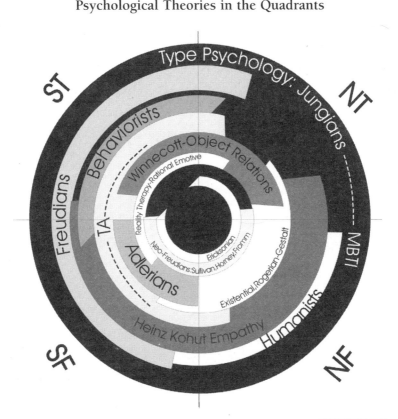

FIGURE 6.5

into the NF quadrant because of its emotionally centered complexes, and because experiences of symbolic transformation, conscious dialogues with the inner images, and the entire individuation process cannot occur without the "emotional value" of the feeling function. Finally, Jung's psychology circles the quadrants because of its typological theory, which is conceived as the Compass of the Soul. Freudian psychoanalysis, as the Osmond group shows, belongs first in the ST quadrant and then extends, with its strong moralistic overtones, into the parental SF place.[20] Transactional Analysis (TA) covers the same range as the Freudians, with its objective Adult Ego State and its

Parental Ego Stage, but also extends, with its Child Ego State, into the NF area. The Ericksonian school, having moved from Freud's psychosexual to a psychosocial view of development with its magnificently imagined eight ages of life, has a central and holistic NT outlook, like Jung's system. It also flows into the NF quadrant, because it recognizes personal virtues in each stage, beginning with trust versus mistrust. Because of the breadth and depth of its eight life crises, it, too, circles the type globe. Object Relations retains Freud's conflict theory and is also psychosocial in its assimilation of outside objects, beginning especially with parenting persons (SF). Kohut and the self psychologists de-emphasize the Freudian/Object Relations inner conflicts, while retaining some of the Freudian terminology (ST). They stress the internalization of the child-parent relations, the therapeutic focus on empathic intervention as the healing tool (SF) and the basic hunger for self-esteem (NF). Adler's system has a particularly strong SF orientation because of its main parental moral injunction, "this is how the world should be"; its emphasis on education and family configurations also extends it into the NF quarters. The Neo-Freudians, such as Sullivan, Horney, and Fromm, were opposed to Freud's drive theory and stressed development based on social relations (SF and NF). Existential, Gestalt, and Rogerian psychologies, all assuming self-unfolding and self-responsibility and grouped under the larger Humanistic school, are centered in the NF quadrant. They also extend into the NT's creative and expansive systems and the SF's caring orientation. The first, Existential psychology, stresses the evolving of a meaningful consciousness as a "being in the world" faced with life's suffering. The second, Gestalt psychology, focuses on processing life in the here and now through interpersonal and intrapsychic dialogues. The third, Rogerian psychology, considers mainly the healing of pathologies through a sensitive articulation of the other's feelings and an accompanying unconditional positive regard, all NF characteristics. Behavioral psychology, Rational Emotive therapy, and Reality therapy, all assuming as they do that irrational belief systems can be overcome through logically cognitive and rational interventions, belong mainly in the ST quadrant.

Throughout this exploration of type and archetype we have stressed the importance of the quaternity, as a skeletal structure for the infinite varieties of human types, experiences, and theories. While writing the last sections of this chapter I had the following dream, which communicated such clarity and numinosity that it demanded serious attention:

> I am observing and commenting on a great crowd that is moving fanlike in every direction from what seems to be a point on the earth. Yet there is also a sense of a quaternity of movement, that in some way the mass of mankind is proceeding in four great sections. The dream people are also eager to hear about these patterns.

An interpretation of the dream might conclude that the point on the earth and out of the earth is the Self or Soul, the unique source of identity and personal power. The fanlike movement feels like the great cone of existence divided into the four directions and into the four functional and archetypal quadrants, reflecting my present preoccupation with the types. Each of us is different and also each of us is one with the whole of being. Further, different general theories in every area of human thought participate in these four archetypal directions.

Now we need to consider the *Myers-Briggs Type Indicator* as the most important explicator of Jung's four archetypal directions of our psychic compass.

Notes

1. C. G. Jung, *CW,* vol. 6, *Psychological Types,* English edition, translated by H. G. Baynes (1923; rpt., Princeton NJ: Princeton University Press, 1971), para. 93.

2. James Hillman, *Egalitarian Typologies versus the Perception of the Unique,* Eranos Foundation, Ascona, Switzerland (Dallas TX: Spring Publications, [1986] c. 1980), pp. 52–53.

3. Abby Whiteside, *Mastering the Chopin Etudes and Other Essays* (New York: Charles Scribner's Sons, 1969), p. 4.

4. Richard Wilhelm, translated by C. F. Baynes, with a foreword by C. G. Jung, *The I Ching or Book of Changes* (London: Routledge and Kegan Paul, 1968), p. 186.

5. Jung, "The Stages of Life," *CW,* vol. 8, *The Structure and Dynamics of the Psyche* (Princeton NJ: Princeton University Press, 1960), para. 795: "In conclusion I would like to come back for a moment to the comparison with the sun. The one hundred and eighty degrees of the arc of life are divisible in four parts. The first quarter, lying to the east, is childhood, that state in which we are a problem for others but are not yet conscious of any problems of our own [SF Parental]. Conscious problems fill out the second and third quarter [ST Structural's pragmatic challenges and the NT Ethereal's ultimate concerns]; while in the last, in extreme old age, we descend again into condition, where, regardless of our state of consciousness, we once more become something of a problem for others [NF Oceanic's childlike place]." In Jung's article, however, on the stages of life, Jung shows that the third quarter involves a chaotic plunge into the intuitive's images and the feeling's emotional values (the NF quadrant), followed by theoretical understandings of these experiences in the NT quadrant. We will take up this process again in chapter 9.

6. Jung, *Memories, Dreams, Reflections* (New York: Pantheon Books, 1961), p. 197.

7. Jung, *Analytical Psychology: Notes of the Seminar Given in 1925* (Princeton NJ: Princeton University Press, 1989), p. 32.

8. Ibid., p. 34.

9. Ibid.

10. Jung, *CW,* vol. 13, *Alchemical Studies* (Princeton NJ: Princeton University Press, 1967), pp. 1–56.

11. For those interested in learning Taoist exercises, particularly the Inner Smile, see the following books, both by Mantak Chia: *Awaken Healing Energy Through the Tao: The Taoist Secret of Circulating Internal Power* (Santa Fe: Aurora Press, 1983); and *Taoist Ways to Transform Stress into Vitality: The Inner Smile, Six Healing Sounds* (Huntington NY: Healing Tao Press, 1985).

12. Hillman, *Egalitarian Typologies versus the Perception of the Unique,* Eranos Foundation, Ascona, Switzerland (Dallas TX: Spring Publications, 1980).

13. Jung, *CW,* vol. 6, *Psychological Types,* para. 851.

14. Hillman, *Egalitarian Typologies versus the Perception of the Unique,* pp. 23–24.

15. Jung, *CW,* vol. 6, *Psychological Types,* para. 986.

16. Ibid., p. xi.

17. Ibid., para. 846.

18. Ibid., para. 959.

19. Ibid., para. 986.

20. Philip Rieff, *Freud, The Mind of the Moralist* (Garden City NY: Anchor Books, Doubleday and Company, 1961). "No more compulsively moral man has ever explored the compulsiveness of morality" (p. xvi).

CHAPTER 7

Strengthening Jung's Typology

The Myers-Briggs Type Indicator® (MBTI®)

---

*Type development is fostered by excellence in almost
anything that children can, with effort, do well. As Jung
once said, if they have planted a cabbage right, they have
saved the world in that spot. The excellence need not be
competitive, except as children try to excel their own past
performance, and virtue need not be its own reward. The
satisfaction earned by the striving can be whatever
furnishes the strongest incentive to the child, for example,
extra pleasures or possessions for a sensing child, special
freedoms or opportunities for an intuitive, new dignity or
authority for a thinker, and more praise or companionship
for a feeling type.[1]*

Isabel Briggs Myers, *Gifts Differing*

NALYSTS HAVE ALWAYS been reluctant to
popularize or see their psychology popularized,
possibly trivialized. Despite this, individual concepts
such as extraversion and introversion are common
knowledge, and Jung's concepts of shadow and
persona and of anima and animus lead healthy separate lives in literary and
philosophical fields. In typology, this reluctance was overcome when
people, including analysts, began to use Jung's theory to develop methods
of identifying individual types. Myers points out how sensitively the
average person can understand the varying needs of different types of
children when those needs are expressed in ordinary language. Her acute

perceptions of human behavior enrich rather than water down Jung's psychology. The *Myers-Briggs Type Indicator*® (*MBTI*®) has been the primary instrument that has popularized Jung's type theory. However, a short history of the various instruments devised to identify types will put this concern in perspective.

THE *MBTI* AND OTHER SURVEYS

In the 1940s, a group of Jungians led by Joseph and Jane Wheelwright developed the Gray-Wheelwright Type Survey (also called the JTS, or the Jungian Type Survey). This was about the same time that Katharine Briggs' daughter, Isabel Briggs Myers, expanded on her mother's observations and began to work on the *MBTI*, now a highly researched instrument taken by millions. Unlike the *MBTI*, the JTS has been minimally researched and used mainly among Jungian analysts. However, a comparative analysis of the JTS and the *MBTI* yields a sufficient correlation to prove that "The two instruments appear to be tapping the same constructs, but more consistently with E–I and S–N than with T–F."[2] The JTS remained faithful to Jung's intrapsychic approach to types by reporting the dominant function and attitude as well as the auxiliary function and attitude, but its major weakness was that it, unlike the *MBTI*, never considered or developed the value of function couplings. Only with Myers' 1962 formulations and Osmond's 1977 article did anyone consider the couplings and their archetypal character. In the late 1970s, June Singer and Mary Loomis developed the Singer Loomis Inventory of Personality (SLIP) that challenged Jung's polar view and therefore both the *MBTI* and the JTS, and also eliminated the type compass and the couplings. (I will discuss this challenge in chapter 10.)

SOME THERAPEUTIC USES OF TYPOLOGY

Before going more fully into the structure of the *MBTI*, I want to briefly review the response of analysts and other psychological practitioners to their personal and clinical use of typology. A. Plaut conducted a survey to determine the extent to which Jungian analysts used the Jungian Type Survey "in the practical work of analysis."[3] Only one-half of the respondents had found any typology instrument useful. Plaut argued that this low level of usage might be due to the fact that 51 percent of the responding analysts considered themselves dominant intuitives while only 8.5 percent said they were dominant sensation types. The other 40.5 percent were either dominant thinkers or feelers. After discussing Plaut's research, Hans Dieckmann argued that rather than valuing the descriptive, factual impact of type on the client-therapist relationship, analysts were more interested in following their intuitive bent in "the interpretation of symbols as a therapeutic method."[4] This seems very logical and would probably be correct if non-Jungian therapists who used the *MBTI* were typologically differ-ent. However, this inference is not valid since NFs and NTs (with their typical intuitive's interest in symbols) outnumber STs and SFs four-to-one among the 4600 members of *MBTI's* Association for Psychological Type (APT).[5]

There are, however, sensitive Jungian analysts who have used and written about the value of typology in analysis—to name a few: John Beebe, June Singer, Mary Loomis, Alex Quenk, Maria Louise von Franz, James Hillman, C. A. Meier, Hans Dieckmann, Daryl Sharp, Tom Lavin, Wayne Detloff, and, deserving of so much praise, Joseph and Jane Wheelwright. Beebe has identified the archetypal significance of each position in the type compass as well as four more archetypal (shadow) constellations that are made up of the same function in each position but with the opposite attitude, and, as I mentioned, Singer and Loomis developed the SLIP. Alex and Naomi Quenk have written an important article on the type uses in analysis,[6] and Naomi Quenk has written a book on the inferior functions, *Besides Ourselves*, as noted in chapter 1. Von Franz and Hillman have written, respectively, "The Inferior Function" and "The Feeling Function," the most significant essays by Jungians expanding on specific aspects of Jung's basic system.[7] Meier has written a book in which he looks at individuation from a typological standpoint,[8] and Dieckmann has given his views about the place of typology in Jung's entire psychology. Sharp provides a concise, lucid description of the eight functions as found in chapter 10 of *Psychological Types* and Lavin, a supporter of the SLIP, has written of his use of that instrument.[9] Finally, Detloff, with both an extensive factual knowledge and a deep experiential discernment, has researched the types for decades.[10] However, only John Beebe and the Quenks have specifically valued or encouraged the use of the *MBTI*.

Overall there are two distinct Jungian communities in the world: Jungian analysts and Jungian-oriented psychotherapists; and a much larger world of *MBTI* practitioners and students of Jung's typology, as well as the millions who have taken the *MBTI*. We will now consider the world of the *MBTI*.

CONTRIBUTIONS OF THE *MBTI* TO TYPE THEORY

Thanks to Briggs and Myers' work and the creative contributions of Mary McCaulley and the staff at the Center for the Applications of Psychological Type (CAPT), the *MBTI* has become the most widely employed inventory in personality assessment in the world of psychology. It is used in education, management, and organizational development; career and occupational guidance; psychology and counseling; assessing of multicultural differences; religious education and spiritual guidance; and research and theory. In 1995, over a million persons took the *MBTI* to identify their typology, and by 1997 the number had jumped to roughly two million annually. Research with the Indicator has been ongoing for many decades, particularly in work areas, the results of which are available in the *MBTI Manual*. The APT's *Journal of Psychological Type,* devoted mainly to research, features statistical measurements of human differences in countless occupations and human situations. The APT's *Bulletin of Psychological*

Type and the independently published *Type Reporter* present a more humanistic and down-to-earth description of types in many different areas of life.

In contrast to the publications of professional Jungian analysts, we find in the world of the *MBTI* that research predominates over life story; tables, statistics, and graphs have replaced the Jungian preference for circles, patterns, and dreams. Although introverted intuitive feeling types, Briggs and Myers worked consciously or unconsciously in a left-brain hemisphere that providentially compensated for the right-brain focus of most students of psychology. We have noted Katharine Briggs' stubborn persistence and inventiveness in pursuing her understanding of typology. When Myers began to develop a type survey in the 1940s, she acknowledged that it was her mother's determination to make Jung's original insights more available to the average person that primarily motivated her in that difficult task. She also felt that she wanted to contribute to the war effort by helping to further the understanding of human differences in various work situations. She began to study statistics under the guidance of Richard Cordray, a Swarthmore College friend and honors graduate in electrical engineering and mathematics. However, Cordray admitted that Myers soon surpassed him in her knowledge of this subject. Myers found the study very difficult, and once humorously characterized a confusing statistical concept as a "nice stubborn little hybrid, [a] cross-bred mule—a son of a statistic," and called the world of statistics "a [very] suspicious world" in which every time "you turn around you have to square yourself"[11]

MBTI research and training continued at the Center for Applications of Psychological Type in Gainesville, Florida, under the leadership of both Isabel Myers and Mary McCaulley. With CAPT sponsorship, the same training began to be offered throughout the country. We have noted that the publication of the *MBTI* was transferred in 1975 to Consulting Psychologists Press (CPP) in Palo

Alto, California. The enthusiastic and intelligent marketing practices of this organization dramatically enhanced sales and uses of the Indicator. In 1981, the Fourth National Conference on the *MBTI* was held at Stanford University; this was the first national conference sponsored by the newly formed Association for Psychological Type.

James Newman noted in his article based on his participation in the 1981 *MBTI* Conference that, because Myers was not a trained psychologist and therefore lacked credentials, "the response from academic psychology was (and in many ways remains) cool, if not hostile. . . . But her greatest obstacle was the nearly total lack of credibility which Jung's ideas enjoyed in academic circles," a lack of credibility still notable to this day.[12] He reported that researchers in clinical psychology made several seemingly serious attempts to evaluate the *MBTI* and its intriguing possibilities, but they finally rejected it. He continued:

> I can only conclude that those authors were simply unable to admit that the *MBTI* might be a valid measure of Jungian type, largely because they could not accept the idea that Jung's original theory had any valid basis.[13]

Newman also contributed to and organized a monograph based on a later symposium from the Tenth Biennial International Conference (July 1993) in which academia's Five Factor Model (FFM) of human types was compared and contrasted with the *MBTI*. (We will discuss the FFM in chapter 10.) It is appropriate to note here that the same reluctance from academics to value anything Jungian appears to be present in the FFM researchers.

A QUESTION OF POPULARITY
In these and other regional and national conferences, it has become apparent that the *MBTI* has attracted large numbers of business and other organizational managers, government officials, vocational and

career counselors, couple and marriage counselors, and secular and religious educators. The growing popularity of the *MBTI* met Myers' goal of making typology more accessible, a goal with which Jung and many Jungians disagreed, fearing that this would reduce typology to a parlor game. However, as Newman pointed out, popularity can befall any Jungian idea, such as anima and animus. Then he continued with a very telling statement:

> But I think this is a false issue. In the long run we have no control over whether ideas or theories become "popular" or not. Concepts which possess a basic universality and usefulness inevitably spread. Whether these ideas are relatively easy to grasp, like Darwin's concept of natural evolution, or as esoteric as Einstein's relativity, they tend to eventually permeate the fabric of society. Jung's typology, like so many other of his conceptions, is an idea with an essential universality. The proof of this for me is in the resonance which I continually experience in talking with the "average" individual about type, despite the skepticism maintained by orthodox psychology.[14]

Newman's term "resonance" is reminiscent of Jung's term "numinal accent," which points to the type's archetypal roots. That is, when we hear a description of our typology, we feel in a deep way that something substantial in our Soul has been touched, and we experience it as our own. The resonance occurs between the *numen* of our Soul—the divinity, Kant's "incomprehensible essence"—and our conscious awareness. Yet even though this idea of resonance is so characteristically Jungian, many of Jung's followers include themselves among the skeptics in the "orthodox" psychological circles that do not value typology. One can suppose that is the case because the types are not seen as archetypes. Despite Newman's suggestion in the above article that the Singer-Loomis instrument might fill this lacuna, there is still no evidence that the SLIP has helped move typology out of the shadow for most depth psychologists. I will evaluate this instrument in chapter 10. One can say that a great many Jungians have scorned typology, while many people in other areas of work, practice, and theory have enthusiastically embraced Jung's contribution.

TYPOLOGY AS A PRACTICAL TOOL
FOR HEALTHFUL EVERYDAY LIVING

The most important book about the *MBTI*, in addition to the type *Manual*, is Isabel Briggs Myers' *Gifts Differing*, completed just before her death. Newman turned to the book to help us get the spirit of the *MBTI* founder. He notes that in "both style and content, Myers' book is almost the antithesis of *Psychological Types*,"[15] where Jung described the various types only in chapter 10. He devoted the first nine chapters to a detailed exploration of type differences discussed or exemplified by many great Western scholars and artists in order to substantiate his typological hypotheses. Although Jung researched the historical evidence for typology, Isabel Briggs Myers adapted, practiced, and popularized Jung's basic ideas. Myers worked with a quiet persistence, a fierce determination and a brilliant creativity for four decades to develop a type inventory based on Jung's discoveries. In the *MBTI*, she precisely sculpted each question after testing its validity many times in order to capture incisively from the rough stone of everyday life and from the hidden veins of the unconscious one's true Self, much like Michelangelo wrested a Moses and a David from his blocks of marble.

In *Gifts Differing*, Myers translated Jung's more obtuse description of the types into a simple language that ordinary people could immediately understand. Myers' and Jung's contrasting typological preferences illuminate their differing approaches. She had a more relational INFP personality, dominated by introverted feeling and an NF Lover archetype, in contrast to Jung's analytical INTJ makeup, which was dominated by introverted intuition and a theoretical NT Magician archetype. Having at her disposal the results of Jung's scholarly research, she devoted most of her book to type descriptions and applications, adding little to existing theory.

Myers was more interested in the positive or psychologically healthy aspects of typology that first of all help persons to understand their authentic type. In a discussion with Mary McCaulley, Myers said, "Mary, type is the cake, and type development is the icing on the cake."[16] My experience with types both in my personal life and my professional work with my clients supports Myers' approach, with qualifications. We must get grounded in all aspects of our own innate identity before we can consider developing those typological resources other than our original preference. Myers assumed, as did Jung, that healthy living was based first of all on consciously realizing our original capacities, such as our native typological endowment. But the idea that development beyond our native types is only "icing" trivializes the importance of the whole circle of the types in the process of individuation. McCaulley then noted in the same article that, according to Myers, learning through experience to develop, nurture, and use auxiliary functions and the nonpreferred attitude depends very much on effective judgment.[17] We have also shown that such development and even the functional realization of one's natural typology may depend on a healthy upbringing. Parents and early environments that are humanly destructive will diminish both inborn capacities and lifetime learning potentials. Myers was reluctant to promote type development before people at least knew and lived their native typology. She wrote McCaulley in a letter dated March 9, 1970, that her reluctance "has been due in large part to the value I have set on the unthreatening character of type per se. So very many personality tests have dealt with a continuum that runs from good to bad."[18] In typological psychology, every member of the personality family has equal value and equal voice. Myers correctly points out that, in general, too much emphasis in psychology has been placed on "what is wrong with people. The *MBTI* is about what's right with people."[19] Typology reveals a person's healthy inborn makeup.

However, we can speculate about a negative consequence of Myers' putting type development on the back burner. She was undoubtedly aware that the Jungian Type Survey was always accompanied by a circular depiction of the dominant function, its auxiliaries, and the inferior function. Such a picture immediately implies potential development beyond the dominant function. Myers chose instead to focus on the distinct separation of each of the sixteen types and even of the four couplings, showing them always in linear or rectangular tables rather than circles. The consequence of her focus on each of the sixteen distinct types was that it hindered the understanding of typology's larger meaning and potential. Such a view also ignores both the resistance encountered when other functions or the other attitudes are called forth, as well as the more destructive consequences of overusing and overvaluing one's dominant function and dominant coupling.

Be that as it may, Myers' emphasis on normalcy was attuned to Jung's similar goal in his general psychology as well as in his typological system. Sonu Shamdasani (1998) gives a good summary of Jung's view in this regard:

> In Jung's life and work, the period between 1912 and 1918 was of critical importance. It was during this period . . . that he formulated his most well-known theories—of psychological types, of the archetypes and the collective unconscious, and of the process of individuation. It was precisely at this time that he began to develop what became known as analytical psychology. In so doing, he re-formulated the practice of psychotherapy. No longer simply concerned with the treatment of the sick, psychotherapy became a means of higher personality development of the healthy. This was to have far-reaching consequences in the subsequent development of humanistic, transpersonal and alternative therapies.[20]

THE PERCEIVING AND JUDGING TYPES
AND THE DOMINANT FUNCTION

The *MBTI's* most important additions to the type picture lay in recognizing the central importance of the couplings, and in delineating the perceiving and judging preferences as separate lifestyle categories. This second contribution has proven to be significant, leading to a better understanding of the dominant and auxiliary functions. We recall that Jung spoke of these two functions, but did not give us a clear idea of how to distinguish which one dominates and which one serves. We recall further his use of the word *compass* to describe the functional circle. This term, *compass,* gives us the key to a further understanding of the dominant function.

Jung's comparison of the compass with its four directions and the type quaternity is brilliantly appropriate. For one thing, "compass" comes from the Old French word *compas,* which means "circle," and the Old French word *compasser,* which means "to go around," "to comprehend," and "to grasp as a whole." All of this emphasizes the endless directions of the compass, and the equally numerous possibilities of types. The circular diagram of the types emphasizes the couplings which are situated on its circumference. The compass indicates direction because its magnetized needle always points to the magnetic North Pole. Typologically, the cluster of related interests that attract and name the dominant function establish the primary axis of orientation, as does the North Pole for the magnetic compass. In turn, the two auxiliary functions make up the Soul's horizontal axis, analogous to the compass' two other major directions, east and west. This also holds true for the dominant couplings and the three other couplings. Again, Jung established the immense significance of type dominance with the compass metaphor, but that did not necessarily help us to recognize which axis or function is dominant. Thus we turn to Briggs and Myers.

Myers acknowledged that all of us must use both judging (J) and perceiving (P), although most people find they prefer one over the other, and use it "as often as possible in dealing with the outer world.[21] Notice how the J and P have "dealing with the outer world" as their specific purpose. How did Briggs and Myers and their co-workers come to the conclusion that J and P point to our way of functioning in the social world? According to Mary McCaulley, Briggs first came up with this view by simply observing individual behavior. Briggs reasoned somewhat as follows: I cannot know what is going on in a person's mind, but I can observe his or her behavior in the world and ascertain whether this person extraverts in a perceptive sensing or intuitive way or in a judging feeling or thinking way. Myers notes that, in reading her mother's discussion of the J–P preference, the perceiving types "are still following the explanation with an open mind" and the judging types "have decided by now whether they agree or disagree." The former feel that "not all the evidence is in; new developments will occur," whereas the latter feel that "all the evidence is in, and anything more is irrelevant and immaterial."[22] Perceiving types are open-ended, adaptable, and seek comprehensive information on any subject, whereas judging types seek "only the essentials to begin their work," and "like to get things settled and finished."[23] At the extreme, perceiving types tend to be too loose and overly liberal in accepting other people's idiosyncracies and new information, but judging types tend in their extremes to be overly rigid and sometimes even moralistic in dealing with personal quirks and new information.

For example, continuing her characterization of the differing ways in which extraverts and introverts show their functions to the world, Myers employs the metaphors of the general and his aide to explain the related tasks of the dominant and auxiliary functions. In an extravert, the general (dominant function) is outside the tent dealing with affairs while the aide (the auxiliary) is respectfully in the background or in the tent. In the case of the Introvert, the roles are reversed:

the aide is outside "fending off interruptions" while the general is inside the tent "working on matters of top priority."[24] In simple and straightforward terms, Myers clarifies our understanding of extraversion and introversion:

> It is easy for people to see that they have a choice of two worlds on which to concentrate their interest. One is an outer world where things happen outside individuals or "without" them, in both senses of the word, and the other is an inner world where the activity is within the individual's mind, so that the individual is an inseparable part of all that goes on.[25]

Myers' "two worlds" aptly describe introversion and extraversion since each of these attitudes can be the primary worldview of an entire culture. There are nations, religions, and philosophies that tend to be either introverted or extraverted. Eastern religions and philosophies promote introversion. Many tribal peoples of the world, such as our Native Americans, tend to be introverted. For this reason they have created internally oriented worldviews with matching sciences, such as medicine, self-defense, and nutrition. The Western nations are more extraverted. Our Judeo-Christian and Greco-Roman roots have looked out at the natural and social worlds rather than inward to the workings of the soul. Accordingly, our extraverted scientific-technological and sociopolitical achievements have focused on understanding, using, and manipulating the objective natural world and societal forces.

Jung supports the distinctions between perceiving and judging. He called the former "irrational" and the latter "rational." By irrational, Jung designates those functions—sensation and intuition—as taking in innumerable impressions from what he calls "the flux of events." The rational functions—thinking and feeling—seek to limit and contain the impressions by virtue of choices that "are in complete harmony with the laws of reason."[26] For Jung, the flux has to do with objects in the external world. In another passage, Jung acknowledged in passing that the dominant and auxiliary functions operate from different attitudes:

> For all the types appearing in practice, the principle holds good that besides the conscious main function there is also a relatively unconscious auxiliary function which is in every respect different from the nature of the main function.[27]

"The operative words," Myers adds, "are 'in every respect.'"[28]

Given that a perceiving (sensation or intuition) or a judging (thinking or feeling) function is immediately visible, is it the dominant or an auxiliary? The answer, according to Briggs and Myers, depends on whether one is decidedly introverted or extraverted. Introverts tend to hide their dominant function and to show their auxiliary or secondary function to the world. Extraverts usually have no secrets, so their manifest function is their dominant function. Introverts feel they must keep secrets in order to survive, and their most important hidden treasure is their greatest strength, their dominant function. How does the *Myers-Briggs* formulation make clear these differences? We will use as an example our dominant cultural family, ESTJ.

Again, the P and J preferences are used "for dealing with the outer world," that is, they are extraverted.[29] When we look at the ESTJ family, for example, we see that the judging function—thinking—is extraverted (E); that is, it operates in relation to the outer world. Further, because the ESTJ type is naturally extraverted, extraverted thinking is clearly this type's dominant function. But what happens when a person is introverted? Let us take, for example, the ISTJ person. Such a person is also oriented to the outer world through the judging's T. However, since introverts never show their best suit to the world, the ISTJ type's dominant function will be the hidden introverted sensing.

Many analysts will say that one ought to be able to figure out one's dominant function (and the other functions' inner dynamics) without the help of the *MBTI*. This is possible. Anyone can understand a person typologically without the Indicator if one pays consistent attention to individual differences in everyday life and in dreams, but it is still helpful to have the *MBTI* schema to work with. If the *MBTI* leads us to a clearer understanding and experience of ourselves and the others with whom we live or work, it will have served its purpose. Of course, such aids are only maps; we should never depend solely on the instrument's results. Our continual observation of and interaction with the living person ultimately yields the richest rewards.

Newman raised an important point in regard to the relationship between the dominant and the auxiliary functions. In the case of the INFP, for example, the preferred attitude is introversion. Some Jungians maintain that both the dominant function (F) and the auxiliary function (N) are introverted. Newman remarked that others, notably the analyst Alex Quenk, disagreed with his Jungian colleagues by supporting the *MBTI* conclusion, that the one function is introverted, the other extraverted.[30] I also agree with the *MBTI* on this. Myers put this issue in disarmingly simple terms:

> Introverts have less choice about participating in both worlds. The outer life is thrust upon them whether they want one or not. Their dominant process is engrossed with the inner world of ideas, and the auxiliary process does what it can about their outer lives. In effect, the dominant process says to the auxiliary, "Go out there and tend to the things that cannot be avoided, and don't ask me to work on them except when it's absolutely necessary."[31]

Newman said he was in a quandary: was the attitude (Myers also calls it the process) of the auxiliary different or the same as the dominant? However, he granted that if the auxiliary, the intuition, somewhat compensates the dominant introverted feeling in the INFP person, the intuition rightly ought to be extraverted to better balance the person. Again, I agree, but with this difference: the dominant attitude casts its peculiar ambience over the entire psyche of an individual. For example, whenever introverted persons extravert, they do so in a subdued way since authentic Introverts tend not to mimic the more outgoing Extraverts. That is to say, introverts will extravert the auxiliary in a quiet manner, as Myers has also written.[32]

The Greek myth of Psyche and Eros supports this viewpoint. In the second test that Aphrodite gives Psyche, she must cross the River Styx, climb up to a high plain where sheep and rams are standing in a state of rage in the noon-day sun, pluck golden fleece from their backs, and escape without injury. Being a shy, introverted, feeling type, Psyche despairs and prepares to throw herself off the cliff into the river. However, the reeds of the river tell her to rest in the shade of a nearby tree and wait till dusk when the sheep and rams are sleeping. Then she can pick the fleece off the nearby thistles against which the animals have been rubbing themselves. She does this and succeeds. We can translate this vignette into type terms. This very introverted young woman performs an extraverted task in the ambience of introversion, that is, at dusk or at night in the moonlight when the human mind and heart are quieter and seek the inwardness of rest and sleep.[33]

It is clear that in observing how extraverts and introverts relate to the outer world, Myers and her co-workers added considerable clarity to the place, task, and characteristic of the auxiliary function in the type mandala. We can also note the incompleteness of Jung's work in this regard. Myers rightfully points out that Jung gave it little consideration until late in *Psychological Types*.[34] In all fairness to Jung, however, we need to repeat that he devoted by far the greater part of *Psychological Types* to developing the theoretical basis for his system by examining Western culture as a whole and its most significant explorers of human differences.

Jung and Myers, both adept explorers of the Soul, valued the obvious as well as the subtle differences and balances that we all hunger to rightfully understand and live. Myers, however, has brought a charming simplicity yet deep meaning to her account of typology that balances Jung's, as well as most Jungians', more turgid and theoretical style in this area.

THE *MBTI'S* SIXTEEN TYPES
AND THE COUPLING ARCHETYPES

In considering the sixteen types, I am again taking up the central thread of this book: the importance of the four couplings as four directional archetypes. Further, since these four couplings are archetypal, the sixteen *MBTI* types also are archetypal. The quaternal mandala itself is an archetype, as are the four type couplings which make up four central archetypes that are psychically directional and significant in societal communication. Within each individual, the four archetypal couplings represent phases both of creative processes and of the larger life journey of individuation. I have also pointed out in many places that our Western patriarchal society can be characterized as one dominated by an ESTJ archetype in its history, the patterns of its societal functions and its values. In the last chapter of this book, I will also show how the societal dominance of the ESTJ archetype rules the first stage of every life, particularly in Western culture, and that this overuse of one typology has created serious societal problems. When one archetypal pattern overshadows all others in a society, it can either complement or distort our individual typology as we seek to live out each stage of life.

We will now consider the sixteen types as developed in the *MBTI* to see how they further strengthen the connections between type and archetype. Jung combined introversion and extraversion with the four dominant functions to conceptualize a maximum of eight types. McCaulley observes a progression in Myers' thinking: to identify a type, Myers first notes the way we perceive the world—that is, whether we see, hear, touch, or smell what is around us (i.e., employ the sensation function), or grasp meanings and possibilities (i.e., relate to the concrete world through our intuition);[35] she then adds the two fundamental ways in which we judge or decide what to do about our accumulated knowledge, either through the logical view of a system in thinking, or through a canon of values that informs the feeling function; and by adding perceiving and judging to the type description and utilizing both the dominant and auxiliary functions, McCaulley has pointed out that the *MBTI* extends the possible combinations to sixteen types. We thus have our four couplings: ST, SF, NF and NT, in that order, according to Myers.

This lineup, ST, SF, NF and NT allows for an interesting observation. Myers, as we have noted, never used the type circle. When the circle is used counterclockwise, it represents the creative process as discussed in chapter 6. By creating a table in this way, Myers constructed, possibly unconsciously, this process. In my view, this alignment represents Myers' innate, brilliant, intuitive, and creative mind. We see below how these four couplings and their order also accounts for the sixteen types and the structure of her type table, as pictured in *Gifts Differing*.[36]

We now have a complex picture of human differences that goes far

		Sensing Types		Intuitive Types	
		Thinking	Feeling	Feeling	Thinking
		–ST–	–SF–	–NF–	–NT–
Intravert	I-J	ISTJ	ISFJ	INFJ	INTJ
	I-P	ISTP	ISFP	INFP	INTP
Extravert	E-P	ESTP	ESFP	ENFP	ENTP
	E-J	ESTJ	ESFJ	ENFJ	ENTJ

beyond the original type structures that Jung conceived. Yet Myers acknowledges that in his creative development of the typological opposites, Jung implied these sixteen types. She writes:

> We did not invent or discover them. They are inherent in Jung's theory of the function types, which is based on many years of observations that seemed to him to synthesize already existing knowledge of personality.[37]

Myers adds a comment that helps us understand the important differences in emphasis between her *MBTI* work on one hand and Jung's position on the other:

> We have been less interested in defining the processes than in describing the *consequences* of each preference as far as we can observe or infer them, and in using the most accessible consequences (not the most important) to develop a means of identifying types.[38]

In effect, she is saying that Jung's development of the types is more theoretical while her *MBTI* approach is more descriptive, based more on observation, and more available for everyday use. Then Myers adds a paragraph that states her and her mother's deep commitment to discovering and articulating the breadth and depth of types as based on Jung's original discoveries:

> Since the more superficial aspects of type are often the easiest to report, many trivial reactions are useful for identification, but these are merely straws to show which way the wind blows. They are not the wind. It would be a mistake to assume that the essence of an attitude or of a perceptive or judging process is defined by its trivial surface effects or by the test items that reflect it or by the words used to describe it. *The essence of each of the four preferences is an observable reality.* [39]

The "observable reality" is made up of all the elements of individual functions and attitudes, and the couplings we have discussed: their archetypal traits and images; life styles; articulations of work, love, play and prayer; their cultural manifestations; their permutations through the stages of life and the creative process; and their ethical demands. With this background, we now have a basis for discussing the archetypal couplings in the *MBTI* in greater depth.

THE ARCHETYPAL COUPLINGS IN THE *MBTI*

In chapter 5 we considered the elegant way in which Myers constructed a phenomenology of the four type couplings in her *Introduction to Type*. The type table shown on page 300 (Myers' figure 2 in *Gifts Differing*) clearly shows the genesis of the sixteen *MBTI* types. We see the four couplings as the basis of the sixteen. Although she never identifies these couplings as archetypal, her descriptions make clear that they are indeed archetypes—fundamental, innate patterns in the human Soul.

Drawing on their familiarity with Myers' formulations of the couplings, the Osmond group recognized their archetypal nature. They called the couplings "umwelts," or "self worlds." They argued that "the functions give one the *contents* of consciousness, the umwelts the *form* of consciousness."[40] Form refers to consistent images and traits that emerge from innate patterns (i.e., archetypes). As I have already indicated, the coupled functions allow us to recognize larger, more extensive archetypal structures or fields of consciousness in addition to the archetypal properties of individual functions. They also consolidate the elements of the type mandala, the symbol of the whole or individuating person. As we have seen, these coupled functions strengthen the Jungian tradition of type/archetype connections first articulated by Toni Wolff and now given new depth and breadth by connecting the work of the Osmond group, the theorizing and research of *MBTI* practitioners, and Moore and Gillette's observations of the adult archetypes in culture and psyche.

In the *MBTI* types, the relationship between the dominant and auxiliary functions is clear. For example, the ESTJ is characterized primarily by its two central functions, sensing and thinking. The judging orientation indicates that in this coupling, the extraverted thinking is dominant and will assert that dominance over its sensing partner. Notice in Myers' diagram how the four couplings each stand at the head of four *MBTI* type families. Our focus will now be on the importance of these four combinations in the *MBTI* theory, literature, and research.

In *Gifts Differing*, Myers carries forward the coupling consciousness, as if she were writing Jung's second book on types. In the section "Combinations of Perception and Judgment," she writes:

> The TF preference (thinking or feeling) is entirely independent of the SN preference (sensation or intuition). Either kind of judgment can team up with either kind of perception. Thus, four combinations occur:
>
> ST Sensing plus thinking
> SF Sensing plus feeling
> NF Intuition plus feeling
> NT Intuition plus thinking[41]

Continuing, she describes these combinations with typical forthrightness and clarity:

> Each of these combinations produces a different kind of personality characterized by *interests, values, needs, habits of mind, and surface traits that naturally result* from the combination. Combinations with a common preference [the dominant function] will share some qualities, but each combination has qualities all of its own, arising from the interaction of the preferred way of looking at life [perceiving] and the preferred way of judging what is seen.[42]

With a simple brilliance, Myers describes the very essence of the four archetypal personalities, each of which "has qualities all of its own," but does not discuss which function is dominant and which is auxiliary in each coupling. She brackets them out, since she assumes that each pairing has an intrinsic, archetypal meaning of its own that she can define in terms of interests, values, needs, habits of mind, and surface traits.[43]

- *Interests* are the motive powers that move us to select congruent careers, avocations, and pastimes;

- *Values* are the human qualities that express our world-views and our personal sense of integrity;

- *Needs*, not wants, are the elemental appetites that forge authentic relationships in which both individual autonomy and mutual surrender are wed;

- *Habits* of mind are the unconscious and conscious constituents of our character;

- *Surface traits* are those typical behaviors which for Jung were circumscribed as personae or social roles and which Myers identified above as "the more superficial aspects of type."

Both the dominant and the auxiliary functions contribute to each of the archetypal personalities and must function in them with some "adequate (but by no means equal)" degree of intensity and consciousness. Myers writes:

> If a person has no useful development of an auxiliary process, the absence is likely to be obvious. An extreme perceptive with no judgment is all sail and no rudder. An extreme judging type with no perception is all form and no content. In addition to supplementing the dominant process in its main field of activity, the auxiliary has another responsibility. It carries the main burden of

supplying adequate balance (but not equality) between extraversion and introversion, between the outer and inner worlds.[44]

She also emphasizes the interpersonal significance of the coupling by noting that those who share "the same combination are apt to be the easiest to understand and like." On the other hand, "people who differ on both preferences will be hard to understand and hard to predict." Further, "Many destructive conflicts arise simply because two people are using opposite kinds of perception and judgment," especially if they are closely involved either at work or at home. When each understands the implications of typology, the conflict between them "becomes less annoying and easier to handle." Finally, if at work (and, certainly by implication, at home), a person is not allowed to use one's natural combination, "an even more destructive conflict" can occur.[45] Myers echoes Jung, who warned about the consequences of ignoring one's type, as well as not honoring a person of a different type because one does not recognize that a different type also constitutes one's undeveloped potential, which Jung called the shadow.

However, Myers compares her typological approach to Jung's, noting that she presents hers "in a less abstruse form" and "states the theory in terms of everyday aspects." Besides, she points out that Jung's description of the types focused on eight as only attitudinal/functional combinations, such as ET and IT. By doing so, Jung was describing "the rare, theoretically 'pure' types, who have little or no development of the auxiliary."[46] We recall that Jung acknowledged the limits of these eight types, discussed the "co-determining influence" of the couplings, and then dropped the subject.[47] Myers continues:

> Jung's approach has several unfortunate effects. By ignoring the auxiliary, he bypasses the combinations of perception and judgment and their broad categories [the four directional archetypes] of interest in business, people,

language, and science. . . . Consequently, other researchers, who have reinvented the categories under different names, were unaware of the parallels between their findings and Jung's theories.[48]

Two such revisionary approaches to the Jung/*MBTI* work with couplings are the Kiersey and Bates model and the Singer Loomis instrument, which I will assess in chapter 10.

Myers points to another negative effect as a result of Jung's failure to develop the combinations. For example, the introvert without an extraverted auxiliary is seemingly "unable to communicate, to use their insights, or to have any impact on the outer world."[49] According to McCaulley, Myers recognized that Jung's oversight pushed his type theory toward more of "a focus on psychopathology," presumably because his typology did not consistently consider the healthy interplay of the perceiving–judging combinations.

Because of this important gap in Jung's theory, Myers concluded, "For decades, therefore, the practical utility of his theory went unexplored."[50] I would add that because Jung did not develop the couplings as a significant aspect of his system, a *substantial* dimension of his theory went unexplored. Myers, on the other hand, put the couplings on center stage in her approach when she identified them as universal patterns of human differences, when she realized their critical interpersonal importance, and when she took them as the basis for both her sixteen types and for her extensive research. Overall, Myers' contributions to and criticisms of Jung's type theory in regard to the couplings constitute the most practical and wise supports for the thesis of this book. Now we can consider the individual couplings.

THE ST COUPLING

Sensing thinking types—that is, the ISTJs, the ISTPs, the ESTPs, and the ESTJs—are fundamentally practical, matter-of-fact folks who differ mainly on E–I and J–P preference. ST types rely on facts because they perceive with their sensing function and "approach their decisions regarding these facts by impersonal analysis" via the thinking function, "with its step-by-step logical process of reasoning from cause to effect, from premise to conclusion."[51] The research tables in the *MBTI®* *Manual* show that, as Structural Warriors, they are the dominant types in management,[52] among finance and commerce students,[53] and in urban police forces.[54] In general, Myers writes, "their best chances of success and satisfaction lie in fields that demand impersonal analysis [T] of concrete facts [S], such as economics, law, surgery, business, accounting, production, and the handling of machines."[55] If we look at the broader range of occupations usually associated with the four ST types, we see the consistent, underlying patterns of these occupations. Of the seventeen discrete occupations that Kroeger and Thuesen list under the four ST types, fifteen of them demand a tough-minded set of traits in which systems and things dominate over relationships and people.[56]

The ST person tends to stand out from the sensing feeling, intuitive thinking, and intuitive feeling types as the one who seizes the most power. The person who prefers sensing and thinking demands to be heard and insists on action. This coupling is predominant in our ESTJ Western culture. While it has limitations, its demands for discipline, reliability, pragmatism, and action are essential to all types for adapting to society in the first stage of life, and especially for our transition from family life to the responsible world of work. It is no wonder that the Osmond group called this type and this facet of our psyche the Structural, and Moore and Gillette named it the Warrior.

An interesting demonstration of the significance of the various couplings, in addition to their relevance for occupations, occurred at a meeting of the Chicago Association for Psychological Type. Peter

Noble (ENFP) and Marci Segal (INTJ) formed groups according to their coupled functions, and asked them to respond to several questions about power.[57] When asked, "How do you define power?" STs responded with: "authority; leadership; rules; organization; control; 'on top' of things." And when asked, "How do you gain power?" the STs said "work hard, get on top of things, get results, and . . . earn power." In other words, the ST Warrior gets power by doing. In dreams as in waking life, the ST acts decisively. For example, an essentially INFP woman who had fully developed her ST side by modeling herself after her ST father consistently killed or defeated aggressive males in her dream. She functions well in the highly competitive world of stock trading, but has begun to realize that her hard ST exterior and her Artemis-like sturdiness seriously throttle her artistic and humanistic NF inclinations and do not attract men in social life.

THE SF COUPLING

The sensing feeling types include the ISFJ, ISFP, ESFP, and ESFJ. By virtue of their central SF structure that Myers called "sympathetic and friendly," these types are "more interested in facts about people than in facts about things and, therefore, they tend to be sociable and friendly." Myers continues:

> They are most likely to succeed and be satisfied in work where their personal warmth [F] can be applied effectively to the immediate situation [S], as in pediatrics, nursing, teaching (especially elementary), social work, selling of tangibles, and service-with-a smile jobs.[58]

Of the seventeen occupations that Kroeger lists under the SFs, every one of them centers on ministering to people in practical areas of life as members of the clergy, home economics professionals, hair dressers, teachers, social workers, and librarians.[59] SFs are pragmatic persons in waking life (as well as in dreams), but they are not tough-minded like the ST Warrior. They bring their genuine feeling for people to bear in practical ways that satisfy people's utilitarian and emotional needs. The Osmond group's name for this archetypal personality—Experial—implies their need to experience a closeness with people while providing hands-on services. The Osmond group's other name for them—the Moralists—denotes the kind of ethical commitment and loyalty that such earthy people are capable of giving others. In family life, SF is the aspect of parenting that is absolutely necessary to help children feel both lovingly contained (F) and reasonably disciplined (S).

Lifted to a more collective level in psyche and society, Moore and Gillette call them Kings and Queens, since as leaders they are the societal equivalent of parents, moral pacesetters, and exemplars of order for states and large private organizations. Within the dynamic of society and the type mandala, the Moralists inspire the allegiance and industry of the STs, the more aggressive initiators and doers. Further, SFs are, in inner work, the reconciling bridges between the ST Warriors and the NF Lovers, as we see from the type mandala. In the Chicago APT workshop mentioned above, the SFs defined power as "strength with self and others; control; exerting influence over others without regard for acceptance; providing positive influence." Concerning ways to gain power, the SFs used an equation: competence + character = trust. Both answers are consistent with the SF parent/leader. In dreams, they often appear as a dream ego or dream figure that demonstrates a leadership power and ethical message that challenges the waking personality to act accordingly.

THE NF COUPLING

The intuition and feeling combination, which Myers describes as "enthusiastic and insightful," is the structural centerpiece of the INFJ, INFP, ENFP, and ENFJ types. NFs share the same warmth as the SFs, but they prefer intuition's visions of possibilities, "such as new projects (things that haven't ever happened but might be made to happen) or new truths (things that are not yet known but might be found out). . . . Often they have a marked gift of language." Myers continues:

> They are most likely to find success and satisfaction in work that calls for creativity to meet a human need. They may excel in teaching (particularly college and high school), preaching, advertising, selling of intangibles, counseling, clinical psychology, psychiatry, writing, and most fields of research.[60]

In Myers' surveys, they, along with the NTs, made up the majority of seventy-one male Rhodes Scholars (39 percent NF and 44 percent NT).[61] Of 118 counselor education students, NFs made up 76 percent, and of thirty-one art education seniors, they represented 65 percent.[62] When I tested eighty MA students in the Creation Spirituality program at Mundelein College in Chicago over a two-year period, 93 percent were NFs. Kroeger shows that NFs tend to choose careers as education consultants, clergy, physicians, media specialists, artists and writers, psychiatrists, psychologists, editors, musicians, composers, and entertainers.[63] All of these occupations call for innovative work that touches people's lives in the areas of health, art, communication, and spirituality.

The Osmond group called NFs Oceanics, apparently because they like to swim in the chaotic and deep waters of change, novelty, risk, and uncertainty in order to come up with creative solutions. Moore and Gillette call them Lovers, for they steep themselves in the intimate and vulnerable realms of human interaction. On the type circle, they form empathic bridges between the SF ruler and NT sage in society, in stories, and in dreams. In our life journey, each of us, no matter what our type, must develop our NF potential in the second stage of life, an inner loving tryst with Soul and an outer embrace of all of mankind, as both Carl Jung and Eric Erikson have shown. In the Chicago APT meeting, the NFs defined power as "being in control of the vision; having the respect of others; having the ability to persuade, influence and energize desired outcomes," thus emphasizing the inventive and relational qualities of the NF. They described gaining power as "developing competence and knowledge" that in turn would presumably attract followers. In dreams, the NF aspect of Soul is often depicted as the wounded child or the healing child, for it is the child in life and in the psyche that radically loves and demands love from birth to death. As representing new life, the inner child also images the dawning of creative insights and happenings. When old patterns and conventions collapse in life crises as well as dreams, it is the NF archetype, with its feminine and childlike qualities, that contains chaos, change, darkness, and confusion, and, if this suffering is endured, becomes the vessel of transformation.

THE NT COUPLING

Myers called the intuitive thinking types "logical and "ingenious."[64] The NT constitutes the center of the INTJs, INTPs, ENTPs, and ENTJs, the Ethereal group. Of all of them Myers says, "Although they focus on possibility [N], they approach it with impersonal analysis [T]." She continues:

> NTs . . . are most successful in solving problems in a field of special interest, whether scientific research, electronic computing, mathematics, the more complex aspects of finance, or any sort of development or pioneering in technical areas.[65]

Kroeger lists them as dominant in law (along with STs), natural and life sciences, computer systems analysis, chemical engineering, university teaching, writing and creative arts (along with NFs), and photography, among other areas. According to the *Manual,* 40 percent of thirty experimental psychologists are informed by this archetype.[66]

According to *Gifts Differing*, 41 percent of 2,248 law students and 44 percent of seventy-one male Rhodes Scholars are NTs.[67] I have worked with nine architects, all of whom have been NTs. NT Ethereals have a difficult time with unexamined authoritative ideas; even as children, they generally report that they never readily swallowed unexamined dogmas. With their gift of intuition that can look beyond the conventional and, given their objective thinking, they are not readily captivated by any rigid system of thought. On the cultural stage, they are most often the great philosophers, scientists, theologians, and psychologists who organize innovative systems and readily challenge old ways.

Named Ethereal types by the Osmond group and Magicians by Moore and Gillette, they stand opposite the rulers of society and challenge them. Because of the breadth and depth of their thought, they are capable of changing the course of history. In their roles in society and in psyche, they invite us to explore the ancient truths in books and libraries and, above all, in the most important source of truth, one's own Book of Life, the immortal Soul. On our inner type circle and in our outer life journey, NT capacities emerge often when the ST Warrior in each of us is exhausted from overwork and over-achievement, or when in depression or entering any critical change in life. At these points, we ask in desperation, "Was it worth it all? Is there any ultimate or deeper meaning to life?"

At the Chicago APT meeting, the NTs defined power as "auton-omy; ability to direct process/outcomes; having control of process, outcomes, and interpretation of outcomes . . . [as] self-perceived; authority." There are intimations here of an expansive and in-depth view of power (i.e., "self-perceived") that corresponds with the NT Magician's holistic view of systems. As to gaining power, the NTs, like the NFs, also spoke of developing competence and knowledge, adding, however, "control of mental resources and information analysis," which also assumes a large systemic approach. Our NT

The Myers-Briggs Compass

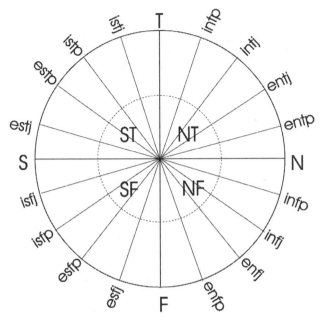

FIGURE 7.1

composites are represented in dreams as inner guides, as wise figures who fill the painful gap produced in those of us who have lacked parental guidance, inspiration or love, or as seemingly evil wizards who challenge us to discover hidden secrets.

In summary, the *MBTI* tradition has consistently provided a solid picture of the four archetypes that clearly emerge from the couplings, especially in vocational areas, an aspect of life that analysts have hardly touched. We can now see what the full type mandala (figure 7.1) looks like after Briggs and Myers developed the sixteen types based on the four couplings.

The work of Myers and Briggs, especially in their research in vocational areas, buttresses Jung's original explorations, Toni Wolff's formulation of the quaternity, the Osmond group's work with type couplings and Moore and Gillette's archetypal researches. In the vast research that Mary McCaulley pursued over the years, the couplings have formed the solid basis for her and her co-workers' statistical compilations and analysis of over one million surveys. As a result, they described an extensive phenomenology of the four archetypes—the primordial images with their hidden, psychosomatic instincts—albeit without being aware of the archetypal nature of their findings. Given this solid work, hundreds and thousands of practitioners have developed their own statistics, interpretations, and expertise with the types, again with their archetypal dimension always implicit in the background. Overall, it is clear that the *MBTI* work has solidified and creatively extended the psychology of types that Jung developed in the first two decades of this century. However, the types' archetypal nature has been neither recognized nor emphasized. With awakening consciousness to the typological archetypes, the cooperation of Jungians and *MBTI* practitioners can be expanded both in theory and practice.

We now have a rich understanding of typology from Jungian analysts and *MBTI* practitioners and researchers. I devote the next chapter to Ned Herrmann's creative explorations of the four quadrants of the brain, which adds independent corroboration and substance to the theory of typology.

Notes

1. Isabel Briggs Myers,with Peter B. Myers, *Gifts Differing* (Palo Alto CA: Consulting Psychologists Press, 1980), p. 188.

2. Isabel Briggs Myers and Mary H. McCaulley, *Manual: A Guide to the Development and Use of the Myers-Briggs Type Indicator* (Palo Alto CA: Consulting Psychologists Press, 1985), p. 209. See also table 11.1, p. 180.

3. A. Plaut, "Analytical Psychology and Psychological Types: Comments on Replies to a Survey," *Journal of Analytical Psychology,* no. 17 (1972).

4. Hans Dieckmann, *Methods in Analytical Psychology* (Wilmette IL: Chiron Publications, 1991), p. 193.

5. *Membership Directory: 1994–1995* (Kansas City MO: Association for Psychological Type) p. 23. Forty-two percent of the members are dominant intuitives, and eighty-two percent are NTs and NFs.

6. Alex T. Quenk and Naomi L. Quenk, "The Use of Psychological Typology in Analysis," in *Jungian Analysis,* edited by Murray Stein (La Salle IL: Open Court, 1982), chapter 8.

7. Marie-Louise von Franz and James Hillman, *Jung's Typology* (1979).

8. C. A. Meier, *Personality: The Individuation Process in the Light of C. G. Jung's Typology* (Einsiedein, Switerland: Daimon, 1995).

9. Thomas P. Lavin, "The Art of Practicing Jung's Psychological Types in Analysis," in *Jungian Analysis,* 2nd ed., edited by Murray Stein (La Salle IL: Open Court, 1995).

10. Wayne Detloff, "Psychological Types: Fifty Years Later," *Psychological Perspectives* 3:1 (Spring 1972).

11. Frances W. Saunders, *Katharine and Isabel: Mother's Light, Daughter's Journey* (Palo Alto CA: Consulting Psychologists Press, 1991), p. 113.

12. James Newman, "The Myers-Briggs Type Indicator and Gifts Differing," *San Francisco Jung Institute Library Journal* 3:1 (Autumn 1981): p. 38.

13. Ibid., p. 39.

14. Ibid., p. 41.

15. Ibid., p. 45.

16. Mary McCaulley, "Isabel Myers: A Double Legacy," *Bulletin of Psychological Type* 20:2 (Spring 1997): p. 24.

17. Ibid., p. 24.

18. Ibid., p. 24.

19. Ibid., p. 24.

20. Sonu Shamdasani, *Cult Fictions: C. G. Jung and the Foundation of Analytical Psychology* (London and New York: Routledge, 1998), p. 20. This book presents a historically sound argument against the views of Richard Noll that Jung had intended to create a cult. See Noll's book, *The Jung Cult: Origins of a Charismatic Movement* (Princeton NJ: Princeton University Press, 1994) (emphasis added).

21. Myers, *Gifts Differing*, p. 14.

22. Ibid., p. 8.

23. Myers, *Introduction to Type: A Description of the Theory and Applications of the Myers-Briggs Type Indicator* (Palo Alto CA: Consulting Psychologists Press, 1962), p. 29.

24. Myers, *Gifts Differing*, p. 13.

25. Ibid., p. 23.

26. Jung, *CW*, vol. 6, *Psychological Types*, English edition, translated by H. G. Baynes (1923; rpt., Princeton NJ: Princeton University Press, 1971), para. 787.

27. Ibid., para. 669.

28. Myers, *Gifts Differing*, p. 19.

29. Ibid., p. 9.

30. Newman, *The San Francisco Jung Institute Library Journal*, p. 46.

31. Myers, *Gifts Differing*, p. 12.

32. Ibid., p. 22: "Briggs [Myers' mother] also found that when the introvert's auxiliary was a perceptive process, it gave rise to a perceptive attitude and an outer personality that resembled in a *quiet way* [italics, mine] the 'spontaneous' personality of the perceptive extravert. When the auxiliary was a judging process, it produced a judging attitude that was the opposite of 'spontaneous' [that is, also quiet]." I did not know this view was held by the *MBTI* founders until recently.

33. In a subsequent book I will interpret this myth from a type standpoint in order to show its relevance to individuals in our present culture. In agreement with many others, I assume that this story, one of the greatest in all of mythology, provides a balance for the present ESTJ culture. For the heroine of this tale, Psyche, is, in my view, a perfect imaginal depiction of the INFP person and of the INFP counterculture that we so desperately need.

34. Myers, *Gifts Differing*, pp. 17–18. By ignoring the significance of the auxiliary, Jung in effect is ignoring the couplings and, implicitly, their archetypal nature, so Myers writes: "Jung's approach has several unfortunate effects. By ignoring the auxiliary, he bypasses the combination of perception and judgment and their broad categories of interest in business, people, language, and science."

35. Ibid., pp. 28–29.

36. Ibid., p. 29.

37. Ibid., p. 23.

38. Ibid., p. 23.

39. Ibid., p. 23 (my emphasis).

40. Humphrey Osmond et al., "Typology Revisited: A New Perspective,"*Psychological Perspectives* (Fall 1977), p. 208.

41. Myers, *Gifts Differing,* p. 4.

42. Ibid., p. 4 (emphasis, Myers).

43. Ibid., p. 4.

44. Ibid., pp. 11–12.

45. Ibid., p. 4.

46. Ibid., p. 17.

47. Jung, CN, vol 6, *Psychological Types,* para. 666.

48. Myers, *Gifts Differing,* p. 17.

49. Ibid., p. 17.

50. Ibid., p. 18. Here is the full text: "Few of Jung's readers realized that his type concepts had a bearing on the familiar daily problems of educating people, of counseling them, employing them, communicating with them, and living in the same family with them. For decades, therefore, the practical utility of his theory went unexplored."

51. Ibid., p. 5.

52. Myers and McCaulley, *Manual,* p. 90.

53. Myers, *Gifts Differing,* p. 42.

54. Ibid., p. 50.

55. Ibid., p. 5.

56. Otto Kroeger and Janet M. Thuesen, *Type Talk: The 16 Personality Types That Determine How We Live, Love, and Work* (New York: Bantam Doubleday Dell, 1988), pp. 194–196. See also 215–218, 230–234, 247–261, 265–269.

57. Julie Benesh, "March Meeting: Type and Power," *Chapter News* (March 1996): pp. 2–3. Noble and Segal based this workshop on the work of Margaret

Hartzler, president of Type Resources of Canada, for which they also work.

58. Myers, *Gifts Differing,* p. 5.

59. Kroeger and Thuesen, *Type Talk,* pp. 194–196. See also 218–222, 234–238, 251–256, 269–272.

60. Myers, *Gifts Differing,* p. 5–6.

61. Ibid., p. 48.

62. Ibid., pp. 46–47.

63. Kroeger and Thuesen, *Type Talk,* pp. 194–196. See also 222–226, 238–243, 256–261, 272–276.

64. Myers, *Gifts Differing,* p. 6.

65. Ibid., p. 6.

66. Myers and McCaulley, *Manual,* p. 86.

67. Myers, *Gifts Differing,* pp. 48–49.

CHAPTER 8

Creative Breakthrough

Herrmann's Metaphorical
Whole Brain Model

The exponential growth of the human brain during the last two hundred and fifty thousand years is unique in the history of evolution. Even today we lack a satisfactory explanation of how it came about.[1]

Richard Restak

If the brain is a computer, then it is the only one that runs on glucose, generates 10 watts of electricity, and is manufactured by unskilled labor.[2]

David Lewis

The fruit of the brain is a natural product and as such must be assumed to contain the general principles of nature. A very wise man could construct the whole world from one apple. . . . Why then should it not be supposed that the brain could produce a perfectly natural fruit which would reproduce all [of] nature.[3]

C. G. Jung

 UNG'S PSYCHOLOGY DEMANDS that we not allow generalities to blind us to the uniqueness of individuals. On the other hand, the realization of an integral personal identity is difficult to achieve given the bewildering complexity of each person, the enormous number of choices available in our contemporary society and,

consequently, the many wrong turns we can take and false facades we can construct. We have seen that the types generally and the four couplings in particular provide needed blueprints for alleviating this difficulty. The structure of the brain provides further evidence of the validity of type preferences. While this is a field that changes almost daily, certain principles of brain structure have become evident.

DISCOVERING THE TWO-HEMISPHERE BRAIN

Brain researchers have shown that the left brain controls the right side of the body and the right brain, the left side. Newman notes that Ernest Rossi was the first Jungian analyst to recognize the possible relationship between psychological type and the brain hemispheres. Acknowledging Jung's view that sensation and intuition were irrational functions, and thinking and feeling rational, Rossi assigned the former to the right brain hemisphere and the latter to the left. However, Newman and another researcher situated the feeling function in the right hemisphere and the sensation function in the left. This fits the classical type structure (see figure 2.2, page 54) that shows sensation centrally located on the left and intuition centrally located on the right.

Ideas about a separation of brain and mind functions have existed since ancient times. In the fifth century B.C., Hippocrates held that within the brain of a patient, there can exist a mental duality. In the thirteenth century, Roger Bacon argued that humans exercised two modes of knowing, one through verbal argument and the other through nonverbal experience. Jung's *Symbols of Transformation,* first published in 1912 as *The Psychology of the Unconscious,* begins with a chapter entitled "Two Kinds of Thinking," by which he meant logical and symbolic expression.[4] Even years ago at the beginning of my analytical studies, I was aware that Jungians recognized a kind of laterality: images and other phenomena that occurred in dreams and spontaneous drawings differed significantly, depending on whether they appeared in the left or the right. Some of the characteristics which were identified—such as conventional images on the right side and the strange or innovative images on the left—agreed with the later brain researchers, beginning with Roger Sperry in the 1960s. Sperry, a psychologist, working with split-brain patients, began to demonstrate that the right and left brain hemispheres were specialized; early in the same decade, Robert Ornstein used the EEG machine in biofeedback research to show that this same brain specialization existed in normal people.

In 1981, James Newman was already doing work in this field on the differentiation between brain hemispheres. He writes:

> One hemisphere, normally the left, is clearly superior in activities involving language and abstract thought in general. The right hemisphere has only rudimentary capacities for linguistic processing, but possesses a superior ability to deal with a number of non-verbal activities. These include such things as the ability to interpret complex visual-spatial relationships; to orient oneself in space, and to appreciate non-linguistic messages in general.[5]

But it is the work of Ned Herrmann that contributes most substantially to our understanding of the relationship between psychological type and brain structure.

TOWARD A FOUR-QUADRANT BRAIN

In *The Creative Brain,* Ned Herrmann lays out a short history of modern brain research along with his personal journey of discovery in this field. Herrmann's artistic breakthroughs in painting during an illness led him to research creativity. In the 1970s, he became aware of the new theory of brain specialization. He learned that some people are right-hemisphere dominant and others left-hemisphere dominant. Here, he realized, was significant anatomical support for the varieties of human difference that first, "gives us an automatic lead response to any situation," and second, gives "us higher skill levels than we could otherwise attain."[6] He also recognized that if we strongly favor one mode of knowing and behaving, we tend to reject the other. He began to organize this research in his model that categorizes human differences. Without apparently knowing it, Herrmann was beginning to point to the language of Jung's typological psychology. He also began to realize the extent to which our culture has emphasized the left brain. He writes:

> The left-brain modes have become especially entrenched in our educational system, which typically emphasizes the "three R's" and neglects—or even attacks—the cognitive capacities of the right brain, such as art, intuition, music and dance. . . . As a result, our right-brain capabilities remain latent, at best, and often atrophy, at great cost to our personal satisfaction as well as our effectiveness as problem-solvers.[7]

Without so expressing it, Hermann was describing the reigning ESTJ emphasis of our Western culture, which Jung saw as already developing in the first centuries of the Christian era.

Along with the left brain/right brain theory, researchers were also developing the triune brain theory that Herrmann incorporated into his model. Beginning at the base of the skull, the brain is structured in three strata, each level lying on top of the other. The lowest level, the reptilian, resembles brains in prehistoric reptiles as well as alligators and lizards today. The middle level is the limbic or mammalian brain that we share with lower animals such as rats, rabbits, and horses. It is the seat of emotions and controls the body's autonomic nervous system. The topmost level, the neocortex or "thinking cap," is the mass of gray matter "that evolved with such rapidity in just the last million years to produce Homo sapiens." The two older brains control "genetic/instinctual behaviors" while the "newer neocortex, in contrast, seems adept at learning new ways of coping and adapting."[8]

Finally, there are interconnections for the two hemispheres as well as cortex/limbic linkages. Concerning behavior, brain researchers have discovered that certain brain areas are also specialized. Given the rich body of information on the brain, Herrmann concludes:

> When the triune brain and left brain/right brain theories are added, and we incorporate the reality of brain dominance [or specialization], we have the essential elements of an organizing principle upon which a working model of brain function can be based.[9]

Herrmann learned to use the EEG, the instrument that measures brain waves, so that he could determine what part of the brain was being activated. Biofeedback specialists were learning to identify these dominant areas by observing what brain waves were present when the subject was presented with a certain task. The brain wave that measures conscious activity is beta, and the two brain waves that measure relatively unconscious activity are alpha and theta. If, for example, the left brain were being used with such specialized exercises as number and language processing, this brain switched into "a beta or active state" and the right brain remained in alpha, or a quiet state. When drawing and visualization exercises were pursued, the right brain recorded beta and the left, alpha.[10]

As corporate manager of management development at General Electric, Hermann began to test volunteers in order to determine their brain hemisphere dominance, the congruencies among those of the same brain preference, and conflicts and misunderstandings between different brain tendencies. In addition to the testing he put together a survey form, requesting data on education, preferred academic subjects and work, and "some adjectives describing different functions of the specialized [two hemisphere] brain."[11] When Herrmann had Kendrik Few of Opinion Research Corporation do a factor analysis of his rudimentary data, he found that certain clusters agreed with reports from people who saw themselves as left-brainers while others correlated with information from people who saw themselves as right-brainers. He had the beginning of a scientific instrument, which in 1978 was expanded and refined into what has become the Herrmann Brain Dominance Instrument (HBDI).[12]

Herrmann's instrument began to reveal four clusters of answers, which he began to see as distinct.[13]

The line describes "two extremes, one for left and one for right, and two intermediate ratings, one for left center and one for right center."[14] These clusters had the following elemental characteristics: two clusters represented the end points of the continuum, the extremes of the dichotomy (logical, analytical, and quantitative on the left; intuitive, artistic, and imaginative on the right); the other two seemed to represent a pair of points centered between the extremes,[15]

Herrmann's Evolving Four Clusters

LEFT   RIGHT

Left/Right Continuum. Two Points

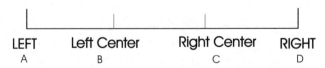

LEFT   Left Center   Right Center   RIGHT
A   B   C   D

Left/Right Continuum. Four points, two added for left center
and right center

FIGURE 8.1

His Figure 3-6: Data Clusters.[16]

which I have called left center and right center. The left center descriptors had to do with planning, organizing, and administering; the right center cluster had to do with emotions, interpersonal aspects, expressiveness, and music.

By this time Herrmann had measured hundreds of people, but he was still working primarily with the left hemisphere/right hemisphere—or dual model—of human preferences as seen in his linear diagrams. He was impressed with the fact that "the overall data seemed equally distributed among the four regions."[17] Meanwhile, he was thinking about how the two-hemisphere theory and the triune brain theory might fit together. While driving between home and the office, he suddenly had a breakthrough:

> I was thinking about how to merge the triune and the left brain/right brain theories. Both theories initially appeared in my mind's eye the way they are always illustrated: the left brain/right brain concept I "saw" was a frontal cross section of the brain indicating two separate hemispheres. The triune brain appeared in a side view cross section cut between the hemispheres rather than through them. Then, in my visualization, the triune brain cross section rotated through 90 degrees, so instead of looking at it from the side, I was seeing it from the back.

> Eureka! There, suddenly, was the connecting link I had been searching for! The limbic system was also divided into two separate halves, and also endowed with a cortex capable of thinking, and also connected by a commissure—just like the cerebral hemispheres. Instead of there being two parts of the specialized brain, there were *four—the number of clusters the data had been showing!*

> Instead of using a straight line with four clusters, I could simply bend the ends up and around to form a circular graph, which would also correspond to a cutaway of the

brain from behind. So, what I had been calling left brain, would now become the *left cerebral hemisphere.* What was the right brain, now became the *right cerebral hemisphere.* What had been left center, would now be *left limbic,* and right center, now *right limbic.* The fact that each quadrant touched the next would reflect the connectors—the two commissures between the left and right sides of the brain, and the association and projection fibers that provide communication between cerebral and limbic on the same side.[18]

Figure 8.2 represents the four quadrants, as described above. The letters, A, B, C, and D designate each quadrant, beginning with the left cerebral and proceeding counterclockwise through the three other quadrants. The letters had come from the four clusters he had identified on the straight line, beginning with A on the far left.[19]

The Whole Brain Model

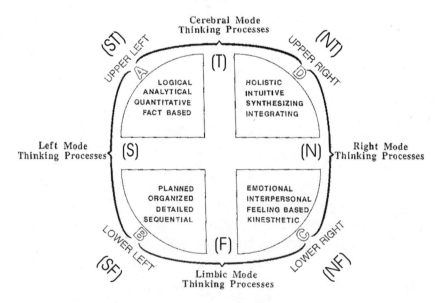

by Ned Hermann, The Creative Brain, p.411
(with individual types and type couplings added by John Giannini)

FIGURE 8.2

Now Herrmann had visualized a mandala, a circle in four parts, similar to Jung's type mandala. Before looking at these connections, we need to reflect on Herrmann's next step: "The shift from the physiological model to the metaphoric," the descriptions of which are already observed in figure 8.2 (page 326). In figure 8.3 (page 328), Herrmann seeks to show the evolution of his theory.

THE METAPHORICAL QUADRANT BRAIN
AND TYPE PREFERENCES

A metaphorical model was necessary, Herrmann argued, for three reasons:

1. Because "determining precisely which part of the brain was doing what was looking more and more difficult and less and less important." In other words, it was not necessary to do EEG brain scans on every person to determine the physical area of the cognition. The actual anatomical area of the brain as the locus of each mental mode is not the issue; rather, it is the consistency of experiences and language associated with each of the quadrants as experienced by people who were tested.[20]

2. Whether the limbic system was the physical basis of the two center clusters or not, the "idea was useful because it provided a means of organizing and clarifying our thinking about modes of knowing." He continued, quoting Ralph Sockman:

> And that, after all, is what metaphors are: ideas that clarify understanding of something else, like—"man's soul is the candle of the Lord" (Proverbs) or "The larger the island of knowledge, the longer the shoreline of wonder."[21]

3. "Finally, 'The data was great! Daily occurrences confirmed that the four quadrant modes-of-knowing model was producing data on human behavior that was consistent enough to have validity in its own right.'"[22]

Evolution to the Metaphorical Model

PHYSIOLOGY➡*ARCHITECTURE* ➡ *METAPHOR* ➡ *APPLICATION*

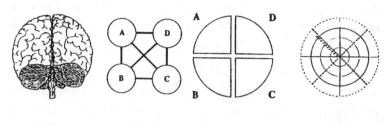

| THE BRAIN | THE ORGANIZING PRINCIPLE | THE WHOLE BRAIN MODEL | THE BRAIN DOMINANCE PROFILE |

*The Evolution to the Metaphorical Model from
The Creative Brain
by Ned Herrmann

FIGURE 8.3

Jung himself would have been particularly pleased by Herrmann's shift to the metaphorical, because in *Psychological Types,* as we recall, he began to connect the archetypal images and language (which are metaphors) of the two attitudes and the four functions with the corresponding bodily instincts that have their roots in the brain. In the second decade of the twentieth century, he had intuited the brain-mind connections that are now being discovered. Further, Jung and Isabel Briggs Myers would have resonated with Herrmann's amplification of the meaning of metaphors. As Hermann writes:

> They can bridge cultures, languages, and brain dominance preferences. A product of the right brain, a metaphor can be thought of as a translation from one mental language to another, from the literal to the analogic. Its power is the instant understanding it brings by reason of the translation.[23]

THE WHOLE BRAIN AS A METAPHOR
OF THE CREATIVE PROCESS

Herrmann sees this model as an extended metaphor for the creative process, just as discussed earlier in examining the type mandala. Herrmann's description of creativity as it proceeds from quadrant to quadrant enables us to connect his brain quadrants with the type couplings. In Herrmann's view, the counterclockwise process begins in quadrant A with interest and the capacity to ask clear and logical questions (that we also find in the ST archetype). *Preparation* draws on the resources of both quadrants A (ST) and B (SF) to gather facts and organize and develop a plan of action. (I have suggested that a more critical typological view of the initial question would be pursued along with aiding the planning characteristic of the SF mentality.) Then follows *incubation,* which, for Herrmann, occurs in the C (NF) and D (NT) quadrants, consisting of contemplation, subconscious processing, reflection, mulling, visualization, and sensory perception. (I suggest here that incubation also occurs in the B quadrant that embraces the parental and reflective mode, and that the NF and NT couplings provide a sharper delineation of the creative process.) The NF/C is the metaphorical place of sudden breakthroughs, since it is the most undifferentiated of the types/archetypes, and consequently was called the Oceanic by the Osmond group. Herrmann indirectly alludes to this same idea when he describes the C quadrant as the "seat of music," which is the most primal of the human arts. The NF quadrant is also the psychophysiological place of emotions, the elemental wellspring of all creativity. Then the more organized NT characteristic of the D quadrant gives deeper order and creative structure to the original breakthrough. *Verification* returns us to the A and B quadrants for the purpose of "checking out to see if it [the creative response] resolves the original problem." The final step for Herrmann is *application,* which may begin in B and involves all four quadrants.[24]

Herrmann makes a particularly strong statement about application in the context of creativity:

creativity in its fullest sense involves both generating an idea and manifesting it—making some thing happen as a result. To strengthen creative ability you need to apply the idea in some form. . . . While ideas can come in seconds, application can take days, years, or even a lifetime to realize . . . application ultimately calls on specialized mental capabilities in all four quadrants of the brain.[25]

Herrmann shows that the dominance of any two adjacent quadrants, such as AB, CD, AD, or BC, creates primary hindrances to any creative achievement.[26] Again, as with Jung, any rigid one-sidedness not only barbarically destroys the human and ecological commonweal but also limits inventive potentials. However, in my opinion, a rigid viewpoint is not easily maintained within a two-quadrant consciousness, since most of us have this mental and attitudinal range. But Herrmann convincingly argues that in the business world, most people generally think that problem-solving is a particularly left-brain process, so that all the creative potentials of the C and D quadrants are ignored, such as "modeling, simulating, doodling, intuiting, thinking metaphorically and synthesizing."[27] The fact that our cultural bias is generally left-brain supports Herrmann's perception of the business world's inflexibility.

Herrmann proceeds to explore the creative process in several venues: how it is furthered in education;[28] how it is experienced in his workshops;[29] and what creative people pay attention to, such as "Albert Einstein dreaming of himself riding on a beam of light as a prelude to conceiving the theory of relativity."[30] The "key to creative living," he writes, lies in "reclaiming our passions,"[31] learning from the idiosyncratic behavior of children,[32] and expanding our preferences beyond specific quadrants.[33]

Herrmann cites examples of differences among quadrant types that appear when they were asked to describe "the most creative person" they knew. Proceeding counterclockwise: the A (ST) type person was unable to offer any description; the B (SF) type's description was factual; the C (NF) rendered a literary prose depiction; and finally the D (NT) created an actual poetic description.[34] Herrmann also shows some of the various telling traits of people from the different quadrants. For example, As dress the most formally and, proceeding again counterclockwise, Ds dress most informally.[35]

In all of this, Herrmann did not give much thought to the parallel work of the *Myers-Briggs Type Indicator®* (*MBTI®*). In turn, most *MBTI* researchers and Jungian analysts have ignored Herrmann's creative contributions to understanding human differences. I suggest that there is one solid reason for this lack of awareness: Herrmann conceptualizes his quadrants in an interactive circle or compass. Herrmann's circle of interactive quadrants is somewhat similar to at least one factor that has separated the two worldwide Jungian communities of analysts and typologists: most typologists perceive the types in separate boxes and lines and as relatively separated from one another, while the Jungian circle portrays the interaction of the four functions and couplings both intrapsychically and socially. In the circular arrangement, the dynamic relationship among the types is more apparent. Unfortunately, few Jungians actualize this theory in practice. As a result, they are as unaware of the work of Herrmann as they are of the *MBTI* typologists.

THE WHOLE BRAIN MODEL AND THE *MBTI*

Herrmann became more aware of the Jung/*MBTI* model when Victor Bunderson, an experienced researcher, began collaborating with him to validate the Herrmann Brain Dominance Indicator (HBDI) in the early 1980s. Bunderson began connecting Jung's types and the *MBTI* research to Herrmann's emerging model. In his work (presented in appendix A of *The Creative Brain*), Bunderson shows considerable knowledge of the *MBTI* and demonstrates a certain congruence between the *MBTI* and the Herrmann whole brain model. Bunderson speaks of the *MBTI* as "highly regarded as a measure of personality type."[36] He integrated his HBDI research and the *MBTI* in several ways. For one thing, he added an introversion–extraversion spectrum to the HBDI itself.[37] His research shows a high correlation of the *MBTI's* individual functions with Herrmann's related quadrants: thinking with A; feeling with C; and intuition with D. The weakest correlation seemed to be between B and sensing. However, an extensive grouping of the B quadrant's characteristics—such as "data collector, conservative, controlled, sequential . . . detailed"—cries out to be identified as the sensation function.[38] If we now look at figure 8.2 (page 326), we see that the functions are correctly opposite one another. Immediately we have a strong additional validation of the thinking and feeling, and sensation and intuition functions as polar behaviors. Further, Bunderson's research shows that there is an interesting and validated grouping of intuition and perception on one hand, and sensation and judging on the other, which supports the *MBTI* researchers' strong correlations of these groupings.[39]

THE FOUR TYPE COUPLINGS
AND THE WHOLE BRAIN MODEL

Bunderson says nothing about the type couplings, even though the relative location of the individual functions in the brain and metaphorical circle makes such a connection possible. Bunderson had obviously neither read the Osmond group's work nor focused on the extensive *MBTI* research based on the four couplings. However, given the alignment of the functions, we can make the following correlations (as already indicated in the earlier discussion of the creative process): ST with the A quadrant; SF with the B quadrant; NF with the C quadrant; and NT with the D quadrant. Sally L. Power and Lorman L. Lundsten's 1997 *MBTI* research project gives statistical support for the connection between the four type couplings and Herrmann's four quadrants.[40] While their focus was on the correlation "between type preferences and left-brain/right-brain cognitive functioning," they also looked at the correlation of the individual types with the cerebral frontal brain's more abstract metaphors and with the limbic back brain's more "emotionally-toned thought process" where "I, S, F, and J are more limbic functions, and E, N, T, and P are more cerebral."[41] Finally, without focusing on this fact, they established the basis for associating the four brain quadrants with the four type couplings when they showed the following high correlations:[42]

> **ISTJ (S dominance and ST coupling) with Cerebral Left (97.5) and Limbic Left (93.1)**
>
> **ESFJ (F dominance and SF coupling) with Limbic Left (90.6) and Limbic Right (72.9)**
>
> **ENFP (N dominance and NF coupling) with Limbic Right (80.5) and Cerebral Right (91.5)**
>
> **INTP (T dominance and NT coupling) with Cerebral Left (87.2) and Cerebral Right (86.9)**

Notice the interrelated flow of the couplings in the counterclockwise circle: ST, SF, NF, and NT.

In looking now at these correlations among functions, couplings, and brain quadrants, we need to consider Herrmann's description of each quadrant and his development of the brain dominance profile that depicts each individual's quadrant preferences. Herrmann's quadrants, the Whole Brain concept, and his metaphorical descriptions of individual preferences developed initially out of physiological studies of the brain. By relating individual preferences to brain anatomy and his conceptual articulations in the four quadrants, Herrmann supports the coupling archetypes that Jung first mentioned and which are found in Toni Wolff's four feminine modalities, in the Osmond group's research, in Moore and Gillette's adult archetypes; and finally in the

MBTI's enormous data bank of more than one million profiles.

The Whole Brain model substantially agrees with the picture that consistently emerges from the many other variations of the four couplings that we have been studying. Referring to figure 8.2 (page 326), we see that the characteristics of the A quadrant—logical, analytical, quantitative, and fact-based—correspond to those of the ST Structural archetype. The defining elements of the B quadrant—planned, organized, detailed, and sequential—agree with the ordered propensities of the SF Moralist combination. Further, the typical features of the C quadrant—emotional, interpersonal, feeling-based, and kinesthetic—are in line with the artistic, harmonizing tendencies of the NF Oceanic/Lover archetype. Finally, the specific traits of the D quadrant—holistic, intuitive, synthesizing, and integrating—match the large picture orientation of the NT Ethereal configuration.

In turn, the four function couplings add depth of meaning to each of Herrmann's quadrants. The A quadrant is enriched by the ST Structural's love of creating maps and designs, and by the Warrior's capacity to finish any task, provide the "doer" energy from the psyche and seek out the inspiration of the Leader. The SF Moralist adds to the B quadrant a practical, warm, ethical, and parental character and sets the moral tone for any organization, from family to nation. Herrmann's picture of the B quadrant person as conservative and attuned to law and order is strengthened by the SF King/Queen's identification with the universal principle of cosmic order. The characteristics of the NF Creative Artist/Lover archetype help us perceive the C quadrant as the psychic place in each of us that spawns original insights. The NF coupling also focuses on human development and relationship, which Herrmann describes so well as human resources, personal growth, and interaction. The added feature of the NT Magician, which Moore and Gillette describe as the one who enters into the in-depth realms of knowledge and wisdom, strengthens the D quadrant's facility for capturing the big picture. Overall, Herrmann's creative work, initially conceived independent of Jungian and *MBTI* influence, dovetails with the other descriptions of the four function couplings. Herrmann's model supports my thesis that the type couplings are archetypes.

THE BRAIN DOMINANCE PROFILE, THE TYPE COUPLINGS AND THE UNCONSCIOUS

Herrmann sought a way to show the various strengths as well as inter-relations of the four quadrants. His solution was the Brain Dominance Profile, a creative depiction of these structures and their contrasting numerical values. The Profile provides a circular configuration that might help *MBTI* practitioners further their consciousness of a circular approach to the types, especially the couplings, which I am advocating in this book. Used together, the two instruments enhance the depiction of functions as dynamically relational. However, Herrmann's quadrants by themselves lack specific identities that probably limit their interactive possibilities. In contrast, the individual functions and their couplings in the Jung/*MBTI* model are related to introversion and extraversion, and to judging and perceiving so as to clearly establish the identity of the dominant, auxiliary, and inferior functions, their respective locations in the compass, their various well-defined tasks, and their many possible interactions. Moreover, the Jung/*MBTI* model takes into account the difficult, chaotic resistance and creative potential found in the activated inferior functions and the inferior couplings, as well as the limited remittances of the auxiliary functions and couplings. This awareness stands in sharp contrast to Herrmann's view that realizing nonpreferred ways of functioning is relatively easy. On the other hand, Herrmann's Profile has a distinct advantage over the typological circle in that it graphically displays the measured strengths of each of the quadrants and, therefore, of the related individual and coupled functions (see figure 8.4, page 336).

Figure 8.4 depicts an ST/A dominant person, a configuration that Herrmann calls an "A Only Profile," in whom the three other quadrants

The Basic Diagram of the Brain Dominance Profile
(Featuring an A/ST Dominance)

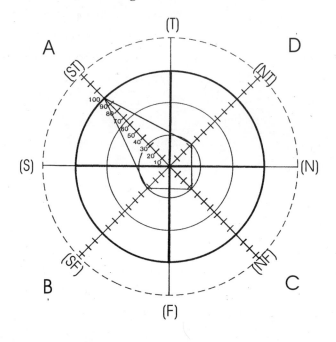

by Ned Herrman, The Creative Brain, Fig 4-2, p.78
(parenthesis added by John Giannini)

FIGURE 8.4

Herrmann's Figure 4-2, p. 78, with all the function types and couplings superimposed

are relatively weak. He subsequently pictures the three other quadrants in a similar way. Then he shows profiles of multiple dominants,[43] and typical profiles of persons in different occupations.[44] In another series of figures,[45] Herrmann suggests that one can move to the opposite of one's dominant preference by consciously relaxing one's preference and simply beginning to value its opposite. For example, he writes that an A-type person shifting toward the C quadrant can "move to the Lower Right: Relax on need for proof of fact. VALUE FEELING." To some extent this is possible, as Jung has indicated, at least as far as switching from the superior function to the first auxiliary. However, Jung warns of serious problems when one encounters the inferior function to which Herrmann is referring, since it is both in, as well as a bridge to, the unconscious, and is the opposite of the superior, conscious dominant. Repercussions arise in dealing with the inferior function because this relatively unused function most often activates volcanolike emotions and frightful images from the unconscious. In some rational or superficial way, one can explore one's opposite, such as an ST Left Cerebral dominant person trying to write poetry or doodle spontaneously. However, no fundamental change occurs in any person without a transformative, emotional shift in conscious values emerging from the depth of the creative unconscious. Paradoxically, one needs the emotional storms that come from the unconscious, specifically from the emerging inferior function or coupling. Difficult, consistent, often very painful work with emotionally volatile dreams, stubborn memory material, and sensitive relationships is necessary in order to fundamentally expand one's function or coupling preference. We need to look again at figure 6.2 (page 247) in chapter 6. It shows the human personality pictured metaphorically as a circular surface (on which the four quadrants are represented), as well as depicting a conelike depth grounded in the Self as the source and container of the person's whole brain and mind. We can imagine that, while all four quadrants could be pictured on the surface, they could also be portrayed as descending to the Soul's depth, beginning with the preferred quadrant, followed by the first auxiliary, the second auxiliary, and finally, the inferior quadrant.

We also need to consider how quadrant dominants other than one's natural dominant can be seriously injurious to physical as well as mental health, as Jung has pointed out and personally experienced. Individuals who, out of necessity, live their lives, as I did, operating from dominant quadrants that are not natural to them inflict upon themselves a certain amount of typological violence. Just as parts of the body are injured when they are misused, so damage occurs when psychic parts are misused. An example will illustrate this dynamic.

John, a middle-aged man, whose case Lawrence LeShan reported in *You Can Fight For Your Life,*[46] was in a midlife crisis and desperately ill with an advanced, massive brain tumor. In the book, LeShan calls him a lawyer, but we know from a 1985 audio tape by LeShan and a personal conversation that he was a surgeon. The profile of a surgeon might look, at least superficially, like the exclusively ST/A dominant person in figure 8.4 (page 336). As a surgeon, John had to fully develop the ST/A quadrant's capabilities of logical proficiency and precise pragmatism. He did so practically to the exclusion of his SF/B caretaker capacities, his NF/C emotionality, and NT/D creativity, although he had been a child prodigy in music. However, his domineering father would not allow any son of his to become a musician—to him, an inferior profession. Nevertheless, John continued to play music on the side. In the course of his adult life, he had come to hate not only his present work but also his marriage. If John had taken the *MBTI* and the HBDI at age twelve, his profile might have looked like figure 8.5.

His innate preferences would be located in his right brain hemisphere, beginning with the musical sensitivity of his NF/C quadrant and the creative expansiveness of his NT/D quadrant. In order to function as a surgeon, John had to develop his ST abilities. The differences between his learned profile, demanded by parental authority, and his natural profile caused him much stress. Similar cases are available from *MBTI* records. My own misuse of the types caused me serious psychological anguish.

Disavowed innate preferences can also become endemic in a given culture. A report on Korean children ages seven to fourteen from the 1995 *MBTI* International Conference showed a wide discrepancy between the natural type patterns and the apparent learned behavior

John's Approximate INFJ Profile
as a Twelve-Year-Old Musical Prodigy

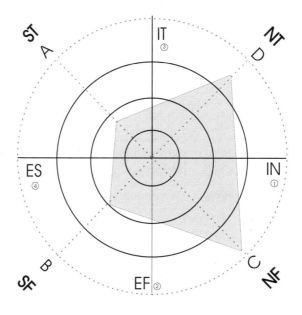

A 2-2-1-1 Profile

FIGURE 8.5

among adult women, male university students, and male employees. For example, while 89 percent of the children preferred feeling, 58 percent of adult women, 61 percent of male university students, and 78 percent of male employees preferred thinking.[47] One wonders about the possibilities of serious psychological damage that such a typological distortion has caused in Korean youth.

John pursued inner work, and his cancer eventually went into remission after he entered fully into his beloved performing with a symphony orchestra. The return to his innately preferred typology and musical gifts facilitated tremendous healing. However, such a recovery does not happen overnight. With reference to inner work, LeShan tells all his patients that their ultimate health depends on achieving a personally felt, imaged relationship with their inner despairing child. Initially, John could interact imaginatively with the child, but could not feel emotionally connected. He had, after all, developed an ST/A Warrior dominance in his twenty years or more of surgical work, which demanded an objective, rational consciousness and excluded any subjective feelings for patients. Now his very survival, as well as his reborn musical genius, demanded an emotional recovery. However, a powerful resistance against any loving feeling for his remembered and inner child continued until he had a dream in which he saw on a dock a small boy who was frightened and crying because he feared falling into the water. The dream continued:

> I was walking out on the dock toward him. I don't know why I was walking there. When I came near him, he started to run toward me. I knelt down and held out my arms. He ran into them and I stood up. As I carried him back toward the shore he stopped crying. I felt that I loved him.[48]

When John told this dream to Dr. LeShan, both men wept. John apparently also recovered the felt connection to his musical ability and a latent, related potential for health because of this loving connection with the inner child. These are NF/C achievements. From the book and the personal conversation with LeShan in 1985, I learned that John had been at that time a successful musician for around two decades, with his cancer in total remission.

It is possible that John, a man in his forties, might have shown a C and D dominance in the HBTI and his natural INFJ in the *MBTI*. However, a phantom profile, developed over the years, would have also been acting as a hidden barrier to realizing his inherent capacity for health and his innate musical talent. Yet if one had asked him about his work passions, he would have revealed his natural inclination toward the musical NF area. Unless we review a person's life history and natural interests, our superficial use of either the *MBTI* and the HBDI can miss a person's real interests.

I have pointed out elsewhere in this book that many *MBTI* practitioners do not pay enough attention to the powerful effects of the inferior function. In a like manner, those practitioners may be slow to perceive a typological preference imposed either by family or collective expectations. Yet both the inferior function and imposed functions, such as John experienced, can cause untold damage to the mind, heart, body, and social attitudes of every person. Because of the shadowy, unconscious demands of imposed and inferior functions that skew people's minds, those who use the *MBTI* and HBDI need to develop a knowledge of the revealing and healing powers of the unconscious.

One of the resources for engaging the unconscious is dream work. In spite of Ned Herrmann's rich inventiveness, he does not pay sufficient attention to the unconscious mind's most primitive creativity: the creation of dreams. In most cases, it is the dream that opens the door to the integration of something of the inferior and ignored functions. In my four decades of work with this nightly innovative output that clients report, I have never encountered a dream that did not add significant, precise meaning to everyday life. This meaning is revealed when we understand the dream's symbolic language in a current or even a lifelong context. Further, dream work has never failed to open emotional doors to other quadrants. After all these years, I continue to be amazed at the new, yet accurate dream images that emerge into consciousness with their emotionally healing insights and consciousness-expanding gifts.

Dreams often show us pathologies, needed corrections, and potentials for a particular type dominance. Here is an example from Marlene, an INFP/C type, whose dream revealed in stark imagery both her life story and the barrier to valuing and then moving beyond her dominant NF quadrant:

I see myself as a four-year-old, standing next to the coffin of my dead mother. There are other members of the family around, including aunts and uncles, but no one notices me. Suddenly, I see myself getting smaller and smaller until I am a two-year-old. At this point, I let my insides go out between my tiny legs. As soon as I do this, my mother awakens from the dead. I know that, in order to keep her alive, I must be her servant for life.

Marlene had been born into a family in which left-hemisphere sensation and thinking typologies characterized her parents and her four siblings. All of them have either ST or SF preferences. No one understood or noticed Marlene, who had an innate right-hemisphere dedication to gentle, harmonious living and to sensitive, creative imaginings. Only in late mid-adulthood, after much inner work, has she learned to appreciate her own typology and creativity, and to understand her antipathy to technology, the product of ST minds. She had felt so vulnerable in the face of this technology and its type preferences, which originated in her family, that she had developed many allergies to petroleum products as well as a generalized loathing of modern science. She has slowly begun to value her rational and logical capacities, as well as to accept and even admire contemporary scientific achievements. Most of all, she has learned to accept herself as an INFP Lover. She recognizes this type's natural gifts and strengths. She recognizes her preference's weaknesses, such as fear of personal power, fear of criticism, and inappropriate generosity—giving without expecting decent treatment in return. True to her type's love of nature and universal harmony, she is also dedicated to preserving the natural environment and fights incessantly against the use of destructive pollutants in her area, even as she is beginning to conquer her allergies.

Herrmann encourages persons to awaken their creativity, especially through the arts, in order to utilize the right-hemisphere possibilities that he feels our culture has generally discouraged. He tells of designing his "Whole Brain House."⁴⁹ He encourages companies to allow employees to imaginatively personalize their work spaces.⁵⁰ He also discusses the need for parents to support the unique development of their children,⁵¹ which, next to the parents' realizing their own intimacy, is the greatest of human challenges. He feels that every person has "some island of potential brilliance still hidden in their mental seascape," pointing, as an example, to the subject of *May's Miracle*, a Canadian-produced documentary about Mary Lempke, a tiny, middle-aged woman called May by everyone.⁵² May believed in the potentials of her adopted son, baby "Leslie," a child born blind and the victim of severe cerebral palsy. Through unremitting care, love, and observation, she encouraged his musical ability in particular, which blossomed into a virtuoso-level skill, despite his limitations.

As adults, we also need to recognize the creativity that exists within us. We need to recognize that the Soul, the principle of life in each of us, is both a sacred mentor and a playwright. Just as a physical injury to the body is really healed by the body's own innate somatic dynamic, as any doctor will agree, so are our psychospiritual wounds healed by the Soul's psychic energies. The psyche is always sending us dreams and synchronistic events that seek to awaken our consciousness to healing and growth, to the necessary realization of our whole mind potential. Repetitive dreams and synchronistic real-life situations continually call us to awaken to life's breadth and depth. Both are karmic and come to us for one deep reason: to help us realize unfulfilled potentials. Most people stubbornly resist these spiritual challenges, but in many ways, we can even work through resistance, especially if we see them for what they are: invitations to make needed changes. We can engage resistance as an inner personality, and address its emotional content in a dialogue, either in words or in nonverbal communications (such as drawing, sculpting, dancing, etc.). We can face resistance before sleep, and ask the unconscious to produce a dream that will reveal its positive value. We must persist in looking for every clue and subtle shift that moves our consciousness forward. Every move forward is a move into an unknown and dark region, into a daring journey of faith, in which we must trust that a map will emerge and that we are contributing to the structure of that map.

This is the depth psychologist's approach. In contrast, Herrmann, following his natural extraverted preference, concentrates on conscious attempts to change preferences. He devotes chapter 8 of his book to this task. His commonsense view is that "frames of reference"—the reality of old habits that serve us well in our dominant choices—block us from seeking new preferences. To expand our personal frame, we need to grasp the value of others' frames. For instance, an ST/A type needs to stop denigrating feeling, and realize that feeling's rationale can "actually improve the value of thought."[53] Herrmann gives a good example of this in the experience of an NT/D artist, who was an excellent painter but a poor manager of his life. He was always late for meetings, he delivered wrong items, and so forth. He was also consistently critical of the organization of art shows. Herrmann talked him into participating in a team that was planning and assembling an art show. The experience touched him significantly; he began to appreciate the gifts and talents of SF/B types and his own new potential in this quadrant. Again, this sanguine view of preferential development is true up to a point. Most *MBTI* practitioners work with a similar assumption—that a conscious development of other preferences is possible and valuable.

However, some of the vast violence in our society—especially the hate and fear stirred up in us by our inferior function and coupling—covers the spectrum from the physical to the psychological and from individual families to international politics, and has its roots in a lack of understanding and valuing typological differences. Jerome Bernstein traces the failed dialogues between the Soviet Republic and the United States in their power struggle under the awesome shadow of a possible atomic war in *Power Politics: The Psychology of Soviet-*

American Partnership. Bernstein gives many examples of misinterpreted communications that arose between the representatives of these nations, due to, among other reasons, cultural type differences that mutually awakened each side's shadowy collective inferior functions.[54] He shows how the Americans spoke in an extraverted thinking language and the Russians in the (opposite) introverted feeling mode. It is not enough, however, that we understand such differences cognitively. Ignorance of typological differences cuts to the instinctual and emotional core of our typological development. We recall what Jung said of the failed communication between Freud and Adler, due to Freud's extraverted and Adler's introverted orientations: that each of them was challenged to find the other in the "principle of imagination," that is, in the creative potential of the Self.[55] The rational mind must enter into a conscious dialogue with the more irrational aspects of the Soul found in the chaotic NF/C quadrant of the right hemisphere, and awaken the light-giving insights of our inferior typological opposites. In the final analysis, we must first rediscover the authority that is within, the divine gift of the widest and deepest possible typological identity that is our birthright.

We cannot do this personal and societal work alone. We need to join groups of dedicated people who search for mind/brain wholeness through acknowledging human differences and creatively work with those differences. Though not so named, such groups often exist in AA and other twelve-step gatherings, in church-related groups, in some professional organizations coming out of depth, humanistic and type psychologies, and in movements dedicated to promoting a free and just society. In working toward individuation, some of us need help from individual and group counseling, and from wise friends.

Even hard-nosed businesses profit from the insights of typology and Herrmann's model. A 1997 article in the *Harvard Business Review* describes the importance of corporate leaders' selecting managers and workers who have different personalities so as to further the creativity and profitability of the company. The authors argue, "Conflict is essential to innovation. The key is make the abrasion creative."[56] They continue:

> Innovate or fall behind; the competitive imperative for virtually all businesses today is that simple. Achieving it is hard, however, because innovation takes place when different ideas, perceptions and ways of processing and judging information collide. That, in turn, often requires collaboration among various players who see the world in inherently different ways.[57]

Accordingly, they recommend both the Herrmann Brain Dominance Instrument and the *Myers-Briggs Type Indicator*® as two significant and related instruments that contribute to maximizing creative conflict in a company. The message is clear: it does indeed take all types to run a business, a government, a religious structure, or a society.

A FOLLOW-UP BOOK ON THE WHOLE BRAIN

Katherine Benziger, with Anne Sohn as a collaborator, has written a book entitled *The Art of Using Your Whole Brain*.[58] Benziger attended one of Herrmann's certification workshops in the early 1980s, and began collaborating with the Whole Brain associates. She had been developing her own management training approaches, and was impressed with Herrmann's work because it agreed with Jung's type psychology. She feels that her model, which is substantially the same as Herrmann's except for some differences in brain theory, owes a debt to both Carl Jung and Karl Pribram.[59] She dedicates her book to "the Tradition of thinking about thinking, especially to the Native American Medicine Wheel and to Carl Jung," and to her maternal grandmother, who had studied with Jung.

Benziger develops the relationship of Herrmann's four modes with various archetypal systems. For example, she connects the quadrants with the four geographical directions of the Native American Medicine Wheel and with the directions' related animals and their characteristics. In my view, the characteristics of the animals, as Benziger describes them, agree roughly with the qualities of each of the four type couplings:

> **The Frontal Left (ST) with the North and the Buffalo, Wisdom, cold without feeling.**
>
> **The Basal Left (SF) with the West and Bear, Introspection, looks-within place.**
>
> **The Basal Right (NF) with the South and the Mouse, Innocence and Trust, Touching.**
>
> **The Frontal Right (NT) with the East and the Eagle, Illumination, clear far-sighted vision, but close to nothing, always above and separated from life.[60]**

Benziger recognizes the correlation of the four individual functions with the four brain areas as in Herrmann's model. She also implicitly connects the four quadrants with the four type couplings when she correctly sees the alignment of the quadrants with the four Moore/Gillette cultural archetypes:

> **Basal Left (SF)—King: stability, order, fecundity**
>
> **Frontal Left (ST)—Warrior: goal-focused, aggressive, strategic, acts decisively, skilled with weapons**
>
> **Basal Right (NF)—Lover: feeling, connected, spiritual, nature lover**
>
> **Frontal Right (NT)—Magician: mystical, pattern-sensitive, insightful[61]**

However, she does not develop these fruitful affinities any further. She also acknowledges quite pointedly the relationship of Herrmann's creative work to Jung's:

> In fact, it would be largely accurate to say that what Herrmann did in the 1970's in terms of describing the contents of the four modes [quadrants] was to ground Jung's theory in what was then known and hypothesized about the actual workings of the brain. As such, it was a major breakthrough and, perhaps because of its scientific aspect, was well received by American and European businesses.[62]

Benziger's work builds on and adds to Herrmann's achievements much in the same way that Briggs and Myers' builds on Jung's. For example, Benzinger shows the difficulty an NF/Basal Right person has with time, because this type values the person more than schedules. Benziger suggests that the NF/Basal Right type person needs a collaborator, a left-hemisphere dominant manager type,[63] an SF/Basal Left who works very much on schedule. However, since the SF/Basal Left person may so overschedule that they do not leave any time for recreation, and because they try to pack too much order into given time frames, they need more time. However, this is not because they are lost in human interactions, as are the Basal Rights. "By contrast, the [ST] Frontal Left is a natural master of time," a person who is especially "adept at listening only for key information, analyzing it quickly, and taking immediate decisive action."[64] "For the [NT] Frontal Right, time management is almost a moot question," as they become completely involved in creative work.[65]

In the area of decision-making, NF/Basal Right people seek out others of a like mind with whom they discuss important issues which require them to make judgments. SF/Basal Lefts, by contrast, seek out procedural guidelines; NT/Frontal Rights make quick intuitive decisions; and ST/Frontal Lefts easily decide by prioritizing important concerns and considering only key facts.[66]

In personal relationships, we tend to choose like-minded friends who even mirror our nonverbal behavior and whom we feel we can trust. People who have the use of two quadrants on the same side of the brain more easily find friends because this pattern "appear[s] most frequently in our society" (p. 123). Multidominant individuals and those who are dominant in only one quadrant find it more difficult since the latter have fewer to draw on, and since the former address so many areas of interest that people cannot keep up.[67] Benziger's results are in line with Jungian and *MBTI* clinical and research experience, as well as her conclusion that we tend to marry our quadrant and hemisphere opposites. Benziger deserves to be quoted in this regard:

> our choice of a spouse is perhaps one of the most rational choices we make. . . . we marry in order to have the best chance to survive as well as to grow. Paradoxically, this means we marry someone who is very different from us. Someone who can handle those problems in life which frighten, baffle, or are otherwise uncomfortable for us. This then is the rule of marriage: we seek a mate who will complement and complete us in order to guarantee our survival. You might say, we marry to get a whole brain.[68]

Following Jung, a related but different way of understanding marriage is that the Self is constantly urging each partner to realize wholeness while mutually encouraging and supporting both partners to become whole. Marriage, in my view, therefore poses a greater challenge and spiritual opportunity for individuation than any other human relationship. Given these possibilities, it is of the utmost importance that the partners know and fully appreciate their own and the other's type.

Benziger's continuing work in brain research led her to differ with Herrmann regarding the brain structures that underlie the conceptual descriptions of the four quadrants. She began to speculate that the limbic system, because it is not a center of thinking, does not in any way form the primary basis for the two back quadrants of the brain. While the limbic system enables us to "store new memories in the cortex" and access existing memories, it focuses our attention and energizes our thinking either by "directing" or "fogging" our thoughts via its emotions.[69] In 1985, she consulted with Karl Pribram, a practicing neurosurgeon and psychologist who headed the Stanford Behavioral Research Labs, and whose book, *Language of the Brain,* was already acknowledged to be a modern classic. Pribram confirmed that the "four modes identified by the model most probably reflected the four cerebral chunks," two frontals and two basals.[70]

Furthermore, Pribram's wide research and theoretical background supports the Jungian view that the four quadrants or modes must always be considered in the larger context of all levels of the psyche, and, most importantly, are embraced and fed by the Soul or what Jung calls the Self (see figure 6.2, page 247). Ken Wilber, writing about Pribram, notes that his brain research later moved to a more visionary outlook when he changed from behaviorism to transpersonal psychology.[71] This shift occurred particularly through his collaboration with the theoretical physicist, David Bohm, and led Pribram, Bohm, and others to perceive the brain as a hologram, a holistic instrument, that mirrored the physical universe as "a gigantic hologram." Wilber continues:

> It was at this point that the "holographic paradigm" was born: the brain is a hologram perceiving and participating in a holographic universe. In the explicate or manifest realm of space and time, things and events are indeed separate and discrete. But beneath the surface, as it were, in the implicate or frequency realm, all things and events are spacelessly, timelessly, intrinsically one and undivided. And Bohm and Pribram reasoned, the quintessential religious experience, the experience of mystical oneness

and "supreme identity," might very well be a *genuine* and *legitimate* experience of this implicate and universal ground.[72]

The part intuits the whole—that is, the whole brain intuits the universe. This is the essence of the holographic paradigm. From this hypothesis has come the invention of holographic photography, or holography. Holography is three-dimensional photography that pictures things as if existing in space. The holographic negative itself does not register the object but only shows a meaningless pattern of swirls. However, when this negative is placed in a coherent light beam like a laser, the original wave pattern is regenerated, and the object appears as if in a three-dimensional space. The process mimics the visible mix of Chaos Science and, in Jung's psychology, the invisible and undifferentiated collective unconscious. As in Chaos Science, the form or pattern appears out of the apparent formless, and in depth psychology, the archetypes appear in types, dreams, and stories out of the dark depths of the unconscious. Further, any piece of the holographic plate will picture the entire photographed object. Similarly, many dreams depict one's entire life, particularly in regard to stable and evolving type preferences and to the unique, lifelong tasks that each of us is challenged to complete and the karmic obstacles we must overcome.

This information sends a powerful message to each of us. It says that when a substantial number of people realize a typological brain wholeness, the world will be drastically improved. It says that while each brain quadrant with its related coupled function archetype and characteristics are "separate and discrete" from the other quadrants on the surface, underneath they are also spaceless, timeless, and "one and undivided" in the Soul's ground. Perhaps this realization will become an absolute, an imperative, as the danger to both the human species and millions of surviving other species exponentially increases.

The lethal opposite of this wholeness is when a person adapts to a wrong preference, which Jung called a "falsification of types." Benziger has written a book-size monograph on this subject, in which, drawing on many authorities, she shows to what extent we suffer many debilitating behaviors, such as hostility and anxiety, alcoholism and other addictions, and even serious illnesses when we do not realize our own identity. She repeatedly reminds us that identity cannot ignore types, so that, "Given that self and identity encompasses type, a search was made to surface corroborating references to: falsification of type; falsification of self; or falsification of identity."[73]

The false use of types includes, in my view, the ineffective or inflated use of one's natural types, particularly if one is utilizing one's preferences to the exclusion of other types. In my last chapter, I show that the falsification of types is a collective problem in our Western and particularly United States societies because our cultural leaders and popular media adopt too consistently an inflated ESTJ Warrior and Left Frontal mode, to the virtual exclusion of the other three quadrants.

SUMMARY: THE COMPLEMENTARY RELATIONSHIP OF THE *MBTI* AND THE HBDI

Let us now summarize how the *MBTI* and the HBDI may complement and thereby strengthen one another. The *MBTI* registers the inner, personal dynamics, not only of the four functions, but also of the four coupled archetypes. Many who have worked on the *MBTI* have intuitively recognized this fact. Like the HBDI, the Indicator shows which quadrant is dominant, but, unlike the HBDI, it also shows which among the other quadrants are most easily accessible for development, beginning with the first auxiliary quadrant and ending with the inferior quadrant.

Consider A-dominant persons, as in figure 8.4 (page 336). Their first preference is ST. If we assume they are ESTJ types, their typological diagram (as pictured in figure 8.4, page 336) would show the ST/A quadrant as dominant. Since thinking (T) is the dominant function, it will be next coupled with intuition (N) so that the second quadrant of preference will be the first coupling auxiliary, NT/D. The third quadrant will be the SF/B, since it is opposite the NT/D in the circle. The fourth or inferior quadrant, the NF/C, must be opposite the first or dominant quadrant, the ST/A. Using the *MBTI* would help the whole-brain practitioner assist these one-quadrant persons to further develop in other modes.

The HBDI profile complements the *MBTI* by showing what the *MBTI* configuration of a type (in this case, the ESTJ) cannot directly show, even though the HBDI is arranged in the classical Jungian mandala. The HBDI profile, in contrast to the *MBTI*, is visibly structured to give a numerical weight to each quadrant, and, therefore, helps the viewer to assess the relative strengths of each quadrant. Let us again consider ESTJ/A quadrant persons. If the measured weight of the first auxiliary, NT/D, is weak, the apparent conclusion is that much hard work is needed to strengthen this quadrant. On the other hand, we could also infer that this quadrant, though quite natural to the ESTJ/A person, may have been devalued in their families or their immediate culture. Because it is naturally accessible as a preference, they can more easily develop it.

The circular HBDI's profile more clearly depicts four-quadrant, creative people, or, in *MBTI* terms, people who indicate a great deal of clarity in every function because their profile diagram so clearly highlights the strong areas in each quadrant. Showing the type polarities as spectrums has been the only diagramming used by *MBTI* practitioners. A spectrum diagram is useful, but, unlike the circle, it does not show the interplay of all the functions. We have here an opportunity to see how the couplings help give clarity to an HBDI personality picture.

Let us take the example of a male client who came out on the Indicator as an ISFJ/P, in which his J and P totals were exactly equal, the E score was close to the I, the N score was close to the S, and some answers showed a preference for T. The S and the F were, practically speaking, equally dominant. Jung determined that one of the functions in any coupling must be dominant and the other, a first auxiliary or first assistant. Focusing on the coupling rather than on individual functions lessens the risk of misidentifying the dominant function, or at least provides a better context in which to consider the dominant function in the coupling, especially when scores are so close. In this example, then, the SF/B is the first preferred quadrant. Because of the strong score on intuition (N), the second preferred quadrant (the NF/C) is practically as significant as the first. Further, because of the strength of the S function, this client also registers a high ST/A quadrant score in an *MBTI* version of this HBDI profile. The only slightly weak quadrant is the NT/D quadrant. Yet in actual work life, this person has developed considerable skill in creatively developing complex computer programs for his company. This shows his high NT proficiency. He is also artistically inclined, has an undergraduate engineering degree and an M.A. in social work. He is presently in the process of obtaining a doctorate in psychology. This example shows how using the Whole Brain Profile diagram to depict his type structure and focusing on the place and dynamic of the couplings adds considerable clarity when the *MBTI* score registers so much strength in all of the functions.

The Benziger study shows that dual quadrant people (people who prefer two side-by-side quadrants or any half of the personality circle) make up a large portion of the human population. The *MBTI* research has hardly considered this kind of insight. On the other hand, the Jung/*MBTI* perspective enriches this insight by noting that each of the dual quadrants as halves of the circle is dominated by one of the functions. Focusing on each of these crucial functions in each of the halves provides a way of describing each of the dual quadrants. Looking at the Whole Brain Model in figure 8.2 (page 326), we see the two frontal or cerebral quadrants are centered in thinking, the two left quadrants in sensation, the two right quadrants in intuition, and the two limbic or basal in feeling. Therefore, the two frontal modes can rightly be said to possess the objective and cool qualities of the T; the two left-brain quadrants, the pragmatic and grounded tenor of the S; the two right-brain quadrants, the inventive and futuristic focus of the N; and the two basal quadrants, the warm and subjectively caring quality of the F.

This last fact—the dominance of feeling in the lower brain quadrants—reminds us of the special significance of the feeling function, and with it, the NF Lover. As we noted earlier, Jung emphasized the crucial importance of the feeling function in the last essay he wrote before he died. He held that this function as "emotional value" is absolutely essential for integrating symbols and achieving individuation. What was said of the F, I again say here of the NF/C quadrant. We recall, in this regard, that a four-quadrant, clockwise view of the entire life cycle culminates in the NF/C Lover. When considered in this context, it is no wonder Moore and Gillette argue that the NF Lover is the most maligned among the four adult archetypes. Why? Because the Lover archetype is the most challenging and most demanding of the Soul's qualities, since it lays the very foundation of the golden rule: the love of self, on which both the love of one's neighbor and the love of God are based.

We can look again at examples of people who illustrate the importance of the feeling function and the NF coupling. Our story of Helen refers to this primal need to love and be loved. Helen stayed in therapy and continued to use the key to open the door to her own self love. The heroic trust and care that Mary Lempke gave the severely damaged "Little Lester" made possible the awakening of his remarkable musical ability. Marlene's dream in which her mother rose from the dead when she, as a two-year-old in her dream, surrendered her own sense of self, refers to the immense damage we suffer when we ignore our own self love. She has been striving to reclaim that love. LeShan's John would have never healed or recovered his musical gifts without experiencing in his mind and body the love of his despairing child and the child's love of him. Finally, the Holographic or Whole Brain and Mind Theory, is, in the deepest sense, a depiction of the all-embracing NF/C Lover in each of us. Type theory is a secular way of restating how all world scriptures represent God, both in the world and in each of us. For example, in the Bible's book of Wisdom, we read:

> In your sight the whole world is like a grain of dust that tips the scales. . . . Yet you are merciful to all, because you can do all things and overlook men's sins so that they can repent.

> Yes, you love all that exists, you hold nothing that you have made in abhorrence, for had you hated anything, you would not have formed it. . . . You spare all things because all things are yours, Lord, lover of life. (Wisdom, 11:22–27)

After four decades of work with the unconscious, I am convinced that what is said in such texts about God, understood cosmically, is also meant of us, understood microcosmically. All that happens to us inwardly and outwardly is finally oriented to our growth in love, the experiential way to wholeness. Outwardly, wholeness culminates in the Lover's relentless push toward a childlike compassion and creativity in the NF/C quadrant, and in effective and visionary social justice in the NT/D quadrant. Inwardly, wholeness depends on realizing a sufficient consciousness and an adequate assimilation of the inferior function, as well as misused or suppressed natural functions. Finally, this same NF/C quadrant is the source of our creativity, including dreams, music, and the great stories of all times.[74] In turn, these stories inspire major philosophies, theologies, and world-embracing systems, all of which are informed by the NT/D mentality.

Thus far in this book I have sought to show that typology metaphorically describes the whole human and divine story with the Soul through its archetypal quadrants. I have developed this story from various sources: (1) from many persons who have experienced the reconciling effects of type opposites in dreams and hence found a Taoistlike path in life; (2) from the theory and research initiated by Jung and the worldwide work of *MBTI* practitioners whom he inspired; (3) from the experiential typologists led by the Osmond group; (4) from the cultural and psychological explorations of Moore and Gillette; and (5) from the brain researches of both Herrmann and Benziger.

While I was in the midst of writing this chapter on the brain metaphors, a young student of the Torah assassinated Israel's great leader, Yitzhak Rabin, the pragmatic old warrior who had become a peace advocate. The solemn burial services for Rabin on November 6, 1995, attended by all the world leaders, sparked my following dream:

> A young, gaunt Jewish man is showing me a skull cap. It is larger than the ones usually worn by Jewish men of faith. It covers the whole of the top of the head, just as the cortex covers the top of the brain as the "thinking cap." I notice that the cap has four strange insignias: one in front, one in the rear and the other two on each side. I am approaching the man to ask him their meaning.

At the least, I can assume that the insignias refer to the type compass with its four functions and quarters. They appear on a sacred Jewish skull cap, the yarmulke. Some yarmulkes cover the entire top of the head, as does the cortex. This dream's context—writing on types in relationship to the brain, the international implications of Rabin's death by a radical Jewish rabbinic student, and the importance of respecting individual and national differences—all point to the importance of this dream's synchronistic message. The four insignias on the yarmulke suggest the overall meaning: our survival, the world's survival, depends on developing a whole mind and whole brain conscious of the sacredness of all of humankind and all of nature. The young man in the dream was about the same age as the young lawyer who, after killing Rabin, said, "justice was served."[75] This tragically myopic vision, which sees other viewpoints different from one's own as blurred, shadowy, and dangerous, spurred Jung, Briggs, Myers and McCaulley, the Osmond group, Moore and Gillette, Herrmann, Benziger, and others to help us see, experience, and value one another's differences. I hope to follow their lead with this book.

Notes

1. Richard Restak, quoted in Ned Herrmann, *The Creative Brain* (Kingsport TN: Quebec or Printing Book Group, 1994), p. 35. Most of the information about brain research will come from this source, unless I indicate otherwise in my text.

2. David Lewis, quoted in Herrmann, *The Creative Brain,* p. 33.

3. C. G. Jung, *Analytical Psychology: Notes of the Seminar Given in 1925* (Princeton NJ: Princeton University Press, 1989), p. 76.

4. Jung, *CW*, vol. 5, *Symbols of Transformation* (Princeton NJ: Princeton University Press, 1956), chapter 2, "Two Kinds of Thinking."

5. James Newman, "The Myers-Briggs Type Indicator and Gifts Differing," *San Francisco Jung Institute Library Journal* 3:1 (Autumn 1981), p. 52.

6. Herrmann, *The Creative Brain,* p. 17.

7. Ibid., p. 22.

8. Ibid., p. 31.

9. Ibid., p. 39.

10. Ibid., pp. 48–49.

11. Ibid., p. 51.

12. Ibid., pp. 52–53.

13. Ibid., pp. 47–60.

14. Ibid., p. 54.

15. Ibid., p. 58.

16. Ibid., p. 54.

17. Ibid., p. 61.

18. Ibid., p. 63 (italics, Herrmann).

19. Ibid., p. 65.

20. Ibid. Victor Bunderson, Herrmann's research specialist, notes in appendix A that Herrmann was criticized by two persons for seemingly holding that he had pinned down the actual locations in the brain of these four modes of knowing and acting. He writes: "These two detractors based their criticism on their impressions that the model is making a statement about the geographical location of functions in specific areas of the brain. Despite impressions these writers may have formed, the four quadrant model explained in this book depends fundamentally on preference [*MBTI* language] clusters and the idea of dominance or avoidance of these clusters by individuals, not on ideas about the location of brain function" (p. 345).

21. Ibid., p. 64.

22. Ibid.

23. Ibid., p. 223.

24. Ibid., p. 190–92.

25. Ibid., p. 186.

26. Ibid., pp. 192–93.

27. Ibid., p. 194.

28. Ibid., p. 218f.

29. Ibid., p. 210f.

30. Ibid., p. 196.

31. Ibid., p. 199f.

32. Ibid., p. 200f.

33. Ibid., p. 255f.

34. Ibid., pp. 92–93.

35. Ibid., pp. 94–95.

36. Ibid., pp. 353–54.

37. Ibid., pp. 67, 349–50.

38. Ibid., p. 425.

39. Ibid., p. 365.

40. Sally J. Power and Lorman L. Lundsten, "Studies That Compare Type Theory and Left Brain/Right Brain Theory," *Journal of Psychological Type* 43 (1997): pp. 22–28.

41. Ibid., pp. 22, 27.

42. Ibid., p. 26.

43. Herrmann, *The Creative Brain*, figure 4.8, p. 78.

44. Ibid., pp. 100–105.

45. Ibid., figure 9–12, p. 264.

46. Lawrence LeShan, *You Can Fight for Your Life: Emotional Factors in the Causation of Cancer* (New York: M. Evans, 1977), pp. 17–19, 136–37.

47. Sally Campbell, "Using Type Across Cultures," *Bulletin of Psychological Type* 18:3 (Summer 1995): pp. 14–17. "The culture values self-composure and controlled behavior, being centered, and not talking too much, respect, rituals, and thoughtful reflection. Behavior as a direct expression of feeling is just not done in Korea." So, for example, ENFP, INFP, and ESFP children tend to become ISTJs in high school, "which may reflect a survival mode in this highly competitive environment" (p. 16). One also wonders if this obedient behavior might also account for the religious cults that have originated in Korea, such that of the Reverend Moon and the University Bible Fellowship.

48. LeShan, *You Can Fight for Your Life,* p. 136.

49. Herrmann, *The Creative Brain,* pp. 298–305. It is impossible in a limited space to describe what Herrmann means by a "Whole Brain House," except to record that he considered the house's larger environment and helped design the house (D/NT), worked out many difficult details and strategies for utilizing solar energy (A/ST), made certain that the house had an aesthetic and practical warmth with the kitchen "as the central core of the house" (B/SF) (p. 303),

and developed the entire project in a creative, loving partnership with his wife (C/NF). He succinctly summarizes such a project as well as his actual work life in a "whole-brain way" as one that honors "the humanitarian values of C quadrant, the vision of D, the logic of A, and the practicality of B" (p. 304).

50. Ibid., p. 305f.

51. Ibid., p. 288.

52. Ibid., pp. 244–46.

53. Ibid., p. 256.

54. Jerome S. Bernstein, *Power and Politics: The Psychology of Soviet-American Partnership,* Boston: Shambhala, 1989). Bernstein writes: "Carl Jung's theory of psychological types offers unique insights into the communication problems between the Soviet Union and the United States and can provide a powerful new tool in solving shadow problems between the two superpowers" (p. 38). "In Jungian terms, the dominant typology of the United States is Extroverted thinking and the dominant typology of the Soviet Union, the Slavs in particular, is introverted feeling," and consequently, these nations "have been talking past one another. As a generalization, the introverted feeling type . . . may appear to his typological counterpart . . . as cold, unemotional or too emotional, easily offended . . . intellectually dull. . . . On the other hand, the extroverted thinking type . . . may appear . . . as heady, a know-it-all, dogmatic, arrogant and glib . . . too abstract, unemotional and insensitive, very materialistic" (p. 40).

55. Jung, *CW,* vol. 6, *Psychological Types,* English edition, translated by H. G. Baynes (1923; rpt., Princeton NJ: Princeton University Press, 1971), paras. 91–93.

56. Dorothy Leonard and Susan Straus, "Putting Your Company's Whole Brain to Work," *Harvard Business Review,* reprint no. 97407 (July–August 1997): p. 111. They advocate that a manager "loosen control to unleash creativity" (p. 116). Further, "To innovate successfully, you must hire, work with, and promote people who are unlike you" (p. 117). "Successful managers spend time getting members of diverse groups to acknowledge their differences" (p. 119), and "Managing the process of creative abrasion means making sure that everyone in the group is talking" (p. 120).

57. Ibid., p. 111.

58. I. Katherine Benziger and Anne Sohn. *The Art of Using Your Whole Brain* (Rockwall TX: KBA Publishing, 1993).

59. Ibid., p. 241.

60. Ibid.

61. Ibid., p. 242.

62. Ibid., p. 239.

63. Ibid., pp. 107–8.

64. Ibid., p. 109.

65. Ibid., p. 110.

66. Ibid., pp. 110–12.

67. Ibid., p. 124.

68. Ibid., p. 127.

69. Ibid., p. 240.

70. Ibid., p. 247.

71. Ken Wilber, ed. *The Holographic Universe, And Other Paradoxes* (Boulder CO: Shambhala, 1982), pp. 2–3.

72. Ibid., p. 6.

73. I. Katherine Benziger, *Falsification of Types: Its Jungian and Physiological Foundations and Mental, Emotional, and Physiological Costs* (Rockwall TX: KBA Publishing, 1995), p. 19. Benziger is publishing a new book entitled *Thriving in Mind* which, drawing on the fruit of her research, gives many thought-provoking examples of the impact on individuals of the wrong use of types. I have read her manuscript.

74. In another book, I want to look deeply into one of these great stories, the Psyche Eros myth, both in its original version and in the C. S. Lewis version, *Till We have Faces.* Both versions pit our dominant ESTJ culture against the INFP subculture, which must come alive in enough individuals and in the culture as a whole in order to ensure the survival of life on our planet.

75. From a public radio report. The report shows that this murder was well planned and was attempted at two other events. There seems to be evidence that others were involved as coconspirators. Before studying the law, the young killer had studied at Bar-Ilan University, the only religious university in Israel, and had also studied in the Institute for Higher Torah Studies. We do not know his typology. Typology itself and all differences are transcended by such religious extremists' evil that, like life itself, is an utter mystery

CHAPTER 9

Enlarging the Archetypes

Walter Lowen's Child Development and Erik Erikson's Ages of Life

---

Every child is an artist.
The problem is how to remain an artist
after he grows up.[1]

Picasso

 NOTHER UNIQUE type venture that uses the Myers model is Walter Lowen's brilliant construction of child development based on the four couplings and the sixteen *Myers-Briggs Type Indicator®* (*MBTI®*) types. This system is described in a difficult book entitled *Dichotomies of the Mind*, written in the early 1980s by Walter Lowen.[2] In 1987 and 1988, Susan Scanlon, the editor of *The Type Reporter,* published a summary of this book in six different issues, the intelligent synthesis of which is very helpful in assimilating this significant but obscure writing.[3] This publication is based on a series of Lowen lectures. When we compare Lowen's system and Erik Erikson's eight ages of life, many similarities emerge that help us better understand the journey of life.

Lowen is an INTJ who has been involved in conceptual designs throughout his work life, first in engineering and then in brain and type psychology. Fate brought him into Jung's ambience when he studied at the Swiss Federal Institute of Technology in Zurich. Afterwards, in 1967, he was invited by the president of State University of New York, a Jungian, to begin a new, high-technology graduate program in SUNY's liberal arts school. Lowen asked Dr. Dieter Baumann, a Jungian analyst and a grandson of Jung, to present a course entitled "Creative Aspects of the Unconscious." These beginnings eventually led Lowen into researching what he refers to as "the man-machine interface problems," which then led him to research the brain structures and dynamics through typology.

LOWEN'S MODEL OF HUMAN DEVELOPMENT AND THE FOUR TYPE ARCHETYPES

At first, this book appears to differ radically from the thesis I have been developing on the type quadrants, because we have been looking at a four-quadrant design intended primarily for adults. Instead, Lowen shows how the sixteen *MBTI* types relate to the linear development of a child's consciousness. He also finds relationships between the four type combinations and the four levels of the brain's cortex. But then Lowen shows that the four developmental levels are available non-linearly to adults. So his work and our focus on the four adult type archetypes are not only reconcilable, but Lowen's consciousness of developmental stages adds significant features to the types as archetypes, especially in illuminating our life journey with the Soul.

His work with the brain and type correlations did not take shape until, after running into many blind alleys, he combined the four functions into our couplings in the following order: SF, ST, NF, and NT. Then he linked each of the brain's four developmental levels with a corresponding coupling, which most clearly represents the child's development of skills at each stage. In a personal correspondence,[4] Lowen describes his arrival at the coupling and child level correspondences through an intensive study of the brain from both a biological and mathematical standpoint. His biological understanding of the brain's complementary opposites, such as between the left and right hemispheres and the frontal and basal parts of the brain, led him to

Lowen's Four Levels of the Mind and the Couplings

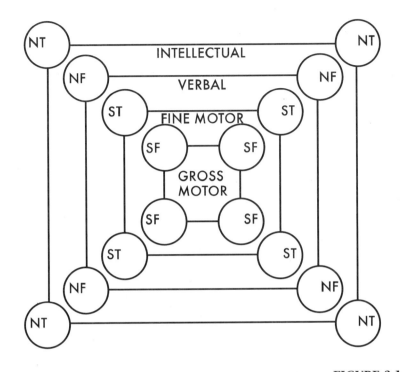

FIGURE 9.1

Walter Lowen, *Type Reporter* 3:1 (Summer 1987, 5)

consider a description of brain development by using the polarity of the type opposites. Notice in figure 9.1 that within each level, there are right brain/left brain and front brain/back brain polarities. He acknowledges in his letter that "this kind of exacting, systematic, cold, rational way of thinking is very difficult for people who are guided by feelings, metaphors, mysteries, and possibilities. But there is also a kind of beauty in the order of things—how everything falls in place."[5] I wish every person in our society had this kind of empathic understanding of typology. Besides, as I began again to explore his complex book, I discovered Lowen's own metaphorical language for the functions harmonize with the *MBTI's* traditional language and which in themselves lucidly account for his coupling and developmental level connections. He ascribes these following characteristics to the four functions: sensation is thing-focused and concrete in approach; feeling is people-focused and concrete; intuition is people-focused and abstract in approach; and thinking is thing-focused and abstract, as noted below:

Concrete	Abstract
People	People
F	N

Concrete	Abstract
Thing	Thing
S	T

By virtue of this approach Lowen was able to correlate the sixteen types with child development. The earliest developments of the child occur on the gross motor level (large muscles in the arms, legs, and trunk) via SF combinations. He shows that this level is closest to the spinal cord and is awakened in the first year of life. He relates the SF coupling to "Concrete," which according to *Webster's,* comes from "con-crescere" meaning "to grow together . . . in a solid mass." In contrast, "abstract comes from 'abstrahere,' meaning 'to draw from or separate,' or 'to be theoretical, not practical.'"

The key, therefore, to Lowen's connection between the SF coupling and the gross motor level is that both S and F are concrete in their approach; they are materially grounded in both perceiving and judging, as befitting a gross motor place.

The second level is the ST fine motor level (hand/eye coordination), which awakens between the ages of one and two. Lowen adds a further description of the four functions that is relevant to an ST congruence with a fine motor development.[6] He notes that the four functions have the following temporal relationships: sensation with the present; feeling with the past; intuition with the future; and thinking with a sequential play of time. This means that the concrete and thing-focused orientation of sensation is correlated with thinking's sense of timing, which is exactly what is needed for the eye/hand correlation that characterizes a fine motor development.

The third level is the NF verbal level (speech and hearing), which emerges between the ages of two and seven. The child's consciousness has now shifted from the very personal efforts of achieving bodily coordination to relating with others through verbal and nonverbal dialogues. It is fitting that intuition and feeling are both people-oriented as one abstractly perceives a sentence and a larger order of thought and concretely applies such thought in everyday situations.

The fourth level is the intellectual level (abstract, logical reasoning), which occurs after the age of eight.[7] This big-picture approach that characterizes an NT consciousness is possible in Lowen terms because both N and T have an abstract approach in both perceiving and judging respectively. The idea of abstraction is perfectly congruent with the very first name given this combination by the Osmond group—the Ethereal, that part of us that comprehensively sees and systematically organizes such large perspectives.

The next creative move by Lowen involved locating extraversion and introversion and judging and perceiving in the brain's geography. The front part of the brain cortex receives messages from the limbic system as to our internal needs, such as hunger, which must be met in the objective world. The internal message translates into "go out and seek food." Lowen connects this type of call for action with extraversion.

The back of the brain receives messages from the outer world through the five senses, and must figure out what those messages mean. Lowen connects this need for inner reflection to introversion.[8]

Perceiving and judging are also located by Lowen in the brain's geography (figure 9.2, page 368). The left side of the brain "can deeply focus on one thing at a time," and the right hemisphere "can broadly process many things simultaneously."[9] Lowen considers the focused processing as connected with judging (J), and the broad processing as connected with perceiving (P). By virtue of these relationships, the following diagram emerges.

Thus, the sixteen types are conceptualized spatially, with the EJs in the left frontal diagonal, the IJs in the left back diagonal, the EPs in the right frontal diagonal and the IPs in the right back.

Four Levels of Child Development and the *MBTI* Types

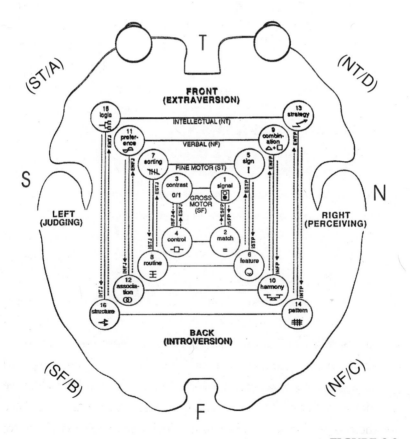

FIGURE 9.2

Walter Lowen, *Type Reporter* 3:1 (Summer 1987, 4)

Lowen then named the main characteristics of each of the sixteen types as mental "capacities," which he now prefers to call "cognitive skills." He knew that these capacities had to develop in children in a sequence from gross motor to fine motor to verbal and, finally, to intellectual. Further, Lowen reasoned that experience precedes naming, so that the right-brain capacities must develop before left-brain capacities. He theorized that any new learning on each of the four levels must begin in the right hemisphere. Finally, he assumed that as infants we are first of all instinctively extraverted in that we at first need food and motherly connections, and only later do we develop reflection. Therefore, he believed that development on each level begins in the right frontal area of the brain.

Using the names based on the mental capacities of each type, and the general experiential priorities we have just noted, he proceeded to number the order of the type capacities, as seen in figure 9.2.

TRANSLATING LOWEN'S MODEL INTO THE ADULT FOUR-FOLD ARCHETYPES

Now we can begin to see the connection between our four-fold approach to the psyche and Lowen's work. Further, Erik Erikson's eight crises of human development can be fitted into Lowen's schema, and thus into our general schema of the archetypes' structures and dynamics.

Lowen describes in detail this inner growth of a child through the first twelve years of life as he or she develops each of the sixteen capacities. However, after childhood, rather than using these capacities in a linear developmental fashion, we adults utilize them as we need them. We favor certain capacities by virtue of our innate preferences; we add to these preferences as needed in the many vicissitudes of life; we develop our inferior capacities in times of crisis; and we can experience all these type abilities in the counterclockwise creative circle as we explore cutting-edge challenges and opportunities. Lowen acknowledges that this happens in adulthood. This makes sense from a depth psychology standpoint that sees the past as a geological layer of the present psychic geography rather than a linear movement back through time. All memories are contained in this present moment, including developmental memories, from gross muscle to intellectual.

Lowen was undoubtedly aware of what Jung says in his autobiography of this adult awareness—that while in childhood "uniform development exists," in our adult years, "There is no linear evolution; there is only circumambulation of the self."[10] This centering on the Self is most often illustrated by a circle. Jung had, in the beginning of that period, begun sketching daily in a notebook "a small circular drawing, a mandala," which seemed to mirror the present state of his Soul: "It became increasingly clear to me that the mandala is the center. . . . It is the path to the center, to individuation."[11]

Jung was creating a more objective mandala intended for all of us at this time: the circle of the four functions, the mandala of typology, which he also called a psychology of individuation. Notice that when Jung speaks of the mandala, he describes it both as a circle and as a center. This can only be understood clearly if we remember that Jung's system is a depth psychological one. That is why, as shown in figure 6.2 (page 247), we have pictured a conelike conception of the Soul or Self. That diagram reminds us that the Self is the center of the circle as well as the creative nadir of the cone. As the creative source, the Self is the generator of the circle's circumference, with all of its types and its corresponding archetypes, and the ground of all development in the various levels of the psyche and brain. Jung's "path to the center" is not only the whole circle, but also the return to the nadir, which we can call the center in-depth; it is a return to roots, to the Soul as the beginning and the end, the alpha and the omega of all of life. We are reminded again that no authentic realization of types other than our innate preferences can occur without evoking them from this center and nadir. We need to keep this in-depth view in mind as we consider Lowen's developmental schema.

Lowen was finding his own center, not only through Jung's typology but also through his vision of brain development on four levels, the four couplings and their sixteen types.

Lowen sketched out the beginnings of a theory and systemic diagramming of an adult brain as a holistic, nonlinear phenomenon.[12] This sketch added substantial clarity to his book. We refer again to figure 9.2 (page 368), where the four-quadrant structure appears. Our focus at this point is on the following coordinates:

SF/B coordinated with the I–J mode

ST/A coordinated with the E–J mode

NF/C coordinated with the I–P mode

NT/D coordinated with the E–P mode

I have added in parentheses the SF/B and the other comparable designations and the four functions to Lowen's diagram. Notice that I have shown the four couplings in the four Lowen areas, and I have added the following: thinking (T) to the front of the brain, feeling (F) to the back, sensation (S) to the left and intuition (N) to the right. This represents the standard type diagram I have used for years, especially since becoming conscious of the left and right hemispheres of the brain. This type lineup of individual functions and the resulting couplings has made possible the connection between the Jung/*MBTI* theory, the Osmond group's archetypes, the four cultural archetypes of Moore and Gillette and the Herrmann Whole Brain quadrants.

These connections in the Lowen model begin easily with the close relationship that has been consistently recorded by both the Herrmann and *MBTI* researchers: namely, J is correlated with S, and P with N. There is also a relationship between the extraverted front part of the brain and the thinking preference. As I have noted before, Jung observed some early type explorers who linked thinking and extraversion in his book, *Psychological Types*. This happens because extraversion seeks to relate to external objects, and thinking does the same, though in a more indirect way. That is, thinking, in contrast to feeling's subjectivity, is characterized by its objectivity in decision-making. According to *Webster's,* the adjective "objective" means "having to do with a known or perceived object as distinguished from something existing only in the mind of the subject." Extraversion orients one to the objective world, and thinking seeks to make decisions about the stuff of the outer world through its objectivity. Further, extraversion has an aggressive quality in interpersonal relations. Thinking demonstrates a similar aggressive and detached quality by virtue of its incisiveness, its quality of conceiving ideas that cuts up and names an otherwise whole and amorphous reality. Thinking retains this detachment even with inner objects. In chapter 3, I symbolized thinking as a straight line and as a sword, as the instrument of division and aggression.

Introversion and feeling also connect. As Jung observes, introversion is that orientation in which inner reflection on outer realities occurs. Both introversion and feeling have a subjective or inward quality. When our feeling function is in charge in decisive actions, we find it difficult to unravel our needs from others' needs. Feeling types are often characterized as "bleeding hearts," while thinking types are often called "cold-blooded." Webster's notes that the term, "subjective" has, therefore, an introverted aspect, in that it focuses on "the feelings or temperament of the subject . . . rather than the attributes of the object thought of." Further, such experiences are "incapable of being checked externally or verified by other persons."

A NEW VIEW OF THE FOUR QUADRANTS BASED ON HUMAN DEVELOPMENT

The SF Gross Motor Level. Lowen adds new clarity to the phenomenology of the four coupling archetypes as well as to the specific sixteen *MBTI* types. He has provided the type conscious person a creative and innovative set of precise terms which link the four couplings to stages of development. Human development then starts with the SF coupling (see figure 9.2, page 368). We can recognize in this diagram a fresh way of describing the SF archetype, called the King/Queen/Moralist. This archetype plays itself out as the parental guide of the social order. Following Lowen's theory, after a child, or eventually an adult, receives a "signal," that is, a "sensory reaction to the environment" (step 1), he or she immediately seeks to "match" it with something similar (step 2) and to "contrast" it with an opposite (step 3), "like right or wrong, do and don't, good and bad." The element of "control" develops (step 4), ensuring that the new behavior has an ordered outcome in relationship to other established human behaviors. Thus, the SF Moralist archetype, with its special attribute for establishing societal order through standards and mores, develops instinctively in the infant.

In child development, the first movements and achievements of the child occur in the context of the mother relationship. In Jungian terms, it is the loving embrace of the real mother in society, amplified by the loving embrace of the inward mother, the containing Self, that ensures healthy development of the child. In the view of Erik Erikson, this empathic containment is mainly made up of the mother's trust in life, and the awakened trust over mistrust in the contained child. Such trust has added somatic benefits for the baby, according to Erikson: "The first demonstration of social trust in the baby is the ease of feeding, the depth of sleep, the relaxation of his bowels."[13]

This elemental social order of the SF Moralist archetype continues in Erikson's second stage, in which autonomy wins over shame and doubt. The child learns to walk and control bowel movements, while imbibing a nurturing environment. If the environment is not favorable, all of society suffers. Thus, the parental SF archetype as the good parent, as the King and Queen of any society, is rooted in this Lowen-Eriksonian consciousness.

Our Eden-like dreams remind us that this earliest childhood

development of trust and initiative is a sublime order that Erikson characterizes as religious: "Trust born of care is, in fact, the touchstone of the *actuality* of a given religion."[14] We recall the person who dreamt that she was in a marvelous garden, at the center of which was a great tree whose branches extended over the entire garden. The tree for her was a cosmic, embracing mother. An SF order, therefore, beyond mere societal conventions, is rooted in a spiritual feeling or a sacred emotional climate that says that all is well with our young world. This spiritual matrix must include the SF/King and Queen's parental blessing of those under them, as reported by Moore and Gillette.

To the extent that our early life is filled with chaos and mistrust, then dreams of suffering, entrapped children will occur in persons of all ages: children as blue babies forgotten in refrigerators, ignored children left to die or remembered at the last moment, or children tied to a bed and orphaned. Many adults who struggle with issues of trust are afraid to consciously experience a sacred mother figure who holds one lovingly in a dream. Such a resistance is the bitter fruit of an early mistrust of the mothering person. A conscious imaginative holding of the inner orphaned child is very helpful, even though this practice has been trivialized in popular psychological literature.

Furthermore, dream symbols and bodily symptoms often manifest as aspects of one another on this gross motor level. Here, mistrust's horror and fear imbeds itself in the reflexes and muscles of the body and emerges as painful muscular knots and tensions and psychically manifests in dreams such as, for example, the dreamer suffering an onslaught of cold-blooded insects or crustaceans or plants. We have learned in depth psychology that the lower the animals and plants in the evolutionary process, the more their dream images symbolize the radical depth of the gross motor injury and its attendant primitive mistrust. A medical researcher with whom I consult, Lawrence Beuret, M.D., is associated with other like scientists in Europe who are investigating gross motor movements in neonates and babies as reenacted in children and adults. Beuret and other scientists are providing exercises based on those movements that are dramatically healing attention deficits.[15] Injuries on this gross motor level, however, may be due to causes other than parental neglect. Dr. Beuret's work with this neuro-developmental remediation agrees with the developmental process described by Lowen. He notes that when difficulties are rooted in the gross motor development, their psychosomatic distortions affect subsequent developmental levels much more globally.

The ST Fine Motor Level. The next stage in child development, the fine motor coordination between the eyes and hands, relates to the capabilities of the ST. Lowen describes the four features of fine muscle development as sign, feature, sorting, and routine. "A sign" (step 5), writes Lowen, "is much more complex than a signal,"[16] which was the first capacity of the SF gross motor development. Lowen continues, "A single sign stands for a complex chain of events." We begin to see on a metaphorical level why the Osmond group called the ST combination the Structuralist, a person who loves to make maps and patterns. Now "the child can link experiences together into more complex structures. It recognizes mother's face over the crib, sees hands reach out, feels itself being lifted, and so forth."[17]

As the "match" capacity on the SF level connects one behavior with another, so the next capacity, "feature" (step 6), does the same in this ST's evolving structure, but on a more much complex level since it involves eye-hand coordination. Feature, writes Lowen, is a capacity to reduce "information content to its essential contrasting differences, the very thing a caricaturist does so well."[18] Scanlon gives the example of the typical ESTP who in an emergency, when others were shouting and getting nothing done, "just stood there with his intense expression, then picked up the phone, or pulled a tool, or gave direction."[19] We recall that Moore and Gillette call the ST Warrior the preeminent "doer."

The next step in the ST phase is "sorting" (step 7). Lowen describes this capacity as one that "we constantly draw on, whether we're figuring out whether to get off at the next subway stop or setting the table for dinner."[20] The specific *MBTI* type here is the ESTJ, who often describe themselves as "being able to get the job done and on time."[21] Following sorting, we establish a "routine" (step 8), which for Lowen means "any fixed, ordered sequence of events, literally like a computer program . . . how to tie a shoelace . . . writing the letter 'A.'"[22] ISTJs, associated by Lowen with this capacity, are the routine-makers par excellence, so it is no accident that these types make such excellent accountants and computer programmers, according to *MBTI* researchers. Overall, the ST Structural/Warrior archetype ensures that we get things done in rational, systemic ways, as also seen in the Herrmann Whole Brain Model and the Moore and Gillette cultural research.

Erickson's third and fourth developmental events, initiative versus guilt and industry versus inferiority, are coordinated with this ST phase. Initiative ensures that we affect others as we conceive and put our plans into action. The child learns to use his little sword—that is, the power of one's assertive actions—to give notice to others that one is present and accounted for in this life. Erikson, in his poetic way, writes that the child (and the adult in corresponding behaviors) "suddenly seems to 'grow together' both in his person and in his body." The child also develops the ability to plan and attack a task as well as a sense of responsibility, possibly feeling guilt if one oversteps assertiveness.[23] In industry versus inferiority, the child becomes a worker in school, and learns to perform assigned tasks within time frames, following "some systemic instruction," and working alongside others.[24]

In dream work in analysis, recognizing again the child in the adult, we watch for dream motives in which an imaged child steps forward to magically solve problems. In one of my own dreams, I received a bunch of keys with an accompanying message to find a room which one of the keys unlocked. I was lost until a young boy selected one key and guided me down a dark street, into a church and to the door of an inner meditation room, which the key unlocked. The latent dream message was clear: I needed more inner quiet for myself.

The negatives of this ST archetype, which for Erikson are guilt (versus initiative) and inferiority (versus industry), were symbolized in a client's dream by a child hiding in a corner and feeling thoroughly impotent, or, in another dream, evil children subverting an emerging creative task. In this latter dream, the woman, who felt abandoned in childhood, dreamt she was reconstructing her house (Self as container), when suddenly a group of young marauders killed the workers and destroyed the new construction. The marauders were, in effect, saying to the dreamer: your sense of inferiority includes the feeling that you do not deserve to be creative. On the other hand, the dream implicitly challenged the dreamer to face these marauders in conscious imaging, and, eventually, by painfully persisting, transform their destructive attitudes into creative energies and images. Another kind of dream motive that devalues this ST development is one in which the dreamer destroys a child's toys or forbids a child's playfulness. These negative dreams reveal the pathology of the ST Warrior, a pathology that can even limit the fine hand-eye development that childhood play awakens.

The NF Verbal Level. The verbal level of development agrees with the qualities of the NF Lover types. Lowen identifies four capacities for this archetypal development: combination, harmony, preference, and association. Combination (step 9) is represented by the ENFP type, which, writes Lowen, joins "odd elements that might not normally be thought of as belonging together. . . . Fantasies, imagination, scenarios and possibilities are all the results of this combining." Lowen recognizes that the extraverted intuitive function is taking the lead here in the NF archetype.[25] The introverted feeling function, as dominant in the INFP, is the main actor in the next capacity, harmony (step 10), which is a sophisticated aspect of matching (step 2). In harmony, we synthesize various combinations. INFPs, attuned as they are to a quiet introversion, seek to overcome social dissonance in subtle verbal discourse. Lowen is sensitive to this introverted feeling dominance when he points out that this capacity wishes to fit events and people with one another in a way that envisions "a bigger whole," and to bring peace on a deep level.[26] Overall, the INFP, representing, as we have suggested, the counterculture in a dominant ESTJ scientific/techno-logical society, is critically needed for its harmonizing capacity in our present culturally and economically split society.

The preference step (step 11) is a sophisticated version of the simpler third capacity, contrast (step 3). At this level we do not compare "merely black and white, but a continuous spectrum of dark and light gray . . . from unacceptable to ideal."[27] Lowen links this capacity to the ENFJ. Clearly its EF preference demands a sensitive, innovative value judgment. Susan Scanlon's summary of Lowen's work clarifies this by showing that the ENFJ, with its extraverted feeling dominance, helps differentiate the various gifts of members in groups, so that each person feels "preferred."[28] Finally, in the association capac-ity (step 12), an INFJ person "looks for what two different things might have in common," such as "mother and love."[29] Scanlon adds that here, because of this NF Lover's dominance of introverted intuition, we seek the one big idea or strategy "that holds a lot of people together."[30] Overall, creative caring and relating, the genius of the NF archetype as a Lover/Creative Artist in Herrmann's C quadrant, are at work.

Erikson's identity versus role confusion and intimacy versus isolation parallel the NF archetype. Identity indicates the teenage challenge of holding together while massive and confusing cognitive and sexual changes occur. Adolescents have to refight many old battles of the past, and integrate these past identifications with "the vicissi-tudes of the libido," natural endowments and social challenges and opportunities.[31] All of Lowen's four NF capacities, in all of their creative and relating abilities, are involved in this crisis and in Erikson's next life crisis, intimacy and isolation.

Intimacy is the greatest of human challenges, as the young adults learn the need to live in a daily loving mix of mutual pleasure, personal autonomy, and interactive surrender. The core of intimacy's challenge is the balancing of a mutual surrender, which includes active listening and a holding of the other's pains and failures as well as joys and successes, with a continuing realization of one's own and the other's autonomy. Considering Lowen's four capacities for this verbal NF level of development, the authenticity of this union depends on the combining (step 9) of masculine and feminine traits and type differences, the harmonizing (step 10) of a complex interactive web of idiosyncracies, weaknesses, strengths, and talents, the valuing of one another's subtle preferences (step 11), and, finally, associating (step 12) so as to meet on common grounds and in a renewed peace pact. The successful intimacy of a couple demands interactive creativity, love, sensuality, and spirituality. To make possible this great human achievement takes all of the NF's capacities in each of us.

However, the obstacles to intimacy emerge from the central pathology of this NF Lover archetype: a fusion with one or both parents. In dreams, therefore, when the pathology takes over, a dreamer beginning a love relationship might find a parent or the entire family walking in and breaching the necessary privacy and the needed autonomy. This NF Lover's pathology constitutes an original addiction to parents or to the family of origin in any one of us, no matter what our ordinary type may be. We must keep in mind here that we are concerned with our childhood development in which all of the types participate. This addicted wounding of the Lover, as Moore and Gillette have written, becomes the seat of other addictions in any one of us, beginning with codependent relations with friends and lovers. For all who seek a healthy love for another, I recommend asking the unconscious with stubborn persistence to provide dreams of inner lovers, of soul mates and soul friends. The power of the damaging parent, as visualized and dreamt, must also be faced and transformed into one's authentic power of presence and identity. One young man in therapy finally stopped his inner mother as she was preaching to him. In this dream, her admonitions were being broadcast in a restaurant so that all could hear. In another dream, he experienced his mother as his wife. Finally, he dreamt that she approached him naked from the waist up and breastless (meaning, no longer narcissistically nourishing him) and saying, "It's about time you claim your own body and your own identity." His inner work was paying off.

The NT Intellectual Level. The NT intellectual level of development manifests four capacities: strategy, pattern, logic, and structure. Strategy (step 13) involves perceiving patterns. Scanlon gives the example of an ENTP consultant who had contracts with four different organizations to do four different kinds of work. He was able to see, through his outer intuitive powers, that they shared a common need. Through strategic planning he was able to satisfy the four easily. NFs combine (step 9) in a similar way to NTs, writes Lowen, but NTs make combinations into "a sequence that constitutes a plan of action or *strategy*." In strategy, Lowen adds, one plays "the game of 'what if,'"[32] in which one sees possibilities (N) and systemically organizes them (T). It is the extraverted intuitive and thinking abilities in the NT Creative Scientist that enables this kind of person to effectively influence organizations. Persons in organizational development often possess this type combination.

The next capacity manifested in the NT is pattern (step 14). The NT finds designs in "a complex display of information." The comparable capacity in the SF level is called match (step 2). The NT's pattern "is a more sophisticated way, a quantified way, of telling one thing from another."[33] The INTP does his work well here, because this type's introverted thinking dominance does the primary work of distinguishing and naming large patterns, such as Jung and Myers did in constructing the types.

The next NT capacity is logic (step 15). Its counterpart on the SF level is contrast (step 3). Logic, like contrast, helps us make distinctions. A typical ENTJ says that she "makes things manageable." This capacity is also related to the ST capacity of sorting (step 7). But the ENTJ cannot operate without first having a vision of the "big picture," unlike the ESTJ Sorter type who "could just walk into an office and organize it" without the gestalt view.[34] The big picture is a combination of the N's large view and the T's systemic connections within the view. One can feel here the more assertive intervention of the ESTJ in contrast to the slower, gentler, and more global intervention of the ENTJ.

With structure (step 16), we come to the finale of the child's developmental process, according to Lowen. It is interesting that this capacity's most precise type representative is the INTJ, the type of both Jung and Lowen. INTJs typically have the uncanny ability even in childhood to challenge collective norms because they see such norms in a larger context and with a critical inner eye. Lowen says that structure must be understood "in the sense of gestalt, some hidden schema that gives systems form, meaning and a framework of reality in this internal representation." A gestalt makes the whole seem larger than the sum of its parts, "like a symphony . . . a thought, an idea."[35]

Here in the NT potential in each of us is the Creative Scientist or, in Moore and Gillette terms, the Magician, whose special gift is an inner inclusive knowing, resulting from the culmination of all of the other capacities of the NT. Opposite to the INTJ are the ESFP Moralists, known for the "speed of their reactions" because the elements they deal with are simpler. A good analogy, writes Scanlon, might be found in comparing reactions to "the taste of a perfect ripe apple just picked off the tree, with a Thanksgiving supper which took days to cook."[36]

Each dream and vision is the conscious and unconscious intuitive product of the NT/Magician when the content of each includes an image of wholeness. Certain dreams give us gestaltlike pictures—mandalas—as symbols of wholeness. We reported one dream of a young client who encountered, first on four mountaintops and then around him, a mandala consisting of the four adult archetypes, imaged as King, Warrior, Magician, and a child as Lover, with a guiding angel representing the Self hovering above.

A potential pathology of the NTs is that they can get totally lost in large visions, and are incapable of relating their cosmic views to everyday life. Even the normal NT/D quadrant type often loses a practical sense of time. A severe pathological loss of time and space awareness that affects practical, everyday functioning is a psychotic symptom.

Erikson's parallel to this NT level of development is found in his last two human life ages, generativity versus stagnation and ego integrity versus despair. Erikson, writing, as he usually does, from an interpersonal standpoint, declares that the generativity stage "is primarily the concern in establishing and guiding the next generation."[37] In intrapsychic terms, he adds, it also means "*productivity* and *creativity*." Without these developments outwardly and inwardly, there is only stagnation, an early biological or spiritual death.

In Lowen's discussion of this capacity of structure (step 16), he helps us see a special tie between "concept" as the internal intellectual form of structure and Erikson's generativity. Structure is the ability to conceptualize in a generative way. Generative, according to *Webster's*, comes from the latin, *generare,* meaning "to beget." Concept is derived from "to conceive" and is associated with "conception." Accordingly, a concept gives birth to a reflective consciousness, one in which I know that I know. This capacity, that Jung often called divine, emerges at the beginning of adolescence, according to Jean Piaget. A beautiful example of this is Helen Keller's famous breakthrough, when she finally identified the feel of water with the word water, communicated through Ann Sullivan's touching her hand. This occurred because, in her internal intellectual maturation, she began to conceive, to experience concepts. In that moment, she received the capacity of making structure, or gestalt. In that gestalt, Keller "saw the light," saw the whole conceptually. In the concept, she experienced the connection between the water and the word.

Finally, following Erikson, we come to the culminating crisis of life, ego integrity versus despair. The Jungian equivalent is a fully realized or at least a "good enough" individuation, a stage, not of separateness, but of wholeness, of a connecting with God and with the mystery of existence. Here, we find the fruit, both sweet and bitter, of all the other seven Eriksonian ages of life, and all the other type capacities. I am quoting Erikson extensively here, because this final goal of life is seminally present in every moment of my life and yours, including in the moment of death. Erikson writes of integrity:

> It is the acceptance of one's one and only life cycle as something that had to be and that, by necessity, permitted of no substitutions: it thus means a new, a different love of one's parents. . . . Although aware of the relativity of all the various life styles which have given meaning to human striving, the possessor of integrity is ready to defend the dignity of his whole life style against all physical and economic threats. . . . The style of integrity developed by his culture or civilization thus becomes the 'patrimony of his soul,' the seal of his moral paternity of himself. . . . In such final consolidation, death loses its sting.

> The lack or loss of this accrued ego integration is signified by fear of death. . . . Despair expresses the feeling that the time is now short, too short for the attempt to start another life. . . .

> Each individual, to become a mature adult, must to a sufficient degree develop all the ego qualities [of all the seven previous crises], so that a wise Indian, a true gentleman, and a mature peasant share and recognize in one another the final stage of integrity. . . .

> *Webster's* dictionary is kind enough to help us complete
> this outline in a circular fashion. Trust (the first of our ego
> values) is here defined as "the assured reliance on
> another's integrity," the last of our values. . . . And it seems
> possible to further paraphrase the relation of adult integ-
> rity and infantile trust by saying that healthy children will
> not fear life if their elders have integrity enough not to fear
> death.[38]

The goal of life, integrity, and the reality of death are seminally
present in each of us in every moment, if we pay attention. Aristotle
put it this way: "The last in execution is the first in intention."
Catherine of Siena said something similar, but in more spiritual terms:
"All the way to heaven is heaven." In accepting death, we more readily accept all of the ups and downs, the peaceful and chaotic moments,
the saintly and sinful acts, in ourselves and in every human being.
Erikson writes in other places that we find wisdom, in which, by virtue
of knowing one's authenticity, one also experiences the potentials and
failures in all others, so that in this crowning achievement of individuation, in Erikson's language, "Mankind is my kind," and in Lowen's
terms, we realize the fullest realization of the intellectual level of the
brain as a gestalt. Thus the archetype of the Magician is manifested, the
inner hidden knower and technologist of this knowing, the one who
leads us back into the dark depth of discovery and wholeness. Jung put
it this way: "One does not become enlightened by imagining figures of
light, but by making the darkness conscious."[39]

The NT Magician in each of us is constantly seeking to present the
light in darkness to us though dreams. When consciousness is in the
dark of sleep, we dream. One person, in the throes of a lover's
argument in waking life, dreamt that a bird suddenly spoke, saying to
him: "God loves you." In the last great writing of the Arthurian legend,
Le Morte d'Arthur, Arthur has a nightmare the night before his final
battle with Mordred, in which both are mortally wounded. In the

dream, he is dressed in kingly array as he stands on a pinnacled platform. He sees below the dark waters filled with treacherous creatures of the deep. In the next instant, Arthur plunges into the water and the creatures rush toward him to tear him to bits.[40]

What is the meaning of this dream? The elemental creatures depict the inner child, whose fundamental emotional needs have been ignored by this Warrior/King. The purpose of such a dream is to awaken us biologically in order to awaken us spiritually. Arthur is being challenged by the dream to face in conscious imaging the frightening creatures depicting his inner child on an instinctual level, so that he may reclaim this ignored child, and with the child, his hidden femininity. Jung has called dreams the "vox dei," the voice of God, or if you will, the voice of the NT Magician. Arthur, as a driven ST Warrior and workaholic SF King, is out of balance with nature, with the divine imperatives, with the totality of his typology. He has ignored the loving needs of Guinevere so that she falls in love with Arthur's beloved friend, Lancelot. The kingdom is falling into despairing disarray, as the king and his knights, interested only in tournaments and jousts, forget their social center, their knightly integrity as protectors of women and children (the NT and NF dimensions). They ignore their spiritual collective wholeness, the totality of the type mandala, as symbolized by the Round Table. At the time the dream occurs, Arthur and his men must face the treacherous Mordred, who is a nightmare in the flesh as Arthur's bastard son and shadowy inner child, as well as a collective symbol of warriors gone berserk.[41] The dream speaks to these social and personal failures of Arthur, whose SF Kingship makes him the symbol and carrier of the collective ego. The dream demonstrates that the NT gestalt capacity never sleeps, as the Soul seeks to awaken us to all the other Lowen capacities and their four enfolding coupling archetypes. Any diverging from that gestalt results in a warning nightmare or a physical illness. A significant dream is a symbolic gestalt and dynamic of the Soul's wholeness, either reveling in its integrity or seeking to correct any violation of that integrity.

IMPLICATIONS OF LOWEN'S WORK
IN OUR ADULT CONSCIOUSNESS

Lowen's brilliant work in relating the sixteen Myers types to the child's developmental levels enriches our understanding of the four coupling archetypes as they constitute our lifelong acquisition and use of skills and knowledge. More important, the compatibility of the Lowen and Erikson theories typologically clarifies the adult journey, especially in the second half of life.

We have explored the four couplings as they occur in each evolving stage: the SF gross motor, the ST fine motor, the NF verbal, and the NT intellectual levels. We are also reminded, as both Lowen and Jung have pointed out, that after our linear development ends in early adolescence, we can begin to use all of our type capacities in more flexible ways. When we are learning any physical procedure that involves unused or seldom used muscles, or rehabilitating injured muscles, we are repeating the gross motor phase of development, to which we must give the concrete attention typical of the SF coupling. In undertaking any activity involving unfamiliar eye/hand coordination, we are reactivating the ST's structural capacities for creating new mental maps. In learning a foreign language or the complex terminologies of a new profession, we succeed to the extent that we experientially enter into the cultural milieu of that particular country or profession in an NF Oceanic way. When we begin to study any philosophical system or any other complex theory, we must bring to the fore the large holistic characteristics of the NT Creative Scientist.

No matter what our type preference is, our success in life often revolves around our ability to use our less preferred type capacities as well as our strengths. An NF musician, for example, can remain grounded in his type because it is so congruent to his profession but needs to sharpen his ST practical capacity to market himself. He might also need NT capacities to build his career and teach new students with both his parenting SF sensitivities and his NF artistic gifts. However, it takes considerable effort to use our less preferred type capacities because of the natural resistance from the preferred couplings.

We have also noted that the creative process often begins with a question in an ST focus, is then incubated in an SF parental containment, subsequently blossoms into a creative breakthrough from the NF Oceanic's depth, and is systematized with NT skills.

Above all, the developmental works of Lowen and Erikson help adults better understand the typical life process. Ideally, people should pass through the first half of life beginning with parental care in the SF quadrant and reaching a zenith in the practical ST world of independent studies and work. Then they sometimes can enter without trauma or crisis into the second half of life's NT Magician's deeper realms of knowledge, pursuing ultimate life meanings in various fields, such as the sciences, humanities, philosophies, and theologies. The fruit of such a pursuit may lead to a new level of love for one's self and others in our final NF quadrant of life.

However, neither the Lowen linear structures nor Erikson's functional and age-related progressions follow this rather utopian plan in life's second half. Recall that in Lowen's levels of childhood development the SF and ST levels are followed first by the NF, not the NT, accompanied by the corresponding Eriksonian phases. However, the Lowen model, like the larger *MBTI* depiction of the types, only minimally takes into account the powerful emotional factors accompanying significant life changes. But Erikson's corresponding ages of life do introduce emotional elements in their respective polar characteristics, beginning with trust versus mistrust. Erikson's lifelong journey with its many milestones ends with the final struggle to realize wholeness over the experience of despair, which accompanies a growing realization of mortality and the nearness of death. Erikson, in parallel with Jung's insistence that there is no individuation without working through life's emotions, asserts that there is no development of the human virtues without working through the turbulent challenges of each life age.

In all of life, whether in the midst of the critical changes and accompanying agonies of the early years, or in the later years' journey that Jung characterized as "circumambulating a Center," we patiently and persistently develop established patterns and logical behaviors, only to subsequently experience a bewildering shattering of those valued patterns and logical behaviors. Most of us are subjected in a lifetime to many psychological and spiritual deaths due to illnesses, the death of beloved relatives and friends, and any of the other countless life changes and conflicts that the Taoists wisely call a continuous process of death and rebirth. The play of the many aspects of life and their related typological demands therefore not only requires a complete circling of the Compass of the Soul, but also a plunge into the conic nadir of that center which depth psychology calls the unconscious. This plunge takes place in the NF Oceanic place, in which the unconscious is the fathomless ocean with its awesome darkness and mystery. Just as the ST Warrior place is the scene of societal adaptation, no matter what our individual typology might be, this Verbal NF depth is the place of death and rebirth, of destruction and reconstruction, of imaged and felt dream language, no matter what our individual preferences may be.

So a combination of the Lowen/Eriksonian/Jungian theories gives us a picture of the second stage of life that is truer to life as a difficult yet deeply spiritual journey, as shown in figure 9.3. The conelike diagram is like that of figure 6.2 (page 247), in which we were showing primarily how the four quadrants of the mandala of life are all under the aegis and control of the Self. Here, we are showing that the Self is also the center and source of the entire journey of life, which for Jung consists of a two-stage process, the first, proceeding out of the Soul, and the second, leaving society and its outer demands and plunging into its dark, emotional depths, followed by new beginnings and insights.[42]

In any life crisis, we plunge from our ST heights into the emotional

Lowen's Child Development/Erikson's Adult Life Development

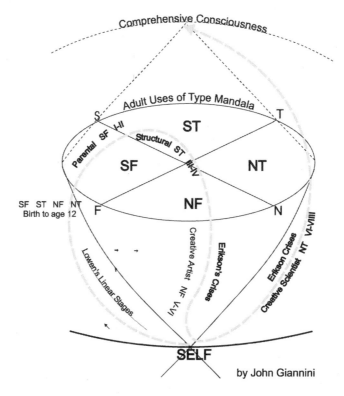

FIGURE 9.3

chaos of the NF/C regions of the psyche and brain. The usual response is like erupting geysers of fear, anger, depression, and self-pity. Psychically, we are in transition, we are crossing a bridge over a gully of primitive, unassimilated feelings and fantasies, which rise up like childhood ghosts. We have learned from Erikson that this reawakening of childhood traumas is typical of the adolescent crisis. So any adult life crisis returns us metaphorically and experientially to the crude and bewildering experiences of the teen years. For example, we often dream about being back in high school, where we are unprepared for an exam, being snubbed by peers, or suffering the loss of a teenage romance. As adults we are often challenged again both symbolically and emotionally by demands of intimacy, in which we must learn anew the art of surrender, the realities of a dependency on others, and the unremitting claims of a mutual love.

When I encountered my first life crisis, it happened because I was trying to function as an ST Warrior to meet the demands of my position as production control manager of a large foundry. I awakened one morning from a frightening dream to find myself still assailed by its fantasies in my waking state. When I got close to the company site, my stomach and legs became so taut with fear that I turned back, called my cousin, who was a nurse, and saw a psychiatrist she recommended. My ignored NF Lover capacities had attacked me with a frightening vengeance that changed the course of my entire life. The remedy the doctor proposed was progressive relaxation, which required a return to gross motor work and consciousness. This, however, was only a beginning. I needed a larger vision, given to me from Jung's psychology, which included these gross motor and emotional readjustments but also the insights and experiences from the primitive nature of the symbolic language. This was followed by improved insights on the intellectual level.

When Jung broke from Freud and from the thinking dominance implicit in Freud's theory, he encountered an avalanche of ignored intuitive powers and related feelings. He practiced yoga until he calmed down. Then he entered again into the maelstrom of feelings and allowed creative images to emerge from their midst. He writes in his autobiography:

> In order to grasp the fantasies which were stirring in me "underground," I knew I had to let myself plummet down into them, as it were. I felt not only violent resistance to this, but a distinct fear. For I was afraid of losing command of myself and becoming a prey to the fantasies—and as a psychiatrist I realized only too well what that meant. After prolonged hesitation, however, I

saw that there was no other way out. I had to take the chance, had to try to gain power over them; for I realized that if I did not do so, I ran the risk of their gaining power over me. A cogent motive for making the attempt was the conviction that I could not expect of my patients something I did not dare to do myself.[43]

Jung is talking about consciously plunging into the NF's emotional depths. It is for this reason that Jung also called his view of the Soul *depth psychology*. The gravitational pull of psyche sucks us down to those same depths when we still have significant life issues to resolve. As Jung often reminds us, the Soul always seeks to return to its primitive yet creative roots.[44] Anyone who has gone through any life crisis knows this experience. In terms of our quaternity, we are pushed to enter the NF quadrant, where raw emotionality mixed with our primal instincts and creative potentials both reside near the Self, the Soul's divine depth and ground. It is up to us to choose whether we remain stuck there, or whether, by virtue of holding the many paradoxes we encounter there, we experience transformation and healing from dreams and conscious fantasy work. If we follow the latter, we are blessed with the gift of a creative and spiritually fruitful life.

Understanding and theorizing about the experiences we have gone through brings us into the NT quadrant of the Creative Scientist. Jung acknowledges in many places that the experiences he had in roughly a four-year period after his break with Freud provided the raw material for his entire theory, the theoretical side of which was shaped by Taoist, Buddhist, Hindu, primitive, and mythic sources, as well as by quantum and Einsteinian physics, all encompassed in his Judaic-Christian heritage.

Thus, when we view the Lowen, Erikson, and Jungian structures from our own common human experiences of crisis, we can see the flow of the life cycle in the context of the type's quaternal mandala. In the next chapter, we shall see how this flow is obstructed in three models of human types that compete with the Jung/*MBTI* type theory.

Notes

1. Ned Herrmann, *The Creative Brain* (Kingsport TN: Quebec or Printing Book Group, 1994), quoting Picasso, p. 207.

2. Walter Lowen, *Dichotomies of the Mind: A Systems Science of the Mind and Personality* (New York: John Wiley and Sons, 1982).

3. Susan Scanlon, ed., "Walter Lowen's Model of the Mind," *The Type Reporter* (Summer 1987–November 1988), published monthly by The Type Reporter, Inc., 524 North Paxton Street, Alexandria, Va., 22304 (703/823-3730). Her outlines and selective graphs of a very complicated book have helped me get to the core of this book more rapidly.

4. A letter dated February 8, 2000, from Walter Lowen to the author. His interest in Jung and in the brain structures made possible his typological description of the child's psychophysiological development. He points to the fact that in the "physical brain . . . the right and left hemispheres do opposite tasks, but complementary when working together" based on the "connecting fibers." The "front and the back of the brain also are cooperating opposites and this is critically germane to your book." He discusses the "billions of networks in the brain, arranged in clusters, sometimes referred to as LAN's—local area networks, which have attributes in common." He found that these "attributes in common" could be designated as SF, ST, NF, and NT. So, "For the purpose of my model I considered only the 16 such LAN's," that is, the sixteen *MBTI* types that are based on the four couplings.

5. In the same letter, Lowen demonstrates his high type sensitivity when he writes: "it is clear to me that my book was written in the typical language of the INTJ, very difficult for you [he knows I am an E/INFP]. . . . Other INTJs as so many rave letters I have received indicate find it refreshingly clear. But such differences in perception are not new to me. I've worked closely with my son, John, an INFP, who knows my model very well after struggling with it for years." It is not within the parameters of this book to describe the details of Lowen's remarkable research. I again refer the reader to his book, which, however, is now out of print. *The Type Reporter* articles do not capture its fine details, though they do provide enough of a structure to make this chapter of my book possible.

6. Lowen, *Dichotomies of the Mind,* pp. 41–42.

7. Scanlon, ed., "Walter Lowen's Model of the Mind," *The Type Reporter,* 3:1, p. 4.

8. Ibid., p. 4.

9. Ibid., p. 7.

10. C. G. Jung, *Memories, Dreams, Reflections* (New York: Vintage Books, 1961), pp. 196–97.

11. Ibid., p. 197.

12. Scanlon, "Walter Lowen's Model of the Mind," *The Type Reporter* 3:1.

13. Erik Erikson, *Childhood and Society,* 2nd ed. (New York: W. W. Norton, 1963), p. 247.

14. Ibid., p. 250.

15. These symptoms are grouped under a more inclusive name, such as MBD or minimum brain dysfunction. Dr. Beuret describes his interventions as neuro-developmental remediation. He began to observe learning difficulties among adolescents when he was in training at the Mayo Clinic. He has since 1985 both trained and lectured at the Institute for Neuro-physiological Psychology in Chester, England. The methods of this institute are centered on recovering primary body movements in neonates and babies, and teaching these to patients.

16. Lowen, *Dichotomies of the Mind,* pp. 128–29.

17. Ibid., p. 129.

18. Ibid., p. 131.

19. Scanlon, "Walter Lowen's Model of the Mind," *The Type Reporter* 3:6, p. 1.

20. Lowen, *Dichotomies of the Mind,* p. 81.

21. Scanlon, "Walter Lowen's Model of the Mind," *The Type Reporter* 3:6, p. 2.

22. Lowen, *Dichotomies of the Mind,* p. 81.

23. Erikson, *Childhood and Society,* pp. 255–56.

24. Ibid., pp. 258–60.

25. Lowen, *Dichotomies of the Mind,* p. 83.

26. Ibid., p. 83.

27. Ibid., p. 84.

28. Scanlon, "Walter Lowen's Model of the Mind," *The Type Reporter* 3:6, p. 4.

29. Lowen, *Dichotomies of the Mind,* pp. 84–85.

30. Scanlon, "Walter Lowen's Model of the Mind," *The Type Reporter* 3:6, p. 4.

31. Erikson, *Childhood and Society,* p. 261.

32. Lowen, *Dichotomies of the Mind,* p. 86.

33. Ibid.

34. Scanlon, Susan. "Walter Lowen's Model of the Mind," *The Type Reporter* 3:5, p. 4.

35. Lowen, *Dichotomies of the Mind,* p. 87.

36. Scanlon, "Walter Lowen's Model of the Mind," *The Type Reporter* 3:5, p. 4.

37. Erikson, *Childhood and Society,* p. 267.

38. Ibid., pp. 268–69.

39. Jung, *CW,* vol. 13, *Alchemical Studies* (Princeton NJ: Princeton University Press, 1967), para. 335.

40. Thomas Malory, *Le Morte d'Arthur,* vol. 2, book 21:3 (Harmondsworth, Middlesex, England: Penguin Books, 1969 and 1985), pp. 510–11. John Boorman in 1981 helped write and direct one of the outstanding movies on the legends called "Excalibur." In one great moment of this movie, Arthur is waiting at night for the next day's battle with Mordred. He awakens, as it were, his old mentor, Merlin, from his sleep of death when he cries out for his help. Arthur pitifully asks the Merlin phantom: "Merlin, will you henceforth only come to me in my dreams?" Merlin, with his cloaked arms outspread against the sky, like a great bird in flight, responds ominously: "In dreams to some, and to others, NIGHTMARES."

41. Ibid., p. 24.

42. "I have called this center the *self.* Intellectually the self is no more than a psychological concept, a construct that serves to express an unknowable essence which we cannot grasp as such, since by definition it transcends our powers of comprehension. It might equally well be called the 'God within us.' The beginnings of our whole psychic life seem to be inextricably rooted in this point, and all our highest and ultimate purposes seem to be striving towards it. This paradox is unavoidable as always, when we try to define something that lies beyond the bourn of our understanding." C. G. Jung, *CW,* vol. 7, *Two Essays on Analytical Psychology* (Princeton NJ: Princeton University Press, 1953), para. 399.

43. Jung, *Memories, Dreams, Reflections* (New York: Vintage Books, 1961), p. 178.

44. Jung et al., eds., *Man and His Symbols* (Garden City NY: Doubleday, 1964), p. 89: "The main task of dreams is to bring back a sort of 'recollection' of the prehistoric as well as the infantile world, right down to the level of the most primitive instincts." This process is consistent with the entire process of individuation. Paradoxically, to find our primitive depths means that we also find our spiritual heights and wholeness.

CHAPTER 10

Freezing and Unfreezing the Compass' Dynamics

The Five Factor Model, the Keirsey-Bates Model, and the Singer-Loomis Model

---

From earliest times, attempts have been made to classify individuals according to types, and so to bring order into chaos. The oldest attempts known to us were made by astrologers who devised the so-called trigons of the four elements—air, water, earth and fire . . .

. . . The Greek classification according to the four physiological temperaments, took as its criteria the appearance and behavior of the individual exactly as we do today in the case of physiological typology. But where shall we seek our criterion for a psychological theory of types?[1]

Carl Jung

HREE SYSTEMS of typology challenge the basic premises of the Jung/*Myers-Briggs Type Indicator®* (*MBTI®*)model and its quaternity of couplings: the Five Factor model, the Keirsey-Bates model and the Singer-Loomis Inventory of Personality (the SLIP). The first takes an academic, cognitive/behavioral position, questioning the entire premise underlying the approach taken by Jung and the *MBTI* researchers. The second posits the four ancient temperaments rather than the psychological function as the basis for human types, and then misuses the four couplings. The third, coming out of the analysts' world, questions Jung's bipolar assumptions, seeks an inclusion of all eight Jungian types based on a spectrum approach, and totally excludes the couplings. My critique of the last two models will, strangely but appropriately, receive support from the ancient four-element view by virtue of their relationship with the four functions: air with thinking, water with feeling, earth with sensing, and fire with intuition.

THE FIVE FACTOR MODEL

I will treat this model briefly because it has a limited application to my overall work on the four coupled archetypes. However, the Five Factor model's static structure helps to highlight the importance of the MBTI's dynamic structure. (The information on this model has been obtained from a 1993 MBTI symposium led by James Newman.)[2]

The Five Factor model (or Trait model) was born independently of the MBTI. Each of the five factors is as static as Keirsey's four archetypal temperaments, which we will discuss next. As a result, the couplings are meaningless in this system. The Five Factor model, originally based on a cognitive/behavior modification approach, was developed sporadically over several decades from the 1880s to the 1960s. Initially, thousands of human characteristics were culled out of dictionaries, and finally correlated in the 1980s under five factors: Extroversion; Openness; Agreeableness; Conscientiousness; and Neuroticism, or Emotional Stability. Newman, drawing on others' research, shows the following correlations between the MBTI types and four factors in the Five Factor model. In the FFM:

1. **Extroversion correlates .70 with Extraversion/Introversion;**

2. **Openness correlates .70 with Sensing/Intuition;**

3. Agreeableness correlates .45 with Thinking/Feeling;

4. Conscientiousness correlates .47 with
   Judging/Perceiving.

These are amazing correlations, since even .3 is considered high. Yet one team of developers of the FFM, McCrae and Costa, are "very critical of the MBTI as a valid measure of Jungian typology" although they grant an "impressive convergence," and they urge MBTI users to "seriously consider abandoning Jungian theory [and] . . . adopt the perspective of the five factor model of personality."[3] The implicit reasons are similar to those that James Newman and others have noted—that is, that most academicians generally reject Jung's dynamic, complex-oriented premises about psychology, and in particular, about the types. These academics opt for their static set of definitions, while finding a dynamic, polar approach too alien to their prevailing methodologies. Besides, we also saw that the Educational Testing Service called Isabel the "little old lady in tennis shoes." They treated Katharine Briggs and Isabel Briggs Myers with less than full respect because they never had the academic credentials that collegiate researchers have demanded.

MBTI researchers see the value of the FFM as extending and expanding the acceptability of personality type among theorists and practitioners. Newman, however, feels that the many negative traits listed under each factor present problems for the more normative descriptions of the MBTI. Yet the greatest difficulty in realizing a comprehensive theory that would incorporate both the FFM and the MBTI is the dynamic developmental aspects of the Jung/Myers model and the assumption that there is an implicit purposeful wholeness of all of the types in each person, an assumption that FFM theorists roundly reject.

Wayne D. Mitchell, one of the researchers in this symposium, undertook a study in which he demonstrated the validity of the

Jung/Myers model by showing specific, statistically significant shifts in some subscales of the various functions in the following ways:[4]

1. The dominant form of a function will have different mean scores compared with the auxiliary form of the same function. This follows from the fact that an *MBTI* functional trait is never separable from its E–I and J–P connections. Thus there is a dynamic shift in the way a given function uses a given trait, because the trait operates in an interactive, holistic psychic field that includes both Introversion and Extraversion, and Judging and Perceiving. The "tough/tender" subscale of the feeling function especially stood out here.

2. Any function used in the extraverted attitude will differ significantly when it is used in the introverted attitude. In the Jung/Myers model, the whole is greater than the sum of the parts, in contrast to the Traits Theory, which, because of its static quality, deals only with parts (i.e., traits). In each function, at least two subscales demonstrated this dynamic.

3. At least in some subtraits, older people will have shifted somewhat from their dominant function toward its opposite, the inferior function. The results here were mixed: some people moved more toward their dominant function, others moved more toward the inferior function and a third group shifted from a first auxiliary to a second. In any case, some dynamic shifts did occur.

Overall, this *MBTI* research, using 1,760 subtraits (110 for each of the sixteen types), randomly selected from a stratified sample and drawn from a database of 9,200 cases, established the value of the qualitative, dynamic, and holistic Jung/Myers model over the quantitative, static, and parts-oriented Traits model. The value of this research is that it underlines the importance of the archetypal couplings, which are based on the structures and dynamics of the individual functions.

THE KEIRSEY-BATES MODEL

The influential Keirsey-Bates model, based on the temperaments, challenges the source, structure, and dynamic of the type circle and its archetypes in a way that the FFM does not, since it uses the *MBTI* types, and yet posits the ancient temperaments rather than the functions as the fundamental ground for human differences. Keirsey and Bates first described their model in the popular *Please Understand Me: An Essay on Temperament Styles.*[5] The authors consider four basic archetypes related to the types, but purportedly more solidly based on the ancient four temperaments. The book became popular, however, because of the authors' clear and imaginative articulation of the individual functions and of the sixteen type families, all based on the pioneering work of Briggs, Myers, and McCaulley. Thereby they contributed significantly to the spread of typological understanding, even before Isabel Briggs Myers published *Gifts Differing.*

However, I have been concerned for years about Keirsey and Bates' rationale and description of their four archetypes, only two of which are based on the couplings we have been exploring. Not only have they radically changed the quaternity of archetypes by basing them on the ancient temperaments, but they have also totally eliminated the inner dynamic of the four functions, and therefore of the interactive archetypes in the type compass.

This model of the archetypes has a considerable following, among whom Linda Berens has been particularly influential since she wrote her dissertation on the temperaments.[6] The Temperament Research Institute in Huntington Beach, California, trains facilitators in type/temperament work, publishes literature on the temperaments, and organizes training seminars throughout the country.[7] The work of Keirsey (Bates is deceased) and now Linda Berens dominates this segment of the typological world, which is concentrated in California. Berens, Giovannoni, and Cooper (1990) have published an *Introduction to Temperament*[8] that somewhat corresponds to the Myers-Briggs *Introduction to Types.* While relying entirely on the Jung/Myers types for its structures, this temperament group denies some of the assumptions originally developed by Jung and extended by *MBTI* research and theory.

TEMPERAMENT BASED

The Keirsey-Bates model is based on the assumption that the ancient four temperaments—the choleric, the phlegmatic, the melancholic, and the sanguine—not the four functions, are the true basis for four fundamental type archetypes. The temperaments were proposed by Hippocrates and Galen as elemental human behaviors in the fifth century B.C. and were popularized by Ernst Kretschmer in the second decade of the twentieth century,[9] according to Keirsey.[10] Berens draws even more from the historical work done by Abraham Roback.[11] Keirsey writes:

> In taking our cue from Kretschmer in the temperament hypothesis we must abandon Jung's idea of "functions." But in giving up Jung's "functions" we must not abandon his behavior descriptions, for they have great predictive value. By knowing a person's type, we can anticipate rather accurately what he will do most of the time. This is not something to give up lightly, so it is not so much that the "function type" is abandoned but rather subordinated to the concept of "temperament," the latter having a much wider range of convenience as an explainer of behavior.[12]

Having acknowledged that he is drawing on Jung's functions as accurate "behavior descriptions," Keirsey then subordinates them to the temperaments, because the latter have "a much wider range of convenience as an explainer of behavior." Thus, Keirsey needs to describe the four temperaments with some kind of clarity that is superior to the functions. He writes that "Only the choleric are concerned with making the Self real. . . . Only the sanguine like themselves better when they live freely and spontaneously. . . . Those who are melancholic hold themselves in high regard when they achieve position and belong to social units . . . phlegmatics look upon themselves with pride as their powers increase."[13] These ideas are quite vague, but it is apparent in what follows that the authors perceive the temperaments to be more physiologically and innately basic than the functions:

> Very simply, temperament determines behavior because behavior is the instrument for getting us what we must have, satisfying our desire for that one thing we live for. The god (or temperament) we were born to has left each of us a hunger that must be fed daily.[14]

Berens is much more specific in describing each temperament.

> In 450 B.C., Hippocrates described four such dispositions he called *temperaments*—a choleric temperament with an ease of emotional arousal and sensitivity; a phlegmatic temperament with a cool detachment and impassivity; a melancholic temperament, with a very serious, dour and downcast nature; and a sanguine temperament full of impulsivity, excitability and quick reactivity.[15]

These descriptions differ somewhat from the traditional dictionary definitions. *Webster's* tells us that the choleric type has a connection with "cholera, a disease of the bile." Therefore choleric means "bilious . . . easily irritated, irascible, inclined to anger." Phlegmatic comes from "phlegm," as "mucus," one of the four humors of the body which was believed to cause sluggishness or dullness. Hence "phlegmatic" means "hard to arouse to action . . . sluggish, dull, calm, cool, imperturbable." Melancholia is also associated with bile, but is black rather than yellow, and "refers to a mental disorder characterized by excessive gloom," so that a melancholic is "one affected with a gloomy state of mind." The sanguine temperament is based on the ancient view that such a person is "one in whom the blood is the predominate humor of the four," and is therefore a "cheerful, confident, optimistic" person. Although differing somewhat, these dictionary descriptions share an inner consistency with those of Keirsey and Berens.

REJECTING THE TEMPERAMENTS

Jung, however, rejected the temperaments as the basis for human differences because they were based only on their primitive physiological qualities. He noted that their "differentiation hardly rates as a psychological typology since the temperaments are scarcely more than psychophysical colorings."[16] Further:

> The four temperaments are obviously differentiations in terms of affectivity, that is, they are correlated with manifest affective reactions. But this is a superficial classification from the psychological point of view; it judges only by appearance.[17]

Jung posits that a man who looks phlegmatic might be profoundly passionate within, "his intense, introverted emotionality expressing itself through the greatest outward calm." He continues this argument, holding that the emotionality that characterizes the temperaments must yield to what he calls a more objective system: "We have, therefore, to find criteria which can be accepted as binding not only by the judging subject but also by the judged object."[18] In this regard it is striking that neither Keirsey nor Berens discusses Jung's objections to the old temperament theory in any of their writings. Furthermore, their descriptions of the four temperaments are as mental or metaphorical as Jung's descriptions of the functions.

Jung begins by comparing the striking differences between extraverted and introverted types, starting with children who manifest from birth marked differences in this regard.[19] Then he introduces the four functions, which perfectly capture our basic cognitive needs:

sensation tells us that something is real; intuition shows us its possibilities; thinking identifies its meaning; and feeling establishes its value for us and others around us.[20] These simple structures have proven to be accurate metaphors for understanding human differences; the *MBTI* has popularized them as reliable bases for the four coupled archetypes this book has been describing.

There is, moreover, sufficient support for making a rudimentary connection between the four functions and the four temperaments: feeling with the choleric's emotional arousal; thinking with the phlegmatic's cool detachment; sensation with the melancholic's dour and sad nature; and intuition with the sanguine's impulsivity and excitability. Jung may have indirectly supported this connection when he noted that the first attempts in our Western culture to classify individuals according to types "were made by oriental astrologers" via "the four elements: air, water, earth, and fire."[21] Jung calls this classification the "ancient cosmological scheme," in which the four temperaments corresponding to the four humours as a "physiological typology," closely connect with the ancient cosmological scheme. In turn, contemporary astrologers such as the Jungian analyst Liz Greene have associated air with thinking (and so, in my view, with the Phlegmatic), water with feeling (and the Choleric), earth with sensation (and with Melancholic), and fire with intuition (and with Sanguine).[22] By connecting the four temperaments with the four elements in the same way that I am proposing here, Berens and associates also implicitly relate the four temperaments with the four functions in *Introduction to Temperament* (1990).[23]

Assuming he knew these connections, Jung argued that the temperaments were too emotionally oriented on a crass physiological level. After noting both the cosmological schema (the four elements) and the physiological system (the four temperaments), he asserted that neither could be the basis of a psychological typology.

GOD METAPHORS

Even Keirsey and Bates recognized the descriptive limitations of the temperaments. They write:

> The Hippocratic names for the four temperaments, however, are misleading. They derive from the four bodily fluids—blood, phlegm, yellow bile and black bile—and so have arcane (and limited) reference. On the other hand, four Greek gods, all of whom Zeus commissioned to make man more like the gods, represent the temperaments quite accurately, albeit metaphorically. These are Apollo, Dionysus, Prometheus and his brother Apimetheus. Myth has it that Apollo was commissioned to give man a sense of spirit, Dionysus to teach man joy, Prometheus to give man science and Epimetheus to convey a sense of duty.[24]

Without making immediate explicit connections, the authors assume the reader will understand that these four gods represent the Sanguine, Choleric, Phlegmatic, and Melancholic temperaments respectively. The stories of the gods, then, become the new metaphors to describe the ancient temperaments. This is a valid attempt to move from body to metaphor, as we saw Jung doing in *Psychological Types,* noting that an instinct for introversion demands a metaphorical explanation, or "a psychic apprehension," which he begins to call an archetype.[25] We also saw Herrmann move from a physiologically measured way of characterizing the brain quadrants to a metaphorical approach. Even as metaphors, however, these descriptions of the temperaments do not provide for the kind of subtle intrapsychic interplay and dynamics that exist between the functions in the Type Compass. The description of the temperaments themselves and their Greek god metaphors are not in any way dynamically related.

The four gods, moreover, suffer the same limitations that Moore and Gillette saw in Toni Wolff's four feminine archetypes, that is, they are too specific for describing what amounts to the four central psychic directions of the mind/brain compass. It is no accident, then, that when it comes to describing the various *MBTI* archetypes that are presumably based on these four temperament-related gods, Keirsey and Bates say little about the gods' characteristics and stories. The authors revert to describing each archetype in terms of the type attitudes and functions that are presumed subservient to the illusive temperaments. The archetypal nature of type patterns gives substance to the archetypal temperaments, not the other way around. One wonders if Jung and Myers together had systematically articulated the individual types and couplings as archetypes whether Keirsey and Bates would have developed their model or, if they had done so, whether it would have attracted any followers.

PROBLEMS WITH THEIR ARCHETYPES

Keirsey and Bates then find couplings within the sixteen *MBTI* families of types they consider a match for the temperaments' structures. Two couplings from the Jung/Myers mandala are the same: NTs are the Phlegmatic/Prometheans and NFs are the Choleric/Apollonians. Two are different: the SPs are the Sanguine/Dionysians and the SJs are the Melancholic/Epimetheans. Why did the authors choose the SJ and SP combinations, instead of the STs and the SFs? They appear to have been influenced by Kretschmer's schizothymes and cyclothymic types, and by four of Eduard Spanger's six human types: religious (or spiritual), theoretical, economic, and aesthetic. Given these, they write:

> Further, the Jungian typology must undergo some rearrangement to conform to these temperaments. What Jung called intuition (N) appears to be equivalent to Kreschmer's schizothymic temperament. The N's or schizothymes, opt either for the Apollonean [NF] spirituality (self-actualization) or Promethean [NT] science

(powers). Sensation (S) seems equivalent to Kretschmer's cyclothymic temperament. The S's or cycloids, choose either the Dionysian [SP] joy (freedom to act) or the Epimethean [SJ] duty (social status).[26]

It is beyond my understanding how the "N's (intuitives) or schizothymes" can be the source of both an NF and an NT combination. How does N by itself translate into these two couplings? This is also the case with the "S's (sensates) choosing either SP and SJ combinations." Keirsey and Bates must have gone first to all of the sixteen types that have these four combinations and worked backward to relate two of them to schizothymes and two of them to cycloids. Compared with Jung's simple plan that posited the four functions as the basic factors in human differences, the Keirsey and Bates process is very difficult to understand.

Be that as it may, since it follows faithfully the NF coupling, the description of the NF Apollonian is perfectly in tune with the Oceanic/Lover archetype. Keirsey and Bates find Carl Rogers, the creator of Rogerian psychology, to be an excellent example of this archetype. Rogers taught that therapeutic healing was based primarily on the therapist's unconditional, loving acceptance of the client, an attitude that fits this Lover Archetype well. The authors write further of Rogers:

> He is increasingly listening to the deepest recesses of his psychological and emotional being, and finds himself increasingly willing to be, with greatest accuracy and depth, that self which he most truly is.[27]

"Apollonian," however, does not suit this type/archetype. Apollo is both the god of music and an aggressive Warrior known for his sharp tongue and rational powers. Apollonian Warrior and rationalist are misleading and incongruous qualities for the NF, whom the Osmond group call the Oceanic. I call this configuration the Creative Artist; Moore and Gillette identify this archetype as the Lover and artist; and Herrmann associates him with the C quadrant as the elemental musician. All these figures and qualities are the opposite of the ST Warrior.

In one specific way, the name Prometheus fits the larger meaning of the NT types that the Osmond group calls Ethereals; that Herrmann and I name the Creative Scientists; and Moore and Gillette recognize as the Magicians. Prometheus seeks the fire of the gods, their secret knowledge. Such a figure is a good exemplar of the Magician. Hence the NF Apollonian and the NT Promethean archetypes, as Keirsey and Bates generally describe them, are in substantial agreement with all the other formulations of the NF and NT in the type quadrant theory.

However, this is not the case with their SP/Dionysian and SJ/Epimethean structures. By virtue of placing the *MBTI* version of the J and the P types into two couplings, they fundamentally change the basic structure of the type mandala. The Keirseyan model eliminates the centrality of both the ST and the SF couplings. This subverts the inner structure and dynamics of the type mandala and its supportive Jung/Myers theory. While the J and P have specific characteristics, their main function, as discovered by Katherine Briggs and Isabel Briggs Myers, is helping specify the dominant function within each type coupling. The J and the P, along with the E and I, are subordinate to the four couplings in terms of basic personality traits. We have shown—beginning with Jung's intimations in the couplings of the dominant/auxiliary, followed through in Briggs and Myers' theory and research, and in the Osmond group's research, buttressed by Moore and Gillette's archetypes and Herrmann's and Lowen's brain research— that the four couplings of the sixteen function-attitude pairings establish the main characteristic of all these types, and they are, therefore, the four fundamental archetypes. They are as inviolable in their individual structures and in their interactive dynamics as are the four functions. They are as absolute in both unique makeup and mutuality of relationships as are the major organs of the human body. When one suffers, they all suffer.

In assembling both the SP/Dionysian and the SJ/Epimethian, Keirsey and Bates conflate the SF and ST couplings of the type mandala. Under the SPs they include the following: ISTP, ESTP, ISFP, and ESFP. Thus the SP/Dionysian is, in the language of the archetypal structures we have been developing, both parent/moralists (SFs) and structural/warriors (STs). This is confusing enough. Then when Keirsey and Bates describe this type, they point out characteristics that belong primarily to the NFs, that is, that they are "great painters, instrumentalists, vocalists."[28] Recall that in the Herrmann model, the NF/C quadrant is the musical one. Thus, Keirsey and Bates invade their own Apollonian type, generally considered to be the musician. Furthermore, the SFs in all the type literature are shown usually to have some hands-on craft skills but are not typically talented in the fine arts. Even more bizarre, STs are said to be in artistic professions, when all available research in the area of type shows that such types are the furthest of all from the fine arts. We recall that Herrmann's ST/A quadrant persons could not begin to describe, with even the slightest modicum of artistry, a creative person. Keirsey and Bates also say that this Dionysian archetype is adept at "construction work, jobs where heavy machinery is employed . . . driving ambulances and racing cars, motorcycles, aircraft." Here Keirsey and Bates are certainly more in line with all reports we have on SFs and STs, especially the latter.

Overall, there is a hopeless confusion of vocational orientations in this Keirsey archetype. Certainly any one person can be a complex mix of several such types and archetypes. However, these are rare combinations, but finding rare combinations is hardly the point here. The SP Dionysian and the other three are supposed to be the four archetypes—sharply distinguished from one another and yet dynamically interrelated—that would constitute the central and guiding elements

The Keirsey-Bates Archetypes

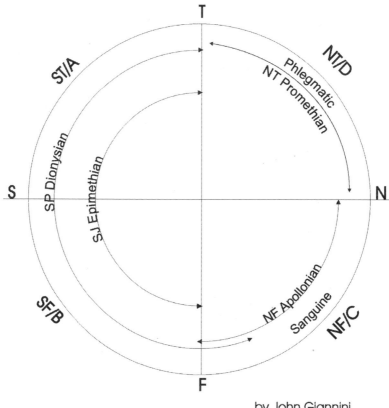

by John Giannini

FIGURE 10.1

of a type compass. But in our typological cross, these Dionysians would occupy more than half of the archetypal quadrants, as we see in figure 10.1, enmeshed as they are in three of the four: the SF/Bs, the ST/As and the NF/Cs. In the Herrmann Whole Brain model, these types are rare individuals who practically embrace the four quadrants.

While pondering the Keirsey-Bates model, I attended the Twelfth International Conference in Boston. There a Mr. Scott Blanchard gave one of the major talks on his experiences as an ESFP Dionysian. By this time, Keirsey and his temperament followers were giving new names to their four archetypes. Their additional name attached to the SF Dionysian was the Artisan. Blanchard was delighted to have better understood himself as an ESFP Artisan. He is a highly enthusiastic and confident individual, a success in business, happy in family life, and claims the love of creative parents, both of whom are ENFPs. He discussed many aspects of his life experience which I began to locate in the four coupled quadrants:

1. ST: his organizational and tough-minded strengths in business, his business acumen even as a youngster and his capacity to stick to a task and finish it;

2. SF: his enjoyment of parenting, his kinglike leadership at work, his need in school and in all of life to find pragmatic, experiential relevancy in any body of knowledge and his love of woodwork, often so typical of SFs who realize their artistry in the crafts;

3. NF: his obviously warm, empathic nature, his need for a meaningful life, his learning often in "random ways," his testing at times as ENFP and the influence of his ENFP parents;

4. NT: his dislike of theory in college courses and in any areas of life.

Mr. Blanchard turned out to be a perfect example of an ESFP Artisan. He fully understood this, and for this reason he embraced the Temperament theory. However, his type, as noted more theoretically above, cannot be one of four directional archetypes in the type circle. He is too rare an individual. He is, however, a very good example of a three quadrant person, as understood in the Jung/MBTI model. See figure 10.2 for how the Artisans look in the MBTI diagram.

This Artisan's dominant coupling is SF, his first auxiliary coupling is ST, and his second auxiliary coupling is NF. Mr. Blanchard, considering both his inborn traits and the upbringing by his ENFP parents, is effective and alive in his first three quadrants. However, he clearly dislikes the theoretical and holistic world of the NT quadrant, which is his inferior coupling.

An SP Sanguine Artisan Mapped as a Three-Quadrant ESFP Type

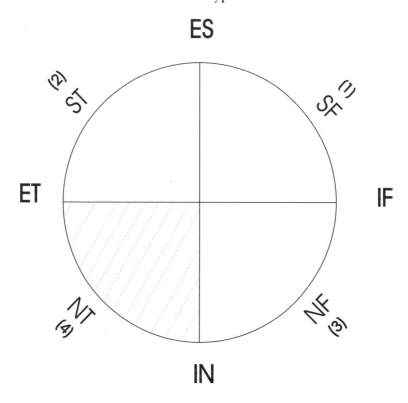

FIGURE 10.2

The SJ Epimethean seems to fit primarily the ST/A/Warrior quadrant of the psyche and brain, since a person here is strong on a "work ethic against a play ethic."[29] But there is also a significant mix of the ST Worker/Warrior and the SF Parent/King, since Keirsey and Bates single out the following *MBTI* types to fit this pattern: ISFJ, ESFJ, ISTJ, and ESTJ. Thus, like the SPs, the central couplings are the same STs and SFs, with E–I and P–J variations. Here, as with the SPs, the SJs usurp the unique centrality of the SF and ST. So the ST's worker ethic is now mixed in with the SF's parental ethic, since they describe this SJ type as also "the caretaker," endowed with a "parental attitude," who feels "bound and obligated" to his or her duties and "supports his parental and responsibility purposes with a belief in and desire for hierarchy."[30] Again, in terms of the four ultimate psychic directions, clarity of direction is lost.

Jung always made clear that we must not get hung up with too sharp divisions in understanding human differences. Yet he stubbornly held that the four functions constituted a precise and distinct gestalt that essentially framed the entire human cognitive process and that made possible "something that has long been lacking, a critical psychology."[31] It is remarkable that Jung's intuitive ingenuity, which created the type mandala in the first two decades of the twentieth century, would be confirmed by Myers' immense research beginning in the 1940s, and provide the metaphorical basis for the emergence of the brain's adult quadrants, as well as the child's brain/mind development in the 1980s and 1990s. For even as the four functions are unalterable and basic, so are their couplings, which form the basis for the systems we have explored.

I am arguing that if Keirsey and Bates were seeking to establish a similarly clear quaternity based purportedly on the temperaments and their use of the Jung and the *MBTI* system, they have not succeeded in doing so. Keirsey and Bates' alternative structures may be interesting and vigorously developed, but they do not meet the criteria for an ultimate psychic compass for human differences. The traits and the vocational preferences of both the SP and the SJ are too mixed and varied for such a psychic compass.

CRITIQUE OF BERENS

As already noted, the other important person in developing the Keirsey model is Linda Berens. Her Ph.D. research, while a comprehensive review of type differences among many persons and systems in history, does not substantially change the above argument. By the time Berens wrote her dissertation and, with the other two authors, completed the *Introduction to Temperaments,* Keirsey had wisely named the four temperaments by more general names: the NF Apollonian becomes the Idealist, a name in its undifferentiated sense that would be close to the Osmond Oceanic; the NT Promethean becomes the Rational, a term too narrow since it excludes the irrational N; the SJ Epimethean becomes the Guardian; and the SP Dionysian, as noted in discussing Mr. Blanchard, the Artisan. While the latter two are apt terms for the archetypes they describe, they (unacceptably) overlap the vocational characteristics of the first two.[32]

Berens' Ph.D. dissertation is totally based on the Keirseyan model. Briefly, she compares an *MBTI* understanding of an introverted thinking type, specifically the ISTP, with the Keirseyan version of that same type, called the SP Artisan temperament. Seeing a basic disagreement between the *MBTI* version and the Keirseyan version of this same type, both of "which purport to describe the same universe," she asks which of the two theories stands up better when a group of ISTP types are measured? The research favored the Keirseyan approach.[33] Given the thesis of this book and our critique of the temperament model, we can see that a well-defined description of the SP Artisan temperament that embraces the ST, SF, and even part of the NF quadrants, in contrast to the description of an ISTP with its introverted sensing thinking dominant and its NT auxiliary, is like comparing apples and oranges. However, win or lose here, the overall reliability of the *MBTI*, acknowledged generally in the psychological field and substantiated even more when the *MBTI* is compared with academia's Five Factor model as discussed above, is not damaged by this research.

However, Berens does make certain important critical comments about Jung's type methodology that need some consideration. Both she and Keirsey make much of Jung's original focus on introversion and extraversion. Berens writes, "The primary polarity in Jung's typology is the concept of attitudes of introversion and extraversion [sic]."[34] Jung never said this. However, he did point out in many places that these human differences are the first, most easily discerned ones. In *Psychological Types* we can follow the process of Jung's discovery in which he first observed the obvious difference between extraverted and introverted individuals and phenomena. The more specific nature of the four functions became apparent to him later. In my view, the primary polarities in Jung's type theory are the function couplings, with all their rich connections and implications which we have been exploring.

Berens also claims that Jung has confused introversion and intuition as well as extraversion and sensation.[35] However, Jung's distinctions are very clear, not only in the text of *Psychological Types* but also four additional papers on psychological typology (contained in the appendix to *Psychological Types*). "Introversion," writes Jung, "means an inward turning of libido. . . . Interest does not move toward the object, but withdraws from it into the subject."[36] Introversion is a psychic direction toward an inner consciousness. Intuition is not a general orientation or attitude, but a mode of cognition that perceives what the "naked eye" cannot—that is, perception through the images of the unconscious. Introversion is not perception; it indicates that attention is drawn to an inner, private consciousness. One can never call introversion a potentially creative attitude. Rather, it is the function of intuition that perceives the endless potentials lying outside of our ordinary consciousness that can be called creative. However, it is true, as Berens shows, that Jung continually linked introversion and intuition, not, however, because he confused them, but rather because both have an inward direction: intuition works through "inner," non-physical senses, especially the imagination, just as introversion directs one to an inward subjectivity.

Berens also points out the closeness of and confusion between extraversion and sensation. Again, extraversion is a psychic direction toward objects in the outer, manifest world, and sensation is the function of perception that utilizes the "outer," physical senses. Because sensation depends on the "outer" senses, it appears to have an extraverted aspect, not as direction but as an awareness of physical reality.

Berens agrees with what other commentators have noted as one of the most important contributions of Briggs and Myers to Jung's theory—namely, the more precise identification of the dominant function effected by including the separate orientations of judging and perception, showing which function extraverts in any one of the sixteen types. However, this feature of the MBTI does not mean anything in the Keirsey-Bates model, because there are no inner dynamics in the Keirsey-Bates model. Considering, on the other hand, the coupling/archetypal thesis I have been developing, I believe that the MBTI's other important contribution has been Isabel Briggs Myers' creative development of Jung's seminal idea of the type couplings (both in her Introduction to Types and in Gifts Differing) and her decision to base her monumental MBTI research on these four couplings.

Closer to the major thrust of this book, we need to look at how Berens, in her dissertation and in Introduction to Temperaments, articulates the rationale for temperaments. Following the Keirsey and Bates premise that the temperaments identify a more fundamental, innate, and physiological phenomenon than Jung's more psychological functions, Berens and her collaborators in Introduction to Temperaments seek natural metaphors to describe the temperaments. They write: "Just as the blueprint for an oak or a pine tree is present in its very seed, so is the temperament completely present at birth."[37] Just as a pine will always remain a pine, so is this true of a temperament. This is certainly in line with the Jungian idea that one's basic preference is inborn. However, the Jung/Myers model supposes and demonstrates an additional premise, also supported by the Herrmann and Lowen researches, that innate type preferences develop naturally, seek to grow within the other functions and then interact with the other functions and attitude inwardly and socially. The temperament theory, in contrast, insists on the enduring, even "static" character of each temperament. A person is born a whole SP Dionysian, and will remain a whole Dionysian. In the temperament model there is no intimation of development among the functions that we find, for example, in Lowen's work. While it is true that a newborn insect, for example, is already a full-blown worker and simply a small adult, this static condition is certainly not true of humans.

Further, Keirsey holds that, in contrast to his static, holistic model, the Jung/*MBTI* model is a dynamic parts model ("function theory"), born of individual functions, beginning with introversion and extraversion, followed by a dominant function, and then inferior functions. Berens, picking up this theme, continues:

> Another difference lies in the basic theoretical perspective of each theory. The functions in Function Theory are constructs of hypothesized psychic processes presumably explanatory of observed actions. The temperaments are also constructs, not of mental processes but of activity patterns. The Jung/Myers conception is said to be "dynamic," and as such the faculties, functions or parts have energy of their own and are thought to combine, interact or even change. Keirsey's is static, the whole having a uniting theme which persists from birth to death. Function Theory, as it is used, is a dynamic parts model, which posits basic psychological "attitudes" and "functions" which can be consciously manipulated. Keirseyan Temperament Theory is a system model which focuses on the configuration of the whole. The first is reductionist, the second, holistic.[38]

STATIC ASPECTS OF THEIR ARCHETYPES AND OTHER INCORRECT ASSUMPTIONS

There you have it: the Keirseyan model is holistic because it is static.

In contrast, because Jung's and Myers' is a "parts model," and because it has an internal structure of parts that are dynamically related to one another, it can also dynamically change and develop. Further, because it has "parts," it is also "reductionist" whereas the Keirseyan model is presumably progressive. It is important to note that the so-called parts are function traits that are related to one another intrapsychically and interpersonally. In addition, the Keirsey model uses the full-blown *MBTI* types, which also are made of "parts" that are now frozen into one another! How can a frozen or static type be progressive?

The Keirsey model overlooks an overall dynamic that transcends the individual functions, couplings and the sixteen *MBTI* types and is represented by the compass of the Soul. This dynamic is operative under the aegis of the Self, or the Soul, as the principle of wholeness and of life, the source and containing archetype of all of the types (see figure 6.2, page 247). In a maternal, Godlike containment, the Self embraces the major polar opposites of consciousness and the unconscious within, and the infinite cosmos and unique person without. As the source of wisdom, the Self is the intelligent connecting principle, the endless and restless dynamo of purposefulness, creativity, and healing. In considering Herrmann's Whole Brain model, we discussed this soulful source as the holographic brain, mind, and universe. Closer to our immediate subject, the Self's dynamic thrust toward wholeness means that one potentially can and eventually must live out all of the typological archetypes, always in varying degrees in different individuals. Following Jung, I showed in chapter 2 the close connection between the Self and the Chinese concept of the Tao. According to Jung, just as the Tao embraces all polarities symbolized by Yin and Yang structures and energies, so does the Self embrace all the typological polarities and their energic dynamism. All the types, therefore, are subject to this overall reality and energy.

Because the Self is the hidden or implicate order in the unconscious, another major dynamic must be noted here in the Jung/Myers model: the inferior function. The inferior function by itself represents a haunting presence and an insistent dynamic, and when it bursts into consciousness, it becomes a chaotic, emotional climate. When contained and worked through, it makes possible at least a beginning wholeness, in which a dialogue between all the types begins to occur.

Presumably none of these dynamisms have any meaning in the static world of the Keirseyan model, and indeed one does not read anything about these function dynamics in any of their archetypal descriptions. It is precisely here where the model, while it may work to some extent in practice, if one sticks with its focus on a fixed whole-ness, suffers significant theoretical and practical limitations in its analogy with nature. Where in nature does one find a whole without parts? To say that the pine tree is a whole from the beginning is to ignore the function of different cells in the tree, some of which function as bark, some as root, some as trunk and branches, and others as leaves, all of which must grow, change, and relate to one another at different times in the tree's development. There are no wholes without the continuous interaction of functional parts. Thus the root cells continue to grow and bring the entire tree the necessary mineral nutrients and water. The trunk and branch cells provide the structure and highways over which these vital substances travel to the buds, which flower, create new seeds, and produce leaves. In turn, the leaves produce chlorophyll cells with which the sun's light interacts to transform water and carbon dioxide into carbohydrates, which in turn feed all the other cells including the root cells.

Because it functions like any organic thing with many type parts, the Jung/Myers model, is, therefore, a *dynamic whole* in contrast to the Keirseyan model's static wholeness. It seems that the theorists of this model have had to come to this static view because there is no inter-relationship among the temperaments in the first place. Similarly, there is no natural interrelationship among the four posited Greek gods or among the final four general types, the Idealist, the Rational, the

Guardian, and the Artisan. Their replacing the ST and SF coupling with, respectively, SP and SJ, destroyed the dynamic interactions of the type circle.

So from the standpoint of the Jung and *MBTI* model, there appears to be an internal inconsistency in the Keirseyan theoretical argument, given that the argument proceeds from a series of wrong assumptions. This series continues to grow, for, after referring to nature itself as the ultimate ground for their model, Berens submits that this system is made up of "activity patterns" (presumably the four bodily liquids of the temperaments) in contrast to "mental processes." But such activity patterns would seem, of necessity, to be involved in mental processes. Besides, are not the functions also activity patterns? For example, an extravert's actions are oriented by the "outer," manifest world of objects, and the introverts informed by "inner" world of pattern. Berens acknowledges in *Introduction to Temperaments* that both theories use type descriptions that consist of mental processes. She concludes that both theories "may be useful. What is remarkable is that the *MBTI*, which was based on one theory, is useful in the application of both."[39] In effect the Keirseyan, static model—based presumably on nature—uses the dynamic Jung's and Myers' mental or metaphorical descriptions of the types based on mental processes. Can one have one's cake and eat it too?

The series of wrong assumptions continue. Berens and her associates also hold that, whereas the Jung and Myers model emphasizes the "intrapsychic" dimension, the Keirseyan model is an "interpsychic, systems-communication model." They continue: "This model leads professionals to focus on the communicational aspects of behavior between rather than within psyches, thus treating the individual as an organized whole."[40] How do the temperaments provide the basis for a "communication model" when each temperament is statically complete in itself and is in no way dynamically related to the other temperaments in a nonexistent compass? But the Jung and Myers model cannot be limited to the intrapsychic dimension, given the interpersonal significance of the types as explored in the *MBTI*, by the Osmond group, Moore and Gillette, and Herrmann. This research explicates the many societal functions of the function types in such areas as specific career choice, teamwork, conflict resolutions in couples, families and other societal groups, management styles, and the larger meaning of the Self that directs us both inwardly and outwardly. (In the final chapter I will show more of the sociopolitical implications of the Jung and Myers model I have been exploring.)

In summary, the Keirsey model suffers from two basic flaws due to discarding Jung's directional and circular type mandala: 1) the loss of precision in both specifying the traits and the occupational areas of their SJ and SP archetypes; and 2) the loss of the many dynamisms among the four archetypes that constitute the Jung and Myers model's Compass of the Soul.

Both the FFM and the Keirsey-Bates suffer from a basic ignorance of Jung's dynamic psychology, which includes the types. As a result, both instruments have eliminated the inner dynamics of the types and thereby have frozen the Soul's compass.

THE SINGER-LOOMIS INVENTORY OF PERSONALITY (SLIP)

Whereas the FFM critiques the *MBTI* based on academia's rejection of Jung's entire psychology, and Keirsey/Bates assumes that the ancient temperaments are more basic than Jung's functions, the Singer-Loomis Inventory of Personality (SLIP) criticizes the Jung/*MBTI* theory and instrument from within Jung's own system. The SLIP—developed by two outstanding Jungian analysts, June Singer and Mary Loomis, beginning in the late 1970s—rejects Jung's bipolar assumption and therefore the *MBTI*, based on the assumption that it restricts the conscious availability of all functions and attitudes. Singer and Loomis have reported their theory, inventory, and results in a 1982 journal article, in the 1986 Berlin International Jungian Congress' proceedings, in Loomis' 1991 book, *Dancing the Wheel of Psychological Types*, and in Singer's 1994 revision of her book, *Boundaries of the Soul*.⁴¹

The SLIP research grew out of Loomis' dissertation on the typology of creative people, for which she and Singer, one of her advisers, found the *MBTI* unsatisfactory. They found the forced choice yes/no approach of the *MBTI* too limiting in its attempt to reflect Jung's theory of bipolarity, holding that his position is more theoretical than practical.

They initially grant some validity to the bipolar hypothesis, but they also believe that the bipolarity can be transcended. Singer uses the analogy that "taking things apart and looking at the pieces," and then putting them back together again in a whole that transcends the pieces, transcends the polarities.⁴² For example, an introverted thinking function and an introverted feeling function can both be the strong aspects of a person's typology. They submit that the forced choices of the *MBTI* too often obliterate these possibilities. Hence instead of the *MBTI*'s forced choices between the attitudes and the perceiving and judging functions, the SLIP measures each of Jung's eight types (ES, IS, EN, IN, ET, IT, EF, and IF) separately.

THE THEORY OF THE SLIP:
REJECTING THE JUNG/*MBTI* OPPOSITES

Singer acknowledges both that "the *MBTI* is the product of extensive research, and has been statistically validated over and over again" and "is used in business and industry throughout the United States and internationally."⁴³ However, Singer and Loomis assume that the bipolar theory is too rigid and, therefore, does not free the psyche, and does not render people sufficiently conscious, because it does not allow for the fullest use of all of the eight Jungian types. They consider the Jung/*MBTI* bipolar theory to be a limited first-stage-of-life viewpoint in which the theory itself, its type circle and cross (as Jung depicts it, figure 1.1, page 34), and its *MBTI* instrument restrict the accessibility and dynamics of all the functions, thereby reducing human freedom and limiting consciousness. As they note in all of their publications, besides finding difficulties with the *MBTI* in the testing of creative people, they also questioned how they themselves were assessed. Singer writes that her analyst thought her "leading cognitive mode was introverted thinking," but felt that she was equally strong in both thinking and feeling.[44] This experience is not new to countless users of the *MBTI* who recognize opposite traits in themselves, or varying degrees of traits on the types' bipolar spectrums, without denying the validity of bipolarity.

Singer and Loomis argue that Jung was originally too rigid in his polar assumptions about the types, and in all of the polarities in his psychology in general. They contend that in his early work, "The two elements in the dualities are always posed against each other as opposites, and considered basically to be mutually exclusive."[45] On one hand, they argue, Jung's polar theory was a "tentative assumption" at the beginning of his career that has become a "cornerstone on typology for many years." On the other hand, pointing especially to his work in *Mysterium coniunctionis, Collected Works,* volume 14, Singer and Loomis assert that supporters of the *MBTI* have ignored Jung's later developments in regard to the fact that his "main thrust was in the direction of harmonizing the opposites"—that is, putting the pieces together again.[46]

THE PERMANENCE OF OPPOSITES

However, just as no one is totally extraverted or totally introverted and everyone lives in the tension between the extraverted and introverted opposites, there is no contradiction between the apparent exclusivity in bipolarization and the dynamic harmonizing of the polarities. All polarities, such as hot and cold and day and night, are gradations, but also distinct as extreme values or conditions. Hot and cold can be luke-warm in water, and night and day can be blended together at dawn and dusk. Yet, hot and cold and night and day have both conceptual validity and reality value. In his first formal seminar in 1925, four years after he completed *Psychological Types,* Jung speaks of an existence without opposites as "grey" or lifeless. Jung clearly recognized very early on that without the differences the opposites create, there would be no energy flow. He continues:

> And that is exactly what life would be if there were no opposites in it; therefore the pairs of opposites are not to be understood as mistakes but as the *origin of life.* For the same thing holds in nature. If there is no difference in high and low, then water can not come down. Modern physics expresses the condition that would ensue were opposites removed from nature by the term entropy: that is, death in an equable tepidity. . . . We are part of the general energic process, and it is psychology looked at with this fact in mind that I have tried to present in the *Types.*[47]

In a letter dated February 18, 1935, Jung criticizes the labeling of people, and writes that he avoids immediately discussing a person's type in analysis, unless "I have to explain to certain patients the one-sidedness of their behavior, their remarkable relations with other people, and such things."[48] But the polarities in human behavior do not go away, simply because, as Singer and Loomis imply, Jung also sought to harmonize them. Certainly, one-sidedness is a barbaric curse, but Jung also implies that the differences in types in a loving relationship can be a sublime blessing.

I perceive the conflict between the *MBTI* and the SLIP as I do the issue of autonomy and surrender in an intimate relationship. Jung's early work and the *MBTI* might represent the distinctive autonomy of each type in a polarity comparable to the autonomy of each person in the relationship. The later work of Jung and the SLIP might represent a blending of the polar opposites, comparable to the surrender in a relationship. But the autonomy and tension between the members of each pair of opposites, like the autonomy and tension between the members of each couple, is absolutely necessary before there can be a surrender and realized unity of the opposites. But an intimate unity does not extinguish the uniqueness and sovereignty of each partner; otherwise an intimate unity becomes an amorphous fusion. It is also possible that the MBTI and the SLIP are as irreconcilable, and yet equally useful, as the two mathematically proven theories in quantum physics: (1) that matter is made up of particles, and (2) that matter is made up of waves.

The authors of the SLIP imply a cultural critique in regard to the rigid opposites. I see our culture as one-sided and stuck in a predominantly extraverted, sensing, thinking, and judging (ESTJ) Warrior consciousness (a view I elaborate in chapter 12). The patriarchal ESTJ Warrior consciousness, like most individuals in the first stage of life, values and emphasizes differentiation, exclusiveness, and externalization over cooperation, inclusiveness, and inward depth. Jung maintained that Freud, while adequately developing the psychological challenge of adapting to society in life's first stage, was also caught up in the pathology of the first stage. Jung submitted that this either/or consciousness leads to overt aggressiveness and competition. Freud saw the polymorphically perverse, childish Id in an eternal battle with the adult superego's collective norms. Even though Singer and Loomis would agree that Jung transcended this cultural and Freudian position, they imply that his type theory, developed early in Jung's post-Freudian career, and even conceived of as an answer to his difficulties with his psychological mentor, subtly continued to carry this first stage tendency toward a rigid and relatively exclusive bipolarity in his typology and other early work.

For example, in various places Singer and Loomis posit that there need not be an opposite such as the inferior function, citing statistics which showed that in 29 percent of people who took both the SLIP and the MBTI, the inferior function was not opposite their dominant function. Unfortunately, this is a less than persuasive argument because it shows that 71 percent of the sample did support the bipolar assumptions of the *MBTI*. Further, the analysis of SLIP profiles of Michigan State University students found that "most of them had cognitive styles which conformed to Jung's hypothesis" of a bipolar development. Singer and Loomis hypothesize that because of the student's first-stage-of-life task of adapting to society, "they need to rely on their most highly developed modes," resulting in "a bi-polar development of their typology."[49] Here, the patriarchal assumption that we always live in an either/or mentality raises its legitimate but limited voice. In the second stage of life, we are challenged to realize a both/and feminine consciousness, but the polar opposites are not extinguished.

Then in the same context Singer and Loomis talk about these students' first-stage-of-life type awareness as if it were not conscious, for they assert:

> Generally, it is not until individuals are working to become conscious that they transcend the bipolar developments of their typology. This change is likely to occur after 35 years of age, when the demands of society usually have been met.[50]

They seem to be saying that consciousness arises only in the second stage of life. In her book's new edition, Singer corrects this impression by pointing out that our development in the first stage of life is a conscious process and that "with the beginning of consciousness comes differentiation, first into opposites—myself and other—and then fragmentation into the many."[51] As a rule, most persons adapt to societal demands in the first stage of life by employing the function and attitude that comes naturally to them. If they adapt by living the wrong type, they will experience the punishing effects of the unconscious, as experienced by me, Jung, and many others.

The research support for the inferior function in the *MBTI* and for the dominance of particular types in the Michigan State University students, as well as the examples of the frightening challenges of the inferior function, such as the case of Carol in chapter 6, remind us that Jung's typology is set within the context of the ultimate polarities—consciousness and the unconscious—that we must face, especially in the second stage of life. In this most comprehensive of polarities in which the dominant function and coupling are developed in the first stage and the inferior function and coupling (especially) in the second stage, the perceiving and judging functions are powerful factors in the monumental play of forces as one attempts to create wholeness, often against mighty resistance from the unconscious. Singer and Loomis seem to imply throughout their writings that the Jung/*MBTI* system is incomplete because the inferior function is seemingly always excluded from consciousness. Are they forgetting the dominant function's immense resistance against the shadowy inferior function as it begins to intrude on consciousness? Yet they end their 1986 workshop by discussing the ultimate task in individuation, that of relating consciousness and the unconscious in the transcendent function, in which "one is willing to stand in the center of one's circle typologically and *bear the tension* of developing the inferior function."[52] To "bear the tension" implies the pull of opposites.

When a mature person takes a "stand in the center," it must be a conscious act. In contrast, when Loomis recounts the "Myth of the Three Feathers" as representing an unconscious development of the inferior function,[53] she implies that the Jung/*MBTI* model describes a relatively unconscious condition. In the "Three Feathers" story, there are four characters rather than eight types: the king, the two bright sons, and the dunce of a son, called the Dumling. Dumling, who represents the inferior function of the father king, wins all the prizes without any conscious effort on his part. Loomis calls this an example of "enantrodromia," the movement toward one's opposite. Jung seems to have inadvertently contributed to the assumption that individuation can be an unconscious process when he spoke of the transcendent function as "a purely natural process, which may *in some cases* pursue its course without the knowledge or assistance of the individual."[54] Loomis is correct in saying that Jung really meant the Self in this statement rather than the transcendent function, which of its very nature is one's conscious relationship to and dialogue with the unconscious.[55] However, we know that we can often consciously encourage and influence a movement to the opposite. Anyone who faces one's own pathology, and, by this homeopathic act, intensifies one's own suffering, consciously contributes to awakening one's healing opposite.

Singer and Loomis hold that a conscious inclusion of the opposites doesn't exist in the *MBTI* model. This conclusion can at least be partially attributed to the lack of communication and minimal understanding between the worlds of certified analysts and professional typologists. Analysts have so generally ignored typologists that they scarcely know how dedicated to Jung and to scientific research the *MBTI's* best practitioners actually are. The typologists, in turn, have focused on tables and measurements—for example, in their research of occupations, ethnicity, age groups, and economic levels—at the expense of ignoring Jung's insistence on the primacy of dynamics over structure in human differences. However, if one carefully reads every one of Myers' sixteen type descriptions (e.g., in *Introduction to Type*), one discovers the quiet but insistent attention she gives to the inferior function. Other *MBTI* practitioners take pains to fill this gap. For example, Angelo Spoto in *Jung's Typology in Perspective* seeks to locate the *MBTI* within the context of Jung's system, and particularly within his polarities; Naomi Quenk in her *Beside Ourselves* lays out the conscious process of developing one's inferior function in all the types.

The concept of individuation—our search for wholeness throughout the two stages of life—has been noticeably absent from the center of the *MBTI* literature. If we check the index of Myers' *Gifts Differing,* we find no reference to the term or to the stages of life. Yet Myers' use of the word archetypes, which she defines as "the universals, the shapes of thought, which bring pattern and meaning out of the overwhelming multiplicity of life," implies the process of individuation.[56] For example, introverts, she writes, tend to be more in touch with these universals that come from the Self, but they are challenged to understand also the demands of extraversion and its societal conventions, which, if ignored, can be disastrous.[57] Aspects of individuation and whole-life consciousness are evident in such thinking, even if only by implication and even if she does not describe the types as archetypal. The broader *MBTI* literature also shows much sensitivity to Jung's general psychological system; for example, the proceedings from their international typology conferences where workshop leaders and lecturers explore typology across cultures, in spirituality and religion, in psychological theory and practice, in management practices and leadership, in organizational development, in career counseling, and in research.

Singer and Loomis emphasize in their theory the dynamics of a personal development throughout the life span, whereas the *MBTI* pragmatically focuses primarily on providing people with a type-characteristics awareness so that they can effectively function in ordinary interactions and in the everyday realms of work and love, again a first-stage-of-life orientation. Loomis' work particularly focuses on individuation and lifelong growth, a subject we will turn to when we consider her Native American wheel.

Overall, in their writings about the process of individuation, Singer and Loomis assume that in its realization, all eight of the functions must be developed. Loomis interprets Jung's statement that "Consciousness rests on the four elements or basic functions"[58] to mean that the four means all eight (the four functions multiplied by the two attitudes). The Jung and *MBTI* model has assumed that the development of one's four primary functions in the type compass is in itself a very significant whole life development. Further, I have been arguing in this book that within this model, a more comprehensive life development is realized through the four archetypal couplings.

THE CROSS OPPOSITES

Singer and Loomis view Jung's type diagram, which they characterize simply as "a cross," as symbolic of the Jung and *MBTI* strictures. As pictured in this model, "interactions could occur between adjacent functions, but not between opposing functions," especially between the dominant function and the inferior function.[59] The "adjacent functions" are the couplings, which, according to Loomis, "would always include a perceiving and a judging function." This is all they say of the couplings, ignoring Myers' seminal descriptions of them, the Osborne group's archetypal development of them, and Myers and McCaulley's extensive research based on these combinations.

Jung's diagram of the types in the form of a cross has become a bugaboo for Singer and Loomis because it graphically illustrates what they reject: the absoluteness of the bipolar hypothesis. In the Berlin workshop they posit that this figure represents an "either/or orientation, rather than a both/and."[60] Immediately this either/or formulation suggests again the "mutual exclusivity" of the Jung/*MBTI* model, which we have already discussed as too simplistic an interpretation of bipolarity. Further, the authors write that the cross, with its "axes . . . equal in length," suggests a serious dynamic problem, that is, "that energy flows in one direction or the other, but not both." They do not explain the basis for this interpretation.

Finally, they suggest another image is needed. Loomis takes up this challenge, specifically in the form of the Native American medicine wheel:

> The oppositional arrangement of the functions as imaged
> by the cross was a teaching device used by Jung to explain

the possible interaction of the functions. Unfortunately it has contributed to the misunderstanding of Jung's theory. The cross is an incomplete symbol. The oppositional arrangement contradicts Jung's basic premise that the aim of psychological growth is the resolution of opposites.[61]

This is an extraordinary statement in the light of what Jung says about the cross within his entire psychological theory, as for example in *Psychology and Religion*.[62] He writes, "The terrors of death on the cross are an indispensable condition for the transformation" of lifeless "substances" into life and "spiritualization."[63] In my view, this transformation includes that of the inferior function, for it, too, is "lifeless" until, through terrors-of-death experiences, it is brought into a relationship with the dominant function that creates both a union and a tension of the opposites. The cross as a "mandala," Jung continues, "has the status of a 'uniting symbol,'" it represents "the union of God and Man," "has the meaning of a boundary stone between heaven and earth," and represents the spiritual center as a symbol "with equal arms."[64] Finally, in a statement which is in tune with the entire thesis of this book—that typology is a creative archetype of order—Jung writes:

> The cross signifies order as opposed to the disorderly chaos of the formless multitude. It is, in fact, one of the prime symbols of order, as I have shown elsewhere. In the domain of psychological processes it functions as an organizing centre, and in states of psychic disorder caused by an invasion of unconscious contents it appears as a mandala divided by four.[65]

In the light of such assertions about the cross as a significant symbol of the Soul's wholeness, of which types are an integral part, it is certain that Jung would not agree that the type cross can be "incomplete," and befitting only an unconscious person.[66] Singer and Loomis' conclusion makes sense if we assume with them that all eight of Jung's types are absolutely necessary for individuation. In this case, the cross, as working with only four functions is, as Loomis writes, a "Procrustean fit for eight cognitive modes" that they consider to be a patriarchal, first-stage image.[67] Singer and Loomis have not proven this eight-type categorization either statistically or in its pragmatic value for a person's life. It is like saying, in terms of the four archetypal couplings, that to be complete one must become perfectly developed as an NF artist, an NT creative scientist, an ST structuralist and an SF parent. This is possible only for some rare individuals.[68] The authors saw this breadth in some artistic persons. They have mistakenly assumed that all of us can easily realize such wholeness.

Not only are Singer and Loomis seeking more type inclusiveness but also, as they perceive it, a more fluid, more flexible, and freer approach than the theoretical and instrumental strictures of the Jung and *MBTI* mode. This is the deep and admirable motive behind their thought and research. Hence they speak of the "independence" of each type, and therefore the need to measure the "eight cognitive modes independently."[69] The cross, as used by Jung, "forces a static interpretation,"[70] and represents for them the forced answer approach that was developed by the *MBTI*. They write, "We concluded that a free response inventory was needed, one that would allow the measurement of typological functioning without imposing a forced polarity."[71] They want to free us from what can best be expressed as the *MBTI's* Warriorlike strictures.

THE DEVELOPMENT OF THE SLIP INSTRUMENT

Let us now consider the development of the SLIP instrument. Singer and Loomis' immediate objection to the *MBTI* was the forced choice, which explained for them why this instrument could not "reveal the typology of a creative individual. Forced choice items would not allow it." However, in this regard, the *MBTI* research shows consistently that writers, fine artists, and architects, as examples of creative persons, favor intuition over sensation, are either NTs and NFs, or a combination of both, and often demonstrate even SF or ST strengths, approaching what Herrmann calls a four-quadrant person.

For example, in order to avoid forced choice in their instrument, Singer and Loomis changed the *MBTI* question, "At a party I like to a) talk or b) listen," to two separate items: (1) "At a party I like to talk" and (2) "At a party I like to listen." The subject responds to these questions by specifying "never, sometimes, half the time, usually, or always." Such a treatment was devised for each of the eight types. At this point, we need to remind our readers what Jung wrote of the eight types that he described in chapter 10 of *Psychological Types*:

> In the foregoing descriptions I have no desire to give my readers the impression that these types occur at all frequently in such pure form in actual life. They are, as it were, only Galonesque family portraits, which single out the common and therefore typical features, stressing them disproportionately, while the individual features are just as disproportionately effaced. Closer investigation shows with great regularity that, besides the most differentiated function, another less differentiated function of secondary importance is invariably present in consciousness and exerts a co-determining influence.[72]

Singer and Loomis created an instrument based on the premise that each type is autonomous, a premise that Jung maintains does not exist in everyday consciousness and behavior. He opted instead for the couplings, without developing their full implication.

The results of an individual's SLIP are indicated in bar graph form, depicting each function independently. When I first took the SLIP in the late 1970s and early 1980s, I could not understand what to do with it. Without the mandala and its interrelated types, I did not know how to appraise the results in terms of my personal developmental tasks, as

I experienced them in the interplay of the Jung/*MBTI*'s dominant, auxiliary, and inferior functions. Neither could I identify myself as I did in the *MBTI* as an ENFP, nor could I envision how archetypal couplings would in any way be manifest in the SLIP system when I began to work with them. Has my resistance been due to the difficulty of readapting, or is it due to something more substantial? I believe Jung's above assertion about the limits of isolating the eight functions points to a more substantive problem.

I recently retook the SLIP, and it yielded the following results, some of which I constructed from the bar structures. My judging function totaled 205 and my perceptive, 175. This is significantly contrary to my natural tendencies of vastly favoring perception. My diploma thesis adviser once said to me, "Giannini, when you write on a subject, you want, like a great mother, to include all things." This remark describes the characteristics of a perceptive type, not a judging type, and undoubtedly accounts for the size of this book. The total of 185 for introversion and 195 for extraversion agreed with comparable *MBTI* scores, although my natural, but limited, extraversion has been overshadowed by much meditation. The total of my EF and IF was 110, of the ET and IT, 95, of the EN and IN, 93, and of the ES and IS, 82. In the *MBTI*, I am definitely less clear in T than F, as well as in S, more in line with my experiences. As to my T, I have found tight syllogistic reasoning difficult, and following my F bent, I prefer stories to logic. As a clear intuitive, and moreover, an intuitive, perceiving type, I continually lose things and forget dates and much detail. In coupling terms, my NF totaled 203, my NT, 188, my SF, 192, and my ST, 177. I come out somewhat a four-quadrant person, but with a dominant NF, an auxiliary SF in the SLIP, a second auxiliary, NT, and with an inferior, ST, which agrees roughly with my personal coupling configuration from the *MBTI*, though my NT is stronger than my SF. However, there is no way to relationally conceptualize these couplings in the SLIP, unless we do so on the typological compass and cross that the SLIP rejects. I am left with eight bars and an amorphous set of numbers.

One client who took both the SLIP and the *MBTI* was clearly an INFP in all of her work and love experiences. In the SLIP, her dominant F was supported, but her Ns were at the bottom of the bar, totally out of keeping with my experience of this clearly NF Creative Artist. Another creative INFJ client came out in the SLIP as high on all four of her introverted functions (figure 10.3), with a big gap separating the four extraverted functions. This makes some sense even from an *MBTI* standpoint, since a strong introvert can cast an inward-looking attitude over several functions on Jung's mandala. As we discussed in the *MBTI* chapter, an introvert authentically extraverts every function in a quiet

A SLIP Diagram of an INFJ Client

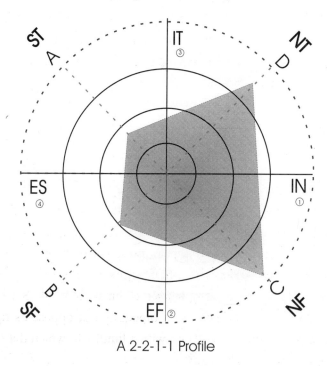

A 2-2-1-1 Profile

FIGURE 10.3

way, so that there is a kind of qualitative coming together of the two attitudes that transcends any quantifying.

Many questions and comparisons emerge as one reflects on the SLIP theory and instrument in relation to the Jung/*MBTI* model. Do most people come out, as my personal experience shows, with a more balanced picture than the *MBTI* presents? Some evidence is mounting in the affirmative, contributing to the conclusion that the SLIP's answers come out too amorphous. And again, are we measuring apples and oranges? The SLIP follows Jung in joining each function with an attitude. In the *MBTI*, the attitudes are tested separately and then joined to the other types in the sixteen type configurations. The SLIP seems to violate common experiences as well as Jung's strong assertion in hypothesizing that the attitudes and functions can be measured independently. Are we not always functioning between opposites in everyday experiences, as in Taoism's "interplay of Yin and Yang," which Jung also calls "the 'mother' and 'father' of everything that happens"?[73] In this matrix, do we not struggle with and choose between the polar tugs of assertiveness and passivity, between tough-mindedness and tender-mindedness, order and chaos, light and dark, masculine and feminine, even life and death, to name just a few? In terms of Erikson's first life crisis—trust versus mistrust—any therapist knows how people wounded in early childhood struggle mightily, fearfully, and often with much anguish to realize a modicum of trust when, in both dreams and waking life, a most trustworthy lover or friend is there for them. The reader is advised at this point to look again at chapter 2, in which the many ways that Yin and Yang play between one another corresponds with the play of type opposites. Are not many of these typological tensions lost with the SLIP, so that the Soul's Compass with its inner polar interactions is simply eliminated? While Singer and Loomis declare their allegiance to bipolarity but oppose its rigidity, their instrument initially ends up with a fluidity in which the play of the types is uncontained in any type structure, such as the figure of the

Compass and crosslike directions. We end up with a series of eight bars. Jung opted for the couplings first described as the superior and first auxiliary combinations.

Hence the SLIP negates the Jung/MBTI assumption that in all human activity we live out the couplings, since we are constantly taking in information (perception) and then deciding its use (judging). Would Singer and Loomis have created their instrument if they had taken the couplings into account, not only as initially discussed by Jung but particularly as creatively developed by Myers and McCaulley in both theory and research?

Order and freedom seem to be opposed in the two instruments. Angelo Spoto correctly points out the possible excesses of each: the MBTI might be "too tidy" a typology, and the SLIP, "too loose."[74] He also lyrically speaks of the proper use of any typology as a balancing of Apollo's bow and Hermes' lyre: an Apollonian order evokes "the excitement as an archer would have hitting the bull's eye," and a Hermetic playfulness, the exciting "spontaneity and subjectivity, boldness and subtlety" of the musician.[75] The MBTI needs a more flexible, dynamic approach to the types, which this book and others are beginning to address. The SLIP has needed more of an ordered dynamic, which the eight types, shown in a bar structure, could not provide. The answer for Singer and Loomis has come with the Native American medicine wheel.

THE NATIVE AMERICAN MEDICINE WHEEL

Over the years, Loomis, who is now dead, was involved with a Cherokee medicine man, Harley Swiftdeer, who taught her the wisdom of several matriarchal Native American tribes, which includes a path of development called the Red Road. Its visual vehicle is the Medicine Wheel, which returns us to the cross and circle as depicted in figure 10.4.[76] The circle is important, writes Loomis, because it represents not only a life cycle that Jung described, but also because it

The Medicine Wheel, the Elements and the
Power of the Four Directions

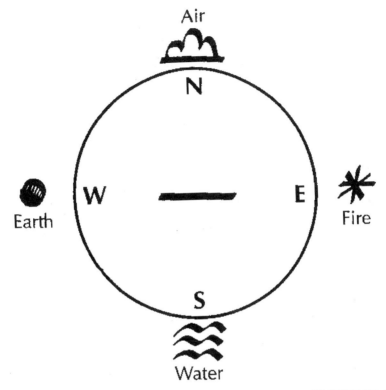

FIGURE 10.4

represents the view that "all things—humans, rocks, stars, trees, animals are interrelated," all within the "Powers of the Four Directions." North is at the top, South at the bottom, West on the left, and East on the Right, and the center of the wheel represents the "Sacred Mystery."[77] In Jung's language, this "Mystery" is the Self archetype, the reconciler of all opposites. In the medicine wheel, the south is "the place of giving," related to water; the west, the place of holding—even as the element "earth holds the energy upon which we stand"; "the north receives energy," as does air; "and the east moves the energy in a determined way," as does the element fire." The center is the place of the catalytic energy."[78] Further, "Human emotions are placed in the South, the physical body in the west, the human mind in the north, the spirit in the east, and sexuality in the center."[79] Only when we are aligned correctly with all of these quadrants do we realize the Powers of the Four Directions, that is, "giving with my emotions, holding with my physical body, receiving with my mind, and determining with my spirit." Misalignments can occur, for example, when we try to hold with the emotions, writes Loomis. There are also wheels within the major wheel; "On the emotions wheel, fear is in the south, depression in the west, anger in the north, and stress—both anxiety and hysteria—in the east."[80] This wheel presents a magnificent picture of humankind in relationship to nature. Will it prove useful for typology? The mind wheel is used for development, as indicated in figure 10.5.

The Mind Wheel

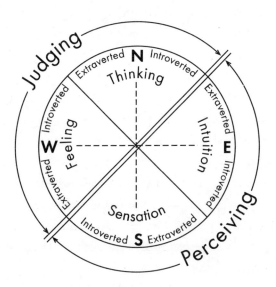

FIGURE 10.5

THE MIND WHEEL

The mind wheel is different from the emotion wheel, writes Loomis, "in that everyone enters the mind wheel from the south," and, "It depicts the process toward wholeness," a process that, surprisingly, moves from south to north, then west to east, then to the center.[81] The south is the place of the "water mind . . . a mind guided by emotions . . . the child mind," always demanding an inner dialogue in adults.[82] The north is the "wind mind . . . the adult mind with intermittent inner dialogue . . . the mind of dualities," where the individual "separates the world into opposites and categorizes everything in order to understand."[83] This is a picture of a nonpathological patriarchal culture. When the "individual begins the difficult process of dissolving the opposites, the developmental process moves him or her to the west, to earth mind. This is where mental processes and bodily knowing merge to form one-mind," a disciplined process that a few, such as Zen masters, might attain.[84] "The fourth stage is the fire mind in the east. . . the spirit mind" that is "capable of holding multiple viewpoints" usually "held by the enlightened ones, those beings like Jesus or Buddha."[85] The final stage is "represented by the center of the circle . . . the place of the void, or no-mind . . . where all things are possible."[86]

This is a beautiful depiction of a process of total individuation, as inspired by the Medicine Wheel, the further description of which is beyond the scope of this book. One wonders if Loomis is saying that the Jung/*MBTI* circle and cross are simply inadequate when faced with this profound view of an ultimate human and divine development, whereas the SLIP is adequate, or whether she is describing a cosmic and mystical picture of the life cycle that includes, yet goes far beyond, any typological approach. No answer to these concerns seems conclusive, since she describes the four directions only in terms of the four functions.

Whatever the outcome, I applaud Loomis' attempt to include such spiritual depth and beauty within the type theory. However, isn't Jung's description of the cross as recorded above similar to this spiritual picture? Such spiritual dimensions, moreover, are not unfamiliar to *MBTI* practitioners, who, in the 1995 International Typology Conference, were able to attend workshops or lectures on gods and goddesses by Jean Bolin, on types in relation to the I Ching and Tarot Cards, on Dostoevski's four brothers Karamasov, on God images, spiritual experiences, religious belief systems, and the type dynamics in Hamlet.[87]

In following chapters of *Dancing the Wheel of Psychological Types,* Loomis writes about the process of individuation with its special task of integrating the shadowy or undeveloped aspects of the psyche (chapter 2). She writes about Jung's descriptions of the attitudes and functions, with his particular distinction between emotions and the feeling function, and generally between emotions and mind, so that Jung finally characterizes the functions as "mental processes" (chapter 3). It is in this chapter that Loomis makes a clearer connection between the four basic functions and the four directions of the medicine wheel's "wind mind wheel (figure 10.6)."

Loomis writes:

> There is an opposition, but it is not between thinking and feeling and sensation and intuition. . . . In this arrangement, sensation is in the south, thinking in the north, feeling in the west, and intuition in the east.

> The reason for placing sensation in the south is that the south is the starting place in teaching wheels, and the place of trust and innocence. Sensation is the first of the functions. It records what is without bias, unselectively, and it is the only function that can work by itself. Thinking is placed in the north because the power of the north has to do with wisdom and logic. Logic is the thinking function. The feeling function is placed in the west. The power of the west connects to the earth and the physical body. It is the place of bodily knowing. . . . The east is the place of fire and the spark of illumination.

It is the place of unlimited imagination. Intuition belongs here.

There is an opposition in this typological mind wheel. It is an opposition between the judging functions and the perceiving functions. Thinking and feeling together are opposed to sensation and intuition. This, I think, is the basic opposition in the typological functions.[88]

Disputing Loomis' description of the functional directions and cosmic signs in this last paragraph, we suddenly come to a sea change in the Singer-Loomis theory. They have acknowledged in other writings that the bipolarities between thinking and feeling and sensation and intuition are still evident in more than half of the population so far tested, and that a person's inferior function in these

The SLIP's Four Functions within the Wind Mind Wheel

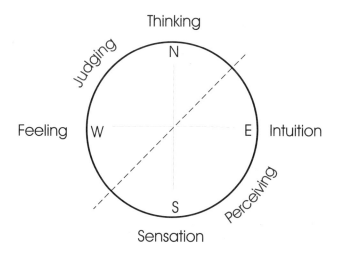

*The Wind Mind Wheel adapted from figure 6
Dancing the Wheel of Psychological Types
by Mary E. Loomis

Figure 10.6

polarities does lead to the unconscious and individuating potentials. Loomis now dismisses these polarities in favor of only a judging (thinking–feeling) versus a perceiving (sensation–intuition) opposition. In addition, by placing the ordering tendencies of judging on the left, and the open-ended aspects of perceiving on the right, they remind us of Herrmann's initial work with the left and right brain. In this formulation of the Singer-Loomis theory, a metaphorical under-standing of the brain is limited to the two hemispheres, as in Herrmann's initial work, without the possibilities of the four-quadrant brain metaphors that Herrmann later explored. This shift happens because the south has now been related by Loomis to sensation, and the west to feeling. This change, moreover, is contrary not only to the Jung/MBTI type theory but also to the corresponding findings of both Herrmann and Lowen.

A more ancient tradition is also violated. We recall that in figure 10.4 (page 439) and also in figure 10.5 (page 440), the medicine wheel's four directions are related to the four cosmological elements: earth in the west, air in the north, fire in the east, and water in the south. We have already seen in the Keirsey-Bates model that these cos-mological elements have been connected in the astrological traditions with the functions in the following ways: earth with sensation, air with thinking, fire with intuition and feeling with water. The Jungian ana-lyst, Liz Greene, develops these connections at length in her book, Relating, as we have noted. Using other Greek analogies, Hillman relates sensation to matter, feeling to soul, intuition to spirit, and thinking to intellect or logos, which substantially corresponds with Greene's elemental connections.[89]

Given these connections of the four elements with both the four directions and the four functions, it follows that the south and water are related to feeling, and the west and earth are related to sensation. The other two, north and east, remain unchanged. Further, figure 10.5 (page 440) shows that in this Native American tradition, the south "gives energy."[90] Giving is associated with feeling as harmonizing energy but can become pathological, either when excessive and dominating or inadequate and subservient. The south is also associated with "trust and innocence" that can just as easily be applied to the feeling as to the sensation function, and is also associated with the "emotional place " and "giving with . . . emotions."[91] I have pointed out in chapter 4 that Jung calls the feeling function "emotional value" in *Man and His Symbols.* He also calls the feeling function "the intelligence of the Heart." Loomis has emphasized the usual Jungian position that emotion or affect is not the same as feeling, but she does not consider that feeling, following Jung, transforms crass emotion into value, just as readily as symbols transform the crass emotions into useful or valuable energy. In Jung's view, without emotion there is no change. "Giving with my emotions," therefore, seems congruent with Jung's description of the feeling function and with human development.

Given that we associate sensation with the west via the earth element, Loomis' assertion that the west is the place of the "physical aspect" but also that it is aligned to "holding with [the] physical body" makes sense.[92] This is fitting for the sensation function, since it perceives the concrete elements of reality that "ground" us, that help keep its opposite, the intuitive function, from flying too high and spreading out too loosely. Dominant sensation types are great nesters and have considerable difficulty making physical changes in details and in living quarters, as well as making psychic changes. They also love to hold to the present moment, rather than consider the past or the future.

Loomis also convincingly emphasizes the flexibility of the medicine wheel's approach to the functions, in that, "sensation can combine with intuition, if the individual's mental energy flows to the right on the wheel. It can combine with feeling if the energy moves to the left, or with thinking if the energy bridges across the circle," and so forth.[93] This movement, however, is modified by the usual resistance that occurs in any person who has certain dominant functions, which even the SLIP acknowledges in the bar graphs. While Loomis beautifully develops ideas about the shadow's stubborn reactions to the light of consciousness, she appears to ignore this when dealing with types. In the Jung/*MBTI* cross, one does not just move across the circle, but also around it, especially given the four archetypal combinations of perceiving and judging functions found there, which are totally ignored in the SLIP. However, whether dealing with individual functions or couplings, the Jung/*MBTI* system takes very seriously the countergravitational, uphill struggle to develop unfamiliar types, the difficulties of adapting to an ESTJ dominant culture for persons other than STs, and finally the suffering one undergoes in developing just the four functions and archetypal couplings in the compass' whole-life process, as discussed in all of the preceding chapters. It seems that both the SLIP and the Jung/*MBTI* model free the types and freeze the compass in different ways.

THE STAR MAIDEN CIRCLE

Now we need to consider the Medicine Wheel's developmental dynamics, called the "Star Maiden Circle" (Loomis, 1991, p. 57ff.). The Star Maiden Circle incorporates the directions and their characteristics, as already described, with the added idea that they participate in the life cycle that begins in the South and proceeds clockwise around the circle.

Loomis describes here a rich life process, beginning with its negative aspects, called "The Dark Dance" and its "Circle of the Foxes." Now the South represents a wounded child and all of the consequences of this woundedness in all of the eight directions of the Soul's compass. Figure 10.7 does not show these, but one can easily imagine the darker aspects of the descriptions. Suffice it to say that what is pictured in this figure, if looked at negatively, depicts an unhappy life

The Star Maiden Circle

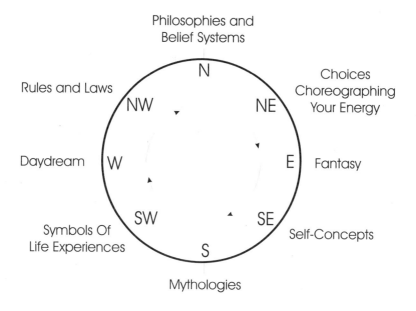

Philosophies and Belief Systems

Rules and Laws

Choices Choreographing Your Energy

Daydream

Fantasy

Symbols Of Life Experiences

Self-Concepts

Mythologies

*The Star Maiden Circle from
Dancing the Wheel of Psychological Types
by Mary E. Loomis

FIGURE 10.7

dominated by the South's "Mythologies of the wounded, needy little child, afraid to change."[94] This is followed by the Southwest as "closed experiences of life;" the West as "being a victim;" the Northwest as "rules and laws that induce guilt, blame, and shame"; the North as "closed, rigid philosophies and belief systems"; the Northeast as "limited restricted choices"; the East as the place of "illusions"; and the Southeast as "self-concept defined by the Seven Dark Arrows," two of which are "attachments" and "dependencies."[95] These describe a richly pertinent and poignantly painful picture of a very damaged journey.

Loomis does not at this point discuss the connection between these pathologies and the individual functions that are associated with the four main directions. However, the South's sensation could be associated with a fear of change that is typical of sensation types, the North's thinking could be tied to closed systems of thought, the West's feeling could be linked to a dislike of "being a victim," and the East's intuitive imagination could be connected with going amuck in "illusions."

Now let us look at Loomis' figure of "The Star Maiden Circle"[96] (page 447) as a positive path laid out in its bare and neutral structures, and imagine in that circle characteristics of the White Dance's "Walk of the Wolves,[97] so that the South's "mythologies" allow us "to learn through pleasure instead of pain"; the SW's "symbols of all life experiences" are "open symbols"; the West's "daydreaming" becomes "actualizing [our] sacred dream"; the NW's "rules and laws" are devoid of "guilt, blame or shame"; the North's "philosophies or belief systems" are either none at all or such that we can apply them flexibly and freely; the NE's "choices, choreographing [our] energy" are translated into our "choosing freely from an inner guidance of balance" and becoming "aligned with sacred law";[98] the East's "fantasy" embraces "unlimited imagination"; and the SE's "self concept" is realized as "loving self—self concept based on the seven light arrows," such as "self-awareness," "self-acceptance," "self-love," and "self-actualization."[99] Loomis does not discuss the typological implications of this life journey at its various points, so the readers are challenged to make the connections by themselves. Most knowledgeable readers would, for example, recognize the East's intuition adequately characterized as "unlimited imagination."

FINDING THE COUPLINGS IN THE OBLIQUE DIRECTIONS OF THE STAR MAIDEN CIRCLE

Loomis does not explicitly consider the typological significance of the four oblique directions: the SW, the NW, the NE, and the SE. This

The Star Maiden Circle (with the Four Archetypal Couplings)

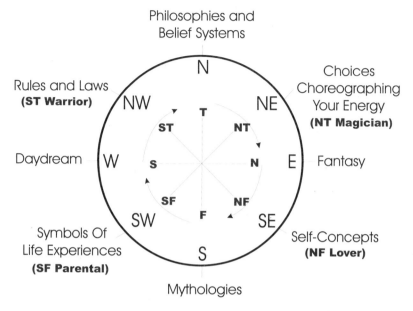

Philosophies and
Belief Systems

Rules and Laws
(ST Warrior)

Choices
Choreographing
Your Energy
(NT Magician)

Daydream

Fantasy

Symbols Of
Life Experiences
(SF Parental)

Self-Concepts
(NF Lover)

Mythologies

*The Star Maiden Circle adapted from figure 11
<u>Dancing the Wheel of Psychological Types</u>
by Mary E. Loomis

Type compass and archetypal couplings added.

FIGURE 10.8

follows from the fact that with the SLIP's elimination of the Soul's Type Compass, the four directional archetypes as type couplings are no longer considered in this system, but readers who have followed this book's explorations of the couplings can find some affinities with the oblique directions. Their subtle, insistent presence is evident in figure 10.8, in which I have added the functions and the couplings.

Let us begin with the Southwest. Whether we ascribe to the South and West as respectively related to sensation and feeling as Loomis does, or vice versa, as I do, the SW is still functionally the place of the SF Coupling, variously called the Parental King or Queen, the

Moralist, the B quadrant and, in Erikson's life stages, the place of trust versus mistrust and of autonomy versus shame and doubt. This is the life quadrant in which we live under the crucial influence of our parents. Loomis very aptly discusses here the personae of children who have suffered too much mistrust, shame, and doubt from their parents and a parenting environment, such as "The Tough Little Kid," "The Girl Who Endures," and "Daddy's Little Darling."[100] These represent survival tactics, emerging from the oppression of the inborn, sacred trust that the child brings to any parental relationship, a stifling that awakens profound existential fears, a deeply ingrained propensity to mistrust any close relationship and a weakened capacity for autonomy. As a result, shame and doubt haunt such a person throughout a life cycle.

We recall that the Northwest direction is called "the mind of dualities" and the psychic place of opposites and categories, surely a solid depiction of a healthy patriarchy (1991, p. 8).[101] This direction is clearly the place of the ST Structural, who translates rules and laws (see figure 10.7, page 447, "The Star Maiden Circle") into maps and systems, the place of the Warrior, who completes tasks and realizes goals, and the place where the healthy young person, according to Erikson, takes initiatives rather than falling prey to guilt, and develops work's industry rather than experiencing inferiority. Loomis specifically names the Warrior in this direction, who may, through discipline and hard work, develop his intellect and hone his competitiveness and "would judge himself harshly, feeling guilty or ashamed, if he were not prepared for the task at hand, or if he saw himself as being weak or incompetent."[102] It is here that the young person, having left the family, seeks to make it in the larger societal world of work, education, technical skills, and professional callings, the world whose conventions, styles, normal expectations, laws, and regulations must be reasonably obeyed, all befitting an ST mentality. Presumably, the SLIP creators, describing as they do the Jung/*MBTI* model as rigid, see this typology as stuck in this psychic place.

Before going further, Loomis makes the following observation about the flexibility of movement in the Medicine Wheel:

> The Dance of the Coyote and the Walk of the Wolf are not limited to moving in a clockwise fashion, repeating the spiral endlessly. In these movements, one can bridge the circle, dancing from side to side. The influence of the opposite on the medicine wheel is always taken into consideration.[103]

This admonition is in line with Walter Lowen's and Jung's remarks about the capacity of the mature adult to play with any type, any direction, any quadrant of the Soul. The directions always remain guidelines. Yet, following the wisdom of Jung's life stages and Erikson's Life Ages, linear development and free circuitry go hand in hand, along with some special imperatives that arise in times of crises.

One of these, as discussed in the previous chapter, is the midlife crisis, which often forces one to plunge into the Southeast direction, whereby the structures and discriminations of the ST and NT places are suddenly invaded by the NF Oceanic's dark and turbulent waters. Out of this emerges a stronger, water-tight self-concept. In this Lover's feeling and intuitive depth, out of which dreams and other hauntings surface into consciousness, one must often face, as Loomis writes, the fact that "the individual is living up to someone else's expectations of who or what he or she should be."[104] As we saw in John's case in chapter 8 when considering Herrmann's Whole Brain model, living another's expectations can be physically as well as psychologically lethal. One must begin to live his or her true identity—in John's case, living as a musician. It was in this often frightful place that Jung, Carol, and I, among countless others, discovered that we were living out the Northwest direction's ESTJ persona, especially its thinking dominance. Others plunge into this NF place of the Creative Artist when, for the first time, they discover the awakening potentials of the healthy inner child, beyond and in spite of their fears. This pristine child is like the many facets of a crystal in dreams told by clients. One is all-knowing. Another picks the correct key that leads to the place of prayer. Another creates kaleidoscopelike mandalas out of broken bits of glass. Another discourses like a hoary wise person. Others discover their NF potentials for the first time, and realize that they have been forced to deny them in our overwhelmingly ST culture. We experience with both awe and fear the exciting powers of reflective consciousness and sensuality in Erikson's Identity versus Identity Diffusion; in Intimacy versus Isolation we surrender with strength to the beloved.

Either after this NF tempering into a stronger and tougher identity or in a peaceful midlife progression, the Northeast's imaginatively conceived larger philosophical views of life, as congruent with the NT's Magician/Creative Scientist's outlook, usually follow. In terms of Erikson's Generativity versus Stagnation age, we find that we can dedicate ourselves to birthing offspring, be they children, ideas, artifacts, or meaningful societies. Finally, we find Erikson's eighth age of life, Integrity versus Despair, in which the question of "to be or not to be," and related ultimately spiritual questions, lead to large visionary constructions that we call philosophies or theologies. Contrary to Loomis, each of us builds and lives in a philosophical or belief system, even those who say there need not be one. The issue is not the system, but how meaningfully, yet lightly, one holds to it and finds resonances with many other philosophies or beliefs. This NT coupling, manifesting, according to Moore and Gillette, as the Magician's "inner knowing," is indicated in the Northeast direction's "choosing freely from an inner guidance of balance."

Singer and Loomis chose freely from their inner guide when they challenged the structure of the typological cross and circle. In doing so they are following in the spirit of James Hillman, who considers the type traits too limiting, and Keirsey and Bates, who feel that the cognitive functions are not as basic as the physically oriented temperaments.

The SLIP research is just getting off of the ground, just as was the case of the *MBTI's* beginnings. As we understand their work now, have they liberated typology and its circles or have they frozen the Soul's Compass in a new way? We have seen that in seeking to work with all eight function-attitude combinations, they believe they have liberated typology. However, in doing so, they have ended up with an amorphous picture of eight separate types on their bar graphs, though they did achieve a more enlightening system when Loomis incorporated the types in the Medicine Wheel. This has had a liberating influence, but the SLIP still ignores the personal dynamics of the dominant, auxiliary, and inferior functions, which Jung viewed as a lifelong individuation process in itself.

We also see, in light of this book's entire thesis, that Singer and Loomis have lost the solid and pervasive intelligence of the archetypal couplings in their system. We have experienced the explicit as well as implicit presence of the four couplings throughout this entire book, beginning with Jung's tentative versions as dominant/first auxiliary duos; Myers' inventive process of identifying each of them "as a different kind of personality"; the Osmond group's calling them "umwelts"; their kinship with the cultural and psychological archetypes reinvented by Moore and Gillette; their correspondence with Herrmann's metaphorical quadrants of the brain; their relationship to Lowen's childhood levels; Erikson's Ages of Humankind and Jung's two stages of life; the four aspects of a creative process; and, finally, their correspondence with the Medicine Wheel's four oblique directions in the cycle of life.

The SLIP's new research group is Moving Boundaries, Inc., of Gresham, Oregon. Led by its directors, Elizabeth and Larry Kirkhart, they have restructured their instrument and have begun to formally train people in it under a new name, SL-TDI, The Singer Loomis Type

Deployment Inventory. They espouse the theory of Singer and Loomis, though their claims of superiority over the *MBTI* have become more emphatic, asserting, for example, that they "have discovered that approximately half of the people who complete a forced type inventory are not provided with accurate information about their personality."[105] I took their one-day workshop, and again took the inventory. Again, my judging functions read higher than my perceiving functions, which is not in line with my experience. My NF coupling is the most dominant, and my ST total reflected correctly my inferior coupling. My SF coupling was too heavily weighted, again counter to my experience. They attempt to recover something of the original dynamics of the Jung/*MBTI* model by considering roughly the first or second type as "dominant," the second two as "auxiliary," the next two as "Mid-Modes," and the last (usually one) as the "Least-Preferred," adding, "sometimes called the Inferior." The most obvious difference between this instrument's underlying theory and the Jung/*MBTI*'s is beautifully illustrated in figure 10.9.

Singer-Loomis Type Modes (The SL-TDI Version)

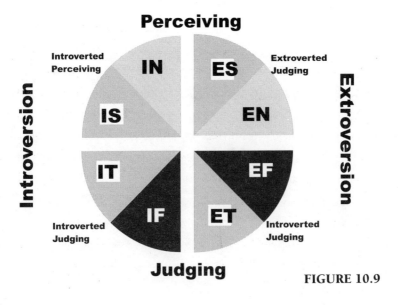

FIGURE 10.9

Notice that not only are the perceiving and judging functions opposites, but also the attitudes of introversion and extraversion. The eight functions are aligned in four quadrants in such a way as to eliminate the Jungian cross and compass with its opposing functions and its four couplings. In a brochure that compares their instrument with the *MBTI*, the SL-TDI authors claim that their instrument measures "thousands" of personality profiles while the *MBTI* measures only sixteen. Such a response ignores the almost infinite variations reported within the sixteen *MBTI* types. This difference between the two inventories also poses to the Singer-Loomis advocates a question: how will they articulate for individuals and corporate groups the ways in which these "thousands" relate to one another intrapsychically and interpersonally in some meaningful order? The sixteen *MBTI* types work wonderfully in corporate groups, they make it easy, with their manageable number, to consider individual differences and dynamics. Further, the couplings, with their perceiving and judging combinations, provide the consistent core and an archetypal order among the innumerable individual typological combinations in and among people as they live out their lives in love and work, in family and company.

In the final analysis, the SLIP's medicine wheel and the SL-TDI model still leave the attitudes and functions in a somewhat amorphous place in identifying human differences. Singer and Loomis personally and theoretically opted for a more flexible approach. Personally and theoretically, I want more definition while still seeking to maximize the creative potentials within the limits of the particular individual and coupled types. I was numinously awakened decades ago when I realized that I was an NF instead of an ST, thus clarifying and overcoming years of confusion, pain, and vocational dead ends. I was equally grateful and happily moved when I experienced my kinship with other ENFPs in an *MBTI* certification class (I also come out as an INFP) through shared traits and life experiences. Sorted by our test scores into sixteen type groups, we each wrote our composite on a large sheet of paper, which was pinned to the wall. This "pinning" did not categorize me; it did not, as Hillman would have, box me in. Rather it located my place within the infinite firmament of human types, much as a dying woman dreamt that she identified with a specific colored star in a sky ablaze with innumerable colored stars and galaxies. She was ready to die, and I, newly aware of my similarity to those who share my typology, was led to live more fully. The awareness of the centrality of the couplings deepened my sense of definition in a vast human cosmos. These experiences of type sharing are no different than some of the common assumptions Jungians share in contrast to other psychological systems.

In Jung's concluding remarks in the epilogue to *Psychological Types*,[106] he reflected on the fact that legislators can provide laws that make possible legal equality and uniformity of opportunity, but they cannot legislate for "all those people whose greatest opportunities lie not without, but within." He continues, "No social legislation will ever be able to overcome the psychological differences between men, this most necessary factor for generating the vital energy of a human society."[107]

Jung implies here that identifying such human differences protects us from uniformity rather than contributes to it. Also, when we were considering various theories in chapter 6, we noted the assertion that every philosophical system "depends on a personal psychological premise," that is, a particular individual with a specific typological preference spawned the system in question; and followers are attracted to its structures and energies because they share with its creator "a *typical* personal attitude."[108] Myers has reminded us that the couplings are most crucial in building these social affinities. Further, Jung and Myers observe that different types with their competing beliefs act as partisans who "attack each other purely externally, always seeking out the chinks in their opponent's armour," instead of looking at the opponents' "psychological realm," from which his viewpoint "arose in the first place." Jung then concludes: "A real understanding can, in my view, be reached only when the diversity of psychological premises is accepted."[109] I hope I have shown sufficient respect in this chapter for these three type systems that differ from the Jung/*MBTI* theory, even as I have disagreed with them.

In conclusion, I want to return to Loomis' view that the West and East directions are the spiritual places of the most sublime mystical searchers and saints whose outlooks transcend partisan bickering and violence. In an added spiritual yet secular view, the Northeast also spawns the NT's pragmatic scientists from quantum physicists to imaginative architects and computer geeks as well as the Merlins who understand the strategies of war and peace within the sacred and dark energies of nature. The Southeast is the realm of the NF Creative Artists, such as Picasso or Mozart, and the Lovers, such as Lancelot and Guinevere. All of these are present in each of us through our passionate participation in the arts and sciences and through awakening the loving potentials within ourselves. I am grateful to Loomis for introducing the typologies into these ultimate realms of the spirit, because if enough of us lived in these realms—if in Jung's words, we were "able to bear the tension of the opposites" on these spiritual levels—then more of us would contribute to ending the horrors of crime and war.

It is no accident, therefore, that Jung was shaping his type theory in the second decade of this century, when such powerful social forces as women's suffrage, labor demands, and German militarism and socialism were alarming the established governments and their ideologies. He was writing *Psychological Types* during and after the First World War, the most violent and bloody human conflict in human history, the seeds of which spawned the Second World War in the 1940s. Briggs and Myers began seriously to construct their Indicator during this latter, terrible event. This second conflict, with its combatants' improved technology and worldwide alliances, was fought in Europe, Africa, and Asia, and awakened an evil as mysterious as grace—the Holocaust. It was during this disastrous war that Pope Pius XII wrote his "Encyclical on the Body of Christ," which affirms the uniqueness of each person in the world within a cosmic spiritual field that we call Christ in Christianity, but that can be called the Law in Judaism, the Tao in China, the Great Spirit among Native Americans, and comparable *Weltanschauung* in all of the religions. Many of us involved in social concerns found a vital inspiration in the socio/spiritual worldview of the "Encyclical." Those of us who were starved for meaning in Christianity fed on the New Testament's metaphors of the trunk and branches in John's Gospel and the Body of Christ theology in Paul, just as equally hungry Jews feasted spiritually on the Passover season and the meal's profound spiritual messages. However, few of us who were later awakened by the numinous knowledge of typology made connections with these spiritual experiences and sources.

Long after this sound and fury of destructive wars and Myers' personal struggles with competing typological theories and practices, when she was faced with the imminent reality of death, she wedded typology with an appropriate quotation from Paul that she placed in the beginning of *Gifts Differing,* and from which she selected its title. This quotation also captures the feminine spirit in Myers, McCaulley, Singer, and Loomis, which, as I suggested in the introduction, Sabina Spielrein carried when Jung was developing his type theory, and which has been needed in the writing of this book on the Soul's four directional archetypes. The quotation reminds us that even as we argue, we must also respect the many type differences in people, organizations, faiths, arts, sciences, ideologies, and psychologies, because there are authentic "gifts differing" among all of these. Myers quotes Paul:

> For as we have many members in one body,
> and all members have not the same office:

So we, being many, are one body . . .
and every member one of another.
Having then gifts differing . . .
(Cor. 12: 4–8)

With this quotation, I have completed the substance of this book on the archetypal couplings and their importance for understanding individuals and some general characteristics of our cultural history. In chapter 11 of section III, "The Couplings in Society," I consider why there are now two separate worldwide Jungian communities that are not relating to one another, and in chapter 12, I examine an ESTJ pathology in the United States in light of the couplings and their related pragmatic as well as spiritual insights, especially in the organizational philosophy of William Edwards Deming.

Notes

1. C. G. Jung, *CW*, vol. 6, *Psychological Types,* English edition, translated by H. G. Baynes (1923; rpt., Princeton NJ: Princeton University Press, 1971), paras. 933–34.

2. James Newman, "Measure of the Five Factor Theory and Psychological Types: A Major Convergence of Research and Theory." This booklet is based on a July 1993 symposium entitled "Recent Trends in Type Theory and Research," as part of the Tenth Biennial International Conference of the Association for Psychological Types. The collaborators in the symposium, James Newman, Thomas Bouchard, Wayne D. Mitchell, Don Johnson, Tommy H. Poling, and Janie Johnson, decided to add research dimensions to their talks for the sake of the publication. All that I know of the Five Factor Theory is taken from this booklet.

3. Ibid., p. 6.

4. Ibid., chap. 3.

5. David Keirsey and Marilyn Bates, *Please Understand Me: An Essay on Temperament Styles* (Del Mar CA: Prometheus Nemesis, 1978).

6. Linda Verdale Berens, "A Comparison of Jungian Function Theory and

Keirseyan Temperament Theory in the Use of the Myers-Briggs Type Indicator," Ph.D. diss., United States International University, San Diego, 1985.

7. The Temperament Research Institute, located at 116152 Beach Boulevard, Suite 179, Huntington Beach, CA 92647, seems to be the basic organizing body of this temperament system, because of the presence of Keirsey and Berens there, and because the *MBTI* has also approved of its teaching its own theory. However, the Keirsey model has produced many other groups, whom I observed selling their wares at the Kansas Conference. One of these calls itself Types and Temperament, Inc, P.O. Box 200, Gladwyne, PA 19035-0200.

8. Louise C. Giovannoni, with Linda V. Berens and Sue A. Cooper, *Introduction to Temperament,* 4th ed. (Huntington Beach CA: Telos Publications, 1990).

9. Ernst Kretschmer, *Physique and Character* (London: Harcourt Brace, 1925).

10. Keirsey and Bates, *Please Understand Me,* pp. 3, 21.

11. Abraham Aaron Roback, *The Psychology of Character* (New York: Arno Press, 1973).

12. Keirsey and Bates, *Please Understand Me,* p. 27.

13. Ibid., p. 29.

14. Ibid., p. 30.

15. Giovannoni, Berens, and Cooper, *Introduction to Temperament,* p. 2.

16. Jung, *CW,* vol. 6, *Psychological Types,* para. 13.

17. Ibid., para. 547.

18. Ibid., para. 888.

19. Ibid., paras. 896–97.

20. Ibid., para. 958.

21. Ibid., para. 933.

22. Liz Greene, *Relating: An Astrological Guide to Living with Others on a Small Planet* (York Beach ME: Samuel Weiser, 1977). Greene, a Jungian analyst from England, shows air as connected with thinking, water with feeling, fire with intuition, and earth with sensation, as I do in the text. However, she differs as to the cosmological and physiological connections, the discussion of which would detract too much from our main thrust in this book.

23. Giovannoni, Berens, and Cooper, *Introduction to Temperament,* p. 2.

24. Keirsey and Bates, *Please Understand Me,* p. 29.

25. Jung, *CW,* vol. 6, *Psychological Types,* para. 624.

26. Keirsey and Bates, *Please Understand Me,* p. 30.

27. Ibid., p. 58.

28. Ibid., pp. 35–36.

29. Ibid., p. 41.

30. Ibid., pp. 40–41.

31. Jung, *CW,* vol. 6, *Psychological Types,* para. 959.

32. Keirsey published a new book in 1987 in which he expands the four archetypes into eight. He writes: "There are *two variations* of each of the four temperaments. Thus there are two different Artisans, two different Guardians, two different Rationals, two different Idealists. These variants are different from each other in the way they communicate about the *kind of relationship* they are willing to have with others." These do not add or detract from the basic discussion we are having in this book about the basic constituents of a type/archetype mandala. David Keirsey, *Portraits of Temperament* (Del Mar CA: Prometheus Nemesis, 1987), p. 12.

33. Berens, "A Comparison of Jungian Function Theory and Keirseyan Temperament Theory in the Use of the Myers-Briggs Type Indicator," pp. 12–13.

34. Ibid., p. 65.

35. Ibid., pp. 67–71.

36. Jung, *CW,* vol. 6, *Psychological Types,* para. 769.

37. Giovannoni, Berens, and Cooper, *Introduction to Temperament,* p. 3.

38. Berens, "A Comparison of Jungian Function Theory and Keirseyan Temperament Theory in the Use of the Myers-Briggs Type Indicator," pp. 9–10.

39. Giovannoni, Berens, and Cooper, *Introduction to Temperaments,* p. 14.

40. Ibid., p. 14.

41. Mary Loomis, "A New Perspective for Jung's Psychology," *Journal of Analytical Psychology,* no. 27 (1982): pp. 39–69; June Singer and Mary Loomis, "The Singer-Loomis Inventory of Personality: An Update on the Measurement of Jung's Typology," a workshop given at the 1986 Berlin Congress; in M. A.

Mattoon, ed., *The Archetype of Shadow in a Split World: The Tenth International Congress of Analytical Psychology* (Einsiedeln, Switzerland: Daimon Verlag, pp. 431–43; Mary E. Loomis, *Dancing the Wheel of Psychological Types* (Wilmette IL: Chiron Publications, 1991); June Singer, revision of the 1972 book *Boundaries of the Soul* (New York: Anchor Books Doubleday, 1994).

42. Singer, *Boundaries of the Soul,* p. 350f.

43. Ibid., p. 348.

44. Ibid., pp. 346–47.

45. Ibid., pp. 345.

46. Singer and Loomis, "The Singer-Loomis Inventory of Personality," p. 433.

47. Jung, *Analytical Psychology: Notes of the Seminar Given in 1925* (Princeton NJ: Princeton University Press, 1989), p. 78.

48. Jung, *Jung Letters,* vol. 1 (Princeton NJ: Princeton University Press, 1973), p. 186.

49. Singer and Loomis, "The Singer-Loomis Inventory of Personality," p. 435.

50. Ibid., p. 435.

51. Singer, *Boundaries of the Soul,* pp. 345.

52. Singer and Loomis, "The Singer-Loomis Inventory of Personality," p. 440 (emphasis added).

53. Loomis, *Dancing the Wheel of Psychological Types,* pp. 50–53.

54. Ibid., p. 49 (emphasis added).

55. Ibid., p. 53.

56. Myers, *Gifts Differing,* p. 53.

57. Ibid., p. 53.

58. Loomis, *Dancing the Wheel of Psychological Types,* p. 49.

59. Ibid., p. 28.

60. Singer and Loomis, "The Singer-Loomis Inventory of Personality," p. 439.

61. Loomis, *Dancing the Wheel of Psychological Types,* p. 31.

62. Jung, *CW*, vol. 11, *Psychology and Religion: West and East* (Princeton NJ: Princeton University Press, 1958).

63. Ibid., para. 338.

64. Ibid., para. 136 and note 36.

65. Ibid., para. 433.

66. Loomis, *Dancing the Wheel of Psychological Types,* pp. 37–38.

67. Ibid., p. 37.

68. John Beebe, M.D., a Jungian analyst, has included the eight functions within the Jung/*MBTI* model by positing a shadow cross, hidden within the four functions of the more conscious cross. For example, in the shadow of the dominant function, which he also characterizes as the Hero, he posits the same function but with its opposite attitude, as the Oppositional Personality; in the shadow of the first auxiliary, called the Parent, he locates the Senex, as the rigid aspect of the Parent, etc. We are waiting for Beebe to publish a book on this subject, which will be one of the most important contributions to the type theory within its bipolar assumptions. See John Beebe, "Psychological Types in Transference, Countertransference and the Therapeutic Interaction," in *Transference Countertransference,* edited by Nathan Schwartz-Salant and Murray Stein, Chiron Clinical Series (Wilmette IL: Chiron Publications, 1992), pp. 147–61. An audio description of Beebe's system, entitled "A New Model for Psychological Types," #317, 4/88, can be obtained from the C. G. Jung Institute of Chicago, Evanston, Illinois.

69. Singer and Loomis, "The Singer-Loomis Inventory of Personality," p. 435.

70. Loomis, *Dancing the Wheel of Psychological Types,* p. 38.

71. Singer and Loomis, "The Singer-Loomis Inventory of Personality," p. 434.

72. Jung, *CW*, vol. 6, *Psychological Types,* para. 666.

73. Jung, *CW*, vol. 8, *The Structure and Dynamic of the Psyche,* para. 865.

74. Angelo Spoto, *Jung's Typology in Perspective,* revised edition (Wilmette IL: Chiron Publications, 1995), pp. 179–82, 187–89.

75. Ibid., p. 170.

76. Loomis, *Dancing the Wheel of Psychological Types.* Loomis writes: "The medicine wheel offers an image of wholeness with the symbol of the circle, encompassing a cross. The cross alone is incomplete because it lacks the circle.

Jung was aware that the image of the cross within a circle was a universal symbol of wholeness, but he did not use it when he first explained his theory" (p. 38). This assertion is contradicted by the evidence we have in the introduction when Jung discusses in a 1918 letter to Spielrein her typology described in terms of a cross and symbol, and the evidence we have of figure 1 and other type circles that Jung developed in his 1925 Seminar.

77. Loomis, *Dancing the Wheel of Psychological Types*, pp. 2–3.

78. Ibid., pp. 3–4.

79. Ibid., p. 4.

80. Ibid., pp. 5–6, 10–11.

81. Ibid., p. 7.

86. Ibid., pp. 7–8.

83. Ibid., p. 8.

84. Ibid.

85. Ibid., pp. 8–9.

86. Ibid., p. 9.

87. Proceedings of the Association for Psychological Type's XI Biennial International Conference, July 11–16, 1995, Kansas City, Missouri, "Diversity and Expression of Type," Kansas City: Association for Psychological Type Publication.

88. Loomis, *Dancing the Wheel of Psychological Types*, pp. 39–40.

. 89. James Hillman, *Egalitarian Typologies versus the Perception of the Unique*, Eranos Foundation, Ascona, Switzerland (Dallas TX: Spring Publications, [1986] c. 1980). Hillman, working from Jung's reflections on the Greek types as matter (hylikoi or physis), soul (psychikoi) and spirit (pneumatikoi) from his *Psychological Types* book, paras. 14 and 964, and adding intellect (nous, logos), arrives at an archetypal basis for each type: sensation as matter; feeling as soul; intuition as spirit; and intellect as thinking (p. 21).

90. Loomis, *Dancing the Wheel of Psychological Types*, pp. 3–4.

91. Ibid., p. 5.

92. Ibid., p. 5.

93. Ibid., p. 41.

94. Ibid., pp. 60–61.

95. Ibid., pp. 60–66.

96. Ibid., p. 58.

97. Ibid., p. 72.

98. Ibid., pp. 72, 74.

99. Ibid., p. 75.

100. Ibid., p. 60.

101. Ibid., p. 8.

102. Ibid., p. 62.

103. Ibid., p. 66.

104. Ibid., p. 62.

105. From their advertising brochure, "What is the SL-TDI?, produced by Moving Boundaries, Inc., 1375 SW Blain Ct., Gresham, OR 97080. Their training packet includes Singer/Loomis articles and the *Interpretive Guide for the Singer-Loomis Deployment Inventory.* They follow closely the same assumption, that all polarities among the functions are out, yet, as will be noted in the text, they retain the polarities of perceiving versus judging and introversion versus extraversion. The most bothersome message comes from a four-page writeup in which they compare the *MBTI* and the SL-TDI, in which no mention is made that the *MBTI* has been reliably proven and is the most used personality instrument in all of psychology. The most offensive statement is as follows: "Who created the initial inventory [*MBTI*]? A pianist and an educator," presumably alluding to Katherine and Isabel, apparently without knowing anything about the brilliance of these two women and with no mention of the Ph.D. clinical psychologist Mary McCaulley and her monumental research work since 1969. This is all in contrast to SL-TDI's creators, "Two Jungian analysts, one of whom trained at the Jung Institute in Zurich; the other at the Chicago C. G. Jung Institute."

106. Jung, *CW,* vol. 11, *Psychological Types,* paras 845–57.

107. Ibid., para. 845.

108. Ibid., para. 846.

109. Ibid., para. 846.

SECTION 3

THE FUNCTION COUPLINGS

IN SOCIETY

CHAPTER 11

Jung's Divided Family

Analysts and Typologists

. . . art is not a separate "profession," but a quality inherent in all work well done. . . . How then do we find value in art? . . . We "tend to select the critical approach appropriate to the psychological type to which we belong." It will come as no surprise to learn that the types are Jung's. Read's way of using them is anything but clumsily deterministic: "Whether the wholly harmonious mind exists—the mind equally balanced between thought and feeling, between intuition and sensation—is perhaps doubtful, but surely that is the ideal toward which we ought to strive." If society makes it impossible for such a "complete and harmonious being to exist, then we should be working to change society to encourage and support that kind of being."[1]

Barry Ulanov

N THE INTRODUCTION, I asked the question, why is it that the two worldwide Jungian communities, the analysts and the *Myers-Briggs Type Indicator®* (*MBTI®*) typologists, have developed into separate entities who are relatively unaware of and indifferent to one another? We recall in the introduction that Jung encouraged Briggs and Myers' work over a period of several decades. Why then did the analysts and the *MBTI* practitioners go their separate ways? This intramural split is

critically important, since a sensible professional alliance of the two communities would significantly advance the influence of Jung's psychology. Moreover, this separation has resulted in serious deficiencies in both organizations, with resulting negative consequences for individuals who participate in both societies.

There are more personally relevant reasons for this chapter. Many of the factors that have split these two communities are played out in each one of us, such as introverted versus extraverted preferences, or intuition versus sensation issues, both of which have subtle roles in this cultural drama. Similar struggles go on among members or factions in a family or a neighborhood. Finally, any societal typological overlay, not only in these Jungian communities, but in our churches, schools, political entities, or companies, can consciously and unconsciously affect our personal understanding and growth. The lessons learned in Jung's divided family apply to all societal and personal differences.

Some intimations of the division between these two parts of the Jungian family appear when one attends conferences of either community. An analyst's conference is usually concerned with work with clients in the closed, introverted situation of analysis. As a rule, analysts will only peripherally and secondarily consider the relationship between their psychology and specific social issues, as Hillman would want analysts to do.[2] The genius of Jung's psychology has thus far been mainly applied to large intellectual, creative, and cultural issues, such as interpreting symbolic themes and stories in myths, fairy tales, novels, theater and the other arts, alchemy, scriptures, and history. These sorts of studies have been applied to the imaged and dreamt experiences of individuals in analysis and have aided their individuation. However, such conferences barely touch on the nuts and bolts of everyday social living, from family to politics; for those issues analysts turn to object relations.[3] When analysts do, they rarely allude to Jung's typology, which can so concretely ground the inner and outer objects of his psychology.

In a typologists' conference, the opposite is true. Practitioners consider in multiple ways the practical impact of types on one's character and on every possible relationship in our society, such as among husbands and wives, children and parents, friends and co-workers, teachers and students, and every kind of superior and subordinate relationship, including therapists and clients. Many typologists have become organizational consultants in such areas as leadership styles, conflict management, and team building. Typologists, moreover, consider how the types inform every kind and expression of collective human situation, for example, research, government, the armed forces, movies, education, cross-cultural issues, business, parishes, sports, and psychological counseling. In addition, there is a concurrent, but faintly emerging interest in Jung's typological views of the interior dynamics of persons and Jung's psychology in general.

Overall, analysts concentrate on the individual and broad cultural concerns, and typologists on the impact of individuals on society as revealed in practical anecdotal experiences and statistical research. In general, the two worldwide communities are not in formal or informal communication with one another. They share neither meetings nor publications. As a result, the potency of Jungian psychology is diminished both in the privacy of analysis and in the public realm.

The following considerations may shed some light on how this vexing situation developed and on its implications for the central theme of this book: the four couplings as archetypal directions for a fuller life.

Jung himself stopped developing his theory of typology. As Jung wrote to Isabel in 1950, he had not paid much attention to typology for decades. He had spent the eight years between 1913 and 1921 writing *Psychological Types* in which he researched every possible person who spoke of human differences in Western thought as well as some pertinent aspects of Eastern thought, particularly the typological significance of the Yin and Yang archetypes in Chinese Taoism. Then he dropped the subject, except occasionally to complain that everyone, even his own followers, ignored the complex and fruitful research he had done in the first nine chapters, and turned instead to the completed summary of the types in chapter 10. Jung was implying that his followers and others were ignoring the fertile archetypal content and promise of the previous chapters that were the bases for his phenomenology of the types.

Jung's Psychological Types *itself has been a problem*. The book satisfied Jung's need to explain his differences from and breakup with Freud as well as to clarify the relationship of his work with Alfred Adler's.[4] But his book went far beyond this concern when he began in his first pages to acutely critique, in his own typological terms, our narrow-minded EST society (Jung did not use the J and P categories). He gave many examples of our historical one-sidedness, such as the favoring of Origen's thinking dominance over Tertullian's feeling preference. He appraised the ninth-century Communion controversy, in which he bewailed the ascendancy of a concretistic sensation-dominant theology, still officially held among many Christians today, that teaches that the bread and wine are transformed into the *actual* body and blood of Christ. Instead, Jung favored the defeated intuition-dominant belief in the symbolic, psychically real existence of Christ in the Eucharist's elements. He examined the typological bias in the ideas of many important thinkers. He plumbed the meaning of types in Friedrich von Schiller's "naive" and "sentimental" attitudes and his idealist and realist types in poetry. He analyzed Nietzsche's view of the Greek opposites, the Dionysian and the Apollonian (respectively EST and INF). In a similar vein, Jung considered the type problem in human character—in the poets Carl Spitteler and Wolfgang von Goethe, and in psychopathology, aesthetics, modern philosophy, and biography. He also began to see the importance of the powerful capacity of the symbol to unite opposites and to relate inner and outer experiences, culminating in his eighteen-page study of "The Relativity of the God-concept in Meister Eckhart." He mentioned in several places, but did not amplify, that typology constituted a "critical psychology," that is, one that establishes the basis for distinguishing among assumptions and viewpoints of different theories in all intellectual fields, including psychology. All of these various strands make *Psychological Types* difficult for beginners in typology or, for that matter, in psychology. *Psychological Types* has proven to be an exceedingly demanding work in its complex ideas and examples, and in tracing Jung's process of discovery that led to the final, relatively clear descriptions of the types. Because of the book's fluid and circular style and the breadth of its demands, because of Jung's failure to systematically identify the types as archetypes, and because of the ambiguity of his views of the role of society in human development, Jung's *Psychological Types* has remained too hard to incorporate into the whole of his psychology, and is thus too easily discarded by most analysts as well as typologists.

Jung never systemically developed the types as archetypes. Jung's *Psychological Types* and his later reflections on the functions and attitudes would have been more accessible and his typology more centrally located in the body of his psychology if Jung had systematically identified types as archetypes. We have explicitly and implicitly considered this issue throughout this book. If Jung had more substantively established the fact that the great images, stories, and dreams of mankind both informed and were informed by the types, he would not have relegated the types to an inferior place, and his followers would have been more responsive to his type theory and the creatively pragmatic contributions of Briggs and Myers. However, as discussed in Section II, and as gleaned from both Jung's and Myers' implicit seeds, each of the four function couplings has been revealed as an individual archetype as well as a constituent of the archetypal Compass of the Soul. But Jung failed to cultivate the coupling seeds, which he both discovered and uncovered in the rich soil of his book. Instead, his ever-exploring mind turned to the evidence of archetypes in cultural stories and personal experiences, particularly to a pursuit of the archetypal substructures of alchemy, beginning in the 1920s and culminating in 1951 in *Mysterium coniunctionis*.

Pierre Ferrand, a highly sensitive typologist as well as a Jungian scholar, has suggested that Jung's failure to so incorporate the types into his total system was due to a *European cultural bias which significantly influenced Jung*.[5] Typology was the most pragmatic and down-to-earth creation of Jung's. It helped heal his painful break with Freud. However, dropping further work with types, with its every-day, prosaic usefulness fit well his education as a typical European intellectual, who was, according to Ferrand, rather scornful of social inferiors, such as manual laborers, servants, and women, or even engineers. To be practical was almost an insult, and European doctors trained around the turn of the century [the twentieth] were likely to be humanists with broad intellectual interests.[6]

The few analysts who have noted the archetypal nature of types have never developed this fact systemically and so for this reason also the types never entered the mainstream of Jungian studies.[7] H. G. Baynes' 1923 English translation of *Psychological Types* included the subtitle "The Psychology of Individuation"—surely an archetypal consideration—which was subsequently dropped. Hillman mentions this early inclusion, as well as the general archetypal nature of each type in his 1980 lecture. Marie Louise von Franz also assumed this quality of types in her important article on the inferior function. In addition, Singer and Loomis wrote of the individuating possibilities of types as they developed the SLIP beginning in the early 1980s. But such implications were never integrated into the body of Jung's psychology. We saw (for example, in chapter 10) how types only elusively and inconclusively entered into the SLIP individuation process when Loomis developed the archetypal potentials of the Native American Wheel.

Another analyst, C. A. Meier, assumed the archetypal nature of the functions and attitudes when he wrote *Personality: The Individuation Process in the Light of C. G. Jung's Typology*.[8] Meier discusses types with sensitive insight and an obvious respect for them as a total structural system. In his third chapter, entitled "The Compass," he follows Jung in identifying the dynamic of the type compass as an archetypal individuating process when he writes:

> With his book, *Psychological Types* (1921), and to the end of his life, his vast clinical experience showed him that with the development of personality, i.e., with individuation, there must be an attempt to make all four functions conscious in the course of time—in other words, differentiate them as much as possible. So his "compass" proved itself in more than one way.[9]

Meier writes in several places about the numinal energy of each type, a characteristic which implies archetype. He even considers the dominant/auxiliary combinations in his chapter 2, but he does not relate them to one another on the Compass. As he develops his overall thesis of individuation in the rest of the book, he fails to include the types in this process' various individuating moments and challenges—namely, the persona, the shadow, the masculine and feminine principles, and the Self as mandala. While he among the analysts comes closest to the goal of reintegrating types as archetypes into Jung's system, Meier still falls short. Only John Beebe is pursuing a new archetypal understanding and method integrating all eight individual types. His book on this subject is forthcoming.

In my view, this failure to holistically harmonize the types with the archetypes by both Jung and Jungian analysts is the central intellectual cause of the split in the Jungian family. The other more extrinsic cause, following from the first, has been the one-sided orientation of Jung and most analysts to individual concerns, which has, in effect, relegated society itself to a shadowy place in their collective psyches, whether in analytic ranks or in the world as a whole. As an analyst, I have also been too often caught up in this private outlook.

Jung's ambivalence regarding the relevance of societal groups and society as a whole as healing agents has contributed to a subsequent narrow use of typology. In his early work after his break with Freud, Jung collaborated with a small group of analysts to construct his own psychology, as discussed in the book, *Cult Fictions,* by Sonu Shamdasani.[10] One of the fruits of this work is found in chapter 11 of *Psychological Types,* entitled "Definitions," where, except for archetypes, Jung defines practically all of his original ideas. Besides working with the group of analysts, Jung also supported the foundation of a psychology club that was made up of analysts, students of analytical psychology, and other interested lay people who were in analysis. After its foundation, many purposes of the club competed for attention, generating a conflict between those who wanted the organization, in Jung's words, to be devoted to "a rigorous conception of the principles of analysis" and others who sought "the emergence of ordinary familiarity" and "much more a social gathering relieved of the compulsion of principles."[11] Jung noted that the majority wanted the latter, that is, "the need for simple conviviality," and these needs, he requested, "will thus form the actual club." Jung recognized here that the more intellectual group had lost out because of their excessive and unbalanced preference for introversion and thinking. Jung's view of types at this time was limited to conflating introversion with thinking and extraversion with feeling,[12] which he later realized was incorrect. The description of the intellectual group with their focus on both rigor and principles connotes for me the qualities of both the introverted ST Warrior and introverted NT Magician, with the former's need for disciplined doing and structured planning, and the latter's inclination toward an inner knowing. The dominant group that desired a social setting would have encouraged these STs and NTs as well as the SFs to express their more underdeveloped extraverted feeling needs. Most of the club members, given the typical Jungian-oriented person's introverted intuitive bent, were seeking to authenticate their NF Lover's preference for meaningful relationships or their NT Magician's need for inventive playfulness in extraverted ways.

On the other hand, as New York analyst Thayer Green and others have discovered, *Jung downplayed the importance of an extraverted participation in society*, and in general considered any society, whether a therapeutic group or a large industry, a hindrance to individuation.[13] Green's associate in New York, the late Edward Whitmont (with Green, a leader among Jungians in group therapy), wrote that Jung "was open and frank about his aversion to group activity," as well as to any large social entity, such as a corporation, as agents of individuation.[14] For Jung, most societal structures were antithetical to the individuating potentials of their participants. Green notes Jung's sensitivity to the shadow potentials of both extraverts and introverts. Introverts often perceive society as too invasive and brutish. Accordingly, the introverted Jung, while recognizing that the persona as the archetype of societal relatedness was a necessary ingredient of our human extraverted makeup, usually described it in negative terms, as for example, "a compromise between individual and society . . . only a secondary reality . . . a mask that *feigns individuality*," by which "one is simply playing a part in which the collective psyche speaks."[15] Both Green and Whitmont show that Jung's bias against extraversion and, as I have suggested, the related ST society, has left its mark on the world of analytical psychology.

The *introverted intuitive orientation of most analysts*, combined with either feeling or thinking, has buttressed and extended Jung's work in the theory and practice with individuals, while at the same time retaining his serious bias against the outer world. A certain amount of this aversion is due to the dominance of the ESTJ behavior and atmosphere in contemporary Western culture, particularly here in the United

States. We reviewed in chapter 3 Jung's perception of this evolving one-sidedness in the earliest Judaic-Christian tradition, and the consequent need for a more inward and deep appreciation of soul. (In the next chapter I will consider the insidious effects of this present one-sided ESTJ culture, which ignores not only the Soul but also the ordinary welfare of so many populations in society.)

Green notes in his critique of Jung and, by extension, most analysts, "Nothing I have to say should be taken as a failure to appreciate Jung's compensatory response to the one-sidedness of Western extraverted materialism."[16] The dangers of such an ESTJ bias have formed a strong subtext of this book, so much so that I have been accused of pathologizing this type. However, exaggerated, compensatory responses from many analysts as introverted NT Magicians, with their gnostic inner knowing, and as introverted NF Oceanics, with their spiritual hunger for connectedness with all things except sociopolitical concerns, are also hurtful. This critique, in Green's words, "might rather be considered a compensation for a compensation," that is, that an extraverted societal exaggeration is being corrected by some analysts' introverted exaggerations. Type statistics of analysts, trainees, and Jungian students consistently show them to be predominantly introverted, intuitive types. My statistics from many classes and from private clients show that analysts, trainees, and people interested in Jung are primarily introverted NFs and NTs.[17]

The problem for analysts, writes Green, arises as the result of this one-sided collective typology, "when in theory we claim to have an understanding of the psyche capable of universality and completeness while in practice we collectively keep stumbling over our inferior attitude and functions. . . . *Our collective inferiority . . . lies in extraverted sensation.*"[18]

I prefer to believe this collective inferiority consists of such left-brain attributes as extraverted ST and extraverted SF types. We seem too often, Green continues, to be incapable of valuing the outer world where "something central, numinous and transformative can be experienced objectively." We need to value outer experiences that are "allowed to remain 'out there.'" We can say with Hillman that we analysts are capable of "a depth psychology of extraversion." These numinous and transformative experiences, occurring, for example, in love-making, child-rearing, helping others in cooperative efforts, and musical, theatrical, and sports events, are as important for individuation as are inner experiences. Further, like Jung, we analysts seem to devalue the persona and its social function. We look with great energy and insight into the "differentiation of the ego and anima/animus," but we attach "little importance . . . to the persona as an agent of education" and individuation.[19] To what extent have analysts been influenced by an overt introverted intellectualism that had influenced Jung?

The analysts' problem with society as a whole is also played out more intimately in their own training institutes. In a workshop at the 1998 Florence Congress of Analytical Psychology entitled "Poison or Panacea: The Group Shadow in Jungian Training," Thayer Green noted that the introverted, intuitive strength that serves analysts so well in their analytical sessions can become tyrannical if analysts do not combine these strengths with virtues of the other types, or at least recognize and deal with their extraverted sensation shadow. Perceiving and acting only from the inner intuitions of the NF and NT combinations becomes destructive when analysts relate with associates and with trainees as if they were still in the analytical hour's fluid consciousness, plumbing the depths. Analysts usually replicate Jung's problem with groups that extend even to the formation of Jungian institutions. Jung, for instance, remarked at the 1947 inauguration of the Zurich Institute, "Thank God I am Jung and not a Jungian." In subsequently absenting "himself from any institutional responsibility," he showed his introverted intuitive bias, writes Green. Since Jung clearly was an INTJ, his introverted NT Magician's focus on inner knowing was evident, and his inferior extraverted SF Parent, with its compulsive need for order and its moralistic fury, lurked in the shadows. On the other hand, as Joseph Wheelwright often told analysts, Jung also feared the usual evolving rigidities of any organization. When Wheelwright told Jung that he was forming an institute in San Francisco, Jung responded, "Keep it loose, Joe, keep it loose."

Green holds that because analysts are so consistently introverted intuitives, they project a "primitive, undeveloped and naive extraverted sensate feeling [SF] shadow" on one another and on trainees. They, like Jung, get caught up in the inferior SF Parental archetypal shadow. The very nature of the analysts' work in the analytical hour, whatever their typologies, demands that they develop a strong NT Magician as they focus in the analytic interactive field on the inner knowing and wisdom of the unconscious and on their love of holistic archetypal images and situations. I suggest further, as an analyst, that because so many of my associates are also introverted NFs who thrive in an empathic therapeutic alliance, we analysts also harbor an undeveloped aggressive ST Warrior in our shadowy psychic armament. Given their (and my) compulsively ordered SF Parental shadows, it is understandable why analysts can quickly marshal moral imperatives if they experience trainees caught in complexes. Their other shadow, the angry ST Warrior, can be readily aroused when they encounter trainees who are not afraid to demonstrate some hostile feelings and challenging viewpoints.[20] Green reads these negative interpersonal reactions as intuitive projections, wherein analysts ignore their own shadowy sensate evaluation of trainees. As a result analysts do not sufficiently value the sensate particulars of trainees' responses, and cannot "listen to feedback from candidates with *discriminating realism,"* and, as a result, many training situations have "obscured and distorted the *real person sitting before us."* Green reminds himself and his associates, "in the institutional training process we . . . are adult professionals training adult professionals." Again, analysts too readily can mix up the introverted, intuitive, interactive field in analysis with the extraverted, sensation, feeling pragmatic societal field in their interactions with associates and trainees.

Further, Green writes that, while the analyst's work with infantile regressions in analysis is fruitful because the analyst assumes a needed parental role, assuming a comparable parental role in training leads almost inevitably to the infantilism of those being trained. In typological terms, analysts responsible for training forget the Compass of the Soul, which demands some degree of consciousness of all four functional quadrants and both introversion and extraversion. The typically introverted analyst needs to recognize in an ST Structural way the societal status and competence of our trainees as adult professionals, honor their SF leadership as parents and as agency and corporate officers, value their mature NF Lover and consider the systematic knowledge and subtly revealed wisdom they demonstrate in worldly NT endeavors.

Analysts have provided the world with an enormous inner blueprint that compensates for the surface superficiality of so much of our human life. They must never lose or denigrate in any way the introverted, intuitive, feeling, and thinking ground that has made this possible. Arwind Vasavada, another analyst who has struggled, as have Green and Whitmont, with the personal/societal issue among analysts, delivered a paper in Chicago in 1995 entitled "Training Process versus the Individuation Process."[21] Vasavada sought to put in perspective the professional development that demands that analysts and trainees learn techniques, take exams, and become state certified to "make a name, earn money, and maintain an image in the world." This is the first stage of life work, and does not touch "the second half of life, the sunset of life, which is the heart of Jung's psychology."[22] He reminded analysts that Jung's greatest gift to humankind was to help recover the Soul and its "Religious Function," which is "unending, undying, and eternal . . . immortal and timeless" in each of us.[23] The religious function plays itself out in society through respecting and loving one another. He writes: "When two people meet with the intention to discover one another's depth, a sacred place is naturally created,"[24] so that individuation is taking place there, too.

Vasavada recognizes the danger of analysts ignoring meaningful social reality as an aspect of individuation, but technique and state licensing do not fit into his view of the outer aspects of the spiritual journey. I believe otherwise—that an analyst must be like the artist who learns techniques, lives realistically in the world, and embraces in his artistic depth both technique and world. The analyst's professional techniques and the art of analysis are not opposed. The inwardness of the religious function is synchronistically present in the things of this world. Jung reminds us that the unconscious, and with it the religious function, "is more like an atmosphere in which we live than something that is found in us . . . in the case of so-called synchronicity, it proves to be a universal substrata present in the environment."[25] Here is the soulful ground for Hillman's writing, in which we are to realize "a depth psychology of extraversion." I would rather call it, synchronistically, an introverted depth approach to the interpersonal and the cosmological. Inwardness is not just under my skin; it is a deeply felt and intuited atmosphere in which we live.

Typologically, Vasavada appears to be saying that extraversion and sensation have little to do with the religious function, with individuation. Richardson's *The Four Spiritualities,* on the other hand, recognizes that the religious function is realized in four different universal patterns based on the four couplings. This perspective on the entire Soul helps pinpoint the strengths as well as the limits of Vasavada's critique of training and individuation. Vasavada embraces the Journey of Unity (NT), the Journey of Harmony (NF), and the Journey of Devotion (SF). What must be added to our Jungian system and its goal of individuation is the Journey of Works (ST). In a holistic atmosphere, in which the Self embraces both the inner person and the world, we must include pragmatic works. Finally, Vasavada alludes to type changes that usually occur in the beginning of a second half of life, when, "Our personality type and functions start to change into their opposites."[26] In type dynamics, however, his statement must mean that the under-developed functions and attitude are always built on and assimilated into, not substituted for, the inborn typological strengths.

Given this deep but difficult ground in which we analysts seek wholeness through inner work as well as through outer practical behavior and consciousness in society, we need to humbly acknowledge that we have ignored, or, worse, misunderstood the undisputed collective impact and the pragmatic societal successes presently enjoyed by the other half of our Jungian family, the worldwide community of type practitioners. In turn, typologists need to recognize the difficult process of initiation that analysts must go through in their many years of intense training. Some typologists undoubtedly have comparable training in their respective professions, besides training in typology, but many do not. They can profit greatly from the analysts' depth consciousness. In turn, analysts can humbly acknowledge that as typologists bring Jung's type theory and practice into many societal places with much wisdom, compassion, and dedication, they are individuating in their own way.

Given the assumption that most analysts have perceived typology to be separate from the archetypes, and given the loss among analysts of typology's more natural and pragmatic social consciousness, *most analysts have reduced this aspect of Jung's psychology simply to an overemphasis on sensation.* This diminution has been historically true. Plaut's 1972 research, as we saw in chapter 6, showed even then that only about 50 percent of Jungian analysts gave much thought to typology. Also, fewer than 10 percent of the analysts considered themselves sensation types. Plaut and others came to the conclusion that intuitively oriented analysts saw typology to be a sensate concern in which detail and categorizing dominated.

Hillman picked up this same theme in 1980 when he observed

that typology's trait consciousness and research lead to generalized labeling and therefore to a psychic entrapment of the human spirit that violates the uniqueness of the individual. Hillman is partially right, in that leading typologists, though strongly preferring intuition, did emphasize trait research and did not understand types as archetypes. However, Hillman has not taken into account all the factors considered above, and the necessary left-brain compensatory dynamic that developed in the *MBTI* founders to balance the analysts' right-brain consciousness, which we will consider below. In Hillman, we have a classical response by a strong intuitive thinking type to the hard-nosed ST research and painstaking articulation of each type by, ironically, the clearly intuitive *MBTI* founders. Hillman also ignores the Jungian imperative for individuation: that each individual must eventually embrace the Soul's entire Compass with all of its functions and both attitudes. We are seeing here a left-brain and right-brain split, given that the left brain is primarily sensation oriented and the right, intuition oriented. One must concede that there is always a natural aversion among intuitive people, including analysts, to their inferior sensation and to any presumably sensation-oriented science that measures and classifies. Also, Hillman, an analyst trained in Zurich and attracted to the Italian Renaissance, seems to share some of Jung's intellectual bias against the prosaic needs of everyday life.

Given this overall picture—that the archetypes are bereft of the type traits and the natural aversion of introverted analysts to ordinary social issues—one can see why most analysts have resisted typology. Besides, they have not known that over 80 percent of the members of the Association for Psychological Type are intuitives. The two big exceptions to analysts' indifference to types are the Gray-Wheelwright type survey (the JTS), which was developed in the 1940s but was never seriously researched and is now no longer used by analysts; and, since 1980, the SLIP. Even in these two cases, Joseph Wheelwright, June Singer, and Mary Loomis are all intuitives.

These two surveys have also presented a problem for this book's theme, since neither survey has valued the function couplings, of which the intellectual and experiential dimensions can minimize the perception of typology as primarily sensate in character. The creators of the JTS paid no attention to the function pairs as such, concentrating instead on the specific and separate value of each individual function; the SLIP developers eliminated these pairs along with the symbol of the circle and cross.

Analysts who have taken typology seriously have been ignorant of, or have ignored, or have even been derogatory toward the MBTI, especially toward its founders' presumed lack of professionalism. Joe Wheelwright, the leading proponent of the Grey-Wheelwright, publicly derided the *MBTI* on several occasions because Briggs and Myers were not psychological professionals. The group that purchased the SLIP from Singer and Loomis devalue the *MBTI* in their promotional material for similar reasons. Singer and Loomis dismissed the *MBTI* because they perceived it to be a limited model for measuring human differences and for actualizing individuation. On the other hand, many Jungian analysts and trainees experienced the excitement of discovering their types through the *MBTI*, but they have been subsequently turned off by the narrow categorizing by some type practitioners, a concern that serious *MBTI* practitioners share.[27] Among leading Jungian teachers, only John Beebe has valued the *MBTI* and its worldwide community of typologists. Beebe has reintroduced the circular dynamic of types and has given archetypal significance to all eight attitude/function combinations by developing a second shadow circle and cross within the usual quartered cross.

As a result of all the above considerations, a sort of Jungian version of a behavioral cognitive approach to types, emphasizing mainly their positive conscious aspects, has evolved among both typologists and analysts. Analysts have simply not considered the type mandala a serious archetypal avenue that leads to Self-realization. Did Jung's occasional reference to typology as a "psychology of consciousness" throw the analysts off course? Jung's statement cannot be taken at its face value if we concede with Jung that the psyche as a whole, in its entire conscious-unconscious spectrum, "is the very thing we know least about."[28] Jung continues, "It is just because the psyche is so close to us that psychology has been discovered so late," hence, "we lack the concepts and definitions, with which to grasp the facts" and "we are surrounded—almost buried—by facts." Yet, because of the nonspatiality of the psyche, "It becomes difficult even to establish the facts."[29] In my view, this illusive understanding of psychic facts applies to the naming and measuring that we do in typology. On the other hand, Jung argues, these facts "are just as objective and just as definite as any other event . . . from the known things we observe outside"; that is, these psychic facts emerge as consistent archetypal patterns in images and traits from the unconscious. In this context, analysts and typologists must not ignore this culminating statement that Jung makes in the context of this discussion:

> My more limited field of work is not the clinical study of external characteristics, but the investigation and classification of the psychic data which may be inferred from them. The first result of this work is a phenomenology of the psyche, which enables us to formulate a corresponding theory about its structure. [Read: his entire psychology as both experienced and intellectually described.] From the empirical application of this structural theory, there is finally developed a psychological typology.[30]

Jung is saying that his type theory is one of the culminating fruits of his entire system.

Typologists have also followed a cognitive/behavioral path similar to the analysts via the leadership of Isabel Myers, who stressed a solid conscious awareness and use of one's innate dominant and auxiliary functions (the couplings), and only gently intimated that wholeness is possible if one integrates the tertiary and inferior types, as well as over-comes one's pathologies. Hence typologists have done little work on the darker unconscious sides of their makeup as revealed in the inferior function and function pair. Yet whenever differences arise among both groups as to theories, policies, and clinical practices, the inferior archetypal functions or the ignored dominant functions are present like ghostly specters lurking in dark corners. The important work that von Franz did on the inferior function is often forgotten among analysts. Recent publications by Spoto, Quenk, and others have begun to turn around this shallowness among typologists. In her important work, Quenk takes our need to integrate the inferior function seriously and, like Spoto, discusses the dynamic quality of this function as a guide and path to the collective unconscious. She never mentions the Self, however, minimally discusses dreams, and never touches on active imagination as the central means whereby the Self makes available to the ego the opportunity to integrate and creatively use the inferior function in consciousness. Spoto and Quenk's books represent the most serious attempt to achieve a reintegration of Jung's holistic depth approach with typology and are most closely aligned with this book. The dark side of the types also appears at least inferentially in the typological literature, filled as it is with discussions via tables, charts, and stories about the interpersonal difficulties we have with those who are typologically at variance with us.

Meanwhile, only the Osmond group of experiential typologists paid attention to Myers' landmark work on the four function couplings. However, this group did not acknowledge that they had borrowed the coupling idea from her, and they remained equally silent about the immense *MBTI* research in vocational areas with the function pairs as the central cores of the sixteen types. Peter Richardson's *Four Spiritualities* draws from the *MBTI* in formulating his four world-encompassing pictures of spiritualities based on the couplings, but he totally ignores the Jung and Myers context and methodology which would make his work so fruitful in a broad sense. Ironically, the two persons who provide the most pragmatic examples of the usefulness of the couplings are the two brain quadrant researchers, Ned Herrmann and Katherine Benziger, though both assume that their formulations are connected only with the four individual functions.

The principle of compensation, so important in Jungian psychology, helps explain the development of the MBTI. This principle holds that when we overdevelop one side of the mind, a balancing compensatory process must occur to overcome what Jung calls a psychic "barbarism," with its covert, as well as obvious, psychic violence. The empirical work of typologists provides a left-brain balance for the intuitively dominant right-brain analysts. Myers and McCaulley, both INFP Creative Artists, a type makeup ardently oriented toward intuitive concerns, have nevertheless heroically committed themselves to a hard-nosed, statistically based scientific research. Such research ordinarily has belonged to STJs, who often intellectually disdain the type preferences of Myers and McCaulley. Thus a statistical, tabular consciousness has emerged in the *MBTI* world, beginning with the *Manual* and continuing in *The Journal of Psychological Type,* as well as in many other type publications. These pragmatic outcomes met Myers' vocational goal of making Jung's theory more practically accessible in down-to-earth terms, and therefore more useful for nonprofessional people in the society. The tightly compartmentalized Type Table that Myers constructed fit this goal perfectly (see figure 11.1). She felt that Jung's turgid, circular writing needed the clarity and neatness of the sharply defined sixteen types, each of which is located in its proper square in the *MBTI* Type Table.

But again, this obvious focus on the sensing and thinking functions has given the impression to those who view the *MBTI* superficially that this statistical, tabular consciousness is all that there is to the type world. This impression has generated a strong resistance

MBTI TYPE TABLE

ISTJ	ISFJ	INFJ	INTJ
ISTP	ISFP	INFP	INTP
ESTP	ESFP	ENFP	ENTP
ESTJ	ESFJ	ENFJ	ENTJ

FIGURE 11.1

to the *MBTI* in intuitive thinking and intuitive feeling analysts. Yet, these typological oppositions are visible in the contrast between the flexible dynamics pictured in Jung's original type circles, and in the more rigid but also eminently clear divisions of endlessly varied adaptations of Myers' Type Table. Overall, most analysts and a large population that have taken the *MBTI* are unaware of the creative explorations that are evident at type conferences and in the larger type literature.

Have analysts become elitists in regard to the obvious widespread use of the *MBTI*? Analysts have been especially afraid of popularizing any aspect of Jung's psychology, fearing that this will transform a depth approach to psyche into a superficial one. On the other hand, to the extent that analysts appear to be elitist in their intellectualism and disengagement from society, they expose themselves to charges of being too gnostic and cultlike.[31] Ironically, a more down-to-earth connection with ordinary people through typology would effectively offset such separatist charges. But as long as analysts see typology as separated from symbolic archetypal systems and the innate powers of the unconscious, their fear of an obvious typological popularity and reluctance to use the MBTI will persist. Despite shuddering over popularization, analysts have seen the popularization of other ideas of Jung in Robert Moore and Douglas Gillette's four cultural archetypes (valued in the men's movement), Thomas Moore's concern for Soul, Jean Bolin's archetypal gods and goddesses, James Hillman's Self designated as the Soul's Code, and Clarissa Pinkola Estes' powerful tales of women's individuation.

Many typologists seem afraid to learn more of Jung's psychology. There is resistance to Jung's comprehensive psychology, because a facile use of the types is easier and more immediately pragmatic. Myers herself said in a 1977 video that typology as a total system could stand alone and did not need the larger context of Jung's work with the types.[32] Myers' statement is true to the extent that the Type Compass is understood as an integral archetypal system. However, her observation does not take into account the fact that the full participation of the type compass in individuation is inseparable from all of Jung's psychic structures and dynamics. The compass' origin is the Self, whose dark and pregnant depth gives birth not only to the natural flow in consciousness of one's type preferences but also to the tempestuous emotions and symbols of the inferior function that demand an acute consciousness and recognition when they appear in societal interactions, dreams, and the great stories of humankind. Myers' innocent statement may have minimally contributed to these two communities' impasse; she may have said this because she had no mentors among analysts in the four decades in which she labored on her instrument.

Her focus on consciously grounding all persons in their strong type, the boxed-in character of her Type Table and the fact that she ignored the birthing of all of the types from the Self all contributed to her unfortunate comment.

Many type practitioners and other kinds of psychologists typically misunderstand and criticize Jung's psychological premises. Myers' experience with the Educational Testing Service (discussed in chapter 1), the evidence given by typology researcher, James Newman (related in chapter 7), and the rejection of the *MBTI* by proponents of the Five Factor Model in academia (recorded in chapter 10) attest to this negative perception of Jung's psychology among many other therapists and academics. Many typologists may consider that identifying the *MBTI* too closely with Jung damages their own credibility. Jung's critics have not understood the breadth and depth, the pragmatic spirituality and sublime realism of Jung's psychology. Even here the integrating of the types into Jung's overall system would help temper other psychologists' perceptions that Jungian psychology is not sufficiently clinical and practical.

However, *many typologists are studying Jung and beginning to develop a more circular understanding* of the archetypal structures and dynamics of the types. I have seen evidence of this broader awareness in international and national conferences and in the more popular literature, such as in the *Bulletin of Psychological Type*. There has been some movement away from the table form of depicting the types. Henry (Dick) Thompson, for example, a leading type theorist and practitioner, has developed the communication wheel. Peter Richardson has constructed a complex circular depiction of the types in his book, *The Four Spiritualities*. Richardson shows this circle again in a 1998 article in the *Bulletin of Psychological Type*.

Richardson suggests that the rectangular presentation of the sixteen types in what is called the type chart or type table too readily reinforces "a reductionist trap."[33] He continues: "we must move from the rectangle to the circle—for the circle leads away from reductionist boxes to type dynamics." He originally developed his mandala "to illustrate the deepening process of the Four Spiritualities" and their interaction with one another.

Richardson wrote his 1998 article in response to another by Ken Green, the editor of the *Bulletin,* entitled "A Modest Proposal: The Type Circle."[34] I find in Green's article some links that resonate strongly with my views in this book. For one thing, his type circle looks almost like my figure 7.1 (page 313) on the *MBTI* in chapter 7, though his layout of the sixteen types is different from mine. Unlike Richardson's circle, and similar to mine, he shows each type's opposite across the circle. Another typologist, Louise A. Hoxworth, develops a similar type circle.[35] Green believes that the type table itself that Myers created too readily gives the impression of type labeling and of "putting people in boxes." Myers would be most grieved by this impression since "one of her greatest concerns was that type would be used as a means of pigeon-holing people." She wrote of the arrangement of types in her table in endearing, typically INFP Lover terms, "that those in specific areas of the Table have certain preferences in common and hence share whatever qualities arise from those preferences. . . . Personalized with the names of friends and family, the Type Table and type differences come to life."[36]

The table is organized vertically according to the four function pairs, and aligned according to the compass' counterclockwise order from left to right: ST, SF, NF, and NT. Horizontally, the top line is made up of IJs and the bottom line of EJs, as if the tough Js provided a protection for their friendly neighbors. The two inner middle horizontal lineups are made up of all Ps. Green's "modest proposal" is that "we let our most enduring symbol [the Type Table] evolve into a much more powerful symbol—the circle," since "as a mandala, after all, the circle is an ancient symbol of wholeness, occurring (as Jung stated so persuasively) in all of the world's cultures nearly from the very beginning of humankind." As a ritual elder in a men's community, Green continues, "I have learned the power of the inclusive circle to heal and contain everyone within it. In a circle there is no favorite place." He writes:

> Jung's research showed that the circle mandala often appears as a quaternity, a square within a circle, divided into four equal parts. To me, the four functions are just such a quaternity, every bit as fundamental as the four elements of the ancients or the four directions of Native American Spirituality. . . . Perhaps this is merely the fanciful musing of a romantic idealist, yet the more I think of it, the more I find myself favoring a circle over a bunch of boxes. No doubt others will find ways to arrange the type circle differently—I make no proprietary claims, only this modest proposal.[37]

I am gratified that Richardson's and Green's strong ideas about the Compass of the Soul support the major theme of this book and strengthen ties with the analysts' view of the circularity as well as the conelike depth of the Soul. However, we need to keep an inclusive and balanced perspective in regard to tables and circles. *The table as a square is also a mandala,* a picture of the Self, as we learn from Jung.[38] This "bunch of boxes" squares the types, and, as a pregnant container, has given birth to an enormous creativity among *MBTI* practitioners. No creation occurs without boundaries, just as the new plant does not emerge without the containing shell of the fertile seed. So within this squared corral, practitioners have explored each type in thousands of variations and styles just as storytellers of every age have told and written endless variations of the major archetypal tales of humankind. We are never bored if the storyteller speaks from the authentic experiences of the heart. Equally the greatly varied stream of books and articles that have flowed from those who know and love the types has deepened our understanding of them and enriched their perceived usefulness. Yet the argument that the Type Table evokes too much of a reductionist box or type labeling still holds. This squaring of the types limits the creative process because it fails to reveal an interactive, fluid, and dynamic approach to human differences that are immediately apparent in the Compass. Green is no "romantic idealist" but a holistic realist when he holds this view.

Some historical perspectives and statistics from Mary McCaulley are fitting at this point.[39] She reports, "In the 1970s the focus for the *MBTI* was individual counseling." This focus shifted in 1987 when Thomas Moore wrote in the March 30, 1987, issue of *Fortune,* "Personality Tests Are Back: The Latest Management Tool Dates to Carl Jung." Corporate interest in the instrument took off after this article. Training of persons in the *MBTI* is now done not just by CAPT and CPP, but by "many other organizations worldwide. In 1976, the year CPP (Consulting Psychologists Press) first advertised the *MBTI*, the *CAPT Bibliography* had 337 entries. Now the *CAPT Bibliography* entries are nearing 8,000." McCaulley noted that during the 1970s, there were no *MBTI* journals. Now there is both the *Bulletin* for popular articles and the *Journal of Psychological Type* for academic researchers. In 1975, a Japanese translation and research of the *MBTI* heralded the instrument's first international development. "Now the *MBTI* is used worldwide," writes McCaulley. In the 1970s, and even into the 1980s, there were only handbooks and reference materials for teaching types. Now there is "an explosion of books to teach type to the general public." Finally, McCaulley observes that "some Jungians are seeking a better understanding of *MBTI.*"[40]

Even the *"bunch of boxes" has metaphorically evolved in the* Bulletin. The front page of the summer 1992 issue showed the type table as a jumbled, incomplete jigsaw puzzle. In an accompanying article entitled "Filling in the Pieces," McCaulley writes:

> I picture our knowledge of type as a gigantic jigsaw puzzle. Jung and Myers put together most of the border

> and enough of the inside sections for us to see the general
> picture. Later researchers have put in more pieces. . . .
> Other sections have gaping holes. . . . Every *MBTI* user is
> part of the jig-saw puzzle team.[41]

This democratic statement invites every type user to make creative contributions. McCaulley explains the interest in the types professed by an enormous variety of persons in many diverse roles and professions by pointing to Jung's theory as based on "*perception* and *judgment,* two words that should be printed with flashing lights around them to remind us how basic they are." According to McCaulley, Jung classified us, not "in terms of the traditional variables of sociology; but instead sorted people by the four tools of our minds"—that is, the two perceiving functions and the two judging functions, which also constitute the four function pairs. She continues, "The reason there are so many applications of psychological type is that every waking hour we are either perceiving or judging—taking in information or making decisions."[42] McCaulley is pointing here to the archetypal work of the function couplings.

Within this seemingly static *MBTI* world of "boxes," there is evidence of a creative thinking attuned to Jung's and of intimations of the couplings. As to creative imaging, the winter 1999 *Bulletin* depicts in many of its pages the Type Table as "The house with the 16 rooms," which looks like a small, inviting hotel with ample windows. For Jung and for analysts, the house is another classical archetype that constantly shows up in myths, fairy tales, and dreams. In the analytical training in symbolism, analysts record the consistent patterns in these stories about the meaning of the various rooms, floors, front sides, and back sides of houses. In dreams, old mansions we have inherited or purchased in this imaginal world reveal wondrous paintings and murals behind layers of dirt, paint, hidden rooms, or secret doors.[43] The house itself as the inclusive container is a symbol of the maternal aspects of the Self.

In this same *Bulletin,* Carolyn Barnes discusses with ingenious charm and beauty her particular room in the *house with sixteen rooms.* Her article is entitled "Rooms of My Mind: Introverted Thinking."[44] She is presumably describing her "room" in IT terms. However, when we reflect on her descriptions, we recognize the strong presence of one of the couplings. Her room is a ballroom on the top floor of the apartment house. In it she has created:

> a miniature working model of the universe . . . a three-dimensional model/map of *my* known universe. All my experiences outside in the world are mapped here, along with all of the concepts I use to make sense out of those experiences. . . . It is not made up of pictures but is more like an architect's blueprint and scale model of an immense resort project. . . . It is important for me for my model/map to be accurate. . . . My map/model room is very close to the library where I store my words. . . . I think this room [the library] is related to my ability to process spatial relationships, because I borrow diagrams and symbols to express myself as much as I borrow words. . . . I also form analogies here to explain the world's diverse domains. The parallels between an atom and the solar system are inescapable when examining my model. . . . It's all interrelated. . . . Sometimes I am so pleased with a part of it that I want to share it. When I do, almost invariably people look at me like I am an alien. . . . Sometimes I am astounded that the models of other people don't warn them of crises that lie ahead. See! It is right here on the map.[45]

A cursory reading of this description of Barnes' room/map articulates a typology beyond introverted thinking. This is a person who also prefers an extraverted, intuitive outlook, who revels in spaces, in wholes, in diagrams and symbols, in analogies, interrelated events, people, and things, and who sees into the future. This is the mind of an NT Magician, a creative scientist, an Ethereal who sees big pictures, who also probes the inner intelligence found within oneself and in others. Faithful to her extraverted intuition, she needs constantly to check out and reorder her inner map to stay in tune with others and with the large events of the world. Her obvious dominant NT coupling feels the accompanying warmth and need for outside connections through her introverted NF auxiliary pair. Her type, she reports, is ENTP. EN, therefore, is her dominant function; IT her auxiliary function; and EF her second auxiliary.

James Newman's article, "Theory and Practice," in the *Bulletin's* spring 1992 issue gives us another implicit view of the four couplings.[46] He believes that, like Einstein's theory, Jung's "inspired theory . . . opens us to a deeper reality. When theory and practice jibe, the potential for powerful applications blossoms." Accordingly, he discusses typology from the standpoint of four "foundation stones," which provide a "solid basis for practical applications of type theory." The first foundation stone is "The Theory itself," an NT Ethereal issue. He notes here how few Jungian analysts have taken it seriously, whereas Myers did in its entirety. The second foundation stone is "a means of empirical verification," which Myers so competently developed in her instrument, thus providing "the 'reality-check' against which the theory must be checked," an ST Structural issue. The third stone is "intuitive inspiration," which leads to a "ferment of new ideas." One example is the MBTI Step II, an instrument in which a number of typical traits that describe each type are each tested in a spectrum with an opposite trait, the results of which add depth and flexibility to our understanding of the basic types. We can see here the NF Oceanic's/Creative Artist's contribution. Finally, the fourth stone is "Ethical Practice," which demands truthful and courageous application of our archetypically given preferences to everyday life. In his autobiography, Jung demanded the same of his dream images, which, if ignored, he warned, could bring about damaging societal and personal consequences.[47] This is clearly the province of the SF Moralist.

These are only a few instances of the implicit presence of the function pairs in type circles, even when they are not consciously considered. But these functional pairs show up everywhere, true to their archetypal nature. For example, Dick Simpson, a political scientist from the University of Illinois Circle campus in Chicago, has identified four kinds of city councils, which he has depicted as a circle with four quadrants. Their placement and characteristics, either positive or negative, agree with the four couplings' quadrants: Council Wars in the ST Warrior quadrant; a Rubber Stamp Council in the SF Parental place, with its need for order; a Fragmented Council in the undifferentiated NF Oceanic quadrant; and a Representative Democratic Council in the NT quadrant.[48]

Both analysts and typologists have suffered several overall damaging consequences as a result of this split in Jungian ranks. Analysts have not been especially interested in societal issues. They can correct this tendency by consciously raising their societal and political sensitivity, especially by becoming more typologically aware. We have seen how Jerome Bernstein has done this in his *Power Politics.* Typologists, on the other hand, have easily plunged into the rough-and-tumble social world. They have recognized that ignorance of human differences has contributed to much suffering and misunderstanding and that knowledge of type differences contributes to health and healing among individuals and groups. Type practitioners have sensitively recorded these facts in fields such as counseling, family dynamics, the classroom, academic research, and cross-cultural studies and in organizations ranging from government and industry to psychology and religion. As a result, typologists are involved in organizational development and management consulting in increasing numbers.

Analysts also have lost out on a substantial validation of Jung's overall psychological theory, since typology as developed by the *MBTI* is the only aspect of his theory that has been subjected to immense statistical research. The *MBTI* is recognized as one of the most reliable and scientifically verifiable instruments for the understanding of personality. Analysts would profit, even if painfully, in assimilating this more tough-minded aspect of our psychology.

In turn, *MBTI* practitioners have suffered their own significant losses by ignoring the fullness of Jung's system, particularly its consciousness of archetypes and individuation. Because a circular or compass awareness has usually been left out of the *MBTI* research and literature, a realization of the dynamic between the types has been mainly limited to the interactive struggles in each type's polar spectrum, in the play of the dominant and auxiliary functions, and finally in the obvious difficulties encountered when any of the different sixteen types encounter one another. Typologists have not fully realized the larger and deeper consequences of ignoring one's personal or collective shadow, the inferior function and coupling, with its difficult, confusing, and often terrifying dream images. They have settled instead for a lesser understanding of the relative consciousness of the dominant function and coupling, and so miss out on the more fulfilling fruits of the lifelong individuation process. Finally, because typologists have not understood the archetypal nature of the types, they have not assimilated the richness of Jung's psychology as it illuminates universal patterns not just in individuals but also within so many human realms, such as anthropology, mythology, literature, biology, physics, philosophy, and theology. Most of all, both analysts and typologists have hardly considered the significance of experiencing and understanding the types as aspects of Jung's depth psychology, depicted as conic structures with the Self as its foundation, source, container, and dynamic (see chapters 6, 9, and 12). Analysts particularly need to consider that Jung depicted his psychological system as a mandala only in typological terms.

Finally, the lack of a consciousness of the couplings themselves among both analysts and typologists, in spite of the seminal work of both Jung and Myers, has contributed significantly to a separation of the two communities. If Jung had rethought his initial work with the couplings, or if an analyst had picked up on their importance, an early connection might have been made between the couplings and Toni Wolff's imaginative work in the 1930s with her four feminine archetypes (discussed in chapter 4). Then, as we have seen (in chapters 5 and 7), after Myers developed her phenomenology of the sixteen types and her extensive research based on the four couplings, analysts and typologists could have more readily connected. A coupling consciousness, we are reminded, includes a larger archetypal outreach than individual types, extending to the four cultural archetypes, the four levels of child development and the eight life stages of an entire human life, as well as the four metaphorical quadrants of the brain, the four moments of a creative process and the four quarters of the life journey. Further, they subliminally and archetypically appear as deep ordering principles, cropping up in such divergent structures as the Native American Medicine Wheel and, as we shall see in the final chapter, in the four disciplines of William Edwards Deming's philosophy of organizations.

Such a consciousness of the function couplings as archetypes in *MBTI* circles would also have made the shortcomings of other type theories (such as that of Keirsey and Bates) instantly noticeable. Also, a recognition of the importance of the couplings among analysts would have made it more difficult for Singer and Loomis to have eliminated the polar relationship of the functions, and, therefore, of the function pairs.

In summary, the historical separation of the two Jungian communities and the related eclipse of the type couplings have significantly limited Jungian psychology's impact on individuals and on society in general. Though we have seen how, in type circles, a growing study of Jung's system and even an appreciation of the Type Compass is occurring, we have ignored the fact that we belong to the same family. Mary McCaulley states the unrealized potential of this family:

> In psychology we talk about the clinician-research model. As clinicians, we see patterns and come up with hunches. As researchers, we turn our hunches into hypotheses and test them. Jung was a good example of this model. . . . Jung began by observing patterns and validating them in his clinical work. [And I would add, among his friends and acquaintances, as he has reported.] Isabel Myers studied Jung's work and tested his observations for twenty years by studying her family and friends. Then she became a researcher. Starting from Jung's work, she set herself the task of creating a tool to validate his work and apply it. *Together, they became one of the most creative clinician-researcher teams in the history of psychology.*[49]

This declaration is an intelligent call to unite an otherwise divided family, the two parts of which have been living apart as strangers to one another. This book has made this reunion one of its goals. Together, analysts and typologists can more wisely and effectively, inwardly and outwardly, personally and collectively, help humankind better understand the nobility of each person, the value of societal institutions, and the reality of the one human and earthly family. When we do not achieve a typological balance, barbarisms occur. We as analysts and typologists within this one family need to take Read's quote in Ulanov's *Jung and the Outside World* at the beginning of this chapter very seriously: "If society makes it impossible for such a 'complete and harmonious being [with the balanced types] to exist, then we should be working to change society to encourage and support that kind of being.'"[50] Also, we need to heal one of the larger societal barbarisms, our ESTJ Western cultural pathology, which we are presently enduring, especially in this country, and which we will now consider.

Notes

1. Barry Ulanov, *Jung and the Outside World* (Wilmette IL: Chiron Publications, 1992), pp. 88–89. Ann Ulanov writes in the foreword: "Much has been written on Jung's life and Jung's work. Little has been written on the effect of the man's work on other thinkers and artists of talent and depth. . . . Jung's perception of the objectivity of the psyche—the collective unconscious— stands out as the signal influence. Next would come the transformation of the Self. . . . Finally the alchemy of the two sexes catches many" (p. ix). Among the many eminent scholars and artists who either incorporated Jung's ideas uncritically or felt compelled to respond to his challenging ideas, the following are worth noting: R. C. Zaehner of Oxford, the eminent historian Arnold Toynbee, the playwright Samuel Beckett, the cultural philosopher Gaston Bachelard, the composer Michael Tippett, the painter Jackson Pollock, the film director Federico Fellini, the poet Robert Bly, among many others. *Jung and the Outside World,* commenting on Herbert Read.

2. James Hillman and Michael Ventura, *We've Had a Hundred Years of Psychotherapy and the World's Getting Worse* (San Francisco: HarperSanFrancisco, 1992), p. 52.

3. There is some limited evidence that a more serious societal concern is growing in these professional ranks. As to societal concerns, the following, for example, are important: *The Political Psyche,* by Andrew Samuels; *Power Politics,* by Jerome Bernstein; *Persona: Where Sacred Meets Profane,* by Robert H. Hopcke; and *We've Had a Hundred Years of Psychotherapy and the World's Getting Worse,* by James Hillman and Michael Ventura. The Chicago Society of Jungian Analysts has also been involved in an organizational development contract with a major industry, after co-sponsoring a conference with organizational development specialists. Ironically, this enterprise seems to have ended because of conflicts between two key analysts. Overall, however, Jungians stay with their central concern, the individuation process of individuals.

In the above books touching on social issues, we have seen that only Bernstein has taken typology seriously. Samuels' book has no reference to the types. Hillman and Ventura provides one shining moment on the types. Hillman holds that our inwardness of soul must embrace the inwardness of the world, that is, a "shifting the idea of depth from the psychology of the inner person to a psychology of things, *a depth psychology of extraversion*" (pp. 52–53, italics added).

As to more intellectual and cultural concerns, the following are worth mentioning: *Jung and the Outside World,* by Barry Ulanov; *The Cambridge Companion to Jung,* edited by Polly Young-Eisendrath and Terence Dawson, and *C. G. Jung and the Humanities,* edited by Karin Barnaby and Pellegrino D'Acierno. In the *Humanities* book, Anne Griswold Tyng proposes an extraverted and introverted interplay in the creation of great architecture (pp. 110–11), and Beverley Zabriskie sees Jung's positive valuing of the unconscious as a feminine/artistic introverted counterbalance to an extraverted patriarchy (p. 272). In the *Companion,* there are similarly short references to typology, such as that Jung and Schopenhauer had been influenced by Schiller's understanding of typology (p. 24). Otherwise, in the section entitled "Part III: Analytical Psychology in Society," there are no formal articles or substantive references to typology.

4. Editorial note in C. G. Jung, *CW,* vol. 6, *Psychological Types,* English edition, translated by H. G. Baynes (1923; rpt., Princeton NJ: Princeton University Press, 1971), p. v.

5. Pierre Ferrand, "Jung, Jungians, and Type Practitioners," *Bulletin of Psychological Type* 21:1 (Winter 1998): pp. 34–37.

6. Ibid., p. 34. Ferrand continues: "Jung's way of handling this break [with Freud] was conceptual and abstract and involved the examination of differing intellectual attitudes all over the map, from Greek mythology to medieval theology, Schiller's esthetics, and Nietzsche's philosophy. . . . Type theory was a by-product, with many of the key concepts merely sketched in an appendix." Ferrand concludes: "Properly understood, the *MBTI* approach has inherited [from Jung] some of the best features of the humanistic tradition, including accepting and valuing diversity and warning against labelling and pigeon-holing" (p. 36).

7. There are no connections shown between the archetypes and the types in the *CW,* vol. 20, *General Index of the Collected Works of C. G. Jung* (Princeton, NJ: Princeton University Press, 1979).

8. C. A. Meier, *Personality: The Individuation Process in the Light of C. G. Jung's Typology* (Einsiedeln, Switzerland: Daimon, Verlag, 1995).

9. Ibid., pp. 56–57.

10. Sonu Shamdasani, *Cult Fictions: C. G. Jung and the Founding of Analytical Psychology* (London and New York: Routledge, 1998), pp. 38–39. Jung writes to the analysts suggesting that in a "democratic form of discussion," they together consider the important concepts which formed the basis of analytical psychology. "The focus that he suggests on the 'definition and application of technical terms' appears to have resulted in the extensive lexicon of psychological concepts that he presented at the end of *Psychological Types.*"

There is a considerable use of typology by the individuals discussed in this book, especially by one of Jung's assistants, Maria Moltzer, who eventually split with Jung and the Psychology Club over its objectives. The many clumsy and idiosyncratic uses, especially of the functions, indicates that typology was still in its infancy.

11. Shamdasani, *Cult Fictions,* p. 45.

12. Ibid., p. 40.

13. Thayer Green, "Confessions of an Extravert," *Quadrant,* the Journal of the C.G. Jung Foundation for Analytical Psychology in New York, vol. 8:2 (Winter 1975): pp. 21–31. Green draws heavily on a London analyst, David Holt, in his diploma thesis for the Zurich Institute, "Persona and Actor." Holt shows that the term *persona* comes from *per* and *sonare,* meaning *to sound through.* Holt continues: "Jung's use of the word *persona* is related to only one, and a very limited, aspect of acting. Most of his analogies are taken from the professions, not the stage. In the professions, the actor in us all is required always to play the same role. Thus, the essence of the actor, which is his ability to change roles, is denied" (p. 27). Green prefers to look beyond the mask as a symbol of the persona and consider, as so many dreams and great stories reveal, the importance of clothes, but, most of all, the significance of the skin, as the most elemental way of relating inside and outside (p. 29).

Readers who want to pursue the excellent thinking of David Holt can go to his 1992 book, *The Psychology of Carl Jung: Essays in Application and Deconstruction* (Lewiston NY: Edwin Mellen Press). His chapter 15, "Jung and the Third Person," contains the most profound discussion I have ever read on extraversion and introversion, the comparable play of body and society, and the ontological/metaphysical ground of these type differences and interactions.

14. Edward Whitmont, "Analysis in a Group Setting," *Quadrant* (Spring 1974). Whitmont points out that "a holistic view of man was Jung's chief concern throughout his entire life and work. His typology, the integration of the inferior function, reconciliation with the shadow, anima and/or animus, the symbolism of the mandala, the integrative demands of the self, are all symbols which bespeak Jung's striving for wholeness. His refusal to value or to recognize the individual's need for encounter with the group, is the one glaring exception" (p. 7). He had seen the need for a club in Zurich, but for Whitmont this was not enough. One following statement by Jung, among so many, illustrates Jung's negativity to even well-defined corporate structures: "A large company that is made up of entirely admirable people, resembles, in respect to its morality and intelligence, an unwieldy stupid animal" (p. 6). From C. G. Jung, *Psychological Perspectives* (New York: Harper Torchbook, Harper and Row, 1961), p. 148.

15. Thayer Green, "Confessions of an Extravert," p. 25.

16. Ibid., p. 21.

17. Ibid., p. 23. Green notes that "Katherine Bradway's study of twenty-eight California analysts reveals seventy-five percent to be introverted

intuitives." In my classes and workshops, I have consistently found that roughly 60 to 75 percent of the participants are NFs, 20 to 40 percent are NTs, a few, up to 15 percent, are SFs, and STs are usually not represented.

18. Ibid.

19. Ibid., p. 27.

20. I have personally experienced such reactions within myself and associates. Too often an offended trainee will remark that he/she has never experienced such harsh criticisms in other areas of their professional training. The breadth and depth of a Jungian's spiritual inner work, like all strengths, has its negative side. One trainee, a brilliant and integrally spiritual person, was once accused of having an "overt sentimental attitude toward religion." Another was told that she was caught in a "soft mother complex" in relating to clients. Both of these trainees are outstanding in their professional field. Both assessments were patently wrong. A few trainees have been eliminated, some for objectively sound reasons and others because of questionable overt responses to similar complexes. Overall, however, as I look at my nineteen years of functioning as a training analyst, I recognize the balanced and broad-based handling of most trainees by my associates. But our shadows remain and as a result we have at times been patently unjust to some trainees.

21. Arwind Vasavada, "Training Process versus the Individuation Process," a paper presented at the October 25-28, 1995, meeting of the Inter-Regional Society of Jungian Analysts at Tucson, Arizona. E-mail, william@boulder.earthnet.net, Donald Williams, LPC, Jungian Analyst, Website Editor, Boulder, Colorado.

22. Ibid., p. 8.

23. Ibid., pp. 12–13.

24. Ibid., p. 7.

25. C. G. Jung, *C. G. Jung Letters,* vol. 1, 1906–1950 (Princeton NJ: Princeton University Press, 1971), p. 433.

26. Vasavada, "Training Process versus the Individuation Process," p. 13.

27. Mary McCaulley, "APT and the Constructive Use of Differences," *Bulletin of Psychological Type* 22:1 (Winter 1999): p. 10. McCaulley laments any misuse of the types, pointing to examples of people, usually new to typology, who use types stereotypically. One person said of another: "Oh, you are an ENTJ—one of those power-hungry people." When Myers and McCaulley set up the Center for Applications of Psychological Type, Myers declared that their mission was to bring about "the constructive use of type." As the world of the

MBTI grew, Myers and then McCaulley, with many supporting actors, have consistently strived for excellence in both research and imaginatively and ethically sound applications of the type theory.

28. Jung, CW, vol. 6, *Psychological Types*, para. 920.

29. Ibid., para. 921.

30. Ibid., para. 922.

31. Victor White, my first analyst, wrote of the danger of a too narrowly gnostic approach in Jung in his 1952/1982 book, *God and the Unconscious* (Dallas TX: Spring Publications). Martin Buber brought a similar charge against Jung. Richard Noll has accused Jung of creating a cult. See his *The Jung Cult: The Origins of a Charismatic Movement* (Princeton NJ: Princeton University Press, 1994). Sonu Shamdasani in his *Cult Fictions: C. G. Jung and the Founding of Analytical Psychology,* quoted above, competently counters Noll's views.

32. *Conversations with Isabel Myers,* originally filmed in 1977 on the campus of Michigan State University. Appearing in the original footage with Myers are Mary McCaulley, Naomi Quenk, Cecil Williams, and Janie Sweet. Mary H. McCaulley, co-founder and president of CAPT, added opening and closing comments. This video can be rented or purchased from CAPT, 2815 NW 13th Street, Suite 401, Gainesville, FL 32609, 1-800-777-2278.

33. Peter T. Richardson, "A Circle of Type," *Bulletin of Psychological Type* 21:4 (Summer 1998): pp. 27–28. His book *The Four Spiritualities* is published by CPP's Davies-Black Publishing.

34. Ken Green, "A Modest Proposal: The Type Circle," *Bulletin of Psychological Type* 21:3 (Late Spring, 1998): p. 18. Green is an INFP, a writer, and a video producer, besides being the editor of the *Bulletin.*

35. Louise A. Hoxworth, in an article entitled, "A Different Way to Introduce Type," *Bulletin of Psychological Type* 20:2 (Spring 1997), has constructed a wheel picturing each of the sixteen *MBTI* types, with the opposites of each located across the circle. After coloring in one's type, one reflects on the value that each of the other fifteen types brings to the world. Hoxworth also suggests that the wheel helps members of a team better appreciate the contributions that other persons of different types bring to the team (pp. 40–41).

36. Isabel Briggs Myers, *Gifts Differing* (Palo Alto CA: Consulting Psychologists Press, 1980), p. 27.

37. Ken Green, "Confessions of an Extravert," p. 18.

38. Jung, CW, vol. 6, *Psychological Types,* para. 790.

39. McCaulley, "Type and the Growth of the MBTI: Then and Now," *Bulletin of Psychological Type* 20:3 (Summer 1998): pp. 48–49.

40. Ibid.

41. McCaulley, "Applications of Type: Filling in the Jig-saw," *Bulletin of Psychological Type* 15:3 (Summer 1992): p. 20.

42. Ibid. McCaulley gives a homey example of the archetypal richness of each type when she gives the example of four ESTJs: "one may enjoy looking at the foundations of a bridge, another at the balance sheet of a business, the third at the carburetor of a car, and the fourth at the broken bone of an athlete. They seem to have chosen widely different careers, but they have a bond: all enjoy the evidence of their senses"(p. 20). I would also add that they all enjoy their structural abilities as STs.

43. Jung, CW, vol. 11, "Psychology and Religion," *Psychology and Religion: West and East* (Princeton NJ: Princeton University Press, 1958). Jung discusses here in various places a house in a dream called "The House of the Gathering" (pp. 35, 38, 51, 74f, 79–80, 83). Gaston Bachelard's book, *The Poetics of Space,* 1958 in French, 1964 in English (New York: Orion Press), is devoted to many aspects of the house archetype.

44. Carolyn Biediger Barnes, "Rooms of My Mind: Introverted Thinking," *Bulletin of Psychological Type* (Winter 1999): pp. 1, 3.

45. Ibid.

46. James Newman, "Theory and Practice," *Bulletin of Psychological Types* (Summer 1992): pp. 27–28.

47. Jung, *Memories, Dreams, Reflections* (New York: Vintage Books, 1961), pp. 192–93. It is not enough, writes Jung, to classify and understand the images from the unconscious. "Insight into them must be converted into an ethical obligation. Not to do so is to fall prey to the power principle, and this produces dangerous effects which are destructive not only to others but even to the knower." Our entire book argues that such archetypal images are also the types. Type readers need to consider here what it means to ignore the inferior function.

48. Dick Simpson, *Rogues, Rebels, and Rubber Stamps: The Politics of the Chicago City Council from 1863 to the Present,* with a preface by Studs Terkel (Boulder CO: Westview Press, 2001), p. 316. The four points of Dick Simpson's cross and circle have the following designations: "Conflict" at thinking's top place, with its implied differentiating symbol, the sword; "Control" at the left

horizontal place of sensing with its love of order; "Acquiescence" at the bottom place of feeling with its capacities for harmony and surrender; and "Participation" at the right horizontal place of intuition with its characteristic of holistic inclusiveness. Simpson acknowledges that he did not plan this arrangement according to the types; it simply happened.

49. McCaulley, "Applications of Type: Filling in the Jig-saw," p. 20. McCaulley quotes Jung from the preface of the 7th edition of the *Types* book, in which he addresses the book's critics, who "commonly fall into the error of assuming that the types were, so to speak, fancy free and were forcibly imposed on the empirical material." Instead he says: "All my formulations are based on the experience in the hard course of my daily professional work. What I have to say in this book, therefore, has been tested a hundredfold." Jung in effect is saying that types have emerged from the soil of the unconscious as archetypes, which his consciousness observed and named, and were not "forcibly imposed" by his ego.

50. Ulanov, *Jung and the Outside World*, p. 89.

CHAPTER 12

Our ESTJ National Pathology and the Healing Possibilities of William Edwards Deming's System of Management

---

To whom shall I speak today?
Brothers are evil.
Friends today cannot be loved.
To whom shall I speak today. . . .
Each man takes his neighbor's goods. . . .
Gentleness is overthrown.
Violence rules all. . . .
To whom shall I speak today?
When vice is greeted as a friend,
the brother who will remonstrate becomes a foe.[1]

From *Rebel in The Soul: An Ancient Egyptian Dialogue Between a Man and His Destiny*

 hidden agenda is at the heart of this book on typology and its soulful, archetypal way. Given Jung's assumption that typology applies to culture as well as to the psyche and body of individuals, this agenda is about the state of our society, particularly in the United States. I am concerned overall with the generally despotic attitude toward those who have relatively limited or no power. The attitude touches a wide

range of populations: women, children, and old people in our typical families; welfare recipients and the poor, especially among black, Latino, and other ethnic minorities; and prisoners and ex-convicts. Today it also touches populations once immune to society's contempt: health care providers, including doctors, and corporate workers in the middle and lower classes caught in downsizing practices of companies. The issues discussed with reference to one population spill over into others.

This mean-spirited attitude characterizes the ESTJ Warrior mentality, which, when uncontrolled and one-sided, functions as a tyrannical force in both individuals and in society. This is not a criticism of the ESTJ type as such, but of its excesses. We know in psychology and in life that one-sidedness and inertia in any mental or emotional position, including any *Myers-Briggs Type Indicator®* (*MBTI®*) type, can result in personal and societal damage. Jung in chapter 3 of this book calls such one-sidedness "barbaric." Our focus here is on the ESTJ makeup because, as we shall try to show in this chapter, it dominates the current cultural orientation. Even when healthy, it illustrates William James' characterization of "tough-minded" persons in contrast to "tender-minded" individuals. When it takes other types into account, it is healthy, but it is often pathologized in leaders and collective attitudes that demand absolute conformity. We can see its distortions in any leader's need to hire underlings who totally agree with his/her aggressive, concretistic, logical, and linear thought processes, and compartmentalized, detailed strategies. Overall, this cultural bias illustrates ESTJ attitudes and values representing a patriarchal philosophy of power and dominance which has characterized human society for the last 5,000 years.[2] This ESTJ cultural climate, whether healthy or pathological, is a collective overlay that characterizes our societal leaders, from politicians to popular TV and movie creators (figure 12.1). It both subtly and blatantly affects each one of us, no matter what our individual typology may be. The one-sidedness

Some Characteristics of Our National ESTJ Pathology

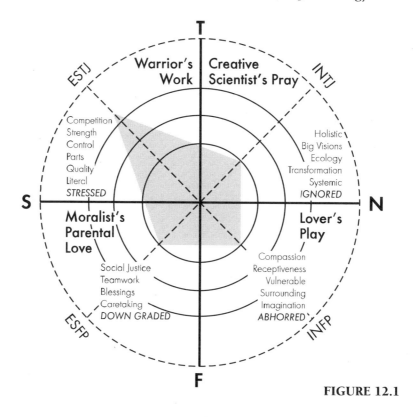

FIGURE 12.1

of this set of values ignores necessary and compensating values in the three other type quadrants.

This ESTJ power pathology is elitist, denies the value of the other type couplings and their congruent representatives, and tends to recognize persons who prefer it as fit to govern.[3] For example, this attitude spawned the Iran-Contra conspiracy that acted covertly against the congressional laws and the American populace. Its contemptuous attitude toward others contributes to the low-level mentality of TV situation comedies, talk shows, and violent dramas, and the typical political campaign based on TV images, sound bites, and negative slogans.[4] This narrow approach to life, including a contempt for fellow creatures, is seen in popular radio and TV personalities, such as Rush Limbaugh saying, "If the spotted owl can't adjust, then screw it."[5]

A consistently cold-hearted attitude toward the weakest members of our nation's family characterizes this ideology, in spite of its political leaders' loud protestation about supporting family values.[6] The damage from this attitude is shown by our high child mortality rate (as compared to other industrialized nations), the number of children living in subhuman economic conditions, our poor child care facilities, our lack of health and life services for old folk, and our poor support for family life and schools.[7] The plight of poor families and their children demands a radical shift from American individualism to the new popular African proverb, "It takes a village to raise a child." Translated into the Compass of the Soul, it takes all the attributes of the whole mind and brain to raise a child and create a just society.[8]

The narrow sensing thinking viewpoint values quantity, as in measurable school facts, observable behaviors, and the limited solutions that follow from a factual approach. Generally, there is an innately shortsighted tendency in the isolated ST Structural, given that the sensing part naturally likes concrete order and dislikes change, and the thinking part values objective systems and devalues subjective relations. This tough-mindedness of the ST Warrior becomes cold and cruel when it loses the SF Parent's compassionate and practical sensitivity to others. By overvaluing ST characteristics, such an attitude tends to encourage the ST potential in each of us, an aspect which often misses the deeper relational powers, the creative energies, and the vital emotionality of the NF Lover. The most damaging aspect of the ST's pathology is that it views its own inner NF Lover's striving for harmony and compromise as inferior and weak. As a result, this warrior mind perceives compassion as weakness toward both one's self and others.[9] When caught in this mentality, we often dream of ignoring or punishing children, feminine figures, or tender-minded males—images of the very aspects which our overly aggressive egos need.

A remarkable book, Philip K. Howard's *The Death of Common Sense: How Law Is Suffocating America,* describes with both theoretical clarity and pointed examples how this national pathology has invaded our legislative processes.[10] Legislation was once characterized by its brevity and simple guidelines, which allowed its executors to apply it with appropriate intelligence, common sense, personal responsibility, and creative execution. However, beginning in the 1960s, a new national climate slowly emerged that has changed the very structures of the law. It is a climate of distrust of ordinary people, as is typical of a ruling elite, which has produced, as Howard writes in his chapter 3, "A Nation of Enemies." As a result, legislative packages have multiplied ten and twenty times, attempting to describe every detail of the law's applications. This attitude opts for a "precision" that presumably will produce "scientific certainty."[11] Instead of stimulating idiosyncratic and creative action, it seeks "uniformity" in order to ensure fairness. However, writes Howard, "Fairness . . . is a far more subtle concept than making all the words on the page apply to everyone."[12] This ST attitude attempts to "anticipate every future contingency."[13] This is the sign of a one-sided sensing function that, in its intuitive shadow, fears the future. Further, this mentality is ruled in the thinking function by a "philosophy of rationalism," which assumes "that a natural order in government could be found similar to the order that Isaac Newton thought he had found in nature."[14] The upshot, as stated by sociologist Max Weber, is the development of bureaucracy that the more it is perfected, "the more it is 'dehumanized'."[15] In rationalism, writes Howard, we try to "make government operate like a Swiss watch. . . . We have cast aside our good sense, and worship an icon of abstract logic and arbitrary words."[16] As an overall result, he points out, "Modern regulatory law resembles central planning." He continues:

> There are differences, of course. The Soviets tried to run their country like a puppeteer pulling millions of strings. In our country, the words of law are like millions of trip wires, preventing us from doing the sensible thing.[17]

In a subtle if unconscious recognition of typological differences, Howard writes: "Human nature seems to lead people, or at least certain kinds of people, down this path."[18]

In Welfare. Welfare agencies too are overwhelmed with this frigid, legalistic mentality. While limiting the amount of time on welfare may be appropriate, the prevailing attitude despises efforts of a poor mother who, alone, cares for her children and depends on public aid. The call for the elimination of welfare without comprehensive attempts to strengthen the family and the school, reduce crime in welfare recipients' neighborhoods, provide better job training, and make available viable work with a decent family-sustaining wage and future security is another result of pathologized ST thinking. The supreme irony in this discussion of welfare for the poor is that its cost is nothing compared to what is now called corporate welfare, such as "enterprise funds" to develop Eastern Europe,[19] and state tax breaks for big companies, particularly those which lure companies to relocate in areas which are less unionized.[20] This latter strategy makes non-union, low-wage jobs available in those states, but those who profit most are "primarily bankers, corporate lawyers, people involved in investment and financial services."[21]

Welfare, in the largest possible sense, includes the care of our natural resources, following the dictum of one of nature's greatest advocates, Theodore Roosevelt: "A nation behaves well if the natural resources and assets which one generation turns over to the next are increased and not impaired in value." Even here corporate welfare is winning out over natural resources:

> Every year, hundreds of millions of dollars, raised through the leasing of Federal lands for mineral, gas and oil extraction, is sent west . . . for the benefit of oil, gas, mining, agriculture, and development interests.[22]

The modern ESTJ Warrior type in his one-sided neurotic form is a new version of the old mercenaries, who would fight any kingdom's battles as long as they were paid for their services. The mercenary does not care for his own ST organizational gifts that align well with the SF Moral Leader's concern for the welfare of a nation's people; he cares only for money and an illusory freedom from all government. Neither does he care for visionary programs from NT types, since such programs cannot be measured in dollars and cents.

Money as power dominates our national life. Kevin Phillips shocked the nation with *The Politics of the Rich and the Poor,* showing how in the Reagan years, the wealthy became increasingly wealthier and the poor increasingly poorer.[23] Phillips followed with another book, entitled *Arrogant Capital,* in which he argues that the American people have lost control of their government to national and international private conglomerates from whose coffers immense amounts of money are dispensed to our political leaders.[24] A sadly ironic parody of the golden rule painfully fits this state of affairs: "Those with the gold make the rules."

This critique is echoed by others. Money is the Pope of our time, argues a *National Catholic Reporter* article. People believe that more money earned and less taxes imposed will be the salvation of our country. Yet money, the writer points out, is ruthless when it wins out over human needs, especially the welfare of the poor. This "hard cash" mentality of our business community is highlighted by its leading guru, Milton Friedman, who preaches that a company has only one "social responsibility . . . to increase its profits so long as it stays within the rules of the game."[25]

While this philosophy fits an old Puritan view that one's financial gains from hard labor are a sign of God's blessing and one's rightful due, both the Bible and history remind us that personal spiritual health and a nation's enduring survival depend upon the quality of its care for the poor. Yet we have shamelessly allowed a growing disparity between the rich and the poor.[26] The wisdom of every culture tells us that, even with millions of dollars in our coffers, we are consigned to a hell on earth if we ignore the holistic demands of Soul and brain, of Self, the human commonweal, and the community of all beings.

In Criminal Justice and Gun Consciousness. Another troublesome topic is that of criminals, prisons, and rehabilitation. Of all the first world nations and third world nations, we have the most prisons, the longest sentences, and the greatest numbers of crimes per capita.[27] It seems obvious that many factors contribute to this. We have the worst welfare and the least medical care for families and children among developed nations. We are the most mobile nation, so more of our nuclear families are separated from their family and neighborhood beginnings. We are also an ethnic melting pot for millions who have left behind their geographical and cultural roots. Whereas at one time criminals, following patterns of immigration, were historically Italians, Irishmen, and Germans, now most are black Americans and Latinos, struggling in impoverished environments. Pressures of poverty lead the dispirited poor to the typical dynamics that often end in violence: an escalation of hunger, abandonment, fear, frustration, rage, and revenge, leading inevitably to jail. The middle class and the wealthy, on the other hand, often play out violence in more socially acceptable ways, as in drinking and psychosomatic illnesses, and also have many more resources beyond prison for rehabilitation.

Our ESTJ culture itself, when too one-sided, contributes to criminality. This type values the most tough-minded, masculine individual, with an extraverted thinking centerpiece within the psyche, and its ST Warrior archetype in society. Each element of this type complex is on the heady side of the psyche and the brain's left hemisphere. Extraversion is assertive. Sensation categorizes experiences and things into parts and facts. Thinking defines, names, categorizes, and decides objectively (i.e., without input from the feeling function). Judging insists on finishing the work. These ESTJ traits are all positive and constructive in themselves, However, when these qualities are pathologized, they become the most cold-blooded of all of the sixteen *MBTI®* types.

European settlers conquered with guns when they brought in black slaves and put Native American in reservations. Today, Americans continue in peacetime to have the most ownership of private guns among first nations. No other Western nation has an organization comparable to our powerful National Rifle Association. The typical NRA member considers the right to bear arms equivalent to the spiritual inward capacity to feel empowered.[28] Socially, this mentality mistrusts the government and totally ignores the poor. This same one-sided ST mentality, seen on the larger stage, also seeks repressive remedies to our national violence. Accordingly, President Clinton's crime bill called for the construction of ten more Federal prisons, established a mandatory life sentence for a third serious felony and designated the death penalty for fifty-two more crimes,[29] even though all criminal justice research shows that the death penalty is not a deterrent, and that most prison experiences only enhance criminality. This ST Warrior tendency, caught on the surface of consciousness, fears the reflective breadth and depth of the NT Magician, the parental concern of the SF Moralist, and the compassion of the NF Lover.

For eight years, I managed a counseling and job-placement program for ex-offenders, run by Chicago's SAFER Foundation. The client population reflects that of the justice system: 95 percent are males mainly from the ages of eighteen to twenty-eight, 85 percent of whom are black, 10 percent Latino, and 5 percent white. Our research also showed that most of our clients were introverted, sensate, thinking types.[30] As introverts, they fear aggressive, extraverted behavior but are pushed into bravado activities in neighborhoods by gang leaders and others.

We learned that finding these ST clients jobs was not enough, unless a much deeper level of rehabilitation of their human needs was realized. Metaphorically and spiritually, this "rehabilitation," this "re-housing," has to be realized in the Soul, in the Self, in one's inner castle where the Magician sees visions, the Creative Artist works, and the Parent cares for the wounded child. This is the only solid grounding for a journey of self-discovery and effective productivity. We learned at SAFER that in our client's life histories, they experienced hurts at a much deeper place than job inefficiency or incompetence. Their woundedness began literally in the bodies and at the breasts of mothers, who worried about the next meal for themselves and their children, who feared abandonment from men who, too often, could not find work but could find violence on the street. As children these ex-offenders had had to repress their fears and rage as well as their hunger for love and community in order to survive. The antisocial behaviors which emerged from their repressions are the same ones that people from all social strata experience: addictive, neurotic, and psychotic behavior. Rehabilitation occurs only when such wounded depths are healed by an ex-offender program that includes understanding of typology, dreams, and emotional patterns, along with educational and work opportunities. Both staff and clients must believe in the Soul's transformative powers.

In Health Concerns. The health care crisis in the United States is another area of concern. The ST Structural bias of our society is reflected in the proliferation of for-profit Health Maintenance Organizations (HMOs) based on typical business practices. The national business attitude, ruled as it is by the Friedman philosophy of industry, promotes a health industry dominated by corporate profits in contrast to the health care of clients. Again, quantity of earnings wins over quality of services. This Friedman ST-dominated goal of private capital becomes particularly perverse in the health care field.

Private companies have in effect created our national health plan. Such a process has led to many significant changes in our national life. "Managed care covered 71 percent of American workers who had health benefits in 1995, up from 52 percent in 1993."[31] This mushrooming of HMOs is now sending up warning signals in many places. Howard Witt writes:

Instead [of a national health-care policy], thousands of corporations and hundreds of health maintenance organizations individually are determining the shape of America's future health care in a loosely regulated marketplace, where the medical interests of patients and the financial interests of doctors increasingly are being placed in direct opposition.[32]

In the final analysis, those who benefit the most from these developments are not the patients but the investors, the company officers, banks and investment counselors, lawyers, and stockholders. For example, the Community Medical Plan's investors in Florida realized a 7,000 percent increase in their investment when the Plan was sold after two years.[33] Yet, contrary to conventional assumptions, these private medical organizations have not contributed to efficient management compared to comparable government functions. In contrast to these for-profit HMOs, the following illustrates the government's comparable efficiency: "Medicare spends an average of two cents on the dollar for administrative overhead, Medicaid about a nickel . . . and private managed care operations a whopping 20 percent overhead."[34]

Meanwhile, the customers of these HMOs often suffer, in contrast to the earnings of these health organizations and their top officers. In a *Time* magazine article of January 22, 1996, the story is told of the immense struggle of the deMeurers family. The family fought to receive appropriate help from their HMO, Health Net of Woodland Hills, California, for the young wife and mother, Christy, who had cancer and eventually died. Their doctors struggled to keep Christy out of the hospital, since the hospital admission, as in many HMOs, cuts into the doctor's income, and they resisted giving her a bone marrow transplant. Ironically, while Christy deMeurer's life was coming to an end, the Chief Officer of Health Net received a lump sum of $1.1 million dollars as the result of a merger, and then, shortly after, exited the organization with a lump-sum payment of $18.1 million, equivalent to the average monthly premiums paid by nearly 134,000 subscribers.[35] "Life is not always fair," retorts the realist. However, this particular unfairness results from skewed ST values. Ironically, the American Medical Association, consistently dominated in the past by these same values, has begun to challenge these HMO developments, because doctors are feeling the strictures in both earnings and patient relations.

In Worker–Management Relations. The story of corporate–patient disparities in the health field mirrors other problems in our last areas of concern: those associated with the average worker and his relationship with management and the relationship between business profits and wages. The prevailing industrial philosophy values work as "bodily or mental effort . . . labor, toil" (*Webster's*), completed with unquestioning obedience to employers. When the Warrior mind is disconnected from the other three archetypes, work means doing with no questions asked, accompanied by perfectionist and workaholic tendencies with the emphasis on quantity of effort and productivity.

However, the verb *"to work"* includes meanings more humanly appropriate to spiritual values, such as "ferment," and "work in the mind," as written in *Webster's,* which suggest the NT Magician's hidden transformative activities in both the individual and in communities. This NT quadrant's meaning of work is also expressed as the general body of achievements of the scientist or artist, such as "the works of Einstein and Shakespeare." Finally, work is perceived spiritually as participating in the Creator's cosmic labors and products, the valuing of which constitutes the essence of prayer. Here, we are in touch with the Soul's inner work.[36]

A distortion of a deep psychology and spirituality of work and valuing only management and stockholders leads to statements such as that in the *Wall Street Journal,* which reported a drop in labor costs as a "welcome development of transcendent importance."[37] This is an ironic use of the word *transcendent* in the face of what lowered wages mean in human suffering. *Webster's* describes *transcendent* as meaning "that [which] exists apart from the physical world: said of God, divine spirit," and of the divine presence in the Soul. By the appalling use of this word, we see how, metaphysically, Big Money is the god of a business mind-set dominated by ESTJ's pathologized preferences.[38]

We can trace the ESTJ pathology through its metaphors that reflect its actions, and trace its dire consequences for workers. The Shadow Warrior values the top dog and looks down on the low man on the totem pole. This is expressed in the typical "downsizing," in which the low-level workers and middle management are cut, and in which top management's salaries and the stockholder's earnings are increased. The ratio of the average salary earned by chief executive officers (CEOs) in comparison to the average worker's salary from 1973 to 1994 starkly highlights our ST valuation of the top dogs: 41 to 1 in 1973–75, 141 to 1 in 1987–89, and 225 to 1 in 1992–94 according to *U.S. News and World Report.*[39] The authors add, "The worst fear is that economic inequality is dividing the nation as well." The decline of American unions in the last three decades has contributed to this economic disparity and danger. After gaining legal status in 1935, unions made available to workers the only recourse for balancing economic forces in our country.[40] With the weakening of unionism in our nation, the standard of living of the average worker has lowered considerably.

A Summary of ESTJ Pathologies. In summary, our society has been overwhelmed by a one-sided and therefore distorted ESTJ patriarchal ideology, characterized by its cruel dominance over the weak and powerless. It maintains its control through many psychological, ethical, and spiritual traits, which become destructive when taken to the extreme. Such traits are fear of diversity, a total-warlike competitiveness, literalism, a need to quantify, masculine characteristics, and visual and outward orientation. They may also be logical, mechanistic, hierarchical, elitist, aggressive, work-driven, acquisitive, controlling, antidemocratic, and antipopulist. The ESTJ patriarchal ideology values parts, organized facts, the surface of reality, binary thinking, and either/or decisions. These values are valid in themselves, but when isolated from the whole of life, they lead to an overall cold and even cruel approach to subordinates, to the weak and poor, to women, children, and the elderly. Politically, given the power of money in both the private and the public sector, this one-sided ST mind-set has, in effect, created an economic tyranny in our country. Our strong democratic structures were developed because the founders of our country recognized the need for a political balance of power among the three branches of government—the legislative, the judicial and the executive—and between the federal government and the states. However, a comparable economic balance of power has not yet been worked out, especially between the wealthy and the poor and the corporate owners and the workers who have been the subject of hit-and-miss, crisis-oriented programs and irregular legislation, judicial decisions, and executive orders.

Moreover, while we experience the destructive effects of this unrestrained ESTJ mentality on our society, we also experience damage to our inner personal lives. Throughout this book I have reported dreams that reveal that this one-sided mentality affects us powerfully in unspoken and hidden ways. Some of the negative dream images signifying the autocracy of this ST Warrior are a faceless child; Nazi or Mafia figures threatening one's freedom; addictive figures showing up in forms such as a serial killer; a machine-like lover; starving, lost children; animals that need rescuing; frightening enemies; lethal atmospheres, such as a killer gas, radiation, or polluted waters; sick and dying plants; bombs ready to explode; cars out of control; conflicted images of children, such as a laughing boy covered with excrement; and revengeful, cruel children, among others. I have also shown in many ways how dream work has led to the dreamers' rediscovery of authentic personal power through claiming ignored types and coupled archetypes.

Patriarchal power continues to haunt us. A dream presented to me by an INFP male as I was writing this chapter dramatically captures the Mafia-like shadow side of the Warrior. The dreamer, a professor, has suffered at the hands of "warriors," such as his father, a despised Marine corporal, his university authorities, ambitious academics, and his ESTJ attorney wife. Here is the dream:

> I am standing on a corner, watching Mafia-type men in a large black car, crazily and clumsily moving the four door windows. They see I am observing their behavior, and that I find it amusing. . . . Suddenly the scene shifts to a countryside. I am walking toward the grounds of a large estate. On my right I see a small lake or swamp, somewhat overrun with weeds and algae. A man is doing some cleaning. I enjoy this lake area and yearn for its natural atmosphere. Then as I look toward the large house I realize I have ventured near the home of the Mafia group that had been in the car. I see a henchman coming toward me with a gun. I can't run. I know I will be shot. I refuse to kneel facing him directly, so I turn to my right and kneel, thus exposing my left side. He promptly shoots me in the heart area. The power of the bullet pierces my body and pushes my heart from its natural center left position to the right side of the rib cage. I do not know whether I will live or die, but I know that I will not surrender.

Since an uptight, machismo mentality like that of his father does not tolerate being laughed at, even in good-natured fun, the dreamer's early life was not a joyful one. In yearning for the dream's lake area, he seeks the earthy, creative atmosphere which is co-natural to his peaceful and literary personality. The shot in the heart that pushes his heart to the right represents the ST Warrior aggressively thrusting its left-brain ideology and values on this gentle NF man. Live or die, he knows he will not let that killer mentality defeat him.

The question arises: what can we do to balance and thereby heal the ESTJs' pathological dominance in the United States?

SEEKING SOLUTIONS

As a therapist, I often work with tough-minded business and professional leaders, who, although successful on the job and honored in society, are often as wounded and dispirited in their hidden sensitive side as the rest of society. Their large homes and incomes do not satisfy their souls. One of the objectives of this book has been to show, within a type psychology, that there is a way to recover the Soul and its sacred way by valuing the wonder and mystery of individuals and their imaginative potentials, by valuing the opportunity in their second-stage-of-life to regain the hidden forces of the heart, the compassionate feelings of our guts, the dark, creative riches of our hidden spiritual treasures. In the typological wholeness of mind and brain, there is a fountain of wisdom, hope, happiness, and spiritual freedom that anyone can tap.

If in some way, the predominance of ESTJ energy makes this the worst of times, it is also the best of times, because many seemingly random and disparate forces, often disparaged as the "new age," are converging to authentically destabilize our old mentality. Strange bedfellows, such as the new physics, ecology, the Gaia earth theory, feminine consciousness, religious ecumenism, depth psychology and theology, and even the World Wide Web, all testify to our recognition of a powerfully connected society, rather than one of lonely warriors. It is imaged most powerfully by the photograph of the earth as seen from the moon, showing our planet to be a single, breathing, holistic organism in space. The physicist Bryan Swimme and the cultural historian Thomas Berry show that all members of the universe are literally cousins to one another. However, they also show that we are destroying this cosmic family.[41] In the past, the old physics and biology, on one end of the human spectrum, and religion and theology on the other end, provided separate bases for understanding ourselves as individuals and as a human society. Now the new sciences and mainline religions have formed an alliance that strongly furthers our understanding of ourselves as cosmically and societally connected, from a theology of creation to organizational leadership.[42]

Jung's psychology has been one of the forerunners of this coming ecological or earth age, particularly in its principle of synchronicity, which we discussed in chapter 4 as an aspect of the intuitive function. Defined as an acausal, universal, potential principle, synchronicity accounts for the intelligent harmonies sometimes experienced between people, and between people and nature, and, according to physicists, also for the critical convergences of certain space/time events that spawned and pushed forward the universe and our earth. A scientist won a Nobel Prize for proving mathematically that certain subatomic particles, under particular circumstances, know what other particles are doing instantaneously across infinite space. So the coming earth age needs to be a holistic, spiritual one that enables each of us to realize with great humility both our existential debt to God and all aspects of the universe, as well as our unique partnership with all of nature and our fellow human beings, who differ from each of us in so many ways, including our typological preferences.

In this book, I have attempted to further typology's contribution to a better understanding of human differences and how those differences touch every aspect of our lives. A poet, David Whyte, has recently published a book that has this same goal, particularly for business leaders: *The Heart Aroused: Poetry and the Preservation of the Soul in Corporate America.*[43] Whyte's first words are:

> The *Heart Aroused* attempts to keep what is tried and true, good and efficient, at the center of our present work life, while opening ourselves to a mature appreciation of the hidden and often dangerous inner seas where our passions

and our creativity lie waiting . . . like Tolkien's character
Gollum, in dark and subterranean caves.[44]

The poet gives his version of the ESTJ biases we have been
discussing when he writes: "Modern business life arises from a love of
the upper world, for material products, of order and organization."[45]
Succinctly showing the positives and limitations of the ESTJ mind, he
continues:

> Work has to do with cornering and controlling conscious
> life. It attempts concrete goals. It loves the linear and the
> defined. But the soul finds its existence through a loss of
> control to those powers greater than human experience.[46]

These insights into the need for change must be linked to a
pragmatic philosophy of societal organization which can foster the
climate needed for such a change. Such a practical understanding of
societal organizations would be applicable in religion, industry,
education, and government, and it would need to resonate with
typology's contributions to both individual differences, as well as
organizational development. Surprisingly, one such pragmatic philosophy that fits this description is already well known for its extraordinary successes. I believe the System of Profound Knowledge as
conceived by William Edwards Deming is one that is also in tune with
the thesis of this entire book.

TYPES' ARCHETYPES IN THE ORGANIZATIONAL SYSTEM
OF WILLIAM EDWARDS DEMING

Deming's History. William Edwards Deming has had a quiet, yet
earth-shaking impact on our world culture by virtue of his organizational system, which, when it has been taken seriously in its depth
and breadth, has stimulated profound corporate changes.
Unfortunately, in many instances, Deming's philosophy has sometimes

been implemented in a shallow, superficial way by opportunistic business leaders, leaving corporations in charge and workers bitter and cynical.

Peter Scholtes and Mary Walton, among many others who have worked with Deming and who have written about his life and work, will be our secondary sources.[47] They represent a small number of teachers and practitioners who seek to increase the use of Deming's system by reporting his successes and by communicating his insights, beginning with his work in Japan. After World War II, the Japanese industry was in total shambles. When General MacArthur needed radios for the country so he could communicate with the people, the American systems analysts adapted MacArthur's attitude that, rather than vengeance and retribution, Americans needed to help the Japanese rebuild their economy. These analysts recommended bringing in a quality control expert, William Edwards Deming.[48]

During the war, Deming had developed a quality control science that he taught to 35,000 engineers and technicians in the U.S. war industries, but, because he had not taught top managers, his ideas were abandoned after the war because of America's overall euphoria. Japan, however, was starting literally from new foundations in 1950. Deming taught top managers as well as technicians many principles: the market place is global; the customer is all-important; quality is determined by enlightened management leadership; production is a system, a chain reaction; and a nation, such as Japan, is a system.[49] Most important, he taught that total worker participation leads to lower costs, increased customer satisfaction and new business. We will explore the relationship of these principles to typology.

Deming made such an impact on Japanese society that one year later, in 1951, the Japanese engineering society established the Deming Prize, which today is a coveted award in Japanese industry. In 1960, he was awarded the Emperor's Medal for making possible Japan's worldwide industrial success. However, it was not until 1980, after an

NBC series of interviews with Deming, that American industrial leaders finally took notice of this man, who was then eighty years old.

Deming was born on October 14, 1900, and died in December 1993 at the age of ninety-three. In typological terms he must have been an ENTJ, one who, in Lowen's terms, focuses on structure and the underlying form in a complex system, and who sees our human interdependence in large configurational pictures. In tune with this makeup, the NT Creative Scientist, he studied undergraduate mathematics, engineering, and physics, and earned a Ph.D. in physics from Yale University. He mastered the science and use of statistical control after he encountered the pioneering work of Walter A. Shewhar.

Deming's other important area of conscious development fit well with his auxiliary coupling in the NF/C Creative Artist and Lover quadrant, wherein one "sops up experience like a sponge" and one's "primary modes are emotional and spiritual."[50] Early on and through-out his life, following his mother's love for music, he played musical instruments, sang in college choirs, composed liturgical music, strug-gled to find a meaningful career, and believed in the fundamental goodness of people.[51] These NF qualities allowed him to love the language and culture of the Japanese people.[52]

Deming was clearly a right-brain person, but his mind and heart also extended strongly into the SF/B Parental Moralist realm. When he worked in Western Electric's Hawthorne plant, he was appalled by the sweatshop conditions and piecework pay that he called "man's lowest degradation."[53] In his work in Japan he was deeply touched by the suffering of the Japanese people, especially the children, after the war.

Deming also developed an ST Warrior's productive ardor, and a passionate single-mindedness about his quality system's pragmatics and its crucial value for mankind. In his latter years, he had to be helped to a podium, but, once there, he could lecture for hours. He never gave up hope that he would influence American industry. In his

1980 television appearance, he decried American industry's lack of determination, insight, and solid goals.[54] Once, when faced with corporate resistance in Philadelphia, he responded with a statement characteristic of his belief in America and of his passion for his work:

> "You say you can't do it?" he thundered at the half-awake executives. . . . "Can't hold up against the Japanese? Such nonsense. You mean Americans can't do it? I don't believe that."[55]

Deming's Philosophy. I first read of Deming's theory of organizations in an article written by Peter Scholtes entitled, "Communities as Systems."[56] Scholtes holds that it is specifically a lack of understanding of community as system that has been "a major inhibitor of the quality movement."[57] When Scholtes wrote about Deming's System of Profound Knowledge, his "final intellectual legacy," consisting of "four important disciplines and areas of insight and the interaction and interdependence between them," I recognized their correspondence to typology's four directional archetypes (see figure 12.2, page 530).

Here is Deming's four-fold corporate mandala overlaid with Jung's congruent four typological areas of the Soul's Compass. Deming's system meshes so perfectly with Jungian typological psychology that it might well be an extension of the typological compass into organizational development. Deming's vision is dominated by a clear sense of the organizational whole, while Jung's general psychology, and typology in particular, is dominated by a clear sense of the Self or Soul as whole. The Soul, in turn, using Deming's terminology, can be described quite accurately as a potential holistic system of profound knowledge. In Deming's terms, the consciousness of this whole occurs first experientially and subliminally as the discipline of "understanding psychology and human behavior," which translates into the NF Lover or Creative Artist's awareness, the hidden psychic place where the individual and the institution begin to realize their identity. This

Deming's System of Profound Knowledge
(with the Types and Couplings Added in Parentheses)

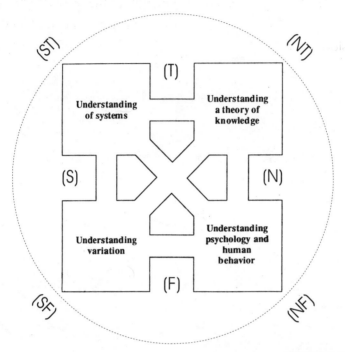

FIGURE 12.2

consciousness is applied and systematized in depth under Deming's discipline "Understanding of a theory of knowledge" and in typology's Compass as the NT Magician or Creative Scientist. It is pragmatically applied as the discipline "Understanding of systems" and as the ST Warrior or Structural, and is monitored by management in the Deming discipline "Understanding variation" and in the SF King/Queen or Moralist.

The NT Theoretical Discipline. Since Deming is a dominant NT Creative Scientist, we begin our consideration of his organizational philosophy with his theoretical vision found in the discipline "Understanding of a theory of knowledge." As a typical Magician,

Deming is "a knower and the master of technology . . . the 'ritual elder' who guides the processes of transformation both within and without."[58] Accordingly, Deming's presentation of the theory begins with the statement "The prevailing style of management must undergo transformation."[59] The "prevailing style" since the 1840s has been the so-called train wreck philosophy of management, developed appropriately by a military officer after a joint government/railroad inquiry into a disastrous train wreck. Its ESTJ beliefs and structures are represented in the typical organizational chart that most of us have seen and worked under. It favors hierarchy, strict authority, clearly defined parts, information flowing from top to bottom, and, overall, "management by results."[60] In contrast, Deming's system is circular, with the four disciplines feeding one another. In his typical flow chart, Deming indicates that feedback for both quality of product and worker life must occur in every phase of the process—from suppliers to key phases of production, to customer reaction, to research, design, and redesign, and to further feedback.[61] The function of management, unlike in the train wreck theory, is to be primarily responsible for the entire system and to maximize communication through participative management and worker teams, all of whom keep in mind the organization as a whole. This is an eminently NT holistic theory.

The basis for this systemic transformation is contained in a puzzling statement: "a system cannot understand itself," so it "requires a view from the outside."[62] What does Deming mean by this "outside"? He means "the first step is the transformation of the individual," who thereby "will perceive new meaning to his life, to events, to numbers, to interactions between people."[63] This conversion occurs personally but is also stimulated through the inspired capacity of management and the entire system to awaken "the intrinsic motivation" in each worker.[64] This fulfilling motivation is an inborn birthright of each person that is "outside" any system, and becomes the ultimate "lens," whereby any organization can be understood and evaluated.[65] Clearly,

Deming's theory is based on his version of depth psychology, which for him means a total respect for every person. Deming, a master of technological quality, was also a master of human quality. We will return to this idea under "The Discipline of Psychology."

The ST Systems Discipline. Deming's next organizational area, "Understanding of *systems*," matches typology's ST Structural realm and Herrmann's A Quadrant. In much of this chapter we have been discussing the societal and personal damages that ensue when this ST aspect is isolated and inflated. Its one-sided attitude looks only at a system's parts, is autocratic rather than cooperative, and is suspicious of psychological ideas. However, in Deming's theory, the ST Structural and Warrior archetype in each of us and in the system occupies a proper place in dignity and value, spelled out in the first of Deming's famous fourteen points for management: "Create constancy of purpose toward improvement of product and service, with the aim to become competitive, to stay in business and to provide jobs."[66] This first objective captures the Warrior's persistence and effort that produces excellence, completes tasks, strives for quality development, and is commited to teamwork. Clearly this is a transformed Warrior who has integrated the King/Queen, the Lover, and the Magician, for Deming says of the Warrior that once intrinsic motivation is awakened, the following changes occur:

> In place of competition for high rating, high grades, to be Number One, there will be cooperation on problems of common interest between peoples, divisions, companies, competitors, governments, countries.[67]

If the reader thinks that this would be an extraordinary transformation of our one-sided ESTJ society, note that Deming also condemns many common business practices to the extent that they duck "the responsibility of management":

automation, new machinery, more computers, gadgets, hard work, best efforts, merit system: annual appraisal; make everybody accountable; (MBO) management by objectives; MBR (management by results); rank people . . . teams . . . divisions, salesmen; reward them at the top, punish them at the bottom; more SQC (statistical quality control); more inspection; establish an office of quality; appoint someone as Vice President in Charge of Quality; incentive pay; work standards (quotas, time standards); zero defects; meet specifications; motivate people.[68]

Deming develops his rationale for modifying these practices in eight out of his fourteen points for management. Anyone who has functioned as a manager might understandably balk at a system which eliminates evaluative measures of individual performances and denigrates new machinery and computers. However, Deming's system does not reject such practices outright; most of them might yet be viable in his philosophy. They will be of little value, unless the system as a whole is sound, involves everyone and is properly taught. In Deming's philosophy, technology is viable only when subordinated to the valuing of people and quality of production. His system assumes that, rather than stimulating performance, fear tactics—such as ranking people and competitive demands by themselves when isolated from teamwork and a holistic view of an organization—only destroy creativity and the motivation intrinsic to it. Such tactics fit perfectly an ESTJ cultural pathology. Deming's system, on the other hand, is grounded in the NF Lover's valuing of each individual and the NT's embracing of a holistic, interactive organization.

In Erikson's terms, Deming's system of profound knowledge translates on a personal level into an inner sense of identity and self-worth, and at the same time a realization that all human beings even at work are "my kind." For both Jung and Erikson, it is the awakened individual who, in his inner work, in his inner dialogue with his Soul, both knows his own worth and is in harmony with the needs of his society.

In Deming's system, therefore, top managers must inspire all other workers to value both themselves and the community of workers.

The SF Leadership Discipline. We turn now to the third of the Deming System's four disciplines, "Understanding *variation.*" Within the type compass, this discipline fits into the SF Moralist's challenge to act justly. Herrmann's view of this B quadrant is congruent with Deming's quality control objectives, in which the manager finds "overlooked flaws" and maintains "a standard of consistency,"[69] but with the imperative Deming adds that the manager first seek to correct the system before correcting units or individuals. The manager attends to two kinds of variations from the productive norm: common causes based on faults in the system itself that can be corrected; and special causes, those outside of the system that usually cannot be corrected. An example of a common cause of accidents on a highway might be an unintelligible road sign.[70] The quality of the sign can be improved. A special cause of an accident would be a patch of ice. Scholtes gives examples of common causes that one might experience at any given moment: "background noise or activity, your own state of mind or health, the condition of the material you are reading, etc.," all usually predictable. Lightning striking a tree and distracting one's reading would be an example of a special cause.[71] Scholtes continues:

> Most variation in our organization is common cause variation built right into the system. But it is a common though misguided managerial reflex to regard anything that goes wrong as a special cause attributable to some persons. . . . If the problem results from common cause variation—and most do—then getting rid of the problem will involve changing the system, process or method of work. If the problem derives from a special cause of variation, then the manager must . . . eliminate that problem at its point of origin.[72]

The manager, archetypally the King or Queen, thereby becomes the moral exemplar who is not afraid to assume the greatest responsibility for correcting errors by changing the system rather than cursing the workers. In such a corporate atmosphere, blaming is minimal, morale is high, and quality work in production and in relationships is maximized.

The manager who blames others and does not assume primary responsibility for the entire system becomes a shadow leader, a destructive parent in any organization. Deming's system, on the other hand, seeks to value each individual and to include every individual in viable teamwork.[73] Deming explains this parental and leadership view:

> A manager of people needs to understand that all people are different. This is not ranking people. He needs to understand that the performance of anyone is governed largely by the system that he works in, the responsibility of management. A psychology that possesses even a crude understanding of variation . . . could no longer participate in refinement of a plan for ranking people.[74]

All can applaud this outlook—but is this an idealistic, far-fetched way of looking at corporate life? At first glance, it seems so, particularly in an ST Warrior culture's assumption that "good guys finish last." Yet it worked so well in Japan under Deming's influence that it transformed entire industries into producers of quality products long unsurpassed by any other nation. The collapse of Japanese economics in the 1990s was in no way due to the Deming method, but to rigid governmental influences on industries. Peter Scholtes believes that Deming's vision can extend also to government, school, and church, and that corporations in any country can become centers of lifetime learning. He believes, too, that managers must see themselves as experimenters who lead learning, not dictators who impose control.[75]

Since 1980, a few American companies have taken the Deming

vision seriously. One of these has been the Ford Motor Company under the leadership of its CEO Donald Petersen, who has written about his work with Deming.[76] Petersen immediately resonated with Deming's message, especially the "emphasis he placed on the importance of people" and the need for a total systems approach. Petersen also recognized the importance of the top managers' affirmation of production segments and being as present as possible in such places. In his view, top managers show "a commitment to the employee involvement process," so as to slowly but relentlessly develop a quality-oriented and participatory culture in the company, overcoming resistance posed by ingrained corporate habits. Whenever possible, he saw it as his role "to praise people, stressing their importance and calling attention to success stories."[77] At the end of his book, Petersen summarizes his experience and expresses his hope:

> In many, many cases, changing to a cooperative culture just takes time. In fact, the ultimate transformation from a top down or autocratic organization to a team-driven dynamo will no doubt be accomplished over several generations of management. I'm hopeful that the young people are now getting comfortable with teamwork and won't dream of doing things any other way as they become the executives of their respective companies.[78]

A large portion of Petersen's efforts at Ford were devoted to teamwork, participative management, and the relentless pursuit of quality in product and environment. As a consequence, Ford's achievement in the 1980s was considered one of the most significant in twentieth-century industry, and earned Petersen the Arbuckle Award from Stanford's Graduate School of Business. Petersen's own vision in valuing his personnel above his products provides a natural lead into the last of the four aspects in Deming's system, "Understanding *Psychology* and Human Behavior." While Deming asserts that each of us is born with intrinsic motivation, he also recognizes that there can be enormous resistance to his method because of entrenched corporate habits characteristic of an ESTJ pathology. Deming calls these aspects "forces of destruction" (see figure 12.3).

We easily recognize these forces as characteristics of the ESTJ style of life, beginning with the "forced distribution of grades in school" to "competition between people, groups, divisions," and "numerical goals without a method." Deming does not indict these practices as

Deming's Diagram of the Forces of Destruction

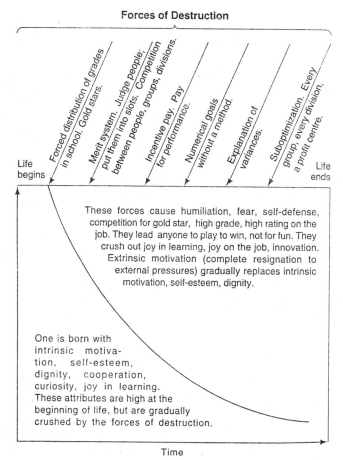

FIGURE 12.3

destructive in themselves, or assert that all grading and numerical goals should be eliminated. If he did, then he would be as one-sided as the pathological ESTJ society. Instead, Deming does say that numerical parameters within a quality control spectrum are necessary, but always within a system where team cooperation and a holistic view of the entire organization dominate. Above all, the pure numerically based and competitive forces of destruction that "rob people and the nation of innovation and applied science" should be eliminated and replaced with a "management that will restore the power of the individual." In Deming's view, the power of the individual is present at birth in each person as "intrinsic motivation, self-esteem, dignity, cooperation, curiosity, joy in learning," all of which can be reawakened by an enlightened management.[79]

The NF Psychological Discipline. We turn now to Deming's final discipline, "understanding psychology and human behavior." Here is the NF/Creative Artist, with which each of us is innately endowed, the "Self Concept" that Loomis saw as the beginning and end of the Medicine Wheel's wise circle of life. Here is Moore and Gillette's Lover Child who knows instinctively at birth that the first law of existence is love of self, the self-fullness of the golden rule that says "Love your neighbor as your *self*." (Don Petersen realized that the Deming system was a pragmatic method for realizing the golden rule, which, practically speaking, means actualizing the full potential of every person in any organization.) As such, Deming is a consummate advocate of individual development as the basis of a successful organization. Further, Deming teaches that awakening each individual can only happen if there is a holistic view of the organization toward which each individual contributes, just as Jung holds that inner development is impossible without an inborn sense of belonging to a community of all humans and all beings. The transformation of individuals and entire organizations must occur in an interdependent and mutual fashion.

We can understand this transformation within a Jungian

psychological context, as illustrated in figure 12.4. We hope this enables us to see Deming's methodology in a larger and deeper perspective.

Deming's System in the Context of the Psyche

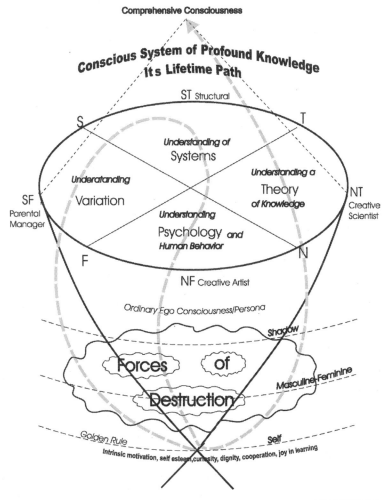

FIGURE 12.4

What Deming calls his system of profound knowledge is implied in Jung's description of the Self, with its psychic pool from which we each uniquely draw. The core of profound knowledge is intrinsic motivation, out of which Deming's system, with its four disciplines, is born into consciousness. Jungian psychology speaks of this core as the innate urge toward individuation, toward becoming all that we potentially can be. As analysts, we call this center the Self, the creative potential in each of us, evidenced in our endlessly innovative metaphorical dream language and a general human inventiveness. In contrast to the forces of destruction that "cause humiliation, fear, self-defense" and "lead anyone to play to win not for fun,"[80] the Self, as the source of the forces of creative constructions, empowers a person to realize from within, "intrinsic motivation, self esteem, curiosity, dignity, cooperation, and joy in learning."

A climate of fear amongst both children and adults destroys creative living on every level, from the family to the corporate life. Eliminating such a climate is a basic plank of Deming's corporate psychology, as stated in point eight of his fourteen points: "Drive out fear, so that everyone may work effectively for the company."[81] However, driving out fear is totally inimical to our pathologized ESTJ culture. The implied ground of this culture's type X authoritarian organization is fear.[82] Maintaining this fear is also the unconscious impetus for Howard's thesis in *The Death of Common Sense,* which describes the massive detailing of laws in public and corporate structures and the collective distrust that has resulted in a "nation of enemies." Further, in an era of corporate downsizing, workers every-where are afraid to take vacations, afraid to speak out, afraid to support unions, and afraid to challenge management, even when the quality of production and company morale might be at stake. In a family or in a society where fear dominates, intrinsic motivation and self-esteem are replaced by an enslaving outward behavior and a desolate sense of powerlessness. In a very substantial sense, all fourteen of Deming's points and all four disciplines making up his system of profound knowledge are designed to overcome fear and restore personal motivation and self-esteem in every person in an organization. With points thirteen and fourteen, "a vigorous program of education and self improvement" and putting "everybody in the company to work to accomplish transformation," the realization of these goals is given more structure and substance.

This vision of corporate life, therefore, demands a profound transformation in both management and workers. Deming begins chapter 4 in his 1994 book, "A System of Profound Knowledge," with the biblical statement: "And the chaff he will burn with unquenchable fire" (Luke 3.17). Deming, like a fiery prophet, is saying that this transformation is no less than a "metanoia" (a term he used in the first edition of this book), a radical inner spiritual change of heart and a painful tempering in the fire of change that overcomes and transforms the forces of destruction. As a result, a new creative energy and positive development is awakened in every individual in an organization.

The developmental line of our figure, which can be said to trace the potential life journey of each of us, as well as, in comparative ways, of any organization, begins with the Soul's inborn traits, proceeds through the SF parental influences, and moves into the ST Warrior's challenge to make it in the outside world. Because we all are afflicted in our early years to some degree with the "forces of destruction," both the SF Parental and the ST Warrior aspects of psyche take on some destructive influences manifesting themselves as fears and inhibitions in individuals and collectives. As a result, the plunge back to the Self's resources usually encounters enormously frightening resistances along the way. Deming's vision, therefore, may be seen as a demanding societal midlife crisis, a collective dark night of the Soul, in which the awakening of all the qualities of the Self, beginning with intrinsic motivation and self-esteem, are slowly and painfully realized in both individual and corporate transformation. It is for this reason that the line of development, the life's journey for each of us, must usually go through the NF's Lover quadrant, with its initial foreboding feelings and emotional darkness, which are also required for creative change in Deming's psychological consciousness. Only then does our path of consciousness, first experienced as a transformation to what is essentially human and spiritual, emerge, like Deming's path, into the NT realm as a spiritual, yet pragmatic, holistic system of organizational life. Deming's method implies that spirituality is practical and efficacious in the workplace. One's new life meaning extends, according to Deming, "to interactions between people," leading to "transformations of the organizations that he belongs to."[83] Management and all employees need to learn "the psychology of individuals, the psychology of a group, the psychology of society and the psychology of change."[84] Individual and corporate consciousness are inseparable in the Deming vision.

The psychology of change is the overarching challenge here, given our rigid ESTJ culture that so fears change. Deming's system is revolutionary, demanding the most acute revitalizing, because he restores "the individual . . . in the complexities of interaction with the rest of the world" in order to "release the power of human resource contained in intrinsic motivation," so that in a "place of competition . . . there will be cooperation on problems of common interest between people, divisions, companies, competitors, governments, countries."[85] Within it all, his vision is identical to the Jungian vision that we have pursued in this entire book: "management of people needs to understand that all people are different," which is "not ranking people." In addition, Jung's typology does not stereotype individuals, but sees each person as discovering and living his or her innate type preference as the basis for both developing and understanding other type preferences and for uniquely contributing to a team and to society.

We know that in the real world, this remarkable organizational system, so in tune with the wisdom tradition of humankind, has run into enormous resistance, given our ancient masculine propensity to value competition over cooperation and our general ESTJ attitudes. It is inevitable that some companies would try elements of Deming's system but fail to really internalize the necessary changes that value the uniqueness and inborn capacities of individuals and the related hunger for community and teamwork. The result is cynicism and the perception of Deming's system as ineffective, especially in a cultural climate that values downsizing, where employees begin to see every company action as a ruse. Here is an example from a man who was downsized:

> At the very least, the short term vision of today's corporate chieftains is creating a generation of people who will never again view the latest company campaign as anything more than a ruse to boost short-term bottom-line performance. "Teamwork," "Empowerment," "Total Quality Control"—I used to spout these out with the best of them. No more. Even if I could believe them, I know no one else would. Five years ago, I thought Deming could be the voice of the corporate world. Now I know it is really Dilbert.[86]

The end goal of both the Deming system and Jung's psychology is transformation and individuation. The book Jung wrote, which resulted in his split from Freud, is now entitled *Symbols of Transformation,* and every practitioner in depth psychology knows that the transformation of both inner images and emotionally grounded attitudes is indispensable for wholeness and spiritual health. Deming has demonstrated that when the goal of an organization agrees with that of depth psychology—that is, the recovery of an individual's motivation and self-esteem—then both individual and corporate health and success follow. I suggest also that any work an individual does to transform negative inner images contained in memories and dreams and symbolizing his or her and society's tyrannical behaviors can help both the individual and the corporation change. For example, earlier I discussed the dream of the woman whose father had abandoned her as a seven-year-old. The rage she felt against him and most others with whom she disagreed haunted her entire private and business life, filling her with explosive and chaotic emotions and dreams of bombs and exploding airplanes. The following dream contained the potential seeds of a transformation:

> I am holding a live bomb that someone has handed me. This time I do not run or drop it. I simply hold it, even though I am afraid. Suddenly it changes into a beautiful piggy bank with money in it. I am puzzled by, yet enjoy this change.

The image and attitude of anger at patriarchal tyranny had slowly begun to change. This change accounted for her dream ego's ability to hold the bomb. In turn, its transformation followed because she did not panic. The piggy bank and the money symbolize respectively creative and practical gains that emerged from her sense of inner identity and self-love. Though she suffered many other inner and outer challenges, she began to feel more in harmony both with her immediate family, and with society in general.

SUMMARY

We are born with many gifts, one of which is our types. Articulated by Jung and lovingly and intelligently researched by Isabel Briggs Myers, each type brings special gifts to fruition in transforming our political, religious, and societal life in the service of all mankind. We have seen, however, to what extent we humans, both societally and individually, resist becoming who we really are and also honoring the authentic typological identity of others. The spiritual implication of this work with human differences, both as to its difficulties and its possibilities, is such that I want to finish with a Pauline quote, both because Deming valued it and because St. Paul, its creator, is an appropriate figure for concluding this book. Paul was born of a Jewish family living in the Roman city of Tarsus. Like his father, Paul was both a Roman citizen and a member of the strict Jewish sect called the Pharisees. He acknowledges that he was a fanatical partisan of the strict observance of the Law and the traditions of the fathers.[87] He was a contemporary Warriorlike representative of an ESTJ autocratic patriarchal view, which despised and feared the nonorthodox but loving spiritual message of Jesus. As Jung puts it, Paul "resented the Christ-complex he could not acknowledge in himself and persecuted the Christians as its representatives."[88] The "Christ-complex" is for Jung another name for the Self, which is a source of our personal identity as well as our social connectedness, and it has many other religious and philosophical names. When Paul was struck down on the road to Damascus by a vision of Christ, who asked "Why do you persecute me?" (Acts, 9.4), he realized that the "me" represented the Christian community. In typological terms, it represents every type function and attitude in the compass of the Soul and every type of person. In Deming's philosophy, it represents the unique potentials of every worker.

Paul's quotation below in turn represents for me how various people have enriched and illustrated for me the fundamentals of a Jungian psychology's spiritual core: Victor White, OP, who first introduced me to Jung through typology; those clients and students who have shared with me the hundreds of dreams and their life stories dealing with types and their archetypal mandala; the many works of Jungian and *MBTI* theorists and practitioners; Isabel Briggs Myers, who first gave archetypal structures to the four type couplings; Mary McCaulley's inspiring work and leadership in both type research and theory; the Osmond group's creative contributions to a coupling consciousness; Moore and Gillette, who provided the fruitful bridge between the type couplings and the four cultural and psychological archetypes; Ned Herrmann and Katherine Benziger, who made possible linking the four archetypes to a whole brain model; Walter Lowen, who through the four couplings established a connection between the sixteen *MBTI* types with the four stages of child development; Erik Erikson, who added much wise humanistic depths to those stages; Singer and Loomis, who perceived new visions to typology particularly through the Native American Medicine Wheel; Keirsey and Bates, who first described a quaternity of archetypes in typological circles; and finally William Edwards Deming, who through the four disciplines of his system of profound knowledge made possible a bridging of the type coupling mandala in each individual to the organizational and sociopolitical realm. Deming quotes the following Pauline passage after he writes: "St. Paul understood a system. Excerpts from 1 Corinthians 12:8":

> A body is not one single organ, but many.
> Suppose that the foot should say,
> "Because I am not a hand,
> I do not belong to the body,"
> it does belong to the body no less.
> Suppose that the ear were to say,
> "Because I am not an eye,
> I do not belong to the body,"
> it does still belong to the body.
> If the body were all eye,
> how could it hear?
> If the body were all ear,
> how could it smell?
> There are many different organs, but one body.
> The eye cannot say to the hand,
> "I do not need you."[89]

Myers would agree with Deming's use of Paul since she drew from a similar Pauline text in *Gifts Differing*, as we saw in chapter 10. In this complex and often violent world which we experience as a war both within and without, and an attainable new and potentially more peaceful world, we all need one another, especially because of our differences in and beyond the type mandala.

Notes

1. Bika Reed, *Rebel in The Soul: An Ancient Egyptian Dialogue Between a Man and His Destiny,* (Rochester VT: Inner Traditions International, 1978/1997), pp. 61–63. The original name of this poem was "A Man Tired of Life in Dispute with His Soul. . . . Some scholars have placed it in the 'Intermediate Period' between the Old and Middle Kingdom (2500–1991 B.C.), others later" (p. 9). This poem, in my view, is very much attuned to our present situation. The author agrees: "Today, in a world where highly developed intellect [read thinking function] is at war with basic social and human needs and where, simultaneously, young intuitive forces are searching for a new way, this initiatic [read initiatory] text is vital. . . . At the peak of its evolution, like the mature fruit, intellect has to face its inevitable transformation, to be able to perpetuate its seed, life itself" (p. 10).

2. Riane Eisler, *The Chalice and the Blade: Our History, Our Future* (Cambridge MA: Harper and Row, 1987). Eisler characterizes this culture as overtly masculine and describes its characteristics as completely in line with an overall ESTJ pathology. The first great civilization, the agricultural Neolithic, developed around 10,000 B.C., and lasted roughly until 3,500. "Its prevailing ideology was gynocentric, or woman-centered." In this atmosphere, "Both men and women—even sometimes as in Catal Huyuk [what is now modern Turkey], people of different racial stock—worked cooperatively for the common good. . . . Symbolized by the feminine Chalice or source of life, the generative, nurturing, and creative powers of nature [In the psyche, the feminine and creative Self]—not the powers to destroy—were . . . given highest values" (p. 43). Then came the invading nomads from the Asiatic and European north. *"The one thing they all had in common was a dominator model of social organization* (italics, author): a social system in which male dominance, male violence, and a general hierarchic and authoritarian social structure was the norm" (p. 45). "Gradually male dominance, warfare, and the enslavement of women and of gentler, more 'effeminate' men became the norm" (p. 48). Recall this chapter's first quotation from ancient Egypt, which includes "Gentleness is overthrown, violence rules all." These are ESTJ pathologized

characteristics found in all cultures, which I will develop in a next book, in contrast to the subject of that book, the INFP counterculture. The title will be *The Sensitive Soul.*

3. Noam Chomsky, *World Orders Old and New* (New York: Columbia University Press, 1994). The author writes about the ideas of Harold Lasswell, "one of the leading figures of modern political science," who began the study of propaganda as a way of keeping people in a democratic society, not controlled by force, in line. He hailed propaganda as this "new technique of control" of the general public, who are a threat to order because of the "ignorance and superstition [of] . . . the masses." As Lasswell explained in the *Encyclopedia of the Social Sciences,* we should not succumb to "democratic dogmatisms about men being the best judges of their own interests. . . . They are not; the best judges are the elite" (p. 85).

4. David Broder, "Millionaires' Club," in the *Chicago Tribune,* January 17, 1996, section 1, p. 19. Broder points out that, because of the cap on presidential contributions by individuals and because of the rising cost of campaigning, personally wealthy politicians are running more and more in both parties. Broder argues that we should get rid of the campaign limits. I say otherwise: do away with all individual contributions, do not allow any advertising of candidates, let contributions go to each party for sponsoring primary debates, and let the government sponsor all TV debates after the primaries for the presidential and congressional candidates.

Generally, our national elective process can be contrasted to those of other first world countries, whose candidates run short, low-cost campaigns in which significant issues are argued on government-paid television and in local assemblies, instead of our combination of multi-million-dollar advertising and limited substantive debates.

5. Kurt Anderson, "Big Mouths," in *Time* magazine, November 1, 1993. "Limbaugh is a more or less conventional pundit whose agenda is the standard public agenda. . . . He has real influence—'the power,' says Clinton White House consultant Paul Bengela, [and as we learned in the subsequent 1994 elections] 'to put something like Zoe Baird on the radar screen. . . .' Howard Stern also epitomizes a similar contemptuous attitude for those who are down, when he said: 'They didn't beat this idiot [Rodney King] enough.'" Anderson continues: "Stern . . . lurches from a convincing take on the New York City mayoral race . . . to leering consideration of Marla Maples' body"(p. 62). My worry is their constituency, who adore them and follow their viewpoints without debate. Limbaugh's legions even call themselves "ditto heads," indicating they support everything that Rush says. This frightening fact proved to be true in the 1992 national election. After the 2000 election, one wonders if we returned to this attitude.

6. Arianna Huffington, "Right has no room for compassion," in the *Chicago Sun Times,* February 3, 1999, p. 35. Huffington discusses the Republican congressional 24-member Renewal Alliance led by Senator Rick Santorum of Pennsylvania. The Alliance is taking seriously an attempt to honestly connect with the American electorate through a *"compassionate conservatism,"* long espoused by Don Eberly. Eberly, speaking to Huffington, said, "The great crying need today is to advance beyond the negative proposition of tearing government down to the positive proposition of building up strong communities and effective local charity." Both Eberly and Santorum were appalled at the negative reaction to the term compassionate conservatism by three Republican presidential candidates, Dan Quayle, Gary Bauer, and Lamar Alexander. Alexander considers the idea "Weasel Words" and "empty shells." Bauer considers the concept "Redundant" and "defensive." Quayle angrily told his staff to "never—EVER—utter the words 'compassionate conservative.'"

7. Garry Wills, "GOP's Breach of Contract," in the *Chicago Sun Times,* January 31, 1996, p. 35N, writes about the recent attempts in Washington to take from our future and so from children "such natural resources as clean air, clean water, safe machines, and national resources in the forests and parks and wetlands of this country."

8. Alex Kotlowitz, "It Takes a Village to Destroy a Child, " in the *New York Times* OP-ED, February 8, 1996, p. A1. The author discusses the case of two Chicago boys, ages 10 and 11, who dropped a five-year-old to his death from a high rise, and the signals that the older boy was giving to family, neighbors, and teachers that he was in serious emotional difficulty because of street violence he had encountered and his father's recent imprisonment. Now 13, he is in an adult prison.

The American child's agony continues. We all know of the Columbine affair that occurred in 1999. The most recent tragedy took place in San Diego where fifteen-year-old Andy Williams killed two school mates and wounded many more. The pattern may be typical: a child harassed and bullied by other children, ignored at home, use of dope and alcohol, his or her threats to kill unreported, and finally, the horrible explosion of gunfire. His story appeared in *Time,* March 19, 2001, p. 22, by Nancy Gibbs, entitled "It's only me," the poignant words he muttered when police captured him. Gibbs writes there: "Don't look for a pattern. . . . Is it the absence of parents, the presence of guns, the cruelty of the culture, the culture of cruelty?" This article is followed by the Williams story and then by a page called "Scorecard of Hatred," showing the many instances of foiled violence by youngsters "in the two years since Columbine" (p. 31). Another article follows called "The Legacy of Columbine." Bob Greene in the *Chicago Tribune* of March 11, 2001, section 1, p. 2, asks, "When will there be zero tolerance for bullying." Bullying is a Shadow Warrior characteristic that can begin at an early age.

9. Even major Church organizations get caught up in this same secular mentality, which plays down, for example, the significance of South and Central America's Liberation Theologians' attempts to make the needs of the poor the primary agenda of Christianity. See here Penny Lernoux, *Cry of the People* (New York: Penguin Books, 1990).

10. Philip K. Howard, *The Death of Common Sense: How Law Is Suffocating America* (New York: Random House, 1994). John Guare writes in the jacket that this book "is a lethal cannonball of a book. It makes me understand why so much of today's government just doesn't make sense." Seventy percent of the American people felt the same way about the impeachment process and trial of President Clinton which occurred in 1998 and 1999. Clinton was wrong in his stupid actions and in his lying about those actions. However, his sin was private, the one sin that can make fools of us all, the one sin that called forth from Jesus of Nazareth, "He who is without [this] sin, cast the first stone." However, an abstractly principled and concretely focused group of legislators pursued their mission with remarkable passion, narrow vision, and a total lack of compassion. Howard saw his views vindicated in this extraordinary national event.

11. Ibid., p. 29.

12. Ibid., p. 34.

13. Ibid., p. 16.

14. Ibid., p. 27.

15. Ibid., p. 28.

16. Ibid., p. 51.

17. Ibid., p. 21.

18. Ibid., p. 26.

19. Leslie Eaton, "Public Money Foots the Bill for 'Privatized' Foreign Aid," *New York Times,* Vol. CXLV, February 7, 1996, pp. A1, C1.

20. John Canham-Clyne, "Message to Congress: Cut Corporate Welfare," *Public Citizen,* July–August, 1995.

21. Chomsky, interviewed by David Barsamian, *Secrets, Lies, and Democracy* (Tuscon AZ: Odonian Press, 1994), pp. 19–20. Chomsky notes that even the conservative Wall Street Journal has stated that these practices have characterized the industrialization of third world countries, in which the average person barely profits, in contrast to a financial elite (pp. 19–20).

22. Eric J. Sly, "They Hate Government, but Love Those Subsidies," *New York Times,* Section A11, January 2, 1996. The writer adds that these Republicans, "while trying in many cases to shut off financing for land and water conservation, are trying to free up more taxpayer-owned resources for the benefit of oil, gas, mining, logging, agricultural, and development interests. See another article in this newspaper, "Grazing Bill to Give Ranchers Vast Control of Public Lands" in the New York Times, Section A1, July 21, 1995.

23. Kevin Phillips, *The Politics of the Rich and the Poor* (New York: Random House, 1990). "In 1986 the Joint Economic Committee released Federal Reserve Board findings, overstated at first and later modified, that the share of wealth held by the naively labeled 'super rich'—the top one half of one percent of U.S. households—had risen significantly in the 1980s after falling during the prior four decades. . . . America's top 420,000 households alone accounted for 26.9 percent of the nation's wealth. The top ten percent of households, meanwhile, controlled approximately 68 percent. Accumulation and concentration would be simultaneous hallmarks of the 1980s" (p. 11).

24. Phillips, *Arrogant Capital: Washington, Wall Street and the Frustration of American Politics* (Boston: Little, Brown, 1994). "The emergence of a rich and privileged capital city is part of a broader transition in America toward social and economic stratification, toward walled-in communities and hardened class structures, toward political, business and financial elites that bail each other out, toward an increasing loss of optimism. . . . As a corollary to the emergence of a fortress-like Washington unswayable by angry winds blowing in from Idaho or Long Island, the U.S. financial sector has also developed its own unprecedented size, power and uncontrollability" (p. xvi).

25. *The National Catholic Reporter,* March 17, 1995.

26. "U.S. Wealth Inequality Seen as Widest in Rich Nations," *New York Times,* April 17, 1995, pp. A1 and C4. For example, "the wealthiest 1 percent of American households—with a net worth of at least $2.3 million each—own nearly 40 per cent of the nation's wealth. By contrast, the wealthiest 1 percent of the British population owns about 18 percent of the wealth there."

27. Jill Smolowe, "And Throw Away the Key," part of the cover story in *Time,* February 7, 1994. The number of inmates in state and federal prisons went up by 180 percent from 1980 to 1993. In contrast to some other nations, our rate of incarceration per 100,000 in 1990–91 was 455, compared to South Africa's 311, Venezuela's 177, Canada's and China's 111, Australia's 79, Denmark's 71, Albania's 55, Ireland's 44, Japan's 42, and India's 34.

28. Phillip Weiss, "A Hoplophobe Among the Gunnies," in the *New York Times Magazine,* Section 8, September 11, 1994. A phobia against the govern-

ment seems to dominate great numbers of the NRA members. A representative statement in this regard is the following: "The agenda of this government is to increase the size of government and to put more and more of our lives under the control of government bureaucrats" (p. 70).

29. Richard Lacayo, "Lock Em Up," part of the cover story in *Time,* February 7, 1994. Prison populations are swelling also because of stupidly rigid drug laws, as reported in another article in this issue, by Jill Smolowe, "And Throw Away the Key." One woman was given $47.50 by a stranger to mail a package. She did not know it contained 232 grams of crack cocaine. Because of the rigidity of the law, a Federal judge was forced to impose a ten-year sentence (p. 55).

30. Hank Cellini, "Final Report: Safer Job Club," Safer Foundation Research paper, Chicago IL (1981–82).

31. Della De Lafuente, "Worker Health Care Cost up 5% in Area," *Chicago Sun Times,* January 30, 1996.

32. Howard Witt, "Quiet Revolution in Health Care," *Chicago Tribune,* October 29, 1995, p. A1.

33. Sydney M. Wolfe, ed., "Republicans Maul Medicare," *Health Letter,* Public Citizen Health Research Group, 1600 20th Street NW, Washington, DC, No. 9, 2000, p. 1. The article adds further that this HMO was spending 51 percent of its income on administration.

34. Ibid., p. 2. In the *Chicago Tribune* of February 14, 1996, the California Medical Association reported that the two biggest for-profit HMOs, PacifiCare and CaliforniaCare, spend in a range of 84 percent to 73 percent on patient care, whereas the "nonprofit HMO Kaiser Permanente spends 97 percent of its revenue on patient care" (section 1, p. 9).

35. Erik Larson, "The Soul of an HMO," *Time,* January 22, 1996, pp. 44–52.

36. Matthew Fox, *The Reinvention of Work: A New Vision of Livelihood for Our Time,* San Francisco: HarperCollins, 1994). Fox is the world leader in reeducating Christians and others of any faith, religious commitment, and humane philosophy in a Creation-centered theology and spirituality. He begins with the reality of existence and its unfolding in the 15 billion year evolutionary story. This is the great work of God; and within this context, all other work finds its meaning as a free commitment and a labor of love.

37. Chomsky, *World Orders Old and New* (New York: Columbia University Press, 1994). "'The major institutional factor that affected the U.S. wage structure is the decline of unions,' U.S. Labor Department chief economist

Lawrence Katz concludes. . . . In 1985, hourly pay in the United States was higher than the other G-7 countries. By 1992, it had fallen to below its wealthy competitors, apart from Britain." Then the author quotes the *Wall Street Journal* as noted in the text (p. 141).

38. A remarkable movie made in 1954, *Executive Suite,* dramatically describes this present situation. It depicts a corporate struggle for power between one man representing finance, efficiency, and the stockholders (played by Fredric March) and another representing the internal stability of the company, the welfare of the workers, and quality production and plant life (William Holden). This movie recognized the dominant values of corporations beholden to Wall Street, the seeds of which, at the dawn of this twenty-first century, have produced such failures as Enron and WorldCom.

39. Don L. Boroughs, with Monika Guttman in Los Angeles, Maria Mallory in Atlanta, Scott McMurry in Chicago, and David Fischer, *U. S. News and World Report,* January 22, 1996, p. 47. The article gives a diagram showing the share of wealth held by the top 1 percent of families. It was 32.4 percent in 1945 and it rose to 42 percent in 1992 (p. 52). The 2003 reported ratio of CEO salary to worker wage is now roughly 500 to 1.

40. Chomsky, *Order Old and New.* When the Wagner Act of 1935 accorded rights to workers "that had been won a half a century earlier in England and elsewhere . . . that victory for working people and for democracy sent a chill through the business community. The National Association of Manufacturers (NAM) warned that 'we are definitely heading for adversity.'" A corporate counteroffensive was quickly launched (pp. 84–85).

41. Brian Swimme and Thomas Berry, *The Universe Story: From the Primordial Flaring Forth to the Ecozoic Era, A Celebration of the Unfolding of the Cosmos* (San Francisco: HarperCollins, 1992). A brilliant achievement, showing that our 15-billion-year evolutionary story is both a scientific reality and a spiritual epiphany. But the authors show that we humans are also demonstrating a lethal demolishing of nature. For example, "We are extinguishing the rainforests, the most luxuriant life system of the entire planet, at the rate of one acre each second of each day. Each year we are destroying a rainforest area the size of Oklahoma" (p. 246).

42. For example, Matthew Fox, *The Coming of the Cosmic Christ* (San Francisco: Harper and Row, 1988), and Margaret J. Wheatley, *Leadership and the New Science* (San Francisco: Berrett-Koehler, 1992).

43. David Whyte, *The Heart Aroused: Poetry and the Preservation of the Soul in Corporate America* (New York: Currency Doubleday, 1994), p. 44. Marion Woodman, an outstanding Jungian analyst, points out on the jacket of the book

that corporate America is learning that losing one's Soul for the sake of corporate profits is not worth it. I agree that some executives have so concluded, but they have not yet significantly influenced our present ESTJ mentality.

44. Ibid., p. 3.

45. Ibid.

46. Ibid., p. 21.

47. Two persons who knew Deming personally, a collaborator and a journalist respectively, are the basis of this section: Peter R. Scholtes, in collaboration with Brian I. Joiner and others, *The Team Handbook* (Madison WI: Joiner Associates, 1988), which has already sold over 750,000 copies, and Peter R. Scholtes, *The Leader's Handbook* (New York: McGraw-Hill, 1998); and Mary Walton, *The Deming Management Method* (New York: Peragee Books, Putnam Publishing Group, 1986). For those who want to research Deming, check out World Wide Web sites dedicated to his work that provide extensive bibliographies.

48. Scholtes, *The Leader's Handbook,* pp. 5–6.

49. Ibid., pp. 6–7.

50. Ned Herrmann, *The Creative Brain* (Kingsport TN: Quebec or Printing Book Group, 1994), pp. 82–83.

51. Stories are told of Deming's love of animals. As a tribute to their father, which is also a testimony of his love for them, his two daughters, Diana Deming Cahill and Linda Deming Ratcliff, are now carrying on his legacy as directors of the W. Edwards Deming Institute in Washington, D.C. See W. Edwards Deming, *The New Economics for Industry, Government, Education* (Cambridge: Massachusetts Institute of Technology, Center for Advanced Engineering Study, 1994), foreword, ix.

52. Mary Walton, *The Deming Management Method,* p. 16.

53. Ibid., p.6.

54. Ibid., p.19.

55. Ibid., pp. 201–2.

56. Scholtes, "Communities as Systems," a mimeograph article published by Scholtes Seminars & Consulting in Madison, Wisconsin. See his figure 1 on p. 4, "Deming's system of profound knowledge." I received this article from Dr. Lawrence Quick, a professor in management at Aurora University, Aurora, Illinois, and a leading Deming scholar, at a time when I was asking: how do I

most meaningfully apply typology to organizational processes? This was for me a synchronistic event.

57. Ibid., p. 2.

58. Robert Moore and Douglas Gillette, *King, Warrior, Magician, Lover: Rediscovering the Archetypes of the Mature Masculine* (San Francisco: HarperSanFrancisco, 1990), p. 98.

59. Deming, *The New Economics*, p. 92.

60. Scholtes, *The Leader's Handbook*, p. 2-4.

61. Walton, *The Deming Management Method*, p. 28.

62. Deming, *The New Economics*, p. 92.

63. Ibid., p. 92.

64. Ibid., p. 123.

65. Ibid., p. 94.

66. Deming, *Out of the Crisis* (Cambridge: Massachusetts Institute of Technology, Center for Advanced Engineering Study, 1986, 20th printing, 1993), p. 23. Deming writes: "The 14 points apply anywhere, to small organizations as well as to large ones."

67. Deming, *The New Economics*, p. 123.

68. Ibid., p. 14.

69. Herrmann, *The Creative Brain*, p. 424.

70. Deming, *The New Economics*, pp. 184–85.

71. Scholtes, *The Leader's Handbook*, p. 28.

72. Scholtes, *The Leader's Handbook*, pp. 27–28.

73. Deming, *The New Economics*, p. 130.

74. Ibid., p. 94.

75, Scholtes, *The Leader's Handbook*, chapter 10.

76. Donald E. Petersen, with John Hillkiak, *A Better Idea: Redefining The Way America Works* (Boston: Houghton Mifflin, 1991). Don Petersen and I graduated from the same high school, Washington High, in Portland, Oregon. After the Second World War, we caught up with one another in 1947 at Stanford University's Graduate School of Business. Don's intellectual brilliance,

common sense, caring attitude, and personal integrity stood out so much in our classrooms, charged as they were with competitive intensity and youthful vigor, that all were certain he would be a top leader in industry. I had the privilege of singing for Don and Jody's wedding. Because of our different types and life stories, we went entirely different routes. Don and I meet now in our common interest in Deming and concern for our country.

77. Ibid., pp. 42–43.

78. Ibid., p. 247. Scholtes drives home this same idea when he writes: "In this book we are presenting what we consider to be a profoundly different and dramatically better approach to leadership. But the old way wasn't all that bad. This may explain why changing is so difficult for so many. There is not all that much wrong with the old way, except that 50 years ago a better way came along." Scholtes, *The Leader's Handbook,* p. 377. The old way is remarkably attuned to our now ancient patriarchal and ESTJ culture. A better ground for the new way is found in Jung's and Myers' immense type theory and practice.

Peterson gave expression to the old way and the difficulty of transformative changes when he addressed Ford's most senior executives on February 10, 1982, two years after introducing the Deming method: "you are the ones who are going to decide whether we are really successful in making a dramatic change in how we do business . . . *it can be very difficult to make significant changes,* especially when you have been in the habit of doing things differently for decades and especially when *the very success that brought you to the positions you now hold was rooted in doing some things, frankly, the wrong way* . . . that you were promoted for the wrong reasons a time or two. [Italics, Scholtes] . . . So I urge you to ask yourselves, do you really understand what we are trying to change." Scholtes, p. 378, quoting from W. W. Scherkenbach, *The Deming Route to Quality and Productivity* (Washington, D.C.: Ceepress Books, 1986).

79. Deming, *The New Economics,* p. 122.

80. Ibid., p. 122.

81. Deming, *Out of the Crisis,* p. 23. See also Thomas Petzinger, Jr. *The New Pioneers: The Men and Women Who are Transforming the Workplace and the Marketplace* (New York: Simon and Schuster, 1999). Petzinger, a journalist for over 20 years with the *Wall Street Journal,* is one of Deming's advocates in this twenty-first century. He notes Deming's "deeply religious belief in human potential," and that after World War II, "he was laughed out of every boardroom he entered" in this country. He then describes his famous success in Japan (pp. 38–39). Those who have avoided new fads, he continues, gained much by staying with Deming. For example, he cites the leadership of Mark Schmink of the Dana Corporation's Stockton, California, factory in inspiring not only technical research but also the cultural development of his workers. His workers

responded: "Worker teams met regularly to question every routine of the plant, right down to the sequencing of individual welds" (pp. 40–42). Petzinger also cites the example of Georg Bauer of Mercedes-Benz Credit Company (pp. 125–29). He told his bosses to let the company "grow from the bottom up," work with teams, and above all, "taking a page out of Deming's book, 'Drive out fear throughout the organization . . . so that everybody may work effectively and more productively for the company'" (p. 127). Result: "By 1998 the firm had swelled its assets to $23 billion" and "was ranked first in the industry for customer satisfaction by J. D. Powers & Associates" (p. 129).

82. D. McGregor, *The Human Side of Enterprise* (New York: McGraw-Hill, 1960, 25th anniversary edition, 1985). McGregor compared the old X autocratic, fear-driven, and "train-wreck" style of management with what he proposed as a type Y philosophy, which describes a democratic and participative style, while retaining a responsible top management.

83. Deming, *The New Economics*, pp. 92–93.

84. Ibid., p. 95.

85. Ibid., p. 123.

86. Tom Scott, one of a series of respondents in a composite article entitled "Downsizing: How It Feels to Be Fired" in the *New York Times*, March 17, 1996, p. E5, in response to a week-long series by that paper entitled "The Downsizing of America," March 3 through March 9, 1996. Dilbert is a weak, somewhat innocuous figure in corporate life in the comic strip of that name, but Scott Adams, Dilbert's creator, is a serious critic of a dehumanized corporate life.

The corrosive downsizing binge that our corporations have been on is in stark contrast to a typical "upsizing" that Deming reports in his 1994 book (p. 27): "In the United States the last ones to suffer are the people at the top. Dividends must not suffer. In Japan, the pecking order is the opposite. A company in Japan that runs into economic hardship takes these steps: 1. Cut the dividend. Maybe cut it out. 2. Reduce salaries and bonuses of top management. 3. Further reduction for top management. 4. Last of all, the rank and file are asked to help out. People who do not need to work may take a furlough. People who can take early retirement may do so, now. 5. Finally, if necessary, a cut in pay for those that stay, but no one loses a job" (from Tsurumi Yoshi, *The Dial*, September 1981).

87. Alexander Jones, general editor, *The Jerusalem Bible* (Garden City NY: Doubleday, 1966), Acts 22:3–5. Paul himself writes there, "I studied under Gamaliel and was taught the exact observance of the Law of our ancestors . . . I even persecuted this Way [the early Christians] to the death, and sent women as well as men to prison in chains."

88. C. G. Jung, "The Psychological Foundations for the Belief in Spirits," *CW,* vol. 8, *The Structure and Dynamics of the Psyche* (Princeton NJ: Princeton University Press, 1960), para. 584.

89. Deming, *The New Economics,* p. 65.

BIBLIOGRAPHY

Anderson, K. (1993, November 1). Big mouths. *Time.*

Barnaby, K. and D'Acierno, P. (1990). *C. G. Jung and the humanities: Towards a hermeneutics of culture.* Princeton, NJ: Princeton University Press.

Beebe, M. D. J. (1992). *Transference countertransference* (N. Schwartz-Salant and M. Stein, Eds.). Wilmette, IL: Chiron Publications.

Benesh, J. (1996). March meeting: Type and power. *Chapter News,* 2–3.

Benziger, K. (1995). *Falsification of type: Its Jungian and physiological foundations and mental, emotional, and physiological costs.* Rockwall, TX: KBA Publishing.

Benziger, K. and Sohn, A. (1993). *The art of using your whole brain.* Rockwall, TX: KBA Publishing.

Berens, L. V., Giovannoni, L. C., and Cooper, S. A. (1990). *Introduction to temperament* (4th ed.). Huntington Beach, CA: Telos Publications.

Bernstein, J. S. (1989). *Power politics: The psychology of Soviet-American partnership.* Boston and Shaftesbury, England: Shambhala Publications.

Bloland, S. E. (1999, November). Fame and the power and cost of fantasy. *The Atlanta Monthly.*

Bolen, J. (1984). *Goddesses in every woman.* New York: Harper and Row.

Bolen, J. (1984). *Gods in every man.* New York: Harper and Row.

Boroughs, D. L., Guttman, M., Mallory, M., and McMurry, S. (1996, January 22). *U.S. News and World Report,* 47, 52.

Briggs, J. and Peat, F. D. (1989). *Turbulent mirror.* New York: Harper and Row.

Broder, D. (1996, January 17). Millionaires' club. *Chicago Tribune,* p. 119.

Campbell, S. (1995). Using type across cultures. *Bulletin of Psychological Type,* 18.3, 14–17.

Canhom-Cline, J. (1995, July/August). Message to Congress: Cut corporate welfare. *Public Citizen.*

Chia, M. (1980). *Transform stress into vitality, the inner smile and the six healing sounds.* Huntington, NY: Healing Tao Books.

Chia, M. (1983). *Awakening healing energies through the Tao.* Santa Fe, NM: Aurora Press.

Chia, M. (1985). *Taoist ways to transform stress into vitality, the inner smile-six healing sounds.* Huntington, NY: Healing Tao Books.

Chomsky, N. (1994). *Secrets, lies, and democracy.* Tuscon, AZ: Odossian Press.

Chomsky, N. (1994). *World orders old and new.* New York: Columbia University Press.

Choquette, S. (1999). *The wise child: A spiritual guide to nourishing your child's intuition.* New York: Rivers Press.

DeLafuente, D. (1995, January 30). Worker health care cost up 5% in area. *Chicago Sun Times.*

Deming, W. E. (1986). *Out of the crisis.* Cambridge, MA: Massachusetts Institute of Technology Center for Advanced Engineering Study.

Deming, W. E. (1994). *The new economics: For industry, government, education.* Cambridge, MA: Massachusetts Institute of Technology Center for Advanced Engineering Study.

Detloff, W. (1972). Psychological types: Fifty years after. *Psychological Perspectives,* 3.1.

Dickinson, E. (1959). *Selected poems and letters of Emily Dickinson.* New York: Doubleday Anchor Books.

Dieckmann, H. (1991). *Methods in analytical psychology.* Wilmette, IL: Chiron Publications.

Eaton, L. (1996, February 7). Public money foots the bill for privatized foreign aid. *The New York Times,* pp. A1, C1.

Eisendrath, P. Y. and Dawson, T. (1997). *The Cambridge companion to Jung.* New York: Cambridge University Press.

Eisler, R. (1987). *The chalice and the blade.* San Francisco: Harper and Row.

Eisler, R. (1995). *Sacred pleasure.* New York: HarperSanFrancisco.

El Saffar, R. A. (1994). *Rapture encaged: The suppression of the feminine in western culture.* New York and London: Rutledge.

Elkind, D. (1981). *The hurried child: Growing up too fast, too soon.* Reading, MA: Addison Westley.

Erikson, E. (1963). *Childhood and society* (Rev. ed.). New York: W.W. Norton.

Final report: Safer job club. (1981–1982). *Chicago Safer Foundation Research Paper.*

Fitzerald, R. (1999). *Journal of Psychological Type,* 51, 34–39.

Flawed trials lead to death. (2000, June 11). *Chicago Tribune,* pp. 116–117.

Fox, M. (1988). *The coming of the cosmic Christ.* San Francisco: Harper and Row.

Fox, M. (1994). *The reinvention of work: A new vision of livelihood for our time.* San Francisco: Harper Collins.

Frame, J. (1989). *Janet Frame: An autobiography.* New York: Braziller.

Friedman, M. and Rosenman, R. H. (1974). *Type A behavior and your heart.* Greenwich, CT: Fawcett Crest.

Gibbs, N. (2001, March 19). It's only me. *Time,* 22.

Gleick, J. (1987). *Chaos: Making a new science.* New York: Viking Penguin.

Goldberg, N. (1986). *Writing down the bones.* Boston: Shambhala.

Green, B. (2001, March 11). When will there be zero tolerence for bullying? *Chicago Tribune,* p. 12.

Green, K. (1998). A modest proposal: The type circle. *Bulletin of Psychological Type,* 21.3, 18.

Green, T. (1998). Poison and panacea: The group shadow in Jungian training. *The Congress of the IAAP.*

Guzie, T. and Guzie, N. M. (1986). *About men and women: How your "great story" shapes your destiny.* New York: Paulist Press.

Hammer, A. and Mitchell, W. D. (1996). The distribution of MBTI types in the U.S. by gender and ethnic group. *Journal of Psychological Type,* 37, 2.

Hartmann, G. V. Typology's distractions and opposites' attractions. *Spring,* 47.

Herrmann, N. (1994). *The creative brain.* Kingsport, TN: Quebecor Printing Book Group.

Hill, G. (1992). *Masculine and feminine: The natural flow of opposites in the psyche.* Boston and London, England: Shambhala.

Hillman, J. (1980/1990). *Egalitarian typologies versus the perception of the unique.* Dallas: Spring Publications.

Howard, P. K. (1994). *The death of common sense: How law is suffocating America.* New York: Random House.

Hoxworth, L. A. (1997). A different way to introduce type. *Bulletin of Psychological Type, 20.2*, 40–41.

Hudson, J. R. (1998). *Natural spirituality: Recovering the wisdom tradition in Christianity.* Danielsville, GA: JRH Publications.

Huffington, A. (1999, February 3). Right has no room for compassion. *Chicago Sun-Times*, p. 35.

Jung, C. G. (1921/1976). *Psychological types.* Princeton, NJ: Princeton University Press.

Jung, C. G. (1953/1956). *Two essays on analytical psychology* (Vol. 7). Princeton, NJ: Princeton University Press.

Jung, C. G. (1953/1968). *Individual dream symbolisms in relation to alchemy: Psychology and alchemy.* Princeton, NJ: Princeton University Press.

Jung, C. G. (1953/1975). *C. G. Jung letters* (Vol. 2). Princeton, NJ: Princeton University Press.

Jung, C. G. (1956). *Symbols of transformation.* (Vol. 5). Princeton, NJ: Princeton University Press.

Jung, C. G. (1958/1969). *Psychology and religion, west and east* (Vol. 11). Princeton, NJ: Princeton University Press.

Jung, C. G. (1959). *Aion.* Princeton, NJ: Princeton University Press.

Jung, C. G. (1959). *The archetypes and the collective unconscious* (Vol. 9). Princeton, NJ: Princeton University Press.

Jung, C. G. (1960). On the nature of the psyche. In *The structure and dynamics of the psyche* (Vol. 8). Princeton, NJ: Princeton University Press.

Jung, C. G. (1960). *Synchronicity: An acausal connecting principle: The structure and dynamic of the psyche.* Princeton, NJ: Princeton University Press.

Jung, C. G. (1961/1989). *Memories, dreams, and reflections.* Princeton, NJ: Princeton University Press.

Jung, C. G. (1963/1970). *Mysterium coniunctionis* (Vol. 14). Princeton, NJ: Princeton University Press.

Jung, C. G. (1964). *Man and his symbols.* New York: Dell.

Jung, C. G. (1967). *Commentary on the secret of the golden flower, alchemical studies* (Vol. 13). Princeton, NJ: Princeton University Press.

Jung, C. G. (1973). *C.G. Jung letters* (Vol. 1). Princeton, NJ: Princeton University Press.

Jung, C. G. (1989). *Analytical psychology: Notes of the seminar given in 1925* (Vol. 49). Princeton, NJ: Princeton University Press.

Keirsey, D. and Bates, M. (1978). *Please understand me: An essay on temperament styles.* Del Mar, CA: Prometheus Nemesis Books.

Keirsey, D. (1987). *Portraits of temperament.* Del Mar, CA: Prometheus Nemesis Books.

Kerr, J. (1993). *A most dangerous method: The story of Jung, Freud and Sabina Spielrein.* New York: Random House.

Kotlowitz, A. (1996, February 8). It takes a village to destroy a child. *The New York Times,* p. A1.

Kretschmer, E. (1925). *Physique and character.* London: Harcourt Brace.

Kroeger, O. and Thuesen, J. M. (1988). *Type talk, the 16 personality types that determine how we live, love, and work.* New York: Dell.

Lacayo, R. (1994, February 7). Lock em up. *Time.*

Lammer, A. (1994). *In God's shadow: The collaboration of Victor White and Carl Jung.* New York: Paulist Press.

Lao-tzu, 1988. *Tao te ching* (Stephen Mitchell. Trans.) New York: Harper Perennial, a Division of Harper Collins.

Larson, E. (1996, January 22). The soul of an HMO. *Time,* 44–52.

Lavin, T. P. *The art of practicing Jung: Psychological types in analysis, Jungian analysis* (2nd ed.). LaSalle. IL: Open Court.

Leonard, D. and Straus, S. (1997, June). Putting your company's whole brain to work. *Harvard Business Review,* 116--120.

Lerner, G. (1986). *The creation of patriarchy.* New York and Oxford, England: Oxford University Press.

Lernoux, P. (1980). *Cry of the people.* New York: Penguin Books.

LeShan, L. (1977). *You can fight for your life: Emotional factors and the causation of cancer.* New York: Jove/HBJ Book.

Loomis, M. (1982). A new perspective for Jung's typology: The Singer-Loomis inventory of personality. *Journal of Analytical Psychology,* 59–69.

Loomis, M. (1991). *Dancing the wheel of psychological types.* Wilmette, IL: Chiron Publications.

Malloy, J. T. (1988). *New dress for success.* New York: Time Warner.

Malone, M. (1977). *Psychetypes.* New York: A Kangaroo Book, Pocket Books, Simon and Schuster.

Malory, T. (1969/1985). *Le morte d'Arthur* (Vol. 2). Middlesex, England: Penguin Books.

Matton, M. A. (1984). *Understanding dreams.* Dallas, TX: Spring Publications.

McCaulley, M. (1992). Applications of type: Filling in the jig-saw. *Bulletin of Psychological Type* 15.3, 20–21.

McCaulley, M. (Spring 1997). Isabel Myers: A double legacy. *Bulletin of Psychological Type,* 20.2, 22–25.

McCaulley, M. (1998). Type and the growth of the MBTI: Then and now. *Bulletin of Psychological Type,* 20.3, 48–49.

McCaulley, M. (1998). Why did C. G. Jung create his typology? *Bulletin of Psychological Type,* 21.5, 20.

McCaulley, M. (1999). APT and the constructive us of differences. *Bulletin of Psychological Type,* 22.1, 10.

McGregor, D. (1960). *The human side of enterprise.* New York: McGraw-Hill.

Meier, C. A. (1995). *Personality: The individuation process in the light of C. G. Jung's typology.* Einsiedein, Switzerland: Daimeon.

Merchant, C. (1980). *The death of nature: Women, ecology, and the scientific revolution.* San Francisco: Harper and Row.

Moore, R. and Gillette, D. (1990). *King, warrior, magician, lover: Rediscovering the archetypes of the mature masculine.* San Francisco: HarperSanFrancisco, a division of Harper Collins.

Myers, I. B. (1962/1987). *Introduction to type.* Palo Alto, CA: Consulting Psychologists Press.

Myers, I. B. and Myers, P. B. (1980). *Gifts differing: Understanding personality type.* Palo Alto, CA: Consulting Psychologists Press.

Myers, I. B. and McCaulley, M. H. (1962/1985). *Manual: A guide to the development and use of the Myers-Briggs type indicator.* Palo Alto: Consulting Psychologists Press.

Neumann, E. (1956). *Armor and Psyche: The psychic development of the feminine, a commentary on the tale by Apuleius.* Princeton, NJ: Princeton University Press.

Newman, J. (Autumn, 1981). The Myers-Briggs type indicator and gifts differing. *The San Francisco Jung Institute Library Journal,* 3:1, 37–54.

Newman, J. (1995). *Measures of the five factor model and psychological types: A major convergency research and theory.* Denver, CO: A monograph.

O'Donohue, J. *Anam cara, a book of Celtic wisdom.* NY: Cliff Street Books, an imprint of Harper Collins.

Osmond, H. (Fall 1977). Typology revisited: A new perspective. *Psychological Perspectives,* 206–219.

Petzingon, T. J. (1999). *The new pioneers: The men and women who are transforming the workplace and marketplace.* New York: Simon and Schuster.

Pfaff, W. (1995, March 17). The health of American plutocracy. *Chicago Tribune,* p. 113.

Phillips, K. (1990). *The politics of the rich and the poor.* New York: Random House.

Phillips, K. (1994). *Arrogant capital. Washington, Wall Street and the frustration of American politics.* Boston: Little Brown.

Power, S. J. and Lundsten, L. L. (1997). Studies that compare type theory and left brain/right brain theory. *Journal of Psychological Type,* 43, 22–28.

Pressman, M. (1999). Discernment, discrimination and judgment in energy medicine. *Bridges: The Quarterly Magazine of the International Society for the Study of Subtle Energies and Energy Medicine,* 10(2), 1,4.

Quenk, A. T. and Quenk, N. L. (1982). The use of psychological typology in analysis. *Jungian Analysis* (M. Stein, Ed.). LaSalle, IL.

Quenk, N. L. (1995). *Beside ourselves: Our hidden personality in everyday.* Palo Alto, CA: Consulting Psychologists Press.

Reed, B. (1978/1997). *Rebel in the soul: An ancient Egyptian dialogue between a man and his destiny.* Rochester, VT: Inner Traditions International.

Richardson, P. T. (1996). *Four spiritualities: Expressions of the self, expressions of the spirit: A psychology of contemporary spiritual choice.* Palo Alto, CA: Davies-Black.

Richardson, P. T. (1998). A circle of type. *Bulletin of Psychological Type, 21*(4), 27–28.

Rieff, P. (1961). *Freud, the mind of the moralist.* Garden City, NY: Anchor Books, Doubleday.

Saunders, F. W. (1991). *Katharine and Isabel, mother's light, daughter's journey: The story of the making of the Myers-Briggs type indicator.* Palo Alto, CA: Consulting Psychologists Press.

Scholtes, P. R. (1995). *Communities as systems.* Madison, WS; Scholtes Seminars and Consulting.

Scholtes, P. R. and Joiner, B. I. (1988). *The team handbook.* Madison, WS: Joiner Associates.

Scholtes, P. R. (1998). *The leader's handbook.* New York: McGraw Hill.

Scott, T. (1996, March 17). Downsizing: How it feels to be fired. *The New York Times,* p. E5.

Sells, B. (1994). *The soul of the law: Understanding lawyers and the law.* Boston: Element Books.

Sharp, D. (1987). *Personality types: Jung's model of typology.* Toronto, Canada: Inner City Books.

Singer, J. (1982). *Boundaries of the soul* (Rev. ed.). New York: Anchor Books, Doubleday.

Singer, J. and Loomis, M. (1986). The Singer-Loomis inventory of personality: An update on the measurement of Jung's typology. *Berlin Congress of the IAAP.*

Sly, E. J. (1995, July 21). Grazing bill to give ranches vast control of public lands. *The New York Times,* p. A1.

Sly, E. J. (1996, January 2). They hate government, but love those subsidies. *The New York Times.*

Smolowe, J. (1994, February 7). And throw away the key. *Time.*

Spoto, A. (1995). *Jung's typology in perspective.* Wilmette, IL: Chiron.

Swimme, B. and Berry, Thomas(1992). *The universe story: From the primoridal flaring forth to the ecozoic era, a celebration of the unfolding of the cosmos.* San Francisco: Harper Collins.

Thompson, H. (1996) *Jung's attitudes-functions explained.* Watkinsville, GA: Wormhole.

Thompson, H. The personality landscape. *Bulletin of Psychological Type,* 21(2), 1–4.

Ulanov, B. (1992). *Jung and the outside world.* Wilmette, IL: Chiron Publications.

von Franz, Marie-Louise and Hillman, J. (1979). *Jung's typology.* Irving, TX: Spring Publications.

Walton, M. (1986). *The Deming management method.* New York: Peragee Books, Putnam Publishing Group.

Weiss, P. (1994, September 11). A hoplophobe among the gunnies. *New York Times,* p. 870.

Wheatley, M. J. (1992). *Leadership and the new science.* San Francisco: Berrett-Koehler.

White, V. (1952/1982). *God and the unconscious.* Dallas, TX: Spring Publications.

Whiteside, A. (1969). *Mastering the Chopin etudes and other essays.* United States and Canada: Charles Scribner's Sons.

Whitmont, E. (1969). *The symbolic quest, basic concepts of analytical psychology.* New York: Harper and Row.

Whyte, D. (1994). *The heart aroused: Poetry and the preservation of the soul in corporate America.* New York: Doubleday.

Wilber, K. (Ed.). (1982). *The holographic universe, and other paradoxes.* Boulder, CO: Shambhala Publications.

Willeford, W. (1976). The primacy of feeling. *Journal of Analytical Psychology,* 21, 115–133.

Willeford, W. (1987). *Feeling, imagination and the self: Transformations of the mother-infant relationship.* Evanston, IL: Northwestern University Press.

Willhelm, R. (1950/1967). *I Ching* (C. F. Baynes, Trans.). London: Routledge and Kegan Paul.

Wills, G. (1996, January 31). GOP's breach of contract. *Chicago Sun Times,* p. 35N.

Witt, H. (1995, September 29). Quiet revolution in health care. *Chicago Tribune,* p. A1.

Wolfe, S. Republicans maul medicine. *Health Letter, Public Citizen Research Group,* 81–82.

Wolff, T. (1995). Structural forms of the feminine psyche. *Psychological Perspectives,* 77–90.

Woodman, M. (1981/88). *Addiction to perfection: The still unravished bride.* Toronto: Inner City Books.

Yankelovich, D. and Barrett, W. (1970). *Ego and instinct: The psychoanalytic view of human nature.* New York: Random House.

INDEX

archetypes. *See also* archetypal nature of types.

first defined by Jung as "the *a priori*, inborn form of intuition" 90

from the Self, the principle of identity and order in the unconscious 10 (*see also* Self.)

inborn forms of psychic apprehensions and primordial images 91–92

instincts in 92–93

invented (in consciousness) and discovered (in the unconscious), according to Jung 138

language of the collective unconscious 67–106

layman's view of: universal patterns existing among all nations and ages 9–10

attitudes. *See* extraversion and introversion.

auxiliary function
controversial aspects 297
Jung on 95–98, 294–299
Myers on 294–299

B

behaviors, four human 82, 236ff

Benziger, Katherine
The Art of Using the Whole Brain 346–352

and Falsification of Type 351–352

most people seek to live out two quadrants 354–355

Via Karl Pribram viewing the compass as a microcosm of the cosmos 350–351

Berens, Linda
criticism of 414–418, 421–422

Keirseyan Temperament Theory in the Use of the Myers–Briggs Type Indicator 418

Bernstein, Jerome
Power and Politics: The Psychology of Soviet-American Partnership 344–345

Berry, Thomas. *See* Swimme, Brian.

body, instincts and psyche. *See also* archetypes; & introversion

SF connection with the gross motor development of the child 372–373

brain. *See also* Herrmann: the Whole Brain Model. *See also* Lowen: the four levels of child development.
two hemispheres of 320–321

Briggs, Katharine. *See also* Myers, Isabel Briggs.
mother of and co–founder with Isabel Briggs Myers of the *MBTI* 36–37, 287, 399

C

Choquette, Sonia
The Wise Child 52

classification of types
basis for the *MBTI* popularity along with its depth meanings 2–4
Jung's and analysts' resistance to (see Jung's divided family)

compass of the soul as mandala or sacred circle
author's view (*see also* couplings)
"compass" name according to Jung 89, 293
dominant coupling acts like north star 293
dream of, by author 357
dream of, by client 203
feminine version of, by Toni Wolff 217–220, 222–227
importance of the couplings 67–106 (*see also* couplings)
Jung and container for the four individual functions 6
means "circle" 293

complexes
as incarnates of archetypes 92–95
includes the learned pragmatics of each type 93–94
and intuition 143
Jung's discovery of 143
meaning of 93
rooted in an archetype 10, 93–94

consciousness

awakening of reflective consciousness 110

conscious role one plays in society (see also persona)

ego as its archetype 70

living a false consciousness in type terms (see also falsification of type)

couplings

constant and universal use of 13

described in various writers and systems:

appearance in the four quadrants of the brain (*see also* Herrmann, Ned)

connection to the four disciplines of Deming's (*see also* Deming, William Edwards)

connection with the four levels of child development (*see also* Lowen, Walter)

implicit in the Native American Medicine Wheel 449–453

Moore and Gillette's four cultural archetypes 204–217

Myers: bases of the *MBTI's* sixteen types 299–300, 303–304

Osmond group (*see also* Osmond group)

philosophy of organizations (*see also* Deming, William Edwards)

relationship with certain vocational areas in the *MBTI* 307–313

religious orientation unique to each (see Peter Tufts Richardson *Four Spiritualities*) 227

as more comprehensive behavioral templates than individual types 186

ST, SF, NF, and NT as the basis of Jung's type system 67, 95–98

the Self as unitying source of 171–172

the unifying theme of this book and the deepest basis for entering types into Jung's archetypal viewpoint 7–8

case studies

Benziger relating couplings/brain quadrants with behaviors toward time, decision–making 349–350

Carol working with her four inner characters as the four couplings 257–264

NF real estate agent, learning to use all four couplings at work 241–242

psychiatrist understanding inner psychic dynamics of a patient in all four quadrants 242

young man in his 20s, learning to use all four couplings in his life 241

creative process

   evidence of in all dreams and creative intuitions (*see also* Dreams and Intuition)

   evidence of in the psyche 195, 235, 245–246, 329–331

   Self as the creative source 246–249

   in the type circle (see figure 6.1) 243–246, 329–331

D

Deming, William Edwards

   author of *The New Economics* and *Out of the Crisis*

   ENTJ Magician type who saw need for deep transformations in organizations 529–530

   four disciplines meshing with the couplings 529–532

   history and development of System of Profound Knowledge 526–544

Dickinson, Emily

   deeply introverted feeling type 124–129

dream(s) (A sample of dreams related in text.)

   birth of inner child 71

   bomb and piggy bank transformation 544

   claiming one's ST warrior power 209

   a client's (John) healing 340, 356

   emerge as intuition but can contain all types 143–144

   Empire State Building triggering ego collapse 85

   four quadrants of brain development 357

   of the four type archetypes 203

   imperative to confront imaged enemy in claiming one's power 57 (*see also* shadow)

   Jung's view of dreams 51

   Mafia-killer 523

   Marlene's dream 341–342, 355

   painful reminder of mother's destructive power in childhood 215

   surrender of her identity keeps controlling mother alive 342

E

Ego

    center of consciousness and includes persona 70 (*see also* consciousness and persona)

Eisler, Riane

    The Chalice and the Blade 119, 527

emotions. *See also* experiences; transformations.

    basis of all growth as per Jung 161–162

    Erik Erikson's eight stages 373–374

    place of, in the lives of Jung and Myers 37–40, 44

    relationship with the feeling function 156–163

    sacred character of (see numinosity)

Erikson, Erik

    Childhood and Society 369, 373–374, 376, 378–379, 382–384, 387

experience. *See also* emotions.

    importance of, in Jung 55, 56, 161–162

    Osmond group as "experiential typologists" 192

extraversion and **extraverts**

    child in classroom 4

    compared with introversion of 116–118, 122

    destructive aspects of: fast life and overwork 120–122

    general characteristics of 5, 118–122

    and Lowen: associated with front lobes of brain 367

ENFJ. *See also* NF (intuitive/feeling coupling).

    NF as center 311–313

    and the presence of J 296, 309–311

    step 2 in Lowen's child development (figure 9.2) 373

ENFP. *See also* NF (intuitive/feeling coupling).

    and John Giannini's typology 256

    NF as center 307–311

    and presence of the P 296

    step 9 in Lowen (figure 9.2) 377

ENTJ. *See also* NT (intuitive/thinking coupling).

> NT as center 311–313
>
> and presence of J
>
> step 15 in Lowen (figure 9.2) 381

ENTP. *See also* NT (intuitive/thinking coupling).

> and case history, of Jason 264–266
>
> NT as center 311–313
>
> and presence of P 293–294
>
> step 2 in Lowen (figure 9.2) 380

ESFJ. *See also* SF (sensate/feeling coupling).

> presence of J 308–309
>
> step 3 in Lowen (figure 9.2) 373

ESFP. *See also* SF (sensate/feeling coupling).

> and presence of P 308–309
>
> step 1 in Lowen (figure 9.2) 377

ESTJ. *See also* ST (sensate/thinking coupling).

> associated with masculine and "tough mindedness" (ch 4)
>
> as the author's adopted (false) typology 43, 70
>
> as basis of our culture's one-sidedness 73–76, 509–524, 526, 532–533, 537, 540, 545
>
> as basis of resistance to Myers and the *MBTI* 39
>
> the ESTJ social collective 112
>
> first stage of life normal challenge 113–114
>
> presence of J 296
>
> step 7 in Lowen (figure 9.2) 376
>
> typical characteristic in hard sciences 79

ESTP. *See also* ST (sensate/thinking coupling).

> and presence of P 283–318
>
> step 5 in Lowen (figure 9.2) 375

F

falsification of type
> author's experience with 42–43
> induced by our one-sided ESTJ culture (see ESTJ type)
> Jung's experience with 30, 34–35
> and Katherine Benziger 5, 352

feeling function
> according to Jung 366
> according to Lowen 366
> in contrast to the thinking function 154
> general characteristics of, 100, 105–106, 155–156
> and growth in consciousness 161
> import of, in brain research 355–356
> and love 155, 178, 355–356
> and NFs (107–181), 355–356 (see *also* NF[intuitive/feeling coupling])
> pathologies of 162–163
> related to Soul and water 157
> and Self 161–162

feminine character of typology 31, 32

Ferrand, Pierre 503

Five Factor Model 399–400

Frame, Janet
> *Janet Frame: An Autobiography* 26–27

Franz, Marie-Louise von, and **James Hillman**
> *Jung's Typology* 19, 41, 100, 247, 429, 475

Freud, Sigmund
> and Adler 80–81
> extraverted 29

Freud, Sigmund, and **Jung, Carl G.**
> founders of psychoanalysis 27, 29
> possible false type per Jung 195–196 (*see also* falsification of type)

Hillman, James

"Egalitarian Typologies versus the Perception of the Unique" 90

holds Jung wrote his book not to distinguish individuals but only theories critique of 274–276

rejection of instruments that measure types critique of 372–373

types as archetypes 90

Howard, Philip K.

The Death of Common Sense 513–514, 540

humility

accepting type opposites 52

as taught by Hinduism 59

I

I Ching

Hexagram 11 (Peace) 60

Hexagram 12 (Standstill) 60–61

Hexagram 48 (the Well) 237–238

internal dynamism of 60–62

structure of based on polarities and the principle of synchronicity 52–53, 57, 60

individuation

an adult life journey with Jung, Lowen and Erik Erikson's 247, 369–391 (*see also* Self; transformations)

Lowen and the child phases of 364–369

typological version in individuals and in organizations 44, 52, 475, 541–544

inferior function. *See also* Quenk, Naomi: *Besides Ourselves.*

included in Jung's concept of shadow 71 (*see also* shadow)

Jung: it is "eruptive in nature" 41, 91

Marie-Louise von Franz, important article on 99–100

and surrender of ego and dominant function 80

instinct. *See also* body, instincts and psyche.

the physiological aspect of each archetype 91–91

purpose in creating typology 4–6, 82, 110, 472

relationship with Katharine Briggs and Isabel Briggs Myers 6–7, 36–38

review of his personal awakening and developing psychology 27–34

and Taoism 49–51

and typology as peripheral 33, 474

See also Jung's psychology

Jung's divided family 469–507

analysts' devaluation of typologists 483

analysts' elitism re typology 474, 489

analysts' societal inferiorities 473, 476–477, 479–481, 503

cognitive behavioral approach to types 485–486, 488

complexity of Jung's book on *types* contributing to split 473

creativity and the couplings within the type "boxes" 493

damage caused by split 473–474, 498, 500

difficulties of Hillman and Singer and Loomis with the MBTI 273–275, 484–485

Jung's own idiocyncracies relative to types and society 473–474

not further developing view of couplings 305–306, 473–474

Jung's psychology. *See also* archetypal nature of types; complex; spiritual nature of types.

autonomy of the unconscious 77–78

biographical essence of history 87

Chinese Taoism's influence on 50–55

Christian heritage of Jung 55

complexes crucially important in 92–94

creative function of symbols 76–86

divine ground of the unconscious 86

four levels of the personal psyche and four levels of culture 68ff

fundamental relationship between conscious and the unconscious 78ff; 80–82

homogeneity of the collective unconscious and heterogeneity of consciousness 273–274 (see *also* Self)

psyche as an energy system (see individuation)

soft, not a hard science 80

sovereignty of the psyche versus Freud's assumption of of physical constitution 67

transformation of negative factors into positive importance of 79

unconscious personal (historical) and collective (transpersonal) 6

K

Keirsey, David

with Marilyn Bates, *Please Understand Me* 124, 401–404

Kerr, John

A Most Dangerous Method 29

Kroeger, Otto, and **Janet M. Thuesen**

Type Talk 308–310

L

Lammer, Ann

In God's Shadow 42

LeShan, Lawrence

You Can Fight for Your Life 30

Loomis, Mary

co-creator of the SLIP with June Singer (see *also* Singer)

Dancing the Wheel of Psychological Types 422, 442

Lowen, Walter

adult use of each level is Self-based 370

assumption that learning begins in the experiential right brain 367

child development in first twelve years 364, 369

Dichotomies of the Mind 363

as an INTJ 363

M

Malloy, John

New Dress for Success 132

Malone, Michael

Psychetypes 192 (*see also* Osmond Group)

McCaulley, Mary

contributions to research and theory of the types 39–40, 286–287, 291

relationship with Consulting Psychologists Press 40

Mandala

Jung's circles contrasted to Myer's type table 488–489

others creating circles 331, 368, 438–452, 530

shared by both Jung and Taoism 53–54

typologists adopting a circular approach 104–105, 491–493

Meier, C. A. 475

Moore, Robert, and **Douglas Gillette**. *See also* Toni Wolff.

four cultural and psychological archetypes: King, Warrior, Magician, Lover 204–217

The Magician Within 223–225

Myers Briggs Type Indicator (*MBTI*) (chap 7)

competing instruments

academia's Five Factor Model 20

Grey-Wheelwright (Jungian Typological Survey or JTS) 284

Singer-Loomis, Inventory of Typology (SLIP) 20, 284, 484–485

construction of the sixteen types 299–306

contributions to Jungian consciousness: his type theory and practice 286–288

developed by Katharine Briggs and Isabel Briggs Myers 8, 37, 287–288

history of 35–39, 286–290

important addition of perceiving (P) and judging (J) 294

increasing practitioner interest in Jung's entire psychology 471

Jung based throughout 283

Myers' focus on the pragmatic *consequences* of each preference 291, 301

popularity of 2

recognizes the archetypal nature of each coupling 302–304

strengthened the archetypal ground of the couplings 306–314

typology poetically grounded by John O'Donohue 3

Myers, Isabel Briggs. *See also* Briggs, Katharine.

creator, with Katharine Briggs, of the *MBTI* 35, 284

Gifts Differing 13–14,229, 283–292, 290–291

Introduction to Type 282–285

Jung's theory simplified and made accessible to the average person 287, 290ff

regarding couplings as combinations of perception and judgment 192

relationship with Jung 36–38

resistance among professionals to instrument based on Jung 38

N

Newman, James

monograph on comparisons between *MBTI* and the Five Factor Model 398–399

supporter of *MBTI* and *Gifts Differing* 288–289

NF (intuitive/feeling coupling)

creative artist 198

Deming's fourth discipline of psychology 539–549

Erik Erikson's stages 377–380

Herrmann's lower right limbic quadrant 326

Lowen's verbal level of child devlopment 367, 377–380

MBTI: choices of vocation 309–311

Moore and Gillette 212–217

most devalued of the four directional archetypes 213, 216

Osmond group's Oceanic 197–198

pathologies 213, 217

Richardson: religion of harmony and experiment 227

Taoist exercise 216

Nietzsche, Friedrich 83

NT (intuitive/thinking coupling)

creative scientist 199

Deming's discipline of theory: organization as organism 530–532

Erikson's final two life stages 382, 386–387

example: introverted NT working out love and work relationship 245–246 examples of, Jung, Einstein, Blake, Emerson 198–199

Herrmann's D quadrant 332–334

Lowen's intellectual level of child development 367, 380

Moore's Magician 207–210

Myers and *MBTI* practitioners: areas of work 194, 311–313

Myers on 193–194

Osmond group's Ethereals 198–200

pathologies 199

power defined as "autonomy" and ability to direct and control processes 312

Richardson on: a religion of unity and clarity 227

tendency to describe a creative person by giving a creative example 331

numinosity. See *also* emotions.

feelings when discovering one's true typology 289

and John O'Donohue (*Anam Cara: A Book of Celtic Wisdom*) 3

"numinal accent" of each type, per Jung 89–90

O

opposites, the types as. See *also* Self as reconciler of all opposites.

Jung: without opposites there is no life. 58

Singer-Loomis Indicator of Personality (SLIP) 423–433

symbols as carriers of polar resolutions, including types 76–77

Taoism's yin and yang as prototypes for Jung's typology 49–50, 52–54, 58–59

Osmond group 189–201, 205, 208, 211,214,487. See *also* couplings.

P

perceiving functions (sensation and intuition)

as distinguished from judging in the *MBTI* 171

extraverts 293–299

how people assimilate knowledge 6

as irrational functions 130

in the *MBTI* influences which function dominates and which function

perceiving/judging combinations

basis of the four couplings 67, 95–98

combination of a principal or dominant function and an auxiliary or helper function 293–299

persona

archetype of social interaction and of mutual expectations between ourselves and others 70–71

Petersen, Donald. *See also* Deming, William Edwards.

A Better Idea: Redefining the Way America Works

CEO of Ford Motor Company 536, 538

Phillips, Kevin

The Politics of the Rich and the Poor and Arrogant Capital 515

Pribram, Karl. *See also* Self.

The Language of the Brain 350

psychic structure

Self and the collective unconscious 91

psychological theories

differences in, as related to the types 277–279

Q

Quenk, Naomi

on the inferior functions 41, 487

R

Richardson, Peter Tufts

Four Spiritualities, based on the four couplings 227, 487

Rosen, David, M.D.

The Tao of Jung: The Influence of Taoism on Jung's Life and Theory 49, 52

S

Scanlon, Susan

> on understanding Walter Lowen 363

Schiller, Friedrich von

> Jung's understanding of sensing and intuition 82–83

Scholtes, Peter

> applications of Deming in *The Leader's Handbook* and *The Team Handbook* 527

Self

> also called "psychic structure" by Jung 91
>
> archetype of identity, source of all archetypes (see *also* figure 3.1) 5, 68, 271
>
> "God within us" as divine influence 44, 90
>
> influence on ntimate partners 349
>
> kinship with all things 160
>
> lifetime journey that Jung calls individuation 68
>
> master playwright within 10
>
> Pribram, Karl and David Bohm (Holographic Universe, Brain and Mind) 350–357
>
> primal source of psychic energy and transformations 5, 250–255 (*see also* transformations)
>
> "reconciler of all opposites" within and in society 16, 88
>
> source of "intrinsic motivation": behaving without fear as one of the basic principles of Deming's organizational philosophy 537, 540
>
> symbolized by a mandala, circle, and cross figure 88
>
> Tao as a Chinese equivalent of 52
>
> true self in contrast to learned identity or false self 70–71
>
> violation of leads to "falsification of type" and illness 5, 351–352
>
> Wilber, Ken: "quintessential religious experiences" 350

Sells, Benjamin

> *The Soul of the Law* 131, 166–167, 180

SF (sensate/feeling coupling)

> Deming's third discipline, top management as "Understanding Variation" 534–539

Jung on: "establishes what is actually present" 6

Lowen on: thing focused, concrete in approach and oriented to the present in time 366

a sensate triumph: the Vietnam War Memorial 135

in Taoist thought and practice 134

shadow

associated with love (wounded child's need for mother love) (figure 3:1) 68

damage when authentic type remains in shadow (*see* falsification of type)

devil as collective symbol of, as in book of Job 78–79

fearful figures in dreams, challenges to claim power or consequences 71, 16, 80–81

Sharp, Daryl

Personality Types 136

Singer, June

creator, with Mary Loomis, of the Singer-Loomis Inventory of Personality (the critique of this instrument by author) 422ff

Jung's and the *MBTI's* polar view of the types rejected 284, 423

Loomis's effort to correct the bar symbol limitations via the Native American Medicine 438–445.

mixed results from the SLIP 435

SLIP. *See* Singer, June.

social/cultural pathology and healing. See *also* ESTJ when pathologized; Deming, William Edwards.

groups from AA to politics need to know human differences 344–345

Jung's divided family: analysts and typologists 509ff

MBTI and Herrmann Brain Dominance Instrument facilitates creative conflict in corporations 346

overcoming gender stereotyping via types 62

typology in

American society's type pathology 509–524

ET language of the United States and EF language of Russia: ignorance of difference during the atomic power crisis 344–345

Jung: EST one-sidedness—naturally destructive 77

spiritual nature of types

> feeling function as connector to the Self and others 155, 160–161
>
> impactful experience when one knows one's own type 3–4, 35, 296
>
> Jung balance outer and inner influences via dynamic of the Self 268–270
>
> Jung's "The Type Problem in Classical and Medieval Thought," the spirituality of Meister Eckhart 73–75, 85–86
>
> Loomis: the spiritual depth of types in the Native American Medicine Wheel 438
>
> Myers' and Deming's use of 1 Corinthians 12:4–8 458–459, 546
>
> Myers and Jung's view of the health and pathology of the psyche 291–292
>
> NF/Lover archetype and feeling function 212–217, 355–356
>
> Richardson's *Four Spiritualities*, based on the four couplings 227
>
> as sacred language 3
>
> type's archetypal nature as numinous (*see* numinosity)
>
> types in dreams, as per Jung "vox dei" or "the voice of God" 151
>
> understanding and tolerance enhanced 3–4; 272–279

Spittler, Carl

> on literary Prometheus as "forethinker" or introvert, and Epimetheus, as "after-thinker" or extravert 83

Spoto, Angelo

> *Typology in Perspective* 2, 41

statistics

> Myers' use of, contrary to her typology 39
>
> statistical equality among introverts and extraverts in the US l990 census 111–112

symbols. *See also* archetypes.

> assimilators of outer and inner experiences in dreams and fantasies 83–84
>
> God symbols highest in stories and in dreams 85–86
>
> images in Jung's system of Self reconciling opposites 84–85
>
> language of the archetypes in dreams, myths, fairy tales, poetry

religion's tendency to stereotype symbols that produce conformity 78

transformers of crass emotions into useful energies 157–159

Synchronicity

abiding principle similar to Providence in religion 53

author's book emerged out of synchronistic events 190–191, 229, 358, 529

as an interpersonal and cosmic extension of the intuitive function 137–138ff

meaningful connections of the "psychic inner world and the physical outer world" 53

psychological and spiritual basis underlying the I Ching 57

Swimme, Brian, and Thomas Berry

The Universe Story: Evolution Understood Scientifically and Spiritually 524–525

T

Taoism as Chinese philosophy and theology. *See also* synchronicity; Rosen, David: *The Tao of Jung.*

Jung: "one of the most perfect formulations" of "psychological principles" 50

Jung personally influenced by Chinese philosophy 49–56, 269–270

meaning of the Tao 56

promotes health and wholeness as in Jung and Myers 49, 51–52, 58

related to Jung's active imagination 57

Self/Soul and the Tao: reconcile opposites and paradoxes 50, 63

shares with typology a circular and polar view of the Soul 49ff

structures of, as in Jung subservient to energies and potential transformations 49ff, 235ff

synchronicity as grounding principle of 53

temperaments. *See also* Keirsey.

Jung's rejection of, as a modern basis for type differences 404–405

limitations of 401–402, 407, 410ff, 419

physiological basis adopted by David Keirsey and Marilyn Bates for identifying human types, used in conjunction with the *MBTI* types 401

origins of such in the Self 251

potentials for in Taoist exercises 269

typologists' difficulties with Jung's overall system 491, 499

U

Ulinov, Barry

Jung and the Outside World: Jung's Impact on Intellectuals 469, 502

V

Vasavada, Arwind

views of analytical training 481–482

Vocation

destiny based on authentic identity (*see* Individuation and Self)

W

White, David

The Heart Aroused: Poetry and the Preservation of the Soul in Corporate America 525–526

Whitmont, Edward

The Symbolic Quest (*see also* Wolff, Toni)

Whole Brain Model and Instrument. *See* Herrmann, Ned.

Wilbur, Ken

The Holographic Universe 350–351

Wolff, Toni

"Structural Forms of the Feminine Archetype" 217

Moore and Gillette's critique of 217–219, 222–226

as picked up by Edward Whitmont and Tad and Noreen Monroe Guzie 220–222

Willeford, William

Feeling, Imagination, and the Self 155–157, 161

Willhelm, Richard

    The I Ching 58–59, 133–134, 140

Y

Yankelovich, Daniel, and **William Barrett**

    Ego and Instinct: The Psychoanalytic View of Human Nature 195

Yin and Yang

    makeup of I Ching 60–62

    as "'mother' and 'father' of everything that happens," per Jung 53

AUTHOR BIOGRAPHY

AUTHOR JOHN L. GIANNINI, MA, MDiv, MBA, has an eclectic background that encompasses engineering, business, theology, philosophy and psychology. He returned from military service in 1946, obtained an MBA from Stanford and became a manager. In 1955, Giannini entered the Dominican Order, where he first experienced Jung's ideas and practices through analytical work with Father Victor White, a Jungian analyst from England. In 1969, Giannini returned to secular life, married and had three children. Meanwhile he received his MA in Religion and Psychology at the University of Chicago and worked as a counselor in community mental health and as a manager and counselor with the SAFER Foundation's ex-offender program in Chicago. In 1980 he obtained his diplomat in Analytical Psychology and has since been in private practice and taught in the C. G. Jung Institute of Chicago in its professional and public programs. He has traveled to throughout the United States to teaching on topics such as inner child, the Arthurian legends, the Psyche-Eros myth, on Job and Jung, intimacy, the life journey in personal stories and dreams, body and psyche, and typology. Besides his Jungian affiliations, he is a member of the Association for Psychological Type, the Association of Humanistic Psychologists, the Association for the Study of Subtle Energy and Energy Medicine, and the National Association for the Advancement of Psychoanalysis.